SQL Server 2014 Design & Programming

Kalman Toth

SQL Server 2014 Design & Programming

Copyright © 2014 by Kalman Toth

ISBN-13: 978-1499529593
ISBN-10: 1499529597

Trademark Notices

Microsoft is a trademark of Microsoft Corporation.
SQL Server 2014 is a program product of Microsoft Corporation.
SQL Server 2012 is a program product of Microsoft Corporation.
SQL Server 2008 is a program product of Microsoft Corporation.
SQL Server 2005 is a program product of Microsoft Corporation.
SQL Server 2000 is a program product of Microsoft Corporation.
SQL Server Management Studio (SSMS) is a program product of Microsoft Corporation.
SQL Server Data Tools (SSDT) is a program product of Microsoft Corporation.
Microsoft Help Viewer is a program product of Microsoft Corporation.
SQL Server Analysis Services (SSAS) is a program product of Microsoft Corporation.
SQL Server Integration Services (SSIS) is a program product of Microsoft Corporation.
SQL Server Reporting Services (SSRS) is a program product of Microsoft Corporation.
SQL Azure is a program product of Microsoft Corporation.
Office Visio is a program product of Microsoft Corporation.
Exam 70-461 is an exam product of Microsoft Corporation.
ORACLE is a trademark of ORACLE Corporation.
Java is a trademark of ORACLE Corporation.
DB2 is a trademark of IBM Corporation.
SYBASE is a trademark of Sybase Corporation.
McAfee is a trademark of McAfee Corporation.
ALL PHOTOS IN THIS BOOK ARE THE COPYRIGHTED PROPERTY OF THE AUTHOR

Warning and Disclaimer

Every effort has been made to ensure accuracy, however, no warranty or fitness implied. The information & programs are provided on an "as is" basis.

SQL Server 2014 Design & Programming

Contents at a Glance

CHAPTER 1: SQL Server Sample & System Databases 1

CHAPTER 2: Installing SQL Server 2014 36

CHAPTER 3: Structure of the SELECT Statement 69

CHAPTER 4: SQL Server Management Studio 87

CHAPTER 5: Basic Concepts of Client-Server Computing 131

CHAPTER 6: Fundamentals of Relational Database Design 161

CHAPTER 7: Normal Forms & Database Normalization 227

CHAPTER 8: Functional Database Design 237

CHAPTER 9: Advanced Database Design Concepts 265

CHAPTER 10: The Art of Database Design 307

CHAPTER 11: New Programming Features in SS 2012 & 2014 352

CHAPTER 12: JOINing Tables with INNER & OUTER JOINs 371

CHAPTER 13: Basic SELECT Statement Syntax & Examples 411

CHAPTER 14: Subqueries in SELECT Statements 471

CHAPTER 15: SELECT INTO Table Creation & Population 497

CHAPTER 16: Modify Data - INSERT, UPDATE, DELETE & MERGE 513

CHAPTER 17: The Magic of Transact-SQL Programming 537

CHAPTER 18: Exporting & Importing Data 554

CHAPTER 19: Maintaining Data Integrity in the Enterprise 601

CHAPTER 20: Query & Stored Procedure Optimization 635

CHAPTER 21: Advanced T-SQL Programming Topics 661

CHAPTER 22: In-Memory OLTP 755

APPENDIX A: Job Interview Questions 773

APPENDIX B: Job Interview Answers 775

INDEX of SQL Server 2014 Design & Programming 777

ABOUT THE AUTHOR

Kalman Toth has been working with relational database technology since 1990. One day his boss at a commodity brokerage firm in Greenwich, Connecticut, had to leave early. He gave his SQL Server login and password to Kalman along with a small SQL task. Kalman was a C/C++ developer fascinated by SQL. Therefore, he studied a Transact-SQL manual 3 times from start to finish "dry", without any server access. His boss was satisfied with the results of the SQL task and a few days later Kalman's dream came true: he got his very own SQL Server login.

Kalman's relational database career since then includes database design, database development, database administration, OLAP architecture, and Business Intelligence development. Applications have included enterprise-level general ledger and financial accounting, bond funds auditing, international stock market feeds processing, broker-dealer firm risk management, derivative instruments analytics, consumer ecommerce database management for online dating, personal finance, physical fitness, and diet and health. His MSDN forum participation in the Transact-SQL and SQL Server Tools was rewarded with the Microsoft Community Contributor award. Kalman has a Master of Arts degree in Physics from Columbia University and a Master of Philosophy degree in Computing Science, also from Columbia. Additionally, he has Microsoft certifications in database administration, development, and Business Intelligence. His dream SQL career took him across the United States and Canada as well as to South America and Europe. SQL also involved him in World History. At one time he worked for Deloitte and Touche on the 96th floor of World Trade Center North. On September 11, 2001, he was an RDBMS consultant at Citibank on 111 Wall Street. After escaping at 10:30 on that fateful Tuesday morning in the heavy dirt and smoke, it took 10 days before he could return to his relational database development job just 1/2 mile from the nearly three thousand victims buried under steel.

What Kalman loves about SQL is that the same friendly, yet powerful, commands can process 2 records or 2 million records or 200 million records in the same easy way. Currently, he is Principal Trainer at www.sqlusa.com. His current interest is Artificial Intelligence. He is convinced that machine intelligence will not only replace human intelligence, but will even surpass it by millions of times in the near future. Kalman's hobby is flying gliders and vintage fighter planes. Kalman is moderator on the following MSDN forums: Database Design, Transact-SQL and Getting Started with SQL Server.

OTHER BOOKS & EBOOKS BY THE AUTHOR:

SQL Server 2014 Database Design

SQL Server 2012 Programming

SQL Server 2012 Database Design

Beginner SQL Programming Using Microsoft SQL Server 2012

Exam 70-461 Bootcamp: Querying Microsoft SQL Server 2012

Beginner Database Design & SQL Programming Using Microsoft SQL Server 2012

SQL Server 2012 SELECT Statement Amazon Instant Video

SQL Server 2012 Administration

1000 Difficult Word Search Puzzles to Improve Your IQ

Brain Puzzles for Adults (IQ BOOST PUZZLES)

CONTENTS

CHAPTER 1: SQL Server Sample & System Databases 1

AdventureWorks Series of OLTP Databases 1
- Diagram of Person.Person & Related Tables 3
- Diagram of Sales.SalesOrderHeader and Related Tables 4

SELECT Query Basics 5
- The Simplest SELECT Statement 5
- SELECT Query with WHERE Clause Predicate 7
- Aggregating Data with GROUP BY Query 8
- GROUP BY Query with 2 Tables & ORDER BY for Sorting 9
- LEN(), DATALENGTH(), LTRIM() & RTRIM() Functions 9
- Finding All Accessories in Production.Product Table 10
- Using Implicit or Explicit Conversion 10
- How Can SQL Work without Looping? 11
- Single-Valued SQL Queries 11
- Data Dictionary Description of Tables in the Sales Schema 12
- NULL Values in Tables & Query Results 13
- NULL Values Generated by Queries 14

Building an FK-PK Diagram in AdventureWorks2012 15

AdventureWorksDW2012 Data Warehouse Database 16
- Diagram of a Star Schema in AdventureWorksDW2012 17

AdventureWorks2008 Sample Database 18

AdventureWorks2012 Sample Database 19
- Production.Product and Related Tables 20
- Descriptions of Columns in Production.Product Table 21
- Mountain Bikes in Production.Product Table 22
- The SOUNDEX() Function to Check Sound Alikes 22

Prior SQL Server Sample Databases 23

Northwind Sample Database 24
- Diagram of Northwind Database 25

pubs Sample Database 26
- Book Titles in pubs Database 27
- Diagram of pubs Database 28

SQL Server System Databases 29
- The master Database 30

The model Database	32
The msdb Database	33
The tempdb Database	34

CHAPTER 2: Installing SQL Server 2014 .... *36*

SQL Server 2014 Express Edition Installation	**36**
SQL Server 2014 Evaluation Edition Installation	**36**
SQL Server 2014 Pay Edition Installation	**37**
Start Menu for SQL Server 2014	**54**
Creating Shortcut for Management Studio on Desktop	54
Launching SQL Server Configuration Manager	**55**
Starting, Restarting & Stopping SQL Server	**56**
Connecting to the New Named SQL Server Instance	**57**
Investigating the New SQL Server Instance	58
Connecting to 2 SQL Server Instances Simultaneously	**59**
BACKUP DATABASE Command	60
Installing Books Online - BOL	**60**
Creating Shortcut for Books Online on Desktop.	63
Installing Developer Reference	**64**
Searching Books Online Contents Mode	**65**
Searching Books Online Index Mode	**66**
Searching the Web for SQL Server MSDN Articles	**66**
Book Online on the Web	**67**
Installing AdventureWorks2012 Sample Database	**68**
Installing Northwind & pubs Sample Databases	**68**

CHAPTER 3: Structure of the SELECT Statement *69*

The SELECT Clause	**69**
SELECT with Search Expression	70
SELECT Statement with Subquery	71
Creating Delimited String List (CSV) with XML PATH	72
Logical Processing Order of the SELECT Statement	73
The TOP Clause	**74**

The DISTINCT Clause to Omit Duplicates 75
The CASE Conditional Expression 76
The OVER Clause 78
FROM Clause: Specifies the Data Source 79
The WHERE Clause to Filter Records (Rows) 80
The GROUP BY Clause to Aggregate Results 81
The HAVING Clause to Filter Aggregates 82
The ORDER BY Clause to Sort Results 83
The EXCEPT & INTERSECT Set Operators 83
CTE - Common Table Expression 84
Combining Results of Multiple Queries with UNION 85
TOP n by Group Query with OVER PARTITION BY 86

CHAPTER 4: SQL Server Management Studio 87

SQL Server Programming, Administration & Management Tool 87

Query Editor 88
Execute All Batches in Query Editor 89
The Significance of GO in T-SQL Scripts 89
Routing Results to Grid, Text or File 92
Routing Results to Text 93
Routing Results to File 94
Saving Results in CSV Flat File Format 95
Copy & Paste Results to Excel 97
Error Handling & Debugging 99
Locating the Error Line in a Query 100
Error Message Pointing to the Wrong Line 101
Parsing a Query for Syntax Errors 102
Deferred Name Resolution Process 103
Executing Single Batch Only 104
Executing Part of a Query 105

Object Explorer 106
Context-Sensitive Right-Click Menu 107
Server Administration & Management Tools 108
SQL Server Agent Jobs to Automate Administration Tasks 109

Graphical Query Designer 111
Designing a GROUP BY Query in Query Designer 112
Graphically Editing of an Existing Query 117

Configuring Line Numbers in Query Editor 119

IntelliSense - Your Smart Assistant 121
IntelliSense Guessing and Completing Object Names 122
IntelliSense Assisting with User-Defined Objects 125
IntelliSense Smart Guessing Partial Word in Middle of Object Names 126
Hovering over Red Squiggly Underline Errors for Explanation 127
Common Error: The multi-part identifier "abc" could not be bound 128

Refreshing IntelliSense Cache for New DB Objects 129

CHAPTER 5: Basic Concepts of Client-Server Computing *131*

Client - Server Relational Database Management System 131

Database Objects on Server-Side 132

Database Related Items on Client-Side 133

SQL Server Profiler to Monitor Client-Server Communications 134

Table - Database Object 135
Tables in Production Schema 136

Index - Database Object 137
Diagram of EmployeeDepartmentHistory and Related Tables 138
Index Description in Data Dictionary 139
Constraint - Database Object 140
PRIMARY KEY & FOREIGN KEY Constraint Descriptions in Data Dictionary 141

View - Database Object 142
View Descriptions in Data Dictionary 143

CREATE Indexed View for Business Critical Queries 143
Graphical View Designer 144

Stored Procedure: Server-Side Program 145
Stored Procedure with Input Parameters 146
Stored Procedure Descriptions in Data Dictionary 147

Trigger: Event Fired Server-Side Program 148

Function: Read-Only Server-Side Program 149
User-Defined Function Descriptions in Data Dictionary 150

Sequence - Database Object 151

ROW_NUMBER() and Ranking Functions 152
    Query to compare RANK, DENSE_RANK & NTILE 153
    RANK & DENSE_RANK Sales By Millions 154

Dynamic SQL To Soar Beyond the Limits of Static SQL 155
    Parameterized Dynamic SQL Query Execution 155

Built-in System Functions 156

Local Variables & Table Variables in T-SQL 157

Constructing T-SQL Identifiers 159

The Use of [] - Square Brackets in Identifiers 160

CHAPTER 6: Fundamentals of Relational Database Design 161

Logical Data Modeling 161

Physical Data Modeling 161
    Column Definitions for the FactInternetSales Table 162

Table Column Data Types 163
    Date Type max_length, precision, scale & collation_name Listing 164

U.S. Default Collation SQL_Latin1_General_CP1_CI_AS 165

DATE & DATETIME Temporal Data Types 166

Two Ways of Commenting in T-SQL Scripts 167

Exploring Database Schemas 168
    SCHEMA_NAME() Function 169
    Tables in HumanResources, Person & Purchasing Schemas 170

The CREATE TABLE Statement 171
    Branch Banking Database with ON DELETE CASCADE 171

Temporary Tables: Workhorses of SQL Server 174

ALTER TABLE for Changing Table Definition 176
    Renaming Tables & Columns with sp_rename 177

DROP TABLE: A Dangerous Statement 178

Table Constraints Inclusion in CREATE TABLE 179

Nullability Column-Level Constraints in CREATE TABLE 180

IX

PRIMARY KEY & FOREIGN KEY Constraints 182
   Single Column & Composite PRIMARY KEY List with XML PATH 184

SSMS GUI Table Designer 185
   Basic GUI Table Design 186
   CHECK Constraint Definition 187
   Managing Indexes and Keys 188
   Setting PRIMARY KEY with a Single Click 189
   Configuring FOREIGN KEY: Declarative Referential Integrity 190
   T-SQL Script Generation from GUI Table Designer 192
   Generated CREATE TABLE & Related Objects Script 193

One-to-Many Relationship Implementation 195

FOREIGN KEY Referencing A UNIQUE KEY 196

FOREIGN KEY Relationship Without Constraint 197

Database Diagram Design Tool in SSMS 198

PRIMARY KEY & FOREIGN KEY as JOIN ON Keys 199

Composite & Indirect FOREIGN KEY 200

NATURAL KEY is a Must in Every Table 201
   CANDIDATE KEY 202

Logical Data Modeling in Visio 203

Relational Database Design with Visio 205

AdventureWorks Database Model in Visio 206

Reverse Engineering a Database with Visio 207
   Reverse Engineered Diagram of Northwind 208

Forward Engineering a Database with Visio 209

Forward Engineering from SSMS Diagram Tool 209
   Generate Change Script Option 214

Scripting Single Database Object with Related Objects 216

Scripting DB Objects With Script Wizard 218

SEQUENCE Objects 223
   SEQUENCE Object Sharing 224
   Cyclical Sequence Objects 225
   Getting the Source Code with sp_helptext 226

CHAPTER 7: Normal Forms & Database Normalization 227

The Goals of Database Normalizaton 227
Orders & Related Tables Diagram in Northwind 228

First Normal Form (1NF) 229

Second Normal Form (2NF) 230

Third Normal Form (3NF) 231

Fourth Normal Form (4NF) 232

Database Denormalizaton 233

Better Alternative to Denormalization 234

Ten Most Common Database Design Mistakes 235
Working for a Company with Messy Database Design 235

Query to List All Table Sizes in a Database 236

CHAPTER 8: Functional Database Design 237

Types of Table Relationships 237

One-To-Many Relationship - FOREIGN KEY Reference 238

Composite PRIMARY KEY 241

Parent-Child Hierarchy 242

Hierarchical Relationship - Multi-Level with FOREIGN KEYs 243

Tree Hierarchy Representation with hierarchyid 244

Many-To-Many Relationship - Junction Table 245

Parent-Child or Master-Detail Tables Design 246
Column Descriptions of SalesOrderHeader & SalesOrderDetail Tables 247
Diagram of PurchaseOrderHeader and Related Tables 248
Multiple FOREIGN KEYs from One Table to Another 249
Parent - Multiple Children Table Design 250

LookupHeader & Lookup Tables for Storing All Lookups 251

History Table Design 253

Implementing One-To-One Relationship 254

One-To-One Relationship between publisher & pub_info Tables 255

SQL Server 2014 Design & Programming

XI

Tables with Computed Columns 256

Building the Data Dictionary 258
    GUI Data Dictionary Maintenance 258
    Data Dictionary Maintenance with T-SQL Scripts 260

Lead Developer as Database Designer 262

Database Design Team at Big Budget Projects 262

Hiring Database Design Consultant where Resources Are Limited 262

Database System Solution Implementation Hierarchy 262

List All Default Constraints with Definition 263

Partitioning Query via Pure SQL - Ye Olde Way 264

CHAPTER 9: Advanced Database Design Concepts *265*

How to Read varbinary(max) Columns 265

FileTable - Integrating Folders with Database 265
    Adding Files to FileTable Using T-SQL 270
    Deleting Files from FileTable Using T-SQL 270

Data Compression: Compressed Table 271

Data Compression: Compressed Index 277

The GUI Data Compression Wizard 278

Partitioned Table, Partition Function & Partition Scheme 282

The GUI Create Partition Wizard 290

Columnstore Index for Data Warehouse Performance 291

DATE Data Type Solves Many Problems with DATETIME 293

Pad with Leading Zeros 293

Database Design & Programming Standards 294
    Database Design Standards 294
    Identifiers 295
    Principles of T-SQL Identifier Architecture 296
    Stored Procedure Outline 297
    User-Defined Function Outline 297

How to Create a Database with T-SQL Script 298

Adding New Column to a Table with ALTER TABLE	299
IDENTITY Column in a Table Variable	300
Partition Data By Country Query	301
Diagram of Sales.SalesPerson & Related Tables	302
Adding IDENTITY Column To Empty Table	303
SET IDENTITY INSERT tablename ON	303
DBCC CHECKIDENT Command	304
ADD Partitioned Sequence Number to Table	305
Add ROW_NUMBER & RANK Columns to Table	306
3-Part Name Table Reference	306

CHAPTER 10: The Art of Database Design 307

The Nature of Connection Between Tables	**307**
Categorical Relationship	307
Information Object Belongs To Relationship	308
Exporting & Presenting XML Data from Production.ProductModel	312
Company Received an Order Relationship	315
Type Relationship	317
When to Use & Not to Use Composite PRIMARY KEYs	**319**
How To Design a Table	**320**
Table-Related Database Objects	**321**
Listing All PRIMARY KEYs	322
UNIQUEIDENTIFIER As PRIMARY KEY	323
List All PK & FK Columns in the Database	324
How to Get Database Object Definition Information	**325**
Scripting Object CREATE Definitions	325
Single Object CREATE & Other Scripts from SSMS Object Explorer	326
Searching for Database Objects in Object Explorer Details	328
OBJECT_DEFINITION() Function for Getting Source Code	329
Scripting Database Objects with PowerShell	**330**
System Views since SQL Server 2005	**331**
Querying Systems Views	332
Listing All System Views	333
SELECT * FROM sys.all_objects where is_ms_shipped=1	334
AND (TYPE_DESC = 'SQL_TABLE_VALUED_FUNCTION' OR	334
TYPE_DESC = 'SQL_SCALAR_FUNCTION' OR	334
TYPE_DESC = 'SQL_INLINE_TABLE_VALUED_FUNCTION')	334
ORDER BY name; -- (96 row(s) affected)	334

XIII

- List of System Tables Prior to SQL Server 2005 334

Other Methods of Metadata Access 335
- Graphical Dependency Information 335
- Scripting GUI Object Change 336
- The sp_helpdb System Procedure 337
- The sp_help and sp_helptext System Procedures 338
- Listing All CHECK Constraints in a Database 340
- Creating a UDF CHECK Constraint 341
- List All DEFAULT Constraint Definitions 342
- Database Object-Definition from sys.sql_modules System View 343

Snowflake Schema Data Warehouse Design 345

Object Explorer Table Editor 346

All Tables Row Count without the COUNT() Function 347
- SQL Server Default Trace 347
- Listing All Columns with PK, FK & IDENTITY Properties 348

The Collation Column Property & the COLLATE Clause 349

Listing All Database & Server Collations 350
- Designing Table for Multi-Language Support with UNICODE 351

CHAPTER 11: New Programming Features in SS 2012 & 2014 352

New Programming Features in SS 2014 352

In-Memory OLTP (In-Memory Optimization) 352

Inline Specification Of Indexes For Disk-Based Tables 353

Improved SELECT … INTO Statement 353

New Programming Features in SS 2012 354

PARSE() Function 354

TRY_CONVERT() Function 356
- TRY_CONVERT() Usage in Adding Column to Table 357

TRY_PARSE() Function 358

FORMAT() Function 359
- Hierarchical DATE Sequence Generation 360

CONCAT() Function 361

CHOOSE() Function 361

THROW Statement.. 362

IIF() Function 363

DATEFROMPARTS() & DATETIMEFROMPARTS() Functions................................ 363

EOMONTH() Function... 364

Result Set Paging with OFFSET & FETCH NEXT 365
    Result Paging Stored Procedure 366

LEAD() & LAG() Functions 367

FIRST_VALUE() & LAST_VALUE() Analytic Functions 368

CUME_DIST() & PERCENT_RANK() Analytic Functions..................................... 369

EXEC New Option: WITH RESULT SETS 370

CHAPTER 12: JOINing Tables with INNER & OUTER JOINs 371

SELECT with INNER JOIN... 371

FOREIGN KEY Constraint as Base for INNER JOIN.. 372
    Diagram of Person.Person and Related Tables 373

EQUI-JOIN BETWEEN FOREIGN KEY & PRIMARY KEY...................................... 374

Diagram of Sales.Customer and Related Tables.. 375

Extracting All or Partial Data from JOINed Tables 376

Table Aliases for Readability 378

Column Aliases for Readability & Presentation 378

Derived Table Alias with a List of Column Aliases 379

INNER JOIN with Additional Conditions 380

Counting Rows in JOINs... 381

INNER JOIN with 3 Tables 382

INNER JOIN with Junction Table 384

NON-EQUI JOINs for Data Analytics 385
    Interchangeability of ON & WHERE Predicates in INNER JOINs 386

SELF-JOIN for Analytics Within a Table.. 387
    Applying SELF-JOIN for Numbering Result Lines 389

INNER JOIN with 5 Tables 390

Creating View as Workaround for "Too Many JOINs" 391

Non-Key INNER JOIN for Analytics 392

JOINing Tables without Relationship for Combinatorics 393
    Cartesian Product 393

SQL OUTER JOIN for Inclusion of Unmatched Rows 394

LEFT JOIN: Include Unmatched Rows from Left Table 395

RIGHT JOIN - Same as LEFT with Tables Switched 396

Cardinality of OUTER JOINs 398

LEFT JOIN & RIGHT JOIN on the Same Table 399

FULL JOIN to Include All Unmatched Rows 400

CROSS JOIN for Cartesian Product 401

CROSS JOIN Generated Multiplication Table 402

INNER JOIN with 7 Tables 403

INNER JOIN with GROUP BY Subquery 404

Making Queries Readable & Results Presentable 405

A 12 Tables JOIN Query 406
    Order of Tables or Predicates Does Not Matter 408

The CROSS APPLY Operator 409
    Using CROSS APPLY with Columns Specified Table Alias 410

CHAPTER 13: Basic SELECT Statement Syntax & Examples 411

Simple SELECT Statement Variations 411

Using the TOP Clause in SELECT Queries 413

Using the WHERE Clause in SELECT Queries 414

Using Literals in SELECT Queries 415

Date & Time Literals in SELECT Queries 416

ymd, dmy & mdy String Date Format Literals 417

Setting DATEFIRST with Literal 418
    Language Setting - SET LANGUAGE 418

The sys.syslanguages System View 419

DBCC USEROPTIONS 420

Easy SELECT Queries for Fun & Learning 421
Cardinality of DISTINCT & GROUP BY Clauses 424
Column Alias Can only Be Used in ORDER BY 425
Workarounds for Column Alias Use Restriction 425
When the Clock Strikes Midnight: datetime Behaviour 426
LEFT(), RIGHT() & SUBSTRING() String Functions 427

Transact-SQL Reserved Keywords 429
Case Sensitive Sort with Latin1_General_CS_AI 430

The ORDER BY Clause for Sorting Query Results 431
Using Column Alias in the ORDER BY Clause 432
Using Multiple Keys in the ORDER BY Clause 438
ORDER BY in Complex Queries 439
ORDER BY with ROW_NUMBER() 440
ORDER BY Clause with CASE Conditional Expression 441
ORDER BY Clause with IIF Conditional Function 444
ORDER BY Clause with the RANK() Function 445
ORDER BY Clause with Custom Mapped Sort Sequence 446
ORDER BY Clause with Custom Alphanumeric Sort Sequence 447

Working with Synonyms 448

Date & Time Conversion To / From String 449
The CONVERT() Function with Style Number Parameter 449
String to Datetime Conversion Without Century 452
Combine Date & Time String into Datetime 453
Date and Time Internal Storage Format 453
Date & Time Operations Using System Operators & Functions 454
Extract Date Only from DATETIME Data Type 454
String Date Formats Without Time 455
DATEADD() and DATEDIFF() Functions 457
Last Date & First Date Calculations 458
BETWEEN Operator for Date Range 459
Date Validation Function ISDATE() 462
Month Sequence Generator 463
The DATEPART() Function to Decompose a Date 465
The DATENAME() Function to Get Date Part Names 466
Extract Date from Text with PATINDEX Pattern Matching 467
Last Week Calculations 469
Specific Day Calculations 470

XVII

CHAPTER 14: Subqueries in SELECT Statements 471

Subqueries 471
- Non-Correlated Subqueries 472
- Subquery returned more than 1 value Error 473
- Correlated Subqueries 474
- Correlated Subqueries with Same Table 476
- CROSS APPLY with Correlated Subquery 476

Derived Tables: SELECT from SELECT 477

The UNION & UNION ALL Set Operators 478

CTE: Common Table Expression for Structured Coding 479
- Multiple CTEs Query 480
- Testing Common Table Expressions 481
- Nested CTEs Queries 482
- Testing Nested CTEs 483
- Recursive CTEs for Tree Hierarchy Processing 485
- Recursive Generation of Date & Month Sequences 486
- Generate Month Names in Different Languages 487
- Graphical Organizational Chart of AdventureWorks Cycles 488

Chain of Command Recursive Query 490
- Graphical Bill of Materials for Mountain-100 Silver, 44 Bike 491

PIVOT Operator to Transform Rows Into Columns 494

UNPIVOT Crosstab View Results 495

Using Subquery in Column List of SELECT 496

CHAPTER 15: SELECT INTO Table Creation & Population 497

Simple SELECT INTO Statement Variations 497

SELECT INTO with IDENTITY Column 502

SELECT INTO From Multiple-Table Queries 503

SELECT INTO with Sorted Table Population 504

SELECT INTO with Random Population 505

Combining SELECT INTO with INSERT SELECT 506

Copy Table into Different Database with SELECT INTO 507

Combining SELECT INTO with UPDATE 507

SELECT INTO Table Create from Complex Query 508

SELECT INTO Table Create from System Procedure Execution 509

SELECT INTO from OPENQUERY Stored Procedure Execution 510

Execution of SELECT INTO from Dynamic SQL 511

SELECT INTO Table Create from View 512

SELECT INTO Data Import from Excel 512

CHAPTER 16: Modify Data - INSERT, UPDATE, DELETE & MERGE 513

INSERT VALUES - Table Value Constructor 513

INSERT VALUES - Ye Olde Way 514

INSERT SELECT 515
INSERT SELECT Literal List 515

INSERT SELECT from Table 516
SCOPE_IDENTITY() for Last-Inserted IDENTITY Value 516
INSERT with Subset of Columns 517
Capturing Last-Inserted IDENTITY Set Values with OUTPUT 517

INSERT EXEC Stored Procedure 518
INSERT EXEC System Procedure 520

INSERT Only New Rows Omit the Rest 521

DELETE - A Dangerous Operation 522

TRUNCATE TABLE & DBCC CHECKIDENT 523

UPDATE - A Complex Operation 525
Checking Cardinality & Changes by UPDATE Prior to Execution 525
ANSI Style UPDATE 526
UPDATE from Table in Another Database 527
UPDATE Syntax Challenges 528
UPDATE with INNER JOIN 529
Capturing Affected Rows with @@ROWCOUNT 529
UPDATE with Common Table Expression 530

Four Methods of UPDATE with GROUP BY Query 531
ANSI UPDATE 531
FROM Clause UPDATE with Derived Table 531
FROM Clause UPDATE with CTE 532
CTE UPDATE 532

MERGE for Combination INSERT, UPDATE or DELETE 533

Using MERGE Instead of UPDATE 536

CHAPTER 17: The Magic of Transact-SQL Programming 537

IF...ELSE Conditional 537

WHILE Looping - UPDATE in Batches 538

WHILE Loop Usage in Cursors 539

WHILE Loop with Table Variable (@tablevariable) 540

T-SQL Transaction 541
    DELETE from 2 Tables with TRANSACTION Control 541

Stored Procedure with Input & Output Parameters 542

Dynamic SQL Stored Procedure to REBUILD Indexes 543

User-Defined Functions 544
    Table-Valued Functions 544
    Table-Valued Function for PRIME Numbers Generation 545
    Inline Functions 546
    Scalar Functions 547

Dynamic PIVOT Script 548

INSERT, UPDATE & DELETE through a View 549

Sensitive Data Audit Trigger 550

Automatic Timestamp Trigger 551

Recursive Product Assembly 552

Percent on Base Calculation 553

CHAPTER 18: Exporting & Importing Data 554

Saving a T-SQL Script as .sql File 554

Executing a .sql Script File Using SQLCMD 555

Making a T-SQL Script Rerunnable 556

bcp Usage for Exporting & Importing Data 558
    Importing Data with the bcp Utility 559

Exporting Data with SQL Server Import and Export Wizard 560

Importing Data with SQL Server Import and Export Wizard 574

Exporting Database Table to Excel 583

Exporting Data Directly into a Flat File 592

Command Prompt Commands List by HELP 593

BULK INSERT Command 595
   Format File Generation with bcp..595
   Export Data with bcp Format File Option 595
   Import Data with BULK INSERT Format File Option 596
   Importing & Exporting Images 597
   Exporting All Images from Table 599

CHAPTER 19: Maintaining Data Integrity in the Enterprise 601

Why is Data Integrity Paramount 601

Entity Integrity 602

How to Remove Duplicates in a Table 603
   Remove Duplicates with CTE & ROW_NUMBER OVER PARTITION BY 605
   Remove Duplicates with GROUP BY 605

Domain Integrity 606
   Domain Integrity Summary Display with sp_help 607
   THE COLUMNPROPERTY() Function 608

Column List Using System Views & Data Dictionary 609

Declarative Referential Integrity 610
   FOREIGN KEY Constraints Represent the Only Connections Among Tables 613

Enterprise-Level Business Rules Enforcement 616
   Special Role of Triggers 616
   Product Reorder Trigger 617
   Trigger Examples In AdventureWorks2012 619

Business Intelligence in the Enterprise 621
   SSRS: Designing Complex Interactive Reports...621
   SSAS: Designing Multi-Dimensional Cubes 624
   Browsing Multidimensional Cube in Management Explorer 626
   Excel PivotTable Report Using AS Cube Datasource 627
   SSIS: Enterprise Level Data Integration 629
   SSAS, SSIS, SSRS in Configuration Manager...630
   ReportServer & ReportServerTempDB Databases 630

Full-Text Index & Full-Text Search 631

SQL Azure - Enterprise in the Clouds 632
   Getting Started with SQL Azure Database 633
   Connecting Azure SQL Server from Management Studio 634

CHAPTER 20: Query & Stored Procedure Optimization 635

Optimization Basics 635

Optimizing a Query by Reengineering 637
   Examining the Actual Execution Plan 639
   Comparing Execution Plan Cost Summary Pop-ups 640
   Optimizing with Multi Statements Query Using Temporary Tables 641
   Optimizing with Covering Index 643

Optimizing with Indexing 644
   The Larger the Table the More Benefits of Indexing 644
   Check Data & Indexes Fragmentation on a Table 645
   Non-SARGable Predicates Force Index Scan 648
   SARGable Predicate Construction 649
   Stored Procedure Parameter Sniffing & Prevention 650

Optimizing with MERGE 650

Stress Testing a View with Include Client Statistics Feature 651

10 Point Optimization Guide 652
   Object Explorer GUI REBUILD Indexes 653
   UPDATE STATISTICS on All Tables Stored Procedure 654
   Blocking of a Query by Another Query 655
   Activity Monitor 656
   Operational Solutions for Performance Problems 656
   Server & Database Standard Reports 657
   Server Dashboard 658

Batching Large INSERT, UPDATE & DELETE 659

Database Engine Tuning Advisor 660

CHAPTER 21: Advanced T-SQL Programming Topics 661

String Pattern Matching & Parsing 661
   The LIKE Operator 661
   The CHARINDEX() Function 662
   The PATINDEX() Function 663

XXII

Composable DML - INSERT into 2 Tables with One Statement **664**

Double Assignment Operator **665**

Running Total & Average Calculation with the OVER Clause **666**
    Running Total with Subquery - Ye Olde Way..667
    Running Total with Multiple Assignment UPDATE 668

Subtotal, Total & Grand Total GROUPING Function **669**

The GROUP BY Clause with GROUPING SETS **670**

SELECT Top N from Each Group **671**
    SELECT Top N from Each Group Ye Olde Way 672

UPDATE PRIMARY KEY & Connecting FK in a Transaction **672**
    Disable & Enable FOREIGN KEY Constraint 672

Table-Valued Parameters **673**

Creating Comma Delimited String from a Column **675**
    Configuring Comma Delimited Result Sets in SSMS..676

Nesting Cursors **677**
    Set Based Operations Equivalent Code 679

Advanced Graphical Query Designer **680**
    Aliasing Tables in the Diagram Pane 680
    Specifying OUTER JOIN in Diagram Pane..681

Template Explorer & Browser **683**
    Create Inline Function Template 684

Entering PowerShell from Object Explorer **687**

PowerShell Command List **688**

TRY...CATCH Block With TRANSACTION **689**

SET TRANSACTION ISOLATION LEVEL Command **690**
    READ UNCOMMITTED Isolation Level - Dirty Reads...691
    READ COMMITTED Isolation Level - Default for SQL Server 692
    REPEATABLE READ Isolation Level 693
    SERIALIZABLE Isolation Level 695
    SNAPSHOT Isolation Level 696
    Tabular Summary of Isolation Levels...697

INSERT Data Into Parent-Child Tables in One Transaction **698**
    ROLLBACK Does Not Roll Back Everything..699

SQL Server 2014 Design & Programming

XXIII

Optimistic Concurrency Control 700

Xquery Examples 705
    The query() Method 705
    value() Method 707
    nodes() Method 707
    exist() Method 708
    modify() Method 710
    Insert (XML DML) 711
    Delete (XML DML) 712

Working with hierarchyid Data Type 713
    Orgchart Based on AdventureWorks2012 713
    Inline User-Defined Function OrgChart at Any Level 715
    hierarchyid System Functions 716
    Sorting Outline Numbers with hierarchyid 716

Calculate Percent Ratios by Groups 717

Dynamic SQL PIVOT 718

Date Range Programming with Datetime Column 720

4-Week 13 Month Calendar 723

DDL Trigger on DATABASE CREATE 724

Spatial Data Types: Geometry & Geography 725
    The POLYGON & STLength() Functions 725
    Polygon Difference & Intersection 726
    Geometry Area & CIRCULARSTRING Functions 727
    The geography Data Type in Map Application 729
    Surveying Spatial Locations in Person.Address with TABLESAMPLE 730

Data Encryption & Decryption 731

Database Backup 732
    Full Database Backup with Verification 732
    Full Database Backup with Datestamp in Filename 732
    Backup of a Single Table 733
    Setting SSMS Query Options to Include Double Quotes with Strings 734

Database Restore 735
    Restore of a Single Table 736

The Database Maintenance Plan Wizard 738

Configure Stored Procedure As SS Agent Job & Schedule 743

SQL Server 2014 Design & Programming

FOR XML Clause 744
    FOR XML RAW 744
    FOR XML AUTO 744
    FOR XML EXPLICIT 745
    FOR XML PATH 746
    Concatenation Loop With XML PATH 747

Interesting T-SQL Scripts 748

Transforming Dynamic SQL Result Set into a View 751
    Accessing a View from Excel 751

Querying the Database from a Client C# Program 753

CHAPTER 22: In-Memory OLTP *755*

SQL Server 2014 RTM In-Memory OLTP Sample 755
    Performance Comparison Of In-Memory & On-Disk Tables 757

Memory Optimization Advisor 758
    Launching the Memory Optimization Advisor 759

Memory Optimized Table Performance 767
    Speed Comparison for GROUP BY Query 769
    Comparing Performance with WHERE Clause Present..771

In-Memory OLTP Highlights 772

APPENDIX A: Job Interview Questions *773*

Selected Database Design Questions 773

Selected Database Programming Questions 774

APPENDIX B: Job Interview Answers *775*

Selected Database Design Answers 775

Selected Database Programming Answers 776

INDEX of SQL Server 2014 Design & Programming *777*

Index of the Most Important Topics 777

INTRODUCTION

SQL Server 2014 programming builds on achievements of decades in advanced relational database technology. Among the new SQL Server 2014 features is prominent: in-memory OLTP tables. Disk was always the slowest part of the computer system. Since memory is abundant, it is logical to place tables into memory to gain in performance. Programming SQL Server 2014 is fun due to the host of marvelous tools available for the developer in SQL Server Management Studio and Visual Studio. Graphical query designer, for example, helps the developer to develop the JOIN structure of a complex query. SQL Server 2014 provides a highly productive environment for database software development.

SQL Server 2014 introduces 3 new database design features: in-memory OLTP tables, inline index declaration in CREATE TABLE statement and updateable clustered columnstore indexes. In-memory OLTP aims to boost performance by reducing disk io as memory capacities are expanding frequently beyond the size of the database. SQL Server 2012 columnstore indexes are static. Updateable columnstore index expands the applicability of the performance feature. Inline index declaration elevates indexes to the level of PRIMARY KEY, FOREIGN KEY, CHECK constraint and DEFAULT constraint which can be declared inline.

Developers across the world face database issues daily. While immersed in procedural languages with loops, RDBMS forces them to think in terms of sets without loops. It takes transition. It takes training. It takes experience. Developers are exposed also to Excel worksheets, or spreadsheets, as they were called in the not so distant past. So, if you know worksheets, how hard can databases be? After all, worksheets look pretty much like database tables, don't they? The big difference is the connections among well-designed tables. A database is a set of connected tables, which represent entities in the real world. A database can be 100 connected tables or 3000. The connection is very simple: row A in table Alpha has affiliated data with row B in table Beta. However, even with 200 tables and 300 connections (FOREIGN KEY references), it takes a good amount of time to become familiar to the point of having an acceptable working knowledge.

"The Cemetery of Computer Languages" is expanding. You can see tombstones like PL/1, Forth, Ada, Pascal, LISP, RPG, APL, SNOBOL, JOVIAL, Algol – the list goes on. For some, the future is in question: PowerBuilder, ColdFusion, FORTRAN and COBOL. On the other hand, SQL is running strong after 3 decades of glorious existence. What is the difference? The basic difference is that SQL can handle large datasets in a consistent manner based on mathematical foundations. You can throw together a computer language easily: assignment statements, looping, if-then conditional, 300 library functions, and voila! Here is the new language: Mars/1, named after the red planet to be fashionable with NASA's new Mars robot. However, can Mars/1 JOIN a table of 1 million rows with a table of 10 million rows in a second? The success of SQL language is so compelling that other technologies are tagged onto it like XML/XQuery, which deals with semi-structured information objects. In SQL you are thinking at a high level. In C# or Java, you are dealing with details – lots of them. That is the major difference.

Why is so much of the book dedicated to database design? Why not plunge into SQL coding and eventually the developer will get a hang of the design? Because high-level thinking requires thinking at the database design level. A farmer has six mules. H how do we model it in the database? We design the Farmer and FarmAnimal tables, and then connect them with FarmerID FOREIGN KEY in FarmAnimal referencing the FarmerID PRIMARY KEY in the Farmer table. What is the big deal about it? It looks so simple. In fact, how about just calling the tables Table1 and Table2 to be more generic. Ouch! Meaningful naming is the very basis of good database design. Relational database design is truly simple for simple well-understood models. The challenge starts in modeling complex objects such as financial derivative instruments, airplane passenger scheduling, or a social network website. When you need to add 5 new tables to a 1000 table database and hook them in (define FOREIGN KEY references) correctly, it is a huge challenge. To begin with, some of the five new tables may already be redundant, but you don't know that until you understand what the 1000 tables are really storing. Frequently, learning the application area is the biggest challenge for a developer when starting a new job.

The SQL language is simple to program and read even when touching 10 tables. Complexities abound though. The very first one: does the SQL statement touch the right data set – 999 records and 1000 or 998? T-SQL statements are turned into Transact-SQL scripts, stored procedures, and user-defined functions, and trigger server-side database objects. They can be short 5 statement programs or long 1000 statement programs. The style of Transact-SQL programming is different from the style in procedural programming languages. There are no arrays, only tables or table variables. Typically, there is no looping, only set-based operation. Error control is different. Testing and debugging is relatively simple in Transact-SQL due to the interactive environment and the magic of selecting and executing a part without recompiling the whole.

WHOM THIS BOOK IS FOR

Developers, programmers, and systems analysts who are new to relational database technology will find this book of value. It is also applicable for developers, designers, and administrators, who know some SQL programming and database design, but wish to expand their RDBMS design and development technology horizons. Familiarity with another computer language is assumed. The book has lots of queries, lots of T-SQL scripts, and plenty to learn. The best way to learn it is to type in the query in your own SQL Server copy and test it, examine it, change it. Wouldn't it be easier just to copy and paste it? It would, but the learning value would diminish. You need to feel the SQL language in your fingers. SQL queries must "pour" out from your fingers into the keyboard. Why is that so important? After all, everything can be found on the web and just be copied and pasted? Well, not exactly. If you want to be an expert, it has to be in your head not on the web. Second, when your supervisor is looking over your shoulder, "Charlie, can you tell me what the total revenue is for March." you have to be able to type in the query without a web search and provide the results to your superior promptly.

ABOUT THIS BOOK

Beginning Relational Database Design and Beginning Transact-SQL Programming is not a reference manual. Rather you will learn by examples: there are over 1,100 SELECT queries in the book. Instead of imaginary tables, the book uses the SQL Server sample databases for explanations and examples: pubs (PRIMARY KEYs 9, FOREIGN KEYs 10), Northwind (PRIMARY KEYs 13, FOREIGN KEYs 13) and the

AdventureWorks family. Among them: AdventureWorks, AdventureWorks2008, AdventureWorks2012 (PRIMARY KEYs 71, FOREIGN KEYs 90), and AdventureWorksDW2012 (PRIMARY KEYs 27, FOREIGN KEYs 44). The book introduces relational database design concepts, and then reinforces them again and again, not to bore the reader, but rather to indoctrinate with relational database design principles. Light weight SQL starts at the beginning of the book, because working with database metadata (not the content of the database, rather data which describes the database) is essential for understanding database design. By the time the reader gets to T-SQL programming, he already knows basic SQL programming from the database design section of the book. The book was designed to be readable in any environment, even on the beach, laptop available or no laptop in sight at all. All queries are followed by results row count and/or full/partial results listing in tabular (grid) format. For full benefits though, the reader should try out the T-SQL queries and scripts as he progresses from page to page, topic to topic. Example for SQL Server 2014 T-SQL query and results presentation:

```
SELECT         V.Name                                    AS Vendor,
               FORMAT(SUM(POH.TotalDue), 'c', 'en-US')   AS [Total Purchase],
               FORMAT(AVG(POH.TotalDue), 'c', 'en-US')   AS [Average Purchase]
FROM AdventureWorks.Purchasing.Vendor AS V
    INNER JOIN AdventureWorks.Purchasing.PurchaseOrderHeader AS POH
        ON V.VendorID = POH.VendorID
GROUP BY V.Name  ORDER BY Vendor;
-- (79 row(s) affected) - Partial results.
```

Vendor	Total Purchase	Average Purchase
Advanced Bicycles	$28,502.09	$558.86
Allenson Cycles	$498,589.59	$9,776.27
American Bicycles and Wheels	$9,641.01	$189.04
American Bikes	$1,149,489.84	$22,539.02

CONVENTIONS USED IN THIS BOOK

- The Transact-SQL queries and scripts (sequence of statements) are shaded.
- The number of resulting rows is displayed as a comment line: -- (79 row(s) affected).
- The results of the queries are usually displayed in grid format.
- Less frequently, the results are enclosed in comment markers: /*...... */.
- When a query is a trivial variation of a previous query, no result is displayed.

While the intention of the book is database design and database development, SQL Server installation and some database administration tasks are included.

"Apparatus Intelligentia

vincet

Humanum Intelligentia"

Dedicated to

JOHN VON NEUMANN

Father of the Digital Computer

CHAPTER 1: SQL Server Sample & System Databases

AdventureWorks Series of OLTP Databases

AdventureWorks sample On Line Transaction Processing (OLTP) database has been introduced with SQL Server 2005 to replace the previous sample database Northwind, a fictional gourmet food items distributor. The intent of the AdventureWorks sample database is to support the business operations of AdventureWorks Cycles, a fictitious mountain, touring and road bike manufacturer. The company sells through dealer network and online on the web. In addition to bikes, it sells frames and parts as well as accessories such as helmets, biking clothes and water bottles. The AdventureWorks2012 database image of Touring-1000 Blue, 50 bike in Production.ProductPhoto table.

T-SQL query to generate the list of tables of AdventureWorks2012 in 5 columns. The core query is simple. Presenting the results in 5 columns instead of 1 column adds a bit of complexity.

```
;WITH cteTableList AS (       SELECT CONCAT(SCHEMA_NAME(schema_id), '.', name)           AS TableName,
   (( ROW_NUMBER() OVER( ORDER BY CONCAT(SCHEMA_NAME(schema_id),'.', name)) ) % 5)     AS Remainder,
   (( ROW_NUMBER() OVER( ORDER BY CONCAT(SCHEMA_NAME(schema_id),'.', name)) - 1 )/ 5)  AS Quotient
                   FROM AdventureWorks2012.sys.tables),
CTE AS (SELECT TableName, CASE WHEN Remainder=0 THEN 5 ELSE Remainder END AS Remainder, Quotient
        FROM cteTableList)
SELECT    MAX(CASE WHEN Remainder = 1 THEN TableName END),
          MAX(CASE WHEN Remainder = 2 THEN TableName END),
          MAX(CASE WHEN Remainder = 3 THEN TableName END),
          MAX(CASE WHEN Remainder = 4 THEN TableName END),
          MAX(CASE WHEN Remainder = 5 THEN TableName END)
FROM  CTE GROUP  BY Quotient ORDER  BY Quotient;
GO
```

The query result set in grid format: tables in AdventureWorks2012

dbo.AWBuildVersion	dbo.DatabaseLog	dbo.ErrorLog	HumanResources.Department	HumanResources.Employee
HumanResources.EmployeeDepartmentHistory	HumanResources.EmployeePayHistory	HumanResources.JobCandidate	HumanResources.Shift	Person.Address
Person.AddressType	Person.BusinessEntity	Person.BusinessEntityAddress	Person.BusinessEntityContact	Person.ContactType
Person.CountryRegion	Person.EmailAddress	Person.Password	Person.Person	Person.PersonPhone
Person.PhoneNumberType	Person.StateProvince	Production.BillOfMaterials	Production.Culture	Production.Document
Production.Illustration	Production.Location	Production.Product	Production.ProductCategory	Production.ProductCostHistory
Production.ProductDescription	Production.ProductDocument	Production.ProductInventory	Production.ProductListPriceHistory	Production.ProductModel
Production.ProductModelIllustration	Production.ProductModelProductDescriptionCulture	Production.ProductPhoto	Production.ProductProductPhoto	Production.ProductReview
Production.ProductSubcategory	Production.ScrapReason	Production.TransactionHistory	Production.TransactionHistoryArchive	Production.UnitMeasure
Production.WorkOrder	Production.WorkOrderRouting	Purchasing.ProductVendor	Purchasing.PurchaseOrderDetail	Purchasing.PurchaseOrderHeader
Purchasing.ShipMethod	Purchasing.Vendor	Sales.CountryRegionCurrency	Sales.CreditCard	Sales.Currency
Sales.CurrencyRate	Sales.Customer	Sales.PersonCreditCard	Sales.SalesOrderDetail	Sales.SalesOrderHeader
Sales.SalesOrderHeaderSalesReason	Sales.SalesPerson	Sales.SalesPersonQuotaHistory	Sales.SalesReason	Sales.SalesTaxRate
Sales.SalesTerritory	Sales.SalesTerritoryHistory	Sales.ShoppingCartItem	Sales.SpecialOffer	Sales.SpecialOfferProduct
Sales.Store	NULL	NULL	NULL	NULL

CHAPTER 1: SQL Server Sample & System Databases

AdventureWorks Series of OLTP Databases

Diagram of Person.Person & Related Tables

Database diagram displays the Person.Person and related tables. PRIMARY KEYs are marked with a gold (in color display) key. The "oo-------->" line is interpreted as many-to-one relationship. For example a person (one) can have one or more (many) credit cards. The "oo" side is the table with **FOREIGN KEY** referencing the gold key side table with the **PRIMARY KEY**.

CHAPTER 1: SQL Server Sample & System Databases

Diagram of Sales.SalesOrderHeader and Related Tables

Database diagram displays Sales.SalesOrderHeader and all tables related with **FOREIGN KEY** constraints. The SalesOrderHeader table stores the general information about each order. Line items, e.g. 5 Helmets at $30 each, are stored in the SalesOrderDetail table.

CHAPTER 1: SQL Server Sample & System Databases

SELECT Query Basics

We have to use "light-weight" SQL (Structured Query Language) in the database design lessons. The reason is that rather difficult to discuss any database related topic without demonstration T-SQL scripts, in fact it would not make sense. **Relational database** and the **SQL language** are "married" to each other forever and ever.

The Simplest SELECT Statement

The simplest SELECT statement is "SELECT * FROM TableNameX" as demonstrated following. The "*" means wildcard inclusion of all columns in the table. Since there is no any other clause in the SELECT statement, it means also to retrieve all rows in the **table in no particular order**. Small tables which were populated in order are usually retrieved in order even though there is no ORDER BY clause. But this behaviour is purely coincidental. **Only ORDER BY clause can guarantee a sorted output.**

SELECT * FROM AdventureWorks2012.HumanResources.Department;
-- (16 row(s) affected)

DepartmentID	Name	GroupName	ModifiedDate
1	Engineering	Research and Development	2002-06-01 00:00:00.000
2	Tool Design	Research and Development	2002-06-01 00:00:00.000
3	Sales	Sales and Marketing	2002-06-01 00:00:00.000
4	Marketing	Sales and Marketing	2002-06-01 00:00:00.000
5	Purchasing	Inventory Management	2002-06-01 00:00:00.000
6	Research and Development	Research and Development	2002-06-01 00:00:00.000
7	Production	Manufacturing	2002-06-01 00:00:00.000
8	Production Control	Manufacturing	2002-06-01 00:00:00.000
9	Human Resources	Executive General and Administration	2002-06-01 00:00:00.000
10	Finance	Executive General and Administration	2002-06-01 00:00:00.000
11	Information Services	Executive General and Administration	2002-06-01 00:00:00.000
12	Document Control	Quality Assurance	2002-06-01 00:00:00.000
13	Quality Assurance	Quality Assurance	2002-06-01 00:00:00.000
14	Facilities and Maintenance	Executive General and Administration	2002-06-01 00:00:00.000
15	Shipping and Receiving	Inventory Management	2002-06-01 00:00:00.000
16	Executive	Executive General and Administration	2002-06-01 00:00:00.000

When tables are JOINed, SELECT * returns all the columns with all the data in the participant tables.

SELECT TOP 3 * FROM Sales.SalesOrderHeader H
         INNER JOIN Sales.SalesOrderDetail D
            ON H.SalesOrderID = D.SalesOrderID;
-- 121,317 rows in the JOIN

CHAPTER 1: SQL Server Sample & System Databases

Query Result Set In Text Format

If no grid format available, text format can be used. While it works, it is a challenge to read it, but computer geeks are used to this kind of data dump.

```
/* SalesOrderID RevisionNumber OrderDate         DueDate          ShipDate           Status
OnlineOrderFlag SalesOrderNumber      PurchaseOrderNumber       AccountNumber   CustomerID
SalesPersonID TerritoryID BillToAddressID ShipToAddressID ShipMethodID CreditCardID
CreditCardApprovalCode CurrencyRateID SubTotal       TaxAmt           Freight          TotalDue
Comment                                                                        rowguid
ModifiedDate        SalesOrderID SalesOrderDetailID CarrierTrackingNumber    OrderQty ProductID
SpecialOfferID UnitPrice         UnitPriceDiscount    LineTotal       rowguid         ModifiedDate
------------ -------------- ----------------------- ----------------------- ---------------------- ------ -------------- --------------------
----- ---------------------- ---------------- ------------ ------------ ------------ ----------------- ----------- ---------
- ---------------------- --------------- --------------------- ------------------- --------------------- ------------------ ----------------
------------------------------------------------------------------------------------------                           ----------------------
-------- ---------------------- -------------- --------------------- -------------------- --------------- ---------- ---------------- ------------
--------- ----------------------- --------------------- --------------------- ---------------------- ----------------------- ------------------

43735       3           2005-07-10 00:00:00.000 2005-07-22 00:00:00.000 2005-07-17 00:00:00.000 5        1
SO43735        NULL             10-4030-016522 16522      NULL       9        25384         25384
1       6526       1034619Vi33896       119       3578.27         286.2616       89.4568
3953.9884        NULL                                                                 98F80245-
C398-4562-BDAF-EA3E9A0DDFAC 2005-07-17 00:00:00.000 43735        391        NULL         1
749     1       3578.27         0.00        3578.270000         74838EF7-FDEB-4EB3-8978-
BA310FBA82E6 2005-07-10 00:00:00.000
43736       3           2005-07-10 00:00:00.000 2005-07-22 00:00:00.000 2005-07-17 00:00:00.000 5        1
SO43736        NULL             10-4030-011002 11002      NULL       9        20336         20336
1       1416       1135092Vi7270       119       3399.99         271.9992       84.9998
3756.989        NULL                                                                  C14E29E7-
DB11-44EF-943E-143925A5A9AE 2005-07-17 00:00:00.000 43736        392        NULL         1
773     1       3399.99         0.00        3399.990000         3A0229FA-0A03-4126-
97CE-C3425968B670 2005-07-10 00:00:00.000
43737       3           2005-07-11 00:00:00.000 2005-07-23 00:00:00.000 2005-07-18 00:00:00.000 5        1
SO43737        NULL             10-4030-013261 13261      NULL       8        29772         29772
1       NULL       NULL             136       3578.27         286.2616       89.4568         3953.9884
NULL                                                                  0B3E274D-E5A8-4E8C-A417-
0EAFABCFF162 2005-07-18 00:00:00.000 43737        393        NULL         1      750       1
3578.27         0.00        3578.270000         65AFCCE8-CA28-41C4-9A07-0265FB2DA5C8
2005-07-11 00:00:00.000                 (3 row(s) affected)    */
```

```
SELECT MatchingRows = COUNT(*) FROM AdventureWorks2012.Sales.SalesOrderHeader H
   INNER JOIN AdventureWorks2012.Sales.SalesOrderDetail D
       ON H.SalesOrderID = D.SalesOrderID;    -- INNER JOIN MatchingRows 121317
```

```
SELECT AllRowsInDetail = COUNT(*) FROM AdventureWorks2012.Sales.SalesOrderDetail
-- AllRowsInDetail 121317
```

CHAPTER 1: SQL Server Sample & System Databases

SELECT Query Basics

SELECT Query with WHERE Clause Predicate

Query to demonstrate how can we be selective with columns, furthermore, filter returned rows (WHERE clause) and sort them (ORDER BY clause).

```sql
SELECT Name AS ProductName,
       ProductNumber,
       ListPrice,
       Color
FROM Production.Product
WHERE Color is not NULL
ORDER BY ProductNumber;
```

#	ProductName	ProductNum...	ListPrice	Color
1	Mountain-500 Black, 40	BK-M18B-40	539.99	Black
2	Mountain-500 Black, 42	BK-M18B-42	539.99	Black
3	Mountain-500 Black, 44	BK-M18B-44	539.99	Black
4	Mountain-500 Black, 48	BK-M18B-48	539.99	Black
5	Mountain-500 Black, 52	BK-M18B-52	539.99	Black
6	Mountain-500 Silver, 40	BK-M18S-40	564.99	Silver
7	Mountain-500 Silver, 42	BK-M18S-42	564.99	Silver
8	Mountain-500 Silver, 44	BK-M18S-44	564.99	Silver
9	Mountain-500 Silver, 48	BK-M18S-48	564.99	Silver
10	Mountain-500 Silver, 52	BK-M18S-52	564.99	Silver
11	Mountain-400-W Silve...	BK-M38S-38	769.49	Silver
12	Mountain-400-W Silve...	BK-M38S-40	769.49	Silver
13	Mountain-400-W Silve...	BK-M38S-42	769.49	Silver
14	Mountain-400-W Silve...	BK-M38S-46	769.49	Silver
15	Mountain-300 Black, 38	BK-M47B-38	1079.99	Black
16	Mountain-300 Black, 40	BK-M47B-40	1079.99	Black
17	Mountain-300 Black, 44	BK-M47B-44	1079.99	Black

256 rows

CHAPTER 1: SQL Server Sample & System Databases

Aggregating Data with GROUP BY Query

The second basic query is GROUP BY aggregation which creates a **summary** of detail data. GROUP BY query can be used to preview, review, survey, assess, and analyze data at a high level.

```sql
-- GROUP BY SELECT with count and average aggregates
SELECT  Color,
        COUNT(*)        AS PrdCnt,
        AVG(ListPrice)  AS AvgPrice
FROM Production.Product
WHERE Color is not null
GROUP BY Color
ORDER BY PrdCnt DESC
GO
```

	Color	PrdCnt	AvgPrice
1	Black	93	725.121
2	Silver	43	850.3053
3	Red	38	1401.95
4	Yellow	36	959.0913
5	Blue	26	923.6792
6	Multi	8	59.865
7	Silver/Black	7	64.0185
8	White	4	9.245
9	Grey	1	125.00

NOTE
GROUP BY aggregate queries can efficiently "fingerprint" (profile) data in tables, even millions of rows. GROUP BY aggregates form the computational base of Business Intelligence.

CHAPTER 1: SQL Server Sample & System Databases

SELECT Query Basics

GROUP BY Query with 2 Tables & ORDER BY for Sorting

JOINing two tables on matching KEYs, FOREIGN KEY to PRIMARY KEY, to combine the data contents in a consistent fashion.

```
-- INNER JOIN of 2 tables; GROUP BY with COUNT & AVG aggregates
SELECT sc.Name          AS Subcategory,
       COUNT(*)         AS PrdCnt,
       AVG(ListPrice)   AS AvgPrice
FROM Production.Product p
    INNER JOIN Production.ProductSubcategory sc
        ON p.ProductSubcategoryID = sc.ProductSubcategoryID
WHERE Color is not NULL
GROUP BY sc.Name
ORDER BY PrdCnt DESC;
GO
```

	Subcategory	PrdCnt	AvgPrice
1	Road Bikes	43	1597.45
2	Road Frames	33	780.0436
3	Mountain Bikes	32	1683.365
4	Mountain Frames	28	678.2535
5	Touring Bikes	22	1425.2481
6	Touring Frames	18	631.4155
7	Wheels	14	220.9292

LEN(), DATALENGTH(), LTRIM() & RTRIM() Functions

The LEN() function counts characters without the trailing spaces. DATALENGTH() counts storage bytes including trailing spaces. LTRIM() trims leading spaces, RTRIM() trims trailing spaces.

```
DECLARE @W varchar(32)= CHAR(32)+'Denver'+CHAR(32);
DECLARE @UW nvarchar(32) = CHAR(32)+N'MEGŐRZÉSE'+CHAR(32);  -- UNICODE 2 bytes per character
SELECT Length=LEN(@W), DLength=DATALENGTH (@W);                                      -- 7  8
SELECT Length=LEN(@UW), DLength=DATALENGTH (@UW);                                    -- 10 22
SELECT Length=LEN(LTRIM(RTRIM(@W))), DLength=DATALENGTH (LTRIM(RTRIM(@W)));          -- 6  6
SELECT Length=LEN(LTRIM(RTRIM(@UW))), DLength=DATALENGTH (LTRIM(RTRIM(@UW)));        -- 9  18
```

CHAPTER 1: SQL Server Sample & System Databases

Finding All Accessories in Production.Product Table

Query to list all accessories (a category) for sale.

USE AdventureWorks2012;

```
SELECT      UPPER(PC.Name) AS Category, PSC.Name              AS Subcategory,
            P.Name AS Product, FORMAT(ListPrice, 'c', 'en-US')  AS ListPrice,
            FORMAT(StandardCost, 'c', 'en-US')                  AS StandardCost
FROM Production.Product AS P
    INNER JOIN Production.ProductSubcategory AS PSC
        ON PSC.ProductSubcategoryID = P.ProductSubcategoryID
    INNER JOIN Production.ProductCategory AS PC
        ON PC.ProductCategoryID = PSC.ProductCategoryID
WHERE PC.Name = 'Accessories'
ORDER BY Category, Subcategory, Product;      -- (29 row(s) affected) - Partial results.
```

Category	Subcategory	Product	ListPrice	StandardCost
ACCESSORIES	Bike Racks	Hitch Rack - 4-Bike	$120.00	$44.88
ACCESSORIES	Bike Stands	All-Purpose Bike Stand	$159.00	$59.47
ACCESSORIES	Bottles and Cages	Mountain Bottle Cage	$9.99	$3.74
ACCESSORIES	Bottles and Cages	Road Bottle Cage	$8.99	$3.36
ACCESSORIES	Bottles and Cages	Water Bottle - 30 oz.	$4.99	$1.87
ACCESSORIES	Cleaners	Bike Wash - Dissolver	$7.95	$2.97

Using Implicit or Explicit Conversion

Implicit conversion results in simpler code and may even be faster. However, if we really need a specific conversion, explicit conversion should be used. In the ShipDate datetime column example, the implicit & explicit conversions yield the same results.

```
SELECT SalesOrderID, OrderDate, ShipDate, CustomerID, SubTotal
FROM Sales.SalesOrderHeader
WHERE ShipDate = '2008-03-08';                         -- Implicit conversion to datetime

/*    WHERE Shipdate = CONVERT(DATETIME, '2008-03-08');   -- Explicit conversion
      WHERE Shipdate = CONVERT(DATE,     '2008-03-08');   -- Explicit conversion */
-- (247 row(s) affected) - Partial results.
```

SalesOrderID	OrderDate	ShipDate	CustomerID	SubTotal
65089	2008-02-29 00:00:00.000	2008-03-08 00:00:00.000	30079	1466.01
65090	2008-02-29 00:00:00.000	2008-03-08 00:00:00.000	29812	98.774
65151	2008-03-01 00:00:00.000	2008-03-08 00:00:00.000	30072	76.20

SELECT Query Basics

How Can SQL Work without Looping?
Looping is implicit in the SQL language. The commands are set oriented and carried out for each member of the set be it 5 or 500 millions in an unordered manner.

SELECT * FROM AdventureWorks2012.Sales.SalesOrderDetail;   (121317 row(s) affected)

SQL Server database engine looped through internally on all rows in SalesOrderDetail table in an unordered way. In fact the database engine may have used some ordering for efficiency, but that behaviour is a blackbox as far as programming concerned. Implicit looping makes SQL statements so simple, yet immensely powerful for information access from low level to high level.

Single-Valued SQL Queries
Single-valued SQL queries are very important because **we can use them where ever the T-SQL syntax requires a single value just by enclosing the query in parenthesis**. The next T-SQL query returns a single value, a cell from the table which is the intersection of a row and a column.

SELECT ListPrice FROM AdventureWorks2012.Production.Product WHERE ProductID = 800;
-- (1 row(s) affected)

ListPrice
1120.49

The "**>**" **comparison operator requires a single value on the right hand side** so we plug in the single-valued query. The WHERE condition is evaluated for each row (implicit looping).

SELECT ProductID, Name AS ProductName, ListPrice
FROM AdventureWorks2012.Production.Product   -- 504 rows
WHERE ListPrice > 2 * (
        SELECT ListPrice FROM AdventureWorks2012.Production.Product
        WHERE ProductID = 800
)
ORDER BY ListPrice DESC, ProductName;   -- (35 row(s) affected) - Partial results.

ProductID	ProductName	ListPrice
750	Road-150 Red, 44	3578.27
751	Road-150 Red, 48	3578.27
752	Road-150 Red, 52	3578.27
753	Road-150 Red, 56	3578.27
749	Road-150 Red, 62	3578.27
771	Mountain-100 Silver, 38	3399.99

Data Dictionary Description of Tables in the Sales Schema

It is not easy to understand a database with 70 tables, even harder with 2,000 tables. Documentation is very helpful, if not essential, for any database. SQL Server provides Data Dictionary facility for documenting tables and other objects in the database. Data which describes the design & structure of a database is called **metadata**. Here is the high level documentation of tables in the Sales schema using the fn_listextendedproperty system function.

```
SELECT
        CONCAT('Sales.', objname COLLATE DATABASE_DEFAULT)      AS TableName,
        value                                                    AS [Description]
FROM fn_listextendedproperty (NULL, 'schema', 'Sales', 'table', default, NULL, NULL)
ORDER BY TableName;
```

TableName	Description
Sales.ContactCreditCard	Cross-reference table mapping customers in the Contact table to their credit card information in the CreditCard table.
Sales.CountryRegionCurrency	Cross-reference table mapping ISO currency codes to a country or region.
Sales.CreditCard	Customer credit card information.
Sales.Currency	Lookup table containing standard ISO currencies.
Sales.CurrencyRate	Currency exchange rates.
Sales.Customer	Current customer information. Also see the Individual and Store tables.
Sales.CustomerAddress	Cross-reference table mapping customers to their address(es).
Sales.Individual	Demographic data about customers that purchase Adventure Works products online.
Sales.SalesOrderDetail	Individual products associated with a specific sales order. See SalesOrderHeader.
Sales.SalesOrderHeader	General sales order information.
Sales.SalesOrderHeaderSalesReason	Cross-reference table mapping sales orders to sales reason codes.
Sales.SalesPerson	Sales representative current information.
Sales.SalesPersonQuotaHistory	Sales performance tracking.
Sales.SalesReason	Lookup table of customer purchase reasons.
Sales.SalesTaxRate	Tax rate lookup table.
Sales.SalesTerritory	Sales territory lookup table.
Sales.SalesTerritoryHistory	Sales representative transfers to other sales territories.
Sales.ShoppingCartItem	Contains online customer orders until the order is submitted or cancelled.
Sales.SpecialOffer	Sale discounts lookup table.
Sales.SpecialOfferProduct	Cross-reference table mapping products to special offer discounts.
Sales.Store	Customers (resellers) of Adventure Works products.
Sales.StoreContact	Cross-reference table mapping stores and their employees.

NULL Values in Tables & Query Results

NULL means no value. If so why do we capitalize it? We don't have to. Somehow, it became a custom in the RDBMS industry, nobody knows anymore how it started. Since the U.S. default collation for server and databases are case insensitive, we can just use "null" as well. **NULL value is different from empty string ('') or 0 (zero) which can be tested by the "=" or "!=" operators.** If a database table does not have a value in a cell for whatever reason, it is marked (flagged) as NULL by the database engine. When a value is entered, the NULL marking goes away. **NULL values can be tested by "IS NULL" or "IS NOT NULL" operators, but not the "=" or "!=" operators.**

The likelihood is high that the color attribute is not applicable to items like tire tube, that is the reason that some cell values were left unassigned (null).

```
SELECT TOP 5   Name                          AS ProductName,
               ProductNumber,
               ListPrice,
               Color
FROM AdventureWorks2012.Production.Product
WHERE Color IS NULL  ORDER BY ProductName DESC;
```

ProductName	ProductNumber	ListPrice	Color
Water Bottle - 30 oz.	WB-H098	4.99	NULL
Touring Tire Tube	TT-T092	4.99	NULL
Touring Tire	TI-T723	28.99	NULL
Touring Rim	RM-T801	0.00	NULL
Touring End Caps	EC-T209	0.00	NULL

We can do random selection as well and get a mix of products with color and null value.

```
SELECT TOP 5   Name AS ProductName,
               ProductNumber,
               ListPrice,
               Color
FROM AdventureWorks2012.Production.Product  ORDER BY NEWID();   -- Random sort
```

ProductName	ProductNumber	ListPrice	Color
Touring-1000 Yellow, 46	BK-T79Y-46	2384.07	Yellow
HL Spindle/Axle	SD-9872	0.00	NULL
ML Mountain Tire	TI-M602	29.99	NULL
Road-650 Red, 60	BK-R50R-60	782.99	Red
Pinch Bolt	PB-6109	0.00	NULL

NULL Values Generated by Queries

NULL values can be generated by queries as well. Typically, LEFT JOIN, RIGHT JOIN and some functions generate NULLs. The meaning of OUTER JOINs: include no-match rows from the left or right table in addition to the matching rows.

```sql
SELECT TOP 5
            PS.Name                     AS Category,
            P.Name                      AS ProductName,
            ProductNumber,
            ListPrice,
            Color
FROM AdventureWorks2012.Production.Product P
    RIGHT JOIN AdventureWorks2012.Production.ProductSubcategory PS
        ON    PS.ProductSubcategoryID = P.ProductSubcategoryID
            AND ListPrice >= 3500.0
ORDER BY newid();
GO
```

Category	ProductName	ProductNumber	ListPrice	Color
Road Bikes	Road-150 Red, 62	BK-R93R-62	3578.27	Red
Road Bikes	Road-150 Red, 52	BK-R93R-52	3578.27	Red
Bib-Shorts	NULL	NULL	NULL	NULL
Socks	NULL	NULL	NULL	NULL
Cranksets	NULL	NULL	NULL	NULL

Some system functions, like the brand new TRY_CONVERT(), can generate NULL values as well. If the PostalCode cannot be converted into an integer, TRY_CONVERT() returns NULL.

```sql
SELECT TOP 5   ConvertedZip = TRY_CONVERT(INT, PostalCode),
            AddressLine1,
            City,
            PostalCode
FROM Person.Address ORDER by newid();
```

ConvertedZip	AddressLine1	City	PostalCode
91945	5979 El Pueblo	Lemon Grove	91945
NULL	7859 Green Valley Road	London	W1V 5RN
3220	6004 Peabody Road	Geelong	3220
NULL	6713 Eaker Way	Burnaby	V3J 6Z3
NULL	5153 Hackamore Lane	Shawnee	V8Z 4N5

CHAPTER 1: SQL Server Sample & System Databases

Building an FK-PK Diagram in AdventureWorks2012

The **FOREIGN KEY - PRIMARY KEY** diagram of AdventureWorks2012 database with over 70 tables can be built just by adding the tables to the diagram. The FK-PK lines are automatically drawn. An FK-PK line represents a predefined referential constraint.

While all tables are important in a database, tables with the most connections play central roles, in a way analogous to the Sun with planets around it.

```
-- PRIMARY KEY tables with the most FOREIGN KEY references
SELECT          schema_name(schema_id)       AS SchemaName,
                o.name                       AS PKTable,
                count(*)                     AS FKCount
FROM sys.sysforeignkeys s   INNER JOIN sys.objects o    ON s.rkeyid = o.object_id
GROUP BY schema_id, o.name   HAVING count(*) >= 5   ORDER BY FKCount DESC;
```

SchemaName	PKTable	FKCount
Production	Product	14
Person	Person	7
HumanResources	Employee	6
Person	BusinessEntity	5
Sales	SalesTerritory	5

CHAPTER 1: SQL Server Sample & System Databases

AdventureWorksDW2012 Data Warehouse Database

AdventureWorksDW series contain second hand data only since they are Data Warehouse databases. All data originates from other sources such as the AdventureWorks OLTP database & Excel worksheets. Tables in the data warehousing database are divided into two groups: dimension tables & fact tables.

Simple data warehouse query.

```
SELECT          D.CalendarYear AS [Year], C.SalesTerritoryCountry AS [Country],
                FORMAT(SUM(S.SalesAmount),'c0','en-US') AS TotalSales
FROM FactInternetSales AS S  INNER JOIN DimDate AS D ON S.OrderDateKey = D.DateKey
       INNER JOIN DimSalesTerritory AS C ON S.SalesTerritoryKey = C.SalesTerritoryKey
GROUP BY D.CalendarYear, C.SalesTerritoryCountry  ORDER BY Year DESC, SUM(S.SalesAmount) DESC;
```

Year	Country	TotalSales
2008	United States	$3,324,031
2008	Australia	$2,563,884
2008	United Kingdom	$1,210,286
2008	Germany	$1,076,891
2008	France	$922,179

CHAPTER 1: SQL Server Sample & System Databases

AdventureWorksDW2012 Data Warehouse Database

Diagram of a Star Schema in AdventureWorksDW2012

The high level star schema diagram in AdventureWorksDW2012 Data Warehouse database with FactResellerSales fact table and related dimension tables. The temporal dimension table DimDate plays a central role in Business Intelligence data analytics.

Distribution of **PRIMARY KEY - FOREIGN KEY** relationships can be generated from metadata (system views) for the entire Data Warehouse.

```
SELECT   schema_name(schema_id) AS SchemaName, o.name AS PKTable, count(*) AS FKCount
FROM sys.sysforeignkeys s  INNER JOIN sys.objects o   ON s.rkeyid = o.object_id
GROUP BY schema_id, o.name  HAVING COUNT(*) > 2 ORDER BY FKCount DESC;
```

SchemaName	PKTable	FKCount
dbo	DimDate	12
dbo	DimCurrency	4
dbo	DimSalesTerritory	4
dbo	DimEmployee	3
dbo	DimProduct	3

CHAPTER 1: SQL Server Sample & System Databases

AdventureWorks2008 Sample Database

There were substantial changes made from the prior version of the sample database. Among them demonstration use of the **hierarchyid** data type which has been introduced with SS 2008 to support sophisticated tree hierarchy processing. In addition employee, customer and dealer PRIMARY KEYs are pooled together and called BusinessEntityID.

CHAPTER 1: SQL Server Sample & System Databases

AdventureWorks2012 Sample Database

There were no apparent design changes made from the prior version of the sample database. A significant content change: dates were advanced 4 years. An OrderDate (Sales.SalesOrderHeader table) of 2004-02-01 in previous versions is now 2008-02-01.

The OrderDate statistics in the two sample databases.

```
SELECT [Year]        = YEAR(OrderDate),   OrderCount   = COUNT(*)
FROM AdventureWorks2008.Sales.SalesOrderHeader GROUP BY YEAR(OrderDate)
ORDER BY [Year];
```

Year	OrderCount
2001	1379
2002	3692
2003	12443
2004	13951

```
SELECT [Year]        = YEAR(OrderDate),   OrderCount   = COUNT(*)
FROM AdventureWorks2012.Sales.SalesOrderHeader GROUP BY YEAR(OrderDate)
ORDER BY [Year];
```

Year	OrderCount
2005	1379
2006	3692
2007	12443
2008	13951

Starting with SQL Server 2012, numeric figures, among others, can be formatted with the FORMAT function.

```
SELECT [Year]        = YEAR(OrderDate),
       OrderCount    = FORMAT(COUNT(*), '###,###')
FROM AdventureWorks2012.Sales.SalesOrderHeader
GROUP BY YEAR(OrderDate)  ORDER BY [Year];
```

Year	OrderCount
2005	1,379
2006	3,692
2007	12,443
2008	13,951

Production.Product and Related Tables

The Product table is the "center" of the database. The reason is that AdventureWorks Cycles is a product base company selling through dealers and directly to consumers through the internet. You may wonder why are we pushing **FOREIGN KEY - PRIMARY KEY** relationship so vehemently? Because there is nothing else to a database just **well-designed tables and their connections which are FK-PK constraints**.

Simple OLTP query.

```
SELECT Color, WOCount=COUNT(*)  FROM Production.WorkOrder W
     INNER JOIN Production.Product P    ON W.ProductID = P.ProductID  WHERE Color != ''
GROUP BY Color ORDER BY WOCount DESC;
```

Color	WOCount
Black	18952
Silver	6620
Yellow	5231
Red	4764
Blue	2319

CHAPTER 1: SQL Server Sample & System Databases

AdventureWorks2012 Sample Database

Descriptions of Columns in Production.Product Table

Queries to list the description of table and columns from Extended Property (data dictionary).

```
USE AdventureWorks2012;
SELECT        objname AS TableName, value   AS [Description]
FROM fn_listextendedproperty( NULL, 'schema', 'Production', 'table', 'Product', NULL, NULL);
```

TableName	Description
Product	Products sold or used in the manfacturing of sold products.

```
SELECT        'Production.Product'      AS TableName,          -- String literal
              objname                   AS ColumnName,
              value                     AS [Description]
FROM fn_listextendedproperty( NULL, 'schema', 'Production', 'table',
                              'Product', 'column', default);
```

TableName	ColumnName	Description
Production.Product	ProductID	Primary key for Product records.
Production.Product	Name	Name of the product.
Production.Product	ProductNumber	Unique product identification number.
Production.Product	MakeFlag	0 = Product is purchased, 1 = Product is manufactured in-house.
Production.Product	FinishedGoodsFlag	0 = Product is not a salable item. 1 = Product is salable.
Production.Product	Color	Product color.
Production.Product	SafetyStockLevel	Minimum inventory quantity.
Production.Product	ReorderPoint	Inventory level that triggers a purchase order or work order.
Production.Product	StandardCost	Standard cost of the product.
Production.Product	ListPrice	Selling price.
Production.Product	Size	Product size.
Production.Product	SizeUnitMeasureCode	Unit of measure for Size column.
Production.Product	WeightUnitMeasureCode	Unit of measure for Weight column.
Production.Product	Weight	Product weight.
Production.Product	DaysToManufacture	Number of days required to manufacture the product.
Production.Product	ProductLine	R = Road, M = Mountain, T = Touring, S = Standard
Production.Product	Class	H = High, M = Medium, L = Low
Production.Product	Style	W = Womens, M = Mens, U = Universal
Production.Product	ProductSubcategoryID	Product is a member of this product subcategory. Foreign key to ProductSubCategory.ProductSubCategoryID.
Production.Product	ProductModelID	Product is a member of this product model. Foreign key to ProductModel.ProductModelID.
Production.Product	SellStartDate	Date the product was available for sale.
Production.Product	SellEndDate	Date the product was no longer available for sale.
Production.Product	DiscontinuedDate	Date the product was discontinued.
Production.Product	rowguid	ROWGUIDCOL number uniquely identifying the record. Used to support a merge replication sample.
Production.Product	ModifiedDate	Date and time the record was last updated.

CHAPTER 1: SQL Server Sample & System Databases

Mountain Bikes in Production.Product Table

Query to list all mountain bikes offered for sale by AdventureWorks Cycles with category, subcategory, list price and standard cost information.

```
USE AdventureWorks2012;
SELECT  UPPER(PC.Name) AS Category, PSC.Name AS Subcategory,
        P.Name AS Product, FORMAT(ListPrice, 'c', 'en-US') AS ListPrice,
        FORMAT(StandardCost, 'c', 'en-US') AS StandardCost
FROM Production.Product AS P
   INNER JOIN Production.ProductSubcategory AS PSC
            ON PSC.ProductSubcategoryID = P.ProductSubcategoryID
   INNER JOIN Production.ProductCategory AS PC
            ON PC.ProductCategoryID = PSC.ProductCategoryID
WHERE PSC.Name = 'Mountain Bikes'
ORDER BY Category, Subcategory, Product;  -- Partial results
```

Category	Subcategory	Product	ListPrice	StandardCost
BIKES	Mountain Bikes	Mountain-100 Black, 38	$3,374.99	$1,898.09
BIKES	Mountain Bikes	Mountain-100 Black, 42	$3,374.99	$1,898.09
BIKES	Mountain Bikes	Mountain-100 Black, 44	$3,374.99	$1,898.09
BIKES	Mountain Bikes	Mountain-100 Black, 48	$3,374.99	$1,898.09
BIKES	Mountain Bikes	Mountain-100 Silver, 38	$3,399.99	$1,912.15
BIKES	Mountain Bikes	Mountain-100 Silver, 42	$3,399.99	$1,912.15
BIKES	Mountain Bikes	Mountain-100 Silver, 44	$3,399.99	$1,912.15
BIKES	Mountain Bikes	Mountain-100 Silver, 48	$3,399.99	$1,912.15
BIKES	Mountain Bikes	Mountain-200 Black, 38	$2,294.99	$1,251.98
BIKES	Mountain Bikes	Mountain-200 Black, 42	$2,294.99	$1,251.98
BIKES	Mountain Bikes	Mountain-200 Black, 46	$2,294.99	$1,251.98
BIKES	Mountain Bikes	Mountain-200 Silver, 38	$2,319.99	$1,265.62

The SOUNDEX() Function to Check Sound Alikes

Soundex function can be used to find names with different spellings.

```
SELECT DISTINCT LastName FROM AdventureWorks2012.Person.Person
WHERE soundex(LastName)  = soundex('Steel');
```

LastName
Seidel
Sotelo
Stahl
Steel
Steele

Prior SQL Server Sample Databases

There are two other sample databases used in the releases of SQL Server: **Northwind** and **pubs**. Northwind has been introduced with SQL Server 7.0 in 1998. That SQL Server version had very short lifetime, replaced with SQL Server 2000 in year 2000. The pubs sample database originates from the time Microsoft & Sybase worked jointly on the database server project around 1990. Despite the relative simplicity of pre-2005 sample databases, they were good enough to demonstrate basic RDBMS SQL queries.

Book sales summary GROUP BY aggregation query.

```
USE pubs;
SELECT pub_name          AS Publisher,
    au_lname             AS Author,
    title                AS Title,
    SUM(qty)             AS SoldQty
FROM   authors
    INNER JOIN titleauthor
        ON authors.au_id = titleauthor.au_id
    INNER JOIN titles
        ON titles.title_id = titleauthor.title_id
    INNER JOIN publishers
        ON publishers.pub_id = titles.pub_id
    INNER JOIN sales
        ON sales.title_id = titles.title_id
GROUP  BY      pub_name,
               au_lname,
               title
ORDER BY Publisher, Author, Title;
-- (23 row(s) affected) - Partial results.
```

Publisher	Author	Title
Algodata Infosystems	Bennet	The Busy Executive's Database Guide
Algodata Infosystems	Carson	But Is It User Friendly?
Algodata Infosystems	Dull	Secrets of Silicon Valley
Algodata Infosystems	Green	The Busy Executive's Database Guide
Algodata Infosystems	Hunter	Secrets of Silicon Valley
Algodata Infosystems	MacFeather	Cooking with Computers: Surreptitious Balance Sheets
Algodata Infosystems	O'Leary	Cooking with Computers: Surreptitious Balance Sheets
Algodata Infosystems	Straight	Straight Talk About Computers
Binnet & Hardley	Blotchet-Halls	Fifty Years in Buckingham Palace Kitchens
Binnet & Hardley	DeFrance	The Gourmet Microwave

Northwind Sample Database

The Northwind database contains well-prepared sales data for a fictitious company called Northwind Traders, which imports & exports specialty gourmet foods & drinks from wholesale suppliers around the world. The company's sales offices are located in Seattle & London. Among gourmet food item products: Carnarvon Tigers, Teatime Chocolate Biscuits, Sir Rodney's Marmalade, Sir Rodney's Scones, Gustaf's Knäckebröd, Tunnbröd & Guaraná Fantástica.

Northwind Sample Database

Diagram of Northwind Database

The basic diagram of Northwind database excluding a few ancillary tables. The Orders table is central since the business is wholesale distribution (reselling) of high-end food products.

CHAPTER 1: SQL Server Sample & System Databases

pubs Sample Database

The pubs database is a very small and simple publishing database, yet it demonstrates the main features of database design such as PRIMARY KEYs, FOREIGN KEYs, and junction table reflecting many-to-many relationship. The main entities (tables) are: (book) titles, authors, titleauthor (junction table), publishers, sales & royalties.

```
USE pubs;
SELECT
    FORMAT(ytd_sales, 'c', 'en-US')                    AS YTDSales,
    CONCAT(a.au_fname, ' ', a.au_lname) AS Author,
    FORMAT((ytd_sales * royalty) / 100, 'c', 'en-US')
                                                       AS AuthorRev,
    FORMAT(ytd_sales - (ytd_sales * royalty) / 100,
            'c', 'en-US')                              AS PublisherRev
FROM titles t
    INNER JOIN titleauthor ta
        ON t.title_id = ta.title_id
    INNER JOIN authors a
        ON ta.au_id = a.au_id
ORDER BY ytd_sales DESC, Author; -- numeric/string sort
GO
```

	YTDSales	Author	AuthorRev	PublisherRev
1	$22,246.00	Anne Ringer	$5,339.00	$16,907.00
2	$22,246.00	Michel DeFrance	$5,339.00	$16,907.00
3	$18,722.00	Marjorie Green	$4,493.00	$14,229.00
4	$15,096.00	Reginald Blotchet-Halls	$2,113.00	$12,983.00
5	$8,780.00	Cheryl Carson	$1,404.00	$7,376.00
6	$4,095.00	Abraham Bennet	$409.00	$3,686.00
7	$4,095.00	Akiko Yokomoto	$409.00	$3,686.00
8	$4,095.00	Ann Dull	$409.00	$3,686.00
9	$4,095.00	Burt Gringlesby	$409.00	$3,686.00

Book Titles in pubs Database

The titles table has the most interesting content in the pubs database as demonstrated by the following T-SQL query.

```
SELECT  TOP 4 title_id AS TitleID, title AS Title, type                   AS Type,
        pub_id AS PubID, FORMAT(price, 'c','en-US')                       AS Price,
        FORMAT(advance, 'c','en-US')                                      AS Advance,
        FORMAT(royalty/100.0, 'p') AS Royalty, FORMAT(ytd_sales, 'c', 'en-US')  AS YTDSales,
        Notes
FROM pubs.dbo.titles
ORDER BY title;
```

TitleID	Title	Type	PubID	Price	Advance	Royalty	YTDSales	Notes
PC1035	But Is It User Friendly?	popular_comp	1389	$22.95	$7,000.00	16.00 %	$8,780.00	A survey of software for the naive user, focusing on the 'friendliness' of each.
PS1372	Computer Phobic AND Non-Phobic Individuals: Behavior Variations	psychology	0877	$21.59	$7,000.00	10.00 %	$375.00	A must for the specialist, this book examines the difference between those who hate and fear computers and those who don't.
BU1111	Cooking with Computers: Surreptitious Balance Sheets	business	1389	$11.95	$5,000.00	10.00 %	$3,876.00	Helpful hints on how to use your electronic resources to the best advantage.
PS7777	Emotional Security: A New Algorithm	psychology	0736	$7.99	$4,000.00	10.00 %	$3,336.00	Protecting yourself and your loved ones from undue emotional stress in the modern world. Use of computer and nutritional aids emphasized.

Diagram of pubs Database

Since pubs is a small database, the diagram conveniently fits on a page.

jobs
- job_id
- job_desc
- min_lvl
- max_lvl

sales
- stor_id
- ord_num
- ord_date
- qty
- payterms
- title_id

stores
- stor_id
- stor_name
- stor_address
- city
- state
- zip

discounts
- discounttype
- stor_id
- lowqty
- highqty
- discount

employee
- emp_id
- fname
- minit
- lname
- job_id
- job_lvl
- pub_id
- hire_date

titles
- title_id
- title
- type
- pub_id
- price
- advance
- royalty
- ytd_sales
- notes
- pubdate

titleauthor
- au_id
- title_id
- au_ord
- royaltyper

authors
- au_id
- au_lname
- au_fname
- phone
- address
- city
- state
- zip
- contract

publishers
- pub_id
- pub_name
- city
- state
- country

pub_info
- pub_id
- logo
- pr_info

roysched
- title_id
- lorange
- hirange
- royalty

Simple JOIN on non-key columns.

```
USE pubs; SELECT p.*, a.* FROM authors AS a
INNER JOIN publishers AS p ON a.city = p.city ORDER BY p.city, a.au_lname;
```

pub_id	pub_name	city	state	country	au_id	au_lname	au_fname	phone	address	city	state	zip	contract
1389	Algodata Infosystems	Berkeley	CA	USA	409-56-7008	Bennet	Abraham	415 658-9932	6223 Bateman St.	Berkeley	CA	94705	1
1389	Algodata Infosystems	Berkeley	CA	USA	238-95-7766	Carson	Cheryl	415 548-7723	589 Darwin Ln.	Berkeley	CA	94705	1

CHAPTER 1: SQL Server Sample & System Databases

SQL Server System Databases

The master, model, tempdb and msdb are system databases for special database server operations purposes. SSMS Object Explorer drill-down listing of system databases.

Query to create a new table in tempdb for development purposes.

```
SELECT * INTO tempdb.dbo.Product  FROM AdventureWorks2012.Production.Product
WHERE ListPrice > 0.0;    -- (304 row(s) affected)
```

The master Database

The master system database is the nerve center of SQL Server. It contains tables and db objects essential for server operations. System tables are accessible only through read-only views. System tables cannot be changed by users. A subset of the system views are called Dynamic Management Views (DMV) which return server state information for monitoring the operational aspects of a SQL Server instance, diagnosing problems, and performance tuning. Dynamic Management Functions (DMF) are applied in conjunction with DMVs.

```
SELECT TOP 5     ST.text,
                 EQS.*
FROM master.sys.dm_exec_query_stats AS EQS                          -- DMV
CROSS APPLY master.sys.dm_exec_sql_text(EQS.sql_handle) as ST       -- DMF
ORDER BY last_worker_time DESC;
```

SQL Server Management Studio Object Explorer display of some objects in the master database and a query listing all databases.

CHAPTER 1: SQL Server Sample & System Databases

SQL Server System Databases

An Important System View In master Database: sys.databases

```
SELECT TOP (10) name, database_id
FROM master.sys.databases
ORDER BY database_id;
```

name	database_id
master	1
tempdb	2
model	3
msdb	4
ReportServer	5
ReportServerTempDB	6
AdventureWorks2012	7
AdventureWorksDW2012	8
pubs	9
Northwind	10

spt_values table in master database can be used for integer sequence with a range of 0 - 2047.

```
-- End of the range - BOTTOM
SELECT TOP 5 number FROM master.dbo.spt_values WHERE TYPE='P'
ORDER BY number DESC;
```

number
2047
2046
2045
2044
2043

Example for using the sequence in spt_values to generate DATE and MONTH sequences.

```
SELECT TOP 5 number,   dateadd(day, number, '20000101')      AS "Date",
                       dateadd(mm, number, '20000101')       AS "Month"
FROM master.dbo.spt_values  WHERE type = 'P'  ORDER BY number;
```

number	Date	Month
0	2000-01-01 00:00:00.000	2000-01-01 00:00:00.000
1	2000-01-02 00:00:00.000	2000-02-01 00:00:00.000
2	2000-01-03 00:00:00.000	2000-03-01 00:00:00.000
3	2000-01-04 00:00:00.000	2000-04-01 00:00:00.000
4	2000-01-05 00:00:00.000	2000-05-01 00:00:00.000

CHAPTER 1: SQL Server Sample & System Databases

The model Database

The model database serves as prototype for a new database. The model database is also the prototype for tempdb when the SQL Server instance started. Upon server shutdown or restart everything is wiped out of tempdb, it starts with a clean slate as a copy of the model database. Therefore we should only place objects into the tempdb can be purged any time.

CHAPTER 1: SQL Server Sample & System Databases

SQL Server System Databases

The msdb Database

The msdb database is used for server internal operations such as support for SQL Server Agent job scheduling facility or keeping track of database the all important backups and restores.

Database backup history query using table in msdb database.

SELECT s.name AS Name, CONVERT(DATE,MAX(b.backup_finish_date)) AS LastGoodBackup,
     b.type AS Type
FROM master.dbo.sysdatabases AS s
LEFT OUTER JOIN msdb.dbo.backupset AS b ON s.name = b.database_name
GROUP BY s.name, b.type ORDER BY Name, Type;

Name	LastGoodBackup	Type
Accounting	2016-11-29	D
AdventureWorks	2016-11-29	D
AdventureWorks2008	2016-11-29	D
AdventureWorks2012	2016-11-29	D

CHAPTER 1: SQL Server Sample & System Databases

The tempdb Database

The tempdb serves as temporary database for system operations such as sorting. Temporary tables (#temp1) and global temporary tables (##globaltemp1) are stored in the tempdb as well. "Permanent" tables can be created in tempdb with a short lifetime which lasts till shutdown or restart.

CHAPTER 1: SQL Server Sample & System Databases

SQL Server System Databases

Sudden Death in tempdb When Server Restarts

Even though a temporary table and a global temporary table are created and queried in the context setting for AdventureWorks2012 database, they are placed into tempdb automatically. Same consideration when a temporary table is created from a stored procedure which is compiled in an application database. Upon server restart everything is wiped out of tempdb, rebirth follows as a copy of model db. We should not place anything into tempdb we cannot afford to lose. tempdb is also used by SQL Server engine for operations such as version control, sorting and more.

> Instead of GUI & mouse use T-SQL scripts which can be saved as .sql disk files.

CHAPTER 1: SQL Server Sample & System Databases

CHAPTER 2: Installing SQL Server 2014

SQL Server 2014 Express Edition Installation

The **Express Edition** is free. It can be installed from the following webpage.

http://www.microsoft.com/en-us/server-cloud/products/sql-server-editions/sql-server-express.aspx

Installation instructions provided.

SQL Server 2014 Evaluation Edition Installation

The **Evaluation Edition** is free for a certain time period like 6 months. It can be installed from the following webpage.

http://www.microsoft.com/en-us/server-cloud/products/sql-server/try.aspx

Installation instructions provided.

SQL Server 2014 Pay Edition Installation

The installation process from the distribution DVD is fairly automatic. Product key (4 x 5 alphanumeric) entry is required near the beginning of the installation.

Planning tab has the preparation steps.

![SQL Server Installation Center screenshot showing Planning tab with options: Hardware and Software Requirements, Security Documentation, Online Release Notes, How to Get SQL Server Data Tools, System Configuration Checker, Install Upgrade Advisor, Online Installation Help, How to Get Started with SQL Server 2014 Failover Clustering, How to Get Started with a PowerPivot for SharePoint Standalone Server Installation]

CHAPTER 2: Installing SQL Server 2014

The Installation tab has the SQL Server and Client Tools (SS Management Studio is a client tool) install options.

[SQL Server Installation Center screenshot showing Installation tab selected, with options: New SQL Server stand-alone installation or add features to an existing installation; New SQL Server failover cluster installation; Add node to a SQL Server failover cluster; Upgrade from SQL Server 2005, SQL Server 2008, SQL Server 2008 R2 or SQL Server 2012.]

SQL Server 2014 Pay Edition Installation

Setup Global Rules page shows the results of preliminary checks for installation readiness. Failed issues require fix.

SQL Server 2014 Setup

Global Rules

Setup Global Rules identify problems that might occur when you install SQL Server Setup support files. Failures must be corrected before Setup can continue.

Global Rules

Operation completed. Passed: 11. Failed 0. Warning 0. Skipped 0.

[Show details >>]   [Re-run]

View detailed report

[OK]   [Cancel]

CHAPTER 2: Installing SQL Server 2014

40   SQL Server 2014 Pay Edition Installation

Setup Install Rules page performs a number of internal system checks.

Install Rules

Setup rules identify potential problems that might occur while running Setup. Failures must be corrected before Setup can continue.

- Product Key
- License Terms
- Global Rules
- Product Updates
- Install Setup Files
- **Install Rules**
- Setup Role
- Feature Selection
- Feature Rules
- Feature Configuration Rules
- Ready to Install
- Installation Progress
- Complete

Operation completed. Passed: 6.   Failed 0.   Warning 1.   Skipped 0.

Hide details <<

View detailed report

Rule	Status
Fusion Active Template Library (ATL)	Passed
Previous releases of SQL Server 2008 Business Intelligence Devel...	Passed
Consistency validation for SQL Server registry keys	Passed
Computer domain controller	Passed
Microsoft .NET Application Security	Passed
Windows Firewall	Warning
Block install when Microsoft SQL Server 2014 CTP1 is present.	Passed

[< Back]   [Next >]   [Cancel]   [Help]

CHAPTER 2: Installing SQL Server 2014

SQL Server 2014 Pay Edition Installation

Installation Type page displays currently installed SQL Server products.

SQL Server 2014 Setup

Setup Role

Click the SQL Server Feature Installation option to individually select which feature components to install, or click a feature role to install a specific configuration.

Product Key
License Terms
Global Rules
Product Updates
Install Setup Files
Install Rules
Setup Role
Feature Selection
Feature Rules
Feature Configuration Rules
Ready to Install
Installation Progress
Complete

○ SQL Server Feature Installation
  Install SQL Server Database Engine Services, Analysis Services, Reporting Services, Integration Services, and other features.

○ SQL Server PowerPivot for SharePoint
  Install PowerPivot for SharePoint on a new or existing SharePoint server to support PowerPivot data access in the farm. Optionally, add the SQL Server relational database engine to use as the new farm's database server.

  ☑ Add SQL Server Database Relational Engine Services to this installation.

○ All Features With Defaults
  Install all features using default values for the service accounts.

[< Back] [Next >] [Cancel] [Help]

CHAPTER 2: Installing SQL Server 2014

Product Key page requests key entry from packaging box inside cover.

SQL Server 2014 Setup

Product Key

Specify the edition of SQL Server 2014 to install.

Global Rules	Validate this instance of SQL Server 2014 by entering the 25-character key from the Microsoft certificate of authenticity or product packaging. You can also specify a free edition of SQL Server, such as Evaluation or Express. Evaluation has the largest set of SQL Server features, as documented in SQL Server Books Online, and is activated with a 180-day expiration. To upgrade from one edition to another, run the Edition Upgrade Wizard.
Product Updates	
Install Setup Files	
Install Rules	
Installation Type	
Product Key	○ Specify a free edition:
License Terms	Evaluation
Setup Role	
Feature Selection	● Enter the product key:
Feature Rules	_____-_____-_____-_____-_____
Feature Configuration Rules	
Ready to Install	
Installation Progress	
Complete	

[< Back] [Next >] [Cancel] [Help]

SQL Server 2014 Pay Edition Installation

License terms page requires acceptance checkmark.

```
SQL Server 2014 Setup

License Terms
    To install SQL Server 2014, you must accept the Microsoft Software License Terms.

Global Rules              MICROSOFT SOFTWARE LICENSE TERMS
Product Updates
Install Setup Files       MICROSOFT SQL SERVER 2014 DEVELOPER
Install Rules             These license terms are an agreement between Microsoft Corporation (or based on where you
Installation Type         live, one of its affiliates) and you. Please read them. They apply to the software named above,
Product Key               which includes the media on which you received it, if any. The terms also apply to any Microsoft
License Terms
Setup Role                    • updates,
Feature Selection             • supplements,
Feature Rules
Feature Configuration Rules                                                                         Copy   Print
Ready to Install          ☐ I accept the license terms.
Installation Progress
Complete                  ☐ Turn on Customer Experience Improvement Program ("CEIP") and Error Reporting to help improve the
                            quality, reliability and performance of Microsoft SQL Server 2014.

                          See the Microsoft SQL Server 2014 Privacy Statement for more information.

                          * Microsoft SQL Server 2014 also includes a Visual Studio component that will have CEIP settings turned
                          off by default. If Visual Studio is installed, this component will use the CEIP settings for Visual Studio.

                                                          < Back      Next >      Cancel      Help
```

CHAPTER 2: Installing SQL Server 2014

Setup Role page lists installation options. "All Features with Defaults" is the easiest to install.

```
SQL Server 2014 Setup

Setup Role
    Click the SQL Server Feature Installation option to individually select which feature components to install, or click a
    feature role to install a specific configuration.

Product Key              ● SQL Server Feature Installation
License Terms
Global Rules                Install SQL Server Database Engine Services, Analysis Services, Reporting Services, Integration Services,
Product Updates             and other features.
Install Setup Files      ○ SQL Server PowerPivot for SharePoint
Install Rules
Setup Role                  Install PowerPivot for SharePoint on a new or existing SharePoint server to support PowerPivot data
Feature Selection           access in the farm. Optionally, add the SQL Server relational database engine to use as the new farm's
                            database server.
Feature Rules
Feature Configuration Rules     [✓] Add SQL Server Database Relational Engine Services to this installation.
Ready to Install
Installation Progress    ○ All Features With Defaults
Complete
                            Install all features using default values for the service accounts.


                                                        < Back    Next >    Cancel    Help
```

CHAPTER 2: Installing SQL Server 2014

SQL Server 2014 Pay Edition Installation

Feature Selection page can be used to pick & choose features.

[Screenshot of SQL Server 2014 Setup - Feature Selection window showing the Features list with Instance Features (Database Engine Services, SQL Server Replication, Full-Text and Semantic Extractions for Search, Data Quality Services, Analysis Services, Reporting Services - Native) and Shared Features (Reporting Services - SharePoint, Reporting Services Add-in for SharePoint Products, Data Quality Client, Client Tools Connectivity, Integration Services) all checked. Left navigation shows: Product Key, License Terms, Global Rules, Product Updates, Install Setup Files, Install Rules, Setup Role, **Feature Selection**, Feature Rules, Instance Configuration, Server Configuration, Database Engine Configuration, Analysis Services Configuration, Reporting Services Configuration, Distributed Replay Controller, Distributed Replay Client, Feature Configuration Rules, Ready to Install, Installation Progress. Feature description panel states prerequisites already installed (Windows PowerShell 2.0, Microsoft .NET Framework 3.5) and Disk Space Requirements: Drive C: 6028 MB required, 584505 MB available. Instance root directory: C:\Program Files\Microsoft SQL Server\; Shared feature directory: C:\Program Files\Microsoft SQL Server\; Shared feature directory (x86): C:\Program Files (x86)\Microsoft SQL Server\.]

CHAPTER 2: Installing SQL Server 2014

Instance Configuration page requires name entrance for the named instance since the default instance is already installed.

The SQL Server reference is [YOURSERVER] for the default instance and [YOURSERVER\INSTANCENAME] for the named instance.

SQL Server 2014 Setup

Instance Configuration

Specify the name and instance ID for the instance of SQL Server. Instance ID becomes part of the installation path.

- Product Key
- License Terms
- Global Rules
- Product Updates
- Install Setup Files
- Install Rules
- Setup Role
- Feature Selection
- Feature Rules
- **Instance Configuration**
- Server Configuration
- Database Engine Configuration
- Analysis Services Configuration
- Reporting Services Configuration
- Distributed Replay Controller
- Distributed Replay Client
- Feature Configuration Rules
- Ready to Install
- Installation Progress

○ Default instance
● Named instance: SQL2014

Instance ID:

SQL Server directory: C:\Program Files\Microsoft SQL Server\MSSQL12.
Analysis Services directory: C:\Program Files\Microsoft SQL Server\MSAS12.
Reporting Services directory: C:\Program Files\Microsoft SQL Server\MSRS12.

Installed instances:

Instance Name	Instance ID	Features	Edition	Version
MSSQLSERVER	MSSQL11.MSSQLS...	SQLEngine,SQLEn...	Developer	11.1.3128.0
SQL12	MSSQL11.SQL12,M...	SQLEngine,SQLEn...	Developer	11.1.3128.0
<Shared Compone...		SSMS, Adv_SSMS, ...		11.1.3128.0
<Shared Compone...		SSDTBI_VS2012		11.1.3360.12
<Shared Compone...		LocalDB, MDS		11.1.3000.0

< Back | Next > | Cancel | Help

SQL Server 2014 Pay Edition Installation

The Server Configuration page covers accounts, startup type and collation.

For example, SQL Server Agent (job management) can be set to automatic instead of manual startup.

SQL Server 2014 Setup

Server Configuration

Specify the service accounts and collation configuration.

- Product Key
- License Terms
- Global Rules
- Product Updates
- Install Setup Files
- Install Rules
- Setup Role
- Feature Selection
- Feature Rules
- Instance Configuration
- **Server Configuration**
- Database Engine Configuration
- Analysis Services Configuration
- Reporting Services Configuration
- Distributed Replay Controller
- Distributed Replay Client
- Feature Configuration Rules
- Ready to Install
- Installation Progress

Service Accounts | Collation

Microsoft recommends that you use a separate account for each SQL Server service.

Service	Account Name	Password	Startup Type
SQL Server Agent	NT Service\SQLAgentSS...		Manual
SQL Server Database Engine	NT Service\MSSQLSSQL...		Automatic
SQL Server Analysis Services	NT Service\MSOLAPSSQ...		Automatic
SQL Server Reporting Services	NT Service\ReportServer...		Automatic
SQL Server Integration Services 12.0	NT Service\MsDtsServer...		Automatic
SQL Server Distributed Replay Client	NT Service\SQL Server D...		Manual
SQL Server Distributed Replay Con...	NT Service\SQL Server D...		Manual
SQL Full-text Filter Daemon Launc...	NT Service\MSSQLFDLa...		Manual
SQL Server Browser	NT AUTHORITY\LOCAL...		Automatic

[< Back] [Next >] [Cancel] [Help]

CHAPTER 2: Installing SQL Server 2014

The Database Engine Configuration page offers administrator accounts, data directories and FILESTREAM setup options.

FILESTREAM is required for FileTable, a new feature starting with SQL Server 2012.

SQL Server 2014 Setup

Database Engine Configuration

Specify Database Engine authentication security mode, administrators and data directories.

Sidebar:
- Product Key
- License Terms
- Global Rules
- Product Updates
- Install Setup Files
- Install Rules
- Setup Role
- Feature Selection
- Feature Rules
- Instance Configuration
- Server Configuration
- **Database Engine Configuration**
- Analysis Services Configuration
- Reporting Services Configuration
- Distributed Replay Controller
- Distributed Replay Client
- Feature Configuration Rules
- Ready to Install
- Installation Progress

Tabs: Server Configuration | Data Directories | FILESTREAM

Specify the authentication mode and administrators for the Database Engine.

Authentication Mode

○ Windows authentication mode
● Mixed Mode (SQL Server authentication and Windows authentication)

Specify the password for the SQL Server system administrator (sa) account.

Enter password: ●●●●●●
Confirm password: ●●●●●●

Specify SQL Server administrators

HPESTAR\Owner (Owner)

SQL Server administrators have unrestricted access to the Database Engine.

[Add Current User] [Add...] [Remove]

[< Back] [Next >] [Cancel] [Help]

SQL Server 2014 Pay Edition Installation

FILESTREAM Configuration

Reporting Services Configuration.

SQL Server 2014 Setup

Reporting Services Configuration

Specify the Reporting Services configuration mode.

Product Key
License Terms
Global Rules
Product Updates
Install Setup Files
Install Rules
Setup Role
Feature Selection
Feature Rules
Instance Configuration
Server Configuration
Database Engine Configuration
Analysis Services Configuration
Reporting Services Configura...
Distributed Replay Controller
Distributed Replay Client
Feature Configuration Rules
Ready to Install
Installation Progress

Reporting Services Native Mode

⦿ Install and configure.
  Installs and configures the report server in native mode. The report server is operational after setup completes.

◯ Install only.
  Installs the report server files. After installation, use Reporting Services Configuration Manager to configure the report server for native mode.

Reporting Services SharePoint Integrated Mode

⦿ Install only.
  Installs the report server files. After installation use SharePoint Central Administration to complete the configuration. Verify the SQL Server Reporting Services service is started and create at least one SQL Server Reporting Services service application. For more information, click Help.

[< Back] [Next >] [Cancel] [Help]

SQL Server 2014 Pay Edition Installation

Ready to Install page shows the action plan.

```
SQL Server 2014 Setup

Ready to Install
    Verify the SQL Server 2014 features to be installed.

Product Key                          Ready to install SQL Server 2014:
License Terms                        ⊟ Summary
Global Rules                            Edition: Developer
Product Updates                         Action: Install (Product Update)
Install Setup Files                   ⊟ Prerequisites
Install Rules                            ⊟ Already installed:
Setup Role                                  Windows PowerShell 2.0
Feature Selection                           Microsoft .NET Framework 3.5
Feature Rules                               Microsoft Visual Studio 2010 Redistributables
Instance Configuration                      Microsoft Visual Studio 2010 Shell
Server Configuration                        Microsoft Visual Studio Tools for Applications 3.0
Database Engine Configuration               Microsoft .NET Framework 4.0
Analysis Services Configuration       ⊟ General Configuration
Reporting Services Configuration         ⊟ Features
Distributed Replay Controller               Database Engine Services
Distributed Replay Client                   SQL Server Replication
Feature Configuration Rules                 Full-Text and Semantic Extractions for Search
Ready to Install                            Data Quality Services
Installation Progress                       Analysis Services

                                     Configuration file path:
                                     C:\Program Files\Microsoft SQL Server\120\Setup Bootstrap\Log\20140423_161954\ConfigurationFile.ini

                                          < Back     Install     Cancel     Help
```

CHAPTER 2: Installing SQL Server 2014

Installation Progress page displays progress messages (this part will take a few minutes).

```
SQL Server 2014 Setup

Installation Progress

Product Key
License Terms
Global Rules                Install_sql_rsshp_Cpu64_Action : InstallFiles. Copying new files
Product Updates
Install Setup Files
Install Rules
Setup Role
Feature Selection
Feature Rules
Instance Configuration
Server Configuration
Database Engine Configuration
Analysis Services Configuration
Reporting Services Configuration
Distributed Replay Controller
Distributed Replay Client
Feature Configuration Rules
Ready to Install
Installation Progress

                                                    Next >      Cancel      Help
```

SQL Server 2014 Pay Edition Installation

The Complete page displays successful installation information or failure.

Feature	Status
Management Tools - Complete	Succeeded
Client Tools Connectivity	Succeeded
Client Tools SDK	Succeeded
Client Tools Backwards Compatibility	Succeeded
Management Tools - Basic	Succeeded
Reporting Services - Native	Succeeded

Viewing Product Documentation for SQL Server

Only the components that you use to view and manage the documentation for SQL Server have been installed. By default, the Help Viewer component uses the online library. After installing SQL Server, you can use the Help Library Manager component to download documentation to your local computer. For more information, see Use Microsoft Books Online for SQL Server (<http://go.microsoft.com/fwlink/?LinkID=299578>).

Summary log file has been saved to the following location:
C:\Program Files\Microsoft SQL Server\120\Setup Bootstrap\Log\20140423_161954\Summary_HPESTAR_20140423_161954.txt

Start Menu for SQL Server 2014
The Start Menu has all the components related to SQL Server including Management Studio and SQL Server Data Tools for Business Intelligence (SSAS, SSIS & SSRS) application design.

Creating Shortcut for Management Studio on Desktop
Management Studio can also be pinned to the Start Menu or Taskbar from the right-click drop-down menu.

CHAPTER 2: Installing SQL Server 2014

Launching SQL Server Configuration Manager

Expand (left click) the Configuration Tools tab on the Start Menu and click on SQL Server Configuration Manager.

SQL Server should be running by itself after installation, if not, it can be started and/or reconfigured.

Starting, Restarting & Stopping SQL Server

Right click on the server name in Configuration Manager launches the control menu. To start the server, click on Start.

Message window pops up.

To stop a running server or restart it, click on the menu item respectively.

CHAPTER 2: Installing SQL Server 2014

Connecting to the New Named SQL Server Instance

The newly installed SS instance is ready for use. Here is how we can connect to it from SSMS Object Explorer. NOTE: on your computer you will see YOURCOMPUTERNAME instead of "HPESTAR".

CHAPTER 2: Installing SQL Server 2014

Investigating the New SQL Server Instance

We can start discovering the new SQL Server instance in Query Editor & Object Explorer.

SELECT @@version; -- Microsoft SQL Server 2014 - 12.0.2000.8 (X64)

SELECT @@SERVERNAME; -- YOURSERVERNAME\SQL12;

-- SS Version, Level (service pack), Edition
SELECT   CONCAT ('Microsoft SQL Server ',convert(varchar, SERVERPROPERTY('ProductVersion')), ' -- ',
convert(varchar, SERVERPROPERTY('ProductLevel')), ' -- ',convert(varchar, SERVERPROPERTY('Edition')));
-- Microsoft SQL Server 12.0.2000.8 -- RTM -- Developer Edition (64-bit)

CHAPTER 2: Installing SQL Server 2014

Connecting to 2 SQL Server Instances Simultaneously

SSMS Object Explorer support multiple SS instances connections. Warning: **Production, QA and Development SS instances may look similar, an opportunity to get confused and carry out actions on the wrong server**. Best prevention: **take regular database backups and connect only to one SQL Server instance at one time**.

The first connection is the named instance, the second is the default instance.

CHAPTER 2: Installing SQL Server 2014

BACKUP DATABASE Command

Database backup command; the backup filename can be changed at will to reflect the backup date.

BACKUP DATABASE [AdventureWorks2012] TO DISK = N'F:\data\backup\AW20161023.bak';

-- Dynamic backup filename with datestamp
DECLARE @Filename nvarchar(64) = CONCAT(N'F:\data\backup\AW', CONVERT(varchar, CONVERT(DATE, getdate())),'.bak');
BACKUP DATABASE [AdventureWorks2012] TO DISK = @Filename;
-- AW2018-08-23.bak

Installing Books Online - BOL

Books Online can be installed from the web or from the distribution DVD. Select Manage Help Settings from the Help menu in Management Studio.

Select **Install content from online** from the pop-up panel.

CHAPTER 2: Installing SQL Server 2014

Installing Books Online - BOL

Add Books Online to the to do list on the dialog box.

Click on UPDATE button to start install. (BOL already installed, Dev. Ref. install pending)

CHAPTER 2: Installing SQL Server 2014

Updating will take a few minutes.

Finish panel. Click in Finish button.

Installing Books Online - BOL

Creating Shortcut for Books Online on Desktop.

Follow the usual process for shortcut creation, start with right click on SQL Server Documentation.

CHAPTER 2: Installing SQL Server 2014

Installing Developer Reference

To install Developer Reference follow the same process as for Book Online.

Click on Update button. Update will take a few minutes. Developer Reference will install into Books Online. At the time of writing this book, there was no SSDT 2014. SSDT 2012 was tested to connect to SQL Server 2014 database correctly.

Desktop segment with SSMS, SSDT and Books Online (includes Developer Reference).

Searching Books Online Contents Mode

Books Online is the complete reference tool for SQL Server. The implementation in Microsoft Help Viewer is new to SQL Server 2014. In the Contents mode, you drill-down in the left pane and read the article in the right pane.

When you drill down in the contents pane, the corresponding article pops up in the right pane.

Searching Books Online Index Mode

In the Index Mode, items are listed alphabetically. When you click on an item, the corresponding article pops up in the right pane.

Searching the Web for SQL Server MSDN Articles

When searching the web for SS documentation use the prefix "SQL SERVER" or "T-SQL" before the keyword.

CHAPTER 2: Installing SQL Server 2014

Book Online on the Web

Books Online is available on the web:

http://msdn.microsoft.com/en-us/library/ms130214(v=sql.120).aspx

Installing AdventureWorks2012 Sample Database

At the writing of this book, no AdventureWorks2014 available. AdventureWorks2012 and other related databases can be installed from the following webpage:
http://msftdbprodsamples.codeplex.com/releases/view/55330

Community Projects & Samples from the Start Menu will bring up the following site:
http://sqlserversamples.codeplex.com/

Installing Northwind & pubs Sample Databases

Here is the download website with instructions. http://www.microsoft.com/en-us/download/details.aspx?displaylang=en&id=23654

CHAPTER 2: Installing SQL Server 2014

CHAPTER 3: Structure of the SELECT Statement

The SELECT Clause

The SELECT clause is the only required clause in a SELECT statement, all the other clauses are optional. The SELECT columns can be literals (constants), expressions, table columns and even subqueries. Lines can be commented with "--".

```
SELECT 15 * 15;                                         -- 225

SELECT Today = convert(DATE, getdate());                -- 2016-07-27   -- getdate() T-SQL only
SELECT Today = convert(DATE, CURRENT_TIMESTAMP);        -- 2016-07-27   -- ANSI SQL

SELECT      Color,
            ProdCnt             = COUNT(*),
            AvgPrice            = FORMAT(AVG(ListPrice),'c','en-US')
FROM AdventureWorks2012.Production.Product p
WHERE Color is not null
GROUP BY Color
        HAVING count(*) > 10
ORDER BY AvgPrice DESC;
```

Color	ProdCnt	AvgPrice
Yellow	36	$959.09
Blue	26	$923.68
Silver	43	$850.31
Black	93	$725.12
Red	38	$1,401.95

```
-- Equivalent with column aliases on the right
SELECT      Color,
            COUNT(*)                                    AS ProdCnt,
            FORMAT(AVG(ListPrice),'c','en-US')          AS AvgPrice
FROM AdventureWorks2012.Production.Product p  WHERE Color is not null
GROUP BY Color HAVING count(*) > 10  ORDER BY AvgPrice DESC;
GO
```

SELECT with Search Expression

SELECT statement can have complex expressions for text or numbers as demonstrated in the next T-SQL query for finding the street name in AddressLine1 column. ISNUMERIC function can be applied to validate text data prior to conversion to numeric format.

```
SELECT  AddressID,
        SUBSTRING(AddressLine1, CHARINDEX(' ', AddressLine1+' ', 1) +1,
        CHARINDEX(' ', AddressLine1+' ', CHARINDEX(' ', AddressLine1+' ', 1) +1) -
        CHARINDEX(' ', AddressLine1+' ', 1) -1)                           AS StreetName,
        AddressLine1,
        City
FROM AdventureWorks2012.Person.Address
WHERE ISNUMERIC (LEFT(AddressLine1,1))=1    AND City = 'Seattle'
ORDER BY AddressLine1;
-- -- (141 row(s) affected)- Partial results.
```

AddressID	StreetName	AddressLine1	City
13079	boulevard	081, boulevard du Montparnasse	Seattle
859	Oak	1050 Oak Street	Seattle
110	Slow	1064 Slow Creek Road	Seattle
113	Ravenwood	1102 Ravenwood	Seattle
95	Bradford	1220 Bradford Way	Seattle
32510	Steven	1349 Steven Way	Seattle
118	Balboa	136 Balboa Court	Seattle
32519	Mazatlan	137 Mazatlan	Seattle
25869	Calle	1386 Calle Verde	Seattle
114	Yorba	1398 Yorba Linda	Seattle
15657	Book	151 Book Ct	Seattle
105	Stillman	1619 Stillman Court	Seattle
18002	Carmel	1635 Carmel Dr	Seattle
19813	Acardia	1787 Acardia Pl.	Seattle
16392	Orchid	1874 Orchid Ct	Seattle
18053	Green	1883 Green View Court	Seattle
13035	Mt.	1887 Mt. Diablo St	Seattle
29864	Valley	1946 Valley Crest Drive	Seattle
13580	Hill	2030 Hill Drive	Seattle
106	San	2144 San Rafael	Seattle

```
-- Search for Crest in the middle of AddessLine1
SELECT * FROM AdventureWorks2012.Person.Address
WHERE AddressLine1 LIKE '% Crest %';
-- (21 row(s) affected)
```

CHAPTER 3: Structure of the SELECT Statement

The SELECT Clause

SELECT Statement with Subquery

Two Northwind category images, Beverages & Dairy Products, from the dbo.Categories table.

The following SELECT statement involves a subquery which is called a derived table. It also demonstrates that INNER JOIN can be performed with a GROUP BY subquery as well not only with another table or view.

```
USE Northwind;
SELECT          c.CategoryName                  AS Category,
                cnum.NoOfProducts               AS CatProdCnt,
                p.ProductName                   AS Product,
                FORMAT(p.UnitPrice,'c', 'en-US') AS UnitPrice
   FROM     Categories c
            INNER JOIN Products p       ON c.CategoryID = p.CategoryID
            INNER JOIN (    SELECT      c.CategoryID,
                                        NoOfProducts = count(* )
                            FROM    Categories c
                            INNER JOIN Products p
                            ON c.CategoryID = p.CategoryID
                            GROUP BY c.CategoryID
                       ) cnum                   -- derived table
            ON c.CategoryID = cnum.CategoryID
   ORDER BY Category, Product;      -- (77 row(s) affected) - Partial results.
```

Category	CatProdCnt	Product	UnitPrice
Dairy Products	10	Mozzarella di Giovanni	$34.80
Dairy Products	10	Queso Cabrales	$21.00
Dairy Products	10	Queso Manchego La Pastora	$38.00
Dairy Products	10	Raclette Courdavault	$55.00
Grains/Cereals	7	Filo Mix	$7.00
Grains/Cereals	7	Gnocchi di nonna Alice	$38.00
Grains/Cereals	7	Gustaf's Knäckebröd	$21.00
Grains/Cereals	7	Ravioli Angelo	$19.50
Grains/Cereals	7	Singaporean Hokkien Fried Mee	$14.00
Grains/Cereals	7	Tunnbröd	$9.00

CHAPTER 3: Structure of the SELECT Statement

Creating Delimited String List (CSV) with XML PATH

The XML PATH clause, the text() function and correlated subquery is used to create a comma delimited string within the SELECT columns. Note: it cannot be done using traditional (without XML) SQL single statement, it can be done with multiple SQL statements only. STUFF() string function is applied to replace the leading comma with an empty string.

```
USE AdventureWorks;

SELECT  Territory        = st.[Name],
        SalesYTD = FORMAT(floor(SalesYTD), 'c', 'en-US'), -- currency format
        SalesStaffAssignmentHistory =

         STUFF((SELECT CONCAT(', ', c.FirstName, SPACE(1), c.LastName)    AS [text()]
              FROM   Person.Contact c
               INNER JOIN Sales.SalesTerritoryHistory sth
               ON c.ContactID = sth.SalesPersonID
               WHERE  sth.TerritoryID =  st.TerritoryID
               ORDER  BY StartDate
               FOR XML Path ('')), 1, 1, SPACE(0))

FROM   Sales.SalesTerritory st
ORDER  BY SalesYTD DESC;
GO
```

Territory	SalesYTD	SalesStaffAssignmentHistory
Southwest	$8,351,296.00	Shelley Dyck, Jauna Elson
Canada	$6,917,270.00	Carla Eldridge, Michael Emanuel, Gail Erickson
Northwest	$5,767,341.00	Shannon Elliott, Terry Eminhizer, Martha Espinoza
Central	$4,677,108.00	Linda Ecoffey, Maciej Dusza
France	$3,899,045.00	Mark Erickson
Northeast	$3,857,163.00	Maciej Dusza, Linda Ecoffey
United Kingdom	$3,514,865.00	Michael Emanuel
Southeast	$2,851,419.00	Carol Elliott
Germany	$2,481,039.00	Janeth Esteves
Australia	$1,977,474.00	Twanna Evans

```
-- Comma delimited list of column names
SELECT CONCAT(',', c.name)  AS [text()]
FROM  sys.columns c   WHERE c.[object_id] = OBJECT_ID('Purchasing.PurchaseOrderDetail')
ORDER BY column_id FOR XML PATH('');
```

Logical Processing Order of the SELECT Statement

The results from the previous step will be available to the next step. The logical processing order for a SELECT statement is the following. Actual processing by the database engine may be different due to performance and other considerations.

1.	FROM
2.	ON
3.	JOIN
4.	WHERE
5.	GROUP BY
6.	WITH CUBE or WITH ROLLUP
7.	HAVING
8.	SELECT
9.	DISTINCT
10.	ORDER BY
11.	TOP

As an example, it is logical to filter with the WHERE clause prior to applying GROUP BY. It is also logical to sort when the final result set is available.

SELECT Color, COUNT(*) AS ColorCount FROM AdventureWorks2012.Production.Product WHERE Color is not NULL GROUP BY Color ORDER BY ColorCount DESC;

Color	ColorCount
Black	93
Silver	43
Red	38
Yellow	36
Blue	26
Multi	8
Silver/Black	7
White	4
Grey	1

CHAPTER 3: Structure of the SELECT Statement

The TOP Clause

The TOP clause filters results according the sorting specified in an ORDER BY clause, otherwise random filtering takes place.

Simple TOP usage to return 10 rows only.

```
SELECT TOP 10 SalesOrderID, OrderDate, TotalDue
FROM AdventureWorks2012.Sales.SalesOrderHeader  ORDER BY TotalDue DESC;
```

SalesOrderID	OrderDate	TotalDue
51131	2007-07-01 00:00:00.000	187487.825
55282	2007-10-01 00:00:00.000	182018.6272
46616	2006-07-01 00:00:00.000	170512.6689
46981	2006-08-01 00:00:00.000	166537.0808
47395	2006-09-01 00:00:00.000	165028.7482
47369	2006-09-01 00:00:00.000	158056.5449
47355	2006-09-01 00:00:00.000	145741.8553
51822	2007-08-01 00:00:00.000	145454.366
44518	2005-11-01 00:00:00.000	142312.2199
51858	2007-08-01 00:00:00.000	140042.1209

TOP function usage: not known in advance how many rows will be returned due to "TIES".

```
SELECT   TOP 1 WITH TIES  coalesce(Color, 'N/A')           AS Color,
         FORMAT(ListPrice, 'c', 'en-US')                   AS ListPrice,
         Name                                              AS ProductName,
         ProductID
FROM     AdventureWorks2012.Production.Product
ORDER BY ROW_NUMBER() OVER(PARTITION BY Color ORDER BY ListPrice DESC);
```

Color	ListPrice	ProductName	ProductID
N/A	$229.49	HL Fork	804
Black	$3,374.99	Mountain-100 Black, 38	775
Red	$3,578.27	Road-150 Red, 62	749
Silver	$3,399.99	Mountain-100 Silver, 38	771
Blue	$2,384.07	Touring-1000 Blue, 46	966
Grey	$125.00	Touring-Panniers, Large	842
Multi	$89.99	Men's Bib-Shorts, S	855
Silver/Black	$80.99	HL Mountain Pedal	937
White	$9.50	Mountain Bike Socks, M	709
Yellow	$2,384.07	Touring-1000 Yellow, 46	954

CHAPTER 3: Structure of the SELECT Statement

The DISTINCT Clause to Omit Duplicates

The DISTINCT clause returns only unique results, omitting duplicates in the result set.

```
USE AdventureWorks2012;
SELECT DISTINCT Color FROM Production.Product
WHERE Color is not NULL
ORDER BY Color;
GO
```

Color
Black
Blue
Grey
Multi
Red
Silver
Silver/Black
White
Yellow

```
SELECT DISTINCT ListPrice
FROM Production.Product
 WHERE ListPrice > 0.0
ORDER BY ListPrice DESC;
GO
-- (102 row(s) affected) - Partial results.
```

ListPrice
3578.27
3399.99
3374.99
2443.35

```
-- Using DISTINCT in COUNT - NULL is counted
SELECT          COUNT(*)                AS TotalRows,
                COUNT(DISTINCT Color)   AS ProductColors,
                COUNT(DISTINCT Size)    AS ProductSizes
FROM AdventureWorks2012.Production.Product;
```

TotalRows	ProductColors	ProductSizes
504	9	18

CHAPTER 3: Structure of the SELECT Statement

The CASE Conditional Expression

The CASE conditional expression evaluates to a **single value of the same data type**, therefore **it can be used anywhere in a query where a single value is required.**

```
SELECT      CASE ProductLine
                WHEN 'R' THEN 'Road'
                WHEN 'M' THEN 'Mountain'
                WHEN 'T' THEN 'Touring'
                WHEN 'S' THEN 'Other'
                ELSE 'Parts'
            END                     AS Category,
            Name                    AS ProductName,
            ProductNumber
FROM AdventureWorks2012.Production.Product
ORDER BY ProductName;
GO
-- (504 row(s) affected) - Partial results.
```

Category	ProductName	ProductNumber
Touring	Touring-3000 Blue, 62	BK-T18U-62
Touring	Touring-3000 Yellow, 44	BK-T18Y-44
Touring	Touring-3000 Yellow, 50	BK-T18Y-50
Touring	Touring-3000 Yellow, 54	BK-T18Y-54
Touring	Touring-3000 Yellow, 58	BK-T18Y-58
Touring	Touring-3000 Yellow, 62	BK-T18Y-62
Touring	Touring-Panniers, Large	PA-T100
Other	Water Bottle - 30 oz.	WB-H098
Mountain	Women's Mountain Shorts, L	SH-W890-L

Query to return different result sets for repeated execution due to newid().

```
SELECT  TOP 3 CompanyName,  City=CONCAT(City, ', ', Country),       PostalCode,
        [IsNumeric] =   CASE    WHEN PostalCode like '[0-9][0-9][0-9][0-9][0-9]'
                        THEN '5-Digit Numeric'   ELSE 'Other'  END
FROM    Northwind.dbo.Suppliers
ORDER BY NEWID();                       -- random sort
GO
```

CompanyName	City	PostalCode	IsNumeric
PB Knäckebröd AB	Göteborg, Sweden	S-345 67	Other
Gai pâturage	Annecy, France	74000	5-Digit Numeric
Heli Süßwaren GmbH & Co. KG	Berlin, Germany	10785	5-Digit Numeric

The CASE Conditional Expression

Same query as above expanded with ROW_NUMBER() and another CASE expression column.

```
SELECT      ROW_NUMBER() OVER (ORDER BY Name)           AS RowNo,
            CASE ProductLine
              WHEN 'R' THEN 'Road'
              WHEN 'M' THEN 'Mountain'
              WHEN 'T' THEN 'Touring'
              WHEN 'S' THEN 'Other'
              ELSE 'Parts'
            END                                         AS Category,
            Name                                        AS ProductName,
            CASE WHEN Color is null THEN 'N/A'
                 ELSE Color END                         AS Color,
            ProductNumber
FROM Production.Product   ORDER BY ProductName;
-- (504 row(s) affected) - Partial results.
```

RowNo	Category	ProductName	Color	ProductNumber
1	Parts	Adjustable Race	N/A	AR-5381
2	Mountain	All-Purpose Bike Stand	N/A	ST-1401
3	Other	AWC Logo Cap	Multi	CA-1098
4	Parts	BB Ball Bearing	N/A	BE-2349
5	Parts	Bearing Ball	N/A	BA-8327
6	Other	Bike Wash - Dissolver	N/A	CL-9009
7	Parts	Blade	N/A	BL-2036
8	Other	Cable Lock	N/A	LO-C100
9	Parts	Chain	Silver	CH-0234
10	Parts	Chain Stays	N/A	CS-2812

Testing PostalCode with ISNUMERIC and generating a flag with CASE expression.

```
SELECT  TOP (4) AddressID,  City,   PostalCode                          AS Zip,
        CASE WHEN ISNUMERIC(PostalCode) = 1 THEN 'Y' ELSE 'N' END    AS IsZipNumeric
FROM    AdventureWorks2008.Person.Address  ORDER BY NEWID();
```

AddressID	City	Zip	IsZipNumeric
16704	Paris	75008	Y
26320	Grossmont	91941	Y
27705	Matraville	2036	Y
18901	Kirkby	KB9	N

CHAPTER 3: Structure of the SELECT Statement

The OVER Clause

The OVER clause defines the partitioning and sorting of a rowset (intermediate result set) preceding the application of an associated window function, such as ranking. Window functions are also dubbed as ranking functions.

```
USE AdventureWorks2012;
-- Query with three different OVER clauses
SELECT   ROW_NUMBER() OVER ( ORDER BY SalesOrderID, ProductID)           AS RowNum
        ,SalesOrderID, ProductID, OrderQty
        ,RANK() OVER(PARTITION BY SalesOrderID ORDER BY OrderQty DESC)   AS Ranking
        ,SUM(OrderQty) OVER(PARTITION BY SalesOrderID)                   AS TotalQty
        ,AVG(OrderQty) OVER(PARTITION BY SalesOrderID)                   AS AvgQty
        ,COUNT(OrderQty) OVER(PARTITION BY SalesOrderID)  AS "Count"  -- T-SQL keyword, use "" or []
        ,MIN(OrderQty) OVER(PARTITION BY SalesOrderID)                   AS "Min"
        ,MAX(OrderQty) OVER(PARTITION BY SalesOrderID)                   AS "Max"
FROM Sales.SalesOrderDetail
WHERE SalesOrderID BETWEEN 61190 AND 61199
ORDER BY RowNum;
-- (143 row(s) affected) - Partial results.
```

RowNum	SalesOrderID	ProductID	OrderQty	Ranking	TotalQty	AvgQty	Count	Min	Max
1	61190	707	4	13	159	3	40	1	17
2	61190	708	3	18	159	3	40	1	17
3	61190	711	5	8	159	3	40	1	17
4	61190	712	12	2	159	3	40	1	17
5	61190	714	3	18	159	3	40	1	17
6	61190	715	5	8	159	3	40	1	17
7	61190	716	5	8	159	3	40	1	17
8	61190	858	4	13	159	3	40	1	17
9	61190	859	7	6	159	3	40	1	17
10	61190	864	8	4	159	3	40	1	17
11	61190	865	3	18	159	3	40	1	17
12	61190	870	9	3	159	3	40	1	17
13	61190	876	4	13	159	3	40	1	17
14	61190	877	5	8	159	3	40	1	17
15	61190	880	1	34	159	3	40	1	17
16	61190	881	5	8	159	3	40	1	17
17	61190	883	2	26	159	3	40	1	17
18	61190	884	17	1	159	3	40	1	17
19	61190	885	3	18	159	3	40	1	17
20	61190	886	1	34	159	3	40	1	17
21	61190	889	2	26	159	3	40	1	17
22	61190	892	4	13	159	3	40	1	17
23	61190	893	3	18	159	3	40	1	17
24	61190	895	1	34	159	3	40	1	17

FROM Clause: Specifies the Data Source

The FROM clause specifies the source data sets for the query such as tables, views, derived tables and table-valued functions. Typically the tables are JOINed together. The most common JOIN is INNER JOIN which is based on equality between FOREIGN KEY and PRIMARY KEY values in the two tables.

PERFORMANCE NOTE
All FOREIGN KEYs should be indexed. PRIMARY KEYs are indexed automatically with unique index.

```
USE AdventureWorks2012;
GO
SELECT
 ROW_NUMBER() OVER(ORDER BY SalesYTD DESC)                          AS RowNo,
 ROW_NUMBER() OVER(PARTITION BY PostalCode ORDER BY SalesYTD DESC)  AS SeqNo,
         CONCAT(p.FirstName, SPACE(1), p.LastName)                  AS SalesStaff,
         FORMAT(s.SalesYTD,'c','en-US')                             AS YTDSales,
         City,
         a.PostalCode                                               AS ZipCode
FROM Sales.SalesPerson AS s
   INNER JOIN Person.Person AS p
     ON s.BusinessEntityID = p.BusinessEntityID
   INNER JOIN Person.Address AS a
     ON a.AddressID = p.BusinessEntityID
WHERE TerritoryID IS NOT NULL    AND SalesYTD <> 0 ORDER BY ZipCode, SeqNo;
```

RowNo	SeqNo	SalesStaff	YTDSales	City	ZipCode
1	1	Linda Mitchell	$4,251,368.55	Issaquah	98027
3	2	Michael Blythe	$3,763,178.18	Issaquah	98027
4	3	Jillian Carson	$3,189,418.37	Issaquah	98027
8	4	Tsvi Reiter	$2,315,185.61	Issaquah	98027
12	5	Garrett Vargas	$1,453,719.47	Issaquah	98027
14	6	Pamela Ansman-Wolfe	$1,352,577.13	Issaquah	98027
2	1	Jae Pak	$4,116,871.23	Renton	98055
5	2	Ranjit Varkey Chudukatil	$3,121,616.32	Renton	98055
6	3	José Saraiva	$2,604,540.72	Renton	98055
7	4	Shu Ito	$2,458,535.62	Renton	98055
9	5	Rachel Valdez	$1,827,066.71	Renton	98055
10	6	Tete Mensa-Annan	$1,576,562.20	Renton	98055
11	7	David Campbell	$1,573,012.94	Renton	98055
13	8	Lynn Tsoflias	$1,421,810.92	Renton	98055

CHAPTER 3: Structure of the SELECT Statement

The WHERE Clause to Filter Records (Rows)

The WHERE clause filters the rows generated by the query. Only rows satisfying (TRUE) the WHERE clause predicates are returned.

> **PERFORMANCE NOTE**
> All columns in WHERE clause should be indexed.

USE AdventureWorks2012;

String equal match predicate - equal is TRUE, not equal is FALSE.

SELECT ProductID, Name, ListPrice, Color
FROM Production.Product WHERE Name = 'Mountain-100 Silver, 38' ;

ProductID	Name	ListPrice	Color
771	Mountain-100 Silver, 38	3399.99	Silver

-- Function equality predicate
SELECT * FROM Sales.SalesOrderHeader WHERE YEAR(OrderDate) = 2008;
-- (13951 row(s) affected)

> **PERFORMANCE NOTE**
> When a column is used as a parameter in a function (e.g. YEAR(OrderDate)), index (if any) usage is voided. Instead of random SEEK, all rows are SCANned in the table. The predicate is not SARGable.

-- String wildcard match predicate
SELECT ProductID, Name, ListPrice, Color
FROM Production.Product WHERE Name LIKE ('%touring%');

-- Integer range predicate
SELECT ProductID, Name, ListPrice, Color
FROM Production.Product WHERE ProductID >= 997 ;

-- Double string wildcard match predicate
SELECT ProductID, Name, ListPrice, Color
FROM Production.Product WHERE Name LIKE ('%bike%') AND Name LIKE ('%44%');

-- String list match predicate
SELECT ProductID, Name, ListPrice, Color FROM Production.Product
WHERE Name IN ('Mountain-100 Silver, 44', 'Mountain-100 Black, 44');

CHAPTER 3: Structure of the SELECT Statement

The GROUP BY Clause to Aggregate Results

The GROUP BY clause is applied to partition the rows and calculate aggregate values. An extremely powerful way of looking at the data from a summary point of view.

```
SELECT
            V.Name                                          AS Vendor,
            FORMAT(SUM(TotalDue), 'c', 'en-US')             AS TotalPurchase,
            A.City,
            SP.Name                                         AS State,
            CR.Name                                         AS Country
FROM Purchasing.Vendor AS V
    INNER JOIN Purchasing.VendorAddress AS VA
            ON VA.VendorID = V.VendorID
    INNER JOIN Person.Address AS A
            ON A.AddressID = VA.AddressID
    INNER JOIN Person.StateProvince AS SP
            ON SP.StateProvinceID = A.StateProvinceID
    INNER JOIN Person.CountryRegion AS CR
            ON CR.CountryRegionCode = SP.CountryRegionCode
    INNER JOIN Purchasing.PurchaseOrderHeader POH
            ON POH.VendorID = V.VendorID
GROUP BY V.Name, A.City, SP.Name, CR.Name
ORDER BY SUM(TotalDue) DESC, Vendor;   -- TotalPurchase does a string sort instead of numeric
GO
-- (79 row(s) affected) - Partial results.
```

Vendor	TotalPurchase	City	State	Country
Superior Bicycles	$5,034,266.74	Lynnwood	Washington	United States
Professional Athletic Consultants	$3,379,946.32	Burbank	California	United States
Chicago City Saddles	$3,347,165.20	Daly City	California	United States
Jackson Authority	$2,821,333.52	Long Beach	California	United States
Vision Cycles, Inc.	$2,777,684.91	Glendale	California	United States
Sport Fan Co.	$2,675,889.22	Burien	Washington	United States
Proseware, Inc.	$2,593,901.31	Lebanon	Oregon	United States
Crowley Sport	$2,472,770.05	Chicago	Illinois	United States
Greenwood Athletic Company	$2,472,770.05	Lemon Grove	Arizona	United States
Mitchell Sports	$2,424,284.37	Everett	Washington	United States
First Rate Bicycles	$2,304,231.55	La Mesa	New Mexico	United States
Signature Cycles	$2,236,033.80	Coronado	California	United States
Electronic Bike Repair & Supplies	$2,154,773.37	Tacoma	Washington	United States
Vista Road Bikes	$2,090,857.52	Salem	Oregon	United States
Victory Bikes	$2,052,173.62	Issaquah	Washington	United States
Bicycle Specialists	$1,952,375.30	Lake Oswego	Oregon	United States

The HAVING Clause to Filter Aggregates

The HAVING clause is similar to the WHERE clause filtering but applies to GROUP BY aggregates.

```
USE AdventureWorks;
SELECT
                V.Name                                   AS Vendor,
                FORMAT(SUM(TotalDue), 'c', 'en-US')      AS TotalPurchase,
                A.City,
                SP.Name                                  AS State,
                CR.Name                                  AS Country
FROM Purchasing.Vendor AS V
   INNER JOIN Purchasing.VendorAddress AS VA
            ON VA.VendorID = V.VendorID
   INNER JOIN Person.Address AS A
            ON A.AddressID = VA.AddressID
   INNER JOIN Person.StateProvince AS SP
            ON SP.StateProvinceID =  A.StateProvinceID
   INNER JOIN Person.CountryRegion AS CR
            ON CR.CountryRegionCode = SP.CountryRegionCode
   INNER JOIN Purchasing.PurchaseOrderHeader POH
            ON POH.VendorID = V.VendorID
GROUP BY  V.Name, A.City, SP.Name, CR.Name
HAVING SUM(TotalDue) < $26000    -- HAVING clause predicate
ORDER BY SUM(TotalDue) DESC,  Vendor;
```

Vendor	TotalPurchase	City	State	Country
Speed Corporation	$25,732.84	Anacortes	Washington	United States
Gardner Touring Cycles	$25,633.64	Altadena	California	United States
National Bike Association	$25,513.90	Sedro Woolley	Washington	United States
Australia Bike Retailer	$25,060.04	Bellingham	Washington	United States
WestAmerica Bicycle Co.	$25,060.04	Houston	Texas	United States
Ready Rentals	$23,635.06	Kirkland	Washington	United States
Morgan Bike Accessories	$23,146.99	Albany	New York	United States
Continental Pro Cycles	$22,960.07	Long Beach	California	United States
American Bicycles and Wheels	$9,641.01	West Covina	California	United States
Litware, Inc.	$8,553.32	Santa Cruz	California	United States
Business Equipment Center	$8,497.80	Everett	Montana	United States
Bloomington Multisport	$8,243.95	West Covina	California	United States
International	$8,061.10	Salt Lake City	Utah	United States
Wide World Importers	$8,025.60	Concord	California	United States
Midwest Sport, Inc.	$7,328.72	Detroit	Michigan	United States
Wood Fitness	$6,947.58	Philadelphia	Pennsylvania	United States
Metro Sport Equipment	$6,324.53	Lebanon	Oregon	United States
Burnett Road Warriors	$5,779.99	Corvallis	Oregon	United States
Lindell	$5,412.57	Lebanon	Oregon	United States
Consumer Cycles	$3,378.17	Torrance	California	United States
Northern Bike Travel	$2,048.42	Anacortes	Washington	United States

The ORDER BY Clause to Sort Results

The ORDER BY clause sorts the result set. It guarantees ordering according to the columns or expressions listed from major to minor keys. Unique ordering requires a set of keys which generate unique data rows. The major key, YEAR(HireDate), in the first example is not sufficient for uniqueness.

```
USE AdventureWorks2012;         -- Sort on 2 keys
SELECT BusinessEntityID AS EmployeeID, JobTitle, HireDate
FROM HumanResources.Employee  ORDER BY YEAR(HireDate) DESC, EmployeeID;
-- (290 row(s) affected) - Partial results.
```

EmployeeID	JobTitle	HireDate
285	Pacific Sales Manager	2007-04-15
286	Sales Representative	2007-07-01
288	Sales Representative	2007-07-01

```
-- Sort on CASE conditional expression
SELECT   BusinessEntityID AS SalesStaffID, CONCAT(LastName, ', ', FirstName) AS FullName,
         CASE CountryRegionName WHEN 'United States' THEN TerritoryName
              ELSE '' END AS TerritoryName, CountryRegionName
FROM Sales.vSalesPerson    WHERE TerritoryName IS NOT NULL        -- view
ORDER BY CASE WHEN CountryRegionName != 'United States' THEN  CountryRegionName
              ELSE TerritoryName  END;
```

SalesStaffID	FullName	TerritoryName	CountryRegionName
286	Tsoflias, Lynn		Australia
278	Vargas, Garrett		Canada
282	Saraiva, José		Canada

The EXCEPT & INTERSECT Set Operators

The EXCEPT operator & the INTERSECT operator require the column lists are compatible for the comparison.

```
USE tempdb; -- Prepare two tables with 400 random(newid()) picks from the Product table
SELECT TOP (400) * INTO Prod1 FROM AdventureWorks2012.Production.Product ORDER BY NEWID();
SELECT TOP (400) * INTO Prod2 FROM AdventureWorks2012.Production.Product ORDER BY NEWID();

-- EXCEPT SET OPERATOR - no match rows
SELECT * FROM PROD1 EXCEPT SELECT * FROM PROD2;  -- (81 row(s) affected)

-- INTERSECT SET OPERATOR - matching rows
SELECT * FROM PROD1 INTERSECT SELECT * FROM PROD2;  -- (319 row(s) affected)
```

CHAPTER 3: Structure of the SELECT Statement

CTE - Common Table Expression

CTE helps with structured programming by the definition of named subqueries at the beginning of the query. It supports nesting and recursion.

```
USE AdventureWorks;
-- Testing CTE
WITH CTE (SalesPersonID, NumberOfOrders, MostRecentOrderDate)
    AS (    SELECT SalesPersonID, COUNT(*), CONVERT(date, MAX(OrderDate))
            FROM Sales.SalesOrderHeader
            GROUP BY SalesPersonID  )
SELECT * FROM CTE;
-- (18 row(s) affected) - Partial results.
```

SalesPersonID	NumberOfOrders	MostRecentOrderDate
284	39	2004-05-01
278	234	2004-06-01
281	242	2004-06-01

```
-- Using CTE in a query
;WITH CTE (SalesPersonID, NumberOfOrders, MostRecentOrderDate)
    AS ( SELECT SalesPersonID, COUNT(*), CONVERT(date, MAX(OrderDate))
        FROM Sales.SalesOrderHeader    GROUP BY SalesPersonID    )
-- Start of outer (main) query
 SELECT         E.EmployeeID,
                OE.NumberOfOrders               AS EmpOrders,
                OE.MostRecentOrderDate          AS EmpLastOrder,
                E.ManagerID,
                OM.NumberOfOrders               AS MgrOrders,
                OM.MostRecentOrderDate          AS MgrLastOrder
  FROM   HumanResources.Employee AS E
            INNER JOIN CTE AS OE                ON E.EmployeeID = OE.SalesPersonID
            LEFT OUTER JOIN CTE AS OM           ON E.ManagerID = OM.SalesPersonID
ORDER BY EmployeeID;
-- (17 row(s) affected) - Partial results.
```

EmployeeID	EmpOrders	EmpLastOrder	ManagerID	MgrOrders	MgrLastOrder
268	48	2004-06-01	273	NULL	NULL
275	450	2004-06-01	268	48	2004-06-01
276	418	2004-06-01	268	48	2004-06-01
277	473	2004-06-01	268	48	2004-06-01
278	234	2004-06-01	268	48	2004-06-01

CHAPTER 3: Structure of the SELECT Statement

Combining Results of Multiple Queries with UNION

UNION and UNION ALL (no duplicates elimination) operators can be used to **stack result sets from two or more queries into a single result set**.

```
-- Column structure of queries must be the same
SELECT Tag='2012', *
FROM AdventureWorks2012.Production.Product

UNION

SELECT Tag='2005', *
FROM AdventureWorks.Production.Product
ORDER BY ProductID, Tag;
GO
```

	Tag	ProductID	Name	ProductNumber	MakeFlag	FinishedGoodsFlag	Color	SafetySt
1	2005	1	Adjustable Race	AR-5381	0	0	NULL	1000
2	2012	1	Adjustable Race	AR-5381	0	0	NULL	1000
3	2005	2	Bearing Ball	BA-8327	0	0	NULL	1000
4	2012	2	Bearing Ball	BA-8327	0	0	NULL	1000
5	2005	3	BB Ball Bearing	BE-2349	1	0	NULL	800
6	2012	3	BB Ball Bearing	BE-2349	1	0	NULL	800
7	2005	4	Headset Ball Bearings	BE-2908	0	0	NULL	800
8	2012	4	Headset Ball Bearings	BE-2908	0	0	NULL	800
9	2005	316	Blade	BL-2036	1	0	NULL	800
10	2012	316	Blade	BL-2036	1	0	NULL	800
11	2005	317	LL Crankarm	CA-5965	0	0	Black	500
12	2012	317	LL Crankarm	CA-5965	0	0	Black	500

```
-- Combining data from OLTP & data warehouse databases
SELECT FirstName,LastName, 0 AS TotalChildren
FROM AdventureWorks2012.Person.Person
UNION ALL
SELECT FirstName,LastName, TotalChildren
FROM AdventureWorksDW2012..DimCustomer;
```

CHAPTER 3: Structure of the SELECT Statement

TOP n by Group Query with OVER PARTITION BY

OVER PARTITION BY method is very convenient for TOP n by group selection. List of top 3 orders placed by resellers (customers of AdventureWorks Cycles).

```sql
USE AdventureWorks2012;

SELECT CustomerID, SalesOrderID, Sale, RecordNo
  FROM  (SELECT CustomerID,
                SalesOrderID,
                FORMAT(TotalDue,'c','en-US')                           AS Sale,
                SUM(TotalDue) OVER(PARTITION BY CustomerID)            AS SalesTotal,
                ROW_NUMBER() OVER
                   (PARTITION BY CustomerID ORDER BY TotalDue DESC)    AS RecordNo
           FROM  Sales.SalesOrderHeader) AS X      -- derived table
 WHERE    X.SalesTotal > 100000
    AND   X.RecordNo <= 3
 ORDER BY CustomerID, RecordNo;
```

	CustomerID	SalesOrderID	Sale	RecordNo
1	29484	50756	$42,379.62	1
2	29484	48395	$36,669.05	2
3	29484	47454	$30,881.77	3
4	29485	71782	$37,497.45	1
5	29485	53459	$33,136.13	2
6	29485	58907	$31,960.09	3
7	29486	44772	$75,865.15	1
8	29486	47409	$69,291.77	2
9	29486	46358	$67,656.45	3
10	29488	53485	$65,910.67	1

762 rows

```sql
-- Row numbering by partitioning view results
SELECT ROW_NUMBER() OVER(PARTITION BY PhoneNumberType ORDER BY SalesYTD DESC) RN,
       CONCAT(FirstName, ' ', LastName) as Name, ROUND(SalesYTD,2,1) AS YTDSales,
       PhoneNumberType
FROM AdventureWorks2012.Sales.vSalesPerson
ORDER BY PhoneNumberType, RN;
```

CHAPTER 3: Structure of the SELECT Statement

CHAPTER 4: SQL Server Management Studio

SQL Server Programming, Administration & Management Tool

SQL Server Management Studio (SSMS) is a GUI (Graphical User Interface) tool for accessing, configuring, managing, administering, and developing all major components of SQL Server with the exception of Business Intelligence components: SSAS (Analysis Services), SSRS (Reporting Services) & SSIS (Integration Services). The two main environments in SSMS: Object Explorer and Query Editor. Object Explorer is used to access servers, databases and db objects. Query Editor is to develop and execute queries. SSMS is used by a DBA (Data Base Administrator) for administrative and programming functions. SSMS can also be used by a database developer to develop application related db objects such as stored procedures, functions and triggers. Some developers prefer to stay in Visual Studio environment which has features to support database development albeit not as extensive as Management Studio. A typical screen display of Management Studio.

CHAPTER 4: SQL Server Management Studio

Query Editor

The Query Editor is used to type in queries, edit them and submit them for execution by the server. Queries can also be loaded from a disk file, typically with .sql extension. In addition to textual query development, a number of special tools available such as graphical query designer, debugger, execution plan display and query analysis in the Database Engine Tuning Advisor.

Query Editor

Execute All Batches in Query Editor

The entire content of the Query Editor is executed when we click on the Execute button. Batches typically separated by "GO" on a separate line.

The Significance of GO in T-SQL Scripts

"GO" is not transmitted to SQL Server. "GO" indicates the end of batch to the client software such as SSMS. "GO" also indicates the end of a logical unit to the human reader. Certain statements must be the first line, or have "GO" preceding them.

```
USE AdventureWorks2012;
CREATE FUNCTION Z () RETURNS TABLE AS
RETURN  SELECT * FROM Production.ProductSubcategory;
GO
/* Msg 111, Level 15, State 1, Line 2   'CREATE FUNCTION' must be the first statement in a query batch. */

USE AdventureWorks2012;
GO
CREATE FUNCTION Z () RETURNS TABLE AS RETURN SELECT * FROM Production.ProductSubcategory;
GO
-- Command(s) completed successfully.
```

CHAPTER 4: SQL Server Management Studio

The Results Pane contains the result rows of the query. It is currently set to Grid format.

Query Editor

The Messages Pane gets the row count values, warning & error messages as well as the output of the PRINT & RAISERROR statements if any.

The client software also gets the same messages following query execution.

```
USE Northwind;

SELECT   A.CustomerID,
         FORMAT(MIN(A.OrderDate), 'd') AS FirstOrder,
         FORMAT(MAX(A.OrderDate), 'd') AS LastOrder,
         FORMAT( (SELECT    TOP 1 B.Freight
           FROM      Orders B
           WHERE     B.CustomerID = A.CustomerID
           ORDER BY OrderDate DESC),'c','en-US')   AS Freight
FROM     Orders A
GROUP BY A.CustomerID
ORDER BY A.CustomerID;
GO
PRINT 'This is a PRINT test message';
```

```
(89 row(s) affected)
This is a PRINT test message
```

CHAPTER 4: SQL Server Management Studio

Routing Results to Grid, Text or File

Results can be routed to Grid, Text or File from the right-click menu or the Query drop-down menu.

Query Editor

Routing Results to Text

The following screen window image displays results in text format. Messages also come to the Results window, following the results rows.

```
SQLQuery30.sql - HPESTAR.Northwind (HPESTAR\Owner (56))* - Microsoft SQL Server Man...

SELECT * FROM Customers ORDER BY CompanyName;

Results
CustomerID  CompanyName                          ContactName
----------  -----------------------------------  --------------------
ALFKI       Alfreds Futterkiste                  Maria Anders
ANATR       Ana Trujillo Emparedados y helados   Ana Trujillo
ANTON       Antonio Moreno Taquería              Antonio Moreno
AROUT       Around the Horn                      Thomas Hardy
BERGS       Berglunds snabbköp                   Christina Berglund
BLAUS       Blauer See Delikatessen              Hanna Moos
BLONP       Blondesddsl père et fils             Frédérique Citeaux
BOLID       Bólido Comidas preparadas            Martín Sommer
BONAP       Bon app'                             Laurence Lebihan
BOTTM       Bottom-Dollar Markets                Elizabeth Lincoln
BSBEV       B's Beverages                        Victoria Ashworth
CACTU       Cactus Comidas para llevar           Patricio Simpson
CENTC       Centro comercial Moctezuma           Francisco Chang
CHOPS       Chop-suey Chinese                    Yang Wang
COMMI       Comércio Mineiro                     Pedro Afonso
CONSH       Consolidated Holdings                Elizabeth Brown
WANDK       Die Wandernde Kuh                    Rita Müller
DRACD       Drachenblut Delikatessen             Sven Ottlieb
DUMON       Du monde entier                      Janine Labrune
EASTC       Eastern Connection                   Ann Devon
ERNSH       Ernst Handel                         Roland Mendel
FAMIA       Familia Arquibaldo                   Aria Cruz
```

Query executed suc... | HPESTAR (11.0 RTM) | HPESTAR\Owner (56) | Northwind | 00:00:00 | 91 rows

CHAPTER 4: SQL Server Management Studio

Routing Results to File

When the routing option is file, the file save window pops up upon query execution.

Part of the file in Notepad.

```
Name                    ListPrice
    ProductNumber       StandardCost
_____
_____    _____
_____

Road-150 Red, 44        $3,578.27
    BK-R93R-44          $2,171.29
Road-150 Red, 48        $3,578.27
    BK-R93R-48          $2,171.29
Road-150 Red, 52        $3,578.27
    BK-R93R-52          $2,171.29
Road-150 Red, 56        $3,578.27
    BK-R93R-56          $2,171.29
```

Query Editor

Saving Results in CSV Flat File Format

Results can also be saved in CSV (comma separated values) format which can be read by Excel and other software.

The saving file dialog box is configured automatically to csv saving.

Part of the file in Notepad window.

```
Chainring,Beaumont Bikes,1602
Chainring,Bike Satellite Inc.,1604
Chainring,Training Systems,1514
Chainring Bolts,Beaumont Bikes,1602
Chainring Bolts,Bike Satellite Inc.,1604
Chainring Bolts,Training Systems,1514
Chainring Nut,Beaumont Bikes,1602
Chainring Nut,Bike Satellite Inc.,1604
Chainring Nut,Training Systems,1514
External Lock Washer 1,Aurora Bike Center,1616
```

Query Editor

Copy & Paste Results to Excel

Using the copy / copy with headers option in SSMS result window, the query results can simply be pasted into an Excel worksheet. Excel may do implicit conversions on some columns.

After pasting into an Excel worksheet some formatting may be necessary such as for datetime columns.

Query Editor

Error Handling & Debugging

Error handling and debugging is a major part of database development work. When there is an error, it is displayed in the Messages area (or returned to the application client software) which automatically becomes active. In the following example, we introduced an invalid column name which resulted in error. The error message line reference starts with the top line of the batch which is the first line after the first "GO" which indicates a new batch. The red wave-underlining comes from optional IntelliSense and not related to the execution attempt error message. IntelliSense gives warning ahead of time if it detects a potential error. Simple errors can be corrected with help from the error message. Complex errors may required web search and/or examining the query in parts.

```
USE Northwind;
GO
SELECT    A.CustomerIDzzzz,
          FORMAT(MIN(A.OrderDate), 'd') AS FirstOrder,
          FORMAT(MAX(A.OrderDate), 'd') AS LastOrder,
          FORMAT( (SELECT   TOP 1 B.Freight
            FROM     Orders B
            WHERE    B.CustomerID = A.CustomerID
            ORDER BY OrderDate DESC),'c','en-US')  AS Freight
FROM      Orders A
GROUP BY  A.CustomerID
ORDER BY  A.CustomerID;
GO
PRINT 'This is a PRINT test message';
GO
```

```
Msg 207, Level 16, State 1, Line 1
Invalid column name 'CustomerIDzzzz'.
This is a PRINT test message
```

CHAPTER 4: SQL Server Management Studio

Locating the Error Line in a Query

Position the cursor on the error and double click. The error line will be highlighted. This method does not work for all errors.

```
USE AdventureWorks2012;

WITH cteLastSalaryChange

    AS (SELECT    BusinessEntityID        AS EmployeeID,
                  Maxi(RateChangeDate)        AS ChangeDate
        FROM      HumanResources.EmployeePayHistory
        GROUP BY BusinessEntityID),

    cteLastSalary
    AS (SELECT    eph.BusinessEntityID      AS EmployeeID,
                  Rate
        FROM      HumanResources.EmployeePayHistory eph
                  INNER JOIN cteLastSalaryChange lsc
                     ON lsc.EmployeeID = eph.BusinessEntityID
                    AND lsc.ChangeDate = eph.RateChangeDate)

-- SELECT * FROM cteLastSalary   -- for testing & debugging

SELECT TOP 1 FORMAT( Rate, 'c', 'en-US') AS SecondHighestPayRate
FROM    (SELECT    TOP 2 Rate
         FROM      cteLastSalary
         ORDER BY Rate DESC) a      -- Derived table
ORDER BY Rate ASC;
```

Messages
Msg 195, Level 15, State 10, Line 6
'Maxi' is not a recognized built-in function name.

CHAPTER 4: SQL Server Management Studio

Query Editor

Error Message Pointing to the Wrong Line

For some errors, the first line of the query (3) is returned by the database engine not the actual error line (13). The error message is still very helpful though in this instance.

```sql
USE AdventureWorks2012;

WITH cteLastSalaryChange
        AS (SELECT    BusinessEntityID        AS EmployeeID,
                      Max(RateChangeDate)     AS ChangeDate
            FROM      HumanResources.EmployeePayHistory
            GROUP BY  BusinessEntityID),

        cteLastSalary
        AS (SELECT    eph.BusinessEntityID    AS EmployeeID,
                      Rate
            FROM      AdventureWorks.HumanResources.EmployeePayHistoryx eph
                      INNER JOIN cteLastSalaryChange lsc
                        ON lsc.EmployeeID = eph.BusinessEntityID
                        AND lsc.ChangeDate = eph.RateChangeDate)

-- SELECT * FROM cteLastSalary  -- for testing & debugging

SELECT TOP 1 FORMAT( Rate, 'c', 'en-US') AS SecondHighestPayRate
FROM    (SELECT   TOP 2 Rate
         FROM     cteLastSalary
         ORDER BY Rate DESC) a      -- Derived table
ORDER BY Rate ASC;
```

Messages
```
Msg 208, Level 16, State 1, Line 3
Invalid object name 'AdventureWorks.HumanResources.EmployeePayHistoryx'.
```

CHAPTER 4: SQL Server Management Studio

Parsing a Query for Syntax Errors

A query (or one or more batches) can be parsed for syntax errors. Parsing catches syntax errors such as using "ORDER" instead of "ORDER BY" for sorting.

```
USE AdventureWorks2012;

WITH cteLastSalaryChange

    AS (SELECT    BusinessEntityID       AS EmployeeID,
                  Max(RateChangeDate)    AS ChangeDate
        FROM      HumanResources.EmployeePayHistory
        GROUP BY BusinessEntityID),

    cteLastSalary
    AS (SELECT    eph.BusinessEntityID    AS EmployeeID,
                  Rate
        FROM      HumanResources.EmployeePayHistory eph
                  INNER JOIN cteLastSalaryChange lsc
                  ON lsc.EmployeeID = eph.BusinessEntityID
                  AND lsc.ChangeDate = eph.RateChangeDate)

-- SELECT * FROM cteLastSalary   -- for testing & debugging

SELECT TOP 1 FORMAT( Rate, 'c', 'en-US') AS SecondHighestPayRate
FROM       (SELECT    TOP 2 Rate
            FROM      cteLastSalary
            ORDER  Rate DESC) a     -- Derived table
ORDER BY Rate ASC;
```

Results
Msg 102, Level 15, State 1, Line 23
Incorrect syntax near 'Rate'.

Query Editor

Deferred Name Resolution Process

Deferred Name Resolution Process: Only syntax errors are caught when parsed, not execution (runtime) errors as shown in the following demo which has an invalid table reference (EmployeePayHistoryx). Similarly, **stored procedures can be compiled without errors with invalid table references**. A table need not exist for stored procedure compilation, only for execution.

```sql
USE AdventureWorks2012;

WITH cteLastSalaryChange

    AS (SELECT     BusinessEntityID       AS EmployeeID,
               Max(RateChangeDate)        AS ChangeDate
        FROM    HumanResources.EmployeePayHistory
        GROUP BY BusinessEntityID),

    cteLastSalary
    AS (SELECT      eph.BusinessEntityID      AS EmployeeID,
                Rate
        FROM    AdventureWorks.HumanResources.EmployeePayHistoryx eph
            INNER JOIN cteLastSalaryChange lsc
              ON lsc.EmployeeID = eph.BusinessEntityID
              AND lsc.ChangeDate = eph.RateChangeDate)

-- SELECT * FROM cteLastSalary   -- for testing & debugging

SELECT TOP 1 FORMAT( Rate, 'c', 'en-US') AS SecondHighestPayRate
FROM    (SELECT    TOP 2 Rate
         FROM    cteLastSalary
         ORDER BY Rate DESC) a    -- Derived table
ORDER BY Rate ASC;
```

Command(s) completed successfully.

CHAPTER 4: SQL Server Management Studio

Executing Single Batch Only

A single batch can be executed by selecting (highlighting) it and clicking on Execute.

```
USE Northwind;
GO
SELECT   A.CustomerID,
         FORMAT(MIN(A.OrderDate), 'd') AS FirstOrder,
         FORMAT(MAX(A.OrderDate), 'd') AS LastOrder,
         FORMAT( (SELECT   TOP 1 B.Freight
           FROM     Orders B
           WHERE    B.CustomerID = A.CustomerID
           ORDER BY OrderDate DESC),'c','en-US')  AS Freight
FROM     Orders A
GROUP BY A.CustomerID
ORDER BY A.CustomerID;
GO
PRINT 'This is a PRINT test message';
GO
```

	CustomerID	FirstOrder	LastOrder	Freight
1	ALFKI	8/25/1997	4/9/1998	$1.21
2	ANATR	9/18/1996	3/4/1998	$39.92
3	ANTON	11/27/1996	1/28/1998	$58.43
4	AROUT	11/15/1996	4/10/1998	$33.80
5	BERGS	8/12/1996	3/4/1998	$151.52
6	BLAUS	4/9/1997	4/29/1998	$31.14
7	BLONP	7/25/1996	1/12/1998	$7.09
8	BOLID	10/10/1996	3/24/1998	$16.16
9	BONAP	10/16/1996	5/6/1998	$38.28
10	BOTTM	12/20/1996	4/24/1998	$24.12

Query executed suc... | HPESTAR (11.0 RTM) | HPESTAR\Owner (57) | Northwind | 00:00:00 | 89 rows

Query Editor

Executing Part of a Query

A part of a query can be executed as long as it is a valid query, otherwise error results. The query part has to be selected (highlighted) and the Execute button has to be pushed. The selected part of the query is considered a batch which is sent to the server. In this example, we executed the subquery (inner query) in the WHERE clause predicate.

```sql
-- Non-correlated subquery
SELECT Name,
       FORMAT(ListPrice, 'c','en-US') AS ListPrice,
       ProductNumber,
       FORMAT(StandardCost, 'c','en-US') AS StandardCost
FROM AdventureWorks2012.Production.Product
WHERE ListPrice >=
    (SELECT ListPrice
     FROM AdventureWorks.Production.Product
     WHERE Name = 'Road-250 Black, 48' )
ORDER BY ListPrice DESC, Name;
GO
```

Results:

	ListPrice
1	2443.35

CHAPTER 4: SQL Server Management Studio

Object Explorer

SSMS Object Explorer functions as:

- ➢ A tree-based directory of all database objects
- ➢ A launching base for graphical user-interface tools
- ➢ An access way to object properties

Context-Sensitive Right-Click Menu

Based on what object the cursor is on, right-click menu changes accordingly, it is context-sensitive. In the following demo the cursor is on table object when we right click on the mouse.

Server Administration & Management Tools

All the available SQL Server administration and management tools can be accessed from the Object Explorer. Usually the Database Administrator (DBA) uses these tools.

CHAPTER 4: SQL Server Management Studio

Object Explorer

SQL Server Agent Jobs to Automate Administration Tasks

SQL Server Agent is a job creation and scheduling facility with notification features. For example, database backup job can be scheduled to execute 2:15AM every night as shown on the following dialog box. Stored procedure execution can also be setup as a job and scheduled for periodic execution.

Job properties panel can be used to create and manage jobs with multiple job steps and multiple schedules.

Job Properties - AW2012MaintenancePlan.Subplan_1

Select a page:
- General
- Steps
- Schedules
- Alerts
- Notifications
- Targets

Script ▼ | Help

Field	Value
Name:	AW2012MaintenancePlan.Subplan_1
Owner:	HPESTAR\Owner
Category:	Database Maintenance
Description:	No description available.

☑ Enabled

Source:

Created: 7/27/2012 2:57:24 AM
Last modified: 7/27/2012 2:57:25 AM
Last executed:

View Job History

Connection
Server: HPESTAR
Connection: HPESTAR\Owner
View connection properties

Progress
Ready

[OK] [Cancel]

Graphical Query Designer

The Design Query in Editor entry on the Query drop-down menu launches the graphical Query Designer which can be used to design the query with GUI method and the T-SQL SELECT code will be generated automatically upon completion.

```
SELECT    Sales.SalesOrderHeader.SalesOrderID AS OrderID, Sales.SalesOrderHeader.OrderDate, Sales.SalesOrderHeader.T
          Product.Name
FROM      Sales.SalesOrderHeader INNER JOIN
          Sales.SalesOrderDetail ON Sales.SalesOrderHeader.SalesOrderID = Sales.SalesOrderDetail.SalesOrderID INNER
          Product ON Sales.SalesOrderDetail.ProductID = Product.ProductID
WHERE     (Sales.SalesOrderHeader.TotalDue >= $10000)
ORDER BY Sales.SalesOrderHeader.OrderDate, OrderID
```

CHAPTER 4: SQL Server Management Studio

Designing a GROUP BY Query in Query Designer

Query Designer can be used to design from simple to complex queries. It can also serve as a starter query for a more complex query. It is really easy to get the tables JOINs graphically.

```
SELECT    Production.Product.ProductNumber
FROM      Purchasing.PurchaseOrderHeader INNER JOIN
          Purchasing.PurchaseOrderDetail ON Purchasing.PurchaseOrderHeader.PurchaseOrderID = Purchasing.Purc
          Production.Product ON Purchasing.PurchaseOrderDetail.ProductID = Production.Product.ProductID
```

Graphical Query Designer

The Production.Product.Name column will also be configured as GROUP BY (drop-down default).

```
SELECT   Production.Product.ProductNumber, Production.Product.Name
FROM     Purchasing.PurchaseOrderHeader INNER JOIN
         Purchasing.PurchaseOrderDetail ON Purchasing.PurchaseOrderHeader.PurchaseOrderID = Purchasing.Purc
         Production.Product ON Purchasing.PurchaseOrderDetail.ProductID = Production.Product.ProductID
GROUP BY Production.Product.ProductNumber, Production.Product.Name
```

We add the TotalDue column and change the summary function to "SUM" from "Group by" and configure sorting on the first column.

Graphical Query Designer

After pressing OK, the query is moved into the Query Editor window. Frequently it requires reformatting.

```sql
SELECT      Production.Product.ProductNumber,
            Production.Product.Name,
            SUM(Purchasing.PurchaseOrderHeader.TotalDue) AS TotalCost
FROM        Purchasing.PurchaseOrderHeader
  INNER JOIN Purchasing.PurchaseOrderDetail
    ON Purchasing.PurchaseOrderHeader.PurchaseOrderID =
       Purchasing.PurchaseOrderDetail.PurchaseOrderID
  INNER JOIN Production.Product
    ON Purchasing.PurchaseOrderDetail.ProductID =
       Production.Product.ProductID
GROUP BY Production.Product.ProductNumber, Production.Product.Name
ORDER BY Production.Product.ProductNumber
```

	ProductNumber	Name	TotalCost
1	AR-5381	Adjustable Race	8553.3242
2	BA-8327	Bearing Ball	6947.575
3	BC-M005	Mountain Bottle Cage	16406.50
4	BC-R205	Road Bottle Cage	16406.50
5	BE-2908	Headset Ball Bearings	9641.0145
6	CA-1098	AWC Logo Cap	30198.96
7	CA-5965	LL Crankarm	4768373.9878
8	CA-6738	ML Crankarm	4768373.9878
9	CA-7457	HL Crankarm	5977657.3143
10	CB-2903	Chainring Bolts	210133.1871
11	CH-0234	Chain	52176.445
12	CL-9009	Bike Wash - Dissolver	59941.75
13	CN-6137	Chainring Nut	210133.1871
14	CR-7833	Chainring	249505.206

CHAPTER 4: SQL Server Management Studio

The only remaining issue with the query is the 3-part column references which is hard to read. We can change the query for readability improvement by using table aliases.

```sql
SELECT          P.ProductNumber,
                P.Name,
                SUM(POH.TotalDue) AS TotalCost
FROM            Purchasing.PurchaseOrderHeader POH
  INNER JOIN    Purchasing.PurchaseOrderDetail POD
    ON POH.PurchaseOrderID = POD.PurchaseOrderID
  INNER JOIN    Production.Product P
    ON POD.ProductID = P.ProductID
GROUP BY P.ProductNumber, P.Name
ORDER BY P.ProductNumber
```

	ProductNumber	Name	TotalCost
1	AR-5381	Adjustable Race	8553.3242
2	BA-8327	Bearing Ball	6947.575
3	BC-M005	Mountain Bottle Cage	16406.50
4	BC-R205	Road Bottle Cage	16406.50
5	BE-2908	Headset Ball Bearings	9641.0145
6	CA-1098	AWC Logo Cap	30198.96
7	CA-5965	LL Crankarm	4768373.9878
8	CA-6738	ML Crankarm	4768373.9878
9	CA-7457	HL Crankarm	5977657.3143
10	CB-2903	Chainring Bolts	210133.1871
11	CH-0234	Chain	52176.445
12	CL-9009	Bike Wash - Dissolver	59941.75
13	CN-6137	Chainring Nut	210133.1871

Graphical Query Designer

Graphically Editing of an Existing Query

An existing query, exception certain complex queries, can be uploaded into the Graphical Query Designer the following way: select (highlight) the query and right-click for the drop-down menu; click on Design Query in Editor.

CHAPTER 4: SQL Server Management Studio

Following screen image shows the query in the Graphical Query Designer after some manual beautifying such as moving the tables for better display.

The query can be edited graphically and upon clicking on "OK", the query text is updated in the Query Editor window.

```
SELECT    UPPER(PC.Name) AS Category, PSC.Name AS Subcategory, P.Name AS Product, FORMAT(P.ListPrice, 'c', 'en-
          AS StandardCost
FROM      Production.Product AS P INNER JOIN
          Production.ProductSubcategory AS PSC ON PSC.ProductSubcategoryID = P.ProductSubcategoryID INNER J
          Production.ProductCategory AS PC ON PC.ProductCategoryID = PSC.ProductCategoryID
WHERE     (PSC.Name LIKE 'Road Frames')
ORDER BY Category, Subcategory, Product
```

CHAPTER 4: SQL Server Management Studio

Configuring Line Numbers in Query Editor

Line numbering is an option which is off by default. Line numbers are helpful to find errors in large queries or T-SQL scripts (a sequence of T-SQL statements) when the error references a line number. Following is an example an error which includes the line number.

The Display Line Numbers option in the query editor can be activated from Options.

IntelliSense - Your Smart Assistant

IntelliSense is a smart agent in Query Editor. It helps completing long object names and pointing out potential errors by red wave-lining them.

The Options configuration screen for IntelliSense.

Underlining with red wave-line potential errors such as misspelling of a column name.

```
SELECT TOP 1000 [BillOfMaterialsID]
      ,[ProductAssemblyID]
      ,[ComponentID]
      ,[StartDate]
      ,[EndDate]
      ,[UnitMeasureCodex]
      ,[BOMLevel]
      ,[PerAssemblyQty]
      ,[ModifiedDate]
  FROM [AdventureWorks2012].[Production].[BillOfMaterials]
```

CHAPTER 4: SQL Server Management Studio

IntelliSense Guessing and Completing Object Names

Screenshots show IntelliSense in action when typing queries.

CHAPTER 4: SQL Server Management Studio

IntelliSense - Your Smart Assistant

IntelliSense drop-down menu for "Prod".

IntelliSense drop-down menu for "ProductS".

CHAPTER 4: SQL Server Management Studio

IntelliSense completion assistance for "ProductN"

```
SELECT * FROM AdventureWorks.Production.Product
WHERE ProductSubcategoryID is not NULL
ORDER BY ProductN
```

    ProductN
    ProductNumber   column ProductNumber(nvarchar, not null)

IntelliSense completion assistance for "Produ"

```
SELECT * FROM AdventureWorks.Production.Product
WHERE ProductSubcategoryID is not NULL
ORDER BY ProductNumber;
GO

INSERT INTO Production.Product (Produ
```

    Produ
    ProductID   column ProductID(PK, int, n
    ProductLine
    ProductModelID
    ProductNumber
    ProductSubcategoryID

CHAPTER 4: SQL Server Management Studio

IntelliSense Assisting with User-Defined Objects

IntelliSense helps out with a user-defined stored procedure execution.

```
USE AdventureWorks2012;
GO
CREATE PROCEDURE sprocProductPaging
(
    @PageNumber int,
    @RowsPerPage int
)
AS
BEGIN
SELECT  ProductNumber,
        Name            AS ProductName,
        ListPrice,
        Color
    FROM Production.Product p
    WHERE ProductSubcategoryID is not NULL
    ORDER BY ProductNumber
    OFFSET (@PageNumber-1) * @RowsPerPage ROWS
    FETCH NEXT @RowsPerPage ROWS ONLY;
END;
GO
-- Command(s) completed successfully.

EXEC sprocProductPaging 10
```

AdventureWorks2012.dbo.sprocProductPaging **@PageNumber int**, @RowsPerPage int
Stored procedures always return INT.

IntelliSense Smart Guessing Partial Word in Middle of Object Names

You don't have to remember how an object name starts. You just have to remember some part of the name. Looking for the system view associated with "waits".

Looking for the SalesOrderHeader table but only remembering "head".

CHAPTER 4: SQL Server Management Studio

IntelliSense - Your Smart Assistant

Hovering over Red Squiggly Underline Errors for Explanation

IntelliSense red wave (squiggly) underlining of errors which is caused, actually, by a single invalid table reference.

CHAPTER 4: SQL Server Management Studio

Common Error: The multi-part identifier "abc" could not be bound.

Hovering over the first error results in an explanation pop-up. This is a distant error, the kind usually the hardest to solve, because, actually, it is a secondary error caused by the primary error which is located on a different line. In this instance, there are few lines difference only, but in a large stored procedure the difference can be 200 lines as an example.

```
PSC.Name AS Subcategory,
```
The multi-part identifier "PSC.Name" could not be bound.

Hovering over the second error yields the cause of all errors: "ProductSubZcategory".

```
Production.ProductSubZcategory AS PSC
```
Invalid object name 'Production.ProductSubZcategory'.

The remaining error messages are all "multi-part..." caused by the solitary invalid table reference.

```
PSC.ProductSubcategoryID = P.ProductSubcategoryID
```
The multi-part identifier "PSC.ProductSubcategoryID" could not be bound.

After fixing the table name, all errors are gone.

```
SELECT          UPPER(PC.Name)                    AS Category,
                PSC.Name                          AS Subcategory,
                P.Name                            AS Product,
                FORMAT(P.ListPrice, 'c', 'en-US') AS ListPrice,
                FORMAT(P.StandardCost, 'c', 'en-US') AS StandardCost,
                P.ProductNumber
FROM     Production.Product AS P
         INNER JOIN  Production.ProductSubcategory AS PSC
                 ON PSC.ProductSubcategoryID = P.ProductSubcategoryID
         INNER JOIN  Production.ProductCategory AS PC
                 ON PC.ProductCategoryID = PSC.ProductCategoryID
WHERE        (PSC.Name LIKE 'Touring Frames')
ORDER BY Category, Subcategory, Product;
```

Refreshing IntelliSense Cache for New DB Objects

IntelliSense cache is not updated real-time. If new objects are created in another connection (session), they will not be seen until exit SSMS/reenter or IntelliSense cache is updated. No red-wave underline for the **newly created object SOD** in the same connection.

In another connection, the query works, but there are red squiggly underlining for the new table & column.

CHAPTER 4: SQL Server Management Studio

Refreshing IntelliSense Local Cache

Squiggly red line goes away in all connections for the new database objects.

CHAPTER 5: Basic Concepts of Client-Server Computing

Client - Server Relational Database Management System

The "server" is SQL Server, operating on a powerful hardware platform, managing databases and related items. The client is application software. The real client is naturally a human user who runs the application software. Automated software which uses the database for one thing or another is also considered a "client". The client computer, in the next room or thousands of miles away, is connected to the server through communications link. The client software sends a request, a query, to SQL Server, after execution the server returns the results to the client. An example for a query sent by the client to the server:

SELECT ListPrice FROM AdventureWorks2012.Production.Product WHERE ProductID = 800;

SQL Server executes the query and returns "1120.49" to the client with a flag indicating successful query execution. A tempting analogy is a restaurant: kitchen is the server, patrons are the clients and the communications / delivery done by waiters & waitresses.

Screenshot displays SQL Server (highlighted) along with other related software such as SQL Server Agent (job scheduling facility), SSIS (data transformation & transfer), SSRS (Reporting), SSAS (OLAP Cube) and other auxiliary software.

CHAPTER 5: Basic Concepts of Client-Server Computing

Database Objects on Server-Side

Screenshot of Object Explorer displays almost all important database objects with the exception of constraints, triggers and indexes.

```
SQLQuery69.sql - HPESTAR.AdventureWorks2012 (HPESTAR\Owner (57)) - Microso...

File  Edit  View  Query  Project  Debug  Tools  Window  Help

New Query
AdventureWorks2012    Execute   Debug

Object Explorer
Connect ▼

☐ AdventureWorks2012
    ⊞ Database Diagrams
    ⊞ Tables
    ⊞ Views
    ⊞ Synonyms
    ☐ Programmability
        ⊞ Stored Procedures
        ⊞ Functions
        ⊞ Database Triggers
        ⊞ Assemblies
        ⊞ Types
        ⊞ Rules
        ⊞ Defaults
        ⊞ Plan Guides
        ⊞ Sequences
    ⊞ Service Broker
    ☐ Storage
        ⊞ Full Text Catalogs
        ⊞ Partition Schemes
        ⊞ Partition Functions
        ⊞ Full Text Stoplists
        ⊞ Search Property Lists
    ⊞ Security
⊞ AdventureWorksDW2012
⊞ CopyOfAdventureWorks
⊞ CopyOfAdventureWorks2012
⊞ CopyOfNorthwind
```

Database Related Items on Client-Side

On the client side the following items:

- SQL Server client libraries to access the server and database
- SQL queries imbedded in application programs
- Stored procedure calls imbedded in application software

Queries by themselves are not database object. To make them database objects we have to build stored procedures, functions or views around them.

The following code segment illustrates database connection and query from ASP to Inventory database. In ANSI SQL terminology catalog means database.

```
' Connect
<%
Dim StrConnInventory
Dim ConnInventory

StrConnInventory = "Provider=SQLOLEDB.1;Data Source=LONDONHEADOFFICE;Initial Catalog=Inventory;User ID=finance;Password=fa$nAnCe#9*"

Set ConnInventory = Server.CreateObject("ADODB.Connection")

ConnInventory.ConnectionTimeout = 4000
ConnInventory.CommandTimeout = 4000
ConnInventory.Open StrConnInventory

' Query
Dim YourQuery As String = "SELECT Name, Price FROM Product"
 Dim YourCommand As New SqlCommand(YourQuery)
 YourCommand.Connection = ConnInventory
 YourConnection.Open()
 YourCommand.ExecuteNonQuery()
 Response.Write(YourCommand)
 YourCommand.Connection.Close()
%>
' Disconnect
<%
ConnInventory.Close
Set ConnInventory = Nothing
%>
```

CHAPTER 5: Basic Concepts of Client-Server Computing

SQL Server Profiler to Monitor Client-Server Communications

SQL Server Profiler, a tool in SSMS, has two modes of operations: interactive GUI and silent T-SQL script based operation. The simplest use of the Profiler is to check what queries are sent to the server (SQL Server) from the client and how long does processing take (duration). The client software sending the queries is SSMS. Even though SSMS appears as the "face of SQL Server", it is only a client software.

```
USE pubs;
GO
SELECT * FROM titles;
GO

USE Northwind;
GO
SELECT * FROM Products ORDER BY ProductName;
GO

USE AdventureWorks2012;
GO
SELECT * FROM Sales.SalesOrderHeader WHERE OrderDate='20080201';
GO
```

EventClass	TextData	A..	L..	CPU	Reads	Writes	Duration
SQL:BatchStarting	USE pubs;	M.	H.				
SQL:BatchCompleted	USE pubs;	M.	H.	0	0	0	7
SQL:BatchStarting	SELECT * FROM tit...	M.	H.				
SQL:BatchCompleted	SELECT * FROM tit...	M.	H.	0	2	0	13
SQL:BatchStarting	USE Northwind;	M.	H.				
SQL:BatchCompleted	USE Northwind;	M.	H.	0	0	0	9
SQL:BatchStarting	SELECT * FROM Produ...	M.	H.				
SQL:BatchCompleted	SELECT * FROM Produ...	M.	H.	0	4	0	4
SQL:BatchStarting	USE AdventureWorks2...	M.	H.				
SQL:BatchCompleted	USE AdventureWorks2...	M.	H.	0	0	0	10
SQL:BatchStarting	SELECT * FROM Sales...	M.	H.				
SQL:BatchCompleted	SELECT * FROM Sales...	M.	H.	0	791	0	75

SELECT * FROM Sales.SalesOrderHeader WHERE OrderDate='20080201';

Trace is running.   Ln 81, Col 1   Rows: 81   Connections: 1

CHAPTER 5: Basic Concepts of Client-Server Computing

Table - Database Object

A database table holds data in tabular format by rows and columns. The main method of connecting tables is FOREIGN KEY referencing PRIMARY KEY. A set of connected tables makes up the database. Screenshot displays the structure and partial content of Northwind database Products table.

CHAPTER 5: Basic Concepts of Client-Server Computing

Tables in Production Schema

The listing and data dictionary description of tables in AdventureWorks2012 Production schema.

```
USE AdventureWorks2012;

SELECT  CONCAT('Production.', objname COLLATE DATABASE_DEFAULT) AS TableName,
        value                                                   AS [Description]
FROM fn_listextendedproperty (          NULL,
                              'schema', 'Production',
                              'table', default,
                              NULL, NULL)
ORDER BY TableName;
```

TableName	Description
Production.BillOfMaterials	Items required to make bicycles and bicycle subassemblies. It identifies the hierarchical relationship between a parent product and its components.
Production.Culture	Lookup table containing the languages in which some AdventureWorks data is stored.
Production.Document	Product maintenance documents.
Production.Illustration	Bicycle assembly diagrams.
Production.Location	Product inventory and manufacturing locations.
Production.Product	Products sold or used in the manfacturing of sold products.
Production.ProductCategory	High-level product categorization.
Production.ProductCostHistory	Changes in the cost of a product over time.
Production.ProductDescription	Product descriptions in several languages.
Production.ProductDocument	Cross-reference table mapping products to related product documents.
Production.ProductInventory	Product inventory information.
Production.ProductListPriceHistory	Changes in the list price of a product over time.
Production.ProductModel	Product model classification.
Production.ProductModelIllustration	Cross-reference table mapping product models and illustrations.
Production.ProductModelProductDescriptionCulture	Cross-reference table mapping product descriptions and the language the description is written in.
Production.ProductPhoto	Product images.
Production.ProductProductPhoto	Cross-reference table mapping products and product photos.
Production.ProductReview	Customer reviews of products they have purchased.
Production.ProductSubcategory	Product subcategories. See ProductCategory table.
Production.ScrapReason	Manufacturing failure reasons lookup table.
Production.TransactionHistory	Record of each purchase order, sales order, or work order transaction year to date.
Production.TransactionHistoryArchive	Transactions for previous years.
Production.UnitMeasure	Unit of measure lookup table.
Production.WorkOrder	Manufacturing work orders.
Production.WorkOrderRouting	Work order details.

Index - Database Object

An index on a table is a B-tree based structure which speeds up random searches. **Typically PRIMARY KEY (automatic), FOREIGN KEY and WHERE clause columns have indexes.** If the index is constructed on more than one column, it is called **composite index**. If all the columns in a query are in the index, it is called **covering index**. Properties dialog box displays the PRIMARY KEY composite index of the EmployeeDepartmentHistory table.

CHAPTER 5: Basic Concepts of Client-Server Computing

Diagram of EmployeeDepartmentHistory and Related Tables

EmployeeDepartmentHistory is a simple junction table with three FOREIGN KEYs to the Employee, Shift and Department tables respectively.

Department (HumanRe...)
- DepartmentID
- Name
- GroupName
- ModifiedDate

Employee (HumanReso...)
- BusinessEntityID
- NationalIDNumber
- LoginID
- OrganizationNode
- OrganizationLevel
- JobTitle
- BirthDate
- MaritalStatus
- Gender
- HireDate
- SalariedFlag
- VacationHours
- SickLeaveHours
- CurrentFlag
- rowguid
- ModifiedDate

EmployeeDepartmentHistory
- BusinessEntityID
- DepartmentID
- ShiftID
- StartDate
- EndDate
- ModifiedDate

Shift (HumanResources...)
- ShiftID
- Name
- StartTime
- EndTime
- ModifiedDate

Index - Database Object

Index Description in Data Dictionary

The indexes listing for Product, SalesOrderHeader & SalesOrderDetail tables.

```
USE AdventureWorks2012;

SELECT  objtype                     AS ObjectType,
        'Sales.SalesOrderHeader'    AS TableName,
        objname                     AS ObjectName,
        value                       AS [Description]
FROM fn_listextendedproperty (NULL, 'schema', 'Sales', 'table', 'SalesOrderHeader', 'index', default)

UNION

SELECT objtype, 'Sales.SalesOrderDetail', objname, value
FROM fn_listextendedproperty (NULL, 'schema', 'Sales', 'table', 'SalesOrderDetail', 'index', default)

UNION

SELECT objtype, 'Production.Product', objname, value
FROM fn_listextendedproperty (NULL, 'schema', 'Production', 'table', 'Product', 'index', default)
ORDER BY TableName;
GO
```

ObjectType	TableName	ObjectName	Description
INDEX	Production.Product	AK_Product_Name	Unique nonclustered index.
INDEX	Production.Product	AK_Product_ProductNumber	Unique nonclustered index.
INDEX	Production.Product	AK_Product_rowguid	Unique nonclustered index. Used to support replication samples.
INDEX	Production.Product	PK_Product_ProductID	Clustered index created by a primary key constraint.
INDEX	Sales.SalesOrderDetail	AK_SalesOrderDetail_rowguid	Unique nonclustered index. Used to support replication samples.
INDEX	Sales.SalesOrderDetail	IX_SalesOrderDetail_ProductID	Nonclustered index.
INDEX	Sales.SalesOrderDetail	PK_SalesOrderDetail_SalesOrderID_SalesOrderDetailID	Clustered index created by a primary key constraint.
INDEX	Sales.SalesOrderHeader	AK_SalesOrderHeader_rowguid	Unique nonclustered index. Used to support replication samples.
INDEX	Sales.SalesOrderHeader	AK_SalesOrderHeader_SalesOrderNumber	Unique nonclustered index.
INDEX	Sales.SalesOrderHeader	IX_SalesOrderHeader_CustomerID	Nonclustered index.
INDEX	Sales.SalesOrderHeader	IX_SalesOrderHeader_SalesPersonID	Nonclustered index.
INDEX	Sales.SalesOrderHeader	PK_SalesOrderHeader_SalesOrderID	Clustered index created by a primary key constraint.

Constraint - Database Object

The PRIMARY KEY constraint ensures that each row has a unique ID. The FOREIGN KEY constraint ensures that the FK points to (references) a valid PK. CHECK constraint enforces formulas (check clauses) defined for a column such as **OrderQty > 0.** If the formula evaluates to TRUE, the CHECK constraint satisfied, otherwise ERROR condition is generated by the database engine. SSMS screenshot shows a CHECK constraints listing query and results in the Northwind database.

```sql
SELECT CONSTRAINT_CATALOG
      ,CONSTRAINT_SCHEMA
      ,CONSTRAINT_NAME
      ,CHECK_CLAUSE
  FROM Northwind.INFORMATION_SCHEMA.CHECK_CONSTRAINTS
```

	CONSTRAINT_CATALOG	CO...	CONSTRAINT_NAME	CHECK_CLAUSE
1	Northwind	dbo	CK_Birthdate	([BirthDate]<getdate())
2	Northwind	dbo	CK_Products_UnitPr...	([UnitPrice]>=(0))
3	Northwind	dbo	CK_ReorderLevel	([ReorderLevel]>=(0))
4	Northwind	dbo	CK_UnitsInStock	([UnitsInStock]>=(0))
5	Northwind	dbo	CK_UnitsOnOrder	([UnitsOnOrder]>=(0))
6	Northwind	dbo	CK_Discount	([Discount]>=(0) AND [Discount]<=(1))
7	Northwind	dbo	CK_Quantity	([Quantity]>(0))
8	Northwind	dbo	CK_UnitPrice	([UnitPrice]>=(0))

CHAPTER 5: Basic Concepts of Client-Server Computing

Index - Database Object

PRIMARY KEY & FOREIGN KEY Constraint Descriptions in Data Dictionary

Query to retrieve constraint descriptions (extended properties) for Product, SalesOrderHeader & SalesOrderDetail tables. Note: *description* not definition.

```
USE AdventureWorks2012;

-- UNION of 3 result sets
SELECT objtype AS ObjectType, 'Sales.SalesOrderHeader' AS TableName,
       objname as ObjectName, value AS [Description]
FROM fn_listextendedproperty (NULL, 'schema', 'Sales', 'table', 'SalesOrderHeader', 'constraint', default)
WHERE left(convert(varchar,value),7)='Foreign' or left(convert(varchar,value),7)='Primary'
UNION
SELECT objtype, 'Sales.SalesOrderDetail', objname, value
FROM fn_listextendedproperty (NULL, 'schema', 'Sales', 'table', 'SalesOrderDetail', 'constraint', default)
WHERE left(convert(varchar,value),7)='Foreign' or left(convert(varchar,value),7)='Primary'
UNION
SELECT objtype, 'Production.Product', objname, value
FROM fn_listextendedproperty (NULL, 'schema', 'Production', 'table', 'Product', 'constraint', default)
WHERE left(convert(varchar,value),7)='Foreign' or left(convert(varchar,value),7)='Primary'
ORDER BY TableName, ObjectName DESC;
GO
```

ObjectType	TableName	ObjectName	Description
CONSTRAINT	Production.Product	PK_Product_ProductID	Primary key (clustered) constraint
CONSTRAINT	Production.Product	FK_Product_UnitMeasure_WeightUnitMeasureCode	Foreign key constraint referencing UnitMeasure.UnitMeasureCode.
CONSTRAINT	Production.Product	FK_Product_UnitMeasure_SizeUnitMeasureCode	Foreign key constraint referencing UnitMeasure.UnitMeasureCode.
CONSTRAINT	Production.Product	FK_Product_ProductSubcategory_ProductSubcategoryID	Foreign key constraint referencing ProductSubcategory.ProductSubcategoryID.
CONSTRAINT	Production.Product	FK_Product_ProductModel_ProductModelID	Foreign key constraint referencing ProductModel.ProductModelID.
CONSTRAINT	Sales.SalesOrderDetail	PK_SalesOrderDetail_SalesOrderID_SalesOrderDetailID	Primary key (clustered) constraint
CONSTRAINT	Sales.SalesOrderDetail	FK_SalesOrderDetail_SpecialOfferProduct_SpecialOfferIDProductID	Foreign key constraint referencing SpecialOfferProduct.SpecialOfferIDProductID.
CONSTRAINT	Sales.SalesOrderDetail	FK_SalesOrderDetail_SalesOrderHeader_SalesOrderID	Foreign key constraint referencing SalesOrderHeader.PurchaseOrderID.
CONSTRAINT	Sales.SalesOrderHeader	PK_SalesOrderHeader_SalesOrderID	Primary key (clustered) constraint
CONSTRAINT	Sales.SalesOrderHeader	FK_SalesOrderHeader_ShipMethod_ShipMethodID	Foreign key constraint referencing ShipMethod.ShipMethodID.
CONSTRAINT	Sales.SalesOrderHeader	FK_SalesOrderHeader_SalesTerritory_TerritoryID	Foreign key constraint referencing SalesTerritory.TerritoryID.
CONSTRAINT	Sales.SalesOrderHeader	FK_SalesOrderHeader_SalesPerson_SalesPersonID	Foreign key constraint referencing SalesPerson.SalesPersonID.
CONSTRAINT	Sales.SalesOrderHeader	FK_SalesOrderHeader_Customer_CustomerID	Foreign key constraint referencing Customer.CustomerID.
CONSTRAINT	Sales.SalesOrderHeader	FK_SalesOrderHeader_CurrencyRate_CurrencyRateID	Foreign key constraint referencing CurrencyRate.CurrencyRateID.
CONSTRAINT	Sales.SalesOrderHeader	FK_SalesOrderHeader_CreditCard_CreditCardID	Foreign key constraint referencing CreditCard.CreditCardID.
CONSTRAINT	Sales.SalesOrderHeader	FK_SalesOrderHeader_Address_ShipToAddressID	Foreign key constraint referencing Address.AddressID.
CONSTRAINT	Sales.SalesOrderHeader	FK_SalesOrderHeader_Address_BillToAddressID	Foreign key constraint referencing Address.AddressID.

CHAPTER 5: Basic Concepts of Client-Server Computing

View - Database Object

A SELECT query, with some restrictions, can be repackaged as view and thus become a server-side object, a coveted status, from "homeless" to "mansion". The creation of view is very simple, basically a name assignment is required as shown in the following demonstration. As soon as the CREATE VIEW statement is executed successfully the query, unknown to the SQL Server so far, becomes an "official" SQL Server database object, stored in the database. A view, a virtual table, can be used just like a table in SELECT queries. A note about the query: **the column aliases FirstAuthor and SecondAuthor cannot be used in the WHERE clause, only in the ORDER BY clause if present.**

SELECT results from views require ORDER BY if sorting is desired. There is no way around it.

```
USE pubs;
GO
```

```
CREATE VIEW vAuthorsInSameCity
AS
SELECT       FirstAuthor     = CONCAT(au1.au_fname,' ', au1.au_lname),
             SecondAuthor    = CONCAT(au2.au_fname,' ', au2.au_lname),
             FirstCity       = au1.city,
             SecondCity      = au2.city
FROM    authors au1
    INNER JOIN authors au2
      ON au1.city = au2.city
WHERE   CONCAT(au1.au_fname,' ', au1.au_lname) < CONCAT(au2.au_fname,' ', au2.au_lname)
GO
```

```
SELECT * FROM vAuthorsInSameCity
ORDER BY FirstAuthor, SecondAuthor
GO
-- (13 row(s) affected) - Partial results.
```

FirstAuthor	SecondAuthor	FirstCity	SecondCity
Abraham Bennet	Cheryl Carson	Berkeley	Berkeley
Albert Ringer	Anne Ringer	Salt Lake City	Salt Lake City
Ann Dull	Sheryl Hunter	Palo Alto	Palo Alto
Dean Straight	Dirk Stringer	Oakland	Oakland
Dean Straight	Livia Karsen	Oakland	Oakland
Dean Straight	Marjorie Green	Oakland	Oakland
Dean Straight	Stearns MacFeather	Oakland	Oakland
Dirk Stringer	Livia Karsen	Oakland	Oakland

CHAPTER 5: Basic Concepts of Client-Server Computing

CREATE Indexed View for Business Critical Queries

View Descriptions in Data Dictionary

Query to list view descriptions in selected schemas.

```
USE AdventureWorks2012;
SELECT   CONCAT('Sales.', objname COLLATE DATABASE_DEFAULT)           AS ViewName,
         value                                                         AS [Description]
FROM fn_listextendedproperty (NULL, 'schema', 'Sales', 'view', default, NULL, NULL)
UNION
SELECT   CONCAT('Production.', objname COLLATE DATABASE_DEFAULT), value
FROM fn_listextendedproperty (NULL, 'schema', 'Production', 'view', default, NULL, NULL)
UNION
SELECT   CONCAT('HumanResources.', objname COLLATE DATABASE_DEFAULT), value
FROM fn_listextendedproperty (NULL, 'schema', 'HumanResources', 'view', default, NULL, NULL)
UNION
SELECT   CONCAT('Person.', objname COLLATE DATABASE_DEFAULT),   value
FROM fn_listextendedproperty (NULL, 'schema', 'Person', 'view', default, NULL, NULL)
ORDER BY ViewName;  -- (18 row(s) affected) - Partial results.
```

ViewName	Description
HumanResources.vEmployee	Employee names and addresses.
HumanResources.vEmployeeDepartment	Returns employee name, title, and current department.
HumanResources.vEmployeeDepartmentHistory	Returns employee name and current and previous departments.
HumanResources.vJobCandidate	Job candidate names and resumes.

CREATE Indexed View for Business Critical Queries

An indexed view is stored like a table unlike a standard view which is a virtual table with a query that is evaluated upon view invocation. Performance is the main benefit of an indexed view, but it comes at a cost: it slows down INSERTs and other operations in the underlying tables.

```
IF OBJECT_ID ('Sales.vSalesByDateByProduct', 'V') IS NOT NULL DROP VIEW Sales.vSalesByDateByProduct ;
GO
CREATE VIEW Sales.vSalesByDateByProduct WITH SCHEMABINDING AS
   SELECT OrderDate, ProductNumber, SUM(LineTotal) AS TotalSales, COUNT_BIG(*) AS Items
   FROM Sales.SalesOrderDetail AS sod INNER JOIN Sales.SalesOrderHeader AS soh
      ON soh.SalesOrderID = sod.SalesOrderID   INNER JOIN Production.Product p ON sod.ProductID=p.ProductID
      GROUP BY OrderDate, ProductNumber;
GO
CREATE UNIQUE CLUSTERED INDEX idxVSalesCI ON Sales.vSalesByDateByProduct (OrderDate, ProductNumber);
GO
SELECT * FROM Sales.vSalesByDateByProduct ORDER BY OrderDate, ProductNumber;
GO  -- (26878 row(s) affected) - Partial results.
```

OrderDate	ProductNumber	TotalSales	Items
2005-07-01 00:00:00.000	BK-M82B-38	44549.868000	7
2005-07-01 00:00:00.000	BK-M82B-42	32399.904000	8
2005-07-01 00:00:00.000	BK-M82B-44	46574.862000	7

Graphical View Designer

A view can be designed graphically or an existing view altered by using the Design option on the View drop-down menu in SSMS Object Explorer. First we create a view, then enter the graphical view designer to take a look.

```
USE [Northwind];
GO
CREATE VIEW [dbo].[ListOfProducts] AS
SELECT Categories.CategoryName as Category, ProductName, CompanyName AS Supplier
FROM Categories        INNER JOIN Products  ON Categories.CategoryID = Products.CategoryID
                       INNER JOIN Suppliers  ON Suppliers.SupplierID = Products.SupplierID
WHERE (((Products.Discontinued)=0));
GO
```

Stored Procedure: Server-Side Program

Stored procedures are T-SQL programs with optional input/output parameters. They vary from very simply to extremely complex. Following is the query which we will transform into a stored procedure, a server-side database object. Typical stored procedure returns table-like results to the client application software just like a SELECT query. That is though not a requirement.

```
USE AdventureWorks2012;
GO
SELECT      P.Name                AS Product,
            L.Name                AS [Inventory Location],
            SUM(PI.Quantity)      AS [Qty Available]
FROM Production.Product AS P
   INNER JOIN Production.ProductInventory AS PI
            ON P.ProductID = PI.ProductID
   INNER JOIN Production.Location AS L
            ON PI.LocationID = L.LocationID
   INNER JOIN Production.ProductSubcategory SC
            ON P.ProductSubcategoryID = SC.ProductSubcategoryID
WHERE SC.Name = 'Touring Bikes'
GROUP BY P.Name, L.Name
ORDER BY P.Name;
GO
-- (44 row(s) affected) - Partial results.
```

Product	Inventory Location	Qty Available
Touring-1000 Blue, 46	Final Assembly	86
Touring-1000 Blue, 46	Finished Goods Storage	99
Touring-1000 Blue, 50	Final Assembly	81
Touring-1000 Blue, 50	Finished Goods Storage	67
Touring-1000 Blue, 54	Final Assembly	60
Touring-1000 Blue, 54	Finished Goods Storage	73
Touring-1000 Blue, 60	Final Assembly	99
Touring-1000 Blue, 60	Finished Goods Storage	30
Touring-1000 Yellow, 46	Final Assembly	83
Touring-1000 Yellow, 46	Finished Goods Storage	65
Touring-1000 Yellow, 50	Final Assembly	62
Touring-1000 Yellow, 50	Finished Goods Storage	75
Touring-1000 Yellow, 54	Final Assembly	40
Touring-1000 Yellow, 54	Finished Goods Storage	35
Touring-1000 Yellow, 60	Final Assembly	100

CHAPTER 5: Basic Concepts of Client-Server Computing

Stored Procedure with Input Parameters

To make the stored procedure even more useful, we replace the literal 'Touring Bikes' with an input parameter.

```sql
CREATE PROC uspProductInventoryLocation @Subcategory nvarchar(50)
AS
BEGIN
SELECT          P.Name                      AS Product,
                L.Name                      AS [Inventory Location],
                SUM(PI.Quantity)            AS [Qty Available]
FROM Production.Product AS P
   INNER JOIN Production.ProductInventory AS PI
            ON P.ProductID = PI.ProductID
   INNER JOIN Production.Location AS L
            ON PI.LocationID = L.LocationID
   INNER JOIN Production.ProductSubcategory SC
            ON P.ProductSubcategoryID = SC.ProductSubcategoryID
WHERE SC.Name = @Subcategory
GROUP BY P.Name, L.Name
ORDER BY P.Name;
END
GO

-- Execute stored procedure with parameter
EXEC uspProductInventoryLocation 'Touring Bikes';
-- (44 row(s) affected)

EXEC uspProductInventoryLocation 'Mountain Bikes';        -- (64 row(s) affected) - Partial results.
```

Product	Inventory Location	Qty Available
Mountain-100 Black, 38	Final Assembly	56
Mountain-100 Black, 38	Finished Goods Storage	99
Mountain-100 Black, 42	Final Assembly	116
Mountain-100 Black, 42	Finished Goods Storage	78
Mountain-100 Black, 44	Final Assembly	100
Mountain-100 Black, 44	Finished Goods Storage	49
Mountain-100 Black, 48	Final Assembly	65
Mountain-100 Black, 48	Finished Goods Storage	88
Mountain-100 Silver, 38	Final Assembly	100
Mountain-100 Silver, 38	Finished Goods Storage	49
Mountain-100 Silver, 42	Final Assembly	65
Mountain-100 Silver, 42	Finished Goods Storage	88
Mountain-100 Silver, 44	Final Assembly	75
Mountain-100 Silver, 44	Finished Goods Storage	83
Mountain-100 Silver, 48	Final Assembly	102

CHAPTER 5: Basic Concepts of Client-Server Computing

Stored Procedure Descriptions in Data Dictionary

Query to list stored procedure descriptions in selected schemas.

```
USE AdventureWorks2012;
```

```
SELECT
        CONCAT('dbo.', objname COLLATE DATABASE_DEFAULT)          AS SprocName,
        value                                                     AS [Description]
FROM fn_listextendedproperty (NULL, 'schema', 'dbo', 'procedure', default, NULL, NULL)
WHERE LEN(convert(nvarchar(max),value)) > 4
UNION
SELECT
        CONCAT('dbo.', objname COLLATE DATABASE_DEFAULT),
        value
FROM fn_listextendedproperty (NULL, 'schema', 'HumanResources', 'procedure', default, NULL, NULL)
ORDER BY SprocName;
```

SprocName	Description
dbo.uspGetBillOfMaterials	Stored procedure using a recursive query to return a multi-level bill of material for the specified ProductID.
dbo.uspGetEmployeeManagers	Stored procedure using a recursive query to return the direct and indirect managers of the specified employee.
dbo.uspGetManagerEmployees	Stored procedure using a recursive query to return the direct and indirect employees of the specified manager.
dbo.uspGetWhereUsedProductID	Stored procedure using a recursive query to return all components or assemblies that directly or indirectly use the specified ProductID.
dbo.uspLogError	Logs error information in the ErrorLog table about the error that caused execution to jump to the CATCH block of a TRY...CATCH construct. Should be executed from within the scope of a CATCH block otherwise it will return without inserting error information.
dbo.uspPrintError	Prints error information about the error that caused execution to jump to the CATCH block of a TRY...CATCH construct. Should be executed from within the scope of a CATCH block otherwise it will return without printing any error information.
dbo.uspUpdateEmployeeHireInfo	Updates the Employee table and inserts a new row in the EmployeePayHistory table with the values specified in the input parameters.
dbo.uspUpdateEmployeeLogin	Updates the Employee table with the values specified in the input parameters for the given BusinessEntityID.
dbo.uspUpdateEmployeePersonalInfo	Updates the Employee table with the values specified in the input parameters for the given EmployeeID.

CHAPTER 5: Basic Concepts of Client-Server Computing

Trigger: Event Fired Server-Side Program

Trigger is like a stored procedure with four differences:

- ➢ Trigger is fired by an event such as table insert not by a call like a stored procedure.
- ➢ Trigger has the deleted (old row copy) and inserted (new row copy) tables available.
- ➢ Trigger does not have input/output parameter option.
- ➢ Trigger never returns table-like results.

Trigger to synchronize data in StateTaxFreeBondArchive table if data is inserted or updated in the StateTaxFreeBond table.

```
CREATE TRIGGER trgFillInMissingCouponRate

ON [dbo].StateTaxFreeBond

FOR INSERT,UPDATE

AS

BEGIN

    UPDATE StateTaxFreeBondArchive

        SET CouponRate = isnull(i.CouponRate,m.CouponRate)

    FROM StateTaxFreeBondArchive m

        INNER JOIN inserted i

            ON m.MBCID = i.MBCID

END
GO
```

Once a trigger is compiled, it is active and working silently in the background whenever insert, update or delete event fires it up.

It is important to note that there is a downside to the trigger "stealth" operation: if a trigger is dropped , it may not be noticed as part of the day-to-day operation. This behaviour is unlike stored procedure whereby if dropped, it causes error in the calling application software which can be noticed by users.

CHAPTER 5: Basic Concepts of Client-Server Computing

Function: Read-Only Server-Side Program

A user-defined function is also a program like a stored procedure, however, **no database change can be performed within a function, read only**. The database can be changed both in a trigger and a stored procedure. The following T-SQL script demonstrates the creation and use of a table-valued user-defined function. The other function type is scalar-valued, returns only a single value.

```sql
CREATE FUNCTION dbo.ufnSplitCommaDelimitedIntegerString (@NumberList nvarchar(max))
RETURNS @SplitList TABLE ( Element INT )
AS
 BEGIN
   DECLARE @Pointer   int,
       @Element nvarchar(32)
   SET @NumberList = LTRIM(RTRIM(@NumberList))
   IF ( RIGHT(@NumberList, 1) != ',' )
    SET @NumberList=@NumberList + ','
   SET @Pointer = CHARINDEX(',', @NumberList, 1)
   IF REPLACE(@NumberList, ',', '') <> ''
    BEGIN
     WHILE ( @Pointer > 0 )
      BEGIN
        SET @Element = LTRIM(RTRIM(LEFT(@NumberList, @Pointer - 1)))
        IF ( @Element <> '' )
         INSERT INTO @SplitList
         VALUES    (CONVERT(int, @Element))
        SET @NumberList = RIGHT(@NumberList,
            LEN(@NumberList) - @Pointer  )
        SET @Pointer = CHARINDEX(',', @NumberList, 1)
      END
    END
   RETURN
 END;
GO
SELECT * FROM  dbo.ufnSplitCommaDelimitedIntegerString ('1, 2, 4, 8, 16, 32, 64, 128, 256');
```

Element
1
2
4
8
16
32
64
128
256

CHAPTER 5: Basic Concepts of Client-Server Computing

User-Defined Function Descriptions in Data Dictionary

Query to list user-defined function descriptions in the default "dbo" schema. "dbo" stands for database owner, a database role.

```
USE AdventureWorks2012;
GO

SELECT
        CONCAT('dbo.', objname COLLATE DATABASE_DEFAULT)              AS UDFName,
        value                                                         AS [Description]
FROM fn_listextendedproperty (NULL, 'schema', 'dbo', 'function', default, NULL, NULL)
WHERE LEN(convert(nvarchar(max),value)) > 4
ORDER BY UDFName;
GO
```

UDFName	Description
dbo.ufnGetAccountingEndDate	Scalar function used in the uSalesOrderHeader trigger to set the starting account date.
dbo.ufnGetAccountingStartDate	Scalar function used in the uSalesOrderHeader trigger to set the ending account date.
dbo.ufnGetContactInformation	Table value function returning the first name, last name, job title and contact type for a given contact.
dbo.ufnGetDocumentStatusText	Scalar function returning the text representation of the Status column in the Document table.
dbo.ufnGetProductDealerPrice	Scalar function returning the dealer price for a given product on a particular order date.
dbo.ufnGetProductListPrice	Scalar function returning the list price for a given product on a particular order date.
dbo.ufnGetProductStandardCost	Scalar function returning the standard cost for a given product on a particular order date.
dbo.ufnGetPurchaseOrderStatusText	Scalar function returning the text representation of the Status column in the PurchaseOrderHeader table.
dbo.ufnGetSalesOrderStatusText	Scalar function returning the text representation of the Status column in the SalesOrderHeader table.
dbo.ufnGetStock	Scalar function returning the quantity of inventory in LocationID 6 (Miscellaneous Storage)for a specified ProductID.
dbo.ufnLeadingZeros	Scalar function used by the Sales.Customer table to help set the account number

Sequence - Database Object

The INT IDENTITY(1,1) function commonly used as **SURROGATE PRIMARY KEY** is limited to the host table. Sequence object, new in SQL Server 2012, can be shared by tables and programs. T-SQL script to demonstrate how two tables can share an integer sequence.

```sql
USE AdventureWorks2012;
GO
CREATE SEQUENCE CustomerSequence as INT
START WITH 1  INCREMENT BY 1;
GO
CREATE TABLE LONDONCustomer
(
        CustomerID      INT PRIMARY KEY,
        Name            NVARCHAR(64) UNIQUE,
        ModifiedDate    DATE default (CURRENT_TIMESTAMP)   );
GO
CREATE TABLE NYCCustomer
(
        CustomerID      INT PRIMARY KEY,
        Name            NVARCHAR(64) UNIQUE,
        ModifiedDate    DATE default (CURRENT_TIMESTAMP)   );
GO
INSERT NYCCustomer (CustomerID, Name)
VALUES
        (NEXT VALUE FOR CustomerSequence, 'Richard Blackstone'),
        (NEXT VALUE FOR CustomerSequence, 'Anna Smithfield');
GO
SELECT * FROM NYCCustomer;
```

CustomerID	Name	ModifiedDate
1	Richard Blackstone	2016-07-18
2	Anna Smithfield	2016-07-18

```sql
INSERT LONDONCustomer (CustomerID, Name)
VALUES
        (NEXT VALUE FOR CustomerSequence, 'Kevin Lionheart'),
        (NEXT VALUE FOR CustomerSequence, 'Linda Wakefield');
GO

SELECT * FROM LONDONCustomer;
```

CustomerID	Name	ModifiedDate
3	Kevin Lionheart	2016-07-18
4	Linda Wakefield	2016-07-18

CHAPTER 5: Basic Concepts of Client-Server Computing

ROW_NUMBER() and Ranking Functions

Ranking functions (window functions), introduced with SQL Server 2005, provide sequencing and ranking items in a partition or all. ROW_NUMBER() (sequence) function is the most used.

```
SELECT  CustomerID,
        CONVERT(date, OrderDate)                            AS OrderDate,
        RANK() OVER (   PARTITION BY CustomerID
                        ORDER BY OrderDate DESC)            AS RankNo
FROM   AdventureWorks2012.Sales.SalesOrderHeader   ORDER  BY CustomerID,  RankNo;
GO  -- (31465 row(s) affected) - Partial results.
```

CustomerID	OrderDate	RankNo
11014	2007-11-01	1
11014	2007-09-24	2
11015	2007-07-22	1
11016	2007-08-13	1

Partition data by CustomerID and rank it OrderDate DESC (most recent orders first).

```
SELECT *
FROM   (SELECT CustomerID,
               CONVERT(date, OrderDate)         AS OrderDate,
               RANK()  OVER (
                   PARTITION BY CustomerID
                   ORDER BY OrderDate DESC)     AS RankNo
        FROM   AdventureWorks2012.Sales.SalesOrderHeader) x -- derived table
WHERE  RankNo  BETWEEN 1 AND 4
ORDER  BY CustomerID;
GO
-- (29383 row(s) affected)  - Partial results.
```

CustomerID	OrderDate	RankNo
11675	2007-08-13	1
11675	2006-04-27	2
11676	2008-06-11	1
11676	2008-02-21	2
11677	2008-06-02	1
11677	2008-03-24	2
11677	2008-03-17	3
11677	2008-03-07	4
11678	2007-08-09	1

CHAPTER 5: Basic Concepts of Client-Server Computing

ROW_NUMBER() and Ranking Functions

Query to compare RANK, DENSE_RANK & NTILE

```
USE AdventureWorks;

SELECT c.AccountNumber                          AS CustAccount,
    FLOOR(h.SubTotal / 1000)                    AS [SubTotal (Thousands $)],
    ROW_NUMBER() OVER(
        ORDER BY FLOOR(h.SubTotal /1000) DESC)  AS RowNumber,
    RANK()  OVER(
        ORDER BY FLOOR(h.SubTotal /1000) DESC)  AS Rank,
    DENSE_RANK()  OVER(
        ORDER BY FLOOR(h.SubTotal /1000) DESC)  AS DenseRank,
    NTILE(5)  OVER(
        ORDER BY FLOOR(h.SubTotal /1000) DESC)  AS NTile
FROM   Sales.Customer c
    INNER JOIN Sales.SalesOrderHeader h
        ON c.CustomerID = h.CustomerID
    INNER JOIN Sales.SalesTerritory t
        ON h.TerritoryID = t.TerritoryID
WHERE  t.Name = 'Germany'
    AND OrderDate >= '20040101' AND OrderDate  <  DATEADD(yy, 1, '20040101' )
    AND SubTotal >= 4000.0
ORDER  BY RowNumber;
```

CustAccount	SubTotal (Thousands $)	RowNumber	Rank	DenseRank	NTile
AW00000230	100.00	1	1	1	1
AW00000230	88.00	2	2	2	1
AW00000302	77.00	3	3	3	1
AW00000320	68.00	4	4	4	1
AW00000536	68.00	5	4	4	1
AW00000536	64.00	6	6	5	1
AW00000266	58.00	7	7	6	1
AW00000302	44.00	8	8	7	2
AW00000687	43.00	9	9	8	2
AW00000482	36.00	10	10	9	2
AW00000176	36.00	11	10	9	2
AW00000464	35.00	12	12	10	2
AW00000320	35.00	13	12	10	2
AW00000176	34.00	14	14	11	2
AW00000464	34.00	15	14	11	3

CHAPTER 5: Basic Concepts of Client-Server Computing

RANK & DENSE_RANK Sales By Millions

Ranking of sales staff by rounding sales down to millions applying the RANK & DENSE_RANK windowing functions.

```
USE AdventureWorks;
GO
SELECT CONCAT(c.FirstName, SPACE(1), c.LastName) AS FullName
   ,RANK() OVER
           (ORDER BY FLOOR(p.SalesYTD/1000000) DESC) AS [Rank]
   ,DENSE_RANK() OVER
           (ORDER BY FLOOR(p.SalesYTD/1000000) DESC) AS [DenseRank]
   ,FORMAT(p.SalesYTD, 'c0','en-US') AS YTDSales
FROM Sales.SalesPerson p
   INNER JOIN Person.Contact c
      ON p.SalesPersonID = c.ContactID
   INNER JOIN Person.Address a
      ON a.AddressID = c.ContactID
WHERE TerritoryID IS NOT NULL AND SalesYTD <> 0
ORDER BY [Rank], FullName;
GO  -- (13 row(s) affected)
```

FullName	Rank	DenseRank	YTDSales
Gail Erickson	1	1	$5,015,682
Shelley Dyck	1	1	$5,200,475
Maciej Dusza	3	2	$4,557,045
Jauna Elson	4	3	$3,018,725
Linda Ecoffey	4	3	$3,857,164
Mark Erickson	4	3	$3,827,950
Michael Emanuel	4	3	$3,189,356
Terry Eminhizer	4	3	$3,587,378
Carol Elliott	9	4	$2,811,013
Janeth Esteves	9	4	$2,241,204
Carla Eldridge	11	5	$1,764,939
Martha Espinoza	11	5	$1,931,620
Twanna Evans	11	5	$1,758,386

Dynamic SQL To Soar Beyond the Limits of Static SQL

Static (regular) T-SQL syntax does not accept variables at all places in a query. With dynamic SQL we can overcome the limitation. Dynamic SQL script uses table list metadata from the INFORMATION_SCHEMA.TABLES system view to build a COUNT() query for all tables. COUNT(*) returns 4 bytes integer. For large values COUNT_BIG() returns an 8 bytes integer.

```
DECLARE @SQL nvarchar(max) = '', @Schema sysname, @Table sysname;
SELECT TOP 20 @SQL = CONCAT(@SQL , 'SELECT "',QUOTENAME(TABLE_SCHEMA),'.',
        QUOTENAME(TABLE_NAME),'"',
        '= COUNT(*) FROM ', QUOTENAME(TABLE_SCHEMA),'.',QUOTENAME(TABLE_NAME) , ';',
        CHAR(10))
FROM INFORMATION_SCHEMA.TABLES  WHERE TABLE_TYPE='BASE TABLE';
PRINT @SQL;          -- Test & debug - Partial results.
```

```
SELECT "[Production].[BillOfMaterials]"= COUNT(*) FROM [Production].[BillOfMaterials];
SELECT "[Production].[Culture]"= COUNT(*) FROM [Production].[Culture];
```

EXEC sp_executesql @SQL   -- Dynamic SQL query execution -- Partial results.

```
[Production].[ScrapReason]
16
```

```
[HumanResources].[Shift]
3
```

Parameterized Dynamic SQL Query Execution

The dynamic SQL string has a parameterized query. It can only be executed if the parameter(s) is supplied when dynamic execution is called. Parameterization of dynamic SQL protects against SQL Injection Attack and offers performance benefits as well. Dynamic SQL & SQL Injection blog: http://blogs.msdn.com/b/raulga/archive/2007/01/04/dynamic-sql-sql-injection.aspx

```
DECLARE @LastName varchar(30) = 'O''Brien';
DECLARE @DynamicSQL nvarchar(max)= 'SELECT BusinessEntityID, FirstName, LastName
           FROM AdventureWorks2012.Person.Person ';
SET @DynamicSQL = CONCAT(@DynamicSQL, 'WHERE LastName = @pLastName');
PRINT @DynamicSQL;   -- testing & debugging
```

EXEC sp_executesql @DynamicSQL, N'@pLastName varchar(40)', @pLastName = @LastName;

BusinessEntityID	FirstName	LastName
1553	Tim	O'Brien

CHAPTER 5: Basic Concepts of Client-Server Computing

Built-in System Functions

SQL Server T-SQL language has a large collection of system functions such as date & time, string and math function. The nested REPLACE string function can be used to remove unwanted characters from a string.

```
DECLARE @text nvarchar(128) = '#1245! $99^@';
SELECT REPLACE(REPLACE(REPLACE(REPLACE(REPLACE(REPLACE(REPLACE(REPLACE(@text,
     '!',''),'@',''),'#',''),'$',''),'%',''),'^',''),'&',''),'*',''),' ','');    -- 124599
```

All the system function are listed in SSMS Object Explorer under the Programmability tab.

CHAPTER 5: Basic Concepts of Client-Server Computing

Local Variables & Table Variables in T-SQL

Local variables with different data types have scope of a batch or a stored procedure/trigger/function. Note that a "GO" in T-SQL script indicates end of batch, therefore the end of scope for local variables. Table variable is a virtual table with similar scope to local variable. Script to demonstrate local and table variables.

```
DECLARE @i INT;  SET @i = 999;

SELECT @i + @i;
-- 1998

SELECT @i = 555;  -- assignment
SELECT @i + @i;
GO
-- 1110

DECLARE @i INT = 999;              -- new in SQL Server 2008
SET @i += 1;                       -- new in SQL Server 2008

SELECT @i;
GO
-- 1000

DECLARE @OrderShipperJunction TABLE                -- Table variable
 (
    ShipperID          SMALLINT IDENTITY ( 1, 1 ) PRIMARY KEY,
    ShipperName        NVARCHAR(64),
    PurchaseOrderID    INT,
    ShipDate           DATE DEFAULT (CURRENT_TIMESTAMP),
    FreightCost        SMALLMONEY
 );
INSERT @OrderShipperJunction
   (ShipperName,
    PurchaseOrderID,
    FreightCost)
VALUES('Custom Motor Bike Distributor',    11111,   177.34)

SELECT * FROM  @OrderShipperJunction
GO
```

ShipperID	ShipperName	PurchaseOrderID	ShipDate	FreightCost
1	Custom Motor Bike Distributor	11111	2016-07-18	177.34

CHAPTER 5: Basic Concepts of Client-Server Computing

Metadata Visibility Through System Views

The system views provide SQL Server and database metadata which can be used just for viewing in SSMS Object Explorer or programmatically in T-SQL scripts. The system views are based on system tables which are no longer accessible since SQL Server 2005. The system view sys.objects contains all the basic info on each and every user objects in the database with the exception of indexes. Query to retrieve partial data form sys.objects system view.

```
select
    s.name                  as [Schema],
    o.name                  as [Name],
    o.type_desc             as [Type],
    o.create_date           as CreateDate
from   sys.objects o
       inner join sys.schemas s
          on s.schema_id = o.schema_id
where is_ms_shipped = 0
order by [Type], [Schema], [Name]
-- (722 row(s) affected)  -  Partial results.
```

Schema	Name	Type	CreateDate
HumanResources	Department	USER_TABLE	2012-03-14 13:14:19.267
HumanResources	Employee	USER_TABLE	2012-03-14 13:14:19.303
HumanResources	EmployeeDepartmentHistory	USER_TABLE	2012-03-14 13:14:19.313
HumanResources	EmployeePayHistory	USER_TABLE	2012-03-14 13:14:19.320
HumanResources	JobCandidate	USER_TABLE	2012-03-14 13:14:19.337
HumanResources	Shift	USER_TABLE	2012-03-14 13:14:19.593
Person	Address	USER_TABLE	2012-03-14 13:14:19.140
Person	AddressType	USER_TABLE	2012-03-14 13:14:19.150
Person	BusinessEntity	USER_TABLE	2012-03-14 13:14:19.183
Person	BusinessEntityAddress	USER_TABLE	2012-03-14 13:14:19.190
Person	BusinessEntityContact	USER_TABLE	2012-03-14 13:14:19.197
Person	ContactType	USER_TABLE	2012-03-14 13:14:19.207
Person	CountryRegion	USER_TABLE	2012-03-14 13:14:19.220
Person	EmailAddress	USER_TABLE	2012-03-14 13:14:19.290
Person	Password	USER_TABLE	2012-03-14 13:14:19.350
Person	Person	USER_TABLE	2012-03-14 13:14:19.357
Person	PersonPhone	USER_TABLE	2012-03-14 13:14:19.370
Person	PhoneNumberType	USER_TABLE	2012-03-14 13:14:19.377
Person	StateProvince	USER_TABLE	2012-03-14 13:14:19.623
Production	BillOfMaterials	USER_TABLE	2012-03-14 13:14:19.170
Production	Culture	USER_TABLE	2012-03-14 13:14:19.237

Constructing T-SQL Identifiers

Identifiers are the names given to SQL Server & database objects such as linked servers, tables, views or stored procedures.

Very simple rule: **do not include any special character in an identifier other than single underscore (_). Double underscore in an identifier inevitably leads to confusion, loss of database developer productivity.**

Creating good identifiers helps with productivity in database development, administration and maintenance. Using names AccountsPayable1 and AccountsPayable2 as variations for AccountsPayable is not good because the 1,2 suffixes are meaningless. On the other hand AccountsPayableLondon & AccountsPayableNYC are good, meaningful names. The list of identifiers can be enumerated from AdventureWorks2012.sys.objects.

SELECT name FROM AdventureWorks2012.sys.objects ORDER BY name; -- (820 row(s) affected)

Selected results with comments.

Identifier(name)	Style Comment
Account	single word
AddressType	double words CamelCase style
BillOfMaterials	CamelCase (also known as Pascal case)
BusinessEntityContact	CamelCase
CK__ImageStore__67152DD3	double underscore separator, CK prefix for CHECK CONSTRAINT
CK_Document_Status	single underscore separator
CK_EmployeeDepartmentHistory_EndDate	mixed - CamelCase and underscore
DF__ImageStor__is_sy__75634D2A	database engine (system) generated name
sp_creatediagram	old-fashioned, sp prefix for system procedure
syscscolsegments	old-fashioned with abbreviations
ufnGetProductDealerPrice	Hungarian naming, ufn stands for user(-defined) function
vSalesPersonSalesByFiscalYears	Hungarian naming, v prefix is for view

CHAPTER 5: Basic Concepts of Client-Server Computing

The Use of [] - Square Brackets in Identifiers

Each identifier can be enclosed in square brackets, but not required. If the identifier is the same as a T-SQL reserved keyword, then it is required. Square brackets are also required when the identifier includes a special character such as space. Double quotes can be used also but that becomes very confusing when single quotes are present. The use of brackets is demonstrated in the following T-SQL script.

```
USE Northwind;
```

```
-- Syntax error without brackets since table name has space
SELECT * FROM Order Details;
/* ERROR
Msg 156, Level 15, State 1, Line 3
Incorrect syntax near the keyword 'Order'.
*/
```

```
-- Valid statement with brackets around table name
SELECT * FROM [Order Details];
-- (2155 row(s) affected)
```

```
-- Create and populate table with SELECT INTO
-- Error since ORDER is a reserved keyword
SELECT * INTO Order FROM Orders;
/* ERROR
Msg 156, Level 15, State 1, Line 1
Incorrect syntax near the keyword 'Order'.
*/
```

```
-- With brackets, query is valid
SELECT * INTO [Order] FROM Orders;
-- (830 row(s) affected)
```

When a database object is scripted out in SSMS Object Explore, the identifiers are surrounded with square brackets even when not needed as shown in the following demonstration.

```
CREATE TABLE [dbo].[Order Details](
        [OrderID] [int] NOT NULL,
        [ProductID] [int] NOT NULL,
        [UnitPrice] [money] NOT NULL,
        [Quantity] [smallint] NOT NULL,
        [Discount] [real] NOT NULL,
 CONSTRAINT [PK_Order_Details] PRIMARY KEY CLUSTERED
(       [OrderID] ASC,
        [ProductID] ASC));
```

CHAPTER 5: Basic Concepts of Client-Server Computing

CHAPTER 6: Fundamentals of Relational Database Design

Logical Data Modeling

Logical data modeling is the first step in database design. The task can be carried out by systems analysts, subject-matter experts, database designers or lead database developers. Small budget projects usually settle for an experienced database developer in the design role. The database design team spends time with the future users (stakeholders) of the database to find out the expectations and requirements for the new database. As soon as the design team has some basic idea of functional requirements, the iterative process continues with discussing entities (corresponds to tables in the database) and their relationships with the users. For example the Order entity has many to many relationship to the Product entity. A Product occurs in many orders, and an Order may hold many products.

Physical Data Modeling

Physical Data Modeling is the process of translating the logical data model into actual database tables and related objects such as PRIMARY KEY and FOREIGN KEY constraints. If a software tool was used to design the logical data model then the forward engineering feature can be applied to generate SQL scripts to create tables and related database objects. **An important step in this process is the design of indexes to support SQL query performance.** Example for Data Warehouse dimension table implementation.

```
dbo.DimDate
  Columns
    DateKey (PK, int, not null)
    FullDateAlternateKey (date, not null)
    DayNumberOfWeek (tinyint, not null)
    EnglishDayNameOfWeek (nvarchar(10), not null)
    SpanishDayNameOfWeek (nvarchar(10), not null)
    FrenchDayNameOfWeek (nvarchar(10), not null)
    DayNumberOfMonth (tinyint, not null)
    DayNumberOfYear (smallint, not null)
    WeekNumberOfYear (tinyint, not null)
    EnglishMonthName (nvarchar(10), not null)
    SpanishMonthName (nvarchar(10), not null)
    FrenchMonthName (nvarchar(10), not null)
    MonthNumberOfYear (tinyint, not null)
    CalendarQuarter (tinyint, not null)
    CalendarYear (smallint, not null)
    CalendarSemester (tinyint, not null)
    FiscalQuarter (tinyint, not null)
    FiscalYear (smallint, not null)
    FiscalSemester (tinyint, not null)
```

Column Definitions for the FactInternetSales Table

Table columns for a fact table in AdventureWorksDW2012 database. PK stands for PRIMARY KEY, FK for FOREGN KEY. The PRIMARY KEY is a composite of 2 columns: SalesOrderNumber and SalesOrderLineNumber.

The screen image is from SSMS Object Explorer.

```
dbo.FactInternetSales
  Columns
    ProductKey (FK, int, not null)
    OrderDateKey (FK, int, not null)
    DueDateKey (FK, int, not null)
    ShipDateKey (FK, int, not null)
    CustomerKey (FK, int, not null)
    PromotionKey (FK, int, not null)
    CurrencyKey (FK, int, not null)
    SalesTerritoryKey (FK, int, not null)
    SalesOrderNumber (PK, nvarchar(20), not null)
    SalesOrderLineNumber (PK, tinyint, not null)
    RevisionNumber (tinyint, not null)
    OrderQuantity (smallint, not null)
    UnitPrice (money, not null)
    ExtendedAmount (money, not null)
    UnitPriceDiscountPct (float, not null)
    DiscountAmount (float, not null)
    ProductStandardCost (money, not null)
    TotalProductCost (money, not null)
    SalesAmount (money, not null)
    TaxAmt (money, not null)
    Freight (money, not null)
    CarrierTrackingNumber (nvarchar(25), null)
    CustomerPONumber (nvarchar(25), null)
    OrderDate (datetime, null)
    DueDate (datetime, null)
    ShipDate (datetime, null)
```

CHAPTER 6: Fundamentals of Relational Database Design

Table Column Data Types

Exact Numerics

bigint	8 byte signed integer	-- Exact Numerics
bit	Boolean	
decimal	5 - 17 bytes decimal number with variable precision	
int	4 byte signed integer	
money	8 byte with ten-thousandth accuracy	
numeric	Same as decimal	
smallint	2 byte signed integer	
smallmoney	4 byte with ten-thousandth accuracy	
tinyint	1 byte signed integer	

Approximate Numerics

float	4 - 8 byte floating point	-- Approximate Numerics
real	4 byte floating point	

Date and Time

date	3 byte date only
datetime	8 byte date & time
datetime2	6 - 8 byte date & time
datetimeoffset	10 byte date & time with time zone
smalldatetime	4 byte date & time
time	5 byte time only

Character Strings

char	Fixed length ASCII character storage - 1 byte for each character -- Character String
text	Variable-length ASCII data with a maximum string length of 2^31-1 (deprecated)
varchar	Variable length ASCII character storage

Unicode Character Strings

nchar	Fixed length UNICODE character storage - 2 bytes for each character
ntext	Variable-length UNICODE data with a maximum string length of 2^30-1 (deprecated)
nvarchar	Variable length UNICODE character storage

Binary Strings

binary	Fixed-length binary data with maximum storage size of 2^31-1 bytes -- Binary String
image	Variable-length binary data with maximum storage size of 2^31-1 bytes (deprecated)
varbinary	Variable-length binary data with maximum storage size of 2^31-1 bytes

Other Data Types

cursor	Contains a reference to a cursor - not for column use
hierarchyid	Represents a position in a tree hierarchy, typically a few bytes up to 892 bytes
sql_variant	Stores values of various SQL Server data types, maximum length of 8016 bytes
table	Store a result set for processing at a later time, not for columns
timestamp	8 byte generated binary number, mechanism for version-stamping table rows
uniqueidentifier	16 byte GUID - Globally Unique Identifier
xml	Stores XML data up to 2GB in size

CHAPTER 6: Fundamentals of Relational Database Design

Date Type max_length, precision, scale & collation_name Listing

Database metadata on data types can be found in types system view.

```
SELECT         name, system_type_id, max_length, precision, scale,
               isnull(collation_name, SPACE(0)) AS collation_name
FROM AdventureWorks2012.sys.types WHERE schema_id = 4 ORDER BY name;
```

name	system_type_id	max_length	precision	scale	collation_name
bigint	127	8	19	0	
binary	173	8000	0	0	
bit	104	1	1	0	
char	175	8000	0	0	SQL_Latin1_General_CP1_CI_AS
date	40	3	10	0	
datetime	61	8	23	3	
datetime2	42	8	27	7	
datetimeoffset	43	10	34	7	
decimal	106	17	38	38	
float	62	8	53	0	
geography	240	-1	0	0	
geometry	240	-1	0	0	
hierarchyid	240	892	0	0	
image	34	16	0	0	
int	56	4	10	0	
money	60	8	19	4	
nchar	239	8000	0	0	SQL_Latin1_General_CP1_CI_AS
ntext	99	16	0	0	SQL_Latin1_General_CP1_CI_AS
numeric	108	17	38	38	
nvarchar	231	8000	0	0	SQL_Latin1_General_CP1_CI_AS
real	59	4	24	0	
smalldatetime	58	4	16	0	
smallint	52	2	5	0	
smallmoney	122	4	10	4	
sql_variant	98	8016	0	0	
sysname	231	256	0	0	SQL_Latin1_General_CP1_CI_AS
text	35	16	0	0	SQL_Latin1_General_CP1_CI_AS
time	41	5	16	7	
timestamp	189	8	0	0	
tinyint	48	1	3	0	
uniqueidentifier	36	16	0	0	
varbinary	165	8000	0	0	
varchar	167	8000	0	0	SQL_Latin1_General_CP1_CI_AS
xml	241	-1	0	0	

CHAPTER 6: Fundamentals of Relational Database Design

U.S. Default Collation SQL_Latin1_General_CP1_CI_AS

Interpretation:

- ➤ SQL collation not Windows
- ➤ Latin 1 alphabet
- ➤ Code page 1 for sorting
- ➤ Case insensitive
- ➤ Accent sensitive

SQL_Latin1_General_CP1_CI_AS is the default collation of SQL Server 2012 in the United States. Only a handful of experts around the world really understand collations. You first encounter with collation will probably be like the following error.

```
SELECT CONCAT('Production.', objname) AS TableName, value AS [Description]
FROM fn_listextendedproperty (NULL, 'schema', 'Production', 'table', default, NULL, NULL);
GO
/* Msg 468, Level 16, State 9, Line 1
Cannot resolve the collation conflict between "SQL_Latin1_General_CP1_CI_AS" and
"Latin1_General_CI_AI" in the concat operation.
*/
```

The easiest fix in most collation error cases is placing COLLATE DATABASE_DEFAULT following the right most operator.

```
SELECT CONCAT('Production.', objname COLLATE DATABASE_DEFAULT) AS TableName,
            value AS [Description]
FROM fn_listextendedproperty (NULL, 'schema', 'Production', 'table', default, NULL, NULL);
```

There are a number of articles on the web which deal extensively with collations.

Collation is a column level property. Server and database collations are only defaults. To change the collation of a column, use ALTER TABLE.

```
-- SQL Server Change Column Collation
SELECT * INTO Product FROM AdventureWorks2012.Production.Product;
GO
ALTER TABLE Product ALTER COLUMN Name nvarchar(50) COLLATE SQL_Latin1_General_CP1_CS_AS null;
GO  -- (504 row(s) affected)
```

CHAPTER 6: Fundamentals of Relational Database Design

DATE & DATETIME Temporal Data Types

DATE data type has been introduced with SQL Server 2008. DATETIME on the other hand is around since the inception of SQL Server. A good deal of programming effort goes into supporting hundreds of different string date & time formats. Each country has its own string date formats adding more to the general confusion. As an example in the United States the mdy string date format is used. In the United Kingdom, the dmy format is used. When one looks at a date like 10/11/2015, it is not apparent which date format is it. In a globalized world the data flows freely from one country to another, frequently without adequate documentation, hence the loss of database developer productivity as related to date & time data issues. List of century (CCYY or YYYY) datetime conversions styles (stylenumber >= 100).

```sql
SELECT convert(datetime, 'Oct 23 2016 11:01AM', 100) -- mon dd yyyy hh:mmAM (or PM)
SELECT convert(datetime, 'Oct 23 2016 11:01AM') -- 2012-10-23 11:01:00.000
SELECT convert(datetime, 'Oct 23 16 11:01AM', 0) -- mon dd yy hh:mmAM (or PM)
SELECT convert(datetime, 'Oct 23 16 11:01AM') -- 2012-10-23 11:01:00.000
SELECT convert(datetime, '10/23/2016', 101) -- mm/dd/yyyy US format
SELECT convert(datetime, '2016.10.23', 102) -- yyyy.mm.dd ANSI date with century
SELECT convert(datetime, '23/10/2016', 103) -- dd/mm/yyyy UK format
SELECT convert(datetime, '23.10.2016', 104) -- dd.mm.yyyy
SELECT convert(datetime, '23-10-2016', 105) -- dd-mm-yyyy
SELECT convert(datetime, '23 OCT 2016', 106) -- dd mon yyyy
SELECT convert(datetime, 'Oct 23, 2016', 107) -- mon dd, yyyy
SELECT convert(datetime, '20:10:44', 108) -- hh:mm:ss
SELECT convert(datetime, 'Oct 23 2016 11:02:44:013AM', 109)
SELECT convert(datetime, '10-23-2016', 110) -- mm-dd-yyyy
SELECT convert(datetime, '2016/10/23', 111) -- yyyy/mm/dd
SELECT convert(datetime, '20161023')
SELECT convert(datetime, '20161023', 112) -- ISO yyyymmdd
SELECT convert(datetime, '23 Oct 2016 11:02:07:577', 113)
SELECT convert(datetime, '20:10:25:300', 114) -- hh:mm:ss:mmm(24h)
SELECT convert(datetime, '2016-10-23 20:44:11', 120)
SELECT convert(datetime, '2016-10-23 20:44:11.500', 121)
SELECT convert(datetime, '2008-10-23T18:52:47.513', 126) -- ISO Datetime
SELECT convert(datetime, N'23 6:52:47:513  1429 شوالPM', 130) -- Islamic/Hijri date
SELECT convert(datetime, '23/10/1429  6:52:47:513PM',    131) -- Islamic/Hijri date
```

CHAPTER 6: Fundamentals of Relational Database Design

Two Ways of Commenting in T-SQL Scripts

Line comment is prefixed by "--". Multiple lines comment has to be enclosed with "/*" and "*/".

```
/*********************************************
 *        COMMENTS IN T-SQL
 *********************************************/

-- Zero divide demonstration
-------------------------------------------------
DECLARE @Amount money = 200.0, @OrderQty int = 0;

SELECT UnitPrice = @Amount / @OrderQty; -- Zero divide will throw error

/* ERROR message from Messages window pasted below

Msg 8134, Level 16, State 1, Line 5
Divide by zero error encountered.

*/
```

Messages:
```
Msg 8134, Level 16, State 1, Line 9
Divide by zero error encountered.
```

CHAPTER 6: Fundamentals of Relational Database Design

Exploring Database Schemas

A schema - introduced in SQL Server 2005 - is a single-level container of database objects to replace database object "owner" in previous SQL Server versions. **The default schema is "dbo", database owner**. Schemas can be used for functional separation of objects which may be essential in large databases with thousands of tables. The application schemas in AdventureWorks: HumanResources, Production, Purchasing, Sales, and Person. The word "schemas" also used in database terminology to mean table definition scripts or database diagram. Screenshot to display all the schemas in AdventureWorks2012 and to demonstrate the use of the CREATE SCHEMA statement. Database object reference in SQL Server 2012 is: "dbname.schemaname.objectname" like "AdventureWorks2012.Sales.SalesOrderheader".

CHAPTER 6: Fundamentals of Relational Database Design

Exploring Database Schemas

SCHEMA_NAME() Function

The SCHEMA_NAME() function can be used to obtain the name of a schema based on the schema_id parameter. Query to list all 3 database objects with the name "Product" in 3 different schemas.

```
SELECT       CONCAT(SCHEMA_NAME(schema_id),'.',name) as ObjectName,
             name, object_id, schema_id, type, type_desc
FROM sys.objects
WHERE name = 'Product' ORDER BY ObjectName;
```

ObjectName	name	object_id	schema_id	type	type_desc
dbo.Product	Product	264388011	1	U	USER_TABLE
Inventory.Product	Product	1533964541	11	U	USER_TABLE
Production.Product	Product	1973582069	7	U	USER_TABLE

T-SQL query to display all the schemas in AdventureWorks2012.

```
SELECT s.*, p.name as PrincipalName
FROM AdventureWorks2012.sys.schemas s
 INNER JOIN AdventureWorks2012.sys.database_principals p   ON s.principal_id = p.principal_id
ORDER BY principal_id, s.name;
```

name	schema_id	principal_id	PrincipalName
Banking	10	1	dbo
dbo	1	1	dbo
HumanResources	5	1	dbo
Inventory	11	1	dbo
Person	6	1	dbo
Production	7	1	dbo
Purchasing	8	1	dbo
Sales	9	1	dbo
guest	2	2	guest
INFORMATION_SCHEMA	3	3	INFORMATION_SCHEMA
sys	4	4	sys
db_owner	16384	16384	db_owner
db_accessadmin	16385	16385	db_accessadmin
db_securityadmin	16386	16386	db_securityadmin
db_ddladmin	16387	16387	db_ddladmin
db_backupoperator	16389	16389	db_backupoperator
db_datareader	16390	16390	db_datareader
db_datawriter	16391	16391	db_datawriter
db_denydatareader	16392	16392	db_denydatareader
db_denydatawriter	16393	16393	db_denydatawriter

CHAPTER 6: Fundamentals of Relational Database Design

Tables in HumanResources, Person & Purchasing Schemas
Query to list tables in the above schemas with data dictionary description.

```
USE AdventureWorks2012;
SELECT   CONCAT('Purchasing.', objname COLLATE DATABASE_DEFAULT)     AS TableName,
         value                                                        AS [Description]
FROM fn_listextendedproperty (NULL, 'schema', 'Purchasing', 'table', default, NULL, NULL)
UNION
SELECT   CONCAT('Person.', objname COLLATE DATABASE_DEFAULT)          AS TableName,
         value                                                        AS [Description]
FROM fn_listextendedproperty (NULL, 'schema', 'Person', 'table', default, NULL, NULL)
UNION
SELECT   CONCAT('HumanResources.', objname COLLATE DATABASE_DEFAULT) AS TableName,
         value                                                        AS [Description]
FROM fn_listextendedproperty (NULL, 'schema', 'HumanResources', 'table', default, NULL, NULL)
ORDER BY TableName;
```

TableName	Description
HumanResources.Department	Lookup table containing the departments within the Adventure Works Cycles company.
HumanResources.Employee	Employee information such as salary, department, and title.
HumanResources.EmployeeDepartmentHistory	Employee department transfers.
HumanResources.EmployeePayHistory	Employee pay history.
HumanResources.JobCandidate	Résumés submitted to Human Resources by job applicants.
HumanResources.Shift	Work shift lookup table.
Person.Address	Street address information for customers, employees, and vendors.
Person.AddressType	Types of addresses stored in the Address table.
Person.BusinessEntity	Source of the ID that connects vendors, customers, and employees with address and contact information.
Person.BusinessEntityAddress	Cross-reference table mapping customers, vendors, and employees to their addresses.
Person.BusinessEntityContact	Cross-reference table mapping stores, vendors, and employees to people
Person.ContactType	Lookup table containing the types of business entity contacts.
Person.CountryRegion	Lookup table containing the ISO standard codes for countries and regions.
Person.EmailAddress	Where to send a person email.
Person.Password	One way hashed authentication information
Person.Person	Human beings involved with AdventureWorks: employees, customer contacts, and vendor contacts.
Person.PersonPhone	Telephone number and type of a person.
Person.PhoneNumberType	Type of phone number of a person.
Person.StateProvince	State and province lookup table.
Purchasing.ProductVendor	Cross-reference table mapping vendors with the products they supply.
Purchasing.PurchaseOrderDetail	Individual products associated with a specific purchase order. See PurchaseOrderHeader.
Purchasing.PurchaseOrderHeader	General purchase order information. See PurchaseOrderDetail.
Purchasing.ShipMethod	Shipping company lookup table.
Purchasing.Vendor	Companies from whom Adventure Works Cycles purchases parts or other goods.

The CREATE TABLE Statement

Creates a table based on column name, data type & size specifications. Constraint and default information can be included as well, or alternately given as a separate ALTER TABLE statement.

Branch Banking Database with ON DELETE CASCADE

T-SQL script to create basic banking application tables. Preceding the first CREATE TABLE, we execute a CREATE SCHEMA to group the tables within one schema.

```sql
USE AdventureWorks2012;
GO
```

```sql
CREATE SCHEMA Banking;
GO
```

```sql
CREATE TABLE Banking.Branch
(
   BranchID     INT IDENTITY ( 1, 1 ),
   BranchName   CHAR(32) NOT NULL UNIQUE,
   BranchCity   CHAR(32) NOT NULL,
   Assets       MONEY NOT NULL,
   ModifiedDate DATETIME DEFAULT (getdate()),
   PRIMARY KEY ( BranchID ),
);

CREATE TABLE Banking.Account
(
   AccountID     INT IDENTITY ( 1, 1 ) UNIQUE,
   BranchID      INT NOT NULL,
   AccountNumber CHAR(20) NOT NULL UNIQUE,
   AccountType   CHAR(12) NOT NULL CONSTRAINT ATC CHECK (AccountType IN ('C', 'S')),
   Balance       MONEY NOT NULL,
   ModifiedDate  DATETIME DEFAULT (getdate()),
   PRIMARY KEY ( AccountID ),
   FOREIGN KEY ( BranchID ) REFERENCES Banking.Branch(BranchID) ON DELETE   CASCADE
);
```

CHAPTER 6: Fundamentals of Relational Database Design

```sql
-- T-SQL script continued

CREATE TABLE Banking.[Transaction]
(
   TransactionID INT IDENTITY ( 1, 1 ) PRIMARY KEY,
   AccountID    INT NOT NULL  REFERENCES Banking.Account    ON DELETE  CASCADE,  -- FK
   TranType    CHAR(1),
   Amount     MONEY,
   ModifiedDate  DATETIME DEFAULT (getdate()),
   UNIQUE ( AccountID, ModifiedDate)
);

CREATE TABLE Banking.Customer
(
   CustomerID   INT IDENTITY ( 1, 1 ) PRIMARY KEY,
   Name       CHAR(32) NOT NULL,
   SSNo       CHAR(9) NOT NULL UNIQUE,
   [Type]     CHAR(20) NOT NULL,
   Street    VARCHAR(32) NOT NULL,
   City      CHAR(32) NOT NULL,
   [State]    CHAR(32) NOT NULL,
   Zip       CHAR(10) NOT NULL,
   Country    CHAR(32) NOT NULL,
   ModifiedDate DATETIME DEFAULT (getdate())
);

CREATE TABLE Banking.Loan
(
   LoanID     INT IDENTITY ( 1, 1 ) PRIMARY KEY,
   BranchID    INT NOT NULL REFERENCES Banking.Branch ON DELETE   CASCADE,  -- FK
   LoanNumber   CHAR(20) NOT NULL UNIQUE,
   LoanType    VARCHAR(30) NOT NULL,
   Amount     MONEY NOT NULL,
   ModifiedDate DATETIME DEFAULT (getdate())
);
```

The CREATE TABLE Statement

-- T-SQL script continued

```sql
CREATE TABLE Banking.Depositor
(
  CustomerID   INT NOT NULL,
  AccountID    INT NOT NULL,
  ModifiedDate DATETIME DEFAULT (getdate()),
  PRIMARY KEY ( CustomerID, AccountID ),
  FOREIGN KEY ( AccountID ) REFERENCES Banking.Account(AccountID) ON DELETE   CASCADE,
  FOREIGN KEY ( CustomerID ) REFERENCES Banking.Customer(CustomerID)
);

CREATE TABLE Banking.Borrower
(
  CustomerID   INT NOT NULL,
  LoanID       INT NOT NULL,
  ModifiedDate DATETIME DEFAULT (getdate()),
  PRIMARY KEY ( CustomerID, LoanID ),
  FOREIGN KEY ( CustomerID ) REFERENCES Banking.Customer(CustomerID),
  FOREIGN KEY ( LoanID ) REFERENCES Banking.Loan(LoanID)
);
```

Note about MONEY data type. While "MONEY" sounds like a magical data type, for calculational accuracy better to use DECIMAL data type such as DECIMAL (20,2).

CHAPTER 6: Fundamentals of Relational Database Design

Temporary Tables: Workhorses of SQL Server

So much so that they even have their own database: tempdb. Temporary tables (example: #Product1) can be applied in queries just like permanent tables. The differences are:

➢ Temporary tables are created in tempdb.

➢ Temporary tables have limited life.

There are two versions:

➢ Temporary tables (#tempA) are multi-user automatically, cannot be shared among connections.

➢ Global temporary tables (##gtempB) is single-user, can be shared among connections.

Global temporary tables are used only for special purposes since they make stored procedures single user only.

Temporary tables can be created by CREATE TABLE or SELECT INTO methods.

```
USE AdventureWorks2012;
GO
-- Command(s) completed successfully.
```

```
-- Create temporary table with CREATE TABLE
CREATE TABLE #Product
(
        ProductID INT,
        ProductName nvarchar(50),
        ListPrice money,
        Color varchar(16)
);
GO
-- Command(s) completed successfully.
```

```
INSERT INTO #Product
SELECT   ProductID,
         Name,
         ListPrice,
         Color
FROM Production.Product ORDER BY Name;
GO  --(504 row(s) affected)
```

CHAPTER 6: Fundamentals of Relational Database Design

ALTER TABLE for Changing Table Definition

Temporary Tables Are Handy When Developing Scripts Or Stored Procedures

```
SELECT TOP 10 * FROM #Product
ORDER BY ProductName;
GO
```

ProductID	ProductName	ListPrice	Color
1	Adjustable Race	0.00	NULL
879	All-Purpose Bike Stand	159.00	NULL
712	AWC Logo Cap	8.99	Multi
3	BB Ball Bearing	0.00	NULL
2	Bearing Ball	0.00	NULL
877	Bike Wash - Dissolver	7.95	NULL
316	Blade	0.00	NULL
843	Cable Lock	25.00	NULL
952	Chain	20.24	Silver
324	Chain Stays	0.00	NULL

```
DROP TABLE #Product;
GO
```

```
-- CREATE temporary table with SELECT INTO
SELECT ProductID, ProductName = Name, ListPrice, StandardCost, Color
INTO #ProductA
FROM Production.Product
ORDER BY ProductName;
GO
```

```
SELECT TOP 10 * FROM #ProductA
ORDER BY ProductName;
```

ProductID	ProductName	ListPrice	StandardCost	Color
1	Adjustable Race	0.00	0.00	NULL
879	All-Purpose Bike Stand	159.00	59.466	NULL
712	AWC Logo Cap	8.99	6.9223	Multi
3	BB Ball Bearing	0.00	0.00	NULL
2	Bearing Ball	0.00	0.00	NULL
877	Bike Wash - Dissolver	7.95	2.9733	NULL
316	Blade	0.00	0.00	NULL
843	Cable Lock	25.00	10.3125	NULL
952	Chain	20.24	8.9866	Silver
324	Chain Stays	0.00	0.00	NULL

```
DROP TABLE #ProductA;
GO
```

CHAPTER 6: Fundamentals of Relational Database Design

ALTER TABLE for Changing Table Definition

An empty table can easily be altered by ALTER TABLE. A populated table change (alter) may require additional operations such as data conversion to the new column data type. Generally increasing the size of a column is a safe change even if the table is populated. If we were to change size from 25 to 10, truncation may occur (data loss), for which we would have to plan by examining what will be lost if any. When decreasing string column size, we can use the LEFT function to truncate the string. T-SQL script to increase the size of a column from 25 to 32, then decrease it 9.

```
USE CopyOfAdventureWorks2012;
-- Sales.SalesOrderDetail columns
/*Name    Policy Health State
SalesOrderID (PK, FK, int, not null)
SalesOrderDetailID (PK, int, not null)
CarrierTrackingNumber (nvarchar(25), null) ..... */
```

```
-- Increase column size of CarrierTrackingNumber
ALTER TABLE Sales.SalesOrderDetail   ALTER COLUMN CarrierTrackingNumber nvarchar(32) null;
```

```
/* Columns after ALTER TABLE
Name    Policy Health State
SalesOrderID (PK, FK, int, not null)
SalesOrderDetailID (PK, int, not null)
CarrierTrackingNumber (nvarchar(32), null) .....        */
```

```
SELECT TOP (1) SalesOrderID, CarrierTrackingNumber FROM Sales.SalesOrderDetail ORDER BY SalesOrderID;
```

SalesOrderID	CarrierTrackingNumber
43659	4911-403C-98

We shall now decrease the size to 9 characters, but first truncate the extra characters. Without the UPDATE, the following error happens.

```
/* Msg 8152, Level 16, State 13, Line 1 String or binary data would be truncated. The statement has been terminated.*/
```

```
UPDATE Sales.SalesOrderDetail SET CarrierTrackingNumber = LEFT (CarrierTrackingNumber,9);
-- (121317 row(s) affected)
```

```
-- Decrease column size of CarrierTrackingNumber
ALTER TABLE Sales.SalesOrderDetail   ALTER COLUMN CarrierTrackingNumber nvarchar(9)  null;
-- Command(s) completed successfully.
```

```
SELECT TOP (1) SalesOrderID, CarrierTrackingNumber FROM Sales.SalesOrderDetail ORDER BY SalesOrderID;
```

SalesOrderID	CarrierTrackingNumber
43659	4911-403C

ALTER TABLE for Changing Table Definition

Renaming Tables & Columns with sp_rename

The system stored procedure sp_rename can be used to rename tables, columns and other user-created database objects.

```
USE tempdb;
GO

-- Create test table
SELECT * INTO Department FROM AdventureWorks2012.HumanResources.Department;
GO
-- (16 row(s) affected)

SELECT TOP 1 * FROM Department;
GO
```

DepartmentID	Name	GroupName	ModifiedDate
1	Engineering	Research and Development	2002-06-01 00:00:00.000

```
-- Rename table column
EXEC sp_rename "Department.Name", "Department";
GO

SELECT TOP 1 * FROM Department;
GO
```

DepartmentID	Department	GroupName	ModifiedDate
1	Engineering	Research and Development	2002-06-01 00:00:00.000

```
-- Rename table
EXEC sp_rename "dbo.Department", "ProfitCenter"
GO

SELECT * FROM ProfitCenter;
GO
```

DepartmentID	Department	GroupName	ModifiedDate
1	Engineering	Research and Development	2002-06-01 00:00:00.000

```
DROP TABLE tempdb.dbo.ProfitCenter;
GO
```

CHAPTER 6: Fundamentals of Relational Database Design

DROP TABLE: A Dangerous Statement

The DROP TABLE statement is to delete a table, including content, for good. It is a very dangerous statement which we don't want to execute accidentally. Therefore, if appropriate we should comment it out in a T-SQL script to prevent unintentional execution.

CHAPTER 6: Fundamentals of Relational Database Design

Table Constraints Inclusion in CREATE TABLE

Table constraints are user-defined database objects that restricts the behaviors of columns. PRIMARY KEY, UNIQUE KEY, FOREIGN KEY, or CHECK constraint, or a DEFAULT constraint can be included in the CREATE TABLE statement on the same line as the column or added as a separate line. In the definition of the Banking.Branch table UNIQUE and DEFAULT constraints are included in the same line while the PRIMARY KEY constraint has its own line at the end of column list. In the definition of Banking.Loan table, the PRIMARY KEY constraint is included with the column definition. FOREIGN KEY constraint definition can include ON DELETE CASCADE action option, meaning if the PRIMARY KEY is deleted all FOREIGN KEYs in the table referencing it should also be deleted.

Nullability Column-Level Constraints in CREATE TABLE

The default is NULL, the column can contain NULL entries, the column is nullable. We have to specifically declare NOT NULL on the column line in CREATE TABLE if we want to add the cardinality constraint to the column. The NULL / NOT NULL constraint cannot be declared on a separate line. In the Production.Product table the Color column is nullable. The ListPrice column is not nullable instead has 0.0 price where there is no price.

PRIMARY KEY & FOREIGN KEY Constraints

PRIMARY KEY constraint on a column automatically implies NOT NULL

The UNIQUE KEY CONSTRAINT allows only one NULL entry in a column since two or more NULL entries would not be unique. Demonstration script:

```sql
USE tempdb;
CREATE TABLE Product   (  ProductID INT UNIQUE,
                          ProductName varchar(64) PRIMARY KEY
                       );

INSERT Product (ProductName) VALUES ('Mobile Phone xZing');
-- (1 row(s) affected)


-- One NULL is OK in ProductID column
-- Second NULL insert attempt errors out

INSERT Product (ProductName) VALUES ('Motor Bike');

/* Msg 2627, Level 14, State 1, Line 7
Violation of UNIQUE KEY constraint 'UQ__Product__B40CC6ECDF4DC6D3'.
Cannot insert duplicate key in object 'dbo.Product'.
The duplicate key value is (<NULL>).
The statement has been terminated. */


-- NULL value in PRIMARY KEY column not allowed

INSERT Product (ProductID) VALUES (2);

/* Msg 515, Level 16, State 2, Line 2
Cannot insert the value NULL into column
'ProductName', table 'tempdb.dbo.Product';
column does not allow nulls. INSERT fails.
The statement has been terminated. */

SELECT * FROM Product;
```

ProductID	ProductName
NULL	Mobile Phone xZing

The PRIMARY KEY constraint is a combination of UNIQUE and NOT NULL constraints.

CHAPTER 6: Fundamentals of Relational Database Design

PRIMARY KEY & FOREIGN KEY Constraints

The PRIMARY KEY constraint is to ensure a referenceable unique address for each row in a table. PK column value cannot be NULL. The underlying mechanism to carry out the enforcement action is a unique index which is clustered by default but in can be nonclustered. PRIMARY KEY constraint can be considered as a UNIQUE constraint with NOT NULL on the column. The typical PRIMARY KEY is the SURROGATE PRIMARY KEY INT IDENTITY(1,1) column. There can only be one PRIMARY KEY defined per table. A PRIMARY KEY can consist of multiple columns, a composite PRIMARY KEY. A PRIMARY KEY cannot be based on part of a column. Production.ProductSubcategory table PRIMARY KEY setup.

The ProductSubcategoryID is the PRIMARY KEY constraint. It is an INT IDENTITY(1,1) surrogate key. ProductCategoryID is a FOREIGN KEY referencing the Production.ProductCategory table ProductCategoryID column. "Name" is the NATURAL KEY. rowguid (used in replication) & ModifiedDate are row maintenance columns. The NATURAL KEY column Name has NOT NULL constraint and unique index defined. As such it can serve as PRIMARY KEY for the table, but we shall see why a meaningless integer number (INT IDENTITY) is better for PRIMARY KEY. Related to this topic: A heap is a table without a clustered index. The implication is if we choose nonclustered PRIMARY KEY, we have to define a clustered index on other column(s) so that the database engine can work with the table as normal. Clustered index speeds up range searches.

> The SURROGATE PRIMARY KEY should not be exposed to end-users, it is for programming use only.

CHAPTER 6: Fundamentals of Relational Database Design

PRIMARY KEY & FOREIGN KEY Constraints

FOREIGN KEY constraint requires that the referenced PK value exists.
FOREIGN KEY column is nullable. FOREIGN KEY can be named differently from the referenced PRIMARY KEY, although for readability purposes usually the same. **Multiple FK columns can reference the same PK column**. In such a case only one FK column can have the same name as the PK column. Invalid FK reference results in error.

```
USE [AdventureWorks2012]
GO
```

```
INSERT INTO Production.ProductSubcategory
    (ProductCategoryID
    ,Name)
  VALUES
    (99
    ,'Inner Tube')
```

```
/*
Msg 547, Level 16, State 0, Line 2
The INSERT statement conflicted with the FOREIGN KEY constraint
"FK_ProductSubcategory_ProductCategory_ProductCategoryID".
The conflict occurred in database "AdventureWorks2012",
table "Production.ProductCategory", column 'ProductCategoryID'.
The statement has been terminated.
*/
```

DELETE attempt on a referenced PRIMARY KEY will give an error unless DELETE CASCADE is defined on the FK:

```
DELETE FROM Production.ProductSubcategory
WHERE ProductSubCategoryID = 4
GO
```

```
/* Msg 547, Level 16, State 0, Line 1
The DELETE statement conflicted with the REFERENCE constraint
"FK_Product_ProductSubcategory_ProductSubcategoryID".
The conflict occurred in database "AdventureWorks2012",
table "Production.Product", column 'ProductSubcategoryID'.
The statement has been terminated.  */
```

CHAPTER 6: Fundamentals of Relational Database Design

Single Column & Composite PRIMARY KEY List with XML PATH

Query to form delimited list for composite PRIMARY KEY columns. STUFF function deletes the leading comma.

```sql
-- Show composite PRIMARY KEYs as a comma-delimited list
USE AdventureWorks2012;
SELECT  K.TABLE_SCHEMA,
        T.TABLE_NAME,
        PK_COLUMN_NAMES =
            STUFF(( SELECT
                            CONCAT(', ',   KK.COLUMN_NAME)                  AS [text()]
                        FROM   INFORMATION_SCHEMA.KEY_COLUMN_USAGE kk
                      WHERE  K.CONSTRAINT_NAME = KK.CONSTRAINT_NAME
                        ORDER BY  KK.ORDINAL_POSITION
                        FOR XML Path ('')), 1, 1, '')
FROM    INFORMATION_SCHEMA.TABLE_CONSTRAINTS T
   INNER JOIN    INFORMATION_SCHEMA.KEY_COLUMN_USAGE K
        ON T.CONSTRAINT_NAME = K.CONSTRAINT_NAME
WHERE           T.CONSTRAINT_TYPE = 'PRIMARY KEY'
            AND K.ORDINAL_POSITION = 1
ORDER BY        K.TABLE_SCHEMA,
                T.TABLE_NAME;
-- (71 row(s) affected) - Partial results
```

TABLE_SCHEMA	TABLE_NAME	PK_COLUMN_NAMES
dbo	AWBuildVersion	SystemInformationID
dbo	DatabaseLog	DatabaseLogID
dbo	ErrorLog	ErrorLogID
HumanResources	Department	DepartmentID
HumanResources	Employee	BusinessEntityID
HumanResources	EmployeeDepartmentHistory	BusinessEntityID, StartDate, DepartmentID, ShiftID
HumanResources	EmployeePayHistory	BusinessEntityID, RateChangeDate
HumanResources	JobCandidate	JobCandidateID
HumanResources	Shift	ShiftID
Person	Address	AddressID
Person	AddressType	AddressTypeID
Person	BusinessEntity	BusinessEntityID
Person	BusinessEntityAddress	BusinessEntityID, AddressID, AddressTypeID
Person	BusinessEntityContact	BusinessEntityID, PersonID, ContactTypeID
Person	ContactType	ContactTypeID
Person	CountryRegion	CountryRegionCode
Person	EmailAddress	BusinessEntityID, EmailAddressID
Person	Password	BusinessEntityID
Person	Person	BusinessEntityID
Person	PersonPhone	BusinessEntityID, PhoneNumber, PhoneNumberTypeID

CHAPTER 6: Fundamentals of Relational Database Design

SSMS GUI Table Designer

SSMS Object Explorer includes a GUI Table Designer which can be launched the following ways for new or existing table from the right-click drop-down menus.

CHAPTER 6: Fundamentals of Relational Database Design

Basic GUI Table Design

The Table Designer provides line-by-line row design including all properties (bottom of dialog box) such as defaults, computed columns, identity and so on.

SSMS GUI Table Designer

CHECK Constraint Definition

CHECK Constraint design window can be launched from toolbox icon: Manage Check Constraints or right-click drop-down menu. We create a constraint on Capital to be greater or equal to $5 billion.

CHAPTER 6: Fundamentals of Relational Database Design

Managing Indexes and Keys

The Manage Indexes and Keys window can be launched by toolbox icon or right-click menu. We add UNIQUE KEY property to the BankName column.

SSMS GUI Table Designer

Setting PRIMARY KEY with a Single Click

PRIMARY KEY can simply be configured just by clicking on the gold key icon. A PRIMARY KEY constraint is created automatically.

CHAPTER 6: Fundamentals of Relational Database Design

Configuring FOREIGN KEY: Declarative Referential Integrity

The Relationships facility can be used to create a FOREIGN KEY link (constraint). NOTE: demo only, BusinessEntityID column in the demo table has no relationship to AdventureWorks tables.

SSMS GUI Table Designer

Tables And Columns Specific Tab Is To Define Mapping From FK To PK

Foreign Key Relationships

Selected Relationship:

FK_Table_1_Table_1*

Editing properties for new relationship. The 'Tables And Columns Specification' property needs to be filled in before the new relationship will be accepted.

- **(General)**
  - Check Existing Data On Creati Yes
  - Tables And Columns Specific
- **Identity**
  - (Name)   FK_Table_1_Table_1
  - Description
- **Table Designer**
  - Enforce For Replication   Yes
  - Enforce Foreign Key Constrair   Yes
  - INSERT And UPDATE Specific

[Add] [Delete]   [Close]

Tables and Columns

Relationship name:

FK_Table_1_BusinessEntity

Primary key table: Foreign key table:

BusinessEntity (Person)   Table_1

BusinessEntityID   BusinessEntityID

[OK] [Cancel]

CHAPTER 6: Fundamentals of Relational Database Design

T-SQL Script Generation from GUI Table Designer
T-SQL code can be generated any time prior to saving the changes.

```
GO
CREATE TABLE dbo.Table_1
    (
    BankID int NOT NULL IDENTITY (1, 1),
    BusinessEntityID int NULL,
    BankName nvarchar(64) NOT NULL,
    City varchar(64) NOT NULL,
    Country varchar(128) NOT NULL,
    Capital money NOT NULL,
    MultiNational bit NOT NULL,
    MainAddress nchar(128) NULL,
    Phone char(16) NULL,
    ModifiedDate date NOT NULL
```

Generated CREATE TABLE & Related Objects Script
Code generated by the Table Designer.

```
/* To prevent any potential data loss issues, you should review this script in detail before running it
outside the context of the database designer.*/
BEGIN TRANSACTION
SET QUOTED_IDENTIFIER ON
SET ARITHABORT ON
SET NUMERIC_ROUNDABORT OFF
SET CONCAT_NULL_YIELDS_NULL ON
SET ANSI_NULLS ON
SET ANSI_PADDING ON
SET ANSI_WARNINGS ON
COMMIT
BEGIN TRANSACTION
GO
CREATE TABLE dbo.Table_1
    (
    BankID int NOT NULL IDENTITY (1, 1),
    BusinessEntityID int NULL,
    BankName nvarchar(64) NOT NULL,
    City varchar(64) NOT NULL,
    Country varchar(128) NOT NULL,
    Capital money NOT NULL,
    MultiNational bit NOT NULL,
    MainAddress nchar(128) NULL,
    Phone char(16) NULL,
    ModifiedDate date NOT NULL
    ) ON [PRIMARY]
GO
ALTER TABLE dbo.Table_1 ADD CONSTRAINT
    CK_Table_1 CHECK (Capital >= $5000000000.0)
GO
ALTER TABLE dbo.Table_1 ADD CONSTRAINT
    DF_Table_1_ModifiedDate DEFAULT CURRENT_TIMESTAMP FOR ModifiedDate
GO
ALTER TABLE dbo.Table_1 ADD CONSTRAINT
    PK_Table_1 PRIMARY KEY CLUSTERED
    (
    BankID
    ) WITH( STATISTICS_NORECOMPUTE = OFF, IGNORE_DUP_KEY = OFF, ALLOW_ROW_LOCKS = ON,
ALLOW_PAGE_LOCKS = ON) ON [PRIMARY]

GO
```

-- T-SQL script continues

```
ALTER TABLE dbo.Table_1 ADD CONSTRAINT
        IX_Table_1 UNIQUE NONCLUSTERED
        (
        BankName
        ) WITH( STATISTICS_NORECOMPUTE = OFF, IGNORE_DUP_KEY = OFF, ALLOW_ROW_LOCKS = ON,
ALLOW_PAGE_LOCKS = ON) ON [PRIMARY]

GO
ALTER TABLE dbo.Table_1 ADD CONSTRAINT
        FK_Table_1_Table_1 FOREIGN KEY
        (
        BankID
        ) REFERENCES dbo.Table_1
        (
        BankID
        ) ON UPDATE  NO ACTION
          ON DELETE  NO ACTION

GO
ALTER TABLE dbo.Table_1 SET (LOCK_ESCALATION = TABLE)
GO
COMMIT
```

Upon Exit or Save, a name can be assigned to the table. In this instance, the Table_1 is changed to MultiNationalBank. The Table Designer automatically replaces all the "Table_1" occurrences in the script with "MultiNationalBank".

CHAPTER 6: Fundamentals of Relational Database Design

One-to-Many Relationship Implementation

The cardinality of relationship implemented with PRIMARY KEY & FOREIGN KEY constraints is one-to-many. Many FKs can reference a single PK value. In the following demo, many products map to a single subcategory value 'Touring Bike'. The matching is not done on the name between tables, rather on the surrogate PK value 3.

```sql
SELECT psc.Name as Subcategory,
       p.Name as Product,
       psc.ProductSubcategoryID as [PRIMARY KEY],
       p.ProductID as [PK in FK Table]
FROM Production.Product p
  INNER JOIN Production.ProductSubcategory psc
    ON p.ProductSubcategoryID = psc.ProductSubcategoryID
WHERE psc.Name = 'Touring Bikes'
ORDER BY Product
```

	Subcategory	Product	PRIMARY KEY	PK in FK Table
1	Touring Bikes	Touring-1000 Blue, 46	3	966
2	Touring Bikes	Touring-1000 Blue, 50	3	967
3	Touring Bikes	Touring-1000 Blue, 54	3	968
4	Touring Bikes	Touring-1000 Blue, 60	3	969
5	Touring Bikes	Touring-1000 Yellow, 46	3	954
6	Touring Bikes	Touring-1000 Yellow, 50	3	955
7	Touring Bikes	Touring-1000 Yellow, 54	3	956
8	Touring Bikes	Touring-1000 Yellow, 60	3	957
9	Touring Bikes	Touring-2000 Blue, 46	3	970
10	Touring Bikes	Touring-2000 Blue, 50	3	971
11	Touring Bikes	Touring-2000 Blue, 54	3	972
12	Touring Bikes	Touring-2000 Blue, 60	3	953
13	Touring Bikes	Touring-3000 Blue, 44	3	978

FOREIGN KEY Referencing A UNIQUE KEY

A FOREIGN KEY can reference a UNIQUE KEY or UNIQUE index column in another table in addition to the PRIMARY KEY. In the following demonstration a FOREIGN KEY is created from ProdNumber column pointing to Production.Product ProductNumber (UNIQUE index) column.

```sql
USE AdventureWorks2012;

CREATE TABLE ProductEmail (
ProdNumber nvarchar(25) PRIMARY KEY
   REFERENCES
   Production.Product(ProductNumber),
EmailSubject nvarchar(255),
EmailBody nvarchar(max),
ModifiedDate date default (getdate()))
GO
```

FOREIGN KEY Relationship Without Constraint

A table can have a FOREIGN KEY which is not supported by server-side constraint. In such instance the client-side application software has to ensure that the relationship is valid. Generally it is undesirable. **Whatever can be done on the server-side should be done there because it is more efficient development wise, maintenance wise and performance wise.**
Demonstration to remove the FK constraint on the ProductID column in the [Order Details] table of the CopyOfNorthwind database.

CHAPTER 6: Fundamentals of Relational Database Design

Database Diagram Design Tool in SSMS

Management Studio Object Explorer includes a diagramming tool for tables and their relationships with each other. While not as sophisticated as independent database design tools, it is excellent for working with a small number of tables.

The diagramming tool has both reverse engineering and forward engineering features. **Reverse engineering**: it creates a diagram based on table and PK/FK constraints definitions. **Forward engineering**: it can change table and constraint setup in the database based on diagram changes. The Gold Key (PRIMARY KEY symbol) end of the connection line points to the PRIMARY KEY table, while the double "o" (infinite symbol in mathematics, here meaning many) end to the FOREIGN KEY table.

CHAPTER 6: Fundamentals of Relational Database Design

PRIMARY KEY & FOREIGN KEY as JOIN ON Keys

When we need data from two related tables we have to JOIN the tables. The typical JOIN keys are the PRIMARY KEY and FOREIGN KEY. In the following demonstration, we want to display the subcategory for each Touring Bike product from the Product table. Since the 'Touring Bike' subcategory value is in the ProductSubcategory table, we have to JOIN it to the Product table. The JOIN keys are: ProductSubcategoryID PRIMARY KEY in the ProductSubcategory table and ProductSubcategoryID FOREIGN KEY in the Product table. Naming the FK same as the PK is helpful with readability, therefore developer productivity.

```sql
SELECT psc.Name as Subcategory,
       p.Name as Product,
       p.ListPrice,
       p.StandardCost,
       FORMAT((ListPrice-StandardCost)/p.ListPrice,'p','en-US') AS Margin
FROM Production.Product p
  INNER JOIN Production.ProductSubcategory psc
    ON p.ProductSubcategoryID = psc.ProductSubcategoryID
WHERE psc.Name = 'Touring Bikes'
      AND p.ListPrice > 0.0
ORDER BY Product
```

	Subcategory	Product	ListPrice	StandardCost	Margin
1	Touring Bikes	Touring-1000 Blue, 46	2384.07	1481.9379	37.84 %
2	Touring Bikes	Touring-1000 Blue, 50	2384.07	1481.9379	37.84 %
3	Touring Bikes	Touring-1000 Blue, 54	2384.07	1481.9379	37.84 %
4	Touring Bikes	Touring-1000 Blue, 60	2384.07	1481.9379	37.84 %
5	Touring Bikes	Touring-1000 Yellow, 46	2384.07	1481.9379	37.84 %
6	Touring Bikes	Touring-1000 Yellow, 50	2384.07	1481.9379	37.84 %
7	Touring Bikes	Touring-1000 Yellow, 54	2384.07	1481.9379	37.84 %
8	Touring Bikes	Touring-1000 Yellow, 60	2384.07	1481.9379	37.84 %
9	Touring Bikes	Touring-2000 Blue, 46	1214.85	755.1508	37.83 %
10	Touring Bikes	Touring-2000 Blue, 50	1214.85	755.1508	37.83 %

The Margin column is calculated with an expression. It is also formatted as percentage with US English culture.

CHAPTER 6: Fundamentals of Relational Database Design

Composite & Indirect FOREIGN KEY

A composite (more than one column) PRIMARY KEY requires matching composite FOREIGN KEY references. In the Sales.SalesOrderDetail table SpecialOfferID & ProductID constitute a composite FOREIGN KEY which references the SpecialOfferProduct table composite PRIMARY KEY. Thus ProductID indirectly references the Production.Product table.

```sql
USE [AdventureWorks2012]
GO

ALTER TABLE [Sales].[SalesOrderDetail]
WITH CHECK ADD  CONSTRAINT
[FK_SalesOrderDetail_SpecialOfferProduct_Spec
FOREIGN KEY([SpecialOfferID],
        [ProductID])
REFERENCES [Sales].[SpecialOfferProduct]
    ([SpecialOfferID], [ProductID])
GO

ALTER TABLE [Sales].[SalesOrderDetail]
CHECK CONSTRAINT
[FK_SalesOrderDetail_SpecialOfferProduct_Spec
GO
```

SalesOrderDetail (Sales)
- OrderQty
- ProductID
- SpecialOfferID
- UnitPrice

SpecialOfferProduct (Sales)
- SpecialOfferID
- ProductID

Product (Production)
- ProductID
- Name
- ProductNumber
- MakeFlag

CHAPTER 6: Fundamentals of Relational Database Design

NATURAL KEY is a Must in Every Table

NATURAL KEY is a unique key which can serve as PRIMARY KEY for identifying data. A product name is a natural key in a product table. A product number is also a NATURAL KEY in a product table. Note that product "number" should better be called product identification since it is frequently not a number rather it is alphanumeric like: AB342BL where BL stands for blue. The Name and ProductNumber columns are NATURAL KEYs in the Production.Product table. **Every table should have a NATURAL KEY**. If it does not, there is a definition problem. Naturally, test tables, work tables and staging tables are exceptions to this rule.

CHAPTER 6: Fundamentals of Relational Database Design

CANDIDATE KEY

A CANDIDATE KEY can be any column or a combination of columns that can qualify as UNIQUE KEY in a table with no NULL value. The ProductID, Name, ProductNumber, rowguid (16 byte random value like FA3C65CD-0A22-47E3-BDF6-53F1DC138C43, hyphens are for readability) are all CANDIDATE KEYs in the Production.Product table. Only one of them can be the PRIMARY KEY. In this instance the selected PRIMARY KEY is ProductID, a SURROGATE (to NATURAL KEY) INT IDENTITY (1,1) PRIMARY KEY.

CHAPTER 6: Fundamentals of Relational Database Design

Logical Data Modeling in Visio

The following screenshots demonstrate logical / conceptual data modeling in Visio using the ORM diagram tool.

Following is the actual implementation of the above relationship.

```
CREATE TABLE [Production].[ProductCategory](
      [ProductCategoryID] [int] IDENTITY(1,1) PRIMARY KEY,
      [Name] [dbo].[Name] NOT NULL,
      [rowguid] [uniqueidentifier] ROWGUIDCOL  NOT NULL,
      [ModifiedDate] [datetime] NOT NULL         );

CREATE TABLE [Production].[ProductSubcategory](
      [ProductSubcategoryID] [int] IDENTITY(1,1) PRIMARY KEY,
      [ProductCategoryID] [int] NOT NULL REFERENCES
Production.ProductCategory(ProductCategoryID) ,
      [Name] [dbo].[Name] NOT NULL,
      [rowguid] [uniqueidentifier] ROWGUIDCOL  NOT NULL,
      [ModifiedDate] [datetime] NOT NULL         );
```

CHAPTER 6: Fundamentals of Relational Database Design

Branch Banking Conceptual Diagram Preparation In Visio ORM Diagram Tool

The actual implementation of Branch - Customer relationship.

CHAPTER 6: Fundamentals of Relational Database Design

Relational Database Design with Visio

Office Visio can be used for physical database modeling and design. Another widely used database modeling tool is ERWIN.

A sample database design diagram in Visio. Lines represent FOREIGN KEY constraints, arrowheads point to the referenced table.

CHAPTER 6: Fundamentals of Relational Database Design

AdventureWorks Database Model in Visio

A segment of the AdventureWorks database design model in Visio. U indicates UNIQUE KEY or unique index.

SalesOrderHeader

PK	SalesOrderID
FK7	ShipMethodID
	RevisionNumber
	OrderDate
	DueDate
	ShipDate
	Status
	OnlineOrderFlag
U2	SalesOrderNumber
	PurchaseOrderNumber
	AccountNumber
FK5	SalesPersonID
FK6	TerritoryID
FK1	BillToAddressID
FK2	ShipToAddressID
FK8	CreditCardID
	CreditCardApprovalCode
FK4	CurrencyRateID
	SubTotal
	TaxAmt
	Freight
	TotalDue
	Comment
U1	rowguid
	ModifiedDate

CurrencyRate

PK	CurrencyRateID
U1	CurrencyRateDate
FK1,U1	FromCurrencyCode
FK2,U1	ToCurrencyCode
-	AverageRate
-	EndOfDayRate
-	ModifiedDate

CreditCard

	CreditCardID
	CardType
	CardNumber
	ExpMonth
	ExpYear
	ModifiedDate

SalesTaxRate

PK	SalesTaxRateID
FK1,U2	StateProvinceID
U2	TaxType
-	TaxRate
	Name
U1	rowguid
-	ModifiedDate

Production

CHAPTER 6: Fundamentals of Relational Database Design

Reverse Engineering a Database with Visio

Visio can reverse engineer a database. Based on PRIMARY KEY & FOREIGN KEY constraints and table definitions, it can construct a database diagram automatically. Here are the first and an intermediate steps.

Reverse Engineered Diagram of Northwind

A section display from the reverse engineered diagram of Northwind sample database (not clear why "Discontinued" displays in bold):

CHAPTER 6: Fundamentals of Relational Database Design

Forward Engineering a Database with Visio

Visio product itself does not have forward engineering feature. Alberto Ferrari developed an Office Addin for generating database scripts from a Visio database model diagram: Visio Forward Engineer Addin for Office 2010 (http://sqlblog.com/blogs/alberto_ferrari/archive/2010/04/16/visio-forward-engineer-addin-for-office-2010.aspx).

Codeplex blog post and free download for the same: Visio Forward Engineer Addin (http://forwardengineer.codeplex.com/).

Forward Engineering from SSMS Diagram Tool

The Database Diagram Tool in SSMS Object Explorer support graphical design and forward engineering.

Screenshot to show the creation of a new table "Automobile" in the Diagram Tool.

The Properties Dialog Box Allows The Individual Configuration Of Each Column
The Right Click drop-down menu has options to Add Indexes/Keys, Add XML Indexes, Add Spatial Indexes, Add Fulltext Indexes, Delete Tables from Database (DANGEROUS!), CHECK constraint and other table related database objects.

Forward Engineering from SSMS Diagram Tool

Forward Engineering Can Be Initiated By Exiting / Saving The Diagram
The save option dialog box activates automatically upon exit.

Save Change Script Panel Pops Up With The Generated T-SQL Change Script

[Screenshot of "Save Change Script" dialog box asking "Do you want to save this change script to a text file?" with the following script content:]

```
ALTER TABLE dbo.Automobile
    DROP CONSTRAINT DF_Automobile_ModifiedDate
GO
CREATE TABLE dbo.Tmp_Automobile
    (
    AutomobileID int NOT NULL IDENTITY (1, 1),
    VIN char(17) NOT NULL,
    Manufacturer varchar(64) NOT NULL,
    Model char(32) NOT NULL,
    Year char(4) NOT NULL,
    Color char(16) NOT NULL,
    BodyStyle varchar(32) NOT NULL,
    Mileage int NOT NULL,
```

☐ Automatically generate change script on every save

[Yes] [No]

The generated T-SQL change script for changing Manufacturer data type to varchar(64).

```
/* To prevent any potential data loss issues, you should review this script in detail before running it
outside the context of the database designer.*/
BEGIN TRANSACTION
SET QUOTED_IDENTIFIER ON
SET ARITHABORT ON
SET NUMERIC_ROUNDABORT OFF
SET CONCAT_NULL_YIELDS_NULL ON
SET ANSI_NULLS ON
SET ANSI_PADDING ON
SET ANSI_WARNINGS ON
COMMIT
BEGIN TRANSACTION
GO
```

Forward Engineering from SSMS Diagram Tool

-- T-SQL script continued

```sql
ALTER TABLE dbo.Automobile
    DROP CONSTRAINT DF_Automobile_ModifiedDate
GO


CREATE TABLE dbo.Tmp_Automobile    (

        AutomobileID int NOT NULL IDENTITY (1, 1),
        VIN char(17) NOT NULL,
        Manufacturer varchar(64) NOT NULL,
        Model char(32) NOT NULL,
        Year char(4) NOT NULL,
        Color char(16) NOT NULL,
        BodyStyle varchar(32) NOT NULL,
        Mileage int NOT NULL,
        ModifiedDate date NOT NULL )  ON [PRIMARY]
GO
ALTER TABLE dbo.Tmp_Automobile SET (LOCK_ESCALATION = TABLE)
GO
ALTER TABLE dbo.Tmp_Automobile ADD CONSTRAINT
        DF_Automobile_ModifiedDate DEFAULT (getdate()) FOR ModifiedDate
GO
SET IDENTITY_INSERT dbo.Tmp_Automobile ON
GO
IF EXISTS(SELECT * FROM dbo.Automobile)
        EXEC('INSERT INTO dbo.Tmp_Automobile (AutomobileID, VIN, Manufacturer, Model, Year, Color, BodyStyle, Mileage, ModifiedDate)
                SELECT AutomobileID, VIN, CONVERT(varchar(64), Manufacturer), Model, Year, Color, BodyStyle, Mileage, ModifiedDate FROM dbo.Automobile WITH (HOLDLOCK TABLOCKX)')
GO
SET IDENTITY_INSERT dbo.Tmp_Automobile OFF
GO
DROP TABLE dbo.Automobile
GO
EXECUTE sp_rename N'dbo.Tmp_Automobile', N'Automobile', 'OBJECT'
GO
ALTER TABLE dbo.Automobile ADD CONSTRAINT
        PK_Automobile PRIMARY KEY CLUSTERED
        ( AutomobileID
        ) WITH( STATISTICS_NORECOMPUTE = OFF, IGNORE_DUP_KEY = OFF, ALLOW_ROW_LOCKS = ON, ALLOW_PAGE_LOCKS = ON) ON [PRIMARY]
GO
COMMIT
```

Generate Change Script Option

Forward Engineering can also be initiated by the Generate Change Script option. The same option can be used when making any changes to the Diagram using the Diagram Tool.

Forward Engineering from SSMS Diagram Tool

The Generated Script Of The Automobile Table By The Diagram Tool

```sql
USE [AdventureWorks2012]
GO

/****** Object:  Table [dbo].[Automobile]    Script Date: 7/22/2016 11:20:17 AM ******/
SET ANSI_NULLS ON
GO

SET QUOTED_IDENTIFIER ON
GO

SET ANSI_PADDING ON
GO

CREATE TABLE [dbo].[Automobile](
	[AutomobileID] [int] IDENTITY(1,1) NOT NULL,
	[VIN] [char](17) NOT NULL,
	[Manufacturer] [char](32) NOT NULL,
	[Model] [char](32) NOT NULL,
	[Year] [char](4) NOT NULL,
	[Color] [char](16) NOT NULL,
	[BodyStyle] [varchar](32) NOT NULL,
	[Mileage] [int] NOT NULL,
	[ModifiedDate] [date] NOT NULL,
 CONSTRAINT [PK_Automobile] PRIMARY KEY CLUSTERED
(
	[AutomobileID] ASC
)WITH (PAD_INDEX = OFF, STATISTICS_NORECOMPUTE = OFF, IGNORE_DUP_KEY = OFF, ALLOW_ROW_LOCKS = ON, ALLOW_PAGE_LOCKS = ON) ON [PRIMARY]
) ON [PRIMARY]

GO

SET ANSI_PADDING ON
GO

ALTER TABLE [dbo].[Automobile] ADD  CONSTRAINT [DF_Automobile_ModifiedDate]  DEFAULT (getdate()) FOR [ModifiedDate]
GO
```

Scripting Single Database Object with Related Objects

The scripting feature works only through the graphical user interface (GUI) in SSMS Object Explorer. **There is no command to script a table.** Start with Right Click on the Banking.Account table.

Generated script for the Banking.Account table and related objects.

```
USE [AdventureWorks2012]
GO
SET ANSI_NULLS ON
GO
SET QUOTED_IDENTIFIER ON
GO
SET ANSI_PADDING ON
GO
```

CHAPTER 6: Fundamentals of Relational Database Design

Scripting DB Objects With Script Wizard

-- T-SQL script continued

```sql
CREATE TABLE [Banking].[Account](
        [AccountID] [int] IDENTITY(1,1) NOT NULL,
        [BranchID] [int] NOT NULL,
        [AccountNumber] [char](20) NOT NULL,
        [AccountType] [char](12) NOT NULL,
        [Balance] [money] NOT NULL,
        [ModifiedDate] [datetime] NULL,
PRIMARY KEY CLUSTERED
(
        [AccountID] ASC
)WITH (PAD_INDEX = OFF, STATISTICS_NORECOMPUTE = OFF, IGNORE_DUP_KEY = OFF, ALLOW_ROW_LOCKS = ON,
ALLOW_PAGE_LOCKS = ON) ON [PRIMARY],
UNIQUE NONCLUSTERED
(
        [AccountID] ASC
)WITH (PAD_INDEX = OFF, STATISTICS_NORECOMPUTE = OFF, IGNORE_DUP_KEY = OFF, ALLOW_ROW_LOCKS = ON,
ALLOW_PAGE_LOCKS = ON) ON [PRIMARY],
UNIQUE NONCLUSTERED
(
        [AccountNumber] ASC
)WITH (PAD_INDEX = OFF, STATISTICS_NORECOMPUTE = OFF, IGNORE_DUP_KEY = OFF, ALLOW_ROW_LOCKS = ON,
ALLOW_PAGE_LOCKS = ON) ON [PRIMARY]   ) ON [PRIMARY]
GO
SET ANSI_PADDING ON
GO
ALTER TABLE [Banking].[Account] ADD  DEFAULT (getdate()) FOR [ModifiedDate]
GO

ALTER TABLE [Banking].[Account]  WITH CHECK ADD FOREIGN KEY([BranchID])
REFERENCES [Banking].[Branch] ([BranchID])
ON DELETE CASCADE
GO

ALTER TABLE [Banking].[Account]  WITH CHECK ADD  CONSTRAINT [ATC]
CHECK  (([AccountType]='S' OR [AccountType]='C'))
GO
```

CHAPTER 6: Fundamentals of Relational Database Design

Scripting DB Objects With Script Wizard

The Script Wizard is a sophisticated tool for scripting out multiple objects, in fact all objects can be scripted in a single setup and execution. The generated script can be saved to single/multiple files, new query window or the Clipboard. The launching sequence of menus starts with Right Click on the database.

CHAPTER 6: Fundamentals of Relational Database Design

Scripting DB Objects With Script Wizard

Script Wizard Optional Description Page

![Generate and Publish Scripts - Introduction screen showing the wizard with steps: 1. Select database objects. 2. Specify scripting or publishing options. 3. Review your selections. 4. Generate scripts, then save or publish them.]

CHAPTER 6: Fundamentals of Relational Database Design

Object Selection Panel For Scripting

Scripting DB Objects With Script Wizard

A number of options can be set for generation, including scripting of related objects.

The script generated by the Script Wizard for the Banking.Loan table and related objects

```
USE [AdventureWorks2012]
GO
SET ANSI_NULLS ON
GO
SET QUOTED_IDENTIFIER ON
GO
SET ANSI_PADDING ON
GO
CREATE TABLE [Banking].[Loan](
        [LoanID] [int] IDENTITY(1,1) NOT NULL,
        [BranchID] [int] NOT NULL,
        [LoanNumber] [char](20) NOT NULL,
        [LoanType] [varchar](30) NOT NULL,
        [Amount] [money] NOT NULL,
        [ModifiedDate] [datetime] NULL,
PRIMARY KEY CLUSTERED
(       [LoanID] ASC
)WITH (PAD_INDEX = OFF, STATISTICS_NORECOMPUTE = OFF, IGNORE_DUP_KEY = OFF,
ALLOW_ROW_LOCKS = ON, ALLOW_PAGE_LOCKS = ON) ON [PRIMARY],
UNIQUE NONCLUSTERED
(
        [LoanID] ASC
)WITH (PAD_INDEX = OFF, STATISTICS_NORECOMPUTE = OFF, IGNORE_DUP_KEY = OFF,
ALLOW_ROW_LOCKS = ON, ALLOW_PAGE_LOCKS = ON) ON [PRIMARY],
UNIQUE NONCLUSTERED
(
        [LoanNumber] ASC
)WITH (PAD_INDEX = OFF, STATISTICS_NORECOMPUTE = OFF, IGNORE_DUP_KEY = OFF,
ALLOW_ROW_LOCKS = ON, ALLOW_PAGE_LOCKS = ON) ON [PRIMARY]
) ON [PRIMARY]

GO
SET ANSI_PADDING ON
GO
ALTER TABLE [Banking].[Loan] ADD  DEFAULT (getdate()) FOR [ModifiedDate]
GO
ALTER TABLE [Banking].[Loan]  WITH CHECK ADD FOREIGN KEY([BranchID])
REFERENCES [Banking].[Branch] ([BranchID])
ON DELETE CASCADE
GO
```

SEQUENCE Objects

Sequence objects are new in SQL Server 2012. They are similar to the INT IDENTITY(1,1) sequence, however, there is a big difference: they don't "live" inside a table. They are table independent database objects. T-SQL demonstration script displays the flexibility of the new method for sequence number management.

```sql
-- Create a sequence object similar to INT IDENTITY(1,1)
CREATE SEQUENCE seqPurchaseOrder
AS INT
START WITH 1   INCREMENT BY 1;
GO

SELECT NEXT VALUE FOR seqPurchaseOrder;
GO 50
/* 1 2 3 .... 50 */

SELECT NEXT VALUE FOR seqPurchaseOrder;
GO
-- 51

SELECT NextOrderNo = NEXT VALUE FOR seqPurchaseOrder;
-- 52

SELECT NEXT VALUE FOR seqPurchaseOrder as NextOrderNo;
-- 54

EXEC sp_help seqPurchaseOrder;
```

Name	Owner	Type	Created_datetime
seqPurchaseOrder	dbo	sequence object	2016-06-27 09:14:32.940

```sql
DECLARE @List TABLE (id int identity(1,1) primary key, i int);
INSERT @List(i) SELECT NEXT VALUE FOR seqPurchaseOrder;
INSERT @List(i) SELECT NEXT VALUE FOR seqPurchaseOrder;
INSERT @List(i) SELECT NEXT VALUE FOR seqPurchaseOrder;
INSERT @List(i) SELECT NEXT VALUE FOR seqPurchaseOrder;
INSERT @List(i) VALUES (NEXT VALUE FOR seqPurchaseOrder);
SELECT * FROM @List
```

id	i
1	55
2	56
3	57
4	58
5	59

CHAPTER 6: Fundamentals of Relational Database Design

SEQUENCE Object Sharing
SEQUENCE is visible in other connections/session as well not only now but until it exists.

Create a new connection to test NEXT VALUE for seqPurchaseOrder.

```
-- Check current value
SELECT current_value
FROM sys.sequences
WHERE name = 'seqPurchaseOrder';
-- 58
```

```
-- Check metadata
SELECT name, object_id, schema_name(schema_id) as SchemaName, type
FROM sys.sequences;
```

name	object_id	SchemaName	type
seqPurchaseOrder	1338487847	dbo	SO

```
DECLARE @List TABLE (id int identity(1,1) primary key,
            i int default (NEXT VALUE FOR seqPurchaseOrder));
INSERT @List(i) DEFAULT VALUES;
INSERT @List(i) DEFAULT VALUES;
INSERT @List(i) DEFAULT VALUES;
INSERT @List(i) DEFAULT VALUES;
INSERT @List(i)DEFAULT VALUES;
SELECT * FROM @List
```

id	i
1	59
2	60
3	61
4	62
5	63

```
DROP SEQUENCE seqPurchaseOrder;
GO
```

```
SELECT NEXT VALUE FOR seqPurchaseOrder;
```

/* Error Message: Msg 208, Level 16, State 1, Line 2

Invalid object name 'seqPurchaseOrder'. */

SEQUENCE Objects

Cyclical Sequence Objects

We can create cyclical sequence objects as well for enumerating cyclical temporal objects such as weekdays or months.

```
CREATE SEQUENCE seqCycleSeven
AS TINYINT
START WITH 1  INCREMENT BY 1  MINVALUE 1   MAXVALUE 7  CYCLE
GO

CREATE TABLE #Weekdays ( ID INT IDENTITY(1,1) PRIMARY KEY, Weekday nchar(20));
GO

-- Populate table with days progressing by addition of cycle number to current day
INSERT INTO #Weekdays
SELECT DATENAME(dw, dateadd(dd,NEXT VALUE for seqCycleSeven,CURRENT_TIMESTAMP));
GO 20

SELECT * FROM #Weekdays ORDER BY ID;
GO
```

ID	Weekday
1	Tuesday
2	Wednesday
3	Thursday
4	Friday
5	Saturday
6	Sunday
7	Monday
8	Tuesday
9	Wednesday
10	Thursday
11	Friday
12	Saturday
13	Sunday
14	Monday
15	Tuesday
16	Wednesday
17	Thursday
18	Friday
19	Saturday
20	Sunday

```
DROP SEQUENCE seqCycleSeven;  DROP TABLE #Weekdays;
```

Getting the Source Code with sp_helptext

The sp_helptext system procedure can be applied to get the source code for some objects, but not all. **Table source code can only be obtained with GUI scripting in Object Explorer.**

```sql
EXEC sp_helptext 'sp_who'
GO
-- Command(s) completed successfully. - 94 rows - Partial results.

CREATE PROCEDURE sys.Sp_who --- 1995/11/28 15:48
 @loginame SYSNAME = NULL --or 'active'
AS
  DECLARE @spidlow  INT,
       @spidhigh INT,
       @spid     INT,
       @sid      VARBINARY(85)

  SELECT @spidlow = 0,
      @spidhigh = 32767

  IF ( @loginame IS NOT NULL
     AND Upper(@loginame COLLATE latin1_general_ci_as) = 'ACTIVE' )
    BEGIN
      SELECT spid,
          ecid,
          status,
          loginame=Rtrim(loginame),
          hostname,
          blk=CONVERT(CHAR(5), blocked),
          dbname = CASE
                WHEN dbid = 0 THEN NULL
                WHEN dbid <> 0 THEN Db_name(dbid)
              END,
          cmd,
          request_id
      FROM   sys.sysprocesses_ex
      WHERE  spid >= @spidlow
          AND spid <= @spidhigh
          AND Upper(cmd) <> 'AWAITING COMMAND'

      RETURN ( 0 )
  END
```

CHAPTER 7: Normal Forms & Database Normalization

The Goals of Database Normalizaton

Database normalization is the design technique of logically organizing data in a database:

➢ Data should uniquely be addressable in a database by table, row and column identification - like x, y, z coordinates in 3D space.

➢ Data redundancy (storing the same data in more than one table) should be avoided.

➢ Data dependency (a property is fully dependent on the PRIMARY KEY) should ensure that a piece of data gets into the right table or if there is none, a new one is created.

The first goal is relatively easy to achieve yet data duplication in a table is a constant issue plaguing database installations. The second goal is simple as well yet it conflicts with deep-seated human insecurity of not seeing all the data together. The third goal on the other hand requires careful design considerations, it can be challenging for complex data relationships or if the database designer is not familiar with the application. If an OLTP database with many data access points is not normalized, the result is inefficiency in database application development and maintenance which can be quite costly to a company for years to come. Metadata query to list all FOREIGN KEYs in NorthWind followed by a high level database diagram.

```
select    fkschema = fk.constraint_schema,  fktable = fk.table_name, fkcolumn = fk.column_name,
          pkcolumn = pk.column_name,   pktable = pk.table_name, pkschema = pk.table_schema,
          fkname = rc.constraint_name
from  northwind.information_schema.referential_constraints rc
      inner join northwind.information_schema.key_column_usage fk
           on fk.constraint_name = rc.constraint_name
      inner join northwind.information_schema.key_column_usage pk
           on pk.constraint_name = rc.unique_constraint_name
where   fk.ordinal_position = pk.ordinal_position order by fkschema, fktable, fkcolumn;
```

fkschema	fktable	fkcolumn	pkcolumn	pktable	pkschema	fkname
dbo	CustomerCustomerDemo	CustomerID	CustomerID	Customers	dbo	FK_CustomerCustomerDemo_Customers
dbo	CustomerCustomerDemo	CustomerTypeID	CustomerTypeID	CustomerDemographics	dbo	FK_CustomerCustomerDemo
dbo	Employees	ReportsTo	EmployeeID	Employees	dbo	FK_Employees_Employees
dbo	EmployeeTerritories	EmployeeID	EmployeeID	Employees	dbo	FK_EmployeeTerritories_Employees
dbo	EmployeeTerritories	TerritoryID	TerritoryID	Territories	dbo	FK_EmployeeTerritories_Territories
dbo	Order Details	OrderID	OrderID	Orders	dbo	FK_Order_Details_Orders
dbo	Order Details	ProductID	ProductID	Products	dbo	FK_Order_Details_Products
dbo	Orders	CustomerID	CustomerID	Customers	dbo	FK_Orders_Customers
dbo	Orders	EmployeeID	EmployeeID	Employees	dbo	FK_Orders_Employees
dbo	Orders	ShipVia	ShipperID	Shippers	dbo	FK_Orders_Shippers
dbo	Products	CategoryID	CategoryID	Categories	dbo	FK_Products_Categories
dbo	Products	SupplierID	SupplierID	Suppliers	dbo	FK_Products_Suppliers
dbo	Territories	RegionID	RegionID	Region	dbo	FK_Territories_Region

Orders & Related Tables Diagram in Northwind

The database diagram clearly shows the central role of the Orders table at a company which is a reseller not a manufacturer.

First Normal Form (1NF)

The first normal form establishes RDBMS basics. The rules make common sense.

- ➢ Each group of related data (entity) should have its own table (no piggybacking data).

- ➢ Each column should be identified with a unique name in a table.

- ➢ Each row should be identified with a unique column or set of columns (PRIMARY KEY).

Selected tables (entities) in Northwind database.

Second Normal Form (2NF)

The Second Normal Form addresses the issue of piggybacking data on a related table.

➢ Tables are in First Normal Form.

➢ Remove subsets of data that apply to multiple rows of a table and create a separate table for them.

➢ Create relationships between these new tables and their predecessors through the use of FOREIGN KEYs.

The tacit assumption here that there was no logical data modeling or that had a mistake. The database designer has created a set of tables and now taking a second look to see if all data belong to that table. Frequently the design starts with lead database developer preparing a first version of the design. Only big companies can afford the "luxury" of logical data modeling and professional database designer. That has to be qualified with a little known fact. Even a small company can hire a professional database designer for a month, surely money well spent. Categories table can easily piggyback on the Products table. Being a separate table increases the usefulness, flexibility and expandability of the design.

CHAPTER 7: Normal Forms & Database Normalization

Third Normal Form (3NF)

The Third Normal Form addresses the issue of storing the data in the appropriate table.

> Tables are in Second Normal Form.

> Remove columns that are not dependent upon the PRIMARY KEY and move them to the correct table.

The royalty and ytd_sales columns are not fully dependent on the title_id PRIMARY KEY. In fact royalty schedule is specified in the roysched table and the dependency includes quantity sold. A view (virtual table) can be setup to return the current royalties based on books sold and the royalty schedule. A more appropriate table for ytd_sales would be saleshist (SalesHistory). The inclusion of the time dependent dynamic ytd_sales column is suspicious right off the bat since all the other columns are static.

CHAPTER 7: Normal Forms & Database Normalization

Fourth Normal Form (4NF)

The Fourth Normal Form addresses the issue of subtle data dependency:

➢ Tables are in Third Normal Form.

➢ A relation should not have multi-valued dependencies.

If we look at "Road-650 Black, 44" and "Road-650 Red, 44" bikes in Production.Product we see that they are the same bike with different color. So it would be sufficient to store only a single row "Road-650, 44" and setup a junction table between the Product table and the (new) Color table to indicate the color variations and other dependent information. We can see that the color occurs in 3 columns: Name, ProductNumber (first letter of color) and Color. By doing 4NF normalization we can remove the color reference from the Name and ProductNumber columns.

CHAPTER 7: Normal Forms & Database Normalization

Database Denormalizaton

Database denormalization is a technique to reduce the number of tables in a normalized database. The author personally disagrees with this process: why would you go into the trouble and expense of creating a normalized database and then ruin it? Regardless of the author's opinion, denormalization is an accepted notion in the database industry. Too many tables require too many JOINs, that is the underlying justification. The trouble with this process is twofold:

> There is no guideline when to stop with denormalization, 10% table reduction, 50%?

> Also, there are no guidelines as to which tables to eliminate when denormalizing.

If you eliminate too many tables you may just end up with a messy database instead of the original neat & efficient 3NF database thus creating a potential disaster for your employer. Typically you would look at the small static tables as candidates for elimination which are not FOREIGN KEY referenced from many tables. There are precise guidelines how to achieve a normalized database. It is a scientific process. Denormalization is not. Performance is another reason mentioned for denormalization, but that is generally not a valid claim. There are much better ways to achieve good performance than denormalizing a well-designed database system. Hypothetically, let's take a look at low population tables in AdventureWorks2012, as candidates for denormalization.

```
SELECT  TOP 10 SCHEMA_NAME(schema_id)+'.'+o.name AS TableName, max(i.rows) AS Rows
FROM    sys.sysobjects o INNER JOIN sys.sysindexes i   ON o.id = i.id
     INNER JOIN sys.objects oo    ON o.id = oo.object_id
WHERE   xtype = 'u' AND OBJECTPROPERTY(o.id,N'IsUserTable') = 1
GROUP BY schema_id, o.name ORDER BY Rows ASC;
```

TableName	Rows
dbo.ErrorLog	0
dbo.AWBuildVersion	1
Person.PhoneNumberType	3
HumanResources.Shift	3
Sales.ShoppingCartItem	3
Production.ProductCategory	4
Production.ProductReview	4
Production.Illustration	5
Purchasing.ShipMethod	5
Person.AddressType	6

Tables like PhoneNumberType, Shift, Shipmethod and SalesReason can likely be eliminated without dire consequences. However, why ruin a well-designed 3NF database such as AdventureWorks2012 just to decrease the number of JOINs with one or two? Is it annoying to have 10 JOINs in a query? Not really. That is how SQL works. Is SQL Server going to be much faster with 8 JOINs as opposed to 10 JOINs? No, there is no such a rule in query optimization.

CHAPTER 7: Normal Forms & Database Normalization

Better Alternative to Denormalization

The best alternative is to use views for frequently used queries to avoid building JOINs again and again. The results of SELECT from a view must be sorted with ORDER BY just like the case for tables. There is no way around it. Demonstration of the powerful method.

```
USE AdventureWorks;
SELECT
            V.Name                                      AS Vendor,
            CONCAT(C.LastName, ', ', C.FirstName)       AS Contact,
            CT.Name                                     AS Title
FROM Person.Contact AS C
   INNER JOIN Purchasing.VendorContact VC
            ON C.ContactID = VC.ContactID
   INNER JOIN Person.ContactType CT
            ON CT.ContactTypeID = VC.ContactTypeID
   INNER JOIN Purchasing.Vendor V
            ON V.VendorID = VC.VendorID
ORDER BY Vendor, Contact;
-- (156 row(s) affected)
```

```
CREATE VIEW vVendorContact
AS
SELECT
            V.Name                                      AS Vendor,
            CONCAT(C.LastName, ', ', C.FirstName)       AS Contact,
            CT.Name                                     AS Title
FROM Person.Contact AS C
   INNER JOIN Purchasing.VendorContact VC    ON C.ContactID = VC.ContactID
   INNER JOIN Person.ContactType CT          ON CT.ContactTypeID = VC.ContactTypeID
   INNER JOIN Purchasing.Vendor V            ON V.VendorID = VC.VendorID
GO
```

```
SELECT TOP 5 * FROM vVendorContact ORDER BY Vendor, Contact;
```

Vendor	Contact	Title
A. Datum Corporation	Pellow, Frank	Assistant Sales Agent
A. Datum Corporation	Wilkie, Jay	Sales Agent
A. Datum Corporation	Yu, Wei	Sales Manager
Advanced Bicycles	Moeller, Jonathan	Sales Associate
Advanced Bicycles	Wilson, James	Sales Manager

We have created from the 4 tables JOIN, a very simple to use, very easy to remember view.

CHAPTER 7: Normal Forms & Database Normalization

Ten Most Common Database Design Mistakes

Along his database career the author found the following list of common design issues:

- Not involving systems analysts and/or subject matter experts in conceptual design.

- Not employing accomplished database designer / lead developer to implement 3NF design standards.

- Denormalizing a well-designed database.

- Not having NATURAL KEY in addition to INT IDENTITY(1,1) SURROGATE PRIMARY KEY.

- Poor documentation & lack of naming convention for the project.

- Not using PRIMARY KEY, FOREIGN KEY, UNIQUE , CHECK & DEFAULT constraints to protect data integrity.

- Using client programs for data management instead of server side stored procedures, functions & views.

- Using triggers to fix design or client software problems.

- Not following the solution implementation hierarchy: constraints -> stored procedures -> triggers -> client SW.

- Lack of formal Quality Assurance process.

Working for a Company with Messy Database Design

In your career you may work for companies with proper 3NF design databases, companies with messy databases or somewhere in the middle. It is a joy to work in 3NF environment. On the other hand, if the database is badly designed, or more accurately lacks design, you have to be careful in criticizing it because you can pick up enemies quickly or even get fired. Badly designed database usually becomes an IT department political issue instead of remaining a technical issue. Most companies don't want to invest in redesigning the database properly. In such a situation you have to accept working with poorly designed databases, enjoy your nice paycheck and wait for an opportunity when new tables or database is needed to create proper 3NF design.

CHAPTER 7: Normal Forms & Database Normalization

Query to List All Table Sizes in a Database

T-SQL script to list all table sizes in AdventureWorks2012 database. Note: the tables are uniquely named in AdventureWorks databases, so there are no duplicates if the schema name is not used. This assumption though not true generally. Objects can be named the same in different schemas.

```
declare @TableSpace table (TableName sysname, RowsK varchar(32), -- table variable
        ReservedMB varchar(32), DataMB varchar(32),
        IndexMB varchar(32), UnusedMB varchar(32));

insert @TableSpace
exec sp_MSforeachtable @command1="exec sp_spaceused '?';" -- undocumented system procedure

update @TableSpace set RowsK = CONVERT(varchar, 1+convert(int, RowsK)/1024)
update @TableSpace set ReservedMB = CONVERT(varchar,
            1+convert(int,LEFT(ReservedMB, charindex(' K', ReservedMB,-1)))/1024);
update @TableSpace set DataMB = CONVERT(varchar,
            1+convert(int,LEFT(DataMB, charindex(' K', DataMB,-1)))/1024);
update @TableSpace set IndexMB = CONVERT(varchar,
            convert(int,LEFT(IndexMB, charindex(' K', IndexMB,-1)))/1024);
update @TableSpace set UnusedMB = CONVERT(varchar,
            convert(int,LEFT(UnusedMB, charindex(' K', UnusedMB,-1)))/1024);

select * from @TableSpace order by convert(int,DataMB) desc;
go
-- (71 row(s) affected) -- Partial results.
```

TableName	RowsK	ReservedMB	DataMB	IndexMB	UnusedMB
Person	20	84	30	51	2
SalesOrderDetail	119	18	10	6	1
DatabaseLog	2	7	7	0	0
TransactionHistory	111	11	7	3	0
WorkOrderRouting	66	8	6	1	0
SalesOrderHeader	31	9	6	2	0
WorkOrder	71	7	5	2	0
TransactionHistoryArchive	88	9	5	3	0
ProductPhoto	1	3	3	0	0
Address	20	6	3	2	0
CreditCard	19	3	2	0	0
EmailAddress	20	4	2	1	0
Password	20	2	2	0	0
PersonPhone	20	3	2	0	0
SalesTerritory	1	1	1	0	0
PhoneNumberType	1	1	1	0	0
Product	1	1	1	0	0
SalesTerritoryHistory	1	1	1	0	0
SalesPersonQuotaHistory	1	1	1	0	0
Employee	1	1	1	0	0

CHAPTER 8: Functional Database Design

Types of Table Relationships

The most frequent relationship is one-to-many (or many-to-one) indicating many FOREIGN KEY references to a single PRIMARY KEY table row. Example: Products & ProductCategories; A product category may have 50 different products. The next most popular one is many-to-many relationship indicating that a single row in Table Alpha can reference multiple rows in Table Beta. Example: Classes & Students at a college; A class may have 20 students and a student may take 5 different classes. In the following pubs table relationship diagram we can see:

- ➢ many-to-many relationship (oo - oo connectors): titleauthor table
- ➢ one-to-one relationship (2 gold keys): publishers & pub_info tables
- ➢ one-to-many: the remaining relationships

CHAPTER 8: Functional Database Design

One-To-Many Relationship - FOREIGN KEY Reference

Northwind example shows that each product belongs to a category. CategoryID column in the Products table (FOREIGN KEY) references CategoryID in Categories table (PRIMARY KEY). One category can have 0 to many products. FK name can be different from PK name. However, if possible, PK name is the best choice for FK name. When multiple FK-s referencing the same PK, we have to choose different names for FK-s.

CHAPTER 8: Functional Database Design

One-To-Many Relationship - FOREIGN KEY Reference

CategoryID in the Products table is a FOREIGN KEY (a pointer) to a PRIMARY KEY in the Categories table

Therefore, we can safely JOIN the two tables using the two ON KEYs.

```sql
SELECT CategoryName, ProductName,
       QuantityPerUnit, UnitPrice
FROM Products p
  INNER JOIN Categories c
    ON p.CategoryID = c.CategoryID
ORDER BY CategoryName, ProductName
```

	CategoryName	ProductName	QuantityPerUnit	UnitPrice
1	Beverages	Chai	10 boxes x 20 bags	18.00
2	Beverages	Chang	24 - 12 oz bottles	19.00
3	Beverages	Chartreuse verte	750 cc per bottle	18.00
4	Beverages	Côte de Blaye	12 - 75 cl bottles	263.50
5	Beverages	Guaraná Fantástica	12 - 355 ml cans	4.50
6	Beverages	Ipoh Coffee	16 - 500 g tins	46.00
7	Beverages	Lakkalikööri	500 ml	18.00
8	Beverages	Laughing Lumberjack Lager	24 - 12 oz bottles	14.00
9	Beverages	Outback Lager	24 - 355 ml bottles	15.00
10	Beverages	Rhönbräu Klosterbier	24 - 0.5 l bottles	7.75
11	Beverages	Sasquatch Ale	24 - 12 oz bottles	14.00

CHAPTER 8: Functional Database Design

The PRIMARY KEY and FOREIGN KEY should not be exposed to the database application user

The Business Intelligence consumer needs meaningful information not meaningless numbers. The software engineer can see the PK and FK values as part of his work.

```
SELECT CategoryName, ProductName,
       QuantityPerUnit, UnitPrice,
       FK=p.CategoryID, PK=c.CategoryID
FROM Products p
  INNER JOIN Categories c
    ON p.CategoryID = c.CategoryID
ORDER BY CategoryName, ProductName
```

	CategoryName	ProductName	QuantityPerUnit	UnitPrice	FK	PK
47	Dairy Products	Raclette Courdavault	5 kg pkg.	55.00	4	4
48	Grains/Cereals	Filo Mix	16 - 2 kg boxes	7.00	5	5
49	Grains/Cereals	Gnocchi di nonna Alice	24 - 250 g pkgs.	38.00	5	5
50	Grains/Cereals	Gustaf's Knäckebröd	24 - 500 g pkgs.	21.00	5	5
51	Grains/Cereals	Ravioli Angelo	24 - 250 g pkgs.	19.50	5	5
52	Grains/Cereals	Singaporean Hokkien Frie...	32 - 1 kg pkgs.	14.00	5	5
53	Grains/Cereals	Tunnbröd	12 - 250 g pkgs.	9.00	5	5
54	Grains/Cereals	Wimmers gute Semmelkn...	20 bags x 4 pieces	33.25	5	5
55	Meat/Poultry	Alice Mutton	20 - 1 kg tins	39.00	6	6
56	Meat/Poultry	Mishi Kobe Niku	18 - 500 g pkgs.	97.00	6	6
57	Meat/Poultry	Pâté chinois	24 boxes x 2 pies	24.00	6	6

We could make the NATURAL KEY ProductName a PRIMARY KEY in the Products table. However, that is a string field (column) nvarchar(40) which can be 80 bytes in size (each UNICODE character is 2 bytes). That would present increased space use and decreased performance in JOINs. It would also present increased maintenance cost if we have to change a product name, for example, "Ravioli Angelo" to "Ravioli Los Angeles". The change would have to be performed in the PRIMARY KEY table and each FOREIGN KEY table. The 4-byte integer SURROGATE PRIMARY KEY ProductID solves all the problems above. Minimal space use, fast in JOINs and since a meaningless number (a database pointer), we never have to change it. If the ProductName changes, it is just a single UPDATE in the PRIMARY KEY table.

Composite PRIMARY KEY

A composite PRIMARY KEY consists of two or more columns. Junction tables typically apply composite PRIMARY KEYs. An example is the Production.ProductProductPhoto junction table.

>ProductID (PK, FK, int, not null)
>ProductPhotoID (PK, FK, int, not null)
>Primary (Flag(bit), not null)
>ModifiedDate (datetime, not null

The PRIMARY KEY is the composite of two FOREIGN KEYs: ProductID and ProductPhotoID.

T-SQL script definition of the above composite PRIMARY KEY.

```
USE [AdventureWorks2012];
GO

ALTER TABLE [Production].[ProductProductPhoto]
ADD  CONSTRAINT [PK_ProductProductPhoto_ProductID_ProductPhotoID]
PRIMARY KEY NONCLUSTERED
(
        [ProductID] ASC,
        [ProductPhotoID] ASC
);
```

A FOREIGN KEY referencing a composite PRIMARY KEY must have the same column structure. Query to display all the data in the table.

```
SELECT  ProductID
        ,ProductPhotoID
        ,[Primary]
        ,ModifiedDate
 FROM AdventureWorks2012.Production.ProductProductPhoto;
-- (504 row(s) affected) - Partial results.
```

ProductID	ProductPhotoID	Primary	ModifiedDate
813	1	1	2006-06-01 00:00:00.000
814	1	1	2006-06-01 00:00:00.000
815	160	1	2006-06-01 00:00:00.000
816	160	1	2006-06-01 00:00:00.000
817	160	1	2006-06-01 00:00:00.000
818	160	1	2006-06-01 00:00:00.000

> NOTE
> Use composite UNIQUE KEY and INT SURROGATE PRIMARY KEY in base tables.
> Composite PRIMARY KEY requires composite FOREIGN KEY!

Parent-Child Hierarchy

When an employee's record includes the manager's ID, it is called self-reference since the manager is an employee also. A simple organizational chart (tree structure) can be established by self-referencing FOREIGN KEYs.

```sql
USE [AdventureWorks]
GO

ALTER TABLE [HumanResources].[Employee]
WITH CHECK ADD  CONSTRAINT
[FK_Employee_Employee_ManagerID]
FOREIGN KEY([ManagerID])
REFERENCES [HumanResources].[Employee]
([EmployeeID])
GO

SELECT EmployeeID, LoginID, ManagerID
FROM HumanResources.Employee;
```

	EmployeeID	LoginID	ManagerID
1	1	adventure-works\guy1	16
2	2	adventure-works\kevin0	6
3	3	adventure-works\roberto0	12
4	4	adventure-works\rob0	3
5	5	adventure-works\thierry0	263
6	6	adventure-works\david0	109
7	7	adventure-works\jolynn0	21

Reading the table: david0 is the supervisor of kevin0, and roberto0 is the supervisor of rob0.

CHAPTER 8: Functional Database Design

Hierarchical Relationship - Multi-Level with FOREIGN KEYs

Product, ProductSubcategory and ProductCategory in AdventureWorks represent multi-level hierarchy which can be implemented with FOREIGN KEYs. To get the hierarchical information, we need to INNER JOIN the tables on the FOREIGN KEYS and PRIMARY KEYS. Column aliases are used to create meaningful column names from the 3 "Name"-s.

```sql
SELECT c.Name as Category,
       s.Name as Subcategory,
       p.Name as ProductName,
       ProductNumber
FROM Production.Product p
  INNER JOIN Production.ProductSubcategory s
    ON p.ProductSubcategoryID = s.ProductSubcategoryID
  INNER JOIN Production.ProductCategory c
    ON s.ProductCategoryID = c.ProductCategoryID
ORDER BY Category, Subcategory, ProductName
```

	Category	Subcategory	ProductName	Pr
59	Bikes	Mountain Bikes	Mountain-500 Silver, 44	B
60	Bikes	Mountain Bikes	Mountain-500 Silver, 48	B
61	Bikes	Mountain Bikes	Mountain-500 Silver, 52	B
62	Bikes	Road Bikes	Road-150 Red, 44	B
63	Bikes	Road Bikes	Road-150 Red, 48	B
64	Bikes	Road Bikes	Road-150 Red, 52	B

CHAPTER 8: Functional Database Design

Tree Hierarchy Representation with hierarchyid

An alternate to using self-referencing FOREIGN KEY is the application of hierarchyid data type introduced with SQL Server 2008.

We can read from the table that ken0 (Ken Sanchez, CEO) is the supervisor of terri0 who in turn is the supervisor of roberto0 who is the supervisor of rob0.

Many-To-Many Relationship - Junction Table

Junction tables have many names, most popular among them are junction table, cross-reference table and bridge table. The titleauthor table in the pubs database is a junction table: a title (book) can have many authors and an author can write many titles. The PRIMARY KEY is a composite of two FOREIGN KEYs referencing the titles and authors tables.

Reading the author - title junction table: book title PC8888 has multiple (two) authors, while author 486-29-1786 wrote multiple (two) books.

CHAPTER 8: Functional Database Design

Parent-Child or Master-Detail Tables Design

In the AdventureWorks series of sample databases, Sales.SalesOrderHeader and Sales.SalesOrderDetail tables are implemented as master-detail tables. Similarly for Purchasing.PurchaseOrderHeader and Purchasing.PurchaseOrderDetail. The PRIMARY KEY of SalesOrderHeader is SalesOrderID (INT IDENTITY(1,1)). The PRIMARY KEY of SalesOrderDetail is composite of SalesOrderID FOREIGN KEY and SalesOrderDetailID (INT IDENTITY(1,1)). The business meaning is that an order from a bicycle reseller can have many line items such mountain bikes, helmets, touring frames and jerseys.

Parent-Child or Master-Detail Tables Design

Column Descriptions of SalesOrderHeader & SalesOrderDetail Tables

UNION query to lists the column descriptions for the above master-detail tables from the data dictionary.

```
SELECT  'Sales.SalesOrderHeader' AS TableName, objname    AS ColumnName,
        value                                              AS [Description]
FROM fn_listextendedproperty (NULL, 'schema', 'Sales', 'table', 'SalesOrderHeader', 'Column', default)

UNION

SELECT  'Sales.SalesOrderDetail' AS TableName, objname    AS ColumnName,
        value                                              AS [Description]
FROM fn_listextendedproperty (NULL, 'schema', 'Sales', 'table', 'SalesOrderDetail', 'Column', default)

ORDER BY TableName DESC, ColumnName;
```

TableName	ColumnName	Description
Sales.SalesOrderHeader	AccountNumber	Financial accounting number reference.
Sales.SalesOrderHeader	BillToAddressID	Customer billing address. Foreign key to Address.AddressID.
Sales.SalesOrderHeader	Comment	Sales representative comments.
Sales.SalesOrderHeader	CreditCardApprovalCode	Approval code provided by the credit card company.
Sales.SalesOrderHeader	CreditCardID	Credit card identification number. Foreign key to CreditCard.CreditCardID.
Sales.SalesOrderHeader	CurrencyRateID	Currency exchange rate used. Foreign key to CurrencyRate.CurrencyRateID.
Sales.SalesOrderHeader	CustomerID	Customer identification number. Foreign key to Customer.BusinessEntityID.
Sales.SalesOrderHeader	DueDate	Date the order is due to the customer.
Sales.SalesOrderHeader	Freight	Shipping cost.
Sales.SalesOrderHeader	ModifiedDate	Date and time the record was last updated.
Sales.SalesOrderHeader	OnlineOrderFlag	0 = Order placed by sales person. 1 = Order placed online by customer.
Sales.SalesOrderHeader	OrderDate	Dates the sales order was created.
Sales.SalesOrderHeader	PurchaseOrderNumber	Customer purchase order number reference.
Sales.SalesOrderHeader	RevisionNumber	Incremental number to track changes to the sales order over time.
Sales.SalesOrderHeader	rowguid	ROWGUIDCOL number uniquely identifying the record. Used to support a merge replication sample.
Sales.SalesOrderHeader	SalesOrderID	Primary key.
Sales.SalesOrderHeader	SalesOrderNumber	Unique sales order identification number.
Sales.SalesOrderHeader	SalesPersonID	Sales person who created the sales order. Foreign key to SalesPerson.BusinessEntityID.
Sales.SalesOrderHeader	ShipDate	Date the order was shipped to the customer.
Sales.SalesOrderHeader	ShipMethodID	Shipping method. Foreign key to ShipMethod.ShipMethodID.
Sales.SalesOrderHeader	ShipToAddressID	Customer shipping address. Foreign key to Address.AddressID.
Sales.SalesOrderHeader	Status	Order current status. 1 = In process; 2 = Approved; 3 = Backordered; 4 = Rejected; 5 = Shipped; 6 = Cancelled
Sales.SalesOrderHeader	SubTotal	Sales subtotal. Computed as SUM(SalesOrderDetail.LineTotal)for the appropriate SalesOrderID.
Sales.SalesOrderHeader	TaxAmt	Tax amount.
Sales.SalesOrderHeader	TerritoryID	Territory in which the sale was made. Foreign key to SalesTerritory.SalesTerritoryID.
Sales.SalesOrderHeader	TotalDue	Total due from customer. Computed as Subtotal + TaxAmt + Freight.
Sales.SalesOrderDetail	CarrierTrackingNumber	Shipment tracking number supplied by the shipper.
Sales.SalesOrderDetail	LineTotal	Per product subtotal. Computed as UnitPrice * (1 - UnitPriceDiscount) * OrderQty.
Sales.SalesOrderDetail	ModifiedDate	Date and time the record was last updated.
Sales.SalesOrderDetail	OrderQty	Quantity ordered per product.
Sales.SalesOrderDetail	ProductID	Product sold to customer. Foreign key to Product.ProductID.
Sales.SalesOrderDetail	rowguid	ROWGUIDCOL number uniquely identifying the record. Used to support a merge replication sample.
Sales.SalesOrderDetail	SalesOrderDetailID	Primary key. One incremental unique number per product sold.
Sales.SalesOrderDetail	SalesOrderID	Primary key. Foreign key to SalesOrderHeader.SalesOrderID.
Sales.SalesOrderDetail	SpecialOfferID	Promotional code. Foreign key to SpecialOffer.SpecialOfferID.
Sales.SalesOrderDetail	UnitPrice	Selling price of a single product.
Sales.SalesOrderDetail	UnitPriceDiscount	Discount amount.

CHAPTER 8: Functional Database Design

Diagram of PurchaseOrderHeader and Related Tables

Database diagram to display the special relationship to the child table PurchaseOrderDetail and PK-FK relationships to other tables.

Employee (HumanRe
- BusinessEntityID
- NationalIDNumb...
- LoginID

PurchaseOrderDetail (P
- PurchaseOrderID
- PurchaseOrderDetai...
- DueDate
- OrderQty
- ProductID
- UnitPrice
- LineTotal
- ReceivedQty
- RejectedQty

PurchaseOrderHeader (
- PurchaseOrderID
- RevisionNumber
- Status
- EmployeeID
- VendorID
- ShipMethodID
- OrderDate
- ShipDate
- SubTotal
- TaxAmt
- Freight
- TotalDue

Vendor (Purchasing)
- BusinessEntityID
- AccountNumber
- Name
- CreditRating
- PreferredVendorStatus
- ActiveFlag
- PurchasingWebService...

ShipMethod (Pur
- ShipMeth...
- Name
- ShipBase
- ShipRate
- rowguid

Parent-Child or Master-Detail Tables Design　　　　　　　　　　　　　　**249**

Multiple FOREIGN KEYs from One Table to Another

Database diagram to illustrate the double FOREIGN KEYs from BillOfMaterials table to the Product table. The FOREIGN KEYs are named **ComponentID and ProductAssemblyID**. In the Product table **SizeUnitMeasureCode & WeightUnitMeasureCode** are double FOREIGN KEYs to the UnitMeasure table.

CHAPTER 8: Functional Database Design

Parent - Multiple Children Table Design

Database design & diagram to represent a parent table with two children table. Notice that in the children table the PRIMARY KEY is a FOREIGN KEY simultaneously.

```
CREATE TABLE Security  (
    Symbol              CHAR(7)  PRIMARY KEY,
    SecurityName        NVARCHAR(64),
    CUSIP               CHAR(9),
    ModifiedDate        DATETIME DEFAULT (CURRENT_TIMESTAMP)   );

CREATE TABLE Stock  (
    Symbol              CHAR(7)  PRIMARY KEY REFERENCES Security ON DELETE CASCADE,
    AuthShares          BIGINT,
    IssuedShares        BIGINT,
    ClosingPrice        DECIMAL(14, 2),
    ModifiedDate        DATETIME DEFAULT (CURRENT_TIMESTAMP)   );

CREATE TABLE Bond  (
    Symbol              CHAR(7)  PRIMARY KEY REFERENCES Security ON DELETE CASCADE,
    Rate                DECIMAL(14, 6),
    FaceValue           DECIMAL(14, 2),
    MaturityDate        DATE,
    ClosingPrice        DECIMAL(14, 2),
    ModifiedDate        DATETIME DEFAULT (CURRENT_TIMESTAMP)   );
```

CHAPTER 8: Functional Database Design

LookupHeader & Lookup Tables for Storing All Lookups

T-SQL script to demonstrate a simple implementation of LookupHeader & Lookup (detail) tables to prevent database "pollution" by many small lookup (code/translate) tables.

```
USE AdventureWorks2012;

CREATE TABLE LookupHeader
(
        LookupHeaderID      INT IDENTITY(1, 1)      PRIMARY KEY,
        [Type]              VARCHAR(80)             UNIQUE,
        ModifiedDate        DATETIME                default ( CURRENT_TIMESTAMP)
);
go

CREATE TABLE Lookup
(
        LookupID            INT IDENTITY(1,1) PRIMARY KEY nonclustered,
        LookupHeaderID      INT NOT NULL REFERENCES LookupHeader(LookupHeaderID),
        Code                VARCHAR(6) NOT NULL,
        [Description]       VARCHAR(255),
        ModifiedDate        DATETIME default ( CURRENT_TIMESTAMP)
);
go

-- composite PRIMARY KEY
ALTER TABLE dbo.Lookup
        ADD CONSTRAINT uq_lookup UNIQUE CLUSTERED ( LookupHeaderID, Code );
go

INSERT LookupHeader ([Type]) VALUES ('Country');
INSERT LookupHeader ([Type]) VALUES ('Department');

SELECT * FROM   LookupHeader ;
go
```

LookupHeaderID	Type	ModifiedDate
1	Country	2016-08-08 07:34:59.077
2	Department	2016-08-08 07:34:59.113

```
-- Populate department code
INSERT INTO LookUp (LookupHeaderID, Code, Description)  VALUES   (2, '1', 'Human Resources');
INSERT INTO LookUp (LookupHeaderID, Code, Description)  VALUES   (2, '2', 'Accounting');
INSERT INTO LookUp (LookupHeaderID, Code, Description)  VALUES   (2, '3', 'Engineering');
GO
```

CHAPTER 8: Functional Database Design

LookupHeader & Lookup Tables for Storing All Lookups

```
-- T-SQL script continued

-- Populate country code lookup
INSERT INTO LookUp (LookupHeaderID, Code, Description)
SELECT 1, [CountryRegionCode],[Name]
 FROM [AdventureWorks2012].[Person].[CountryRegion]
ORDER BY CountryRegionCode;
go

-- Check lookup table content
SELECT * FROM   Lookup ORDER  BY LookupHeaderID, Code;
```

Partial display of the Lookup table content.

	LookupHeaderID	Type	ModifiedDate
1	1	Country	2012-07-04 17:17:03.343
2	2	Department	2012-07-04 17:17:03.353

	LookupHeaderID	Code	Description	ModifiedDate
229	1	VI	Virgin Islands, U.S.	2012-07-04 17:17:03.437
230	1	VN	Vietnam	2012-07-04 17:17:03.437
231	1	VU	Vanuatu	2012-07-04 17:17:03.437
232	1	WF	Wallis and Futuna	2012-07-04 17:17:03.437
233	1	WS	Samoa	2012-07-04 17:17:03.437
234	1	YE	Yemen	2012-07-04 17:17:03.437
235	1	YT	Mayotte	2012-07-04 17:17:03.437
236	1	ZA	South Africa	2012-07-04 17:17:03.437
237	1	ZM	Zambia	2012-07-04 17:17:03.437
238	1	ZW	Zimbabwe	2012-07-04 17:17:03.437
239	2	1	Human Resources	2012-07-04 17:17:03.400
240	2	2	Accounting	2012-07-04 17:17:03.413
241	2	3	Engineering	2012-07-04 17:17:03.423

History Table Design

AdventureWorks2012 EmployeeDepartmentHistory table follows the career of an employee from department to department each with StartDate and EndDate. If EndDate is NULL, that is the employee's current department. For employee ID 250 (BusinessEntityID) the current department is 5. The PRIMARY KEY is composite of BusinessEntityID (employee ID), DepartmentID, ShiftID and StartDate. The first 3 columns in the PRIMARY KEY are FOREIGN KEYs also. BusinessEntityID references (points to) the Employee table, DepartmentID the Department table and ShiftID the Shift table.

Implementing One-To-One Relationship

In a one-to-one relationship, a row in the main table can have no more than one matching row in the secondary table, and vice versa. **A one-to-one relationship requires that both of the related columns are primary keys.** One-to-one relationship tables are not very common because most of the time a single table is used. Nonetheless, we might use a one-to-one relationship tables to: Vertically partition a table with many columns; Vertically divide a table to a narrow and wide part for performance reasons - example: email header & email body; Isolate sensitive columns in a table for security reasons; Store information that applies only to a subset of the main table thus avoiding lots of NULLs in the rows. Demonstration to show the one-to-one relationship between Product and ProductInventory tables.

```sql
-- Dynamic information is separated from static information
-- One-to-one relationship

CREATE TABLE dbo.Product (
    ProductID int identity(1,1) PRIMARY KEY
  , ProductName nchar(32) NOT NULL UNIQUE
  , Color nvarchar(32)
  , Size varchar(64)
  , ModifiedDate datetime default (CURRENT_TIMESTAMP)
)
GO

CREATE TABLE dbo.ProductInventory (
    ProductID int REFERENCES Product(ProductID) PRIMARY KEY
  , QtyOnHand int
  , ReorderPoint int NOT NULL
  , UnitPrice money
  , InventoryCostValue AS QtyOnHand * UnitPrice PERSISTED
  , InventoryCVDEC AS CAST(QtyOnHand * UnitPrice AS DECIMAL(14,2))
  , ModifiedDate datetime default (CURRENT_TIMESTAMP)
)
GO
```

One-To-One Relationship between publisher & pub_info Tables

The intent of the database designer was to separate the bulk data (logo image, PR description) from the regular size columns which likely are more frequently used as well. The implementation: pub_id in pub_info table is PRIMARY KEY and FOREIGN KEY to publishers pub_id.

Tables with Computed Columns

A column can be automatically generated by a formula/expression involving other columns. The generation is "on the fly" when needed. To persist the column the PERSISTED property must be used. That is a requirement for some use such as indexing. All computed columns can be listed by a simple query.

```
SELECT object_name(object_id) as TableName, name AS ComputedColumn,
        definition AS Expression FROM sys.computed_columns ORDER BY name;
```

The demonstration introduces 2 computed columns into the ProductInventory table.

```
USE tempdb;
```

```
CREATE TABLE dbo.Product (
        ProductID int identity(1,1) PRIMARY KEY
      , ProductName nchar(32) NOT NULL UNIQUE
      , Color nvarchar(32)
      , Size varchar(64)
      , ModifiedDate datetime default (CURRENT_TIMESTAMP) );
```

```
-- Table with two computed columns
CREATE TABLE dbo.ProductInventory (
        ProductID int REFERENCES Product(ProductID) PRIMARY KEY
      , QtyOnHand int
      , ReorderPoint int NOT NULL
      , UnitPrice money
      , InventoryCostValue AS QtyOnHand * UnitPrice PERSISTED
      , InventoryCVDEC AS CAST(QtyOnHand * UnitPrice AS DECIMAL(14,0))
      , ModifiedDate datetime default (CURRENT_TIMESTAMP) );
GO
```

```
INSERT Product(ProductName, Color, Size) SELECT 'MusicMobile', 'White', '2" x 3"';
INSERT Product(ProductName, Color, Size) SELECT 'ReaderMobile', 'Black', '5" x 9"';
INSERT Product(ProductName, Color, Size) SELECT 'PhoneMobile', 'Blue', '2 1/2" x 4"';
INSERT Product(ProductName, Color, Size) SELECT 'DELTA laptop', 'Gray', '12" x 16" x 2"';
GO
```

```
SELECT * from dbo.Product;
```

ProductID	ProductName	Color	Size	ModifiedDate
1	MusicMobile	White	2" x 3"	2016-07-08 10:05:53.943
2	ReaderMobile	Black	5" x 9"	2016-07-08 10:05:53.947
3	PhoneMobile	Blue	2 1/2" x 4"	2016-07-08 10:05:53.947
4	DELTA laptop	Gray	12" x 16" x 2"	2016-07-08 10:05:53.947

CHAPTER 8: Functional Database Design

Tables with Computed Columns

-- T-SQL script continued

```
INSERT ProductInventory (ProductID, QtyOnHand, ReorderPoint, UnitPrice) SELECT 1, 105, 30, $99.99;
INSERT ProductInventory (ProductID, QtyOnHand, ReorderPoint, UnitPrice) SELECT 2, 105, 40, $299.99;
INSERT ProductInventory (ProductID, QtyOnHand, ReorderPoint, UnitPrice) SELECT 3, 208, 30, $399.99;
INSERT ProductInventory (ProductID, QtyOnHand, ReorderPoint, UnitPrice) SELECT 4, 103, 30, $599.99;
GO

SELECT * FROM ProductInventory;
GO
```

ProductID	QtyOnHand	ReorderPoint	UnitPrice	InventoryCostValue	InventoryCVDEC
1	105	30	99.99	10498.95	10499
2	105	40	299.99	31498.95	31499
3	208	30	399.99	83197.92	83198
4	103	30	599.99	61798.97	61799

Combination query with INNER JOIN and formatting.

```
SELECT      ProductName                                AS [Product Name],
            QtyOnHand                                  AS [Quantity On Hand],
            ReorderPoint                               AS [Reorder Point],
            FORMAT(UnitPrice,'c','en-US')              AS [Unit Price],
            FORMAT(InventoryCostValue, 'c','en-US')    AS [ Inventory Cost Value],
            FORMAT(InventoryCVDEC, 'c','en-US')        AS [Inventory Cost Rounded]
FROM Product P
     INNER JOIN ProductInventory PI
        ON P.ProductID = PI.ProductID
ORDER BY ProductName;
GO
```

Product Name	Quantity On Hand	Reorder Point	Unit Price	Inventory Cost Value	Inventory Cost Rounded
DELTA laptop	103	30	$599.99	$61,798.97	$61,799.00
MusicMobile	105	30	$99.99	$10,498.95	$10,499.00
PhoneMobile	208	30	$399.99	$83,197.92	$83,198.00
ReaderMobile	105	40	$299.99	$31,498.95	$31,499.00

```
-- Cleanup - FOREIGN KEY table must be dropped first
DROP TABLE tempdb.dbo.ProductInventory;
DROP TABLE tempdb.dbo.Product;
```

CHAPTER 8: Functional Database Design

Building the Data Dictionary

The best way to build the data dictionary is the same time when the database objects are created. It can also be done in the final phases of the database development project when changes are rare to the object designs.

GUI Data Dictionary Maintenance

As an example, right click on a table column name and choose Properties.

Building the Data Dictionary

Extended Properties page can be used for Data Dictionary entry

[Screenshot: Column Properties - Assets dialog showing Extended Properties page with Database: AdventureWorks2012, Collation: SQL_Latin1_General_CP1_CI_AS, and a property Name "Data Dictionary" with Value "Approximate branch assets entered manually in January."]

Check the new entry in the Data Dictionary with a query.

```
SELECT *
FROM fn_listextendedproperty (NULL, 'schema', 'Banking', 'table', 'Branch', 'Column', NULL);
GO
```

objtype	objname	name	value
COLUMN	Assets	Data Dictionary	Approximate branch assets entered manually in January.

CHAPTER 8: Functional Database Design

Data Dictionary Maintenance with T-SQL Scripts

The advantage of using T-SQL scripts for Data Dictionary maintenance is that the script can be saved as a .sql file and rerun when necessary as is or after editing. BOL Data Dictionary web page: http://msdn.microsoft.com/en-us/library/ms124438(v=sql.100).aspx .

```
USE [AdventureWorks2012];
GO
```

```
-- Delete Data Dictionary entry
EXEC sys.sp_dropextendedproperty @name=N'Data Dictionary' ,
        @level0type=N'SCHEMA',@level0name=N'Banking',
        @level1type=N'TABLE',@level1name=N'Branch',
        @level2type=N'COLUMN',@level2name=N'Assets';
GO
```

```
-- Add Data Dictionary entry
EXEC sys.sp_addextendedproperty @name=N'Data Dictionary',
        @value=N'Approximate branch assets entered manually in January each year.' ,
        @level0type=N'SCHEMA',@level0name=N'Banking', @level1type=N'TABLE',
        @level1name=N'Branch', @level2type=N'COLUMN',@level2name=N'Assets';
GO
```

```
-- Check new Data Dictionary entry
SELECT *
FROM fn_listextendedproperty (NULL, 'schema', 'Banking', 'table', 'Branch', 'Column', NULL);
```

objtype	objname	name	value
COLUMN	Assets	Data Dictionary	Approximate branch assets entered manually in January each year.

```
-- Data Dictionary entry for BranchName
EXEC sys.sp_addextendedproperty @name=N'Data Dictionary',
        @value=N'Name of the branch. Updated by supervisor only.' ,
        @level0type=N'SCHEMA',@level0name=N'Banking', @level1type=N'TABLE',
        @level1name=N'Branch', @level2type=N'COLUMN',@level2name=N'BranchName';
GO
```

CHAPTER 8: Functional Database Design

Lead Developer as Database Designer

Updating an Existing Data Dictionary Entry

```
-- Update Data Dictionary entry
EXEC sys.sp_updateextendedproperty @name=N'Data Dictionary',
@value=N'Approximate branch assets entered in January each year by an automated process.',
@level0type=N'SCHEMA',@level0name=N'Banking',
@level1type=N'TABLE',@level1name=N'Branch',
@level2type=N'COLUMN',@level2name=N'Assets'
GO

SELECT *
FROM fn_listextendedproperty (NULL, 'schema', 'Banking', 'table', 'Branch', 'Column', NULL);
GO
```

objtype	objname	name	value
COLUMN	Assets	Data Dictionary	Approximate branch assets entered in January each year by an automated process.

```
-- Data Dictionary entry for BranchCity
EXEC sys.sp_addextendedproperty @name=N'Data Dictionary',
     @value=N'City & State where branch is located.',
     @level0type=N'SCHEMA',@level0name=N'Banking', @level1type=N'TABLE',
     @level1name=N'Branch', @level2type=N'COLUMN',@level2name=N'BranchCity';
GO

-- Listing all Data Dictionary entries for table
SELECT *
FROM fn_listextendedproperty (NULL, 'schema', 'Banking', 'table', 'Branch', 'Column', NULL)
ORDER BY objname;
```

objtype	objname	name	value
COLUMN	Assets	Data Dictionary	Approximate branch assets entered in January each year by an automated process.
COLUMN	BranchCity	Data Dictionary	City & State where branch is located.
COLUMN	BranchName	Data Dictionary	Name of the branch. Updated by supervisor only.

CHAPTER 8: Functional Database Design

Lead Developer as Database Designer
A senior database developer should be able to design a modest business application database. The reason is that he worked with a number of databases so well-familiar with the concept of 3NF relational database design. Naturally if the lead developer is not familiar with the business, then it is rather difficult, there is a steep learning curve. But then it is difficult also for a professional database designer. Getting a systems analyst on board is the best approach to work with the database designer.

Database Design Team at Big Budget Projects
Large companies for important projects may setup the following design team:

> - 1-2 database designers
> - 1-3 systems analysts
> - 1-4 subject matter experts

Hiring Database Design Consultant where Resources Are Limited
Even a small company or a small project at large company should consider hiring a professional database designer on a consulting basis for a month or so to design the database. A well-designed 3NF database may reduce development from 50 man-months to 35 man-months, thus the payback may start before the project is completed. The payback continues after production deployment due to lower cost of future application software development and database maintenance. Once this author was consulting in stored procedure development at a small organization which was the fund raiser for a Connecticut seminary. Only one full-time manager/dba/developer, with consultants help. Quite shockingly, the database was excellent 3NF design. Only big-budget places can afford such a good 3NF design so goes the common wisdom. The manager explained that he hired a consultant expert database designer for a month. An excellent choice indeed.

Database System Solution Implementation Hierarchy
Frequently solutions can be implemented more than one way in a relational database system. For example, the constraint OrderQty > 0 can be implemented as CHECK constraint, stored procedure, trigger and as code in application software. There are great advantages to implement a solution at the lowest possible level of the following hierarchy.

> - Table design
> - Constraint
> - Stored procedure
> - Trigger
> - Client software

CHAPTER 8: Functional Database Design

List All Default Constraints with Definition

T-SQL metadata query to enumerate all column defaults with definition using a system view.

```sql
SELECT  SCHEMA_NAME(schema_id)                              AS SCHEMA_NAME,
        OBJECT_NAME(PARENT_OBJECT_ID)                       AS TABLE_NAME,
        COL_NAME (PARENT_OBJECT_ID, PARENT_COLUMN_ID)       AS COLUMN_NAME,
        Definition                                          AS DEFAULT_DEFINITION,
        NAME                                                AS DEFAULT_CONSTRAINT_NAME
FROM AdventureWorks2012.SYS.DEFAULT_CONSTRAINTS
ORDER BY 1, 2;  -- column numbers
-- (152 row(s) affected) - Partial results.
```

SCHEMA_NAME	TABLE_NAME	COLUMN_NAME	DEFAULT_DEFINITION	DEFAULT_CONSTRAINT_NAME
dbo	AWBuildVersion	ModifiedDate	(getdate())	DF_AWBuildVersion_ModifiedDate
dbo	ErrorLog	ErrorTime	(getdate())	DF_ErrorLog_ErrorTime
HumanResources	Department	ModifiedDate	(getdate())	DF_Department_ModifiedDate
HumanResources	Employee	SalariedFlag	((1))	DF_Employee_SalariedFlag
HumanResources	Employee	VacationHours	((0))	DF_Employee_VacationHours
HumanResources	Employee	SickLeaveHours	((0))	DF_Employee_SickLeaveHours
HumanResources	Employee	CurrentFlag	((1))	DF_Employee_CurrentFlag
HumanResources	Employee	rowguid	(newid())	DF_Employee_rowguid
HumanResources	Employee	ModifiedDate	(getdate())	DF_Employee_ModifiedDate
HumanResources	EmployeeDepartmentHistory	ModifiedDate	(getdate())	DF_EmployeeDepartmentHistory_ModifiedDate
HumanResources	EmployeePayHistory	ModifiedDate	(getdate())	DF_EmployeePayHistory_ModifiedDate
HumanResources	JobCandidate	ModifiedDate	(getdate())	DF_JobCandidate_ModifiedDate
HumanResources	Shift	ModifiedDate	(getdate())	DF_Shift_ModifiedDate
Person	Address	rowguid	(newid())	DF_Address_rowguid
Person	Address	ModifiedDate	(getdate())	DF_Address_ModifiedDate
Person	AddressType	rowguid	(newid())	DF_AddressType_rowguid
Person	AddressType	ModifiedDate	(getdate())	DF_AddressType_ModifiedDate
Person	BusinessEntity	rowguid	(newid())	DF_BusinessEntity_rowguid
Person	BusinessEntity	ModifiedDate	(getdate())	DF_BusinessEntity_ModifiedDate

The sp_helpconstraints system procedure to list all constraints (including default) on a table.

```
EXEC sp_helpconstraint 'Sales.SalesOrderHeader';
```

Object Name: Sales.SalesOrderHeader

#	constraint_type	constraint_name	delete_action	update_action	status_enable
1	CHECK Table Level	CK_SalesOrderHeader_DueDate	(n/a)	(n/a)	Enabled
2	CHECK on column Freight	CK_SalesOrderHeader_Freight	(n/a)	(n/a)	Enabled
3	CHECK Table Level	CK_SalesOrderHeader_ShipDate	(n/a)	(n/a)	Enabled

Table is referenced by foreign key
1 AdventureWorks2012.Sales.SalesOrderDetail: FK_Sales...

Query executed s... | HPESTAR (11.0 RTM) | HPESTAR\Owner (58) | AdventureWorks2012 | 00:00:00 | 35 rows

CHAPTER 8: Functional Database Design

Partitioning Query via Pure SQL - Ye Olde Way

Add new sequence numbering column for subsets(partition by OrderID) with standard SQL only. Note that the old way is not very efficient, the ROW_NUMBER() OVER PARTITION is better performing.

```
USE Northwind;
SELECT  OD.OrderID,
        SeqNo                                                   AS LineItem,
        OD.ProductID,
        UnitPrice,
        Quantity                                                AS Qty,
        CONVERT(NUMERIC(3, 2), Discount)                        AS Discount,
        CONVERT(NUMERIC(12, 2), UnitPrice * Quantity * ( 1.0 - Discount ))  AS LineTotal
FROM    [Order Details] OD
    INNER JOIN (SELECT count(*) SeqNo,   a.OrderID,   a.ProductID
          FROM   [Order Details] A
             INNER JOIN [Order Details] B
                ON A.ProductID >= B.ProductID   AND A.OrderID = B.OrderID
          GROUP  BY A.OrderID,
                 A.ProductID) a
         ON OD.OrderID = a.OrderID
            AND OD.ProductID = a.ProductID
WHERE  OD.OrderID < 10300
ORDER  BY OD.OrderID, OD.ProductID, SeqNo;
-- (140 row(s) affected) - Partial results.
```

OrderID	LineItem	ProductID	UnitPrice	Qty	Discount	LineTotal
10255	1	2	15.20	20	0.00	304.00
10255	2	16	13.90	35	0.00	486.50
10255	3	36	15.20	25	0.00	380.00
10255	4	59	44.00	30	0.00	1320.00
10256	1	53	26.20	15	0.00	393.00
10256	2	77	10.40	12	0.00	124.80
10257	1	27	35.10	25	0.00	877.50
10257	2	39	14.40	6	0.00	86.40
10257	3	77	10.40	15	0.00	156.00
10258	1	2	15.20	50	0.20	608.00
10258	2	5	17.00	65	0.20	884.00
10258	3	32	25.60	6	0.20	122.88
10259	1	21	8.00	10	0.00	80.00
10259	2	37	20.80	1	0.00	20.80
10260	1	41	7.70	16	0.25	92.40
10260	2	57	15.60	50	0.00	780.00
10260	3	62	39.40	15	0.25	443.25

CHAPTER 8: Functional Database Design

CHAPTER 9: Advanced Database Design Concepts

How to Read varbinary(max) Columns

Usually the binary objects such as images or Word documents in varbinary(max) columns have to be exported to the file system and the appropriate software is used to "read" them. Clean plain text is readable after conversion to varchar(max) or nvarchar(max).

```
SELECT  Title AS DocTitle, LEN(Document) AS Length,
        CONVERT(varchar(max), substring(Document,1806, 60)) AS DocumentSegment
FROM Production.Document WHERE DocumentNode = 0x6B40;
```

DocTitle	Length	DocumentSegment
Lubrication Maintenance	22528	NG: Do not over lubricate parts. If oil gets on the wheel ri

FileTable - Integrating Folders with Database

Storing large number of binary files such as images was a challenge until SQL Server 2012: FileTable integrates files in a folder into the database, yet keep them accessible at Windows file system level. In the past, there were two solutions:

- ➢ Keep only the filenames in the database table.
- ➢ Keep both the filenames and binary file objects (varbinary(max)) in the table.

Using the first method, the files were not backed up with the database since they were not part of the database. Applying the second method, the binary objects were in the database, but as a deadweight, since not much can be done with them. FileTable is the best of both worlds: files are backed up / restored with the database, yet they remain visible at the file system level. So if a new file is dropped (copied) into the folder, it becomes visible to SQL Server instantaneously. FileTable requires the FILESTREAM feature as shown on the Server Properties dialog box.

The CREATE TABLE statement for a FileTable

```
-- Create FileTable  -- new to SQL Server 2012
CREATE TABLE ImageStore
AS FileTable
   WITH (
```

```
        FileTable_Directory = 'ImageStore',
        FileTable_Collate_Filename = database_default
     );
GO
-- (1 row(s) affected)
```

We can determine the FileTable folder name which is visible at the file system level the following way.

```
SELECT DBName=DB_NAME ( database_id ), directory_name
   FROM sys.database_filestream_options
       WHERE directory_name is not null;
GO
```

DBName	directory_name
AdventureWorks2012	FSDIR

FileTable directory(path):

\\YOURSERVER\MSSQLSERVER\FSDIR\ImageStore

FileTable - Integrating Folders with Database   267

The dialog box for database options setup as related to FILESTREAM
"hpestar" is the name of the SQL Server instance (default instance, same name as the computer).

CHAPTER 9: Advanced Database Design Concepts

FileTable - Integrating Folders with Database

The FileTable folder is currently empty.

We shall now copy 3 photos in the ImageStore folder using Windows Copy & Paste operation.

CHAPTER 9: Advanced Database Design Concepts

FileTable - Integrating Folders with Database

The photos are "visible" from the database side as well.

[Screenshot of SQL Server Management Studio showing query `SELECT * FROM ImageStore` with 3 result rows containing stream_id, file_stream, name (IMG_1134.JPG, IMG_1139.JPG, IMG_1149.JPG), and path_locator columns.]

The INSERT, UPDATE and DELETE commands are operational on FileTable, however, a new column cannot be added as demonstrated in the following script:

```
SELECT * FROM ImageStore;
GO
UPDATE ImageStore SET name='RollerCoaster.jpg'
WHERE stream_id='E73EA731-AAAA-E111-9078-D8D3857FC43E';
GO
SELECT * FROM ImageStore;
```

CHAPTER 9: Advanced Database Design Concepts

Adding Files to FileTable Using T-SQL
There are two T-SQL methods available.

```
-- Adding files from T-SQL - method 1 xp_cmdshell copy
EXEC xp_cmdshell 'copy "C:\photo\000Test\xBermuda.jpg"
"\\HPESTAR\mssqlserver\FSDIR\ImageStore\xBermuda.jpg"'
GO
```

```
-- Adding files from T-SQL - method 2 OPENROWSET
INSERT INTO [dbo].[ImageStore] ([name],[file_stream])
SELECT 'Bermuda9.jpg', * FROM
    OPENROWSET(BULK N'C:\photo\2012\BERMUDA\BERMUDA\IMG_1154.jpg', SINGLE_BLOB)
        AS FileUpload
```

Deleting Files from FileTable Using T-SQL

```
SELECT * FROM ImageStore
GO
```

```
DELETE ImageStore
WHERE stream_id = '62F55342-ABAA-E111-9078-D8D3857FC43E'
GO
```

```
SELECT * FROM ImageStore
GO
```

```
-- Column(s) cannot be added to a FileTable
ALTER TABLE ImageStore
ADD AddDate smalldatetime NULL
CONSTRAINT AddDateDflt
DEFAULT CURRENT_TIMESTAMP WITH VALUES ;
GO
/* Msg 33422, Level 16, State 1, Line 2
The column 'AddDate' cannot be added to table 'ImageStore' as it is a FileTable.
Adding columns to the fixed schema of a FileTable object is not permitted.
*/
```

```
DROP TABLE ImageStore
GO
```

Data Compression: Compressed Table

The table compression option has been introduced with SQL Server 2008. Data is compressed inside a database table, and it reduces the size of the table. Performance benefit in addition to space saving: "reads" reduction; queries need to read fewer pages from the disk. Sufficient CPU resources are required for the SQL Server instance to compress and decompress table data, when data is read (SELECT) or written (INSERT, UPDATE, MERGE). Analysis is required to ensure that table compression has no adverse effect on business critical query performance. Data compression may not be available in all editions of SQL Server. In the demonstration, first we create a new table for testing.

```sql
SELECT * INTO SOD FROM AdventureWorks2012.Sales.SalesOrderDetail;
GO

CREATE CLUSTERED INDEX idxPKSOD on SOD(SalesOrderID, SalesOrderDetailID);
GO

EXEC sp_spaceused 'dbo.SOD'
GO
```

name	rows	reserved	data	index_size	unused
SOD	121317	12464 KB	12064 KB	80 KB	320 KB

CHAPTER 9: Advanced Database Design Concepts

Switching to PAGE-LEVEL Compression

```
/*************** TABLE PAGE-LEVEL COMPRESSION ***************
ALTER TABLE SOD
REBUILD WITH (DATA_COMPRESSION = PAGE);
GO

EXEC sp_spaceused SOD
GO
```

name	rows	reserved	data	index_size	unused
SOD	121317	5552 KB	5192 KB	80 KB	280 KB

Data storage size decreased from around 12 MB to around 5 MB.

Data Compression: Compressed Table

Testing ROW-LEVEL Compression

```
/***************** TABLE DATA ROW-LEVEL COMPRESSION *****************
ALTER TABLE SOD
REBUILD WITH (DATA_COMPRESSION = ROW);
GO

EXEC sp_spaceused SOD
GO
```

name	rows	reserved	data	index_size	unused
SOD	121317	7920 KB	7528 KB	80 KB	312 KB

We can see the space reduction from 12MB to around 7.5MB.

CHAPTER 9: Advanced Database Design Concepts

Space reduction can be estimated with a system stored procedure.

```
/************* TABLE COMPRESSION SPACE REDUCTION ESTIMATE *************/

exec sp_estimate_data_compression_savings
    'Sales', 'SalesOrderDetail', null, null, 'PAGE'

exec sp_estimate_data_compression_savings
    'Sales', 'SalesOrderDetail', null, null, 'ROW'
```

_id	partition_number	size_with_current_compression_setting(KB)	size_with_requested_compression
1	1	11600	5616
2	1	4256	4576
3	1	2552	1688

_id	partition_number	size_with_current_compression_setting(KB)	size_with_requested_compression
1	1	11600	8152
2	1	4256	4576
3	1	2552	1928

Careful and extensive considerations are required to decide to apply row, page or no compression to a table.

Data Compression: Compressed Table

Query To Check How Many Rows Are Stored In An 8K Page In The Original Non-Compressed Table

```sql
-- Table rows stored in each page (8K size)
SELECT    PARSENAME(t1.[PageName],2) AS PageNumber,
          PARSENAME(t1.[PageName],3) AS FileNumber,
          RecordCount = COUNT(*)
FROM      AdventureWorks2012.Sales.SalesOrderDetail t
          CROSS APPLY (SELECT
          REPLACE(REPLACE(REPLACE(sys.fn_PhysLocFormatter(%% Physloc %%),
              ':', '.'),'(',''),')','') AS PageName) t1
GROUP BY  PARSENAME(t1.[PageName],2),
          PARSENAME(t1.[PageName],3)
ORDER BY  RecordCount DESC
```

	PageNumber	FileNumber	RecordCount
1	26554	1	102
2	26655	1	102
3	26816	1	102
4	26256	1	102
5	26466	1	102
6	26362	1	102
7	26658	1	102

Query to check the same for the compressed table SOD

```sql
-- Table rows stored in each page (8K size)
SELECT   PARSENAME(t1.[PageName],2) AS PageNumber,
         PARSENAME(t1.[PageName],3) AS FileNumber,
         RecordCount = COUNT(*)
FROM     AdventureWorks2012.dbo.SOD t
         CROSS APPLY (SELECT
         REPLACE(REPLACE(REPLACE(sys.fn_PhysLocFormatter(%% Physloc %%),
             ':', '.'),'(',''),')','') AS PageName) t1
GROUP BY PARSENAME(t1.[PageName],2),
         PARSENAME(t1.[PageName],3)
ORDER BY RecordCount DESC
```

	PageNumber	FileNumber	RecordCount
1	13463	1	149
2	13467	1	149
3	13465	1	149
4	13469	1	149
5	13466	1	149
6	13471	1	149
7	13462	1	149

We can see that the best record (rows) count is 149 per page as opposed to 102 when the rows are not compressed. Since compression and decompression are processing intensive, we are trading CPU load vs. disk load. Which one to choose? PAGE compression is the true compression with maximum space saving. Choose PAGE compression for best disk IO reduction. As mentioned earlier careful preparation is required to make sure there are no undesirable side effects.

CHAPTER 9: Advanced Database Design Concepts

Data Compression: Compressed Index

Index can also be compressed. The following script creates and compresses an index with included columns.

```sql
/*************** INDEX COMPRESSION ******************/
SELECT TOP (1) * FROM SOD
GO

CREATE INDEX idxTEST on SOD(rowguid)
INCLUDE (CarrierTrackingNumber, LineTotal, UnitPrice)
GO

EXEC sp_spaceused 'SOD'

ALTER INDEX idxTEST on SOD
REBUILD WITH ( DATA_COMPRESSION = PAGE )

EXEC sp_spaceused 'SOD'
GO

DROP INDEX SOD.idxTEST
GO
```

	CarrierTrackingNumber	O...	Pro...	Sp...	UnitPrice	U...	LineTotal	rowguid
1	4911-403C-98	1	776	1	2024.994	0...	2024.994000	B207C96D-D9E6-402

	name	rows	reserved	data	index_size	unused
1	SOD	121317	16792 KB	7528 KB	8656 KB	608 KB

	name	rows	reserved	data	index_size	unused
1	SOD	121317	14240 KB	7528 KB	6096 KB	616 KB

We can observe the index size reduction. Note that index_size includes all indexes.

The GUI Data Compression Wizard

The wizard can be started with Right Click on the table in SSMS Object Explorer.

The GUI Data Compression Wizard

Space Saving Calculation Wizard Page
The figures include table & indexes total size.

Output Panel Offers Scripting And Execution Options

CHAPTER 9: Advanced Database Design Concepts

Testing the generated script with the sp_spaceused system stored procedure

```
USE [AdventureWorks2012];
EXEC sp_spaceused SOD;
GO
ALTER TABLE [dbo].[SOD] REBUILD PARTITION = ALL
WITH
(DATA_COMPRESSION = PAGE
)
GO
EXEC sp_spaceused SOD;
```

	name	rows	reserved	data	index_size	unused
1	SOD	121317	12040 KB	11968 KB	8 KB	64 KB

	name	rows	reserved	data	index_size	unused
1	SOD	121317	5448 KB	5232 KB	8 KB	208 KB

Indexes Can Be Compressed With The Wizard As Well

Partitioned Table, Partition Function & Partition Scheme

The generated script follows with measurement before and after index compression

```
EXEC sp_spaceused SOD

ALTER INDEX [idxTEST] ON [dbo].[SOD]
REBUILD PARTITION = ALL
WITH (PAD_INDEX = OFF, STATISTICS_NORECOMPUTE = OFF,
SORT_IN_TEMPDB = OFF, ONLINE = OFF,
ALLOW_ROW_LOCKS = ON, ALLOW_PAGE_LOCKS = ON,
DATA_COMPRESSION = PAGE)

EXEC sp_spaceused SOD
```

	name	rows	reserved	data	index_size	unused
1	SOD	121317	14360 KB	5192 KB	8656 KB	512 KB

	name	rows	reserved	data	index_size	unused
1	SOD	121317	11872 KB	5192 KB	6088 KB	592 KB

We can observe that the index size has been reduced from 8656KB to 6088 KB.

Articles
Data Compression: Strategy, Capacity Planning and Best Practices http://msdn.microsoft.com/en-us/library/dd894051(v=sql.100).aspx
Data Compression http://msdn.microsoft.com/en-us/library/cc280449.aspx

CHAPTER 9: Advanced Database Design Concepts

Partitioned Table, Partition Function & Partition Scheme

When data is stored from New York, Chicago, Houston, London and Hong Kong operations in a table, it makes you wonder if the server trips over NYC data when looking for London information. Analogous, 95% of the time in a typical business the last 30 days data may be accessed in a table, yet the dominant storage is for the 5% access of the 5 years prior data. The solution is logical: partition the data according to a usage-based scheme. Partitioning can improve performance, the scalability and manageability of large tables and tables that have varying query access patterns. **Gains with partitioning is not automatic.** Careful design studies are necessary for a successful table partitioning implementation.

In order to carry out a demonstration, first we create a copy of AdventureWorks2012 database from a backup file.

```
/* RESTORE script to create a new copy of AdventureWorks2012
 * Folder  FS1 should exist; FSBeta should not exist; AW12 should exist
 * Folder Backup should exist */
USE [master]
GO
```

```
BACKUP DATABASE [AdventureWorks2012] TO
DISK = N'C:\Data\Backup\AW12.bak'
GO
```

```
RESTORE DATABASE [CopyOfAdventureWorks2012]
FROM  DISK = N'C:\Data\Backup\AW12.bak'
WITH  FILE = 1,  MOVE N'FSAlpha' TO N'F:\data\FS1\FSBeta',
MOVE N'AdventureWorks2012_Data' TO N'F:\AW12\xAdventureWorks2012_Data.mdf',
MOVE N'AdventureWorks2012_Log' TO N'F:\AW12\xAdventureWorks2012_log.ldf',
NOUNLOAD,  STATS = 5
GO
```

We will partition a table with SalesOrderDetail subset information. First a partition function is created.

```
USE CopyOfAdventureWorks2012;
GO

CREATE PARTITION FUNCTION pfSOD (int)
AS RANGE LEFT FOR VALUES (1, 20000, 40000, 60000, 80000, 150000) ;
GO
```

CHAPTER 9: Advanced Database Design Concepts

Partitioned Table, Partition Function & Partition Scheme

The next step is to test the partition function to make sure it works as intended.

```
SELECT $PARTITION.pfSOD (60000) ;   -- 4
SELECT $PARTITION.pfSOD (-10) ;     -- 1
SELECT $PARTITION.pfSOD (0) ;       -- 1
SELECT $PARTITION.pfSOD (1) ;       -- 1
SELECT $PARTITION.pfSOD (2) ;       -- 2
SELECT $PARTITION.pfSOD (80000) ;   -- 5
SELECT $PARTITION.pfSOD (80001) ;   -- 6
SELECT $PARTITION.pfSOD (150000) ;  -- 6
SELECT $PARTITION.pfSOD (150001) ;  -- 7
SELECT $PARTITION.pfSOD (200000) ;  -- 7
GO
```

Results:

(No column name)
4

(No column name)
1

(No column name)
1

(No column name)
1

CHAPTER 9: Advanced Database Design Concepts

T-SQL scripts to create FILEGROUPs for the partitions

```sql
USE [master]
GO
```

```sql
ALTER DATABASE [CopyOfAdventureWorks2012] ADD FILEGROUP [Test1FileGroup]
ALTER DATABASE [CopyOfAdventureWorks2012] ADD FILEGROUP [Test2FileGroup]
ALTER DATABASE [CopyOfAdventureWorks2012] ADD FILEGROUP [Test3FileGroup]
ALTER DATABASE [CopyOfAdventureWorks2012] ADD FILEGROUP [Test4FileGroup]
ALTER DATABASE [CopyOfAdventureWorks2012] ADD FILEGROUP [Test5FileGroup]
ALTER DATABASE [CopyOfAdventureWorks2012] ADD FILEGROUP [Test6FileGroup]
ALTER DATABASE [CopyOfAdventureWorks2012] ADD FILEGROUP [Test7FileGroup]
GO
```

```sql
ALTER DATABASE [CopyOfAdventureWorks2012]
ADD FILE ( NAME = N'Test1', FILENAME = N'F:\UTIL\Microsoft\sampledatabases\Test1.ndf' ,
SIZE = 3072KB , FILEGROWTH = 1024KB ) TO FILEGROUP [Test1FileGroup]
ALTER DATABASE [CopyOfAdventureWorks2012]
ADD FILE ( NAME = N'Test2', FILENAME = N'F:\UTIL\Microsoft\sampledatabases\Test2.ndf' ,
SIZE = 3072KB , FILEGROWTH = 1024KB ) TO FILEGROUP [Test2FileGroup]
ALTER DATABASE [CopyOfAdventureWorks2012]
ADD FILE ( NAME = N'Test3', FILENAME = N'F:\UTIL\Microsoft\sampledatabases\Test3.ndf' ,
SIZE = 3072KB , FILEGROWTH = 1024KB ) TO FILEGROUP [Test3FileGroup]
ALTER DATABASE [CopyOfAdventureWorks2012]
ADD FILE ( NAME = N'Test4', FILENAME = N'F:\UTIL\Microsoft\sampledatabases\Test4.ndf' ,
SIZE = 3072KB , FILEGROWTH = 1024KB ) TO FILEGROUP [Test4FileGroup]
ALTER DATABASE [CopyOfAdventureWorks2012]
ADD FILE ( NAME = N'Test5', FILENAME = N'F:\UTIL\Microsoft\sampledatabases\Test5.ndf' ,
SIZE = 3072KB , FILEGROWTH = 1024KB ) TO FILEGROUP [Test5FileGroup]
ALTER DATABASE [CopyOfAdventureWorks2012]
ADD FILE ( NAME = N'Test6', FILENAME = N'F:\UTIL\Microsoft\sampledatabases\Test6.ndf' ,
SIZE = 3072KB , FILEGROWTH = 1024KB ) TO FILEGROUP [Test6FileGroup]
ALTER DATABASE [CopyOfAdventureWorks2012]
ADD FILE ( NAME = N'Test7', FILENAME = N'F:\UTIL\Microsoft\sampledatabases\Test7.ndf' ,
SIZE = 3072KB , FILEGROWTH = 1024KB ) TO FILEGROUP [Test7FileGroup]
GO
```

Partitioned Table, Partition Function & Partition Scheme

T-SQL scripts to create a partition scheme, a partitioned table and populate the new table with INSERT SELECT

```sql
USE CopyOfAdventureWorks2012;
GO

CREATE PARTITION SCHEME psSOD
AS PARTITION pfSOD
TO (Test1FileGroup, Test2FileGroup, Test3FileGroup, Test4FileGroup,
Test5FileGroup, Test6FileGroup, Test7FileGroup) ;
GO

CREATE TABLE SODPartitioned   (col1 int, col2 char(30))  ON psSOD (col1) ;
GO

insert SODPartitioned
select    SalesOrderDetailID, 'Unit Price: '+convert(varchar,UnitPrice)
from AdventureWorks2012.Sales.SalesOrderDetail;
GO

insert SODPartitioned
select SalesOrderDetailID+1, 'Unit Price: '+convert(varchar,UnitPrice+1)
from AdventureWorks2012.Sales.SalesOrderDetail;
GO

insert SODPartitioned select SalesOrderDetailID+2, 'Unit Price: '+convert(varchar,UnitPrice+2)
from AdventureWorks2012.Sales.SalesOrderDetail;
```

CHAPTER 9: Advanced Database Design Concepts

Query To Check The Data Distribution Within The Partitions

```sql
-- Count of rows in each partition
SELECT $PARTITION.pfSOD(col1) AS Partition,
COUNT(*) AS [COUNT]
FROM SODPartitioned
GROUP BY $PARTITION.pfSOD(col1)
ORDER BY Partition ;
GO
```

	Partition	COUNT
1	1	1
2	2	59996
3	3	60000
4	4	60000
5	5	60000
6	6	123954

Partitioned Table, Partition Function & Partition Scheme

A few more counting queries to check entire table and a single partition population

```sql
-- Total rows
SELECT TotalCount=count(*) from SODPartitioned
go
-- 363951
-- Entire table content
SELECT * from SODPartitioned
go

-- Count of rows in partition 4
SELECT COUNT(*) AS [COUNT]
FROM SODPartitioned
WHERE $PARTITION.pfSOD(col1) = 4
GO
```

Results:

	TotalCount
1	363951

	col1	col2
1	1	Unit Price: 2024.99
2	2	Unit Price: 2024.99
3	3	Unit Price: 2024.99

	COUNT
1	60000

CHAPTER 9: Advanced Database Design Concepts

System views with "partition" prefix contain metadata on partitions.

```sql
-- Partition related system views - metadata
SELECT '[dbo].[SODPartitioned]' AS TableName,
       ps.Name                  AS PartitionScheme,
       pf.name                  AS PartitionFunction
FROM   sys.indexes i
       INNER JOIN sys.partition_schemes ps
         ON ps.data_space_id = i.data_space_id
       INNER JOIN sys.partition_functions pf
         ON pf.function_id = ps.function_id
WHERE  i.object_id = object_id('[dbo].[SODPartitioned]')
```

	TableName	PartitionScheme	PartitionFunction
1	[dbo].[SODPartitioned]	psSOD	pfSOD

Partitioned Table, Partition Function & Partition Scheme

In the following example, we partition for "UK", "US" and other countries.

```sql
CREATE PARTITION FUNCTION pfCountry (char(256)) AS
RANGE left FOR VALUES ('UJ','UK', 'UL', 'UR','US','UT');
GO
CREATE PARTITION SCHEME psCountry AS
PARTITION pfCountry ALL TO ([primary]);
GO
CREATE TABLE Members (
    ID int identity(1, 1),
    Name varchar(200),
    Country char(256)
) on psCountry(Country)
GO
INSERT INTO Members (Name, Country)
SELECT CompanyName, Country
FROM Northwind.dbo.Customers
GO
SELECT * , PartitionNo=$Partition.pfCountry(Country)
FROM Members ORDER BY PartitionNo
```

	ID	Name	Country	PartitionNo
86	82	Trail's Head Gourmet Provisioners	USA	6
87	89	White Clover Markets	USA	6
88	33	GROSELLA-Restaurante	Venezuela	7
89	35	HILARION-Abastos	Venezuela	7

CHAPTER 9: Advanced Database Design Concepts

The GUI Create Partition Wizard

SSMS Object Explorer Create Partition Wizard provides GUI environment for partition design and setup.

Columnstore Index for Data Warehouse Performance

Columnstore index for static tables, new to SQL Server 2012, is designed for Data Warehouse performance enhancement. The first script is a timing script for a GROUP BY summary query, and the second script is the creation of the columnstore index.

```sql
-- Timing before creating Columnstore index (5th timing)
USE AdventureWorksDW2012;
dbcc dropcleanbuffers;
declare @start datetime = getdate()
SELECT SalesTerritoryKey, SUM(ExtendedAmount) AS SalesByTerritory
FROM FactResellerSales    GROUP BY SalesTerritoryKey;
select [Timing]=datediff(millisecond, @Start, getdate());
GO 5
-- 190 msec

CREATE NONCLUSTERED COLUMNSTORE INDEX [idxColStoreResellerSales]
ON [FactResellerSales]
(
  [ProductKey],
  [OrderDateKey],
  [ShipDateKey],
  [EmployeeKey],
  [PromotionKey],
  [CurrencyKey],
  [SalesTerritoryKey],
  [SalesOrderNumber],
  [SalesOrderLineNumber],
  [OrderQuantity],
  [UnitPrice],
  [ExtendedAmount],
  [UnitPriceDiscountPct],
  [DiscountAmount],
  [ProductStandardCost],
  [TotalProductCost],
  [SalesAmount],
  [TaxAmt],
  [Freight],
  [CarrierTrackingNumber],
  [CustomerPONumber],
  [OrderDate],
  [DueDate],
  [ShipDate]
);
```

CHAPTER 9: Advanced Database Design Concepts

Checking the same query after creating the index.

```sql
-- Timing after creating Columnstore index (5th timing)
dbcc dropcleanbuffers
declare @start datetime = getdate()
SELECT SalesTerritoryKey, SUM(ExtendedAmount) AS SalesByTerritory
FROM FactResellerSales
GROUP BY SalesTerritoryKey;
select [Timing]=datediff(millisecond, @Start, getdate())
GO 5
```

	Timing
1	16

	SalesTerritoryKey	SalesByTerritory
1	9	1622869.4219
2	3	7932851.6095
3	6	14463280.151
4	7	4647454.2071
5	1	12523062.9392
6	10	4311126.886
7	4	18598026.9798
8	5	7908318.2562

	Timing
1	16

The performance gain on this particular query: from 190 msec to 16 msec. Generally columnstore index leads to significant query performance improvement in Data Warehouse environment.

DATE Data Type Solves Many Problems with DATETIME

DATE columns should be DATE type (3 bytes) not DATETIME type (8 bytes) with exception when time is needed for the record such as credit card or online banking transaction.

Example: Sales.Customer table create with one computed column which has unique index defined on AccountNumber(computed).

```
CREATE TABLE Sales.Customer(
    CustomerID int IDENTITY(1,1) PRIMARY KEY,
    PersonID int            REFERENCES Person.Person,
    StoreID int             REFERENCES Sales.Store,
    TerritoryID int         REFERENCES Sales.SalesTerritory,
    AccountNumber  AS (isnull('AW'+dbo.ufnLeadingZeros(CustomerID),'')) ,
    RowGuid uniqueidentifier ROWGUIDCOL  NOT NULL default (newid()),
    ModifiedDate DATE  NOT NULL default (CURRENT_TIMESTAMP));

SELECT TOP 2 * FROM Sales.Customer  ORDER BY AccountNumber;
```

CustomerID	PersonID	StoreID	TerritoryID	AccountNumber	rowguid	ModifiedDate
1	NULL	934	1	AW00000001	3F5AE95E-B87D-4AED-95B4-C3797AFCB74F	2008-10-13
2	NULL	1028	1	AW00000002	E552F657-A9AF-4A7D-A645-C429D6E02491	2008-10-13

Pad with Leading Zeros

Padding with leading zeros is a frequent business requirement. The ufnLeadingZeros() scalar-valued user-defined function converts the number into a string and pads it with leading zeros. The new **FORMAT command** can be utilized as well for leading zeros.

```
SELECT [dbo].[ufnLeadingZeros] (999);   -- 00000999

-- T-SQL script to pad with leading zeros
USE AdventureWorks2012;  DECLARE @Len tinyint=8;
SELECT   BusinessEntityID AS EmployeeID,   Rate,
         RIGHT(REPLICATE('0',@Len) + CAST(Rate AS VARCHAR(20)),@Len) AS PaddedRate
FROM   HumanResources.EmployeePayHistory;
```

EmployeeID	Rate	PaddedRate
1	125.50	00125.50
2	63.4615	00063.46
3	43.2692	00043.27

```
SELECT TOP(1) FORMAT(ProductID, '00000') FROM Production.Product;  -- 00980
SELECT FORMAT(999, '00000'); -- 00999
```

CHAPTER 9: Advanced Database Design Concepts

Database Design & Programming Standards

Standards have multiple purposes:

> ➢ Increase the productivity of the database developer.
> ➢ Increase the productivity of the project team.
> ➢ Decrease future maintenance cost of the RDBMS system.

Standards are about communications among project team members and among future software engineers who will come in contact with the work done presently by the software project team. Software standards are simple ordinary rules which should be followed. It is like when you turn on the left-turn signal in your car, the driver behind you anticipates you slowing down and making the next left turn. The situation is a little bit different though with software standards: there is no enforcing authority like the state authority in case of traffic rules. Many times argument can break out within the project team: "I like it this way", "it is really stupid to do it that way", "database expert Q says to do it this way in a blog" and so on. The following standards are pretty reasonable, and are based on industry acceptance, albeit not universal acceptance. The project manager has to enlist the support of all of the project team members for successful standards implementation. Database Design & Programming Standards to aid in optimal usability of SQL Server schema, scripts and stored procedures, user defined functions developed for applications by defining a reasonable, consistent and effective coding style. The identifier segment of the standard will formalize naming conventions. Without standards, database design, function, stored procedure and script development may become sloppy and unreadable, resulting in diminished productivity, usability, reusability, maintainability and extendibility.

Database Design Standards

Base design is normalized to 3NF or higher. History, log, Data Warehouse and reporting tables, containing second-hand data, need not be normalized. Similar considerations for staging and lookup tables. Each OLTP table has the following layout:

```
TableNameID (PRIMARY KEY) - commonly int identity(1,1) SURROGATE PRIMARY KEY
TableNameAlphaID (FOREIGN KEY if any)
TableNameBetaID (FOREIGN KEY if any)
natural-key column(s)
non-key columns
row maintenance columns
  RowGuid          uniqueidentifier
  IsActive         maintenance flag (bit 0 = not active, 1 = active)
  CreateDate       maintenance date (datetime if necessary)
  ModifiedDate     maintenance date (datetime if necessary)
  ModifiedByUser   last user who modified the record
```

CHAPTER 9: Advanced Database Design Concepts

Database Design & Programming Standards

Identifiers

CamelCase (Pascal case) naming convention: OrderDetail, ShippingCompany

With prefix example: vInvoiceHistory (view - Hungarian naming after Charles Simonyi)

Old-style naming example: sales_order_detail

Space usage is not a good idea in identifier: confusing & forces square brackets or double quotation marks use (delimited identifier).

Using spaces example: [sales order detail]

PREFIX ASSIGNMENT

Primary Key Clustered	pk
Primary Key Nonclustered	pknc
Index Clustered	idxc
Index Nonclustered	idxnc
Foreign Key	fk
Unique Constraint	uq
Check Constraint	chk
Column Default	dflt
Synonym	syn

Passed Parameter @p (input/output parameter) or @ - Example: @pStartDate, @StartDate

Local Variable @ - Example: @WeekOfTransaction

Table   usually no prefix; exception large number of tables

Reporting table	rpt
Log table	log
History table	hist or arch
Date Warehouse table	dw, dim, fact
Common Table Expression	cte
View	v or view
User Defined Scalar Function	udf or fns or ufn or fn
User Defined Table Function	udf or fnt or ufn or fn
Stored Procedure	usp, sproc, or none

CHAPTER 9: Advanced Database Design Concepts

Principles of T-SQL Identifier Architecture

Each word in the naming must be functional. The first word must be the highest level category or action indicator. Examples for stored procedure names:

    uspAccountPayableSummary
    uspInsertAccountPayableTransaction
    uspUpdateStockPrice
    sprocInsertInventoryItem
    sprocAccountReceivableSummary
    AccountReceivableMonthly

Commonly accepted or easily understood abbreviations are allowed. Examples for business abbreviations usage in view naming:

    vAPSummary
    vAPDetail
    vARSummary
    vARMonthly
    vGLTrialBalance

AdventureWorks2012 long stored procedure and view names.

```
SELECT name, type FROM sys.objects WHERE LEN(name) > 20 AND type in ('V', 'P') ORDER BY name;
```

name	type
uspGetBillOfMaterials	P
uspGetEmployeeManagers	P
uspGetManagerEmployees	P
uspGetWhereUsedProductID	P
uspSearchCandidateResumes	P
uspUpdateEmployeeHireInfo	P
uspUpdateEmployeeLogin	P
uspUpdateEmployeePersonalInfo	P
vAdditionalContactInfo	V
vEmployeeDepartmentHistory	V
vJobCandidateEducation	V
vJobCandidateEmployment	V
vProductAndDescription	V
vProductModelCatalogDescription	V
vProductModelInstructions	V
vSalesPersonSalesByFiscalYears	V
vStateProvinceCountryRegion	V
vStoreWithDemographics	V

CHAPTER 9: Advanced Database Design Concepts

Database Design & Programming Standards

Stored Procedure Outline

```
use {DatabaseName};
if (objectProperty(object_id('{schema}.{ProcedureName}'),
'IsProcedure') is not null)
    drop procedure {schema}.{ProcedureName}
go

create procedure {schema}.{ProcedureName}
  [{parameter} {data type}]....
as
/*******************************************************************
* PROCEDURE: {ProcedureName}
* PURPOSE: {brief procedure description}
* NOTES: {special set up or requirements, etc.}
* CREATED:  {developer name} {date}
* LAST MODIFIED: {developer name} {date}

* DATE          AUTHOR              DESCRIPTION
------------------------------------------------------------------
* {date}       {developer} {brief modification description}
********************************************************************/
BEGIN
[declare {variable name} {data type}....
[{set session}] e.g. SET NOCOUNT ON
[{initialize variables}]

{body of procedure - comment only what is not obvious}

return (Value if any)

{error handler}
return (Value if any)
END
 go
```

User-Defined Function Outline

Similar to stored procedure outline

CHAPTER 9: Advanced Database Design Concepts

How to Create a Database with T-SQL Script

Database can be created by a script (CREATE DATABASE) or in SSMS Object Explorer using GUI. Here is a T-SQL script version.

```
-- SQL CREATE DATABASE
USE master;
GO
```

```
-- F:\DB\DATA\ folder should exist

CREATE DATABASE [Finance]
ON  PRIMARY
( NAME = N'Finance_Data',
FILENAME = N'F:\DB\DATA\Finance.mdf' , SIZE = 217152KB ,
MAXSIZE = UNLIMITED, FILEGROWTH = 16384KB )
LOG ON
( NAME = N'Finance_Log',
FILENAME = N'F:\DB\DATA\Finance_1.ldf' ,
SIZE = 67584KB , MAXSIZE = 2048GB , FILEGROWTH = 16384KB )
GO
```

```
-- SQL compatibility level 110 is SQL Server 2012
ALTER DATABASE [Finance] SET COMPATIBILITY_LEVEL = 110
GO
```

```
USE Finance;
-- SQL select into table create
SELECT * INTO POH
FROM AdventureWorks2012.Purchasing.PurchaseOrderHeader;
GO
```

```
-- SQL select query for 3 random records
SELECT TOP (3) * FROM POH ORDER BY NEWID()
GO
```

PurchaseOrderID	RevisionNumber	Status	EmployeeID	VendorID
3506	1	4	261	1666
233	1	4	257	1578
84	1	3	261	1654

CHAPTER 9: Advanced Database Design Concepts

Adding New Column to a Table with ALTER TABLE

It happens quite often that a table in production for years needs a new column. While adding a new column to a populated table is relatively simple, there is a downside: application software needs to be retested to make sure it still works with the new table. One offending statement is "SELECT * FROM". The application software was programmed, let's say for example, 6 columns, after the addition SELECT * is sending 7 columns which causes error in the application. T-SQL scripts to demonstrate the addition of a new column to a table for sequencing or other purposes.

```
USE AdventureWorks2012;

SELECT NewProductID = ROW_NUMBER()    OVER (  ORDER BY ProductID),
    *
INTO   #Product
FROM   AdventureWorks.Production.Product
GO
-- (504 row(s) affected)
```

```
ALTER TABLE #Product ADD CountryOfOrigin nvarchar(32) not null DEFAULT ('USA');
GO
-- Command(s) completed successfully.
```

```
SELECT          ProductID,
                Name                    AS ProductName,
                ProductNumber,
                ListPrice,
                COALESCE(Color,'')      AS Color,
                CountryOfOrigin
FROM   #Product
ORDER BY ProductName;
GO
```

ProductID	ProductName	ProductNumber	ListPrice	Color	CountryOfOrigin
1	Adjustable Race	AR-5381	0.00		USA
879	All-Purpose Bike Stand	ST-1401	159.00		USA
712	AWC Logo Cap	CA-1098	8.99	Multi	USA
3	BB Ball Bearing	BE-2349	0.00		USA
2	Bearing Ball	BA-8327	0.00		USA
877	Bike Wash - Dissolver	CL-9009	7.95		USA
316	Blade	BL-2036	0.00		USA
843	Cable Lock	LO-C100	25.00		USA
952	Chain	CH-0234	20.24	Silver	USA
324	Chain Stays	CS-2812	0.00		USA
322	Chainring	CR-7833	0.00	Black	USA
320	Chainring Bolts	CB-2903	0.00	Silver	USA

```
-- Cleanup
DROP TABLE #Product
```

CHAPTER 9: Advanced Database Design Concepts

IDENTITY Column in a Table Variable

Using IDENTITY function for row numbering in new column with table variable. Statements must be in one batch, that is the scope of table variable.

```
DECLARE @Product TABLE
 (
   ID        INT IDENTITY(1, 1),   -- new column
   ProductID   int,
   ProductName varchar(64),
   ListPrice   money,
   Color     varchar(32)
 );

INSERT @Product
    (ProductID,
     ProductName,
     ListPrice,
     Color)
SELECT ProductID,
    Name,
    ListPrice,
    Color
FROM   AdventureWorks2012.Production.Product
WHERE  ListPrice > 0
    AND Color IS NOT NULL
ORDER BY Name;

SELECT TOP(7) *
FROM   @Product
ORDER BY ID;
GO
```

ID	ProductID	ProductName	ListPrice	Color
1	712	AWC Logo Cap	8.99	Multi
2	952	Chain	20.24	Silver
3	866	Classic Vest, L	63.50	Blue
4	865	Classic Vest, M	63.50	Blue
5	864	Classic Vest, S	63.50	Blue
6	948	Front Brakes	106.50	Silver
7	945	Front Derailleur	91.49	Silver

Note: the above "GO" (ending the batch) terminated the scope of @Product table variable.

```
SELECT TOP(7) * FROM  @Product ;
/* Msg 1087, Level 15, State 2, Line 1    Must declare the table variable "@Product" */
```

CHAPTER 9: Advanced Database Design Concepts

Adding New Column to a Table with ALTER TABLE 301

Partition Data By Country Query

Partition sales data by country and sequence sales staff from best to worst.

NOTE: ROW_NUMBER() only sequencing; to rank use the RANK() function.

```
SELECT CONCAT(LastName,', ', FirstName)           AS SalesPerson,
       CountryRegionName                           AS Country,
       ROW_NUMBER() OVER(
                    PARTITION BY CountryRegionName
                    ORDER BY SalesYTD DESC)        AS 'Row Number',
       FORMAT( SalesYTD, 'c', 'en-US')             AS SalesYTD
INTO  #SalesPersonRank
FROM  AdventureWorks2012.Sales.vSalesPerson
WHERE TerritoryName IS NOT NULL
      AND SalesYTD <> 0;
```

```
-- Add new column StarRank, which is 1 "*" for each $1,000,000 of sales
ALTER TABLE #SalesPersonRank ADD StarRank varchar(32) NOT NULL DEFAULT ('');
--Command(s) completed successfully.
```

```
-- New column empty so far, population follows with UPDATE
UPDATE #SalesPersonRank SET StarRank =
REPLICATE ('*', FLOOR(CONVERT(Money, REPLACE(SalesYTD,',',''))  / 1000000.0));
-- (14 row(s) affected)
```

```
SELECT * FROM  #SalesPersonRank  ORDER BY Country,   [Row Number];
```

SalesPerson	Country	Row Number	SalesYTD	StarRank
Tsoflias, Lynn	Australia	1	$1,421,810.92	*
Saraiva, José	Canada	1	$2,604,540.72	**
Vargas, Garrett	Canada	2	$1,453,719.47	*
Varkey Chudukatil, Ranjit	France	1	$3,121,616.32	***
Valdez, Rachel	Germany	1	$1,827,066.71	*
Pak, Jae	United Kingdom	1	$4,116,871.23	****
Mitchell, Linda	United States	1	$4,251,368.55	****
Blythe, Michael	United States	2	$3,763,178.18	***
Carson, Jillian	United States	3	$3,189,418.37	***
Ito, Shu	United States	4	$2,458,535.62	**
Reiter, Tsvi	United States	5	$2,315,185.61	**
Mensa-Annan, Tete	United States	6	$1,576,562.20	*
Campbell, David	United States	7	$1,573,012.94	*
Ansman-Wolfe, Pamela	United States	8	$1,352,577.13	*

```
DROP TABLE #SalesPersonRank;
```

CHAPTER 9: Advanced Database Design Concepts

Adding New Column to a Table with ALTER TABLE

Diagram of Sales.SalesPerson & Related Tables

The sales staff is crucial in any business organization. It is reflected on the following diagram.

CHAPTER 9: Advanced Database Design Concepts

Adding IDENTITY Column To Empty Table

Add IDENTITY column to a table for sequential unique numbering (autonumber).

```
USE tempdb;
CREATE TABLE Department
(
  Name       varchar(32) UNIQUE,
  GroupName  varchar(256),
  ModifiedDate date default (CURRENT_TIMESTAMP)
);
GO -- Command(s) completed successfully.


-- Add new IDENTITY column
ALTER TABLE Department   ADD DepartmentID smallint IDENTITY(1, 1) PRIMARY KEY;
GO
-- Command(s) completed successfully.


-- Only one identity column per table
ALTER TABLE Department
 ADD SecondIdentity smallint IDENTITY(1, 1);
GO
/* Msg 2744, Level 16, State 2, Line 1
Multiple identity columns specified for table 'Department'. Only one identity column per table is allowed.
*/

INSERT INTO Department ( DepartmentID, Name, Groupname) VALUES (17, 'Student Affairs', 'Executive');
/* Msg 544, Level 16, State 1, Line 1
Cannot insert explicit value for identity column in table 'Department'  when IDENTITY_INSERT is set to OFF. */
```

SET IDENTITY INSERT tablename ON

```
-- SQL identity insert enabled
SET IDENTITY_INSERT Department ON;

INSERT INTO Department ( DepartmentID, Name, Groupname) VALUES (17, 'Student Affairs', 'Executive');
-- (1 row(s) affected)

-- SQL identity insert disabled (default)
SET IDENTITY_INSERT Department OFF;
GO
```

CHAPTER 9: Advanced Database Design Concepts

DBCC CHECKIDENT Command
DBCC CHECKIDENT can be used to check and reseed IDENTITY parameters.

```
DBCC CHECKIDENT('Production.Product');
/*Checking identity information: current identity value '999', current column value '999'.
DBCC execution completed. If DBCC printed error messages, contact your system administrator. */
```

```
-- SQL reseeding identity column; reset identity column
DBCC CHECKIDENT ("dbo.Department", RESEED, 999);
/*Checking identity information: current identity value '17'.
DBCC execution completed. If DBCC printed error messages, contact your system administrator. */
```

```
INSERT INTO Department (Name, Groupname) VALUES ( 'Alumni Affairs', 'Executive');
```

```
SELECT * FROM Department;
```

Name	GroupName	ModifiedDate	DepartmentID
Student Affairs	Executive	2016-07-19	17
Alumni Affairs	Executive	2016-07-19	1000

```
-- Add more records to table with INSERT SELECT
INSERT INTO Department (Name, Groupname)
SELECT Name, GroupName FROM AdventureWorks2012.HumanResources.Department;
```

```
SELECT * FROM Department ORDER BY DepartmentID;
```

Name	GroupName	ModifiedDate	DepartmentID
Student Affairs	Executive	2012-07-19	17
Alumni Affairs	Executive	2012-07-19	1000
Engineering	Research and Development	2012-07-19	1001
Tool Design	Research and Development	2012-07-19	1002
Sales	Sales and Marketing	2012-07-19	1003
Marketing	Sales and Marketing	2012-07-19	1004
Purchasing	Inventory Management	2012-07-19	1005
Research and Development	Research and Development	2012-07-19	1006
Production	Manufacturing	2012-07-19	1007
Production Control	Manufacturing	2012-07-19	1008
Human Resources	Executive General and Administration	2012-07-19	1009
Finance	Executive General and Administration	2012-07-19	1010
Information Services	Executive General and Administration	2012-07-19	1011
Document Control	Quality Assurance	2012-07-19	1012
Quality Assurance	Quality Assurance	2012-07-19	1013
Facilities and Maintenance	Executive General and Administration	2012-07-19	1014
Shipping and Receiving	Inventory Management	2012-07-19	1015
Executive	Executive General and Administration	2012-07-19	1016

```
DROP TABLE tempdb.dbo.Department;
```

CHAPTER 9: Advanced Database Design Concepts

Adding New Column to a Table with ALTER TABLE

ADD Partitioned Sequence Number to Table

Partition table by subcategory (ProductSubcategoryID) by applying ROW_NUMBER for sequencing within each partition.

```
SELECT ROW_NUMBER()    OVER ( PARTITION BY p.ProductSubcategoryID
                              ORDER BY ProductID)         AS RowID,
    ps.Name                                               AS SubCategory,
    p.Name                                                AS ProductName,
    ProductNumber,
    Color,
    ListPrice
INTO   #ProductsByCategory
FROM   AdventureWorks.Production.Product p
    INNER JOIN AdventureWorks.Production.ProductSubcategory ps
        ON p.ProductSubcategoryID = ps.ProductSubcategoryID ;
GO
```

```
-- Add new column for display in currency format
ALTER TABLE #ProductsByCategory ADD Dollar varchar(32) not null DEFAULT ('');
GO
-- Command(s) completed successfully.
```

```
-- Populate new column with UPDATE
UPDATE #ProductsByCategory  SET Dollar = FORMAT(ListPrice, 'c', 'en-US');
GO
-- (295 row(s) affected)
```

```
SELECT * FROM  #ProductsByCategory  ORDER BY Subcategory,  RowID;
```

RowID	SubCategory	ProductName	ProductNumber	Color	ListPrice	Dollar
1	Bib-Shorts	Men's Bib-Shorts, S	SB-M891-S	Multi	89.99	$89.99
2	Bib-Shorts	Men's Bib-Shorts, M	SB-M891-M	Multi	89.99	$89.99
3	Bib-Shorts	Men's Bib-Shorts, L	SB-M891-L	Multi	89.99	$89.99
1	Bike Racks	Hitch Rack - 4-Bike	RA-H123	NULL	120.00	$120.00
1	Bike Stands	All-Purpose Bike Stand	ST-1401	NULL	159.00	$159.00
1	Bottles and Cages	Water Bottle - 30 oz.	WB-H098	NULL	4.99	$4.99
2	Bottles and Cages	Mountain Bottle Cage	BC-M005	NULL	9.99	$9.99
3	Bottles and Cages	Road Bottle Cage	BC-R205	NULL	8.99	$8.99
1	Bottom Brackets	LL Bottom Bracket	BB-7421	NULL	53.99	$53.99
2	Bottom Brackets	ML Bottom Bracket	BB-8107	NULL	101.24	$101.24
3	Bottom Brackets	HL Bottom Bracket	BB-9108	NULL	121.49	$121.49
1	Brakes	Rear Brakes	RB-9231	Silver	106.50	$106.50
2	Brakes	Front Brakes	FB-9873	Silver	106.50	$106.50
1	Caps	AWC Logo Cap	CA-1098	Multi	8.99	$8.99
1	Chains	Chain	CH-0234	Silver	20.24	$20.24

```
-- Cleanup
DROP TABLE #ProductsByCategory
```

CHAPTER 9: Advanced Database Design Concepts

Add ROW_NUMBER & RANK Columns to Table

Add row number and rank number to SELECT INTO table create without partitioning and rank (dense ranking) high price items to low price items.

```
SELECT ROW_NUMBER()
    OVER(
      ORDER BY Name ASC)                    AS ROWID,
    DENSE_RANK()
    OVER(
      ORDER BY ListPrice DESC)              AS RANKID,
    ListPrice                               AS Price,
    *
INTO   tempdb.dbo.RankedProduct
FROM   AdventureWorks2012.Production.Product
ORDER  BY      RANKID,
               ROWID;
GO
-- (504 row(s) affected)
```

```
SELECT * FROM   tempdb.dbo.RankedProduct;
GO
-- (504 row(s) affected) - Partial results.
```

ROWID	RANKID	Price	ProductID	Name	ProductNumber	MakeFlag	FinishedGoodsFlag	Color
376	1	3578.27	750	Road-150 Red, 44	BK-R93R-44	1	1	Red
377	1	3578.27	751	Road-150 Red, 48	BK-R93R-48	1	1	Red
378	1	3578.27	752	Road-150 Red, 52	BK-R93R-52	1	1	Red
379	1	3578.27	753	Road-150 Red, 56	BK-R93R-56	1	1	Red
380	1	3578.27	749	Road-150 Red, 62	BK-R93R-62	1	1	Red
332	2	3399.99	771	Mountain-100 Silver, 38	BK-M82S-38	1	1	Silver
333	2	3399.99	772	Mountain-100 Silver, 42	BK-M82S-42	1	1	Silver
334	2	3399.99	773	Mountain-100 Silver, 44	BK-M82S-44	1	1	Silver

```
DROP TABLE tempdb.dbo.RankedProduct;
GO
```

3-Part Name Table Reference

The above script can be executed from any database on this server instance since we are using three-part name as table reference. Referencing a table on a linked server requires 4-part name. Double dot in table reference means default value between dots. Example:

[LONDONPROD1].TranMaster..OnlineOrderDetail is equivalent to
[LONDONPROD1].TranMaster.dbo.OnlineOrderDetail .

CHAPTER 9: Advanced Database Design Concepts

CHAPTER 10: The Art of Database Design

The Nature of Connection Between Tables

There is only **one kind of connection between tables** which is defined as FOREIGN KEY **references** the PRIMARY KEY or UNIQUE KEY. Nonetheless, the application functional meaning of the connections can be many, for example, star schema in a data warehouse.

Categorical Relationship

```
USE AdventureWorks2012;

CREATE TABLE Production.ProductSubcategoryTest(
      ProductSubcategoryID int IDENTITY(1,1) PRIMARY KEY,
      ProductCategoryID int NOT NULL
              REFERENCES Production.ProductCategory(ProductCategoryID),
      Name dbo.Name NOT NULL,
      rowguid uniqueidentifier ROWGUIDCOL  NOT NULL DEFAULT( NEWID() ),
      ModifiedDate datetime NOT NULL DEFAULT( CURRENT_TIMESTAMP ));
-- (1 row(s) affected)
```

Based on the naming, with the help of our Human Intelligence, we conclude the connection is **categorization**, from subcategory to (super)category. The example clearly illustrates the importance of good naming in database design. SQL Server would work equally well with Table1 and Table2, but that would make the design practically unreadable.

The connection between Production.Product and Production.ProductSubcategory is also categorization at the bottom level of the Product --> Subcategory --> Category hierarchy.

```
ALTER TABLE Production.Product
      WITH CHECK
      ADD  CONSTRAINT FK_Product_ProductSubcategory_ProductSubcategoryID
      FOREIGN KEY(ProductSubcategoryID)
      REFERENCES Production.ProductSubcategory (ProductSubcategoryID)
GO
```

Information Object Belongs To Relationship

Since we are working with information in the data processing industry, it may not come as a big surprise that frequently we are dealing with information object rather than real world objects. The products in the AdventureWorks2012 database have information objects associated with them: photos, documents and reviews for example. The relationship is many information objects to one product.

The Nature of Connection Between Tables

Checking Out Information Objects

Let's take a look at the ProductReview table. The information object is customer review about a product.

```
SELECT  P.Name                          AS ProductName,
        R.ReviewerName,
        LEFT(R.Comments,256)            AS Comments
FROM Production.ProductReview R
     INNER JOIN Production.Product P
         ON P.ProductID = R.ProductID
ORDER BY  ProductName,
          ReviewerName;
GO
```

ProductName	ReviewerName	Comments
HL Mountain Pedal	David	A little on the heavy side, but overall the entry/exit is easy in all conditions. I've used these pedals for more than 3 years and I've never had a problem. Cleanup is easy. Mud and sand don't get trapped. I would like them even better if there was a w
HL Mountain Pedal	Jill	Maybe it's just because I'm new to mountain biking, but I had a terrible time getting use to these pedals. In my first outing, I wiped out trying to release my foot. Any suggestions on ways I can adjust the pedals, or is it just a learning curve thing?
Mountain Bike Socks, M	John Smith	I can't believe I'm singing the praises of a pair of socks, but I just came back from a grueling 3-day ride and these socks really helped make the trip a blast. They're lightweight yet really cushioned my feet all day. The reinforced toe is nearly bulle
Road-550-W Yellow, 40	Laura Norman	The Road-550-W from Adventure Works Cycles is everything it's advertised to be. Finally, a quality bike that is actually built for a woman and provides control and comfort in one neat package. The top tube is shorter, the suspension is weight-tuned and th

CHAPTER 10: The Art of Database Design

The Bike Photo Information Object

The digital bike photo is stored in binary format in the Production.ProductPhoto table. Visualization requires Reporting Services report or external graphics software. SSMS cannot display the image, only the binary content.

```
SELECT          P.Name                                  AS ProductName,
                PP.ThumbnailPhotoFilename,
                PP.LargePhotoFilename
FROM Production.ProductProductPhoto PPP
    INNER JOIN Production.Product P
        ON P.ProductID = PPP.ProductID
    INNER JOIN Production.ProductPhoto PP
        ON PPP.ProductPhotoID = PP.ProductPhotoID
WHERE P.Name = 'Road-550-W Yellow, 40'
ORDER BY        ProductName;
GO
```

ProductName	ThumbnailPhotoFilename	LargePhotoFilename
Road-550-W Yellow, 40	racer02_yellow_f_small.gif	racer02_yellow_f_large.gif

The photo of the yellow road bike.

CHAPTER 10: The Art of Database Design

The Nature of Connection Between Tables

XML Diagram Object

The AdventureWorks2012 sample database includes a number of XML data type columns. These columns cannot be displayed in a formatted fashion using Management Studio, rather they require special software for formatting or visualization.

SELECT Diagram FROM AdventureWorks2012.Production.Illustration WHERE IllustrationID = 4;
-- Partial results

```xml
<Canvas>
    <!-- Layer 1/<Path> -->
    <Path StrokeThickness="0.500000" Stroke="#ff656565" StrokeMiterLimit="1.000000" Fill="#ff656565" Data="F1 M 111.049805,46.655762 L 114.526367,48.509766 L 112.671875,52.911621 L 109.694336,51.374512 L 111.049805,46.655762 Z" />
    <!-- Layer 1/<Path> -->
    <Path StrokeThickness="1.202600" Stroke="#ff989898" StrokeMiterLimit="1.000000" Data="F1 M 155.380859,314.981934" />
    <!-- Layer 1/<Path> -->
    <Path StrokeThickness="1.000000" Stroke="#ff000000" StrokeMiterLimit="1.000000" Data="F1 M 88.621094,132.691406 C 88.621094,132.691406 89.542969,135.905762 88.029785,130.630371 C 86.841797,126.486328 88.501953,126.418457 91.141113,125.661621 C 93.777832,124.904785 116.826172,118.705566 120.486328,117.249512 C 124.144531,115.791504 125.061523,117.566406 125.819336,120.205566 C 126.576172,122.842285 126.205078,121.554688 126.205078,121.554688 L 122.169922,123.121582 L 164.131836,264.715332 L 161.495117,268.324707 L 163.008789,273.599121 L 141.530273,279.757324 L 139.910156,274.105957 L 134.900391,272.280762 L 93.264160,131.816406 L 88.621094,132.691406 Z">
        <Path.Fill>
            <LinearGradientBrush MappingMode="Absolute" StartPoint="87.639160,198.240234" EndPoint="164.131836,198.240234">
                <LinearGradientBrush.GradientStops>
                    <GradientStop Offset="0.000000" Color="#ffffffff" />
                    <GradientStop Offset="0.258800" Color="#fffcfcfc" />
                    <GradientStop Offset="0.396200" Color="#ffff4f4f4" />
```

The diagram can be visualized by special XAML software.

CHAPTER 10: The Art of Database Design

Exporting & Presenting XML Data from Production.ProductModel

XML columns contain semi-structured data. There is no general software which can make the XML data presentable. Each XML data requires specialized software for presentation. The Production.ProductModel table contains 2 XML columns. We export one cell from the first XML column, CatalogDescription, using bcp into an xhtml fil.

```
bcp "SELECT CatalogDescription FROM AdventureWorks2012.Production.ProductModel WHERE ProductModelID=19" queryout f:\data\xml\Product19.xhtml -c -t -S yourserver -T
```

When we double click on the new .xhtml file, the information appears in a presentable format without the XML tags.

Our top-of-the-line competition mountain bike. Performance-enhancing options include the innovative HL Frame, super-smooth front suspension, and traction for all terrain.

AdventureWorks2002HTTP://www.Adventure-works.comThese are the product highlights. 3 yearsparts and labor10 yearsmaintenance contract available through your dealer or any AdventureWorks retail store.High performance wheels.*Anatomic design* and made from durable leather for a full-day of riding in comfort.**Top-of-the -line** clipless pedals with adjustable tension.Each frame is hand-crafted in our Bothell facility to the optimum diameter and wall-thickness required of a premium mountain frame. The heat-treated welded aluminum frame has a larger diameter tube that absorbs the bumps. Triple crankset; alumunim crank arm; flawless shifting. frontsmall118 These are the product specifications. Almuminum AlloyAvailable in most colorsMountain bikeUnisexAdvanced to Professional riders

The Nature of Connection Between Tables

Product, ProductPhoto & ProductProductPhoto Tables Diagram

The ProductProductPhoto is a junction table representing many to many relationship between the Product and ProductPhoto. A product may have many photos and a photo may belong to many products.

CHAPTER 10: The Art of Database Design

Graphical Query Design Using the Product & Photo Tables

The good database design lends itself to easy query building with Query Designer. To alias a table requires right click on the table and setting the Alias property.

```
SELECT  P.Name AS ProductName, PP.ThumbnailPhotoFileName, PP.LargePhotoFileName
FROM    Production.Product AS P INNER JOIN
        Production.ProductProductPhoto AS PPP ON P.ProductID = PPP.ProductID INNER JOIN
        Production.ProductPhoto AS PP ON PPP.ProductPhotoID = PP.ProductPhotoID
WHERE   (P.Name = N'Road-550-W Yellow, 40')
ORDER BY ProductName
```

The Nature of Connection Between Tables

Company Received an Order Relationship

Vendor is a company supplying parts or finished product to AdventureWorks Cycles. Here is the relationship diagram. The purchase order to vendor FOREIGN KEY means a sale for the vendor. The detail to header FOREIGN KEY means the detail belongs to the header.

CHAPTER 10: The Art of Database Design

Querying the Vendor & Purchase Order Tables

The query list all purchase orders issued by AdventureWorks Cycles on a particular day.

```
SELECT V.Name, POH.PurchaseOrderID, POH.OrderDate, POH.TotalDue, POD.ProductID, POD.OrderQty
FROM    Purchasing.Vendor AS V INNER JOIN
        Purchasing.PurchaseOrderHeader AS POH ON V.BusinessEntityID = POH.VendorID INNER JOIN
        Purchasing.PurchaseOrderDetail AS POD ON POH.PurchaseOrderID = POD.PurchaseOrderID
WHERE   (POH.OrderDate = CONVERT(DATETIME, '2008-02-07 00:00:00', 102))
ORDER BY V.Name, POH.PurchaseOrderID, POD.ProductID
```

Upon execution the query returns 34 rows. Partial results.

Name	PurchaseOrderID	OrderDate	TotalDue	ProductID	OrderQty
Advanced Bicycles	1641	2008-02-07 00:00:00.000	555.9106	369	3
Allenson Cycles	1642	2008-02-07 00:00:00.000	9776.2665	530	550
American Bicycles and Wheels	1643	2008-02-07 00:00:00.000	189.0395	4	3

CHAPTER 10: The Art of Database Design

The Nature of Connection Between Tables

Type Relationship

A very frequent FOREIGN KEY representing an attribute of an object. For example a celebrity is a singer, actor, fashion model, writer, talk show host, sports figure and so on.

CHAPTER 10: The Art of Database Design

Obtaining Model Information for a Bike
We use the graphical query designer to see Model information for high-priced bikes.

Query Designer

Column	Alias	Table	Output	Sort Type	Sort Order	Filter
Name	Product	Product (Pr...)	✓	Ascending	2	
Name	Model	ProductMo...	✓	Ascending	1	
Name	Culture	Culture (Pr...)	✓	Ascending	3	
ListPrice		Product (Pr...)	✓			> 3000.0
Color		Product (Pr...)	✓			

```
SELECT Production.Product.Name AS Product, Production.ProductModel.Name AS Model, Production.Culture.Name AS Cultu
       Production.Product.Color
FROM   Production.ProductModelProductDescriptionCulture INNER JOIN
       Production.ProductModel ON Production.ProductModelProductDescriptionCulture.ProductModelID = Production.
       Production.Culture ON Production.ProductModelProductDescriptionCulture.CultureID = Production.Culture.Culture
       Production.Product ON Production.ProductModel.ProductModelID = Production.Product.ProductModelID
WHERE  (Production.Product.ListPrice > 3000.0)
ORDER BY Model, Product, Culture
```

Partial results from the generated query.

Product	Model	Culture	ListPrice	Color
Mountain-100 Silver, 48	Mountain-100	English	3399.99	Silver
Mountain-100 Silver, 48	Mountain-100	French	3399.99	Silver
Mountain-100 Silver, 48	Mountain-100	Hebrew	3399.99	Silver
Mountain-100 Silver, 48	Mountain-100	Thai	3399.99	Silver
Road-150 Red, 44	Road-150	Arabic	3578.27	Red
Road-150 Red, 44	Road-150	Chinese	3578.27	Red

When to Use & Not to Use Composite PRIMARY KEYs

A composite PRIMARY KEY can be used in a junction table if it is unlikely that FOREIGN KEY reference needed from other tables. AdventureWorks2012 example of composite PRIMARY KEY with 4 columns in a junction table.

Composite PRIMARY KEY should not be used if FOREIGN KEY reference is necessary today or in the future: ineffective to have FOREIGN KEYs consisting of multiple columns & subtle violation of 3NF rules by duplication of PK table content in other tables as FKs. **The bottom line: COMPOSITE PRIMARY KEYs should not be used in regular tables.** Instead of the composite PRIMARY KEY design:

```
CREATE TABLE AlbumSong(
  AlbumTitle NVARCHAR(64) not null,
  DiskNo INTEGER not null,
  TrackNo INTEGER not null,
  PRIMARY KEY (AlbumTitle, DiskNo, TrackNo),
  Song NVARCHAR(128) not null,
  ModifiedDate DATE default(CURRENT_TIMESTAMP));
```

Design with **SURROGATE PRIMARY KEY** and apply composite **UNIQUE KEY** constraint:

```
CREATE TABLE AlbumSong(
  AlbumSongID INT IDENTITY(1,1) PRIMARY KEY NONCLUSTERED,
  AlbumTitle NVARCHAR(64) not null,
  DiskNo INTEGER not null,
  TrackNo INTEGER not null,
  UNIQUE CLUSTERED (AlbumTitle, DiskNo, TrackNo),
  Song NVARCHAR(128) not null,
  ModifiedDate DATE default(CURRENT_TIMESTAMP));
```

Where to place the clustered index should be based on performance considerations.

CHAPTER 10: The Art of Database Design

How To Design a Table

It is very important that we follow in order. Rules are with reference to the Celebrity table.

- Identify the NATURAL KEY column(s) (LastName, FirstName) & set it as UNIQUE (KEY)
- Design the non-key columns (BirthDate, BirthPlace, NameAtBirth)
- Design the row maintenance columns (CreatedDate)
- Configure the FOREIGN KEY(s) (CountryID)
- Configure the IDENTITY SURROGATE PRIMARY KEY (CelebrityID)

```
CREATE TABLE Profession (
    ProfessionID TINYINT IDENTITY(1,1) PRIMARY KEY,
    Name varchar(50) NOT NULL UNIQUE,
    CreatedDate DATETIME DEFAULT(CURRENT_TIMESTAMP) );
```

```
CREATE TABLE Country (
    ID TINYINT IDENTITY(1,1) PRIMARY KEY,
    Name varchar(128) NOT NULL UNIQUE,
    CreatedDate DATETIME DEFAULT(CURRENT_TIMESTAMP) );
```

```
CREATE TABLE Celebrity(
    CelebrityID SMALLINT IDENTITY(1,1) PRIMARY KEY nonclustered,
    CountryID TINYINT REFERENCES Country(ID),
    LastName nvarchar(40) NOT NULL CHECK( LEN(LastName) > 4),
    FirstName nvarchar(40),
    UNIQUE clustered (LastName, FirstName),
    BirthDate DATE NOT NULL,
    BirthPlace nvarchar(50),
    NameAtBirth nvarchar(60),
    CreatedDate DATETIME DEFAULT(CURRENT_TIMESTAMP) );
```

```
CREATE TABLE CelebrityProfessionXref(
    CelebrityID SMALLINT NOT NULL REFERENCES Celebrity(CelebrityID),
    ProfessionID TINYINT NOT NULL REFERENCES Profession(ProfessionID),
    PRIMARY KEY (CelebrityID, ProfessionID),
    CreatedDate DATETIME DEFAULT(CURRENT_TIMESTAMP) );
```

Without NATURAL KEY we don't have a table. The NATURAL KEY can be set as UNIQUE KEY or PRIMARY KEY. We can tentatively move the clustered index away from the PRIMARY KEY (default), however, final decision point is when we identify the business critical queries. Clustered index is helpful with range query performance.

CHAPTER 10: The Art of Database Design

Table-Related Database Objects

Table is the content object in a database. It has a number of supporting objects to keep the content accurate and accessible. The list of database object types in sys.objects system view.

```
SELECT SeqNo=ROW_NUMBER() OVER (ORDER BY type_desc),
    *
FROM ( SELECT DISTINCT type, type_desc
        FROM sys.objects ) x
ORDER BY SeqNo;
```

SeqNo	type	type_desc
1	C	CHECK_CONSTRAINT
2	D	DEFAULT_CONSTRAINT
3	F	FOREIGN_KEY_CONSTRAINT
4	IT	INTERNAL_TABLE
5	PK	PRIMARY_KEY_CONSTRAINT
6	SO	SEQUENCE_OBJECT
7	SQ	SERVICE_QUEUE
8	IF	SQL_INLINE_TABLE_VALUED_FUNCTION
9	FN	SQL_SCALAR_FUNCTION
10	P	SQL_STORED_PROCEDURE
11	TF	SQL_TABLE_VALUED_FUNCTION
12	TR	SQL_TRIGGER
13	S	SYSTEM_TABLE
14	TT	TYPE_TABLE
15	UQ	UNIQUE_CONSTRAINT
16	U	USER_TABLE
17	V	VIEW

Indexes have their own system view.

```
SELECT      OBJECT_NAME(object_ID)    AS TableName,
            name                       AS IndexName,
            index_id,
            type_desc
FROM AdventureWorks2012.sys.indexes  ORDER BY TableName, index_id;
-- (333 row(s) affected) - Partial Results
```

TableName	IndexName	index_id	type_desc
Address	PK_Address_AddressID	1	CLUSTERED
Address	AK_Address_rowguid	2	NONCLUSTERED
Address	IX_Address_AddressLine1_AddressLine2_City_StateProvinceID_PostalCode	3	NONCLUSTERED
Address	IX_Address_StateProvinceID	4	NONCLUSTERED

CHAPTER 10: The Art of Database Design

Listing All PRIMARY KEYs

Getting database object information can start in sys.objects system view.

```
SELECT  SCHEMA_NAME(schema_id)          AS SchemaName,
        OBJECT_NAME(parent_object_id)   AS TableName,
        name                            AS PKName
FROM AdventureWorks2012.sys.objects WHERE type = 'PK'
ORDER BY SchemaName, TableName;
GO
```

SchemaName	TableName	PKName
dbo	AWBuildVersion	PK_AWBuildVersion_SystemInformationID
dbo	DatabaseLog	PK_DatabaseLog_DatabaseLogID
dbo	ErrorLog	PK_ErrorLog_ErrorLogID
HumanResources	Department	PK_Department_DepartmentID
HumanResources	Employee	PK_Employee_BusinessEntityID
HumanResources	EmployeeDepartmentHistory	PK_EmployeeDepartmentHistory_BusinessEntityID_StartDate_DepartmentID
HumanResources	EmployeePayHistory	PK_EmployeePayHistory_BusinessEntityID_RateChangeDate
HumanResources	JobCandidate	PK_JobCandidate_JobCandidateID
HumanResources	Shift	PK_Shift_ShiftID
Person	Address	PK_Address_AddressID
Person	AddressType	PK_AddressType_AddressTypeID
Person	BusinessEntity	PK_BusinessEntity_BusinessEntityID
Person	BusinessEntityAddress	PK_BusinessEntityAddress_BusinessEntityID_AddressID_AddressTypeID
Person	BusinessEntityContact	PK_BusinessEntityContact_BusinessEntityID_PersonID_ContactTypeID
Person	ContactType	PK_ContactType_ContactTypeID
Person	CountryRegion	PK_CountryRegion_CountryRegionCode
Person	EmailAddress	PK_EmailAddress_BusinessEntityID_EmailAddressID
Person	Password	PK_Password_BusinessEntityID
Person	Person	PK_Person_BusinessEntityID
Person	PersonPhone	PK_PersonPhone_BusinessEntityID_PhoneNumber_PhoneNumberTypeID
Person	PhoneNumberType	PK_PhoneNumberType_PhoneNumberTypeID
Person	StateProvince	PK_StateProvince_StateProvinceID
Production	BillOfMaterials	PK_BillOfMaterials_BillOfMaterialsID
Production	Culture	PK_Culture_CultureID
Production	Document	PK_Document_DocumentNode
Production	Illustration	PK_Illustration_IllustrationID
Production	Location	PK_Location_LocationID
Production	Product	PK_Product_ProductID
Production	ProductCategory	PK_ProductCategory_ProductCategoryID
Production	ProductCostHistory	PK_ProductCostHistory_ProductID_StartDate
Production	ProductDescription	PK_ProductDescription_ProductDescriptionID
Production	ProductDocument	PK_ProductDocument_ProductID_DocumentNode
Production	ProductInventory	PK_ProductInventory_ProductID_LocationID
Production	ProductListPriceHistory	PK_ProductListPriceHistory_ProductID_StartDate
Production	ProductModel	PK_ProductModel_ProductModelID
Production	ProductModelIllustration	PK_ProductModelIllustration_ProductModelID_IllustrationID
Production	ProductModelProductDescriptionCulture	PK_ProductModelProductDescriptionCulture_ProductModelID_ProductDescriptionID_CultureID
Production	ProductPhoto	PK_ProductPhoto_ProductPhotoID
Production	ProductProductPhoto	PK_ProductProductPhoto_ProductID_ProductPhotoID
Production	ProductReview	PK_ProductReview_ProductReviewID
Production	ProductSubcategory	PK_ProductSubcategory_ProductSubcategoryID
Production	ScrapReason	PK_ScrapReason_ScrapReasonID
Production	TransactionHistory	PK_TransactionHistory_TransactionID
Production	TransactionHistoryArchive	PK_TransactionHistoryArchive_TransactionID
Production	UnitMeasure	PK_UnitMeasure_UnitMeasureCode
Production	WorkOrder	PK_WorkOrder_WorkOrderID
Production	WorkOrderRouting	PK_WorkOrderRouting_WorkOrderID_ProductID_OperationSequence
Purchasing	ProductVendor	PK_ProductVendor_ProductID_BusinessEntityID
Purchasing	PurchaseOrderDetail	PK_PurchaseOrderDetail_PurchaseOrderID_PurchaseOrderDetailID
Purchasing	PurchaseOrderHeader	PK_PurchaseOrderHeader_PurchaseOrderID
Purchasing	ShipMethod	PK_ShipMethod_ShipMethodID
Purchasing	Vendor	PK_Vendor_BusinessEntityID
Sales	CountryRegionCurrency	PK_CountryRegionCurrency_CountryRegionCode_CurrencyCode
Sales	CreditCard	PK_CreditCard_CreditCardID

CHAPTER 10: The Art of Database Design

Table-Related Database Objects

Sales	Currency	PK_Currency_CurrencyCode
Sales	CurrencyRate	PK_CurrencyRate_CurrencyRateID
Sales	Customer	PK_Customer_CustomerID
Sales	PersonCreditCard	PK_PersonCreditCard_BusinessEntityID_CreditCardID
Sales	SalesOrderDetail	PK_SalesOrderDetail_SalesOrderID_SalesOrderDetailID
Sales	SalesOrderHeader	PK_SalesOrderHeader_SalesOrderID
Sales	SalesOrderHeaderSalesReason	PK_SalesOrderHeaderSalesReason_SalesOrderID_SalesReasonID
Sales	SalesPerson	PK_SalesPerson_BusinessEntityID
Sales	SalesPersonQuotaHistory	PK_SalesPersonQuotaHistory_BusinessEntityID_QuotaDate
Sales	SalesReason	PK_SalesReason_SalesReasonID
Sales	SalesTaxRate	PK_SalesTaxRate_SalesTaxRateID
Sales	SalesTerritory	PK_SalesTerritory_TerritoryID
Sales	SalesTerritoryHistory	PK_SalesTerritoryHistory_BusinessEntityID_StartDate_TerritoryID
Sales	ShoppingCartItem	PK_ShoppingCartItem_ShoppingCartItemID
Sales	SpecialOffer	PK_SpecialOffer_SpecialOfferID
Sales	SpecialOfferProduct	PK_SpecialOfferProduct_SpecialOfferID_ProductID
Sales	Store	PK_Store_BusinessEntityID

UNIQUEIDENTIFIER As PRIMARY KEY

For most applications INT IDENTITY(1,1) (SURROGATE) PRIMARY KEY is the perfect choice. However, some enterprise applications require the generation of a random rowid without any reference to a database. For those, UNIQUEIDENTIFIER can be used with NEWID() or NEWSEQUENTIALID() fill. **The latter is faster but not completely random therefore should not be used for secure applications.** INT IDENTITY() is fastest of the three (not in following test).

```
USE tempdb; SET NOCOUNT ON;
DECLARE @MaxCount Int = 100000,@START DATETIME,@END DATETIME, @i INT
CREATE TABLE TESTID ( ID UNIQUEIDENTIFIER DEFAULT NEWID() PRIMARY KEY,
-- CREATE TABLE TESTID ( ID UNIQUEIDENTIFIER DEFAULT NEWSEQUENTIALID() PRIMARY KEY,
COL1 CHAR(256) DEFAULT 'Everglades', COL2 CHAR(256) DEFAULT 'Everglades',
COL3 CHAR(256) DEFAULT 'Everglades', COL4 CHAR(256) DEFAULT 'Everglades',
COL5 CHAR(256) DEFAULT 'Everglades', COL6 CHAR(256) DEFAULT 'Everglades',
COL7 CHAR(256) DEFAULT 'Everglades', COL8 CHAR(256) DEFAULT 'Everglades',
COL9 CHAR(256) DEFAULT 'Everglades', COL10 CHAR(256) DEFAULT 'Everglades');
SELECT TOP(0) * INTO #Result FROM TESTID;
DBCC DROPCLEANBUFFERS;  SET @START = GETDATE(); SET @i = 1;
WHILE (@i < @MaxCount)
BEGIN INSERT TESTID DEFAULT VALUES; SET @i += 1; END
INSERT #Result SELECT t1.* FROM TESTID t1 INNER JOIN TESTID t2 ON t1.ID=t2.ID
SELECT  DATEDIFF(ms,@START,GETDATE());  DROP TABLE #Result; DROP TABLE TESTID;

-- Test with newid(): 22,436 msec
-- Test with newid(): 14,866 msec
-- Test with newid(): 14,576 msec


-- Test with newsequentialid(): 12,126 msec
-- Test with newsequentialid(): 11,290 msec
-- Test with newsequentialid(): 10,713 msec
```

CHAPTER 10: The Art of Database Design

List All PK & FK Columns in the Database

We can use INFORMATION_SCHEMA metadata system views for the task. The position indicates the placement of the column within a composite key.

```
USE AdventureWorks2012;
SELECT  k.table_schema              AS SchemaName,
        k.table_name                AS TableName,
        k.column_name               AS ColumnName,
        k.ordinal_position          AS Position,
        c.constraint_type           AS KeyConstraint
FROM    information_schema.table_constraints c
    INNER JOIN information_schema.key_column_usage k
    ON c.table_name = k.table_name
       AND c.constraint_name = k.constraint_name
ORDER BY SchemaName, TableName, KeyConstraint DESC, Position, ColumnName;
GO
-- (194 row(s) affected) - Partial results
```

SchemaName	TableName	ColumnName	Position	KeyConstraint
HumanResources	Department	DepartmentID	1	PRIMARY KEY
HumanResources	Employee	BusinessEntityID	1	PRIMARY KEY
HumanResources	Employee	BusinessEntityID	1	FOREIGN KEY
HumanResources	EmployeeDepartmentHistory	BusinessEntityID	1	PRIMARY KEY
HumanResources	EmployeeDepartmentHistory	StartDate	2	PRIMARY KEY
HumanResources	EmployeeDepartmentHistory	DepartmentID	3	PRIMARY KEY
HumanResources	EmployeeDepartmentHistory	ShiftID	4	PRIMARY KEY
HumanResources	EmployeeDepartmentHistory	BusinessEntityID	1	FOREIGN KEY
HumanResources	EmployeeDepartmentHistory	DepartmentID	1	FOREIGN KEY
HumanResources	EmployeeDepartmentHistory	ShiftID	1	FOREIGN KEY
HumanResources	EmployeePayHistory	BusinessEntityID	1	PRIMARY KEY
HumanResources	EmployeePayHistory	RateChangeDate	2	PRIMARY KEY
HumanResources	EmployeePayHistory	BusinessEntityID	1	FOREIGN KEY
HumanResources	JobCandidate	JobCandidateID	1	PRIMARY KEY
HumanResources	JobCandidate	BusinessEntityID	1	FOREIGN KEY
HumanResources	Shift	ShiftID	1	PRIMARY KEY
Person	Address	AddressID	1	PRIMARY KEY
Person	Address	StateProvinceID	1	FOREIGN KEY
Person	AddressType	AddressTypeID	1	PRIMARY KEY
Person	BusinessEntity	BusinessEntityID	1	PRIMARY KEY
Person	BusinessEntityAddress	BusinessEntityID	1	PRIMARY KEY
Person	BusinessEntityAddress	AddressID	2	PRIMARY KEY
Person	BusinessEntityAddress	AddressTypeID	3	PRIMARY KEY
Person	BusinessEntityAddress	AddressID	1	FOREIGN KEY
Person	BusinessEntityAddress	AddressTypeID	1	FOREIGN KEY
Person	BusinessEntityAddress	BusinessEntityID	1	FOREIGN KEY
Person	BusinessEntityContact	BusinessEntityID	1	PRIMARY KEY
Person	BusinessEntityContact	PersonID	2	PRIMARY KEY
Person	BusinessEntityContact	ContactTypeID	3	PRIMARY KEY
Person	BusinessEntityContact	BusinessEntityID	1	FOREIGN KEY
Person	BusinessEntityContact	ContactTypeID	1	FOREIGN KEY
Person	BusinessEntityContact	PersonID	1	FOREIGN KEY
Person	ContactType	ContactTypeID	1	PRIMARY KEY

How to Get Database Object Definition Information

There are alternate ways of getting object definition metadata.

Scripting Object CREATE Definitions

This is the easiest and most reliable way. Start with a right click on the object in Object Explorer.

Single Object CREATE & Other Scripts from SSMS Object Explorer

Some of the scripts are generated complete. Others are just templates which require completion and testing.

Index CREATE Script

```
USE [AdventureWorks2012]
GO


/****** Object:  Index [IX_EmployeeDepartmentHistory_ShiftID]    Script Date: ..... ******/
CREATE NONCLUSTERED INDEX [IX_EmployeeDepartmentHistory_ShiftID]
ON [HumanResources].[EmployeeDepartmentHistory]
(
       [ShiftID] ASC
)
WITH (PAD_INDEX = OFF, STATISTICS_NORECOMPUTE = OFF, SORT_IN_TEMPDB = OFF,
DROP_EXISTING = OFF, ONLINE = OFF, ALLOW_ROW_LOCKS = ON, ALLOW_PAGE_LOCKS = ON,
FILLFACTOR = 85) ON [PRIMARY]
GO

EXEC sys.sp_addextendedproperty @name=N'MS_Description',
@value=N'Nonclustered index.' ,
@level0type=N'SCHEMA',@level0name=N'HumanResources',
@level1type=N'TABLE',@level1name=N'EmployeeDepartmentHistory',
@level2type=N'INDEX',@level2name=N'IX_EmployeeDepartmentHistory_ShiftID'
GO
```

Index DROP Script

```
/****** Object:  Index [IX_EmployeeDepartmentHistory_ShiftID]    Script Date: ...... ******/
DROP INDEX [IX_EmployeeDepartmentHistory_ShiftID] ON
[HumanResources].[EmployeeDepartmentHistory]
GO
```

View DELETE Script

```
USE [AdventureWorks2012]
GO

DELETE FROM [Person].[vStateProvinceCountryRegion]
      WHERE <Search Conditions,,>
GO
```

How to Get Database Object Definition Information

View UPDATE Script

```sql
USE [AdventureWorks2012]
GO
UPDATE [Production].[vProductAndDescription]
   SET [ProductID] = <ProductID, int,>
      ,[Name] = <Name, Name,>
      ,[ProductModel] = <ProductModel, Name,>
      ,[CultureID] = <CultureID, nchar(6),>
      ,[Description] = <Description, nvarchar(400),>
 WHERE <Search Conditions,,>
GO
```

Inline Table-Valued User-Defined Function ALTER Script

```sql
USE [AdventureWorks2012]
GO
/****** Object:  UserDefinedFunction [Sales].[ufnStaffSalesByFiscalYear]    Script Date: ...... ******/
SET ANSI_NULLS ON
GO
SET QUOTED_IDENTIFIER ON
GO
ALTER FUNCTION [Sales].[ufnStaffSalesByFiscalYear] (@OrderYear INT)
RETURNS TABLE  AS
RETURN
SELECT
     CONVERT(date, soh.OrderDate)                                     AS OrderDate
    ,CONCAT(p.FirstName, ' ', COALESCE(p.MiddleName, ''), ' ', p.LastName)   AS FullName
    ,e.JobTitle
    ,st.Name                                                          AS SalesTerritory
    ,FORMAT(soh.SubTotal, 'c', 'en-US')                               AS SalesAmount
    ,YEAR(DATEADD(mm, 6, soh.OrderDate))                              AS FiscalYear
FROM Sales.SalesPerson sp
    INNER JOIN Sales.SalesOrderHeader soh
        ON sp.BusinessEntityID = soh.SalesPersonID
    INNER JOIN Sales.SalesTerritory st
        ON sp.TerritoryID = st.TerritoryID
    INNER JOIN HumanResources.Employee e
        ON soh.SalesPersonID = e.BusinessEntityID
    INNER JOIN Person.Person p
        ON p.BusinessEntityID = sp.BusinessEntityID
WHERE         soh.OrderDate >= datefromparts(@OrderYear, 1, 1)
          AND soh.OrderDate < dateadd(yy,1, datefromparts(@OrderYear, 1, 1));
GO
```

CHAPTER 10: The Art of Database Design

Searching for Database Objects in Object Explorer Details

We start by positioning on AdventureWorks2012 in Object Explorer. We activate the Object Explorer Details window from the Views tab. Enter the keyword or wildcard in the search box and press the Enter key.

OBJECT_DEFINITION() Function for Getting Source Code

The OBJECT_DEFINITIION() function can be used to retrieve the database object definition source text for some objects such as view, stored procedure, trigger & function.

SELECT OBJECT_DEFINITION(object_id('INFORMATION_SCHEMA.TABLES'));

```
CREATE VIEW INFORMATION_SCHEMA.TABLES
AS
SELECT
        DB_NAME()                      AS TABLE_CATALOG,
        s.name                         AS TABLE_SCHEMA,
        o.name                         AS TABLE_NAME,
        CASE o.type
                WHEN 'U' THEN 'BASE TABLE'
                WHEN 'V' THEN 'VIEW'
        END                            AS TABLE_TYPE
FROM
        sys.objects o LEFT JOIN sys.schemas s
        ON s.schema_id = o.schema_id
WHERE
                o.type IN ('U', 'V')
```

SELECT OBJECT_DEFINITION(object_id('Sales.vSalesPersonSalesByFiscalYears'));

```
CREATE VIEW [Sales].[vSalesPersonSalesByFiscalYears] AS
SELECT   pvt.[SalesPersonID]
  ,pvt.[FullName]
  ,pvt.[JobTitle]
  ,pvt.[SalesTerritory]
  ,pvt.[2006]
  ,pvt.[2007]
  ,pvt.[2008]
FROM (SELECT     soh.[SalesPersonID]
     ,p.[FirstName] + ' ' + COALESCE(p.[MiddleName], '') + ' ' + p.[LastName] AS [FullName]
     ,e.[JobTitle]
     ,st.[Name] AS [SalesTerritory]
     ,soh.[SubTotal]
     ,YEAR(DATEADD(m, 6, soh.[OrderDate])) AS [FiscalYear]
   FROM [Sales].[SalesPerson] sp
     INNER JOIN [Sales].[SalesOrderHeader] soh
     ON sp.[BusinessEntityID] = soh.[SalesPersonID]
     INNER JOIN [Sales].[SalesTerritory] st
     ON sp.[TerritoryID] = st.[TerritoryID]
     INNER JOIN [HumanResources].[Employee] e
     ON soh.[SalesPersonID] = e.[BusinessEntityID]
                INNER JOIN [Person].[Person] p
                ON p.[BusinessEntityID] = sp.[BusinessEntityID]  ) AS soh
PIVOT (
  SUM([SubTotal])
  FOR [FiscalYear]
  IN ([2006], [2007], [2008])
) AS pvt;
```

CHAPTER 10: The Art of Database Design

Scripting Database Objects with PowerShell

PowerShell script can be used to script database object including tables. Scripting tables in the Purchasing schema of AdventureWorks2012 sample database. In all Command Prompt scripts the lines must be without carriage return or new line breaks (CR/NL).

```
sqlps
Set-Location SQLSERVER:\SQL\HPESTAR\DEFAULT\Databases\AdventureWorks2012\Tables;
ForEach ($item in Get-ChildItem  | Where-Object { $_.Schema -eq "Purchasing" }) {$item.Script()}
```

Instead of the console the scripting output can be piped to a .sql file.

```
ForEach ($item in Get-ChildItem  | Where-Object { $_.Schema -eq "Purchasing" }) {$item.Script() | Out-File "f:data\sql\PurchasingTables.sql" -Append }
```

CHAPTER 10: The Art of Database Design

System Views since SQL Server 2005

SQL Server 2005 has introduced a large collection, 400 in SS 2012, of system views providing detail metadata and operational data which was not available before. As an example, the full-text index & full-text search functionalities have a number of supporting system views. The system tables are no longer accessible. System views cannot be altered or updated. **System views are read only**. The head of systems views list.

```
AdventureWorks2012
    Database Diagrams
    Tables
    Views
        System Views
            INFORMATION_SCHEMA.CHECK_CONSTRAINTS
            INFORMATION_SCHEMA.COLUMN_DOMAIN_USAGE
            INFORMATION_SCHEMA.COLUMN_PRIVILEGES
            INFORMATION_SCHEMA.COLUMNS
            INFORMATION_SCHEMA.CONSTRAINT_COLUMN_USAGE
            INFORMATION_SCHEMA.CONSTRAINT_TABLE_USAGE
            INFORMATION_SCHEMA.DOMAIN_CONSTRAINTS
            INFORMATION_SCHEMA.DOMAINS
            INFORMATION_SCHEMA.KEY_COLUMN_USAGE
            INFORMATION_SCHEMA.PARAMETERS
            INFORMATION_SCHEMA.REFERENTIAL_CONSTRAINTS
            INFORMATION_SCHEMA.ROUTINE_COLUMNS
            INFORMATION_SCHEMA.ROUTINES
            INFORMATION_SCHEMA.SCHEMATA
            INFORMATION_SCHEMA.SEQUENCES
            INFORMATION_SCHEMA.TABLE_CONSTRAINTS
            INFORMATION_SCHEMA.TABLE_PRIVILEGES
            INFORMATION_SCHEMA.TABLES
            INFORMATION_SCHEMA.VIEW_COLUMN_USAGE
            INFORMATION_SCHEMA.VIEW_TABLE_USAGE
            INFORMATION_SCHEMA.VIEWS
            sys.all_columns
            sys.all_objects
            sys.all_parameters
            sys.all_sql_modules
            sys.all_views
            sys.allocation_units
```

Querying Systems Views

Querying system views is not a trivial task. Frequently a group of tables involved and a Dynamic Management Function (DMF) CROSS APPLY may be necessary for useful results.

> Download site for SQL Server 2008 R2 System Views Map:
> http://www.microsoft.com/en-us/download/details.aspx?id=722 .

```
USE AdventureWorks2012;
SELECT ReferencedObject = CONCAT(SCHEMA_NAME(o2.schema_id), '.',
                        ed.referenced_entity_name),
    ReferencedObjectType = o2.type,
    ReferencingObjectType = o1.type,
    ReferencingObject = CONCAT(SCHEMA_NAME(o1.schema_id), '.', o1.name)
FROM  sys.sql_expression_dependencies ed
    INNER JOIN sys.objects o1
        ON ed.referencing_id = o1.object_id
    INNER JOIN sys.objects o2
        ON ed.referenced_id = o2.object_id
WHERE  o1.type IN ( 'P', 'TR', 'V', 'TF' )
ORDER BY     ReferencedObjectType, ReferencedObject, ReferencingObject;
-- (163 row(s) affected) - Partial results
```

ReferencedObject	ReferencedObjectType	ReferencingObjectType	ReferencingObject
HumanResources.Department	U	V	HumanResources.vEmployeeDepartment
HumanResources.Department	U	V	HumanResources.vEmployeeDepartmentHistory
HumanResources.Employee	U	TF	dbo.ufnGetContactInformation
HumanResources.Employee	U	P	dbo.uspGetEmployeeManagers
HumanResources.Employee	U	P	dbo.uspGetManagerEmployees
HumanResources.Employee	U	P	HumanResources.uspUpdateEmployeeHireInfo
HumanResources.Employee	U	P	HumanResources.uspUpdateEmployeeLogin
HumanResources.Employee	U	P	HumanResources.uspUpdateEmployeePersonalInfo
HumanResources.Employee	U	V	HumanResources.vEmployee
HumanResources.Employee	U	V	HumanResources.vEmployeeDepartment
HumanResources.Employee	U	V	HumanResources.vEmployeeDepartmentHistory
HumanResources.Employee	U	V	Sales.vSalesPerson
HumanResources.Employee	U	V	Sales.vSalesPersonSalesByFiscalYears
HumanResources.EmployeeDepartmentHistory	U	V	HumanResources.vEmployeeDepartment
HumanResources.EmployeeDepartmentHistory	U	V	HumanResources.vEmployeeDepartmentHistory
HumanResources.EmployeePayHistory	U	P	HumanResources.uspUpdateEmployeeHireInfo
HumanResources.JobCandidate	U	P	dbo.uspSearchCandidateResumes
HumanResources.JobCandidate	U	V	HumanResources.vJobCandidate
HumanResources.JobCandidate	U	V	HumanResources.vJobCandidateEducation
HumanResources.JobCandidate	U	V	HumanResources.vJobCandidateEmployment

CHAPTER 10: The Art of Database Design

System Views since SQL Server 2005

Listing All System Views

Since SQL Server 2005 system tables are off limits, replaced by system views, 400 in SS 2012 ahd 425 in SS 2014. The dm_ prefix indicates **Dynamic Management View** (DMV) such as dm_exec_requests.

```
SELECT * FROM master.sys.system_views;  -- (425 row(s) affected)
```

To list all system views in 3-column layout, use the following query.

```
;WITH cteTableList AS (        SELECT CONCAT(SCHEMA_NAME(schema_id), '.', name)           AS TableName,
  (( ROW_NUMBER() OVER( ORDER BY CONCAT(SCHEMA_NAME(schema_id),'.', name)) ) % 3)    AS Remainder,
  (( ROW_NUMBER() OVER( ORDER BY CONCAT(SCHEMA_NAME(schema_id),'.', name)) – 1 )/ 3) AS Quotient
              FROM AdventureWorks2012.sys.system_views),
CTE AS (SELECT TableName, CASE WHEN Remainder=0 THEN 3 ELSE Remainder END AS Remainder, Quotient
        FROM cteTableList)
SELECT   MAX(CASE WHEN Remainder = 1 THEN TableName END),
         MAX(CASE WHEN Remainder = 2 THEN TableName END),
         MAX(CASE WHEN Remainder = 3 THEN TableName END)
FROM  CTE GROUP  BY Quotient ORDER  BY Quotient;   -- Partial results
```

sys.change_tracking_databases	sys.change_tracking_tables	sys.check_constraints
sys.column_store_dictionaries	sys.column_store_row_groups	sys.column_store_segments
sys.column_type_usages	sys.column_xml_schema_collection_usages	sys.columns
sys.computed_columns	sys.configurations	sys.conversation_endpoints
sys.conversation_groups	sys.conversation_priorities	sys.credentials
sys.crypt_properties	sys.cryptographic_providers	sys.data_spaces
sys.database_audit_specification_details	sys.database_audit_specifications	sys.database_files
sys.database_filestream_options	sys.database_mirroring	sys.database_mirroring_endpoints
sys.database_mirroring_witnesses	sys.database_permissions	sys.database_principals
sys.database_recovery_status	sys.database_role_members	sys.databases

---

FREE Downloads
SQL Server Dynamic Management Views Poster
http://www.quest.com/techbrief/sql-server-dynamic-management-views-poster813218.aspx

SQL Server 2008 System Views Map
http://www.microsoft.com/en-us/download/details.aspx?id=9301

CHAPTER 10: The Art of Database Design

List of master database System Functions
Some are internal and undocumented functions. Some are used for special tasks: fn_listextendedproperty, fn_trace_getinfo, fn_my_permissions & fn_varbintohexstr. The dm_ prefix indicates **Dynamic Management Function** (DMF) such as dm_exec_sql_text.

```
SELECT * FROM sys.all_objects where is_ms_shipped=1
           AND    ( TYPE_DESC = 'SQL_TABLE_VALUED_FUNCTION'          OR
                    TYPE_DESC = 'SQL_SCALAR_FUNCTION'                OR
                    TYPE_DESC = 'SQL_INLINE_TABLE_VALUED_FUNCTION')
ORDER BY name;  -- (96 row(s) affected)
```

List of System Tables Prior to SQL Server 2005
Some of the system tables were updatable in SQL Server 2000 and previous versions. SS 2005 introduced system views which are not updatable and barred access to system tables.

CHAPTER 10: The Art of Database Design

Other Methods of Metadata Access

Graphical Dependency Information

Object dependencies can be launched by a right click on the object.

The dependency chart for the uspGetBillOfMaterials stored procedure.

CHAPTER 10: The Art of Database Design

Scripting GUI Object Change

Most of the dialog panels have scripting options. In fact we don't even have to perform the action, we can just script it and execute the script in a (new) connection. The advantage of this approach that the generated script can be modified and saved for future use or reference. We start an index change with right click and properties.

The generated script.

```
USE [AdventureWorks2012]
GO
SET ANSI_PADDING ON
GO
CREATE UNIQUE NONCLUSTERED INDEX [AK_Product_Name] ON [Production].[Product] (
[Name] ASC )
INCLUDE (      [ProductNumber]) WITH (PAD_INDEX = OFF, STATISTICS_NORECOMPUTE = OFF,
SORT_IN_TEMPDB = OFF,
IGNORE_DUP_KEY = OFF, DROP_EXISTING = ON, ONLINE = OFF, ALLOW_ROW_LOCKS = ON,
ALLOW_PAGE_LOCKS = ON, FILLFACTOR = 85) ON [PRIMARY]
GO
```

The sp_helpdb System Procedure

The sp_helpdb system procedure returns information on all or a specified database.

```
EXEC sp_helpdb;
-- Partial results
```

| Accounting | 3.88 MB | HPESTAR\Owner | 17 | May 24 2012 | Status=ONLINE, Updateability=READ_WRITE, UserAccess=MULTI_USER, Recovery=FULL, Version=706, Collation=SQL_Latin1_General_CP1_CI_AS, SQLSortOrder=52, IsAutoCreateStatistics, IsAutoUpdateStatistics, IsFullTextEnabled | 110 |
| AdventureWorks | 213.94 MB | HPESTAR\Owner | 16 | May 24 2012 | Status=ONLINE, Updateability=READ_WRITE, UserAccess=MULTI_USER, Recovery=SIMPLE, Version=706, Collation=SQL_Latin1_General_CP1_CI_AS, SQLSortOrder=52, IsAnsiNullsEnabled, IsAnsiPaddingEnabled, IsAnsiWarningsEnabled, IsArithmeticAbortEnabled, IsAutoCreateStatistics, IsAutoUpdateStatistics, IsFullTextEnabled, IsNullConcat, IsQuotedIdentifiersEnabled, IsRecursiveTriggersEnabled | 90 |

```
EXEC sp_helpdb AdventureWorks2012;
```

name	db_size	owner	dbid	created	status	compatibility_level
AdventureWorks2012	3118.38 MB	sa	7	May 19 2012	Status=ONLINE, Updateability=READ_WRITE, UserAccess=MULTI_USER, Recovery=SIMPLE, Version=706, Collation=SQL_Latin1_General_CP1_CI_AS, SQLSortOrder=52, IsAnsiNullsEnabled, IsAnsiPaddingEnabled, IsAnsiWarningsEnabled, IsArithmeticAbortEnabled, IsAutoCreateStatistics, IsAutoUpdateStatistics, IsFullTextEnabled, IsNullConcat, IsQuotedIdentifiersEnabled	110

The sp_help and sp_helptext System Procedures

The sp_help and sp_helptext provides database metadata in various formats including multiple result sets.

```
EXEC sp_help 'Production.ProductPhoto'
```

Name	Own...	Type	Created_datetime
ProductPhoto	dbo	user table	2012-03-14 13:14:19.490

Column_name	Type	Comput...	Len...	Pr...	Sc...	Nulla...	TrimTrailingB
ProductPhotoID	int	no	4	10	0	no	(n/a)
ThumbNailPhoto	varbinary	no	-1			yes	no
ThumbnailPhotoFileName	nvarchar	no	100			yes	(n/a)
LargePhoto	varbinary	no	-1			yes	no
LargePhotoFileName	nvarchar	no	100			yes	(n/a)

Identity	Se...	Increm...	Not For Replicat...
ProductPhotoID	1	1	0

RowGuidCol
No rowguidcol column defined.

Data_located_on_filegr...
PRIMARY

index_name	index_description	index_key
PK_ProductPhoto_ProductPhotoID	clustered, unique, primary key located on PRIMARY	ProductPh

constraint_type	constraint_name	delete_acti...	update_act...
DEFAULT on column ModifiedDate	DF_ProductPhoto_ModifiedDate	(n/a)	(n/a)
PRIMARY KEY (clustered)	PK_ProductPhoto_ProductPh...	(n/a)	(n/a)

Table is referenced by foreign key
AdventureWorks2012.Production.ProductProductPhot...

CHAPTER 10: The Art of Database Design

Other Methods of Metadata Access

Using sp_helptext for Obtaining Definition
sp_helptext works only for some database objects. Table definition cannot be obtained by command, any command.

```
EXEC sp_helptext 'dbo.uspLogError';   -- stored procedure

EXEC sp_helptext 'Sales.vSalesPerson'; -- view
```

Results:

	Text
1	
2	-- uspLogError logs error information in the Error...
3	-- error that caused execution to jump to the CAT...
4	-- TRY...CATCH construct. This should be execut...
5	-- of a CATCH block otherwise it will return without...
6	-- information.
7	CREATE PROCEDURE [dbo].[uspLogError]
8	@ErrorLogID [int] = 0 OUTPUT -- contains the ...
9	AS -- by uspLogError in the Er...
10	BEGIN
11	SET NOCOUNT ON;

	Text
1	
2	CREATE VIEW [Sales].[vSalesPerson]
3	AS
4	SELECT
5	s.[BusinessEntityID]
6	,p.[Title]
7	,p.[FirstName]
8	,p.[MiddleName]
9	,p.[LastName]
10	,p.[Suffix]
11	,e.[JobTitle]

CHAPTER 10: The Art of Database Design

Listing All CHECK Constraints in a Database

We can use INFORMATION_SCHEMA views to perform this task.

```
USE AdventureWorks2012;
GO


SELECT          cc.CONSTRAINT_SCHEMA                AS SCHEMA_NAME,
                TABLE_NAME,
                COLUMN_NAME,
                CHECK_CLAUSE,
                cc.CONSTRAINT_NAME
FROM    INFORMATION_SCHEMA.CHECK_CONSTRAINTS cc
            INNER JOIN INFORMATION_SCHEMA.CONSTRAINT_COLUMN_USAGE c
                ON cc.CONSTRAINT_NAME = c.CONSTRAINT_NAME
ORDER BY        SCHEMA_NAME,
                TABLE_NAME,
                COLUMN_NAME;
-- (105 row(s) affected) - Partial results.
```

SCHEMA_NAME	TABLE_NAME	COLUMN_NAME	CHECK_CLAUSE	CONSTRAINT_NAME
HumanResources	Employee	BirthDate	([BirthDate]>='1930-01-01' AND [BirthDate]<=dateadd(year,(-18),getdate()))	CK_Employee_BirthDate
HumanResources	Employee	Gender	(upper([Gender])='F' OR upper([Gender])='M')	CK_Employee_Gender
HumanResources	Employee	HireDate	([HireDate]>='1996-07-01' AND [HireDate]<=dateadd(day,(1),getdate()))	CK_Employee_HireDate
HumanResources	Employee	MaritalStatus	(upper([MaritalStatus])='S' OR upper([MaritalStatus])='M')	CK_Employee_MaritalStatus
HumanResources	Employee	SickLeaveHours	([SickLeaveHours]>=(0) AND [SickLeaveHours]<=(120))	CK_Employee_SickLeaveHours
HumanResources	Employee	VacationHours	([VacationHours]>=(-40) AND [VacationHours]<=(240))	CK_Employee_VacationHours
HumanResources	EmployeeDepartmentHistory	EndDate	([EndDate]>=[StartDate] OR [EndDate] IS NULL)	CK_EmployeeDepartmentHistory_EndDate
HumanResources	EmployeeDepartmentHistory	StartDate	([EndDate]>=[StartDate] OR [EndDate] IS NULL)	CK_EmployeeDepartmentHistory_EndDate
HumanResources	EmployeePayHistory	PayFrequency	([PayFrequency]=(2) OR [PayFrequency]=(1))	CK_EmployeePayHistory_PayFrequency
HumanResources	EmployeePayHistory	Rate	([Rate]>=(6.50) AND [Rate]<=(200.00))	CK_EmployeePayHistory_Rate
Person	Person	EmailPromotion	([EmailPromotion]>=(0) AND [EmailPromotion]<=(2))	CK_Person_EmailPromotion

CHAPTER 10: The Art of Database Design

Other Methods of Metadata Access

Creating a UDF CHECK Constraint

UDF CHECK constraint relies on a user-defined function for logic rather than the simple constraint expression. Demonstration script creates a test table with UDF check constraint.

WARNING: UDF CHECK constraint may present performance issues.

```sql
USE tempdb;
SELECT TOP 10  P.BusinessEntityID, FirstName, LastName,        -- Create test table
            Email=convert(varchar(64),EmailAddress)
INTO Person FROM AdventureWorks2012.Person.Person P
            INNER JOIN AdventureWorks2012.Person.EmailAddress E
                ON E.BusinessEntityID = P.BusinessEntityID;
GO
-- Create user-defined function (UDF) for checking
CREATE FUNCTION ufnEmailValidityCheck (@Email varchar(64))  RETURNS BIT  AS
BEGIN
IF EXISTS(SELECT 1 WHERE
    CHARINDEX('.',@Email,CHARINDEX('@',@Email))-CHARINDEX('@',@Email)>1
    AND CHARINDEX('.',REVERSE(LTRIM(RTRIM(@Email)))) > 2
    AND CHARINDEX('@',LTRIM(@Email)) > 2) RETURN(1)
RETURN (0)
END;
GO
 -- Create UDF check constraint
ALTER TABLE [dbo].[Person]  WITH CHECK
ADD CONSTRAINT [EmailCheck] CHECK (   dbo.ufnEmailValidityCheck (Email) = 1);
GO
 -- SQL check constraint violated missing . (period)
INSERT Person (BusinessEntityID, FirstName, LastName, Email)
VALUES (100000, 'Elvis', 'Presley', 'elvispresley@thekingcom');
/*  Msg 547, Level 16, State 0, Line 5
The INSERT statement conflicted with the CHECK constraint "EmailCheck". The conflict occurred
in database "tempdb", table "dbo.Person", column 'Email'.*/
 -- SQL check constraint met
INSERT Person (BusinessEntityID, FirstName, LastName, Email)
VALUES (100000, 'Elvis', 'Presley', 'elvispresley@theking.com');
GO   -- (1 row(s) affected)
 SELECT * FROM Person ORDER BY Email;  -- Partial results.
```

BusinessEntityID	FirstName	LastName	Email
8	Diane	Margheim	diane1@adventure-works.com
7	Dylan	Miller	dylan0@adventure-works.com
100000	Elvis	Presley	elvispresley@theking.com

CHAPTER 10: The Art of Database Design

List All DEFAULT Constraint Definitions
We can use system views to carry out the task.

```
USE AdventureWorks2012;

SELECT
    SCHEMA_NAME(o.schema_id)    AS SchemaName,
    o.name                      AS TableName,
    c.name                      AS ColumnName,
    d.definition                AS DefaultDefinition,
    d.name                      AS ConstraintName
FROM sys.default_constraints d
    INNER JOIN sys.columns c
        ON d.parent_object_id = c.object_id
        AND d.parent_column_id = c.column_id
    INNER JOIN sys.objects o
        ON o.object_id = c.object_id
ORDER BY SchemaName, TableName, ColumnName;
-- (152 row(s) affected) - Partial results.
```

SchemaName	TableName	ColumnName	DefaultDefinition	ConstraintName
dbo	AWBuildVersion	ModifiedDate	(getdate())	DF_AWBuildVersion_ModifiedDate
dbo	ErrorLog	ErrorTime	(getdate())	DF_ErrorLog_ErrorTime
HumanResources	Department	ModifiedDate	(getdate())	DF_Department_ModifiedDate
HumanResources	Employee	CurrentFlag	((1))	DF_Employee_CurrentFlag
HumanResources	Employee	ModifiedDate	(getdate())	DF_Employee_ModifiedDate
HumanResources	Employee	rowguid	(newid())	DF_Employee_rowguid
HumanResources	Employee	SalariedFlag	((1))	DF_Employee_SalariedFlag
HumanResources	Employee	SickLeaveHours	((0))	DF_Employee_SickLeaveHours
HumanResources	Employee	VacationHours	((0))	DF_Employee_VacationHours
HumanResources	EmployeeDepartmentHistory	ModifiedDate	(getdate())	DF_EmployeeDepartmentHistory_ModifiedDate
HumanResources	EmployeePayHistory	ModifiedDate	(getdate())	DF_EmployeePayHistory_ModifiedDate
HumanResources	JobCandidate	ModifiedDate	(getdate())	DF_JobCandidate_ModifiedDate
HumanResources	Shift	ModifiedDate	(getdate())	DF_Shift_ModifiedDate
Person	Address	ModifiedDate	(getdate())	DF_Address_ModifiedDate
Person	Address	rowguid	(newid())	DF_Address_rowguid
Person	AddressType	ModifiedDate	(getdate())	DF_AddressType_ModifiedDate
Person	AddressType	rowguid	(newid())	DF_AddressType_rowguid
Person	BusinessEntity	ModifiedDate	(getdate())	DF_BusinessEntity_ModifiedDate
Person	BusinessEntity	rowguid	(newid())	DF_BusinessEntity_rowguid
Person	BusinessEntityAddress	ModifiedDate	(getdate())	DF_BusinessEntityAddress_ModifiedDate
Person	BusinessEntityAddress	rowguid	(newid())	DF_BusinessEntityAddress_rowguid
Person	BusinessEntityContact	ModifiedDate	(getdate())	DF_BusinessEntityContact_ModifiedDate
Person	BusinessEntityContact	rowguid	(newid())	DF_BusinessEntityContact_rowguid
Person	ContactType	ModifiedDate	(getdate())	DF_ContactType_ModifiedDate
Person	CountryRegion	ModifiedDate	(getdate())	DF_CountryRegion_ModifiedDate

Database Object-Definition from sys.sql_modules System View

The sys.sql_modules systems view contains definition for stored procedures, triggers, functions and views. Prior to SQL Server 2005 the sys.syscomments table was used to obtain object definition source code.

USE AdventureWorks2012;
GO

SELECT object_id, LEFT(definition,64) AS DefinitionPrefix
FROM sys.SQL_Modules ORDER BY object_id;
GO
-- (52 row(s) affected) - Partial results.

object_id	DefinitionPrefix
7671075	CREATE VIEW [Sales].[vStoreWithContacts] AS SELECT s.[
23671132	CREATE VIEW [Sales].[vStoreWithAddresses] AS SELECT s.
39671189	CREATE VIEW [Purchasing].[vVendorWithContacts] AS SELECT
55671246	CREATE VIEW [Purchasing].[vVendorWithAddresses] AS SELECT
71671303	CREATE FUNCTION [dbo].[ufnGetAccountingStartDate]() RETURNS [
87671360	CREATE FUNCTION [dbo].[ufnGetAccountingEndDate]() RETURNS [da
103671417	CREATE FUNCTION [dbo].[ufnGetContactInformation](@PersonID int
119671474	CREATE FUNCTION [dbo].[ufnGetProductDealerPrice](@ProductI
135671531	CREATE FUNCTION [dbo].[ufnGetProductListPrice](@ProductID [int
151671588	CREATE FUNCTION [dbo].[ufnGetProductStandardCost](@ProductID [

CHAPTER 10: The Art of Database Design

Retrieving the Full Definition of a Stored Procedure

```sql
SELECT          schema_name(schema_id)       AS SchemaName,
                object_Name(m.object_ID)     AS ObjectName,
                definition                   AS ObjectDefinition
FROM   sys.SQL_Modules m
  INNER JOIN sys.objects o      ON m.object_id=o.object_id
WHERE  object_Name(m.object_ID) = 'uspGetBillOfMaterials'
GO
```

SchemaName	ObjectName	ObjectDefinition
dbo	uspGetBillOfMaterials	CREATE PROCEDURE [dbo].[uspGetBillOfMaterials]

```sql
    @StartProductID [int],
    @CheckDate [datetime]
AS
BEGIN
  SET NOCOUNT ON;

  -- Use recursive query to generate a multi-level Bill of Material (i.e. all level 1
  -- components of a level 0 assembly, all level 2 components of a level 1 assembly)
  -- The CheckDate eliminates any components that are no longer used in the product on this date.
  WITH [BOM_cte]([ProductAssemblyID], [ComponentID], [ComponentDesc], [PerAssemblyQty], [StandardCost], [ListPrice],
[BOMLevel], [RecursionLevel]) -- CTE name and columns
    AS (
      SELECT b.[ProductAssemblyID], b.[ComponentID], p.[Name], b.[PerAssemblyQty], p.[StandardCost], p.[ListPrice], b.[BOMLevel],
0 -- Get the initial list of components for the bike assembly
      FROM [Production].[BillOfMaterials] b
        INNER JOIN [Production].[Product] p
        ON b.[ComponentID] = p.[ProductID]
      WHERE b.[ProductAssemblyID] = @StartProductID
        AND @CheckDate >= b.[StartDate]
        AND @CheckDate <= ISNULL(b.[EndDate], @CheckDate)
      UNION ALL
      SELECT b.[ProductAssemblyID], b.[ComponentID], p.[Name], b.[PerAssemblyQty], p.[StandardCost], p.[ListPrice], b.[BOMLevel],
[RecursionLevel] + 1 -- Join recursive member to anchor
      FROM [BOM_cte] cte
        INNER JOIN [Production].[BillOfMaterials] b
        ON b.[ProductAssemblyID] = cte.[ComponentID]
        INNER JOIN [Production].[Product] p
        ON b.[ComponentID] = p.[ProductID]
      WHERE @CheckDate >= b.[StartDate]
        AND @CheckDate <= ISNULL(b.[EndDate], @CheckDate)
    )
  -- Outer select from the CTE
  SELECT b.[ProductAssemblyID], b.[ComponentID], b.[ComponentDesc], SUM(b.[PerAssemblyQty]) AS [TotalQuantity] ,
b.[StandardCost], b.[ListPrice], b.[BOMLevel], b.[RecursionLevel]
  FROM [BOM_cte] b
  GROUP BY b.[ComponentID], b.[ComponentDesc], b.[ProductAssemblyID], b.[BOMLevel], b.[RecursionLevel], b.[StandardCost],
b.[ListPrice]
  ORDER BY b.[BOMLevel], b.[ProductAssemblyID], b.[ComponentID]     OPTION (MAXRECURSION 25)
END;
```

Snowflake Schema Data Warehouse Design

If the following DW design were Star Schema, the DimProduct would be a flat dimension including DimProductSubcategory and DimProductCategory. In Snowflake Schema the dimension tables follow 3NF relational design.

Object Explorer Table Editor

A table editor is available for directly editing data in a table. It is designed for limited use. First we create a test table, Department, then we launch the editor.

We added row 17 just by typing it in, then investigated the right click drop-down menu.

CHAPTER 10: The Art of Database Design

All Tables Row Count without the COUNT() Function
Here is quick way to get a row count, not exact like COUNT(*) but really fast.

```sql
USE AdventureWorks2012;
SELECT  CONCAT(SCHEMA_NAME(schema_id),'.',o.name )        AS TableName,
        FORMAT(max(i.rows),'###,###,###')                 AS Rows
FROM    sys.sysobjects o       INNER JOIN sys.sysindexes i    ON o.id = i.id
    INNER JOIN sys.objects oo      ON o.id = oo.object_id
WHERE   xtype = 'u'         AND OBJECTPROPERTY(o.id,N'IsUserTable') = 1
GROUP BY schema_id, o.name ORDER BY max(i.rows) DESC, TableName;
GO -- (71 row(s) affected)  -- Partial results.
```

TableName	Rows
Sales.SalesOrderDetail	121,317
Production.TransactionHistory	113,443
Production.TransactionHistoryArchive	89,253
Production.WorkOrder	72,591
Production.WorkOrderRouting	67,131
Sales.SalesOrderHeader	31,465

SQL Server Default Trace
Default trace can be used to trace basic database object history such as CREATE, DROP & ALTER.

```sql
EXEC sp_configure 'default trace enabled'; -- Check if default trace is enabled
EXEC sp_configure 'default trace enabled', 1; -- Enable default trace
RECONFIGURE;     SELECT * FROM sys.traces; -- Trace file information
-- Current default trace rollover file
DECLARE @Path varchar(256) = (SELECT CONVERT(varchar(256),VALUE )
        FROM  ::fn_trace_getinfo(0) WHERE  property = 2 );   SELECT @Path;
-- C:\Program Files\Microsoft SQL Server\MSSQL10.SQL2008\MSSQL\Log\log_122.trc
SELECT loginname AS LoginName,  loginsid, spid,  -- Query the default trace rollover file
    hostname AS HostName, applicationname, servername AS ServerName,
    databasename AS DatabaseName,  objectName, e.category_id,
    cat.name AS CategoryName, textdata, starttime,   e.name  AS EventName
FROM ::fn_trace_gettable(@Path, 0)
    INNER JOIN sys.trace_events e  ON eventclass = trace_event_id
    INNER JOIN sys.trace_categories AS cat ON e.category_id = cat.category_id
WHERE  databasename = 'AdventureWorks2008' AND objectname IS NULL
    AND e.name ='Object:Altered';
/* LoginName    loginsid    spid HostName    applicationname   ServerName  DatabaseName
objectName  category_id CategoryName    textdata   starttime   EventName
HPESTAR\SQLAdmin   0x010500000000000515000000083A66141640B5ED2C6FD4509E9030000  54
HPESTAR    Microsoft SQL Server Management Studio   HPESTAR\SQL2008   AdventureWorks2008
NULL  5    Objects     NULL 2017-03-27 05:49:05.043 Object:Altered */
```

CHAPTER 10: The Art of Database Design

Listing All Columns with PK, FK & IDENTITY Properties

There are various ways for retrieving column properties including the COLUMNPROPERTY() function.

```sql
USE AdventureWorks2012;

SELECT c.TABLE_CATALOG                                              AS DatabaseName,
    c.TABLE_SCHEMA                                                  AS SchemaName,
    c.TABLE_NAME                                                    AS TableName,
    c.COLUMN_NAME                                                   AS ColumnName,
    Columnproperty(Object_id(CONCAT(c.TABLE_SCHEMA,'.',c.TABLE_NAME)),
                c.COLUMN_NAME, 'ISIDENTITY')                        AS IsIdentity,
    CASE
      WHEN CONSTRAINT_NAME IN (SELECT NAME
              FROM   sys.objects
              WHERE  TYPE = 'PK') THEN 1
      ELSE 0   END                                                  AS IsPrimaryKey,
    CASE
      WHEN CONSTRAINT_NAME IN (SELECT NAME
              FROM   sys.objects
              WHERE  TYPE = 'F') THEN 1
      ELSE 0   END                                                  AS IsForeignKey
FROM   INFORMATION_SCHEMA.TABLES t
    INNER JOIN INFORMATION_SCHEMA.COLUMNS c
        ON c.TABLE_CATALOG = t.TABLE_CATALOG
        AND c.TABLE_SCHEMA = t.TABLE_SCHEMA
        AND c.TABLE_NAME = t.TABLE_NAME
    LEFT JOIN INFORMATION_SCHEMA.KEY_COLUMN_USAGE u
        ON c.TABLE_CATALOG = u.TABLE_CATALOG
        AND c.TABLE_SCHEMA = u.TABLE_SCHEMA
        AND c.TABLE_NAME = u.TABLE_NAME
        AND c.COLUMN_NAME = u.COLUMN_NAME
WHERE  TABLE_TYPE = 'BASE TABLE'
ORDER  BY SchemaName,   TableName,   c.ORDINAL_POSITION;
GO
-- (534 row(s) affected) - Partial results.
```

DatabaseName	SchemaName	TableName	ColumnName	IsIdentity	IsPrimaryKey	IsForeignKey
AdventureWorks2012	Person	EmailAddress	BusinessEntityID	0	0	1
AdventureWorks2012	Person	EmailAddress	BusinessEntityID	0	1	0
AdventureWorks2012	Person	EmailAddress	EmailAddressID	1	1	0
AdventureWorks2012	Person	EmailAddress	EmailAddress	0	0	0

The Collation Column Property & the COLLATE Clause

Each text column requires the collation property. The server & databases also have collation property as defaults only. When the database collation is changed, the actual column collations remain the same. New table columns will inherit the database default collation. New databases inherit the server collation. A column collation can be changed with ALTER TABLE. To change all text collations in a database may prove to be a big task.

```
USE tempdb;

SELECT * INTO Product FROM AdventureWorks2012.Production.Product;
-- (504 row(s) affected)

ALTER TABLE Product ALTER COLUMN Name nvarchar(50)
            COLLATE SQL_Latin1_General_CP1_CS_AS null;
-- Command(s) completed successfully.
```

Text operations with different collations result in error.

```
SELECT COUNT(*) FROM Product p
            INNER JOIN AdventureWorks2012.Production.Product aw12
                ON p.Name = aw12.Name;
GO
```

```
/*  Msg 468, Level 16, State 9, Line 3
Cannot resolve the collation conflict between "SQL_Latin1_General_CP1_CI_AS" and
"SQL_Latin1_General_CP1_CS_AS" in the equal to operation.    */
```

We can correct it in the query with the COLLATE clause. We can use a specific collation on one side of the expression, or the easy to remember DATABASE_DEFAULT.

```
SELECT COUNT(*) FROM Product p
            INNER JOIN AdventureWorks2012.Production.Product aw12
                ON p.Name = aw12.Name COLLATE DATABASE_DEFAULT;
-- 504
```

Restoring the original column collation.

```
ALTER TABLE Product alter column ProductName varchar(40)
            COLLATE SQL_Latin1_General_CP1_CI_AS null;
```

CHAPTER 10: The Art of Database Design

Listing All Database & Server Collations

Database collations can be enumerated by a query, while there is special function for server collations. QUOTENAME() function forms proper object names.

```
USE AdventureWorks2012;
GO
```

```
SELECT CONCAT(QUOTENAME(s.name), '.', QUOTENAME(t.name),
              '.', QUOTENAME(c.name))                    AS ColumnName,
       c.collation_name                                  AS Collation
FROM sys.schemas s
  INNER JOIN sys.tables t
    ON t.schema_id = s.schema_id
  INNER JOIN sys.columns c
    ON c.object_id = t.object_id
WHERE collation_name is not null
ORDER BY ColumnName;
-- (104 row(s) affected) - Partial results.
```

ColumnName	Collation
[HumanResources].[Employee].[NationalIDNumber]	SQL_Latin1_General_CP1_CI_AS
[HumanResources].[Shift].[Name]	SQL_Latin1_General_CP1_CI_AS
[Person].[Address].[AddressLine1]	SQL_Latin1_General_CP1_CI_AS
[Person].[Address].[AddressLine2]	SQL_Latin1_General_CP1_CI_AS

All server collations can be obtained from a table-valued system function.

```
use master;
select  name                                   AS Name,
        COLLATIONPROPERTY(name, 'CodePage')    AS CodePage,
        LEFT(description,80)                   AS Description
from sys.fn_HelpCollations() order by Name;
-- (3885 row(s) affected) - Partial results;
```

Name	CodePage	Description
Modern_Spanish_CS_AS_KS_WS	1252	Modern-Spanish, case-sensitive, accent-sensitive, kanatype-sensitive, width-sens
Modern_Spanish_CS_AS_WS	1252	Modern-Spanish, case-sensitive, accent-sensitive, kanatype-insensitive, width-se
Mohawk_100_BIN	1252	Mohawk-100, binary sort
Mohawk_100_BIN2	1252	Mohawk-100, binary code point comparison sort
Mohawk_100_CI_AI	1252	Mohawk-100, case-insensitive, accent-insensitive, kanatype-insensitive, width-in

CHAPTER 10: The Art of Database Design

Designing Table for Multi-Language Support with UNICODE

Let's script the DimProductSubcategory table from AdventureWorks2012 to demonstrate multi-language support. nvarchar data type is for UNICODE data with each character 2 bytes. It has sufficient capacity to hold even Chinese, Japanese and Korean letters among others.

```sql
CREATE TABLE dbo.DimProductSubcategory(
        ProductSubcategoryKey int IDENTITY(1,1) NOT NULL,
        ProductSubcategoryAlternateKey int NULL,
        EnglishProductSubcategoryName nvarchar(50) NOT NULL,
        SpanishProductSubcategoryName nvarchar(50) NOT NULL,
        FrenchProductSubcategoryName nvarchar(50) NOT NULL,
        ProductCategoryKey int NULL,
        CONSTRAINT PK_DimProductSubcategory_ProductSubcategoryKey
              PRIMARY KEY CLUSTERED (ProductSubcategoryKey ASC),
        CONSTRAINT AK_DimProductSubcategory_ProductSubcategoryAlternateKey
              UNIQUE NONCLUSTERED (ProductSubcategoryAlternateKey ASC ) );
```

Since there are no COLLATE clauses for the English, Spanish & French names, the collation is the database default. The DATABASEPROPERTYEX() function can be used to retrieve it.

```sql
SELECT DATABASEPROPERTYEX('AdventureWorksDW2012', 'Collation');
-- SQL_Latin1_General_CP1_CI_AS
```

To get a Spanish language sort, we have to add the COLLATE clause to the ORDER BY clause.

```sql
SELECT * FROM DimProductSubcategory
ORDER BY SpanishProductSubcategoryName COLLATE Modern_Spanish_CI_AS_WS;
-- (37 row(s) affected) - Partial results.
```

ProductSubcategoryKey	ProductSubcategoryAlternateKey	EnglishProductSubcategoryName	SpanishProductSubcategoryName	FrenchProductSubcategoryName	ProductCategoryKey
4	4	Handlebars	Barra	Barre d'appui	2
2	2	Road Bikes	Bicicleta de carretera	Vélo de route	1
1	1	Mountain Bikes	Bicicleta de montaña	VTT	1
3	3	Touring Bikes	Bicicleta de paseo	Vélo de randonnée	1
8	8	Cranksets	Bielas	Pédalier	2
36	36	Pumps	Bomba	Pompe	4

Find all collations for a culture.

```sql
SELECT name, description = LEFT(description, 60) FROM   sys.fn_HelpCollations()
WHERE  name LIKE '%german%'  ORDER BY name;   -- (52 row(s) affected)
```

CHAPTER 10: The Art of Database Design

CHAPTER 11: New Programming Features in SS 2012 & 2014

New Programming Features in SS 2014

In-Memory OLTP (In-Memory Optimization)

BOL reference page: http://msdn.microsoft.com/en-us/library/dn133186(v=sql.120).aspx

Sample download: http://msftdbprodsamples.codeplex.com/releases/view/114491

SQL Server 2014 RTM In-Memory OLTP Sample creates a few in-memory tables with the _inmem suffix in AdventureWorks2012. Following is a performance comparison.

```
DBCC DROPCLEANBUFFERS;
SET STATISTICS IO ON; SET STATISTICS TIME ON;
SELECT OrderQty, Freq=count(*) from Sales.SalesOrderDetail_inmem GROUP BY OrderQty
ORDER BY Freq DESC;
SET STATISTICS TIME OFF; SET STATISTICS IO OFF;
```

```
/* Table 'Worktable'. Scan count 0, logical reads 0, physical reads 0, read-ahead
reads 0, lob logical reads 0, lob physical reads 0, lob read-ahead reads 0.
Table 'Workfile'. Scan count 0, logical reads 0, physical reads 0, read-ahead
reads 0, lob logical reads 0, lob physical reads 0, lob read-ahead reads 0.

 SQL Server Execution Times:   CPU time = 47 ms,  elapsed time = 54 ms. */
```

```
DBCC DROPCLEANBUFFERS;
SET STATISTICS IO ON; SET STATISTICS TIME ON;
SELECT OrderQty, Freq=count(*) from Sales.SalesOrderDetail GROUP BY OrderQty
ORDER BY Freq DESC;
SET STATISTICS TIME OFF; SET STATISTICS IO OFF;
```

```
/* Table 'Worktable'. Scan count 0, logical reads 0, physical reads 0, read-ahead
reads 0, lob logical reads 0, lob physical reads 0, lob read-ahead reads 0.
Table 'Workfile'. Scan count 0, logical reads 0, physical reads 0, read-ahead
reads 0, lob logical reads 0, lob physical reads 0, lob read-ahead reads 0.
Table 'SalesOrderDetail'. Scan count 1, logical reads 1246, physical reads 3,
read-ahead reads 1277, lob logical reads 0, lob physical reads 0, lob read-ahead
reads 0.

 SQL Server Execution Times:   CPU time = 78 ms,  elapsed time = 204 ms. */
```

Inline Specification Of Indexes For Disk-Based Tables

The default index for PRIMARY KEY is CLUSTERED, for UNIQUE KEY NONCLUSTERED. In the example below, we place the CLUSTERED index inline on a non-key column.

```
CREATE TABLE Celebrity (
        CelebrityID INT IDENTITY(1,1) PRIMARY KEY NONCLUSTERED,
        Name varchar(70) NOT NULL UNIQUE NONCLUSTERED,
        BirthDate DATE NOT NULL INDEX idxName CLUSTERED,
        ModifiedDate datetime2 default (sysdatetime())
);
-- Command(s) completed successfully.
```

Improved SELECT ... INTO Statement

Comparing SQL Server 2014 vs. SQL Server 2012 we notice performance improvement in the new version.

```
USE tempdb;
GO
DBCC DROPCLEANBUFFERS;
SET STATISTICS IO ON; SET STATISTICS TIME ON;
SELECT * INTO SOD
FROM AdventureWorks2012.Sales.SalesOrderDetail;
SET STATISTICS TIME OFF; SET STATISTICS IO OFF;
GO
DROP TABLE SOD;
/*
SQL Server 2014

Table 'SalesOrderDetail'. Scan count 5, logical reads 1371, physical reads 3, read-ahead reads 1277, lob logical reads 0, lob physical reads 0, lob read-ahead reads 0.

SQL Server Execution Times:  CPU time = 218 ms,  elapsed time = 169 ms.

(121317 row(s) affected)

SQL Server 2012

SQL Server Execution Times:  CPU time = 265 ms,  elapsed time = 378 ms.

*/
```

New Programming Features in SS 2012

PARSE() Function

T-SQL script to demonstrate the use of the PARSE() function. The culture parameter provides support for languages & countries beyond the CONVERT() function available in past versions.

```sql
-- PARSE() returns the result of expression translated to requested data type - String to datetime
SELECT PARSE('SAT, 13 December 2014' AS datetime USING 'en-US') AS [Date&Time];
-- 2014-12-13 00:00:00.000

SELECT PARSE('Saturday, 13 December 2014' AS datetime USING 'en-US') AS [Date&Time];
-- 2014-12-13 00:00:00.000

SELECT PARSE('Saturday 13 December 2014' AS datetime USING 'en-US') AS [Date&Time];
-- 2014-12-13 00:00:00.000

SELECT PARSE('Saturday December 13 2014' AS datetime USING 'en-US') AS [Date&Time];
-- 2014-12-13 00:00:00.000

SELECT PARSE('Saturday December 13, 2014' AS datetime USING 'en-US') AS [Date&Time];
-- 2014-12-13 00:00:00.000

-- Inconsistent string date
SELECT PARSE('Monday, 13 December 2014' AS datetime USING 'en-US') AS [Date&Time];
/*Msg 9819, Level 16, State 1, Line 1
Error converting string value 'Monday, 13 December 2014' into data type datetime using culture 'en-US'*/

-- German culture
SELECT PARSE('Samstag December 13, 2014' AS datetime USING 'DE') AS [Date&Time];
-- 2014-12-13 00:00:00.000

-- Spanish
SELECT PARSE('Sábado December 13, 2014' AS datetime USING 'ES') AS [Date&Time];
-- 2014-12-13 00:00:00.000

-- Hungarian
SELECT PARSE('Szombat December 13, 2014' AS datetime USING 'HU') AS [Date&Time];
-- 2014-12-13 00:00:00.000

SELECT PARSE('Cumartesi December 13, 2014' AS datetime USING 'TR') AS [Date&Time];  -- Turkish
```

TRY_CONVERT() Function

PARSE() Function Usage for Currency Conversion

```
-- German culture - Euro currency conversion
SELECT PARSE('€9999,95' AS money USING 'DE') AS Currency;
-- 9999.95


SELECT PARSE('€9999,95' AS money USING 'de-DE') AS Currency;
-- 9999.95

-- Italian culture - Euro currency conversion
SELECT PARSE('€9999,95' AS money USING 'IT') AS Currency;
-- 9999.95

-- Netherland culture - Euro currency conversion
SELECT PARSE('€9999,95' AS money USING 'NL') AS Currency;
-- 9999.95

-- Slovakian culture - Euro currency conversion
SELECT PARSE('€9999,95' AS money USING 'SK') AS Currency;
-- 9999.95

-- United States - Euro is not US currency
SELECT PARSE('€9999,95' AS money USING 'US') AS Currency;
/*
Msg 9818, Level 16, State 1, Line 1
The culture parameter 'US' provided in the function call is not supported.
*/

-- Italian
SELECT CONVERT(DECIMAL (12,0), PARSE('€99999,95' AS money USING 'IT')) AS DecimalValue;
-- 100000

-- PARSE with variable parameters
DECLARE @AMOUNT AS VARCHAR(12) = '$9999.00';   DECLARE @CULTURE AS CHAR(5) = 'EN-US';
SELECT DOLLAR = PARSE(@AMOUNT AS MONEY USING @CULTURE) ;
GO
-- 9999.00

-- PARSE invalid data
DECLARE @AMOUNT AS VARCHAR(12) = '$9999A.00';   DECLARE @CULTURE AS CHAR(5) = 'EN-US';
SELECT DOLLAR = PARSE(@AMOUNT AS MONEY USING @CULTURE);
GO
/*
Msg 9819, Level 16, State 1, Line 4
Error converting string value '$9999A.00' into data type money using culture 'EN-US'.
*/
```

CHAPTER 11: New Programming Features in SS 2012 & 2014

TRY_CONVERT() Function

The TRY_CONVERT() function augments the CONVERT function to handle invalid data without giving an error. It is a revolutionary new feature which makes invalid data handling significantly easier in T-SQL.

```sql
-- CONVERT returns error on invalid data
SELECT [City]
       ,[PostalCode]
       ,CONVERT(INT, PostalCode)
 FROM AdventureWorks2012.Person.Address
 ORDER BY PostalCode;
/* Msg 245, Level 16, State 1, Line 1
Conversion failed when converting the nvarchar value '7L' to data type int.
*/
```

```sql
-- TRY_CONVERT() returns NULL for invalid data
SELECT DISTINCT [City]
       ,[PostalCode]
       ,TRY_CONVERT(INT, PostalCode) AS INTValue
 FROM AdventureWorks2012.Person.Address
 ORDER BY PostalCode;
```

City	PostalCode	INTValue
Union Gap	98903	98903
Ellensburg	98926	98926
Spokane	99202	99202
Kennewick	99337	99337
Walla Walla	99362	99362
Stoke-on-Trent	AS23	NULL
Birmingham	B29 6SL	NULL
Cambridge	BA5 3HX	NULL
W. York	BD1 4SJ	NULL
London	C2H 7AU	NULL
Cambridge	CB4 4BZ	NULL
Billericay	CM11	NULL

```sql
-- String date conversion to date data type
SET DATEFORMAT dmy;  -- US date format
SELECT TRY_CONVERT(date, '31/12/2016') AS Result;
-- 2016-12-31
```

```sql
-- Invalid date
SELECT TRY_CONVERT(date, '12/31/2016') AS Result;
-- NULL
GO
```

TRY_CONVERT() Usage in Adding Column to Table

Add new column as sequential row number (rowid) to table using the identity(int,1,1) function.

> NOTE
> The IDENTITY values usually follow the ORDER BY specifications sequentially, but there is no guarantee. If ordering is important, create an empty table first with IDENTITY column and populate it with INSERT SELECT ORDER BY.

```
 USE tempdb;

SELECT TRY_CONVERT(int, [SalesOrderID]) AS [NewSalesOrderID],  -- disable IDENTITY inheritance
    *
INTO  SOH
FROM   AdventureWorks.Sales.SalesOrderHeader  ORDER  BY OrderDate,  CustomerID;
GO
-- (31465 row(s) affected)
```

```
-- Take out duplicate SalesOrderID with the IDENTITY property
ALTER TABLE SOH DROP COLUMN SalesOrderID;
GO
```

```
-- Rename NewSalesOrderID to SalesOrderID
EXEC sp_rename 'dbo.SOH.NewSalesOrderID', 'SalesOrderID';
GO
```

```
-- Add IDENTITY function as new first column  for sequence generation - sequential ID
SELECT RowNumber = IDENTITY(INT, 1, 1),      *
INTO  #SOH   FROM  SOH  ORDER  BY OrderDate,  CustomerID;
GO
```

```
 SELECT * INTO  SalesOrderHeader  FROM  #SOH ;  -- Create a permanent table
GO
SELECT TOP (5) *  FROM   SalesOrderHeader  ORDER  BY RowNumber ;
GO
```

RowNumber	SalesOrderID	RevisionNumber	OrderDate	DueDate	ShipDate
1	43676	1	2001-07-01 00:00:00.000	2001-07-13 00:00:00.000	2001-07-08 00:00:00.000
2	43695	1	2001-07-01 00:00:00.000	2001-07-13 00:00:00.000	2001-07-08 00:00:00.000
3	43674	1	2001-07-01 00:00:00.000	2001-07-13 00:00:00.000	2001-07-08 00:00:00.000
4	43660	1	2001-07-01 00:00:00.000	2001-07-13 00:00:00.000	2001-07-08 00:00:00.000
5	43672	1	2001-07-01 00:00:00.000	2001-07-13 00:00:00.000	2001-07-08 00:00:00.000

```
DROP TABLE SOH ;
DROP TABLE #SOH ;
DROP TABLE tempdb.dbo.SalesOrderHeader ;
```

TRY_PARSE() Function

The TRY_PARSE() function returns NULL instead of error in case of invalid data. T-SQL script to demonstrate the various uses of TRY_PARSE.

```sql
-- TRY_PARSE() parses or returns NULL if cast fails
SELECT TRY_PARSE('Monday, 13 December 2014' AS datetime USING 'en-US') AS [Date&Time];
-- NULL
```

```sql
SELECT TRY_PARSE('SAT, 13 December 2014' AS datetime USING 'en-US') AS [Date&Time];
-- 2014-12-13 00:00:00.000
```

```sql
-- Using the new feature with CASE Conditional.
SELECT CASE WHEN TRY_PARSE('Monday, 13 December 2014' AS datetime USING 'en-US') is NULL
        THEN (SELECT CONVERT(datetime, '19000101'))
     ELSE  (SELECT PARSE('Monday, 13 December 2014' AS datetime USING 'en-US')) END;
-- 1900-01-01 00:00:00.000
```

```sql
-- TRY_PARSE with variable parameters and IIF conditional
DECLARE @AMOUNT AS VARCHAR(12) = '$9999.00', @CULTURE AS CHAR(5) = 'EN-US';

SELECT RESULT = IIF(TRY_PARSE(@AMOUNT AS MONEY USING @CULTURE) IS NOT NULL
                        ,PARSE(@AMOUNT AS MONEY USING @CULTURE) ,-1.0);
-- 9999.0000
```

```sql
DECLARE @AMOUNT AS VARCHAR(12) = '$9999A.00'; DECLARE @CULTURE AS CHAR(5) = 'EN-US';

SELECT RESULT = IIF(TRY_PARSE(@AMOUNT AS MONEY USING @CULTURE) IS NOT NULL
                        ,PARSE(@AMOUNT AS MONEY USING @CULTURE) ,-1.0);
-- -1.0000
```

```sql
DECLARE @AMOUNT AS VARCHAR(12) = '$9999A.00', @CULTURE AS CHAR(5) = 'EN-US';

SELECT RESULT = IIF(TRY_PARSE(@AMOUNT AS MONEY USING @CULTURE) IS NOT NULL
                        ,PARSE(@AMOUNT AS MONEY USING @CULTURE) ,NULL);
GO
-- NULL
```

```sql
-- Note the multiplication by 100 using the German culture
DECLARE @AMOUNT AS VARCHAR(12) = '€77777.00'; DECLARE @CULTURE AS CHAR(5) = 'de-DE';

SELECT RESULT = IIF(TRY_PARSE(@AMOUNT AS MONEY USING @CULTURE) IS NOT NULL
                        ,PARSE(@AMOUNT AS MONEY USING @CULTURE) ,NULL);
GO
-- 7777700.00
```

FORMAT() Function

FORMAT() function is borrowed from the .NET languages. It augments the CONVERT function. T-SQL scripts to demonstrate some of the functionalities.

SELECT FORMAT(1111.22,'c','en-us');	$1,111.22
SELECT FORMAT(1111.22,'c','en-gb');	£1,111.22
SELECT FORMAT(1111.22,'c','de');	1.111,22 €
SELECT FORMAT(1111.22,'c','it');	€ 1.111,22
SELECT FORMAT(1111.22,'c','hu');	1 111,22 Ft
SELECT FORMAT(1111.22,'c','tr');	1.111,22 TL
SELECT FORMAT(1111.22,'c','es');	1.111,22 €
SELECT FORMAT(1111.22,'c','nl');	1.111,22 €
SELECT FORMAT(1111.22,'c','pl');	1 111,22 zł
SELECT FORMAT(1111.22,'c','ru');	1 111,22p.
SELECT FORMAT(1111.22,'c','se');	kr 1 111,22

DECLARE @culture char(2)='fr' ; SELECT FORMAT(1111.22, 'c', @culture); -- 1 111,22 €

SELECT FORMAT(1111.22,'c','gr');   /* Msg 9818, Level 16, State 1, Line 1
The culture parameter 'gr' provided in the function call is not supported. */

SELECT FORMAT (getdate(), 'yyyy/MM/dd hh:mm:ss tt', 'en-US');   -- 2016/06/03 09:56:44 AM
SELECT FORMAT (getdate(), 'MMM dd, yyyy hh:mm:ss tt', 'en-US');   -- Jun 03, 2016 09:57:45 AM
SELECT FORMAT(getdate(), 'MMMM d yyyy dddd','en-US'); -- April 28 2020 Monday

SELECT FORMAT (getdate(), 'y', 'en-US') ;   -- July, 2016
SELECT FORMAT (getdate(), 'M', 'en-US') ;   -- July 10
SELECT FORMAT (getdate(), 'd', 'en-US') ;   -- 7/10/2016

-- Percent formatting
SELECT TOP (4) ProductNumber, ListPrice, StandardCost, Markup = FORMAT(ListPrice / StandardCost, 'p', 'en-us')
FROM AdventureWorks2012.Production.Product WHERE ListPrice > 0.0 ORDER BY ProductNumber;

ProductNumber	ListPrice	StandardCost	Markup
BB-7421	53.99	23.9716	225.22 %
BB-8107	101.24	44.9506	225.22 %
BB-9108	121.49	53.9416	225.22 %
BC-M005	9.99	3.7363	267.37 %

CHAPTER 11: New Programming Features in SS 2012 & 2014

Hierarchical DATE Sequence Generation

Frequently a continuous date sequence is necessary even when the data may have gaps. Using recursive CTE, arbitrary long data sequence can be generated. Other alternative is a calendar table which has the granularity of day not minutes. The following date dimension (Data Warehouse terminology) hierarchy implemented: quarter hour, hour, day, month, quarter, year.

```
DECLARE @ReferenceDate datetime = '20100101';
WITH seqCTE ( SeqQtrHr, SeqNo) AS
(
    SELECT @ReferenceDate, 0
    UNION ALL
    SELECT DATEADD(n, 15, SeqQtrHr), SeqNo+1
    FROM seqCTE
    WHERE SeqQtrHr <= CURRENT_TIMESTAMP
)
SELECT
QtrHourDate  = FORMAT(SeqQtrHr, 'yyyy-MM-dd HH:mm'),
HourDate     = FORMAT(DATEADD(hour,    DATEDIFF(hour,    0, SeqQtrHr), 0),'yyyy-MM-dd HH'),
DayDate      = FORMAT(DATEADD(day,     DATEDIFF(day,     0, SeqQtrHr), 0),'yyyy-MM-dd'),
MonthDate    = FORMAT(DATEADD(month,   DATEDIFF(month,   0, SeqQtrHr), 0),'yyyy-MM-dd'),
QuarterDate  = FORMAT(DATEADD(quarter, DATEDIFF(quarter, 0, SeqQtrHr), 0),'yyyy-MM-dd'),
YearDate     = FORMAT(DATEADD(year,    DATEDIFF(year,    0, SeqQtrHr), 0),'yyyy-MM-dd')
FROM seqCTE ORDER BY QtrHourDate
OPTION ( MAXRECURSION 0);
GO
```

Partial results

QtrHourDate	HourDate	DayDate	MonthDate	QuarterDate	YearDate
2014-04-28 03:30	2014-04-28 03	2014-04-28	2014-04-01	2014-04-01	2014-01-01
2014-04-28 03:45	2014-04-28 03	2014-04-28	2014-04-01	2014-04-01	2014-01-01
2014-04-28 04:00	2014-04-28 04	2014-04-28	2014-04-01	2014-04-01	2014-01-01
2014-04-28 04:15	2014-04-28 04	2014-04-28	2014-04-01	2014-04-01	2014-01-01
2014-04-28 04:30	2014-04-28 04	2014-04-28	2014-04-01	2014-04-01	2014-01-01
2014-04-28 04:45	2014-04-28 04	2014-04-28	2014-04-01	2014-04-01	2014-01-01
2014-04-28 05:00	2014-04-28 05	2014-04-28	2014-04-01	2014-04-01	2014-01-01

CONCAT() Function

The CONCAT() function concatenates two or more strings. Previously the + operator was the only available way to concatenate. **NOTE: CONCAT treats NULL as an empty string, this is different from the + operator concatenation.** T-SQL scripts to demonstrate usage.

```
-- Using + string concatenation operator
SELECT  'New'+SPACE(1)+'York'+SPACE(1)+'City' ;        -- New York City
```

```
-- Using the new CONCAT() function
SELECT  CONCAT('New', SPACE(1),'York', SPACE(1), 'City'); -- New York City
```

```
-- Concatenating string columns with CONCAT()
SELECT CONCAT(FirstName, ' ', LastName) AS FullName
FROM AdventureWorks2012.Person.Person
ORDER by FullName;
/* FullName
...
Blake Wright
Blake Young
Bob Alan
Bob Chapman
Bob Fernandez ... */
```

CHOOSE() Function

The CHOOSE() function returns an item from a list of values as specified by an index. T-SQL scripts to demonstrate usage.

```
SELECT CHOOSE ( 3, 'NYC', 'LA', 'Chicago', 'Houston' ) AS City;
-- Chicago
```

```
SELECT CHOOSE ( 3, 'one', 'two', 'three', 'four', 'five' ) AS Number;
-- three
```

```
DECLARE @weekday as tinyint=6;
SELECT CHOOSE(@weekday, 'Sunday', 'Monday', 'Tuesday', 'Wednesday', 'Thursday', 'Friday', 'Saturday');
-- Friday
```

```
-- Random weekday selection using newid() and rand() functions
DECLARE @weekday as tinyint=Round(Rand(Cast(Newid() AS VARBINARY)) * 6+1,0);
SELECT CHOOSE(@weekday, 'Sunday', 'Monday', 'Tuesday', 'Wednesday', 'Thursday', 'Friday', 'Saturday');
GO 10
-- Friday  Sunday  Tuesday .....
```

CHAPTER 11: New Programming Features in SS 2012 & 2014

THROW Statement

The THROW statement passes the error incurred in TRY - CATCH to the application. Demonstration T-SQL script follows.

> The **THROW** statement complies with **XACT_ABORT** setting, RAISERROR does not. New applications should use **THROW** instead of **RAISERROR**.

```
CREATE TABLE Alpha
(
        ID INT PRIMARY KEY
);
GO
```

```
BEGIN TRY
   INSERT Alpha(ID) VALUES(7);
   INSERT Alpha(ID) VALUES(7); -- Force error by attempting duplicate insert
END TRY
BEGIN CATCH
   PRINT 'In CATCH';
  -- The error message encountered will be passed down to the client software application
   THROW;
END CATCH;
/*
In CATCH

Msg 2627, Level 14, State 1, Line 7
Violation of PRIMARY KEY constraint 'PK__Alpha__3214EC272A076B44'. Cannot insert
duplicate key in object 'dbo.Alpha'. The duplicate key value is (1).
*/
```

```
-- No THROW catch - Error message not materialized
BEGIN TRY
   INSERT Alpha(ID) VALUES(7);
END TRY
BEGIN CATCH
   PRINT 'In CATCH';
END CATCH;
/*
(0 row(s) affected)
In CATCH.
*/
```

```
-- Cleanup
DROP TABLE Alpha
GO
```

CHAPTER 11: New Programming Features in SS 2012 & 2014

IIF() Function

The IIF() function returns one of two values based on a condition. Here is a T-SQL demonstration script.

```
SELECT TOP 10  ProductID, ListPrice,
               IIF ( Color is not null, Color, 'N/A' ) AS [Color]
FROM AdventureWorks2012.Production.Product
ORDER BY ProductID DESC;
GO
```

ProductID	ListPrice	Color
999	539.99	Black
998	539.99	Black
997	539.99	Black
996	121.49	N/A
995	101.24	N/A
994	53.99	N/A
993	539.99	Black
992	539.99	Black
991	539.99	Black
990	539.99	Black

DATEFROMPARTS() & DATETIMEFROMPARTS() Functions

The DATEFROMPARTS() & DATETIMEFROMPARTS() functions generate date / datetime value from date parts. Demonstration T-SQL script.

```
SELECT DATEFROMPARTS ( 2016, 10, 23 ) AS RealDate;
GO
-- 2016-10-23
```

```
SELECT DATETIMEFROMPARTS ( 2016, 10, 23, 10, 10, 10, 500 ) AS RealDateTime;
GO
-- 2016-10-23 10:10:10.500
```

```
DECLARE @Year smallint = 2016, @Month tinyint = 10, @Day tinyint = 23;
SELECT DATEFROMPARTS(@Year, @Month, @Day);
GO
-- 2016-10-23
```

CHAPTER 11: New Programming Features in SS 2012 & 2014

EOMONTH() Function

The EOMONTH() function returns the last day of the month for the given input date parameter.
T-SQL script to demonstrate usage.

```
SELECT EOMONTH('20140201') -- 2014-02-28
```

```
SELECT EOMONTH('20160201') -- 2016-02-29
GO
```

```
-- Future/past months optional parameter
DECLARE    @anydate DATE = '20161023';
SELECT
        CurrentMonthEnd    = EOMONTH(@anydate),
        NextMonthEnd       = EOMONTH(@anydate,  1),
        PrevMonthEnd       = EOMONTH(@anydate, -1);
GO
```

CurrentMonthEnd	NextMonthEnd	PrevMonthEnd
2016-10-31	2016-11-30	2016-09-30

```
-- Span 12 months of last day of month by using the sequence from spt_values
DECLARE    @anydate DATE = '20161023';
SELECT  TOP 12   LastDayOfMonth= EOMONTH(@anydate, number)
FROM master.dbo.spt_values WHERE type = 'P'  ORDER BY number;
GO
```

LastDayOfMonth
2016-10-31
2016-11-30
2016-12-31
2017-01-31
2017-02-28
2017-03-31
2017-04-30
2017-05-31
2017-06-30
2017-07-31
2017-08-31
2017-09-30

Result Set Paging with OFFSET & FETCH NEXT

Frequently a query produces a large results set. On the client side usually it has to be presented in small segments such as 20 lines at a time.

```
USE AdventureWorks2012;

SELECT ProductNumber, Name, ListPrice, Color
FROM Production.Product  ORDER BY ProductNumber
      OFFSET 0 ROWS    FETCH NEXT 10 ROWS ONLY;
-- (10 row(s) affected)
```

ProductNumber	Name	ListPrice	Color
AR-5381	Adjustable Race	0.00	NULL
BA-8327	Bearing Ball	0.00	NULL
BB-7421	LL Bottom Bracket	53.99	NULL
BB-8107	ML Bottom Bracket	101.24	NULL
BB-9108	HL Bottom Bracket	121.49	NULL
BC-M005	Mountain Bottle Cage	9.99	NULL
BC-R205	Road Bottle Cage	8.99	NULL
BE-2349	BB Ball Bearing	0.00	NULL
BE-2908	Headset Ball Bearings	0.00	NULL
BK-M18B-40	Mountain-500 Black, 40	539.99	Black

```
SELECT ProductNumber, Name, ListPrice, Color
FROM Production.Product  ORDER BY ProductNumber
      OFFSET 10 ROWS    FETCH NEXT 10 ROWS ONLY;
-- (10 row(s) affected)
```

ProductNumber	Name	ListPrice	Color
BK-M18B-42	Mountain-500 Black, 42	539.99	Black
BK-M18B-44	Mountain-500 Black, 44	539.99	Black
BK-M18B-48	Mountain-500 Black, 48	539.99	Black
BK-M18B-52	Mountain-500 Black, 52	539.99	Black
BK-M18S-40	Mountain-500 Silver, 40	564.99	Silver
BK-M18S-42	Mountain-500 Silver, 42	564.99	Silver
BK-M18S-44	Mountain-500 Silver, 44	564.99	Silver
BK-M18S-48	Mountain-500 Silver, 48	564.99	Silver
BK-M18S-52	Mountain-500 Silver, 52	564.99	Silver
BK-M38S-38	Mountain-400-W Silver, 38	769.49	Silver

```
SELECT ProductNumber, Name, ListPrice, Color
FROM Production.Product   ORDER BY ProductNumber OFFSET 500 ROWS    FETCH NEXT 10 ROWS ONLY;
-- (4 row(s) affected)
```

ProductNumber	Name	ListPrice	Color
VE-C304-L	Classic Vest, L	63.50	Blue
VE-C304-M	Classic Vest, M	63.50	Blue
VE-C304-S	Classic Vest, S	63.50	Blue
WB-H098	Water Bottle - 30 oz.	4.99	NULL

Result Paging Stored Procedure

The OFFSET FETCH functionality can be wrapped into a stored procedure.

```
USE AdventureWorks2012;
GO
```

```
CREATE PROCEDURE sprocProductPaging   (   @PageNumber int,   @RowsPerPage int   )
AS
BEGIN
SELECT        ProductNumber,
              Name AS ProductName,
              ListPrice,
              Color
 FROM Production.Product p
 WHERE ProductSubcategoryID is not NULL
 ORDER BY ProductNumber
 OFFSET (@PageNumber-1) * @RowsPerPage ROWS
 FETCH NEXT @RowsPerPage ROWS ONLY;
END;
GO
-- Command(s) completed successfully.
```

```
EXEC sprocProductPaging 10, 20
GO
-- (20 row(s) affected)
```

ProductNumber	ProductName	ListPrice	Color
FR-T67Y-44	LL Touring Frame - Yellow, 44	333.42	Yellow
FR-T67Y-50	LL Touring Frame - Yellow, 50	333.42	Yellow
FR-T67Y-54	LL Touring Frame - Yellow, 54	333.42	Yellow
FR-T67Y-58	LL Touring Frame - Yellow, 58	333.42	Yellow
FR-T67Y-62	LL Touring Frame - Yellow, 62	333.42	Yellow
FR-T98U-46	HL Touring Frame - Blue, 46	1003.91	Blue
FR-T98U-50	HL Touring Frame - Blue, 50	1003.91	Blue
FR-T98U-54	HL Touring Frame - Blue, 54	1003.91	Blue
FR-T98U-60	HL Touring Frame - Blue, 60	1003.91	Blue
FR-T98Y-46	HL Touring Frame - Yellow, 46	1003.91	Yellow
FR-T98Y-50	HL Touring Frame - Yellow, 50	1003.91	Yellow
FR-T98Y-54	HL Touring Frame - Yellow, 54	1003.91	Yellow
FR-T98Y-60	HL Touring Frame - Yellow, 60	1003.91	Yellow
FW-M423	LL Mountain Front Wheel	60.745	Black
FW-M762	ML Mountain Front Wheel	209.025	Black
FW-M928	HL Mountain Front Wheel	300.215	Black
FW-R623	LL Road Front Wheel	85.565	Black
FW-R762	ML Road Front Wheel	248.385	Black
FW-R820	HL Road Front Wheel	330.06	Black
FW-T905	Touring Front Wheel	218.01	Black

LEAD() & LAG() Functions
THE LEAD() & LAG() analytical functions belong to the **OVER** family of functions.

```
USE AdventureWorks2012;
GO
 SELECT
        SalesOrderID,
        OrderQty,
        FORMAT(LineTotal, 'c', 'en-US')                              AS LineTotal,
        LEAD(SalesOrderDetailID) OVER (ORDER BY SalesOrderDetailID ) AS [LEAD],
        SalesOrderDetailID                                           AS SODID,
        LAG(SalesOrderDetailID) OVER (ORDER BY SalesOrderDetailID )  AS [LAG]
 FROM Sales.SalesOrderDetail sod
 WHERE SalesOrderID IN   (SELECT SalesOrderID FROM Sales.SalesOrderHeader
                          WHERE TotalDue >= 180000)
 ORDER BY SalesOrderDetailID;
 --(111 row(s) affected) - Partial results.
```

SalesOrderID	OrderQty	LineTotal	LEAD	SODID	LAG
51131	11	$337.57	36817	36816	NULL
51131	12	$368.25	36818	36817	36816
51131	9	$5,421.11	36819	36818	36817
51131	2	$400.10	36820	36819	36818
51131	15	$200.76	36821	36820	36819
51131	2	$567.90	36822	36821	36820
51131	6	$8,582.65	36823	36822	36821
51131	4	$1,135.80	36824	36823	36822
51131	16	$12,206.44	36825	36824	36823
51131	8	$4,818.77	36826	36825	36824

.....

SalesOrderID	OrderQty	LineTotal	LEAD	SODID	LAG
55282	2	$76.20	55443	55442	55441
55282	4	$1,781.64	55444	55443	55442
55282	10	$146.94	55445	55444	55443
55282	3	$600.16	55446	55445	55444
55282	3	$1,807.04	55447	55446	55445
55282	28	$800.10	55448	55447	55446
55282	15	$18,685.15	55449	55448	55447
55282	8	$239.95	55450	55449	55448
55282	3	$1,336.23	55451	55450	55449
55282	7	$33.39	NULL	55451	55450

FIRST_VALUE() & LAST_VALUE() Analytic Functions

The FIRST_VALUE() and LAST_VALUE() analytic functions can be applied in conjunction with the OVER clause.

```
USE AdventureWorks2012;
GO
;WITH CTE AS
        (SELECT   PSC.Name AS Subcategory,
   FIRST_VALUE(P.Name) OVER (PARTITION BY PSC.Name ORDER BY ListPrice ASC) AS LeastExpensive,
        MIN(ListPrice) OVER (PARTITION BY PSC.Name ORDER BY ListPrice ASC)        AS LowPrice,
   LAST_VALUE(P.Name)  OVER (PARTITION BY PSC.Name ORDER BY ListPrice ASC) AS MostExpensive,
        MAX(ListPrice) OVER (PARTITION BY PSC.Name ORDER BY ListPrice ASC)        AS HighPrice,
        ROW_NUMBER() OVER (PARTITION BY PSC.Name ORDER BY ListPrice DESC)       AS RN
        FROM Production.Product P
        INNER JOIN Production.ProductSubcategory PSC
                ON P.ProductSubcategoryID = PSC.ProductSubcategoryID)
SELECT * FROM CTE WHERE RN = 1 ORDER BY Subcategory;
```

Subcategory	LeastExpensive	LowPrice	MostExpensive	HighPrice	RN
Bib-Shorts	Men's Bib-Shorts, S	89.99	Men's Bib-Shorts, L	89.99	1
Bike Racks	Hitch Rack - 4-Bike	120.00	Hitch Rack - 4-Bike	120.00	1
Bike Stands	All-Purpose Bike Stand	159.00	All-Purpose Bike Stand	159.00	1
Bottles and Cages	Water Bottle - 30 oz.	4.99	Mountain Bottle Cage	9.99	1
Bottom Brackets	LL Bottom Bracket	53.99	HL Bottom Bracket	121.49	1
Brakes	Rear Brakes	106.50	Front Brakes	106.50	1
Caps	AWC Logo Cap	8.99	AWC Logo Cap	8.99	1
Chains	Chain	20.24	Chain	20.24	1
Cleaners	Bike Wash - Dissolver	7.95	Bike Wash - Dissolver	7.95	1
Cranksets	LL Crankset	175.49	HL Crankset	404.99	1
Derailleurs	Front Derailleur	91.49	Rear Derailleur	121.46	1
Fenders	Fender Set - Mountain	21.98	Fender Set - Mountain	21.98	1
Forks	LL Fork	148.22	HL Fork	229.49	1
Gloves	Half-Finger Gloves, S	24.49	Full-Finger Gloves, L	37.99	1
Handlebars	LL Road Handlebars	44.54	HL Mountain Handlebars	120.27	1
Headsets	LL Headset	34.20	HL Headset	124.73	1
Helmets	Sport-100 Helmet, Blue	34.99	Sport-100 Helmet, Black	34.99	1
Hydration Packs	Hydration Pack - 70 oz.	54.99	Hydration Pack - 70 oz.	54.99	1
Jerseys	Long-Sleeve Logo Jersey, S	49.99	Short-Sleeve Classic Jersey, XL	53.99	1
Lights	Taillights - Battery-Powered	13.99	Headlights - Weatherproof	44.99	1
Locks	Cable Lock	25.00	Cable Lock	25.00	1
Mountain Bikes	Mountain-500 Black, 40	539.99	Mountain-100 Silver, 48	3399.99	1
Mountain Frames	LL Mountain Frame - Black, 40	249.79	HL Mountain Frame - Silver, 46	1364.50	1
Panniers	Touring-Panniers, Large	125.00	Touring-Panniers, Large	125.00	1
Pedals	LL Mountain Pedal	40.49	Touring Pedal	80.99	1
Pumps	Minipump	19.99	Mountain Pump	24.99	1
Road Bikes	Road-750 Black, 44	539.99	Road-150 Red, 56	3578.27	1
Road Frames	LL Road Frame - Black, 44	337.22	HL Road Frame - Red, 58	1431.50	1
Saddles	LL Mountain Seat/Saddle	27.12	HL Touring Seat/Saddle	52.64	1
Shorts	Men's Sports Shorts, S	59.99	Women's Mountain Shorts, L	69.99	1
Socks	Racing Socks, M	8.99	Mountain Bike Socks, L	9.50	1
Tights	Women's Tights, S	74.99	Women's Tights, L	74.99	1
Tires and Tubes	Patch Kit/8 Patches	2.29	HL Mountain Tire	35.00	1
Touring Bikes	Touring-3000 Blue, 44	742.35	Touring-1000 Blue, 60	2384.07	1
Touring Frames	LL Touring Frame - Blue, 50	333.42	HL Touring Frame - Yellow, 60	1003.91	1
Vests	Classic Vest, S	63.50	Classic Vest, L	63.50	1
Wheels	LL Mountain Front Wheel	60.745	HL Road Rear Wheel	357.06	1

CUME_DIST() & PERCENT_RANK() Analytic Functions

CUME_DIST() and PERCENT_RANK() analytic functions work in conjunction with the OVER clause.

```
SELECT  Department,
        CONCAT(LastName,', ', FirstName)                                          AS FullName,
        Rate,
        FORMAT(CUME_DIST () OVER (PARTITION BY Department ORDER BY Rate),'p')    AS CumuDist,
        FORMAT(PERCENT_RANK()  OVER (PARTITION BY Department ORDER BY Rate ),'p') AS PctRnk
FROM HumanResources.vEmployeeDepartmentHistory AS edh   -- view
   INNER JOIN HumanResources.EmployeePayHistory AS e
            ON e.BusinessEntityID = edh.BusinessEntityID
ORDER BY Department, Rate DESC;
-- (334 row(s) affected) - Partial results.
```

Department	FullName	Rate	CumuDist	PctRnk
Facilities and Maintenance	Altman, Gary	24.0385	100.00 %	100.00 %
Facilities and Maintenance	Kleinerman, Christian	20.4327	85.71 %	83.33 %
Facilities and Maintenance	Hedlund, Magnus	9.75	71.43 %	66.67 %
Facilities and Maintenance	Penor, Lori	9.25	57.14 %	0.00 %
Facilities and Maintenance	Macrae, Stuart	9.25	57.14 %	0.00 %
Facilities and Maintenance	Berry, Jo	9.25	57.14 %	0.00 %
Facilities and Maintenance	Coleman, Pat	9.25	57.14 %	0.00 %
Finance	Norman, Laura	60.0962	100.00 %	100.00 %
Finance	Norman, Laura	48.5577	92.31 %	91.67 %
Finance	Kahn, Wendy	43.2692	84.62 %	83.33 %
Finance	Norman, Laura	39.06	76.92 %	75.00 %
Finance	Liu, David	34.7356	69.23 %	66.67 %
Finance	Moreland, Barbara	26.4423	61.54 %	50.00 %
Finance	Seamans, Mike	26.4423	61.54 %	50.00 %
Finance	Tomic, Dragan	19.00	46.15 %	8.33 %
Finance	Sheperdigian, Janet	19.00	46.15 %	8.33 %
Finance	Poe, Deborah	19.00	46.15 %	8.33 %
Finance	Spoon, Candy	19.00	46.15 %	8.33 %
Finance	Walton, Bryan	19.00	46.15 %	8.33 %
Finance	Barber, David	13.4615	7.69 %	0.00 %
Human Resources	Barreto de Mattos, Paula	27.1394	100.00 %	100.00 %
Human Resources	Johnson, Willis	18.2692	83.33 %	60.00 %
Human Resources	Luthra, Vidur	18.2692	83.33 %	60.00 %
Human Resources	Martin, Mindy	16.5865	50.00 %	40.00 %
Human Resources	Culbertson, Grant	13.9423	33.33 %	0.00 %
Human Resources	Chen, Hao	13.9423	33.33 %	0.00 %

EXEC New Option: WITH RESULT SETS

The WITH RESULT SETS clause can be used to remap the result set of a stored procedure or system procedure execution.

```
EXEC sp_who;
GO
-- (145 row(s) affected) - Partial results.
```

spid	ecid	status	loginame	hostname	blk	dbname	cmd	request_id
1	0	background	sa		0	NULL	LOG WRITER	0
2	0	background	sa		0	NULL	RECOVERY WRITER	0
3	0	background	sa		0	NULL	LAZY WRITER	0
4	0	background	sa		0	master	SIGNAL HANDLER	0
5	0	background	sa		0	NULL	LOCK MONITOR	0

```
EXEC sp_who
 WITH RESULT SETS
(
(
 SPID INT,
 ECID INT,
 STATUS VARCHAR(32),
 LOGINAME SYSNAME,
 HOSTNAME SYSNAME,
 BLK TINYINT,
 DBNAME SYSNAME,
 CMD VARCHAR(64),
 REQUESTID INT
)
);
-- (145 row(s) affected) - Partial results.
```

SPID	ECID	STATUS	LOGINAME	HOSTNAME	BLK	DBNAME	CMD	REQUESTID
47	0	background	sa		0	master	BRKR TASK	0
48	0	background	sa		0	master	BRKR TASK	0
51	0	sleeping	HPESTAR\Owner	HPESTAR	0	master	AWAITING COMMAND	0
52	0	sleeping	HPESTAR\Owner	HPESTAR	0	master	AWAITING COMMAND	0
53	0	sleeping	HPESTAR\Owner	HPESTAR	0	AdventureWorks2012	AWAITING COMMAND	0
54	0	sleeping	HPESTAR\Owner	HPESTAR	0	AdventureWorks2008	AWAITING COMMAND	0
55	0	sleeping	HPESTAR\Owner	HPESTAR	0	AdventureWorks2008	AWAITING COMMAND	0
56	0	sleeping	NT SERVICE\ReportServer	HPESTAR	0	ReportServer	AWAITING COMMAND	0
57	0	sleeping	HPESTAR\Owner	HPESTAR	0	AdventureWorks2008	AWAITING COMMAND	0
58	0	runnable	HPESTAR\Owner	HPESTAR	0	AdventureWorks2012	SELECT	0
59	0	sleeping	NT SERVICE\ReportServer	HPESTAR	0	ReportServer	AWAITING COMMAND	0
60	0	runnable	HPESTAR\Owner	HPESTAR	0	master	SELECT	0

CHAPTER 12: JOINing Tables with INNER & OUTER JOINs

SELECT with INNER JOIN

The SELECT statement is used to retrieve data from table(s). An INNER JOIN is a join in which the values in the columns being joined are compared using a comparison operator. Inner join also known as equi-join when equality condition is applied. Equi-join: PRIMARY KEY (table a) = FOREIGN KEY (table b).

FOREIGN KEY Constraint as Base for INNER JOIN

The INNER JOIN is based on HumanResources.Employee.BusinessEntityID (PRIMARY KEY) is a FOREIGN KEY to Person.Person.BusinessEntityID. The Employee table is in one-to-one relationship with a subset of the Person table.

```sql
USE [AdventureWorks2012]
GO
ALTER TABLE [HumanResources].[Employee]
WITH CHECK ADD  CONSTRAINT
[FK_Employee_Person_BusinessEntityID]
FOREIGN KEY([BusinessEntityID])
REFERENCES [Person].[Person]
([BusinessEntityID])
GO
ALTER TABLE [HumanResources].[Employee]
CHECK CONSTRAINT
[FK_Employee_Person_BusinessEntityID]
GO

EXEC sys.sp_addextendedproperty
@name=N'MS_Description',
@value=N'Foreign key constraint
referencing Person.BusinessEntityID.' ,
@level0type=N'SCHEMA',
@level0name=N'HumanResources',
@level1type=N'TABLE',
@level1name=N'Employee',
@level2type=N'CONSTRAINT',
@level2name=N'FK_Employee_Person_Busines
GO
```

FOREIGN KEY Constraint as Base for INNER JOIN

Diagram of Person.Person and Related Tables

The population of Person.Person includes all employees, contacts, and customers, therefore a key table in the database.

```
-- INNER JOIN ON PRIMARY KEY & FOREIGN KEY
SELECT * FROM Person.Person AS P
            INNER JOIN Person.PersonPhone AS PH
                ON P.BusinessEntityID = PH.BusinessEntityID;
-- (19972 row(s) affected)
```

CHAPTER 12: JOINing Tables with INNER & OUTER JOINs

EQUI-JOIN BETWEEN FOREIGN KEY & PRIMARY KEY

EQUI JOIN means the equality operator is used to match the left and right keys. The reason for the popularity: the goal of most query is to gather information from related tables records (rows). Query to demonstrate why are 3 tables necessary to get a meaningful business report with just a few columns.

```
USE AdventureWorks;
GO

SELECT          CONCAT(LastName, ', ', FirstName)       AS Consumer,
                EmailAddress,
                Phone,
                CU.AccountNumber,
                C.ContactID,
                I.CustomerID
FROM Person.Contact AS C
   INNER JOIN Sales.Individual AS I
     ON C.ContactID = I.ContactID
   INNER JOIN Sales.Customer AS CU
     ON I.CustomerID = CU.CustomerID
WHERE CU.CustomerType = 'I'
ORDER BY LastName, FirstName ;
GO
-- (18484 row(s) affected) - Partial results.
```

Consumer	EmailAddress	Phone	AccountNumber	ContactID	CustomerID
Pal, Yolanda	yolanda11@adventure-works.com	1 (11) 500 555-0110	AW00023748	2837	23748
Palit, Punya	punya0@adventure-works.com	164-555-0118	AW00017574	14759	17574
Parker, Adam	adam29@adventure-works.com	808-555-0157	AW00018228	14771	18228
Parker, Alex	alex26@adventure-works.com	613-555-0123	AW00029252	14783	29252
Parker, Alexandra	alexandra50@adventure-works.com	974-555-0142	AW00016866	8977	16866
Parker, Allison	allison30@adventure-works.com	750-555-0124	AW00026501	9021	26501
Parker, Amanda	amanda51@adventure-works.com	978-555-0167	AW00018081	8985	18081
Parker, Amber	amber7@adventure-works.com	1 (11) 500 555-0198	AW00023959	8999	23959
Parker, Andrea	andrea23@adventure-works.com	612-555-0113	AW00020091	8461	20091
Parker, Angel	angel21@adventure-works.com	815-555-0120	AW00014273	14779	14273
Parker, Bailey	bailey28@adventure-works.com	604-555-0112	AW00019529	9007	19529
Parker, Blake	blake44@adventure-works.com	432-555-0151	AW00015008	3413	15008
Parker, Caleb	caleb28@adventure-works.com	593-555-0116	AW00026318	14760	26318
Parker, Carlos	carlos25@adventure-works.com	937-555-0143	AW00020676	14778	20676
Parker, Charles	charles43@adventure-works.com	266-555-0118	AW00021267	4105	21267
Parker, Chloe	chloe5@adventure-works.com	360-555-0121	AW00027480	8965	27480
Parker, Connor	connor28@adventure-works.com	936-555-0177	AW00028839	14763	28839
Parker, Courtney	courtney5@adventure-works.com	266-555-0176	AW00017612	9002	17612
Parker, Dalton	dalton42@adventure-works.com	535-555-0190	AW00013064	3722	13064
Parker, Devin	devin40@adventure-works.com	897-555-0155	AW00011684	4192	11684
Parker, Eduardo	eduardo41@adventure-works.com	131-555-0192	AW00012939	4269	12939

CHAPTER 12: JOINing Tables with INNER & OUTER JOINs

Diagram of Sales.Customer and Related Tables

Customer is the source of revenue for any business. Therefore, proper table design is paramount.

```
-- INNER JOIN ON PRIMARY KEY & FOREIGN KEY - NOTE: PK & FK named differently
SELECT * FROM Sales.Store AS S
         INNER JOIN Sales.Customer AS C   ON S.BusinessEntityID = C.StoreID;
-- (1336 row(s) affected)
```

CHAPTER 12: JOINing Tables with INNER & OUTER JOINs

Extracting All or Partial Data from JOINed Tables

T-SQL scripts to demonstrate how to JOIN two tables and extract all or subset of the information.

```
USE AdventureWorks2012;

-- SELECT all columns from the JOINed tables
SELECT *
FROM   HumanResources.Employee          AS E      -- E is a table alias
    INNER JOIN Person.Person             AS P      -- P is a table alias
        ON E.BusinessEntityID = P.BusinessEntityID
ORDER  BY P.LastName;
-- (290 row(s) affected)  - Partial results.
```

FirstName	MiddleName	LastName
Syed	E	Abbas
Kim	B	Abercrombie
Hazem	E	Abolrous
Pilar	G	Ackerman
Jay	G	Adams

```
SELECT E.*                           -- SELECT Employee columns from the JOINed tables
FROM   HumanResources.Employee AS E
    INNER JOIN Person.Person AS P    ON E.BusinessEntityID = P.BusinessEntityID
ORDER  BY P.LastName;
-- Partial results.
```

JobTitle	BirthDate	MaritalStatus	Gender
Pacific Sales Manager	1969-02-11	M	M
Production Technician - WC60	1961-01-14	M	F
Quality Assurance Manager	1971-11-27	S	M
Shipping and Receiving Supervisor	1966-10-11	S	M

```
-- SELECT Person columns from the JOINed tables
SELECT P.* FROM   HumanResources.Employee AS E
           INNER JOIN Person.Person AS P    ON E.BusinessEntityID = P.BusinessEntityID
ORDER  BY P.LastName;
-- Partial results.
```

BusinessEntityID	PersonType
285	SP
38	EM
211	EM

CHAPTER 12: JOINing Tables with INNER & OUTER JOINs

Table Aliases for Readability

SELECT All Columns From The Joined Tables Using Table Alias And Wildcard

```
SELECT E.*, P.*
FROM   HumanResources.Employee          AS E      -- E is a table alias
       INNER JOIN Person.Person          AS P      -- P is a table alias
         ON E.BusinessEntityID = P.BusinessEntityID
ORDER BY P.LastName;
-- Same results as SELECT * FROM
```

```
-- Count JOINed rows
SELECT count(*)
FROM   HumanResources.Employee AS E
    INNER JOIN Person.Person AS P
       ON E.BusinessEntityID = P.BusinessEntityID
-- 290
```

```
-- Vertically output reduction: eliminate columns from the available pool
SELECT   E.BusinessEntityID              AS EmployeeID,   -- column alias
         E.JobTitle,
         P.FirstName,
         P.LastName
FROM   HumanResources.Employee AS E
    INNER JOIN Person.Person AS P    ON E.BusinessEntityID = P.BusinessEntityID
ORDER BY P.LastName;
-- (290 row(s) affected) - Partial results.
```

EmployeeID	JobTitle	FirstName	LastName
285	Pacific Sales Manager	Syed	Abbas
38	Production Technician - WC60	Kim	Abercrombie
211	Quality Assurance Manager	Hazem	Abolrous
121	Shipping and Receiving Supervisor	Pilar	Ackerman

```
-- Create a new output column from the available pool of columns
SELECT   E.BusinessEntityID                       AS EmployeeID,
         E.JobTitle,
         CONCAT(P.FirstName, ' ', P.LastName)     AS NAME
FROM   HumanResources.Employee AS E
    INNER JOIN Person.Person AS P    ON E.BusinessEntityID = P.BusinessEntityID
ORDER BY P.LastName;
-- (290 row(s) affected) - Partial results.
```

EmployeeID	JobTitle	NAME
285	Pacific Sales Manager	Syed Abbas
38	Production Technician - WC60	Kim Abercrombie
211	Quality Assurance Manager	Hazem Abolrous
121	Shipping and Receiving Supervisor	Pilar Ackerman

CHAPTER 12: JOINing Tables with INNER & OUTER JOINs

Table Aliases for Readability

The table alias serves as shorthand for table name to improve the **readability of queries**. It should be as short as possible and as meaningful as possible when we have to use a few letters. The next T-SQL query applies four table aliases: c, soh, sod, p.

```
USE AdventureWorks;
SELECT DISTINCT SalesPerson = CONCAT(c.FirstName,SPACE(1), c.LastName)
FROM   Person.Contact c
     INNER JOIN Sales.SalesOrderHeader soh
       ON soh.SalesPersonId = c.ContactID
     INNER JOIN Sales.SalesOrderDetail sod
       ON soh.SalesOrderId = sod.SalesOrderId
     INNER JOIN Production.Product p
       ON sod.ProductID = p.ProductID     AND p.Name LIKE ('%Touring Frame%');
GO /*     SalesPerson
          Carla Eldridge
          Carol Elliott
          Gail Erickson  ....*/
```

Column Aliases for Readability & Presentation

The column alias serves as a meaningful column name either replacing a column name or filling in when there is no column name. In the previous example the = sign was used to establish the column alias. Alternate setting follows applying "AS" (it can be skipped) after the column. If the alias has spaces it has to be included in square brackets like [Bond Sales] or double quotes.

```
USE AdventureWorks;
SELECT DISTINCT  CONCAT(c.FirstName,' ', c.LastName)             AS SalesPerson
FROM   Person.Contact c
     INNER JOIN Sales.SalesOrderHeader soh
       ON soh.SalesPersonId = c.ContactID
     INNER JOIN Sales.SalesOrderDetail sod
       ON soh.SalesOrderId = sod.SalesOrderId
     INNER JOIN Production.Product p
       ON sod.ProductID = p.ProductID    AND p.Name LIKE ('%Touring Frame%');
-- (17 row(s) affected) - Partial results.
```

SalesPerson
Carla Eldridge
Carol Elliott
Gail Erickson
Gary Drury
Janeth Esteves
Jauna Elson
John Emory

Derived Table Alias with a List of Column Aliases

Optionally column alias list can be specified for derived tables just like in CTE definition. T-SQL query demonstrates nested derived tables with table-column aliases (P & J).

```
SELECT DISTINCT ProdID, ProdName, ProdPrice, OrderQuantity
FROM    (
            SELECT  ID, ProductName, Price,        -- Derived table columns
                    OrderQty                        -- SOD column
            FROM AdventureWorks2012.Sales.SalesOrderDetail SOD
            INNER JOIN
                (SELECT ProductID, Name, ListPrice
                 FROM AdventureWorks2012.Production.Product
                ) P(ID, ProductName, Price)         -- inner derived table
            ON SOD.ProductID = P.ID
        ) J (ProdID, ProdName, ProdPrice, OrderQuantity)    -- outer derived table
ORDER BY ProdPrice DESC, ProdName;
-- (2667 row(s) affected) - Partial results.
```

ProdID	ProdName	ProdPrice	OrderQuantity
750	Road-150 Red, 44	3578.27	3
750	Road-150 Red, 44	3578.27	6
750	Road-150 Red, 44	3578.27	1
750	Road-150 Red, 44	3578.27	4
750	Road-150 Red, 44	3578.27	2
750	Road-150 Red, 44	3578.27	5
751	Road-150 Red, 48	3578.27	6
751	Road-150 Red, 48	3578.27	3
751	Road-150 Red, 48	3578.27	2
751	Road-150 Red, 48	3578.27	5
751	Road-150 Red, 48	3578.27	4
751	Road-150 Red, 48	3578.27	1
752	Road-150 Red, 52	3578.27	5
752	Road-150 Red, 52	3578.27	3
752	Road-150 Red, 52	3578.27	6
752	Road-150 Red, 52	3578.27	1
752	Road-150 Red, 52	3578.27	4
752	Road-150 Red, 52	3578.27	2
753	Road-150 Red, 56	3578.27	6
753	Road-150 Red, 56	3578.27	3

INNER JOIN with Additional Conditions

The ON clause of a JOIN can include additional conditions as the following demonstration shows. The INNER JOIN is still based on FOREIGN KEY relationship, but only a subset of records (rows) returned due to the additional conditions, or JOIN predicates. The first query returns the distinct set of cases where the Selling Price was below the ListPrice for ProductID 800 which is a yellow road bike. The second query covers the remaining range where the Selling Price was equal or above the ListPrice.

```
USE AdventureWorks2012;
SELECT DISTINCT( P.ProductID ),
        ProductName = P.Name,           -- column alias
        P.ListPrice,
        SOD.UnitPrice AS 'Selling Price' -- column alias
FROM   Sales.SalesOrderDetail AS SOD    -- table alias
   INNER JOIN  Production.Product AS P  -- table alias
    ON SOD.ProductID = P.ProductID
    AND SOD.UnitPrice < P.ListPrice              -- JOIN predicate
    AND  P.ProductID = 800;                      -- JOIN predicate
```

ProductID	ProductName	ListPrice	Selling Price
800	Road-550-W Yellow, 44	1120.49	600.2625
800	Road-550-W Yellow, 44	1120.49	672.294
800	Road-550-W Yellow, 44	1120.49	1000.4375

```
SELECT DISTINCT( P.ProductID ),
        ProductName = P.Name,
        P.ListPrice,
        SOD.UnitPrice AS 'Selling Price'
FROM   Sales.SalesOrderDetail AS SOD
   INNER JOIN  Production.Product AS P
    ON SOD.ProductID = P.ProductID
    AND SOD.UnitPrice >= P.ListPrice
    AND  P.ProductID BETWEEN 800 AND 900
ORDER BY ProductName;
-- (26 row(s) affected) - Partial results.
```

ProductID	ProductName	ListPrice	Selling Price
879	All-Purpose Bike Stand	159.00	159.00
877	Bike Wash - Dissolver	7.95	7.95
866	Classic Vest, L	63.50	63.50
865	Classic Vest, M	63.50	63.50
864	Classic Vest, S	63.50	63.50
878	Fender Set - Mountain	21.98	21.98
860	Half-Finger Gloves, L	24.49	24.49
859	Half-Finger Gloves, M	24.49	24.49
858	Half-Finger Gloves, S	24.49	24.49
876	Hitch Rack - 4-Bike	120.00	120.00

Counting Rows in JOINs

As the T-SQL script following shows, the basic FOREIGN KEY based JOIN returns 121,317 rows which is all the rows in Sales.SalesOrderDetail table. The additional condition P.ProductID = 800 selects a subset of 495 rows which is then divided between the < and >= conditions.

```
USE AdventureWorks2012;
SELECT Rows = count(*)
FROM   Sales.SalesOrderDetail AS SOD
    INNER JOIN  Production.Product AS P    ON SOD.ProductID = P.ProductID
-- 121317
```

```
SELECT Rows = count(*)
FROM   Sales.SalesOrderDetail AS SOD
    INNER JOIN  Production.Product AS P   ON SOD.ProductID = P.ProductID   AND P.ProductID = 800;
-- 495
```

```
SELECT Rows = count(*)
FROM   Sales.SalesOrderDetail AS SOD
   INNER JOIN  Production.Product AS P
     ON SOD.ProductID = P.ProductID
        AND SOD.UnitPrice < P.ListPrice
        AND P.ProductID = 800;
-- 285
```

```
SELECT Rows = count(*)
FROM   Sales.SalesOrderDetail AS SOD
   INNER JOIN  Production.Product AS P
     ON SOD.ProductID = P.ProductID
        AND SOD.UnitPrice >= P.ListPrice
        AND P.ProductID = 800;
-- 210
```

```
SELECT COUNT(P.ProductID)
FROM   Sales.SalesOrderDetail AS SOD
   INNER JOIN  Production.Product AS P
     ON SOD.ProductID = P.ProductID
        AND SOD.UnitPrice >= P.ListPrice
        AND  P.ProductID BETWEEN 800 AND 900;
-- 21085
```

```
SELECT COUNT(DISTINCT P.ProductID)
FROM   Sales.SalesOrderDetail AS SOD
   INNER JOIN  Production.Product AS P
     ON SOD.ProductID = P.ProductID   AND SOD.UnitPrice >= P.ListPrice
        AND  P.ProductID BETWEEN 800 AND 900;
```

INNER JOIN with 3 Tables

T-SQL query to demonstrate JOINing three tables. Due to the application of the FORMAT function, column name is lost. Therefore we have to alias the formatted column with the original column name or something else. Both INNER JOINs are based on FOREIGN KEY relationships. PV.ProductID is an FK to the Production.Product table, and the PV.VendorID is an FK to the Purchasing.Vendor table. The Purchasing.ProductVendor table is a junction table representing many-to-many relationships between products and vendors: a vendor may supply many products (see Beaumont Bikes in results) and a product may be supplied by many vendors (see Chainring in results).

```
USE AdventureWorks;
GO
SELECT      P.ProductNumber,
            P.Name                                    AS Product,
            V.Name                                    AS Vendor,
            FORMAT (PV.LastReceiptCost, 'c', 'en-US') AS LastReceiptCost
FROM Production.Product AS P
  INNER JOIN Purchasing.ProductVendor AS PV
       ON P.ProductID = PV.ProductID
  INNER JOIN Purchasing.Vendor AS V
       ON V.VendorID = PV.VendorID
ORDER BY Product;
GO
-- (406 row(s) affected) - Partial results.
```

ProductNumber	Product	Vendor	LastReceiptCost
AR-5381	Adjustable Race	Litware, Inc.	$50.26
BA-8327	Bearing Ball	Wood Fitness	$41.92
CH-0234	Chain	Varsity Sport Co.	$15.74
CR-7833	Chainring	Beaumont Bikes	$25.42
CR-7833	Chainring	Bike Satellite Inc.	$26.37
CR-7833	Chainring	Training Systems	$28.70
CB-2903	Chainring Bolts	Beaumont Bikes	$47.47
CB-2903	Chainring Bolts	Bike Satellite Inc.	$45.37
CB-2903	Chainring Bolts	Training Systems	$49.64
CN-6137	Chainring Nut	Beaumont Bikes	$42.80
CN-6137	Chainring Nut	Bike Satellite Inc.	$40.49
CN-6137	Chainring Nut	Training Systems	$44.32
RA-7490	Cone-Shaped Race	Midwest Sport, Inc.	$44.22
CR-9981	Crown Race	Business Equipment Center	$50.26
RA-2345	Cup-Shaped Race	Bloomington Multisport	$48.76
DC-8732	Decal 1	SUPERSALES INC.	$0.21
DC-9824	Decal 2	SUPERSALES INC.	$0.21
LE-6000	External Lock Washer 1	Pro Sport Industries	$41.24
LE-6000	External Lock Washer 1	Aurora Bike Center	$43.27
LE-6000	External Lock Washer 1	Expert Bike Co	$41.17

INNER JOIN with Junction Table

T-SQL Query To Return All Road Frames Offered For Sale By AdventureWorks Cycles

```
USE AdventureWorks2012;
SELECT          UPPER(PC.Name)       AS Category,   PSC.Name             AS Subcategory,
                P.Name          AS Product,   FORMAT(ListPrice, 'c', 'en-US')    AS ListPrice,
                FORMAT(StandardCost, 'c', 'en-US')                               AS StandardCost
FROM Production.Product AS P
   INNER JOIN Production.ProductSubcategory AS PSC
          ON PSC.ProductSubcategoryID = P.ProductSubcategoryID
   INNER JOIN Production.ProductCategory AS PC
          ON PC.ProductCategoryID = PSC.ProductCategoryID
WHERE PSC.Name like 'Road Frames'  ORDER BY Category, Subcategory, Product;
```

Category	Subcategory	Product	ListPrice	StandardCost
COMPONENTS	Road Frames	HL Road Frame - Black, 44	$1,431.50	$868.63
COMPONENTS	Road Frames	HL Road Frame - Black, 48	$1,431.50	$868.63
COMPONENTS	Road Frames	HL Road Frame - Black, 52	$1,431.50	$868.63
COMPONENTS	Road Frames	HL Road Frame - Black, 58	$1,431.50	$1,059.31
COMPONENTS	Road Frames	HL Road Frame - Black, 62	$1,431.50	$868.63
COMPONENTS	Road Frames	HL Road Frame - Red, 44	$1,431.50	$868.63
COMPONENTS	Road Frames	HL Road Frame - Red, 48	$1,431.50	$868.63
COMPONENTS	Road Frames	HL Road Frame - Red, 52	$1,431.50	$868.63
COMPONENTS	Road Frames	HL Road Frame - Red, 56	$1,431.50	$868.63
COMPONENTS	Road Frames	HL Road Frame - Red, 58	$1,431.50	$1,059.31
COMPONENTS	Road Frames	HL Road Frame - Red, 62	$1,431.50	$868.63
COMPONENTS	Road Frames	LL Road Frame - Black, 44	$337.22	$204.63
COMPONENTS	Road Frames	LL Road Frame - Black, 48	$337.22	$204.63
COMPONENTS	Road Frames	LL Road Frame - Black, 52	$337.22	$204.63
COMPONENTS	Road Frames	LL Road Frame - Black, 58	$337.22	$204.63
COMPONENTS	Road Frames	LL Road Frame - Black, 60	$337.22	$204.63
COMPONENTS	Road Frames	LL Road Frame - Black, 62	$337.22	$204.63
COMPONENTS	Road Frames	LL Road Frame - Red, 44	$337.22	$187.16
COMPONENTS	Road Frames	LL Road Frame - Red, 48	$337.22	$187.16
COMPONENTS	Road Frames	LL Road Frame - Red, 52	$337.22	$187.16
COMPONENTS	Road Frames	LL Road Frame - Red, 58	$337.22	$187.16
COMPONENTS	Road Frames	LL Road Frame - Red, 60	$337.22	$187.16
COMPONENTS	Road Frames	LL Road Frame - Red, 62	$337.22	$187.16
COMPONENTS	Road Frames	ML Road Frame - Red, 44	$594.83	$352.14
COMPONENTS	Road Frames	ML Road Frame - Red, 48	$594.83	$352.14
COMPONENTS	Road Frames	ML Road Frame - Red, 52	$594.83	$352.14
COMPONENTS	Road Frames	ML Road Frame - Red, 58	$594.83	$352.14
COMPONENTS	Road Frames	ML Road Frame - Red, 60	$594.83	$352.14
COMPONENTS	Road Frames	ML Road Frame-W - Yellow, 38	$594.83	$360.94
COMPONENTS	Road Frames	ML Road Frame-W - Yellow, 40	$594.83	$360.94
COMPONENTS	Road Frames	ML Road Frame-W - Yellow, 42	$594.83	$360.94
COMPONENTS	Road Frames	ML Road Frame-W - Yellow, 44	$594.83	$360.94
COMPONENTS	Road Frames	ML Road Frame-W - Yellow, 48	$594.83	$360.94

CHAPTER 12: JOINing Tables with INNER & OUTER JOINs

INNER JOIN with Junction Table

Three tables INNER JOIN includes the titleauthor junction table which represent many-to-many relationship. All JOINs are EQUI-JOINs with FOREIGN KEYs and PRIMARY KEYs.

```
USE pubs;

SELECT      FORMAT(ytd_sales, 'c', 'en-US')                        AS YTDSales,
            CONCAT(au.au_fname, ' ', au.au_lname)                  AS Author,
            FORMAT((ytd_sales * royalty) / 100,'c','en-US')        AS AuthorRev,
            FORMAT((ytd_sales - (ytd_sales * royalty) / 100),'c','en-US')  AS PublisherRev
FROM titles t
     INNER JOIN titleauthor ta
         ON t.title_id = ta.title_id
     INNER JOIN authors au
         ON ta.au_id = au.au_id
ORDER BY    YTDSales DESC,          -- Major sort key
            Author ASC;             -- Minor sort key
GO
```

YTDSales	Author	AuthorRev	PublisherRev
$8,780.00	Cheryl Carson	$1,404.00	$7,376.00
$4,095.00	Abraham Bennet	$409.00	$3,686.00
$4,095.00	Akiko Yokomoto	$409.00	$3,686.00
$4,095.00	Ann Dull	$409.00	$3,686.00
$4,095.00	Burt Gringlesby	$409.00	$3,686.00
$4,095.00	Dean Straight	$409.00	$3,686.00
$4,095.00	Marjorie Green	$409.00	$3,686.00
$4,095.00	Michael O'Leary	$409.00	$3,686.00
$4,095.00	Sheryl Hunter	$409.00	$3,686.00
$4,072.00	Johnson White	$407.00	$3,665.00
$375.00	Livia Karsen	$37.00	$338.00
$375.00	Stearns MacFeather	$37.00	$338.00
$375.00	Sylvia Panteley	$37.00	$338.00
$3,876.00	Michael O'Leary	$387.00	$3,489.00
$3,876.00	Stearns MacFeather	$387.00	$3,489.00
$3,336.00	Charlene Locksley	$333.00	$3,003.00
$22,246.00	Anne Ringer	$5,339.00	$16,907.00
$22,246.00	Michel DeFrance	$5,339.00	$16,907.00
$2,045.00	Albert Ringer	$245.00	$1,800.00
$2,045.00	Anne Ringer	$245.00	$1,800.00
$2,032.00	Innes del Castillo	$243.00	$1,789.00
$18,722.00	Marjorie Green	$4,493.00	$14,229.00
$15,096.00	Reginald Blotchet-Halls	$2,113.00	$12,983.00
$111.00	Albert Ringer	$11.00	$100.00
NULL	Charlene Locksley	NULL	NULL

NON-EQUI JOINs for Data Analytics

We can use not equal operators in JOIN predicates as demonstrated in the next query. The second predicate in the JOIN is less than JOIN.

```
USE AdventureWorks2012;
GO
-- List of "red" products sold at a discount
SELECT DISTINCT      p.ProductNumber,
                     p.Name                                AS ProductName,
                     FORMAT(p.ListPrice,'c','en-US')       AS ListPrice,
                     FORMAT(sod.UnitPrice,'c','en-US')     AS SellPrice
FROM Sales.SalesOrderDetail AS sod
   INNER JOIN Production.Product AS p
       ON sod.ProductID = p.ProductID
       AND sod.UnitPrice < p.ListPrice
WHERE Color = 'Red'
ORDER BY p.ProductNumber;
--(86 row(s) affected) - Partial results.
```

ProductNumber	ProductName	ListPrice	SellPrice
BK-R50R-44	Road-650 Red, 44	$782.99	$234.90
BK-R50R-44	Road-650 Red, 44	$782.99	$419.46
BK-R50R-44	Road-650 Red, 44	$782.99	$430.64
BK-R50R-44	Road-650 Red, 44	$782.99	$454.13
BK-R50R-44	Road-650 Red, 44	$782.99	$469.79
BK-R50R-44	Road-650 Red, 44	$782.99	$563.75
BK-R50R-44	Road-650 Red, 44	$782.99	$699.10
BK-R50R-48	Road-650 Red, 48	$782.99	$419.46
BK-R50R-48	Road-650 Red, 48	$782.99	$430.64
BK-R50R-48	Road-650 Red, 48	$782.99	$454.13
BK-R50R-48	Road-650 Red, 48	$782.99	$469.79
BK-R50R-48	Road-650 Red, 48	$782.99	$563.75

To resolve the duplicate issue which makes DISTINCT usage necessary, we have to include the SalesOrderID column.

```
SELECT               p.ProductNumber,
                     p.Name                                AS ProductName,
                     FORMAT(p.ListPrice,'c','en-US')       AS ListPrice,
                     FORMAT(sod.UnitPrice,'c','en-US')     AS SellPrice,
                     sod.SalesOrderID
FROM Sales.SalesOrderDetail AS sod
   INNER JOIN Production.Product AS p
       ON sod.ProductID = p.ProductID
       AND sod.UnitPrice < p.ListPrice
WHERE Color = 'Red'   ORDER BY p.ProductNumber;
-- (8408 row(s) affected)
```

Interchangeability of ON & WHERE Predicates in INNER JOINs

We can freely place the predicates to either the ON clause or the WHERE clause in an INNER JOIN. This is not true for OUTER JOINs such as LEFT JOINs.

```sql
USE AdventureWorks2012;
-- List of "blue" products sold at a discount
SELECT DISTINCT  p.ProductNumber, p.Name                    AS ProductName,
                 FORMAT(p.ListPrice,'c','en-US')            AS ListPrice,
                 FORMAT(sod.UnitPrice,'c','en-US')          AS SellPrice
FROM Sales.SalesOrderDetail AS sod
   INNER JOIN Production.Product AS p
       ON sod.ProductID = p.ProductID
       AND sod.UnitPrice < p.ListPrice
WHERE Color = 'Blue'  ORDER BY p.ProductNumber;
--(57 row(s) affected)
```

```sql
SELECT DISTINCT  p.ProductNumber, p.Name                    AS ProductName,
                 FORMAT(p.ListPrice,'c','en-US')            AS ListPrice,
                 FORMAT(sod.UnitPrice,'c','en-US')          AS SellPrice
FROM Sales.SalesOrderDetail AS sod
   INNER JOIN Production.Product AS p
       ON sod.ProductID = p.ProductID
       AND sod.UnitPrice < p.ListPrice
       AND Color = 'Blue'
ORDER BY p.ProductNumber;
--(57 row(s) affected)
```

```sql
SELECT DISTINCT  p.ProductNumber, p.Name                    AS ProductName,
                 FORMAT(p.ListPrice,'c','en-US')            AS ListPrice,
                 FORMAT(sod.UnitPrice,'c','en-US')          AS SellPrice
FROM Sales.SalesOrderDetail AS sod
   INNER JOIN Production.Product AS p
     ON sod.ProductID = p.ProductID
WHERE sod.UnitPrice < p.ListPrice    AND Color = 'Blue'  ORDER BY p.ProductNumber;
--(57 row(s) affected)
```

```sql
-- Old-style INNER JOIN with table list and WHERE clause
SELECT DISTINCT  p.ProductNumber, p.Name                    AS ProductName,
                 FORMAT(p.ListPrice,'c','en-US')            AS ListPrice,
                 FORMAT(sod.UnitPrice,'c','en-US')          AS SellPrice
FROM Sales.SalesOrderDetail AS sod,  Production.Product AS p
WHERE sod.ProductID = p.ProductID
       AND sod.UnitPrice < p.ListPrice
       AND Color = 'Blue'
ORDER BY p.ProductNumber;         --(57 row(s) affected)
```

SELF-JOIN for Analytics Within a Table

When a table is JOINed to itself, it is a called a self-join. The purpose of such a JOIN is to examine data relations within the table. The Production.Product table is self-joined to itself on the ProductSubcategoryID FOREIGN KEY(not on a PRIMARY KEY), a many-to-many JOIN. Subsequently, we made the query "friendlier" by using subcategory names as opposed to ID-s.

```
SELECT DISTINCT  P1.ProductSubcategoryID,
                 P1.ListPrice              AS ListPrice1,
                 P2.ListPrice              AS ListPrice2
FROM   Production.Product P1
  INNER JOIN Production.Product P2
    ON P1.ProductSubcategoryID = P2.ProductSubcategoryID
    AND P1.ListPrice < P2.ListPrice
    AND P1.ListPrice < $15
    AND P2.ListPrice < $15;
```

ProductSubcategoryID	ListPrice1	ListPrice2
23	8.99	9.50
28	4.99	8.99
28	4.99	9.99
28	8.99	9.99
37	2.29	3.99
37	2.29	4.99
37	3.99	4.99

```
SELECT DISTINCT  PS.Name AS Subcategory,
                 P1.ListPrice     AS ListPrice1,
                 P2.ListPrice     AS ListPrice2
FROM   Production.ProductSubcategory PS
    INNER JOIN Production.Product P1
       ON PS.ProductSubcategoryID = P1.ProductSubcategoryID
    INNER JOIN Production.Product P2
       ON P1.ProductSubcategoryID = P2.ProductSubcategoryID
       AND P1.ListPrice < P2.ListPrice              -- To prevent duplicate processing
       AND P1.ListPrice < $15
       AND P2.ListPrice < $15;
```

Subcategory	ListPrice1	ListPrice2
Bottles and Cages	4.99	8.99
Bottles and Cages	4.99	9.99
Bottles and Cages	8.99	9.99
Socks	8.99	9.50
Tires and Tubes	2.29	3.99
Tires and Tubes	2.29	4.99
Tires and Tubes	3.99	4.99

T-SQL SELF-JOIN Query Lists The Competing Suppliers For Each Product Purchased From Vendor

Since the ProductID in the ProductVendor table is part of a composite PRIMARY KEY, we can conclude that it is a many-to-many JOIN.

```
SELECT DISTINCT
            Vendor = V.[Name],
            P1.BusinessEntityID,
            Product = P.[Name],
            P1.ProductID
FROM   Production.Product P
    INNER JOIN Purchasing.ProductVendor P1
        ON P.ProductID = P1.ProductID
    INNER JOIN Purchasing.Vendor V
        ON P1.BusinessEntityID = V.BusinessEntityID
    INNER JOIN Purchasing.ProductVendor P2
        ON P1.ProductID = P2.ProductID
WHERE  P1.BusinessEntityID <> P2.BusinessEntityID
ORDER  BY Product, Vendor
-- (347 row(s) affected) - Partial results.
```

Vendor	BusinessEntityID	Product	ProductID
Beaumont Bikes	1602	Chainring	322
Bike Satellite Inc.	1604	Chainring	322
Training Systems	1514	Chainring	322
Beaumont Bikes	1602	Chainring Bolts	320
Bike Satellite Inc.	1604	Chainring Bolts	320
Training Systems	1514	Chainring Bolts	320
Beaumont Bikes	1602	Chainring Nut	321
Bike Satellite Inc.	1604	Chainring Nut	321
Training Systems	1514	Chainring Nut	321
Aurora Bike Center	1616	External Lock Washer 1	409
Expert Bike Co	1672	External Lock Washer 1	409
Pro Sport Industries	1686	External Lock Washer 1	409
Aurora Bike Center	1616	External Lock Washer 2	411
Pro Sport Industries	1686	External Lock Washer 2	411
Aurora Bike Center	1616	External Lock Washer 3	403
Expert Bike Co	1672	External Lock Washer 3	403
Pro Sport Industries	1686	External Lock Washer 3	403
Aurora Bike Center	1616	External Lock Washer 4	404
Expert Bike Co	1672	External Lock Washer 4	404
Pro Sport Industries	1686	External Lock Washer 4	404
Aurora Bike Center	1616	External Lock Washer 5	406
Expert Bike Co	1672	External Lock Washer 5	406
Pro Sport Industries	1686	External Lock Washer 5	406
Aurora Bike Center	1616	External Lock Washer 6	408
Expert Bike Co	1672	External Lock Washer 6	408

Applying SELF-JOIN for Numbering Result Lines

T-SQL script to demonstrate how SELF-JOIN can be used for numbering lines in query results. Note that in these days we would use **ROW_NUMBER()** function which has been introduced with SQL Server 2005.

```
USE Northwind ;
GO

SELECT   OD.OrderID,
         SeqNo                             AS LineItem,
         OD.ProductID,
         FORMAT(UnitPrice,'c','en-US')     AS UnitPrice,
         Quantity,
         FORMAT(Discount, 'p')             AS Discount
FROM     [Order Details] OD
  INNER JOIN (SELECT   count(*) AS SeqNo,
                       a.OrderID,
                       a.ProductID
              FROM     [Order Details] A
              INNER JOIN [Order Details] B
                ON A.ProductID >= B.ProductID          -- Prevent duplicates
                AND A.OrderID = B.OrderID
              GROUP BY A.OrderID,    A.ProductID) a
    ON OD.OrderID = a.OrderID
    AND OD.ProductID = a.ProductID
WHERE    OD.OrderID < 10400
ORDER BY OD.OrderID,
         LineItem
-- (405 row(s) affected) - Partial results.
```

Vendor	AddressLine1	AddressLine2	City	State	Country
A. Datum Corporation	2596 Big Canyon Road		New York	New York	United States
Advanced Bicycles	7995 Edwards Ave.		Lynnwood	Washington	United States
Allenson Cycles	4659 Montoya		Altadena	California	United States
American Bicycles and Wheels	1667 Warren Street		West Covina	California	United States
American Bikes	7179 Montana		Torrance	California	United States
Anderson's Custom Bikes	9 Guadalupe Dr.		Burbank	California	United States
Aurora Bike Center	65 Park Glen Court		Port Orchard	Washington	United States
Australia Bike Retailer	28 San Marino Ct.		Bellingham	Washington	United States
Beaumont Bikes	2472 Alexander Place		West Covina	Idaho	United States
Bergeron Off-Roads	9830 May Way		Mill Valley	Montana	United States
Bicycle Specialists	1286 Cincerto Circle		Lake Oswego	Oregon	United States
Bike Satellite Inc.	2141 Delaware Ct.		Downey	Tennessee	United States
Bloomington Multisport	218 Fall Creek Road		West Covina	California	United States
Burnett Road Warriors	5807 Churchill Dr.		Corvallis	Oregon	United States
Business Equipment Center	6061 St. Paul Way		Everett	Montana	United States
Capital Road Cycles	628 Muir Road		Los Angeles	California	United States
Carlson Specialties	2313 B Southampton Rd		Missoula	Montana	United States
Chicago City Saddles	3 Gehringer Drive		Daly City	California	United States
Chicago Rent-All	15 Pear Dr.		Newport Beach	California	United States
Circuit Cycles	1 Mt. Dell Drive		Portland	Oregon	United States

INNER JOIN with 5 Tables

It takes accessing five tables to get the vendor name & address information in AdventureWorks. In fact this is the main complaint against 3NF relational database design: too many JOINs required to extract data. True, but the benefits of 3NF design are overwhelming. A way to overcome the "too many JOINs" issue is creating views which are pre-canned SELECT queries.

```
USE AdventureWorks;
GO

SELECT V.Name                    AS Vendor,
    A.AddressLine1,
    isnull(A.AddressLine2, '')   AS AddressLine2,
    A.City,
    SP.Name                      AS State,
    CR.Name                      AS Country
FROM   Purchasing.Vendor AS V
    INNER JOIN Purchasing.VendorAddress AS VA
        ON VA.VendorID = V.VendorID
    INNER JOIN Person.Address AS A
        ON A.AddressID = VA.AddressID
    INNER JOIN Person.StateProvince AS SP
        ON SP.StateProvinceID = A.StateProvinceID
    INNER JOIN Person.CountryRegion AS CR
        ON CR.CountryRegionCode = SP.CountryRegionCode
ORDER BY Vendor;
GO
-- (104 row(s) affected) - Partial results.
```

Vendor	AddressLine1	AddressLine2	City	State	Country
A. Datum Corporation	2596 Big Canyon Road		New York	New York	United States
Advanced Bicycles	7995 Edwards Ave.		Lynnwood	Washington	United States
Allenson Cycles	4659 Montoya		Altadena	California	United States
American Bicycles and Wheels	1667 Warren Street		West Covina	California	United States
American Bikes	7179 Montana		Torrance	California	United States
Anderson's Custom Bikes	9 Guadalupe Dr.		Burbank	California	United States
Aurora Bike Center	65 Park Glen Court		Port Orchard	Washington	United States
Australia Bike Retailer	28 San Marino Ct.		Bellingham	Washington	United States
Beaumont Bikes	2472 Alexander Place		West Covina	Idaho	United States
Bergeron Off-Roads	9830 May Way		Mill Valley	Montana	United States
Bicycle Specialists	1286 Cincerto Circle		Lake Oswego	Oregon	United States
Bike Satellite Inc.	2141 Delaware Ct.		Downey	Tennessee	United States
Bloomington Multisport	218 Fall Creek Road		West Covina	California	United States
Burnett Road Warriors	5807 Churchill Dr.		Corvallis	Oregon	United States
Business Equipment Center	6061 St. Paul Way		Everett	Montana	United States
Capital Road Cycles	628 Muir Road		Los Angeles	California	United States

Creating View as Workaround for "Too Many JOINs"

It is so simple to create a view, that counterproductive if not done for queries which are used again and again. Given that large database systems may have a great number of views, meaningful long names are paremount.

```
-- No implicit ORDER BY can be included in a view - no trick around it either
CREATE VIEW vVendorAddress  AS
SELECT V.Name               AS Vendor,
    A.AddressLine1,
    isnull(A.AddressLine2, '')   AS AddressLine2,
    A.City,
    SP.Name                 AS State,
    CR.Name         AS Country
FROM   Purchasing.Vendor AS V
    INNER JOIN Purchasing.VendorAddress AS VA    ON VA.VendorID = V.VendorID
    INNER JOIN Person.Address AS A               ON A.AddressID = VA.AddressID
    INNER JOIN Person.StateProvince AS SP        ON SP.StateProvinceID = A.StateProvinceID
    INNER JOIN Person.CountryRegion AS CR        ON CR.CountryRegionCode = SP.CountryRegionCode
ORDER  BY Vendor;
GO  /* Msg 1033, Level 15, State 1, Procedure vVendorAddress, Line 18
The ORDER BY clause is invalid in views, inline functions, derived tables, subqueries, and common table
expressions, unless TOP, OFFSET or FOR XML is also specified.  */
```

```
CREATE VIEW vVendorAddress  AS
SELECT V.Name               AS Vendor,
    A.AddressLine1,
    isnull(A.AddressLine2, '')   AS AddressLine2,
    A.City,
    SP.Name                 AS State,
    CR.Name         AS Country
FROM   Purchasing.Vendor AS V
    INNER JOIN Purchasing.VendorAddress AS VA    ON VA.VendorID = V.VendorID
    INNER JOIN Person.Address AS A               ON A.AddressID = VA.AddressID
    INNER JOIN Person.StateProvince AS SP        ON SP.StateProvinceID = A.StateProvinceID
    INNER JOIN Person.CountryRegion AS CR        ON CR.CountryRegionCode = SP.CountryRegionCode
GO
```

SELECT TOP 5 * FROM vVendorAddress ORDER BY Vendor;

Vendor	AddressLine1	AddressLine2	City	State	Country
A. Datum Corporation	2596 Big Canyon Road		New York	New York	United States
Advanced Bicycles	7995 Edwards Ave.		Lynnwood	Washington	United States
Allenson Cycles	4659 Montoya		Altadena	California	United States
American Bicycles and Wheels	1667 Warren Street		West Covina	California	United States
American Bikes	7179 Montana		Torrance	California	United States

CHAPTER 12: JOINing Tables with INNER & OUTER JOINs

Non-Key INNER JOIN for Analytics

So far we have seen INNER JOINs based on FOREIGN KEY to PRIMARY equality relationships. The next INNER JOIN is based on the equality of the first 5 letters of last names. It is also a SELF-JOIN. In addition to the last name part equality, two more conditions are reducing the result set. The < condition is intended to reduce duplicates and the first letter of last name is 'S' limits the query results further. This is a many-to-many JOIN.

```
USE AdventureWorks2012;

SELECT  DISTINCT
    CONCAT( A.FirstName, space(1), A.LastName)      AS Person,
    CONCAT( B.FirstName, space(1), B.LastName)      AS LastNameNeighbor
FROM   Person.Person A
    INNER JOIN  Person.Person B
      ON LEFT(A.LastName, 5) = LEFT(B.LastName, 5)
        AND A.LastName < B.LastName
        AND LEFT(A.LastName, 1) = 'S'
ORDER  BY        Person,
                 LastNameNeighbor;
-- (169 row(s) affected) - Partial results.
```

Person	LastNameNeighbor
Abigail Smith	Lorrin Smith-Bates
Adriana Smith	Lorrin Smith-Bates
Alexander Smith	Lorrin Smith-Bates
Alexandra Smith	Lorrin Smith-Bates
Alexis Smith	Lorrin Smith-Bates
Allen Smith	Lorrin Smith-Bates
Alyssa Smith	Lorrin Smith-Bates
Andre Smith	Lorrin Smith-Bates
Andrew Smith	Lorrin Smith-Bates
Arthur Smith	Lorrin Smith-Bates
Ashley Smith	Lorrin Smith-Bates
Austin Smith	Lorrin Smith-Bates
Barry Srini	Sethu Srinivasan
Ben Smith	Lorrin Smith-Bates
Benjamin Smith	Lorrin Smith-Bates
Beth Srini	Sethu Srinivasan
Brandon Smith	Lorrin Smith-Bates
Brandy Srini	Sethu Srinivasan
Brett Srini	Sethu Srinivasan
Brianna Smith	Lorrin Smith-Bates

JOINing Tables without Relationship for Combinatorics

SQL Server will execute such a JOIN on any pair of compatible columns as demonstrated by the next T-SQL query. Note this is only a demo, there is no business meaning to it unless the combinatorial results are useful for some application. A more practical example in the pubs database matching author city with publisher city using a JOIN.

```
USE Northwind;   -- Cross database JOIN query
SELECT   P.ProductID,
         P.ProductName            AS NorthwindProduct,
         PP.Name                  AS AWProduct
FROM dbo.Products P
         INNER JOIN AdventureWorks2008.Production.Product PP     ON P.ProductID = PP.ProductID
ORDER BY P.ProductID;
```

ProductID	NorthwindProduct	AWProduct
1	Chai	Adjustable Race
2	Chang	Bearing Ball
3	Aniseed Syrup	BB Ball Bearing
4	Chef Anton's Cajun Seasoning	Headset Ball Bearings

Cartesian Product

When all rows in one table combined with all rows of another table it is called a Cartesian product. The cardinality of such a JOIN is (Table 1 Rows) x (Table 2 Rows).

```
-- Old-fashioned no JOIN predicate 2-table query - Cardinality 4x4 = 16
SELECT Category1 = A.Name, Category2 = B.Name
FROM Production.ProductCategory A, Production.ProductCategory B ORDER BY Category1, Category2;
```

```
-- Equivalent CROSS JOIN
SELECT Category1 = A.Name, Category2 = B.Name
FROM Production.ProductCategory A  CROSS JOIN Production.ProductCategory B
ORDER BY Category1, Category2;
```

Category1	Category2
Accessories	Accessories
Accessories	Bikes
Accessories	Clothing
Accessories	Components
Bikes	Accessories
Bikes	Bikes
Bikes	Clothing
Bikes	Components
Clothing	Accessories
Clothing	Bikes
Clothing	Clothing
Clothing	Components
Components	Accessories
Components	Bikes
Components	Clothing
Components	Components

SQL OUTER JOIN for Inclusion of Unmatched Rows

We have seen that INNER JOINs return rows only when there is at least one row from both tables that satisfies the join condition or conditions such as FOREIGN KEY matching the referenced PRIMARY KEY. Inner join queries do not return the rows that do not meet the ON condition with a row from the other table.

OUTER JOINs, however, return all rows from one or both tables in the JOIN. All rows are returned from the left table in a LEFT OUTER JOIN (including non-matching rows), and all rows are returned from the right table in a RIGHT OUTER JOIN. All rows from both tables are returned in a FULL OUTER JOIN. LEFT OUTER JOIN is totally equivalent to RIGHT OUTER JOIN. LEFT OUTER JOIN is mostly used by programmers in countries where the writing is left to right. **RIGHT OUTER JOIN is typically used by developers in countries where the writing is right to left**. **The non-matching rows in an OUTER JOIN are returned with NULL value fields**, therefore, they can be distinquished from the matching rows with a null test.

The following are synonyms:

LEFT JOIN - LEFT OUTER JOIN

RIGHT JOIN - RIGHT OUTER JOIN

FULL JOIN - FULL OUTER JOIN

The legacy syntax for outer joins *= (left join) or =* (right join) is not supported anymore. T-SQL example script lists products (left table) even if they are not being sold such as assembly parts.

```
USE AdventureWorks2012;
SELECT          P.Name,         SOD.SalesOrderID,
          CASE    WHEN SalesOrderID is null THEN 'Non-matching'
                  ELSE 'Matching' END              AS JoinInfo
FROM   Production.Product P
    LEFT OUTER JOIN Sales.SalesOrderDetail SOD    ON P.ProductID = SOD.ProductID
ORDER BY P.Name;   -- (121555 row(s) affected)  - Partial results.
```

Name	SalesOrderID	JoinInfo
Adjustable Race	NULL	Non-matching
All-Purpose Bike Stand	51179	Matching
All-Purpose Bike Stand	51488	Matching
All-Purpose Bike Stand	51520	Matching
All-Purpose Bike Stand	51558	Matching
All-Purpose Bike Stand	51882	Matching
All-Purpose Bike Stand	51903	Matching
All-Purpose Bike Stand	51970	Matching
All-Purpose Bike Stand	52010	Matching
All-Purpose Bike Stand	52032	Matching

LEFT JOIN: Include Unmatched Rows from Left Table

In the LEFT JOIN example, the Vendor table is LEFT JOINed to the PurchaseOrderHeader table to find out which vendors did not supply anything. The LEFT JOIN is based on FOREIGN KEY relationship.

```
USE AdventureWorks2012;

SELECT Vendor = V.Name
FROM   Purchasing.Vendor V
    LEFT JOIN Purchasing.PurchaseOrderHeader POH
        ON V.BusinessEntityID = POH.VendorID
WHERE  POH.VendorID IS NULL          -- Test if POH columns are null
ORDER by Vendor;   -- (18 row(s) affected) - Partial results.
```

Vendor
A. Datum Corporation
Cycling Master
Electronic Bike Co.
GMA Ski & Bike
Holiday Skate & Cycle
Illinois Trek & Clothing

T-SQL query to check which pedal products for sale were reviewed and which ones not.

```
SELECT   p.Name          AS ProductName,
         ProductNumber,
         pr.ProductReviewID,
         pr.ReviewerName,
         pr.Rating
FROM Production.Product p
   LEFT JOIN Production.ProductReview pr
        ON p.ProductID = pr.ProductID
WHERE p.ProductSubcategoryID is not null    AND p.Name like '%pedal%'  ORDER BY ProductNumber;
-- (8 row(s) affected)
```

ProductName	ProductNumber	ProductReviewID	ReviewerName	Rating
LL Mountain Pedal	PD-M282	NULL	NULL	NULL
ML Mountain Pedal	PD-M340	NULL	NULL	NULL
HL Mountain Pedal	PD-M562	2	David	4
HL Mountain Pedal	PD-M562	3	Jill	2
LL Road Pedal	PD-R347	NULL	NULL	NULL
ML Road Pedal	PD-R563	NULL	NULL	NULL
HL Road Pedal	PD-R853	NULL	NULL	NULL
Touring Pedal	PD-T852	NULL	NULL	NULL

CHAPTER 12: JOINing Tables with INNER & OUTER JOINs

RIGHT JOIN - Same as LEFT with Tables Switched

The RIGHT JOIN is totally equivalent, including performance, to the corresponding LEFT JOIN. RIGHT JOIN is more frequently used in countries where they write right to left.

```
USE AdventureWorks2012;

SELECT Vendor = V.Name
FROM   Purchasing.PurchaseOrderHeader POH
    RIGHT JOIN Purchasing.Vendor V
      ON V.BusinessEntityID = POH.VendorID
WHERE  POH.VendorID IS NULL
ORDER by Vendor;
-- (18 row(s) affected) - Partial results.
```

Vendor
A. Datum Corporation
Cycling Master
Electronic Bike Co.
GMA Ski & Bike
Holiday Skate & Cycle

T-SQL RIGHT JOIN examples progress toward a query to provide users with a good report.

```
USE AdventureWorks2012;

SELECT ST.Name AS  Territory,
    SP.BusinessEntityID
FROM   Sales.SalesTerritory ST
    RIGHT OUTER JOIN Sales.SalesPerson SP
      ON ST.TerritoryID = SP.TerritoryID;
-- (17 row(s) affected)
```

```
SELECT   isnull(ST.Name, ' ')                     AS Territory,
       SP.BusinessEntityID,
       CONCAT (C.FirstName, ' ', C.LastName)    AS Name
FROM   Sales.SalesTerritory ST
    RIGHT OUTER JOIN Sales.SalesPerson SP
     ON ST.TerritoryID = SP.TerritoryID
    INNER JOIN Person.Person C
     ON SP.BusinessEntityID = C.BusinessEntityID;
-- (17 row(s) affected)
```

RIGHT JOIN - Same as LEFT with Tables Switched

Add a WHERE condition filter on Sales.SalesPerson SalesYTD column
The NULLs indicate the no match rows in the RIGHT OUTER JOIN.

```
SELECT   ST.CountryRegionCode,
         ST.Name                                    AS Territory,
         SP.BusinessEntityID                        AS EmployeeID,
         CONCAT(C.FirstName, ' ', C.LastName )      AS Name
FROM   Sales.SalesTerritory ST
   RIGHT OUTER JOIN Sales.SalesPerson SP
     ON ST.TerritoryID = SP.TerritoryID
   INNER JOIN Person.Person C
     ON SP.BusinessEntityID = C.BusinessEntityID
WHERE SP.SalesYTD > 1000.0
ORDER BY       CountryRegionCode,
               Territory;
GO
-- (17 row(s) affected)
```

CountryRegionCode	Territory	EmployeeID	Name
NULL	NULL	274	Stephen Jiang
NULL	NULL	285	Syed Abbas
NULL	NULL	287	Amy Alberts
AU	Australia	286	Lynn Tsoflias
CA	Canada	278	Garrett Vargas
CA	Canada	282	José Saraiva
DE	Germany	288	Rachel Valdez
FR	France	290	Ranjit Varkey Chudukatil
GB	United Kingdom	289	Jae Pak
US	Central	277	Jillian Carson
US	Northeast	275	Michael Blythe
US	Northwest	283	David Campbell
US	Northwest	284	Tete Mensa-Annan
US	Northwest	280	Pamela Ansman-Wolfe
US	Southeast	279	Tsvi Reiter
US	Southwest	276	Linda Mitchell
US	Southwest	281	Shu Ito

```
-- Counting the RIGHT JOIN  match rows using a ProductSubcategory column
SELECT COUNT( S.Name)
FROM Production.ProductSubcategory S RIGHT JOIN Production.Product P
   ON S.ProductSubcategoryID = P.ProductSubcategoryID;
-- 295
```

Cardinality of OUTER JOINs

The number of rows returned in an OUTER JOIN is equal to the matching rows plus the non-matching rows from either or both tables. **To identify the non-matching rows (the ones with the NULLs) in an outer join we have to choose a not-nullable column like the PRIMARY KEY column.** T-SQL script demonstrates the cardinality involved with a LEFT JOIN.

```
USE AdventureWorks2012;
```

```
-- Rows in LEFT JOIN
SELECT Rows = count(*)
FROM   Production.Product P
    LEFT OUTER JOIN Sales.SalesOrderDetail SOD
         ON P.ProductID = SOD.ProductID
-- 121555
```

```
-- Rows in right table
SELECT Rows = count(*)
FROM Sales.SalesOrderDetail
-- 121317
```

```
-- Non-matching rows in left table
SELECT Rows = count(*)
FROM   Production.Product P
    LEFT OUTER JOIN Sales.SalesOrderDetail SOD
         ON P.ProductID = SOD.ProductID
WHERE SalesOrderID is NULL
-- 238
```

```
-- Right table rows + non-matching left table rows = rows returned by left join
SELECT 121317 + 238
-- 121555
```

Since the count queries are single valued, we can do the following summation.

```
SELECT (SELECT Rows = count(*)  FROM Sales.SalesOrderDetail )
+
(SELECT Rows = count(*)
FROM   Production.Product P
    LEFT OUTER JOIN Sales.SalesOrderDetail SOD
         ON P.ProductID = SOD.ProductID
WHERE SalesOrderID is NULL);
GO  -- 121555
```

CHAPTER 12: JOINing Tables with INNER & OUTER JOINs

LEFT JOIN & RIGHT JOIN on the Same Table

LEFT JOIN & RIGHT JOIN can be combined on the same table to keep all rows from that table even if they don't match the other two tables. The Production.Product table has a FOREIGN KEY referencing the ProductSubcategory table and another FOREIGN KEY referencing the UnitMeasure table.

```sql
SELECT * FROM Production.ProductSubcategory PSC
            RIGHT JOIN Production.Product P
              ON P.ProductSubcategoryID = PSC.ProductSubcategoryID
            LEFT JOIN Production.UnitMeasure UM
              ON P.SizeUnitMeasureCode = UM.UnitMeasureCode;
-- (504 row(s) affected)
SELECT * FROM Production.ProductSubcategory PSC
            INNER JOIN Production.Product P
              ON P.ProductSubcategoryID = PSC.ProductSubcategoryID
            LEFT JOIN Production.UnitMeasure UM
              ON P.SizeUnitMeasureCode = UM.UnitMeasureCode;
-- (295 row(s) affected)
SELECT * FROM Production.ProductSubcategory PSC
            INNER JOIN Production.Product P
              ON P.ProductSubcategoryID = PSC.ProductSubcategoryID
            INNER JOIN Production.UnitMeasure UM
              ON P.SizeUnitMeasureCode = UM.UnitMeasureCode;
-- (176 row(s) affected)
```

	ProductSubcategor...	ProductCategor...	Name	rowg...	ModifiedD...	Produc...	Name
1	NULL	NULL	NULL	NULL	NULL	1	Adjustable R
2	NULL	NULL	NULL	NULL	NULL	2	Bearing Ball

CHAPTER 12: JOINing Tables with INNER & OUTER JOINs

FULL JOIN to Include All Unmatched Rows

The operation FULL JOIN combines LEFT JOIN and RIGHT JOIN, therefore it does not matter which is the left table or right table, it is a fully symmetrical set operation. T-SQL script demonstrates FULL OUTER JOIN.

```
USE tempdb;
-- Create tables for demo
SELECT distinct Color INTO Color
FROM AdventureWorks2012.Production.Product
WHERE Color is not null;
GO
```

```
SELECT ID=IDENTITY(int, 1, 1), * INTO NormalColor
FROM Color;
SELECT ID=IDENTITY(int, 1, 1), Color=CONCAT('Light', Color)  INTO LightColor
FROM Color;
```

```
DELETE NormalColor WHERE Color = 'Red';
```

```
DELETE LightColor WHERE Color = 'LightBlue';
```

```
-- Demo tables ready - full join query
SELECT   NormalColor      = n.Color,
         LightColor       = l.Color
FROM   NormalColor n      FULL OUTER JOIN LightColor l     ON n.ID = l.ID
ORDER BY NormalColor;
```

NormalColor	LightColor
NULL	LightRed
Black	LightBlack
Blue	NULL
Grey	LightGrey
Multi	LightMulti
Silver	LightSilver
Silver/Black	LightSilver/Black
White	LightWhite
Yellow	LightYellow

```
DROP TABLE  tempdb.dbo.Color;   DROP TABLE tempdb.dbo.NormalColor;
DROP TABLE tempdb.dbo.LightColor;
GO
```

CROSS JOIN for Cartesian Product

A CROSS JOIN with no connecting columns for joining produces a Cartesian product: combines all rows of the left table with all rows of the right tables. If the left table has x rows and the right table y rows, the CROSS JOIN is going to have x*y rows. That is called Cartesian explosion as it happens sometimes unintentionally in database development. In fact, a huge CROSS JOIN can bring SQL Server "to its knees", overwhelming CPU and disk resources. On the same note, no matter how powerful is the hardware platform, a bad runaway query can make SQL Server unresponsive to normal queries from other connections. T-SQL script to demonstrate CROSS JOIN.

```
USE AdventureWorks2012;

-- Cardinality of CROSS JOIN
SELECT count(*) from HumanResources.Employee;        -- 290
SELECT count(*) from HumanResources.Department;      -- 16
SELECT 16 * 290;                                     -- 4640

SELECT      E.BusinessEntityID        AS EMPLOYEEID,
            D.Name                    AS DEPARTMENT
FROM  HumanResources.Employee E  CROSS JOIN HumanResources.Department D
ORDER BY      EMPLOYEEID,    DEPARTMENT;
-- (4640 row(s) affected) - Partial results.
```

EMPLOYEEID	DEPARTMENT
1	Production Control
1	Purchasing
1	Quality Assurance
1	Research and Development
1	Sales
1	Shipping and Receiving
1	Tool Design
2	Document Control
2	Engineering
2	Executive
2	Facilities and Maintenance
2	Finance
2	Human Resources
2	Information Services
2	Marketing
2	Production

CROSS JOIN Generated Multiplication Table

A CROSS JOIN can be used to create combinatorical results. In the next example, a multiplication table is created using a CROSS JOIN which is also a SELF-JOIN. CTE stands for Common Table Expression, which can be used as a table in SELECT and other queries. The master database spt_values table is used to get a sequence of numbers. The ".." in the table reference means: use the default schema which is "dbo".

```
; WITH cteNumber                            -- cte for numbers 1 to 10
    AS (SELECT NUMBER
     FROM   master..spt_values
     WHERE  TYPE = 'P'
        AND NUMBER BETWEEN 1 AND 10)
SELECT MULTIPLICATION=CONCAT( ltrim(str(B.NUMBER)) , ' * '
         , ltrim(str(A.NUMBER)) , ' = '
         , ltrim(str(A.NUMBER * B.NUMBER)) )
FROM   cteNumber A   CROSS JOIN cteNumber B;
-- (100 row(s) affected) - Partial results.
```

MULTIPLICATION
1 * 1 = 1
1 * 2 = 2
1 * 3 = 3
1 * 4 = 4
1 * 5 = 5
1 * 6 = 6
1 * 7 = 7
1 * 8 = 8
1 * 9 = 9
1 * 10 = 10
2 * 1 = 2
2 * 2 = 4
2 * 3 = 6
2 * 4 = 8
2 * 5 = 10
2 * 6 = 12
2 * 7 = 14
2 * 8 = 16
2 * 9 = 18
2 * 10 = 20
3 * 1 = 3
3 * 2 = 6
3 * 3 = 9
3 * 4 = 12
3 * 5 = 15

INNER JOIN with 7 Tables

T-SQL query lists AdventureWorks Cycles retail (web) customers with total purchase amount and order dates. The name & address displays multiple times if a customer did multiple purchases. Generally, that is undesirable, and requires end-user report design considerations how to resolve it. The sorting uses Sales.SalesOrderHeader OrderDate which is datetime data type, instead of the mdy format string report date. mdy string format dates do not sort in chronological order.

```
USE AdventureWorks;
GO

SELECT CONCAT(C.LastName, ', ', C.FirstName)     AS CustomerName,
       A.City,
       SP.Name                                    AS State,
       CR.Name                                    AS Country,
       A.PostalCode,
       FORMAT(SOH.TotalDue, 'c','en-US')          AS SalesAmount,
       FORMAT(SOH.OrderDate,'d')                  AS OrderDate
FROM Person.Contact AS C
   INNER JOIN Sales.Individual AS I
        ON C.ContactID = I.ContactID
   INNER JOIN Sales.CustomerAddress AS CA
        ON CA.CustomerID = I.CustomerID
   INNER JOIN Person.Address AS A
        ON A.AddressID = CA.AddressID
   INNER JOIN Person.StateProvince SP
        ON SP.StateProvinceID = A.StateProvinceID
   INNER JOIN Person.CountryRegion CR
        ON CR.CountryRegionCode = SP.CountryRegionCode
   INNER JOIN Sales.SalesOrderHeader SOH
        ON C.ContactID = SOH.CustomerID
ORDER BY CustomerName, soh.OrderDate ;
-- (16493 row(s) affected)  - Partial results.
```

CustomerName	City	State	Country	PostalCode	SalesAmount	OrderDate
Adams, Aaron	Downey	California	United States	90241	$734.70	3/4/2004
Adams, Adam	Newport Beach	California	United States	92625	$2,566.12	4/16/2004
Adams, Alex	Lake Oswego	Oregon	United States	97034	$2,410.63	3/18/2003
Adams, Alex	Lake Oswego	Oregon	United States	97034	$1,293.38	12/9/2003
Adams, Alex	Lake Oswego	Oregon	United States	97034	$2,643.12	2/1/2004
Adams, Angel	Burlingame	California	United States	94010	$865.20	5/24/2003
Adams, Angel	Burlingame	California	United States	94010	$2,597.81	3/1/2004
Adams, Carlos	Langford	British Columbia	Canada	V9	$44.18	6/28/2004
Adams, Connor	Westminster	British Columbia	Canada	V3L 1H4	$183.74	4/14/2004
Adams, Elijah	Seattle	Washington	United States	98104	$8.04	11/2/2003

INNER JOIN with GROUP BY Subquery

We have to make the GROUP BY subquery into a derived table first. Subsequently, we can apply it just like any other table in a query.

```
USE AdventureWorks2012;
GO

SELECT  Subcategory = Name,
        Color,
        ColorCount,
        AvgListPrice
FROM   (
        SELECT ProductSubcategoryID,                     -- grouping column
         Color = COALESCE(Color, 'N/A'),                 -- grouping column with transformation
         ColorCount = COUNT(*),                          -- aggregate function
         AvgListPrice = AVG(COALESCE(ListPrice, 0.0))    -- aggregate function
         FROM    AdventureWorks2008.Production.Product
         GROUP  BY       ProductSubcategoryID,
                        Color) x                         -- derived table (subquery)
    INNER JOIN Production.ProductSubcategory psc
         ON psc.ProductSubcategoryID = x.ProductSubcategoryID
ORDER  BY Subcategory,
        Color;
GO
-- (48 row(s) affected) - Partial results.
```

Subcategory	Color	ColorCount	AvgListPrice
Bib-Shorts	Multi	3	89.990000
Bike Racks	N/A	1	120.000000
Bike Stands	N/A	1	159.000000
Bottles and Cages	N/A	3	7.990000
Bottom Brackets	N/A	3	92.240000
Brakes	Silver	2	106.500000
Caps	Multi	1	8.990000
Chains	Silver	1	20.240000
Cleaners	N/A	1	7.950000
Cranksets	Black	3	278.990000
Derailleurs	Silver	2	106.475000
Fenders	N/A	1	21.980000

Making Queries Readable & Results Presentable

A database developer has to make a query readable for productivity gain in development and ease of maintenance. At the same time the results must be readable to the user. The next query with results demonstrates how to achieve both objectives.

```
USE AdventureWorks2012;
GO
```

```
SELECT  PC.Name                            AS Category,
        PSC.Name                           AS Subcategory,
        PM.Name                            AS Model,
        P.Name                             AS ProductName,
        FORMAT(ListPrice,'c','en-US')      AS Price
FROM Production.Product AS P
   INNER JOIN Production.ProductModel AS PM
       ON PM.ProductModelID = P.ProductModelID
   INNER JOIN Production.ProductSubcategory AS PSC
       ON PSC.ProductSubcategoryID = P.ProductSubcategoryID
   INNER JOIN Production.ProductCategory AS PC
       ON PC.ProductCategoryID = PSC.ProductCategoryID
ORDER BY Category, Subcategory, ProductName;
GO
-- (295 row(s) affected) - Partial results.
```

The confusing 4 "Name" columns are clarified by well-chosen column aliases. The meaningful column aliases are used in the ORDER BY clause even though not required. To help the user, the list price is currency formatted.

Category	Subcategory	Model	ProductName	Price
Accessories	Bike Racks	Hitch Rack - 4-Bike	Hitch Rack - 4-Bike	$120.00
Accessories	Bike Stands	All-Purpose Bike Stand	All-Purpose Bike Stand	$159.00
Accessories	Bottles and Cages	Mountain Bottle Cage	Mountain Bottle Cage	$9.99
Accessories	Bottles and Cages	Road Bottle Cage	Road Bottle Cage	$8.99
Accessories	Bottles and Cages	Water Bottle	Water Bottle - 30 oz.	$4.99
Accessories	Cleaners	Bike Wash	Bike Wash - Dissolver	$7.95
Accessories	Fenders	Fender Set - Mountain	Fender Set - Mountain	$21.98
Accessories	Helmets	Sport-100	Sport-100 Helmet, Black	$34.99
Accessories	Helmets	Sport-100	Sport-100 Helmet, Blue	$34.99
Accessories	Helmets	Sport-100	Sport-100 Helmet, Red	$34.99

A 12 Tables JOIN Query
The next query JOINs 11 tables, some of the tables occur more than once in the query.

```
USE AdventureWorks;

DECLARE        @Year  int,
               @Month int

SET @Year      = 2004;
SET @Month     = 1;

SELECT SOH.SalesOrderNumber                        AS SON,
    SOH.PurchaseOrderNumber                        AS PO,
    S.Name                                         AS Store,
    CONVERT(VARCHAR, SOH.OrderDate, 110)           AS OrderDate,
    CONVERT(VARCHAR, SOH.ShipDate, 110)            AS ShipDate,
    FORMAT(TotalDue,'c','en-US')                   AS [Total Due],
    CONCAT(C.FirstName,' ',C.LastName)             AS SalesStaff,
    SM.Name                                        AS ShpngMethod,
    BA.AddressLine1                                AS BlngAddress1,
    Isnull(BA.AddressLine2, '')                    AS BlngAddress2,
    BA.City                                        AS BlngCity,
    BSP.Name                                       AS BlngStateProvince,
    BA.PostalCode                                  AS BlngPostalCode,
    BCR.Name                                       AS BlngCountryRegion,
    SA.AddressLine1                                AS ShpngAddress1,
    Isnull(SA.AddressLine2, '')                    AS ShpngAddress2,
    SA.City                                        AS ShpngCity,
    SSP.Name                                       AS ShpngStateProvince,
    SA.PostalCode                                  AS ShpngPostalCode,
    SCR.Name                                       AS ShpngCountryRegion,
    CONCAT(CC.FirstName,' ',CC.LastName)           AS CustomerContact,
    CC.Phone                                       AS CustomerPhone,
    SOH.AccountNumber
FROM   Person.Address SA
    INNER JOIN Person.StateProvince SSP
        ON SA.StateProvinceID = SSP.StateProvinceID
    INNER JOIN Person.CountryRegion SCR
        ON SSP.CountryRegionCode = SCR.CountryRegionCode
    INNER JOIN Sales.SalesOrderHeader SOH
        INNER JOIN Person.Contact CC
            ON SOH.ContactID = CC.ContactID
        INNER JOIN Person.Address BA
            INNER JOIN Person.StateProvince BSP
                ON BA.StateProvinceID = BSP.StateProvinceID
            INNER JOIN Person.CountryRegion BCR
```

A 12 Tables JOIN Query

```
-- T-SQL query continued
                    ON BSP.CountryRegionCode =
                       BCR.CountryRegionCode
                 ON SOH.BillToAddressID = BA.AddressID
              ON SA.AddressID = SOH.ShipToAddressID
        INNER JOIN Person.Contact C
           INNER JOIN HumanResources.Employee E
              ON C.ContactID = E.ContactID
           ON SOH.SalesPersonID = E.EmployeeID
        INNER JOIN Purchasing.ShipMethod SM
           ON SOH.ShipMethodID = SM.ShipMethodID
        INNER JOIN Sales.Store S
           ON SOH.CustomerID = S.CustomerID
WHERE  SOH.OrderDate >= datefromparts(@Year, @month, 1)
    AND  SOH.OrderDate < dateadd(mm,1,datefromparts(@Year, @month, 1))
ORDER  BY Store,   OrderDate DESC;
GO
-- (96 row(s) affected) - Partial results.
```

SON	PO	Store	OrderDate	ShipDate	Total Due	SalesStaff	ShpngMethod	BlngAddress1
SO61257	PO3741176337	Activity Center	01-01-2004	01-08-2004	$12,764.08	Tsvi Reiter	CARGO TRANSPORT 5	Factory Stores Of America
SO61256	PO1421187796	All Cycle Shop	01-01-2004	01-08-2004	$201.08	Tete Mensa-Annan	CARGO TRANSPORT 5	25111 228th St Sw
SO61251	PO6380165323	All Seasons Sports Supply	01-01-2004	01-08-2004	$2,863.30	Michael Blythe	CARGO TRANSPORT 5	Ohms Road
SO61263	PO5452121402	Amalgamated Parts Shop	01-01-2004	01-08-2004	$39,103.04	Rachel Valdez	CARGO TRANSPORT 5	Brunnenstr 422
SO61227	PO10730172247	Area Bike Accessories	01-01-2004	01-08-2004	$75,916.89	Shu Ito	CARGO TRANSPORT 5	6900 Sisk Road
SO61187	PO13978135025	Basic Bike Company	01-01-2004	01-08-2004	$72.92	David Campbell	CARGO TRANSPORT 5	15 East Main
SO61190	PO12441157171	Best Cycle Store	01-01-2004	01-08-2004	$49,337.61	Rachel Valdez	CARGO TRANSPORT 5	Berliner Platz 45
SO61221	PO15399128383	Best o' Bikes	01-01-2004	01-08-2004	$5,872.73	Michael Blythe	CARGO TRANSPORT 5	250880 Baur Blvd
SO61173	PO522171689	Better Bike Shop	01-01-2004	01-08-2004	$38,511.29	Tsvi Reiter	CARGO TRANSPORT 5	42525 Austell Road
SO61254	PO4872176154	Bicycle Exporters	01-01-2004	01-08-2004	$10,665.06	Rachel Valdez	CARGO TRANSPORT 5	Hellweg 4934
SO61243	PO7859152962	Bike Dealers Association	01-01-2004	01-08-2004	$18,976.48	Shu Ito	CARGO TRANSPORT 5	9952 E. Lohman Ave.
SO61250	PO4930183869	Bikes for Kids and Adults	01-01-2004	01-08-2004	$3,852.87	Jae Pak	CARGO TRANSPORT 5	9900 Ronson Drive
SO61209	PO11484136165	Casual Bicycle Store	01-01-2004	01-08-2004	$37,314.33	Jillian Carson	CARGO TRANSPORT 5	Westside Plaza
SO61204	PO15312134209	Citywide Service and Repair	01-01-2004	01-08-2004	$29,797.18	Jae Pak	CARGO TRANSPORT 5	Box 99354 300 Union Street
SO61192	PO10092119585	Classic Cycle Store	01-01-2004	01-08-2004	$3,691.57	Jillian Carson	CARGO TRANSPORT 5	630 Oldgate Lane

Order of Tables or Predicates Does Not Matter

Frequent question: does the order of tables matter in a JOIN? Should I put BETWEEN predicate before LIKE predicate? Valid syntax variations do not matter. The database engine translates the query to an internal form prior to creating an execution plan. Thus the different variations get translated to the same internal form. The only way we have some control over the database engine if we rewrite a single statement complex query to a multi-statements script.

Nondeterministic CTE

CTE is evaluated for every reference, therefore it may return different results if certain functions are used such as newid(), thus yielding a nondeterministic CTE.

```
;WITH CTE AS (SELECT Random = NEWID()),
CTE1 AS (SELECT * FROM CTE),
CTE2 AS (SELECT * FROM CTE),
CTE3 AS (SELECT * FROM CTE),
CTE4 AS (SELECT * FROM CTE),
CTE5 AS (SELECT * FROM CTE)
SELECT * FROM CTE1
UNION ALL
SELECT * FROM CTE2
UNION ALL
SELECT * FROM CTE3
UNION ALL
SELECT * FROM CTE4
UNION ALL
SELECT * FROM CTE5
UNION ALL
SELECT * FROM CTE
UNION ALL
SELECT * FROM CTE
UNION ALL
SELECT * FROM CTE;
```

Random
08D45FE2-52C6-4E15-83A3-0B2F27837887
D6A094E6-0C8A-43E4-B6C4-8821F6EE8E73
281A5852-3D9A-4F2A-99FA-F60EE28FD2E0
C327ED19-5C03-4D9B-A8E8-6ACABAA08F1C
80DDE508-A6AA-4F2B-AB2F-CEEF7EC5E163
5F611B03-46F4-4EED-A8E0-76020527899D
FF8DAE17-65F6-4D80-8AF5-29EBAEBD2FEB
CF342DC9-4CF9-46FD-87F0-3213106C447D

The CROSS APPLY Operator

The APPLY (CROSS APPLY & OUTER APPLY) operators were introduced with SQL Server 2005. The CROSS APPLY operator merges rows from tables (or views) with rows from table-valued function, a form of JOIN.

```
USE AdventureWorks2012;
SELECT
        q.last_execution_time                AS LastRun,
        t.TEXT                               AS QueryText,
        q.sql_handle                         AS SQLHandle
FROM    sys.dm_exec_query_stats AS q                         -- system view
            CROSS APPLY
            sys.dm_exec_sql_text(q.sql_handle) AS t          -- table-valued system function
WHERE LEFT(t.TEXT,8)='SELECT *'  ORDER BY LastRun DESC;
```

LastRun	QueryText
2016-08-01 14:46:12.537	SELECT * FROM Sales.SalesOrderHeader
2016-08-01 14:44:54.257	SELECT * FROM Production.Product
2016-08-01 13:29:25.213	SELECT * FROM sys.dm_os_wait_stats
2016-08-01 09:36:57.980	select * from sys.sysforeignkeys s
2016-08-01 09:36:39.077	select * from sysforeignkeys s

```
-- Return the top N purchase order by amount - inline table-valued function
CREATE FUNCTION dbo.ufnGetTopNPurchases(@VendorID AS INT, @N AS INT)
RETURNS TABLE AS
RETURN
 SELECT TOP ( @N ) *   FROM Purchasing.PurchaseOrderHeader
 WHERE VendorID = @VendorID   ORDER BY TotalDue DESC;
GO  -- Command(s) completed successfully.
```

```
-- List the top 5 highest purchases from vendors
SELECT V.VendorID,
       P.PurchaseOrderID,
       FORMAT(P.TotalDue, 'c','en-US')    AS TotalDue
FROM   Purchasing.Vendor AS V  CROSS APPLY  dbo.ufnGetTopNPurchases(V.VendorID, 5) AS P
ORDER BY V.VendorID, TotalDue DESC
-- (395 row(s) affected) - Partial results.
```

VendorID	PurchaseOrderID	TotalDue
74	325	$1,654.75
74	1727	$855.22
74	2517	$855.22
74	3307	$855.22
74	167	$785.61

CHAPTER 12: JOINing Tables with INNER & OUTER JOINs

Using CROSS APPLY with Columns Specified Table Alias

A regular table alias would result in error in the following delimited string list query. Table alias with column(s) specifications "o(list)" works, the table alias is "o", it has one column "list".

```
USE AdventureWorks;

SELECT  Dealer = st.Name,
        [SalesOrders] = LEFT(o.list,LEN(o.list) - 1)
FROM    Sales.Customer c
        INNER JOIN Sales.Store st
          ON c.CustomerID = st.CustomerID
        CROSS APPLY (SELECT   CONVERT(VARCHAR(14),SalesOrderID) + ',' AS [text()]
                     FROM     Sales.SalesOrderHeader s
                     WHERE    s.CustomerID = c.CustomerID
                     ORDER BY SalesOrderID
                     FOR XML PATH('')
                     ) o(list)
ORDER BY st.Name;
```

#	Dealer	SalesOrders
1	A Bicycle Association	NULL
2	A Bike Store	43860,44501,45283,46042
3	A Cycle Shop	NULL
4	A Great Bicycle Company	44125,44793,45569,46378,49537,59009
5	A Typical Bike Shop	44092,44755,45536,46343
6	Acceptable Sales & Service	43893,46075
7	Accessories Network	53559,58936,71870
8	Acclaimed Bicycle Company	53618,59070,65259,71883
9	Ace Bicycle Supply	46982,48007,49056,51801,63208,69428

701 rows

CROSS APPLY: Most Popular Sales Products Info

```
CREATE FUNCTION ufnProductDetails (@ProductID INT) RETURNS TABLE  AS RETURN
(       SELECT ProductNumber, ListPrice, Color
        FROM Production.Product WHERE ProductID = @ProductID  );
GO
;WITH CTE AS (    SELECT ProductID FROM Sales.SalesOrderDetail
                            GROUP BY ProductID HAVING COUNT(*) > 1000)
SELECT ProductNumber, ListPrice, Color
FROM CTE CROSS APPLY ufnProductDetails (ProductID)
WHERE Color is not null ORDER BY ProductNumber;  -- (15 row(s) affected);
```

CHAPTER 12: JOINing Tables with INNER & OUTER JOINs

CHAPTER 13: Basic SELECT Statement Syntax & Examples

Simple SELECT Statement Variations

SELECT is the most famous statement in the SQL language. It is used to query tables, and generate reports for users. Although SQL Server Reporting Services and other 3rd party packages available for reporting purposes, frequently reports are generated straight from the database with SELECT queries. The next query returns all rows, all columns sorted on DepartmentID.

```
USE AdventureWorks2012;
```

```
SELECT * FROM  HumanResources.Department  ORDER BY DepartmentID;
-- (16 row(s) affected)
```

DepartmentID	Name	GroupName	ModifiedDate
1	Engineering	Research and Development	1998-06-01 00:00:00.000
2	Tool Design	Research and Development	1998-06-01 00:00:00.000
3	Sales	Sales and Marketing	1998-06-01 00:00:00.000
4	Marketing	Sales and Marketing	1998-06-01 00:00:00.000
5	Purchasing	Inventory Management	1998-06-01 00:00:00.000
6	Research and Development	Research and Development	1998-06-01 00:00:00.000
7	Production	Manufacturing	1998-06-01 00:00:00.000
8	Production Control	Manufacturing	1998-06-01 00:00:00.000
9	Human Resources	Executive General and Administration	1998-06-01 00:00:00.000
10	Finance	Executive General and Administration	1998-06-01 00:00:00.000
11	Information Services	Executive General and Administration	1998-06-01 00:00:00.000
12	Document Control	Quality Assurance	1998-06-01 00:00:00.000
13	Quality Assurance	Quality Assurance	1998-06-01 00:00:00.000
14	Facilities and Maintenance	Executive General and Administration	1998-06-01 00:00:00.000
15	Shipping and Receiving	Inventory Management	1998-06-01 00:00:00.000
16	Executive	Executive General and Administration	1998-06-01 00:00:00.000

Since the time part of ModifiedDate is not being used, and that makes business sense, we can format it just as date.

```
SELECT TOP (3) DepartmentID, Name, GroupName, CONVERT(DATE, ModifiedDate) AS ModifiedDate
FROM  HumanResources.Department  ORDER BY DepartmentID;
-- (16 row(s) affected)
```

DepartmentID	Name	GroupName	ModifiedDate
1	Engineering	Research and Development	1998-06-01
2	Tool Design	Research and Development	1998-06-01
3	Sales	Sales and Marketing	1998-06-01

SELECT query with sort on EnglishProductName in DESCending order
ASCending sort is the default.

```
USE AdventureWorksDW2012
GO

SELECT  *
FROM    DimProduct
ORDER BY EnglishProductName DESC
GO
-- (606 row(s) affected) - Partial results.
```

EnglishProductName	SpanishProductName	FrenchProductName	StandardCost
Women's Tights, S	Mallas para mujer, P	Collants pour femmes, taille S	30.9334
Women's Tights, M	Mallas para mujer, M	Collants pour femmes, taille M	30.9334
Women's Tights, L	Mallas para mujer, G	Collants pour femmes, taille L	30.9334
Women's Mountain Shorts, S			26.1763
Women's Mountain Shorts, M			26.1763
Women's Mountain Shorts, L			26.1763
Water Bottle - 30 oz.			1.8663
Touring-Panniers, Large	Cesta de paseo, grande	Sacoches de vélo de randonnée, grande capacité	51.5625
Touring-3000 Yellow, 62	Paseo: 3000, amarilla, 62	Vélo de randonnée 3000 jaune, 62	461.4448
Touring-3000 Yellow, 58	Paseo: 3000, amarilla, 58	Vélo de randonnée 3000 jaune, 58	461.4448

The next query sorts on the SpanishProductName column in ascending order.

```
SELECT  *
FROM    DimProduct
ORDER BY SpanishProductName ASC
GO
-- (606 row(s) affected) - Partial results.
```

EnglishProductName	SpanishProductName
HL Crankset	Bielas GA
LL Crankset	Bielas GB
ML Crankset	Bielas GM
Mountain Pump	Bomba de montaña
Cable Lock	Cable antirrobo
Chain	Cadena
Mountain Bike Socks,	Calcetines para bicicleta de montaña, G

Sorting on FrenchProductName, if empty, use EnglishProductName.

```
SELECT  * FROM    DimProduct ORDER BY FrenchProductName, EnglishProductName;
GO
```

CHAPTER 13: Basic SELECT Statement Syntax & Examples

Using the TOP Clause in SELECT Queries

The TOP clause limits the number of rows returned as specified in the TOP expression according the sorted order if any. In the following query, the sorting is based on a major key (LastName) and a minor key (FirstName).

USE AdventureWorks2012
GO

SELECT TOP 100 *
FROM Person.Person ORDER BY LastName, FirstName
-- (100 row(s) affected) - Partial results.

BusinessEntityID	PersonType	Title	FirstName	LastName	EmailPromotion
285	SP	Mr.	Syed	Abbas	0
293	SC	Ms.	Catherine	Abel	1
295	SC	Ms.	Kim	Abercrombie	0
2170	GC	NULL	Kim	Abercrombie	2
38	EM	NULL	Kim	Abercrombie	2
211	EM	NULL	Hazem	Abolrous	0
2357	GC	NULL	Sam	Abolrous	1
297	SC	Sr.	Humberto	Acevedo	2
291	SC	Mr.	Gustavo	Achong	2
299	SC	Sra.	Pilar	Ackerman	0

The total population of the Person.Person table is 19,972 rows.

SELECT * FROM Person.Person ORDER BY LastName, FirstName
-- (19972 row(s) affected)

We can also count the rows applying the COUNT function.

SELECT RowsCount = count(*) FROM Person.Person
-- 19972

When counting, it is safe to count the PRIMARY KEY (ProductID) values.

SELECT RowsCount = count(ProductID) FROM Production.Product;
-- 504

SELECT RowsCount = count(Color) FROM Production.Product;   -- 256

CHAPTER 13: Basic SELECT Statement Syntax & Examples

Using the WHERE Clause in SELECT Queries

The WHERE clause filters the rows to be returned according the one or more predicates. The next T-SQL scripts demonstrate simple WHERE clause predicates, including multiple WHERE conditions.

```
-- Last name starts with S
SELECT *
FROM    Person.Person
WHERE   LEFT(LastName,1) = 'S'
ORDER BY LastName;
-- (2130 row(s) affected)
```

```
-- First name is Shelly
SELECT  *
FROM    Person.Person
WHERE   FirstName = 'Shelly'
ORDER BY LastName;
-- (1 row(s) affected)
```

```
-- First name is John
SELECT  *
FROM    Person.Person
WHERE   FirstName = 'John'
ORDER BY LastName;
-- (58 row(s) affected)
```

```
-- First name John, last name starts with S - Multiple WHERE conditions
SELECT  *
FROM    Person.Person
WHERE   FirstName = 'John'
     AND LEFT(LastName,1) = 'S'
ORDER BY LastName ;
-- (2 row(s) affected)
```

```
-- Last name starts with S OR first name starts with J
SELECT  *
FROM    Person.Person
WHERE   LEFT(FirstName,1) = 'J'   OR LEFT(LastName,1) = 'S'
ORDER BY LastName;
-- (4371 row(s) affected)
```

```
-- Last name starts with S AND first name starts with J
SELECT  *
FROM    Person.Person  WHERE    LEFT(FirstName,1) = 'J'    AND LEFT(LastName,1) = 'S'
ORDER BY LastName;   -- (221 row(s) affected)
```

Using Literals in SELECT Queries

Literals or constants are used commonly in T-SQL queries, also as defaults for columns, local variables, and parameters. The format of a literal depends on the data type of the value it represents. The database engine may perform implicit conversion to match data types. Explicit conversion of literals can be achieved with the CONVERT or CAST functions. T-SQL scripts demonstrate literal use in WHERE clause predicates.

```
USE AdventureWorks2012;
-- Integer literal  in WHERE clause predicate
SELECT * FROM Production.Product
WHERE ProductID = 800;
-- (1 row(s) affected)
```

```
-- String literal in WHERE clause predicate
SELECT * FROM Production.Product WHERE Color = 'Blue';
-- (26 row(s) affected)
```

```
USE AdventureWorksDW2012;
-- UNICODE (2 bytes per character) string literal
SELECT * FROM DimProduct
WHERE SpanishProductName = N'Jersey clásico de manga corta, G';
-- (1 row(s) affected)
```

```
-- UNICODE string literal
SELECT * FROM DimProduct
WHERE FrenchProductName = N'Roue arrière de vélo de randonnée';
-- (1 row(s) affected)
```

```
USE AdventureWorks2012;
-- Money literal in WHERE clause predicate
SELECT * FROM Production.Product
WHERE ListPrice > = $2000.0;
-- (35 row(s) affected)
```

```
-- Floating point literal with implicit conversion to MONEY
SELECT * FROM Production.Product  WHERE ListPrice > = 2.000E+3;
-- (35 row(s) affected)
```

```
-- Hex (binary) literal
SELECT * FROM Production.Product  WHERE rowguid >= 0x23D89CEE9F444F3EB28963DE6BA2B737
-- (302 row(s) affected)
```

```
-- The rest of the 504 products
SELECT * FROM Production.Product  WHERE rowguid < 0x23D89CEE9F444F3EB28963DE6BA2B737
-- (202 row(s) affected)
```

CHAPTER 13: Basic SELECT Statement Syntax & Examples

Date & Time Literals in SELECT Queries

Date and time literals appear to come from an infinite pool. Every country has tens of string date & time variations. Despite the many external string representation, **date, datetime, datetime, time, smalldatetime** and other temporal data types have unique, well-defined representation within the database engine.

ymd date literal format is the cleanest. There is eternal confusion about the North American mdy string date format and the European dmy string date format. The date and time format with "T" separator (last one) is the ISO date time format literal. ANSI Date literal - YYYYMMDD - the best choice since it work in any country.

CONVERT or CAST Date Time Literal	Result
SELECT [Date] = CAST('20160228' AS date)	2016-02-28
SELECT [Datetime] = CAST('20160228' AS datetime)	2016-02-28 00:00:00.000
SELECT [SmallDatetime] = CAST('20160228' AS smalldatetime)	2016-02-28 00:00:00
SELECT [Datetime] = CONVERT(datetime,'2016-02-28')	2016-02-28 00:00:00.000
SELECT [Datetime2] = CONVERT(datetime2,'2016-02-28')	2016-02-28 00:00:00.0000000
SELECT [Datetime] = CONVERT(datetime, '20160228')	2016-02-28 00:00:00.000
SELECT [Datetime2] = CONVERT(datetime2,'20160228')	2016-02-28 00:00:00.0000000
SELECT [Datetime] = CAST('Mar 15, 2016' AS datetime)	2016-03-15 00:00:00.000
SELECT [Datetime2] = CAST('Mar 15, 2016' AS datetime2)	2016-03-15 00:00:00.0000000
SELECT [Date] = CAST('Mar 15, 2016' AS date)	2016-03-15
SELECT CAST('16:40:31' AS datetime)	1900-01-01 16:40:31.000
SELECT CAST('16:40:31' AS time)	16:40:31.0000000
SELECT [Datetime] = CAST('Mar 15, 2016 12:07:34.444' AS datetime)	2016-03-15 12:07:34.443
SELECT [Datetime2] = CAST('Mar 15, 2016 12:07:34.4445555' AS datetime2)	2016-03-15 12:07:34.4445555
SELECT [Datetime] = CAST('2016-03-15T12:07:34.513' AS datetime)	2016-03-15 12:07:34.513

CHAPTER 13: Basic SELECT Statement Syntax & Examples

ymd, dmy & mdy String Date Format Literals

Date and time string literals are the least understood part of the T-SQL language by database developers. It is a constant source of confusion and frustration, in addition huge economic cost of lost programmer's productivity. ymd, dmy & mdy are the main string date formats. Some countries use ydm format. Setting dateformat overrides the implicit setting by language.

The basic principles:

> - **There is only one DATETIME data type internal format**, independent where SQL Server is operated: New York, London, Amsterdam, Berlin, Moscow, Hong Kong, Singapore, Tokyo, Melbourne or Rio de Janeiro.
> - There are hundreds of national string date & time formats which have nothing to do with SQL Server.
> - String date must be properly converted to DATETIME format.

```
SET DATEFORMAT ymd
SELECT convert(datetime,'16/05/08')            -- 2016-05-08 00:00:00.000

-- Setting DATEFORMAT to UK-Style (European)
SET DATEFORMAT dmy
SELECT convert(datetime,'20/05/16')            -- 2016-05-20 00:00:00.000

-- Setting DATEFORMAT to US-Style
SET DATEFORMAT mdy
SELECT convert(datetime,'05/20/16')            -- 2016-05-20 00:00:00.000
SELECT convert(datetime,'05/20/2016')          -- 2016-05-20 00:00:00.000
```
Interestingly we can achieve the same implicit conversion action by setting language.

```
-- Setting DATEFORMAT ymd  via language
SET LANGUAGE Japanese;  SELECT convert(datetime,'16/05/08') ;     -- 2016-05-08 00:00:00.000

-- Setting DATEFORMAT to UK-Style (European) via language
SET LANGUAGE British;  SELECT convert(datetime,'20/05/16');       -- 2016-05-20 00:00:00.000
SELECT convert(datetime,'05/20/16');
/* Msg 242, Level 16, State 3, Line 3
The conversion of a varchar data type to a datetime data type resulted in an out-of-range value.  */

-- Setting DATEFORMAT to US-Style via language
SET LANGUAGE English;  SELECT convert(datetime,'05/20/16');       -- 2016-05-20 00:00:00.000
SELECT convert(datetime,'05/20/2016');                            -- 2016-05-20 00:00:00.000
SELECT convert(datetime,'20/05/2016');
/* Msg 242, Level 16, State 3, Line 4
The conversion of a varchar data type to a datetime data type resulted in an out-of-range value.  */
```

Setting DATEFIRST with Literal

DATEFIRST indicates the first day of the week which may vary by country, culture or business. The next T-SQL script demonstrates how it can be set by integer literal 1-7. It overrides the implicit setting by language. @@DATEFIRST is a system (SQL Server database engine) variable.

```
SET DATEFIRST 7  -- Sunday as first day of the week
SELECT DATEPART(dw, '20160315');            -- 3
SELECT DATENAME(dw, '20160315');            -- Tuesday
SELECT @@DATEFIRST                          -- 7
```

```
SET DATEFIRST 1  -- Monday as first day of the week
SELECT DATEPART(dw, '20160315');            -- 2
SELECT DATENAME(dw, '20160315');            -- Tuesday
SELECT @@DATEFIRST                          -- 1
```

Language Setting - SET LANGUAGE

DATEFIRST is tied to the language setting, just the like the date format (ymd, dmy, or mdy).

```
SET LANGUAGE us_english
SELECT DATEPART(dw, '20160315');            -- 3
SELECT DATENAME(dw, '20160315');            -- Tuesday
SELECT @@DATEFIRST                          -- 7
```

```
SET LANGUAGE german
SELECT DATEPART(dw, '20160315');            -- 2
SELECT DATENAME(dw, '20160315');            -- Dienstag
SELECT @@DATEFIRST                          -- 1
```

```
SET LANGUAGE british
SELECT DATEPART(dw, '20160315');            -- 2
SELECT DATENAME(dw, '20160315');            -- Tuesday
SELECT @@DATEFIRST                          -- 1
```

```
SET LANGUAGE hungarian
SELECT DATEPART(dw, '20160315');            -- 2
SELECT DATENAME(dw, '20160315');            -- kedd
SELECT @@DATEFIRST                          -- 1
```

```
SET LANGUAGE spanish
SELECT DATEPART(dw, '20160315');            -- 2
SELECT DATENAME(dw, '20160315');            -- Martes
SELECT @@DATEFIRST                          -- 1
```

CHAPTER 13: Basic SELECT Statement Syntax & Examples

The sys.syslanguages System View

The syslanguages table contains not only language related information, but date related settings as well.

```
SELECT
        langid,
        dateformat,
        datefirst,
        name                            AS native_language,
        alias                           AS english,
        left(shortmonths, 15)           AS shortmonths,
        left(days,15)                   AS days
FROM AdventureWorks2012.sys.syslanguages
ORDER BY langid;
GO
-- (34 row(s) affected)  -  Partial results.
```

langid	dateformat	datefirst	native_language	english	shortmonths	days
0	mdy	7	us_english	English	Jan,Feb,Mar,Apr	Monday,Tuesday,
1	dmy	1	Deutsch	German	Jan,Feb,Mär,Apr	Montag,Dienstag
2	dmy	1	Français	French	janv,févr,mars,	lundi,mardi,mer
3	ymd	7	日本語	Japanese	01,02,03,04,05,	月曜日,火曜日,水曜日,木曜日
4	dmy	1	Dansk	Danish	jan,feb,mar,apr	mandag,tirsdag,
5	dmy	1	Español	Spanish	Ene,Feb,Mar,Abr	Lunes,Martes,Mi
6	dmy	1	Italiano	Italian	gen,feb,mar,apr	lunedì,martedì,
7	dmy	1	Nederlands	Dutch	jan,feb,mrt,apr	maandag,dinsdag
8	dmy	1	Norsk	Norwegian	jan,feb,mar,apr	mandag,tirsdag,
9	dmy	7	Português	Portuguese	jan,fev,mar,abr	segunda-feira,t
10	dmy	1	Suomi	Finnish	tammi,helmi,maa	maanantai,tiist
11	ymd	1	Svenska	Swedish	jan,feb,mar,apr	måndag,tisdag,o
12	dmy	1	čeština	Czech	I,II,III,IV,V,V	pondělí,úterý,s
13	ymd	1	magyar	Hungarian	jan,febr,márc,á	hétfő,kedd,szer
14	dmy	1	polski	Polish	I,II,III,IV,V,V	poniedziałek,wt
15	dmy	1	română	Romanian	Ian,Feb,Mar,Apr	luni,marţi,mier
16	ymd	1	hrvatski	Croatian	sij,vel,ožu,tra	ponedjeljak,uto
17	dmy	1	slovenčina	Slovak	I,II,III,IV,V,V	pondelok,utorok
18	dmy	1	slovenski	Slovenian	jan,feb,mar,apr	ponedeljek,tore
19	dmy	1	ελληνικά	Greek	Ιαν,Φεβ,Μαρ,Απρ	Δευτέρα,Τρίτη,Τ
20	dmy	1	български	Bulgarian	януари,февруари	понеделник,втор
21	dmy	1	русский	Russian	янв,фев,мар,апр	понедельник,вто
22	dmy	1	Türkçe	Turkish	Oca,Şub,Mar,Nis	Pazartesi,Salı,
23	dmy	1	British	British English	Jan,Feb,Mar,Apr	Monday,Tuesday,
24	dmy	1	eesti	Estonian	jaan,veebr,märt	esmaspäev,teisi
25	ymd	1	latviešu	Latvian	jan,feb,mar,apr	pirmdiena,otrdi
26	ymd	1	lietuvių	Lithuanian	sau,vas,kov,bal	pirmadienis,ant
27	dmy	7	Português (Brasil)	Brazilian	Jan,Fev,Mar,Abr	Segunda-Feira,T
28	ymd	7	繁體中文	Traditional Chinese	01,02,03,04,05,	星期一,星期二,星期三,星期四
29	ymd	7	한국어	Korean	01,02,03,04,05,	월요일,화요일,수요일,목요일
30	ymd	7	简体中文	Simplified Chinese	01,02,03,04,05,	星期一,星期二,星期三,星期四
31	dmy	1	Arabic	Arabic	Jan,Feb,Mar,Apr	Monday,Tuesday,
32	dmy	7	ไทย	Thai	ม.ค.,ก.พ.,มี.ค.	จันทร์,อังคาร,พ
33	dmy	1	norsk (bokmål)	Bokmål	jan,feb,mar,apr	mandag,tirsdag,

CHAPTER 13: Basic SELECT Statement Syntax & Examples

DBCC USEROPTIONS

The DBCC USEROPTIONS command displays some of the connection (session) settings. As we have seen these settings play an important part on how date literals are interpreted by the system such as dateformat.

	Set Option	Value
1	textsize	2147483647
2	language	us_english
3	dateformat	mdy
4	datefirst	7
5	lock_timeout	-1
6	quoted_identifier	SET
7	arithabort	SET
8	ansi_null_dflt_on	SET
9	ansi_warnings	SET
10	ansi_padding	SET
11	ansi_nulls	SET
12	concat_null_yields_null	SET
13	isolation level	read committed

CHAPTER 13: Basic SELECT Statement Syntax & Examples

Easy SELECT Queries for Fun & Learning

T-SQL scripts to demonstrate simple, easy-to-read SELECT query variations. Important note: alias column names cannot be reused in successive computed columns by expressions or anywhere else in the query except the ORDER BY clause.

```
-- Datetime range with string literal date
SELECT  *  FROM    Person.Person
WHERE   ModifiedDate <= '2002-08-09 00:00:00.000'  ORDER BY LastName;
-- (38 row(s) affected)
```

> **NOTE**
> The string literal above looks like datetime, but it is not. It is only a string literal. The database engine will try to convert it to datetime data type at runtime (implicit conversion), and if successful the query will be executed.
> The syntax of the following query is OK, however, it will fail at execution time.
> SELECT * FROM   Person.Person WHERE   ModifiedDate <= 'New York City' ORDER BY LastName;
> /* Msg 241, Level 16, State 1, Line 1 Conversion failed when converting date and/or time from character string. */

```
-- Complimentary (remaining) datetime range specified again with string literal
SELECT * FROM    Person.Person WHERE   ModifiedDate > '2002-08-09 00:00:00.000'  ORDER BY LastName;
-- (19934 row(s) affected)
```

```
-- Total rows in Person.Person
SELECT ( 38 + 19934 ) AS TotalRows;    -- 19972
```

```
SELECT count(* ) FROM   Person.Person -- 19972
```

```
SELECT TableRows = count(* ),  Calc = 38 + 19934  FROM   Person.Person; -- 19972     19972
```

```
-- Get prefix left of comma or entire string if there is no comma present
SELECT TOP 4                                                                     ProductNumber,
       LEFT(Name, COALESCE(NULLIF(CHARINDEX(',',Name)-1,-1),LEN(Name)))  AS NamePrefix,
       Name                                                                      AS ProductName
FROM AdventureWorks2012.Production.Product   WHERE CHARINDEX(',',Name) > 0
ORDER BY ProductName;
```

ProductNumber	NamePrefix	ProductName
VE-C304-L	Classic Vest	Classic Vest, L
VE-C304-M	Classic Vest	Classic Vest, M
VE-C304-S	Classic Vest	Classic Vest, S
GL-F110-L	Full-Finger Gloves	Full-Finger Gloves, L

CHAPTER 13: Basic SELECT Statement Syntax & Examples

NULL refers to no information available. Note: "=" and "!=" operators are not used with NULL; "IS" or "IS NOT" operators are applicable.

```
SELECT *
FROM    Person.Person
WHERE   AdditionalContactInfo IS NOT NULL
ORDER BY LastName;
-- (10 row(s) affected)
```

```
SELECT *
FROM    Person.Person
WHERE   AdditionalContactInfo IS NULL
ORDER BY LastName;
-- (19962 row(s) affected)
```

```
SELECT   DISTINCT FirstName
FROM     Person.Person
ORDER BY FirstName;      -- (1018 row(s) affected)
```

```
-- Summary revenue by product, interesting sort
USE AdventureWorks2012;
GO
SELECT  TOP 10 p.Name                                              AS ProductName,
   FORMAT(SUM(((OrderQty * UnitPrice) * (1.0 - UnitPriceDiscount))),'c','en-US') AS SubTotal
FROM Production.Product AS p
INNER JOIN Sales.SalesOrderDetail AS sod
ON p.ProductID = sod.ProductID
GROUP BY p.Name
ORDER BY REVERSE(p.Name);
```

ProductName	SubTotal
Water Bottle - 30 oz.	$28,654.16
Hydration Pack - 70 oz.	$105,826.42
LL Mountain Frame - Black, 40	$1,198.99
ML Mountain Frame - Black, 40	$14,229.41
Mountain-300 Black, 40	$501,648.88
Mountain-500 Black, 40	$101,734.12
LL Mountain Frame - Silver, 40	$69,934.28
ML Mountain Frame-W - Silver, 40	$195,826.39
Mountain-500 Silver, 40	$145,089.43
Mountain-400-W Silver, 40	$323,703.82

Easy SELECT Queries for Fun & Learning

DISTINCT & GROUP BY operations are generally "expensive".

```
SELECT   DISTINCT LastName FROM    Person.Person ORDER BY LastName;   -- (1206 row(s) affected)
```

```
-- LastName popularity descending
SELECT LastName,    Frequency = count(*)
FROM    Person.Person
GROUP BY LastName
ORDER BY Frequency DESC;
GO
```

LastName	Frequency
Diaz	211
Hernandez	188
Sanchez	175
Martinez	173
Torres	172
Martin	171
Perez	170
Gonzalez	169
Lopez	168
Rodriguez	166

```
-- Sort on column not in SELECT list - Note: demo only, confusing to end user
SELECT   LastName
FROM    Person.Person
ORDER BY FirstName;
-- (19972 row(s) affected)
```

```
-- Sort on column not in SELECT list
SELECT   Name = CONCAT(LastName, ', ', FirstName )
FROM    Person.Person
ORDER BY LastName;
-- (19972 row(s) affected)
```

```
-- Sort on column alias
SELECT   Name = CONCAT(LastName, ', ', FirstName )
FROM    Person.Person
ORDER BY Name;
-- (19972 row(s) affected)
```

```
SELECT   CONCAT(LastName, ', ', FirstName ) AS FullName
FROM    Person.Person
WHERE    LastName >= 'K'  ORDER BY LastName;
-- (12057 row(s) affected)
```

CHAPTER 13: Basic SELECT Statement Syntax & Examples

The NULLIF Function Actually Creates A NULL

```
SELECT   CONCAT(LastName, ', ', FirstName ) AS FullName
FROM     Person.Person  WHERE   LastName < 'K'  ORDER BY LastName;
-- (7915 row(s) affected)
```

```
-- Cardinality check
SELECT Difference= ((count(*)) - (12057 + 7915)) FROM  Person.Person; -- 0
```

```
-- Using the NULLIF function in counting
-- Count of all list prices - no NULLs in column
SELECT COUNT(ListPrice) FROM   AdventureWorks2012.Production.Product
-- 504
```

```
-- Counts only when ListPrice != 0 - does not count NULLs (ListPrice = 0.0)
SELECT COUNT(NULLIF(ListPrice,0.0)) FROM   AdventureWorks2012.Production.Product
-- 304
```

```
SELECT COUNT(ListPrice)   FROM   AdventureWorks2012.Production.Product   WHERE ListPrice = 0;
-- 200
```

Cardinality of DISTINCT & GROUP BY Clauses

The cardinality of DISTINCT and the cardinality of GROUP BY are the same with the same column(s).

```
-- FirstName by popularity descending
SELECT FirstName,
       Freq = count(* )
FROM    Person.Person
GROUP BY FirstName
ORDER BY Freq DESC;
-- (1018 row(s) affected)
```

FirstName	Freq
Richard	103
Katherine	99
Marcus	97
James	97
Jennifer	96
Dalton	93
Lucas	93
Alexandra	93
Morgan	92
Seth	92

```
SELECT  DISTINCT FirstName  FROM    Person.Person  ORDER BY FirstName;  -- (1018 row(s) affected)
```

Column Alias Can only Be Used in ORDER BY

Column aliases cannot be used in other computed columns (expressions), neither in the WHERE clause or GROUP BY clause.

```
SELECT  TableRows = count(*),
        Calculated = 38 + 19934,
        Difference = (count(*) - 38 - 19934)
FROM    Person.Person;
```

TableRows	Calculated	Difference
19972	19972	0

Workarounds for Column Alias Use Restriction

There is a simple workaround for recycling column aliases in other clauses than just the ORDER BY: make the query into a derived table (x) and include it in an outer query. Similarly, CTEs can be used instead of derived tables.

```
-- Derived table workaround
SELECT TableRows, Calculated, Difference = TableRows - Calculated
FROM (
        SELECT  TableRows = count(*),   Calculated = 38 + 19934,
        FROM    Person.Person
     ) x ;  -- Derived table
GO
```

TableRows	Calculated	Difference
19972	19972	0

```
-- CTE workaround
;WITH CTE AS (
        SELECT  TableRows = count(*),   Calculated = 38 + 19934
        FROM    Person.Person)
-- Outer query
SELECT TableRows, Calculated, Difference = TableRows - Calculated
FROM CTE;
```

TableRows	Calculated	Difference
19972	19972	0

CHAPTER 13: Basic SELECT Statement Syntax & Examples

When the Clock Strikes Midnight: datetime Behaviour

This is one of the most troublesome issues in T-SQL programming (midnight bug, Cinderella syndrom): the predicate YYYYMMDD (date string literal) = DatetimeColumn does not include the entire day, only records with time at midnight: 00:00:00.000 .

```
USE AdventureWorks2012;

-- Note: only midnight 2003-08-09 included
-- Even a second after midnight is not included like 2003-08-09 00:00:01.000
SELECT  *
FROM    Person.Person
WHERE      ModifiedDate BETWEEN '2002-08-09 00:00:00.000'
           AND '2003-08-09 00:00:00.000'
ORDER BY LastName;
GO
-- (396 row(s) affected)
```

```
-- Entire day of 2003-08-09 included
-- The count same as before because no records after midnight 2003-08-09
SELECT  *
FROM    Person.Person
WHERE      ModifiedDate >= '2002-08-09 00:00:00.000'
           AND ModifiedDate <  '2003-08-10 00:00:00.000'
ORDER BY LastName;
GO
-- (396 row(s) affected)
```

CHAPTER 13: Basic SELECT Statement Syntax & Examples

Easy SELECT Queries for Fun & Learning

LEFT(), RIGHT() & SUBSTRING() String Functions

```sql
SELECT  FirstCharOfFirstName = LEFT(FirstName,1),         -- column alias
        FirstCharOfLastName  = LEFT(LastName,1),          -- column alias
        LastCharOfLastName  = RIGHT(LastName,1),          -- column alias
        FullName = CONCAT(FirstName, SPACE(1), LastName), -- column alias
        *                                                  -- wild card, all columns
FROM    Person.Person
WHERE   SUBSTRING(FirstName,1,1) = 'J'
    AND SUBSTRING (LastName,1,1) = 'S'
    AND (RIGHT(LastName,1) = 'H' OR RIGHT(LastName,1) = 'Z')
ORDER BY LastName;
-- (59 row(s) affected) - Partial result.
```

FirstCharOfFirstName	FirstCharOfLastName	LastCharOfLastName	FullName	BusinessEntityID
J	S	z	Jacqueline Sanchez	8975
J	S	z	Jada Sanchez	9499
J	S	z	Jade Sanchez	9528
J	S	z	Janelle Sanchez	18590
J	S	z	Jared Sanchez	15266
J	S	z	Jarrod Sanchez	2948
J	S	z	Jay Sanchez	10298
J	S	z	Jennifer Sanchez	20440
J	S	z	Jeremiah Sanchez	15292
J	S	z	Jermaine Sanchez	8040

```sql
-- Sort on first column
SELECT BusinessEntityID, JobTitle, SUBSTRING(JobTitle, 5, 7)  AS MiddleOfJobTitle
FROM   HumanResources.Employee
WHERE  BirthDate <= '1960/12/31'    -- date literal (constant)
ORDER BY 1;
-- (27 row(s) affected) - Partial results.
```

BusinessEntityID	JobTitle	MiddleOfJobTitle
5	Design Engineer	gn Engi
6	Design Engineer	gn Engi
12	Tool Designer	Design
15	Design Engineer	gn Engi
23	Marketing Specialist	eting S
27	Production Supervisor - WC60	uction

```sql
-- String functions usage in formatting
DECLARE @SSN char(9) = '123456789';
SELECT SSN=CONCAT(LEFT(@SSN,3),'-', SUBSTRING(@SSN,4,2),'-', RIGHT(@SSN,4));
-- 123-45-6789
```

CHAPTER 13: Basic SELECT Statement Syntax & Examples

ASCII value range is 0-127. Extended ASCII: 128-255. Size is 8-bit, one byte.

```
SELECT TOP 5    ProductNumber,
                SUBSTRING(ProductNumber,9,1)         AS MiddleSubstring,
                ASCII(SUBSTRING(ProductNumber,9,1))  AS ASCIIValue
FROM AdventureWorks2008.Production.Product
WHERE LEN(ProductNumber) > 8
ORDER BY Name;                        - OK syntax, but does not make sense
```

ProductNumber	MiddleSubstring	ASCIIValue
VE-C304-L	L	76
VE-C304-M	M	77
VE-C304-S	S	83
GL-F110-L	L	76
GL-F110-M	M	77

NOTE
Table columns and columns by expressions (computed) can be mixed in a query at will.

```
-- Computed (expressions) & table columns
SELECT FirstCharOfFirstName = LEFT(FirstName,1),      -- string expression
       FirstCharOfLastName  = LEFT(LastName,1),       -- string expression
       FullName = CONCAT(LastName, ', ', FirstName ), -- string expression
       SquareOfID = SQUARE(BusinessEntityID),         -- math expression
       *                                              -- wild card, all table columns
FROM    Person.Person
WHERE   LEFT(FirstName,1) = 'J'
    AND LEFT(LastName,2) = 'Sm'
ORDER BY FullName;
-- (14 row(s) affected)   - Partial results.
```

FirstCharOfFirstName	FirstCharOfLastName	FullName	SquareOfID	BusinessEntityID
J	S	Smith, Jacob	348680929	18673
J	S	Smith, James	308986084	17578
J	S	Smith, Jasmine	129572689	11383
J	S	Smith, Jeff	3139984	1772
J	S	Smith, Jennifer	122699929	11077
J	S	Smith, Jeremiah	20511841	4529
J	S	Smith, Jessica	145829776	12076
J	S	Smith, John	332041284	18222
J	S	Smith, Jonathan	312228900	17670
J	S	Smith, Jose	300710281	17341
J	S	Smith, Joseph	357474649	18907
J	S	Smith, Joshua	351825049	18757
J	S	Smith, Julia	121616784	11028
J	S	Smith, Justin	324900625	18025

Transact-SQL Reserved Keywords

List of reserved keywords in SQL Server 2012 Transact-SQL. Keywords can only be used as delimited identifiers such as [Inner] or "Order".

ADD	EXTERNAL	PROCEDURE
ALL	FETCH	PUBLIC
ALTER	FILE	RAISERROR
AND	FILLFACTOR	READ
ANY	FOR	READTEXT
AS	FOREIGN	RECONFIGURE
ASC	FREETEXT	REFERENCES
AUTHORIZATION	FREETEXTTABLE	REPLICATION
BACKUP	FROM	RESTORE
BEGIN	FULL	RESTRICT
BETWEEN	FUNCTION	RETURN
BREAK	GOTO	REVERT
BROWSE	GRANT	REVOKE
BULK	GROUP	RIGHT
BY	HAVING	ROLLBACK
CASCADE	HOLDLOCK	ROWCOUNT
CASE	IDENTITY	ROWGUIDCOL
CHECK	IDENTITY_INSERT	RULE
CHECKPOINT	IDENTITYCOL	SAVE
CLOSE	IF	SCHEMA
CLUSTERED	IN	SECURITYAUDIT
COALESCE	INDEX	SELECT
COLLATE	INNER	SEMANTICKEYPHRASETABLE
COLUMN	INSERT	SEMANTICSIMILARITYDETAILSTABLE
COMMIT	INTERSECT	SEMANTICSIMILARITYTABLE
COMPUTE	INTO	SESSION_USER
CONSTRAINT	IS	SET
CONTAINS	JOIN	SETUSER
CONTAINSTABLE	KEY	SHUTDOWN
CONTINUE	KILL	SOME
CONVERT	LEFT	STATISTICS
CREATE	LIKE	SYSTEM_USER
CROSS	LINENO	TABLE
CURRENT	LOAD	TABLESAMPLE
CURRENT_DATE	MERGE	TEXTSIZE
CURRENT_TIME	NATIONAL	THEN
CURRENT_TIMESTAMP	NOCHECK	TO
CURRENT_USER	NONCLUSTERED	TOP
CURSOR	NOT	TRAN
DATABASE	NULL	TRANSACTION
DBCC	NULLIF	TRIGGER
DEALLOCATE	OF	TRUNCATE
DECLARE	OFF	TRY_CONVERT
DEFAULT	OFFSETS	TSEQUAL
DELETE	ON	UNION
DENY	OPEN	UNIQUE
DESC	OPENDATASOURCE	UNPIVOT
DISK	OPENQUERY	UPDATE
DISTINCT	OPENROWSET	UPDATETEXT
DISTRIBUTED	OPENXML	USE
DOUBLE	OPTION	USER
DROP	OR	VALUES
DUMP	ORDER	VARYING
ELSE	OUTER	VIEW
END	OVER	WAITFOR
ERRLVL	PERCENT	WHEN
ESCAPE	PIVOT	WHERE
EXCEPT	PLAN	WHILE
EXEC	PRECISION	WITH
EXECUTE	PRIMARY	WITHIN GROUP
EXISTS	PRINT	WRITETEXT
EXIT	PROC	

CHAPTER 13: Basic SELECT Statement Syntax & Examples

Case Sensitive Sort with Latin1_General_CS_AI

For case sensitive sort on a column with case insensitive collation, we have use a case sensitive (CS) collation such as Latin1_General_CS_AI.

```sql
-- CASE INSENSITIVE sort using default collation
SELECT lname FROM
        (SELECT TOP 5 UPPER (LastName) AS lname FROM Person.Person ORDER BY FirstName) x
UNION ALL   SELECT lname FROM
        (SELECT TOP 5 LOWER (LastName) AS lname FROM Person.Person ORDER BY FirstName) y
ORDER BY lname;
-- ADAMS, adams, alexander, ALEXANDER, leonetti, LEONETTI, WRIGHT, WRIGHT, wright, wright
```

```sql
-- CASE SENSITIVE sort using %CS% collation
SELECT lname FROM ( SELECT lname FROM
   (SELECT TOP 5 UPPER (LastName) AS lname FROM Person.Person ORDER BY FirstName) x
   UNION ALL  SELECT lname FROM
   (SELECT TOP 5 LOWER (LastName) AS lname FROM Person.Person ORDER BY FirstName) y  ) z
ORDER BY lname COLLATE Latin1_General_CS_AI;
-- adams,ADAMS,alexander,ALEXANDER,leonetti,LEONETTI,wright,wright,WRIGHT,WRIGHT
```

The ORDER BY Clause for Sorting Query Results

The ORDER BY clause is located at the very end of the query. In fact the sorting itself takes place after the query executed and generated **an unordered result set**. Although frequently, especially for small sets, the results appear to be sorted, **only an ORDER BY clause can guarantee proper sorting**. INSERT, UPDATE, DELETE & MERGE statement do not support sorting, **the database engine performs all set operations unordered**. T-SQL scripts demonstrate the many variations of the ORDER BY clause. Table alias can be used in an ORDER BY clause.

```sql
USE AdventureWorks2012;

-- A column can be used for sorting even though not explicitly used in the SELECT list
SELECT *
FROM   Production.Product
ORDER  BY Name ASC;
GO

-- Sort on the second column, whatever it may be
SELECT *
FROM   Production.Product
ORDER  BY 2 DESC;
GO

-- ASCending is the default sort order, it is not necessary to use
SELECT  Name AS ProductName,
        *
FROM   Production.Product
ORDER  BY ProductName ASC;
GO

SELECT  TOP (10) Name AS ProductName,          *
FROM   Production.Product   ORDER  BY 1 ASC;
```

ProductName	ProductID	Name	ProductNumber	MakeFlag	FinishedGoodsFlag	Color	SafetyStockLevel
Adjustable Race	1	Adjustable Race	AR-5381	0	0	NULL	1000
All-Purpose Bike Stand	879	All-Purpose Bike Stand	ST-1401	0	1	NULL	4
AWC Logo Cap	712	AWC Logo Cap	CA-1098	0	1	Multi	4
BB Ball Bearing	3	BB Ball Bearing	BE-2349	1	0	NULL	800
Bearing Ball	2	Bearing Ball	BA-8327	0	0	NULL	1000
Bike Wash - Dissolver	877	Bike Wash - Dissolver	CL-9009	0	1	NULL	4
Blade	316	Blade	BL-2036	1	0	NULL	800
Cable Lock	843	Cable Lock	LO-C100	0	1	NULL	4
Chain	952	Chain	CH-0234	0	1	Silver	500
Chain Stays	324	Chain Stays	CS-2812	1	0	NULL	1000

CHAPTER 13: Basic SELECT Statement Syntax & Examples

Using Column Alias in the ORDER BY Clause

Column alias can be used in an ORDER BY clause. In fact, it should be used to make the query more readable.

```
-- ProductName is a column alias, it can only be used in the ORDER BY clause, not anywhere before
SELECT ProductName = Name, *
FROM Production.Product
WHERE ProductName like '%glove%'
ORDER BY ProductName ASC ;
GO
/* ERROR
Msg 207, Level 16, State 1, Line 3
Invalid column name 'ProductName'.
*/
```

```
-- The TOP clause uses the ORDER BY sorting to select the 5 rows
SELECT TOP (5) ProductName = Name, *
FROM Production.Product
WHERE Name like '%glove%'
ORDER BY ProductName ASC ;
```

ProductName	ProductID	Name	ProductNumber	MakeFlag	FinishedGoodsFlag	Color	SafetyStockLevel
Full-Finger Gloves, L	863	Full-Finger Gloves, L	GL-F110-L	0	1	Black	4
Full-Finger Gloves, M	862	Full-Finger Gloves, M	GL-F110-M	0	1	Black	4
Full-Finger Gloves, S	861	Full-Finger Gloves, S	GL-F110-S	0	1	Black	4
Half-Finger Gloves, L	860	Half-Finger Gloves, L	GL-H102-L	0	1	Black	4
Half-Finger Gloves, M	859	Half-Finger Gloves, M	GL-H102-M	0	1	Black	4

```
-- Descending sort on name which is string data type
SELECT TOP (10) ProductName = Name, *
FROM Production.Product
WHERE Name like '%road%'
ORDER BY ProductName DESC ;
```

ProductName	ProductID	Name	ProductNumber	MakeFlag	FinishedGoodsFlag	Color	SafetyStockLevel
Road-750 Black, 58	977	Road-750 Black, 58	BK-R19B-58	1	1	Black	100
Road-750 Black, 52	999	Road-750 Black, 52	BK-R19B-52	1	1	Black	100
Road-750 Black, 48	998	Road-750 Black, 48	BK-R19B-48	1	1	Black	100
Road-750 Black, 44	997	Road-750 Black, 44	BK-R19B-44	1	1	Black	100
Road-650 Red, 62	761	Road-650 Red, 62	BK-R50R-62	1	1	Red	100
Road-650 Red, 60	760	Road-650 Red, 60	BK-R50R-60	1	1	Red	100
Road-650 Red, 58	759	Road-650 Red, 58	BK-R50R-58	1	1	Red	100
Road-650 Red, 52	764	Road-650 Red, 52	BK-R50R-52	1	1	Red	100
Road-650 Red, 48	763	Road-650 Red, 48	BK-R50R-48	1	1	Red	100
Road-650 Red, 44	762	Road-650 Red, 44	BK-R50R-44	1	1	Red	100

The ORDER BY Clause for Sorting Query Results

Eliminate NULL in result with COALESCE or ISNULL functions

```
SELECT [type] = type,
       AvgPrice = COALESCE(FORMAT(AVG(price),'c', 'en-US') ,'')
FROM  titles  GROUP  BY [type]  ORDER  BY [type] desc;
```

type	AvgPrice
UNDECIDED	
trad_cook	$15.96
psychology	$13.50
popular_comp	$21.48
mod_cook	$11.49
business	$13.73

```
SELECT           pub_name                               Publisher,
                 FORMAT(AVG(price),'c', 'en-US')        AvgPrice
FROM  titles
    INNER JOIN publishers
     ON  titles.pub_id = publishers.pub_id
GROUP  BY pub_name
ORDER  BY pub_name;
```

Publisher	AvgPrice
Algodata Infosystems	$18.98
Binnet & Hardley	$15.41
New Moon Books	$9.78

```
SELECT TOP(3) * FROM   titles ORDER  BY title;
```

title_id	title	type	pub_id	price	advance	royalty	ytd_sales	notes	pubdate
PC1035	But Is It User Friendly?	popular_comp	1389	22.95	7000.00	16	8780	A survey of software for the naive user, focusing on the 'friendliness' of each.	1991-06-30 00:00:00.000
PS1372	Computer Phobic AND Non-Phobic Individuals: Behavior Variations	psychology	0877	21.59	7000.00	10	375	A must for the specialist, this book examines the difference between those who hate and fear computers and those who don't.	1991-10-21 00:00:00.000
BU1111	Cooking with Computers: Surreptitious Balance Sheets	business	1389	11.95	5000.00	10	3876	Helpful hints on how to use your electronic resources to the best advantage.	1991-06-09 00:00:00.000

```
SELECT TOP(3) * FROM   publishers ORDER  BY pub_name;
```

pub_id	pub_name	city	state	country
1389	Algodata Infosystems	Berkeley	CA	USA
0877	Binnet & Hardley	Washington	DC	USA
1622	Five Lakes Publishing	Chicago	IL	USA

CHAPTER 13: Basic SELECT Statement Syntax & Examples

Sorting Products by Attributes

```
USE Northwind;

SELECT      UnitsInStock,
            ProductID,
            ProductName,
            QuantityPerUnit,
            FORMAT( UnitPrice, 'c', 'en-US') AS UnitPrice  -- Column alias is same as column
FROM   Northwind.dbo.Products WHERE  UnitsInStock BETWEEN 15 AND 25  ORDER  BY UnitsInStock;
```

UnitsInStock	ProductID	ProductName	QuantityPerUnit	UnitPrice
15	7	Uncle Bob's Organic Dried Pears	12 - 1 lb pkgs.	$30.00
15	26	Gumbär Gummibärchen	100 - 250 g bags	$31.23
15	48	Chocolade	10 pkgs.	$12.75
15	70	Outback Lager	24 - 355 ml bottles	$15.00
17	38	Côte de Blaye	12 - 75 cl bottles	$263.50
17	43	Ipoh Coffee	16 - 500 g tins	$46.00
17	62	Tarte au sucre	48 pies	$49.30
17	2	Chang	24 - 12 oz bottles	$19.00
19	60	Camembert Pierrot	15 - 300 g rounds	$34.00
20	24	Guaraná Fantástica	12 - 355 ml cans	$4.50
20	35	Steeleye Stout	24 - 12 oz bottles	$18.00
20	51	Manjimup Dried Apples	50 - 300 g pkgs.	$53.00
21	54	Tourtière	16 pies	$7.45
21	56	Gnocchi di nonna Alice	24 - 250 g pkgs.	$38.00
22	11	Queso Cabrales	1 kg pkg.	$21.00
22	64	Wimmers gute Semmelknödel	20 bags x 4 pieces	$33.25
24	13	Konbu	2 kg box	$6.00
24	63	Vegie-spread	15 - 625 g jars	$43.90
25	19	Teatime Chocolate Biscuits	10 boxes x 12 pieces	$9.20

```
-- A second key is necessary for unique ordering
SELECT TOP(8)   UnitsInStock,
                ProductID,
                ProductName,
                QuantityPerUnit,
                FORMAT( UnitPrice, 'c', 'en-US') AS UnitPrice
FROM   Northwind.dbo.Products
WHERE  UnitsInStock BETWEEN 15 AND 25 ORDER  BY UnitsInStock, ProductName;
```

UnitsInStock	ProductID	ProductName	QuantityPerUnit	UnitPrice
15	48	Chocolade	10 pkgs.	$12.75
15	26	Gumbär Gummibärchen	100 - 250 g bags	$31.23
15	70	Outback Lager	24 - 355 ml bottles	$15.00
15	7	Uncle Bob's Organic Dried Pears	12 - 1 lb pkgs.	$30.00
17	2	Chang	24 - 12 oz bottles	$19.00
17	38	Côte de Blaye	12 - 75 cl bottles	$263.50
17	43	Ipoh Coffee	16 - 500 g tins	$46.00
17	62	Tarte au sucre	48 pies	$49.30

CHAPTER 13: Basic SELECT Statement Syntax & Examples

The ORDER BY Clause for Sorting Query Results

Changing WHERE condition changes the cardinality of result set

```
SELECT      UnitsInStock,
            ProductID,
            ProductName,
            QuantityPerUnit,
            FORMAT( UnitPrice, 'c', 'en-US')        AS UnitPrice
FROM   Northwind.dbo.Products
WHERE  UnitsInStock = 15 or UnitsInStock = 25  -- same as UnitsInStock IN (15, 25)
ORDER  BY UnitsInStock, ProductName;
```

UnitsInStock	ProductID	ProductName	QuantityPerUnit	UnitPrice
15	48	Chocolade	10 pkgs.	$12.75
15	26	Gumbär Gummibärchen	100 - 250 g bags	$31.23
15	70	Outback Lager	24 - 355 ml bottles	$15.00
15	7	Uncle Bob's Organic Dried Pears	12 - 1 lb pkgs.	$30.00
25	19	Teatime Chocolate Biscuits	10 boxes x 12 pieces	$9.20

```
SELECT  TOP(7)  UnitsInStock,
                ProductID,
                ProductName,
                QuantityPerUnit,
                FORMAT( UnitPrice, 'c', 'en-US')        AS UnitPrice
FROM   Northwind.dbo.Products  ORDER  BY UnitsInStock DESC, ProductName ASC;
```

UnitsInStock	ProductID	ProductName	QuantityPerUnit	UnitPrice
125	75	Rhönbräu Klosterbier	24 - 0.5 l bottles	$7.75
123	40	Boston Crab Meat	24 - 4 oz tins	$18.40
120	6	Grandma's Boysenberry Spread	12 - 8 oz jars	$25.00
115	55	Pâté chinois	24 boxes x 2 pies	$24.00
113	61	Sirop d'érable	24 - 500 ml bottles	$28.50
112	33	Geitost	500 g	$2.50
112	36	Inlagd Sill	24 - 250 g jars	$19.00

```
SELECT  TOP(5)  UnitsInStock, ProductID, ProductName,    QuantityPerUnit,
                FORMAT( UnitPrice, 'c', 'en-US') AS UnitPrice
FROM   Northwind.dbo.Products
WHERE  UnitsInStock > 15  AND UnitsInStock < 25  ORDER  BY UnitsInStock DESC, ProductName ASC;
```

UnitsInStock	ProductID	ProductName	QuantityPerUnit	UnitPrice
24	13	Konbu	2 kg box	$6.00
24	63	Vegie-spread	15 - 625 g jars	$43.90
22	11	Queso Cabrales	1 kg pkg.	$21.00
22	64	Wimmers gute Semmelknödel	20 bags x 4 pieces	$33.25
21	56	Gnocchi di nonna Alice	24 - 250 g pkgs.	$38.00

CHAPTER 13: Basic SELECT Statement Syntax & Examples

The "Tricky" BETWEEN & NOT BETWEEN Operators
They are very English-like, but results should be verified to make sure they work as intended.

```sql
SELECT  TOP(5)   UnitsInStock, ProductID, ProductName,    QuantityPerUnit,
            FORMAT( UnitPrice, 'c', 'en-US') AS UnitPrice
FROM   Northwind.dbo.Products
WHERE  UnitsInStock BETWEEN 15 AND 25
ORDER  BY UnitsInStock DESC, ProductName ASC;
GO
```

UnitsInStock	ProductID	ProductName	QuantityPerUnit	UnitPrice
25	19	Teatime Chocolate Biscuits	10 boxes x 12 pieces	$9.20
24	13	Konbu	2 kg box	$6.00
24	63	Vegie-spread	15 - 625 g jars	$43.90
22	11	Queso Cabrales	1 kg pkg.	$21.00
22	64	Wimmers gute Semmelknödel	20 bags x 4 pieces	$33.25

```sql
SELECT  TOP(5)   UnitsInStock, ProductID, ProductName,    QuantityPerUnit,
            FORMAT( UnitPrice, 'c', 'en-US') AS UnitPrice
FROM   Northwind.dbo.Products
WHERE  UnitsInStock NOT BETWEEN 15 AND 25
ORDER  BY UnitsInStock DESC, ProductName ASC;
```

UnitsInStock	ProductID	ProductName	QuantityPerUnit	UnitPrice
125	75	Rhönbräu Klosterbier	24 - 0.5 l bottles	$7.75
123	40	Boston Crab Meat	24 - 4 oz tins	$18.40
120	6	Grandma's Boysenberry Spread	12 - 8 oz jars	$25.00
115	55	Pâté chinois	24 boxes x 2 pies	$24.00
113	61	Sirop d'érable	24 - 500 ml bottles	$28.50

```sql
SELECT          Orders.OrderID,
                Shippers.*
FROM   Shippers
    INNER JOIN Orders
      ON ( Shippers.ShipperID = Orders.ShipVia )
ORDER  BY Orders.OrderID;
GO
-- (830 row(s) affected) - Partial results.
```

OrderID	ShipperID	CompanyName	Phone
10248	3	Federal Shipping	(503) 555-9931
10249	1	Speedy Express	(503) 555-9831
10250	2	United Package	(503) 555-3199
10251	1	Speedy Express	(503) 555-9831
10252	2	United Package	(503) 555-3199
10253	2	United Package	(503) 555-3199

The ORDER BY Clause for Sorting Query Results

A second key is frequently required in sorting exception is PRIMARY KEY column.

```
SELECT   OrderID,
         ProductID,
         FORMAT( UnitPrice, 'c', 'en-US')           AS UnitPrice,
         Quantity,
         Discount
FROM     [Order Details] ORDER BY OrderID ASC, ProductID ASC;
GO
-- (2155 row(s) affected) - Partial results.
```

OrderID	ProductID	UnitPrice	Quantity	Discount
10248	11	$14.00	12	0
10248	42	$9.80	10	0
10248	72	$34.80	5	0
10249	14	$18.60	9	0
10249	51	$42.40	40	0
10250	41	$7.70	10	0
10250	51	$42.40	35	0.15
10250	65	$16.80	15	0.15

```
-- Sort keys are different from expression column EmployeeName
SELECT   CONCAT(LastName,', ', FirstName) AS EmployeeName ,
         Title, City, Country
FROM     Northwind.dbo.Employees ORDER BY LastName, FirstName ASC;
```

EmployeeName	Title	City	Country
Buchanan, Steven	Sales Manager	London	UK
Callahan, Laura	Inside Sales Coordinator	Seattle	USA
Davolio, Nancy	Sales Representative	Seattle	USA
Dodsworth, Anne	Sales Representative	London	UK
Fuller, Andrew	Vice President, Sales	Tacoma	USA
King, Robert	Sales Representative	London	UK
Leverling, Janet	Sales Representative	Kirkland	USA
Peacock, Margaret	Sales Representative	Redmond	USA
Suyama, Michael	Sales Representative	London	UK

```
-- Equivalent sort
SELECT TOP(3)    CONCAT(LastName,', ', FirstName) AS EmployeeName ,    Title, City, Country
FROM   Northwind.dbo.Employees ORDER BY EmployeeName ASC;
```

EmployeeName	Title	City	Country
Buchanan, Steven	Sales Manager	London	UK
Callahan, Laura	Inside Sales Coordinator	Seattle	USA
Davolio, Nancy	Sales Representative	Seattle	USA

CHAPTER 13: Basic SELECT Statement Syntax & Examples

Using Multiple Keys in the ORDER BY Clause

If a single sort key does not result in unique ordering, multiple keys can be used. In the next example the Price (major) key is based on a column which is not unique. If we add Name as a second (minor) key, unique ordering will be guaranteed since Name is a unique column, it has a unique index and not null. It's worth noting if Name would allow nulls, we would need a third key for unique ordering.

```
-- Single key sort
SELECT   P.Name,
         P.ProductNumber,
         P.ListPrice              AS PRICE
FROM   Production.Product  P
WHERE  P.ProductLine = 'R'   AND P.DaysToManufacture < 4    ORDER  BY  P. ListPrice DESC;
```

Name	ProductNumber	PRICE
HL Road Frame - Black, 58	FR-R92B-58	1431.50
HL Road Frame - Red, 58	FR-R92R-58	1431.50
HL Road Frame - Red, 62	FR-R92R-62	1431.50
HL Road Frame - Red, 44	FR-R92R-44	1431.50
HL Road Frame - Red, 48	FR-R92R-48	1431.50
HL Road Frame - Red, 52	FR-R92R-52	1431.50
HL Road Frame - Red, 56	FR-R92R-56	1431.50
HL Road Frame - Black, 62	FR-R92B-62	1431.50
HL Road Frame - Black, 44	FR-R92B-44	1431.50
HL Road Frame - Black, 48	FR-R92B-48	1431.50
HL Road Frame - Black, 52	FR-R92B-52	1431.50
ML Road Frame-W - Yellow, 40	FR-R72Y-40	594.83

```
-- Double key sort - PRICE is the major key, Name is the minor key
SELECT   P.Name,
         P.ProductNumber,
         P.ListPrice              AS PRICE
FROM   Production.Product  P
WHERE  P.ProductLine = 'R'   AND P.DaysToManufacture < 4   ORDER  BY  PRICE DESC, Name;
```

Name	ProductNumber	PRICE
HL Road Frame - Black, 44	FR-R92B-44	1431.50
HL Road Frame - Black, 48	FR-R92B-48	1431.50
HL Road Frame - Black, 52	FR-R92B-52	1431.50
HL Road Frame - Black, 58	FR-R92B-58	1431.50
HL Road Frame - Black, 62	FR-R92B-62	1431.50
HL Road Frame - Red, 44	FR-R92R-44	1431.50
HL Road Frame - Red, 48	FR-R92R-48	1431.50
HL Road Frame - Red, 52	FR-R92R-52	1431.50
HL Road Frame - Red, 56	FR-R92R-56	1431.50
HL Road Frame - Red, 58	FR-R92R-58	1431.50
HL Road Frame - Red, 62	FR-R92R-62	1431.50
ML Road Frame - Red, 44	FR-R72R-44	594.83

The ORDER BY Clause for Sorting Query Results

ORDER BY in Complex Queries

An ORDER BY can be in a complex query and/or ORDER BY can be complex itself. T-SQL scripts demonstrate complex ORDER BY usage.

```
-- We cannot tell just by query inspection if the second key is sufficient for unique ordering or not
-- If we inspect the result set it becomes obvious that we need a third key at least (SalesOrderID unsorted)
SELECT  ProductName         = P.Name,
        NonDiscountSales    = ( OrderQty * UnitPrice ),
        Discounts           = ( ( OrderQty * UnitPrice ) * UnitPriceDiscount ),
        SalesOrderID
FROM   Production.Product P
    INNER JOIN Sales.SalesOrderDetail SOD
        ON P.ProductID = SOD.ProductID
ORDER  BY       ProductName DESC,
                NonDiscountSales DESC;
GO
```

ProductName	NonDiscountSales	Discounts	SalesOrderID
Women's Tights, S	1049.86	104.986	47355
Women's Tights, S	824.89	41.2445	46987
Women's Tights, S	783.6455	39.1823	47400
Women's Tights, S	742.401	37.1201	50206
Women's Tights, S	701.1565	35.0578	46993
Women's Tights, S	701.1565	35.0578	46671
Women's Tights, S	701.1565	35.0578	50688
Women's Tights, S	701.1565	35.0578	49481
Women's Tights, S	659.912	32.9956	48295
Women's Tights, S	659.912	32.9956	46967
Women's Tights, S	618.6675	30.9334	46652
Women's Tights, S	608.9188	12.1784	46672
Women's Tights, S	608.9188	12.1784	47365
Women's Tights, S	565.4246	11.3085	47004
Women's Tights, S	565.4246	11.3085	50663

> **NOTE**
> Even though SELECT DISTINCT results may appear to be sorted, **only ORDER BY clause can guarantee sort**. This holds true for any kind of SELECT statement, simple or complex.

```
SELECT DISTINCT JobTitle   FROM   HumanResources.Employee ;
```

```
SELECT DISTINCT JobTitle   FROM   HumanResources.Employee ORDER  BY JobTitle;
```

CHAPTER 13: Basic SELECT Statement Syntax & Examples

ORDER BY with ROW_NUMBER()

T-SQL queries demonstrate sorting with not matching and matching ROW_NUMBER() sequence number.

```sql
SELECT
   ROW_NUMBER() OVER( PARTITION BY CountryRegionName  ORDER BY SalesYTD ASC) AS SeqNo,
   CountryRegionName AS Country,   FirstName,  LastName,   JobTitle,
   FORMAT(SalesYTD, 'c', 'en-US') AS SalesYTD,
   FORMAT(SalesLastYear, 'c', 'en-US') AS SalesLastYear
FROM   Sales.vSalesPerson         ORDER BY JobTitle,   SalesYTD DESC;
```

SeqNo	Country	FirstName	LastName	JobTitle	SalesYTD	SalesLastYear
2	United States	Amy	Alberts	European Sales Manager	$519,905.93	$0.00
3	United States	Stephen	Jiang	North American Sales Manager	$559,697.56	$0.00
1	United States	Syed	Abbas	Pacific Sales Manager	$172,524.45	$0.00
11	United States	Linda	Mitchell	Sales Representative	$4,251,368.55	$1,439,156.03
1	United Kingdom	Jae	Pak	Sales Representative	$4,116,871.23	$1,635,823.40
10	United States	Michael	Blythe	Sales Representative	$3,763,178.18	$1,750,406.48
9	United States	Jillian	Carson	Sales Representative	$3,189,418.37	$1,997,186.20
1	France	Ranjit	Varkey Chudukatil	Sales Representative	$3,121,616.32	$2,396,539.76
2	Canada	José	Saraiva	Sales Representative	$2,604,540.72	$2,038,234.65
8	United States	Shu	Ito	Sales Representative	$2,458,535.62	$2,073,506.00
7	United States	Tsvi	Reiter	Sales Representative	$2,315,185.61	$1,849,640.94
1	Germany	Rachel	Valdez	Sales Representative	$1,827,066.71	$1,307,949.79
6	United States	Tete	Mensa-Annan	Sales Representative	$1,576,562.20	$0.00
5	United States	David	Campbell	Sales Representative	$1,573,012.94	$1,371,635.32
1	Canada	Garrett	Vargas	Sales Representative	$1,453,719.47	$1,620,276.90
1	Australia	Lynn	Tsoflias	Sales Representative	$1,421,810.92	$2,278,548.98
4	United States	Pamela	Ansman-Wolfe	Sales Representative	$1,352,577.13	$1,927,059.18

```sql
-- ROW_NUMBER() ORDER BY in synch with sort ORDER BY
SELECT   ROW_NUMBER() OVER( ORDER BY JobTitle, SalesYTD DESC) AS SeqNo,
    CountryRegionName AS Country,   FirstName,  LastName,   JobTitle,
    FORMAT(SalesYTD, 'c', 'en-US') AS SalesYTD,  FORMAT(SalesLastYear, 'c', 'en-US') AS SalesLastYear
FROM   Sales.vSalesPerson  ORDER BY      SeqNo;
```

SeqNo	Country	FirstName	LastName	JobTitle	SalesYTD	SalesLastYear
1	United States	Amy	Alberts	European Sales Manager	$519,905.93	$0.00
2	United States	Stephen	Jiang	North American Sales Manager	$559,697.56	$0.00
3	United States	Syed	Abbas	Pacific Sales Manager	$172,524.45	$0.00
4	United States	Linda	Mitchell	Sales Representative	$4,251,368.55	$1,439,156.03
5	United Kingdom	Jae	Pak	Sales Representative	$4,116,871.23	$1,635,823.40
6	United States	Michael	Blythe	Sales Representative	$3,763,178.18	$1,750,406.48
7	United States	Jillian	Carson	Sales Representative	$3,189,418.37	$1,997,186.20
8	France	Ranjit	Varkey Chudukatil	Sales Representative	$3,121,616.32	$2,396,539.76
9	Canada	José	Saraiva	Sales Representative	$2,604,540.72	$2,038,234.65
10	United States	Shu	Ito	Sales Representative	$2,458,535.62	$2,073,506.00
11	United States	Tsvi	Reiter	Sales Representative	$2,315,185.61	$1,849,640.94
12	Germany	Rachel	Valdez	Sales Representative	$1,827,066.71	$1,307,949.79
13	United States	Tete	Mensa-Annan	Sales Representative	$1,576,562.20	$0.00
14	United States	David	Campbell	Sales Representative	$1,573,012.94	$1,371,635.32
15	Canada	Garrett	Vargas	Sales Representative	$1,453,719.47	$1,620,276.90
16	Australia	Lynn	Tsoflias	Sales Representative	$1,421,810.92	$2,278,548.98
17	United States	Pamela	Ansman-Wolfe	Sales Representative	$1,352,577.13	$1,927,059.18

The ORDER BY Clause for Sorting Query Results

ORDER BY Clause with CASE Conditional Expression

Sort by LastName, MiddleName if exists else FirstName, and FirstName in case MiddleName is used.

```
USE AdventureWorks;

SELECT      FirstName,
            COALESCE(MiddleName, '')        AS MName,   -- ISNULL can also be used
            LastName,
            AddressLine1,
            COALESCE(AddressLine2, '')      AS Addr2,
            City,
            SP.Name                         AS [State],
            CR.Name                         AS Country,
            I.CustomerID
FROM   Person.Contact AS C
    INNER JOIN Sales.Individual AS I
        ON C.ContactID = I.ContactID
    INNER JOIN Sales.CustomerAddress AS CA
        ON CA.CustomerID = I.CustomerID
    INNER JOIN Person.[Address] AS A
        ON A.AddressID = CA.AddressID
    INNER JOIN Person.StateProvince SP
        ON SP.StateProvinceID = A.StateProvinceID
    INNER JOIN Person.CountryRegion CR
        ON CR.CountryRegionCode = SP.CountryRegionCode
ORDER BY LastName,
    CASE
      WHEN MiddleName != '' THEN MiddleName
      ELSE FirstName
    END,
    FirstName;
-- (18508 row(s) affected) -Partial results.
```

FirstName	MName	LastName	AddressLine1	Addr2	City	State	Country	CustomerID
Chloe	A	Adams	3001 N. 48th Street		Marysville	Washington	United States	19410
Eduardo	A	Adams	4283 Meaham Drive		San Diego	California	United States	25292
Kaitlyn	A	Adams	3815 Berry Dr.		Westminster	British Columbia	Canada	11869
Mackenzie	A	Adams	9639 Ida Drive		Langford	British Columbia	Canada	14640
Sara	A	Adams	7503 Hill Drive		Milwaukie	Oregon	United States	16986
Adam		Adams	9381 Bayside Way		Newport Beach	California	United States	13323
Amber		Adams	9720 Morning Glory Dr.		Brisbane	Queensland	Australia	26746
Angel		Adams	9556 Lyman Rd.		Burlingame	California	United States	18504
Aaron	B	Adams	4116 Stanbridge Ct.		Downey	California	United States	28866
Noah	B	Adams	6738 Wallace Dr.		El Cajon	California	United States	16977
Bailey		Adams	1817 Adobe Drive		Kirkland	Washington	United States	13280
Ben		Adams	1534 Land Ave		Bremerton	Washington	United States	28678
Alex	C	Adams	237 Bellwood Dr.		Lake Oswego	Oregon	United States	21139
Courtney	C	Adams	6089 Santa Fe Dr.		Torrance	California	United States	18075
Ian	C	Adams	7963 Elk Dr	#4	Versailles	Yveline	France	29422

CHAPTER 13: Basic SELECT Statement Syntax & Examples

Special Sorting, Like United States On Top Of The Country Pop-Up List
It requires CASE or IIF conditional expression.

```
-- Major sort key is Color if not null, else product name
-- Minor sort on ProductNumber
SELECT ProductID,
    ProductNumber,
    Name AS ProductName,
    FORMAT(ListPrice, 'c', 'en-US')  AS ListPrice,
    Color
FROM   Production.Product
WHERE  Name LIKE ( '%Road%' )
ORDER  BY       CASE
                    WHEN Color IS NULL THEN Name
                    ELSE Color
                END,
                ProductNumber DESC;
-- (103 row(s) affected) - Partial results.
```

ProductID	ProductNumber	ProductName	ListPrice	Color
768	BK-R50B-44	Road-650 Black, 44	$782.99	Black
977	BK-R19B-58	Road-750 Black, 58	$539.99	Black
999	BK-R19B-52	Road-750 Black, 52	$539.99	Black
998	BK-R19B-48	Road-750 Black, 48	$539.99	Black
997	BK-R19B-44	Road-750 Black, 44	$539.99	Black
813	HB-R956	HL Road Handlebars	$120.27	NULL
512	RM-R800	HL Road Rim	$0.00	NULL
519	SA-R522	HL Road Seat Assembly	$196.92	NULL
913	SE-R995	HL Road Seat/Saddle	$52.64	NULL
933	TI-R982	HL Road Tire	$32.60	NULL
811	HB-R504	LL Road Handlebars	$44.54	NULL
510	RM-R436	LL Road Rim	$0.00	NULL
517	SA-R127	LL Road Seat Assembly	$133.34	NULL
911	SE-R581	LL Road Seat/Saddle	$27.12	NULL
931	TI-R092	LL Road Tire	$21.49	NULL
812	HB-R720	ML Road Handlebars	$61.92	NULL
511	RM-R600	ML Road Rim	$0.00	NULL
518	SA-R430	ML Road Seat Assembly	$147.14	NULL
912	SE-R908	ML Road Seat/Saddle	$39.14	NULL
932	TI-R628	ML Road Tire	$24.99	NULL
717	FR-R92R-62	HL Road Frame - Red, 62	$1,431.50	Red
706	FR-R92R-58	HL Road Frame - Red, 58	$1,431.50	Red
721	FR-R92R-56	HL Road Frame - Red, 56	$1,431.50	Red

The ORDER BY Clause for Sorting Query Results

T-SQL queries demonstrate complex sorting with the CASE expression usage.
CASE expression returns a SINGLE SCALAR VALUE of the same data type.

```
SELECT  SellStartDate,
        SellEndDate,
        *
FROM    Production.Product
WHERE   Name LIKE ( '%mountain%' )
ORDER   BY CASE
              WHEN SellEndDate IS NULL THEN SellStartDate
              ELSE SellEndDate
           END DESC, Name;
GO
-- (94 row(s) affected) -Partial results.
```

SellStartDate	SellEndDate	ProductID	Name	ProductNumber
2007-07-01 00:00:00.000	NULL	986	Mountain-500 Silver, 44	BK-M18S-44
2007-07-01 00:00:00.000	NULL	987	Mountain-500 Silver, 48	BK-M18S-48
2007-07-01 00:00:00.000	NULL	988	Mountain-500 Silver, 52	BK-M18S-52
2007-07-01 00:00:00.000	NULL	869	Women's Mountain Shorts, L	SH-W890-L
2007-07-01 00:00:00.000	NULL	868	Women's Mountain Shorts, M	SH-W890-M
2007-07-01 00:00:00.000	NULL	867	Women's Mountain Shorts, S	SH-W890-S
2006-07-01 00:00:00.000	2007-06-30 00:00:00.000	817	HL Mountain Front Wheel	FW-M928
2006-07-01 00:00:00.000	2007-06-30 00:00:00.000	825	HL Mountain Rear Wheel	RW-M928
2006-07-01 00:00:00.000	2007-06-30 00:00:00.000	815	LL Mountain Front Wheel	FW-M423
2006-07-01 00:00:00.000	2007-06-30 00:00:00.000	823	LL Mountain Rear Wheel	RW-M423
2006-07-01 00:00:00.000	2007-06-30 00:00:00.000	814	ML Mountain Frame - Black, 38	FR-M63B-38
2006-07-01 00:00:00.000	2007-06-30 00:00:00.000	830	ML Mountain Frame - Black, 40	FR-M63B-40

```
-- 2 keys descending sort
SELECT          PRODUCTNAME  = P.Name,
                SALETOTAL    = ( OrderQty * UnitPrice ),
                NETSALETOTAL = ( ( OrderQty - RejectedQty ) * UnitPrice )
FROM   Production.Product P
    INNER JOIN Purchasing.PurchaseOrderDetail SOD
       ON P.ProductID = SOD.ProductID
ORDER BY PRODUCTNAME DESC, SALETOTAL DESC;

-- Column alias sorting of GROUP BY aggregation results
SELECT [YEAR]=YEAR(OrderDate), Orders = COUNT(*)
FROM AdventureWorks2012.Sales.SalesOrderHeader
GROUP BY YEAR(OrderDate)  ORDER BY [YEAR];
```

YEAR	Orders
2005	1379
2006	3692
2007	12443
2008	13951

CHAPTER 13: Basic SELECT Statement Syntax & Examples

ORDER BY Clause with IIF Conditional Function

Sort by LastName, MiddleName if exists else FirstName, and FirstName in case MiddleName is used.

```
USE AdventureWorks;

SELECT      FirstName,
            COALESCE(MiddleName, '')        AS MName,   -- ISNULL can also be used
            LastName,
            AddressLine1,
            COALESCE(AddressLine2, '')      AS Addr2,
            City,
            SP.Name                         AS [State],
            CR.Name                         AS Country,
            I.CustomerID
FROM   Person.Contact AS C
   INNER JOIN Sales.Individual AS I
      ON C.ContactID = I.ContactID
   INNER JOIN Sales.CustomerAddress AS CA
      ON CA.CustomerID = I.CustomerID
   INNER JOIN Person.[Address] AS A
      ON A.AddressID = CA.AddressID
   INNER JOIN Person.StateProvince SP
      ON SP.StateProvinceID = A.StateProvinceID
   INNER JOIN Person.CountryRegion CR
      ON CR.CountryRegionCode = SP.CountryRegionCode
ORDER  BY   LastName,
            IIF( MiddleName != '',
                  MiddleName,             -- TRUE condition return value
                  FirstName),             -- FALSE condition return value
            FirstName;
GO
-- (18508 row(s) affected) -Partial results.
```

FirstName	MName	LastName	AddressLine1	Addr2	City	State	Country	CustomerID
Chloe	A	Adams	3001 N. 48th Street		Marysville	Washington	United States	19410
Eduardo	A	Adams	4283 Meaham Drive		San Diego	California	United States	25292
Kaitlyn	A	Adams	3815 Berry Dr.		Westminster	British Columbia	Canada	11869
Mackenzie	A	Adams	9639 Ida Drive		Langford	British Columbia	Canada	14640
Sara	A	Adams	7503 Hill Drive		Milwaukie	Oregon	United States	16986
Adam		Adams	9381 Bayside Way		Newport Beach	California	United States	13323
Amber		Adams	9720 Morning Glory Dr.		Brisbane	Queensland	Australia	26746
Angel		Adams	9556 Lyman Rd.		Burlingame	California	United States	18504
Aaron	B	Adams	4116 Stanbridge Ct.		Downey	California	United States	28866
Noah	B	Adams	6738 Wallace Dr.		El Cajon	California	United States	16977
Bailey		Adams	1817 Adobe Drive		Kirkland	Washington	United States	13280
Ben		Adams	1534 Land Ave		Bremerton	Washington	United States	28678
Alex	C	Adams	237 Bellwood Dr.		Lake Oswego	Oregon	United States	21139
Courtney	C	Adams	6089 Santa Fe Dr.		Torrance	California	United States	18075
Ian	C	Adams	7963 Elk Dr	#4	Versailles	Yveline	France	29422

CHAPTER 13: Basic SELECT Statement Syntax & Examples

The ORDER BY Clause for Sorting Query Results

ORDER BY Clause with the RANK() Function

T-SQL query demonstrates the combination of CASE expression and RANK() function in an ORDER BY clause. Note that while such a complex sort is technically impressive, ultimately it has to make sense to the user, the Business Intelligence consumer.

```sql
-- SQL complex sorting
USE AdventureWorks;

SELECT      ContactID,
            FirstName,
            LastName,
            COALESCE(Title, '') AS Title
FROM   Person.Contact
WHERE  LEFT(FirstName, 1) = 'M'
ORDER BY CASE
            WHEN LEFT(LastName, 1) = 'A' THEN RANK()
                    OVER( ORDER BY CONCAT(FirstName, SPACE(1), LastName))
            WHEN LEFT(LastName, 1) = 'M' THEN RANK()
                    OVER( ORDER BY CONCAT(LastName,', ', FirstName), Title)
            WHEN LEFT(LastName, 1) = 'U' THEN RANK()
                    OVER( ORDER BY CONCAT(LastName,', ', FirstName)   DESC)
            ELSE RANK()
                    OVER( ORDER BY LastName ASC, FirstName DESC)
    END;
```

ContactID	FirstName	LastName	Title
9500	Mackenzie	Adams	
10144	Mackenzie	Allen	
10128	Madeline	Allen	
11708	Madison	Alexander	
11527	Madison	Anderson	
19872	Morgan	Bailey	
8059	Michelle	Bailey	
8080	Melissa	Bailey	
18291	Megan	Bailey	
8070	Mariah	Bailey	
2432	Maria	Bailey	
14378	Marcus	Bailey	
8063	Makayla	Bailey	
8032	Mackenzie	Bailey	
9521	Morgan	Baker	
3320	Miguel	Baker	
15437	Mason	Baker	
9546	Mary	Baker	
1082	Mary	Baker	
9539	Maria	Baker	

CHAPTER 13: Basic SELECT Statement Syntax & Examples

ORDER BY Clause with Custom Mapped Sort Sequence

Typically we rely on alphabets or numbers for sorting. What if, for example, we don't want United States way down on a website drop-down menu, rather than on the top with Canada and United Kingdom just above "lucky" Australia? We have to do custom mapping for such a sort in the ORDER BY clause.

```
USE AdventureWorks;
SELECT          AddressLine1,
                City,
                SP.StateProvinceCode            AS State,
                PostalCode,
                CR.Name                         AS  Country
FROM   Person.[Address] A
    INNER JOIN Person.StateProvince SP          ON A.StateProvinceID = SP.StateProvinceID
    INNER JOIN Person.CountryRegion CR          ON SP.CountryRegionCode = CR.CountryRegionCode
ORDER  BY (     CASE    WHEN CR.Name = 'United States' THEN 0
                        WHEN CR.Name = 'Canada' THEN 1
                        WHEN CR.Name = 'United Kingdom' THEN 2   ELSE 3  END ),
                Country,
                City
                AddressLine1;
-- (19614 row(s) affected) - Partial results.
```

AddressLine1	City	State	PostalCode	Country
9355 Armstrong Road	York	ENG	YO15	United Kingdom
939 Vista Del Diablo	York	ENG	YO15	United Kingdom
9458 Flame Drive	York	ENG	YO15	United Kingdom
9557 Steven Circle	York	ENG	Y03 4TN	United Kingdom

Sorting on the Last Word of a String

```
USE tempdb;
SELECT BusinessEntityID, FULLNAME = CONCAT(FirstName , SPACE(1), LastName )
INTO   People FROM   AdventureWorks2012.Person.Person ORDER  BY BusinessEntityID ;

SELECT *  FROM   People
ORDER  BY REVERSE(LEFT(REVERSE(FullName), charindex(' ', REVERSE(FullName) + ' ' ) - 1)),
       FullName ;
GO -- (19972 row(s) affected) - Partial results.
```

BusinessEntityID	FULLNAME
285	Syed Abbas
293	Catherine Abel
295	Kim Abercrombie

CHAPTER 13: Basic SELECT Statement Syntax & Examples

The ORDER BY Clause for Sorting Query Results

ORDER BY Clause with Custom Alphanumeric Sort Sequence

A frequent requirement is custom sorting on alphanumeric field (column). The next T-SQL query demonstrates special alphanumeric sorting.

```
USE AdventureWorks;

SELECT AddressLine1,
            isnull(AddressLine2, '')     AS Addressline2,
            City,
            SP.StateProvinceCode         AS State,
            PostalCode,
            CR.Name                      AS Country
FROM   Person.[Address] A
    INNER JOIN Person.StateProvince SP
      ON A.StateProvinceID = SP.StateProvinceID
    INNER JOIN Person.CountryRegion CR
      ON SP.CountryRegionCode = CR.CountryRegionCode
ORDER  BY (    CASE
                    WHEN Ascii([AddressLine1]) BETWEEN 65 AND 90 THEN 0 -- Upper case alpha
                    WHEN Ascii([AddressLine1]) BETWEEN 48 AND 57 THEN 1 -- Digits
                    ELSE 2
               END ),
           AddressLine1,
           City;
GO
-- (19614 row(s) affected) - Partial results.
```

AddressLine1	Addressline2	City	State	PostalCode	Country
Zur Lindung 46		Leipzig	NW	04139	Germany
Zur Lindung 6		Saarlouis	SL	66740	Germany
Zur Lindung 6		Solingen	NW	42651	Germany
Zur Lindung 609		Sulzbach Taunus	SL	66272	Germany
Zur Lindung 7		Berlin	HE	14129	Germany
Zur Lindung 7		Neunkirchen	SL	66578	Germany
Zur Lindung 764		Paderborn	HH	33041	Germany
Zur Lindung 78		Berlin	HH	10791	Germany
Zur Lindung 787		München	NW	80074	Germany
00, rue Saint-Lazare		Dunkerque	59	59140	France
02, place de Fontenoy		Verrieres Le Buisson	91	91370	France
035, boulevard du Montparnasse		Verrieres Le Buisson	91	91370	France
081, boulevard du Montparnasse		Saint-Denis	93	93400	France
081, boulevard du Montparnasse		Seattle	WA	98104	United States
084, boulevard du Montparnasse		Les Ulis	91	91940	France
1 Corporate Center Drive		Miami	FL	33127	United States
1 Mt. Dell Drive		Portland	OR	97205	United States
1 Smiling Tree Court	Space 55	Los Angeles	CA	90012	United States
1, allée des Princes		Courbevoie	92	92400	France

CHAPTER 13: Basic SELECT Statement Syntax & Examples

Working with Synonyms

A synonym is a shorthand name for a longer name including multi-part names. **While prefix like "sn" or "syn" is not required, it is a good practice since otherwise a synonym can be confused with a (real) table for example, leading to loss of DBA or developer productivity.**

```sql
USE tempdb;
GO


-- Create synonyms for a 3-part names
CREATE SYNONYM snCustomerAW    FOR AdventureWorks.Sales.Customer;
CREATE SYNONYM snCustomerAW12  FOR AdventureWorks2012.Sales.Customer;


-- Create a synonym for 4-part name linked server
CREATE SYNONYM snCustomerLDNAW12  FOR
       [LONDONPROD8].AdventureWorks2012.Sales.Customer;
GO -- Command(s) completed successfully.


-- Query the Customer tables by using the synonyms
SELECT * FROM snCustomerAW ORDER BY AccountNumber;     -- (19185 row(s) affected)
SELECT * FROM snCustomerAW12 ORDER BY AccountNumber;   -- (19820 row(s) affected)
GO


-- Delete a synonym
DROP SYNONYM snCustomerAW;   -- Command(s) completed successfully.
GO


-- Enumerating all synonyms in database
SELECT  name                              AS "Name"
       ,base_object_name                  AS "Definition"
       ,PARSENAME(base_object_name, 4)    AS "Server"
       ,PARSENAME(base_object_name, 3)    AS "Database"
       ,PARSENAME(base_object_name, 2)    AS "Schema"
       ,PARSENAME(base_object_name, 1)    AS "Object"
  FROM sys.synonyms ORDER BY Definition;
```

Name	Definition	Server	Database	Schema	Object
CustomerAW12	[AdventureWorks2012].[Sales].[Customer]	NULL	AdventureWorks2012	Sales	Customer
CustomerLNDAW12	[LONDONPROD8].[AdventureWorks2012].[Sales].[Customer]	LONDONPROD8	AdventureWorks2012	Sales	Customer

CHAPTER 13: Basic SELECT Statement Syntax & Examples

Date & Time Conversion To / From String

While there are only a few internal representation of date and time, string representations are many, even not deterministic since they may change from one country to another such as weekday and month names. T-SQL scripts demonstrate the myriad of date and time conversion possibilities.

The CONVERT() Function with Style Number Parameter

```
-- String source  format: mon dd yyyy hh:mmAM (or PM)
-- 100 is the style number parameter for CONVERT
SELECT [Date&Time] = convert(datetime, 'Oct 23 2020 11:01AM', 100)
```

Date&Time
2020-10-23 11:01:00.000

```
-- Default without style number
SELECT convert(datetime, 'Oct 23 2020 11:01AM')          -- 2020-10-23 11:01:00.000


-- Without century (yy) string date conversion with style number 0
-- Input format: mon dd yy hh:mmAM (or PM)
SELECT [Date&Time] = convert(datetime, 'Oct 23 20 11:01AM', 0)
```

Date&Time
2020-10-23 11:01:00.000

```
-- Default without style number
SELECT convert(datetime, 'Oct 23 20 11:01AM')            -- 2020-10-23 11:01:00.000
```

Convert string date & time to datetime (8-bytes internal representation) data type.

```
SELECT convert(datetime, '10/23/2016', 101)       -- mm/dd/yyyy

SELECT convert(datetime, '2016.10.23', 102)       -- yyyy.mm.dd ANSI date with century

SELECT convert(datetime, '23/10/2016', 103)       -- dd/mm/yyyy

SELECT convert(datetime, '23.10.2016', 104)-- dd.mm.yyyy

SELECT convert(datetime, '23-10-2016', 105)       -- dd-mm-yyyy

-- mon (month) types are nondeterministic conversions, dependent on language setting.
SELECT convert(datetime, '23 OCT 2016', 106)      -- dd mon yyyy
```

String Datetime Formats With "Mon" Are Nondeterministic, Language Dependent

```
SELECT [Date&Time] = convert(datetime, 'Oct 23, 2016', 107)  -- mon dd, yyyy
```

Date&Time
2016-10-23 00:00:00.000

```
SELECT [Date&Time ]=convert(datetime, '20:10:44', 108)       -- hh:mm:ss
```

Date&Time
1900-01-01 20:10:44.000

```
SELECT [Date&Time ]=convert(datetime, 'Oct 23 2016 11:02:44:013AM', 109) --  mon dd yyyy hh:mm:ss:mmmAM (or PM)
```

Date&Time
2016-10-23 11:02:44.013

```
SELECT convert(datetime, '10-23-2016', 110)         -- mm-dd-yyyy
SELECT convert(datetime, '2016/10/23', 111)         -- yyyy/mm/dd
```

```
-- YYYYMMDD ISO date format works at any language setting - international standard
SELECT [Date&Time ]=convert(datetime, '20161023')
```

Date&Time
2016-10-23 00:00:00.000

```
SELECT [Date&Time ]=convert(datetime, '20161023', 112)       -- ISO yyyymmdd
```

Date&Time
2016-10-23 00:00:00.000

```
SELECT [Date&Time ]=convert(datetime, '23 Oct 2016 11:02:07:577', 113)  -- dd mon yyyy hh:mm:ss:mmm
```

Date&Time
2016-10-23 11:02:07.577

```
SELECT [Date&Time ]=convert(datetime, '20:10:25:300', 114)        -- hh:mm:ss:mmm(24h)
```

Date&Time
1900-01-01 20:10:25.300

```
SELECT [Date&Time ]=convert(datetime, '2016-10-23 20:44:11', 120)   -- yyyy-mm-dd hh:mm:ss(24h)
```

Date&Time
2016-10-23 20:44:11.000

Date & Time Conversion To / From String

Style 126 Is ISO 8601 Format: International Standard; Works With Any Language Setting

SELECT [Date&Time]=convert(datetime, '2018-10-23T18:52:47.513', 126) -- yyyy-mm-ddThh:mm:ss(.mmm)

Date&Time
2018-10-23 18:52:47.513

SELECT [Date&Time]=convert(datetime, '2016-10-23 20:44:11.500', 121)   -- yyyy-mm-dd hh:mm:ss.mmm

Date&Time
2016-10-23 20:44:11.500

-- Islamic / Hijri date conversion

SELECT CONVERT(nvarchar(32), convert(datetime,'2016-10-23'), 130);
-- 22 محرم 1438 12:00:00:000AM

SELECT [Date&Time]=convert(datetime, N'23 شوال 1441 6:52:47:513PM', 130)

Date&Time
2020-06-14 18:52:47.513

SELECT [Date&Time]=convert(datetime, '23/10/1441 6:52:47:513PM',   131)

Date&Time
2020-06-14 18:52:47.513

-- Convert DDMMYYYY format to datetime with intermediate conversion using STUFF().

SELECT STUFF(STUFF('31012016',3,0,'-'),6,0,'-');
-- 31-01-2016

SELECT [Date&Time]=convert(datetime, STUFF(STUFF('31012016',3,0,'-'),6,0,'-'), 105)

Date&Time
2016-01-31 00:00:00.000

-- Equivalent
SELECT STUFF(STUFF('31012016',3,0,'/'),6,0,'/');   -- 31/01/2016
SELECT [Date&Time]=convert(datetime, STUFF(STUFF('31012016',3,0,'/'),6,0,'/'), 103)

CHAPTER 13: Basic SELECT Statement Syntax & Examples

String to Datetime Conversion Without Century

String to datetime conversion without century - some exceptions. Nondeterministic means language setting (also regional setting) dependent such as Mar/Mär/mars/márc .

SELECT [Date&Time]=convert(datetime, 'Oct 23 16 11:02:44AM')   -- Default

Date&Time
2016-10-23 11:02:44.000

SELECT convert(datetime, '10/23/16', 1)	mm/dd/yy	U.S.
SELECT convert(datetime, '16.10.23', 2)	yy.mm.dd	ANSI
SELECT convert(datetime, '23/10/16', 3)	dd/mm/yy	UK/FR
SELECT convert(datetime, '23.10.16', 4)	dd.mm.yy	German
SELECT convert(datetime, '23-10-16', 5)	dd-mm-yy	Italian
SELECT convert(datetime, '23 OCT 16', 6)	dd mon yy	non-det.
SELECT convert(datetime, 'Oct 23, 16', 7)	mon dd, yy	non-det.
SELECT convert(datetime, '20:10:44', 8)	hh:mm:ss	
SELECT convert(datetime, 'Oct 23 16 11:02:44:013AM', 9)	Default with msec	
SELECT convert(datetime, '10-23-16', 10)	mm-dd-yy	U.S.
SELECT convert(datetime, '16/10/23', 11)	yy/mm/dd	Japan
SELECT convert(datetime, '161023', 12)	yymmdd	ISO
SELECT convert(datetime, '23 Oct 16 11:02:07:577', 13)	dd mon yy hh:mm:ss:mmm EU dflt	
SELECT convert(datetime, '20:10:25:300', 14)	hh:mm:ss:mmm(24h)	
SELECT convert(datetime, '2016-10-23 20:44:11',20)	yyyy-mm-dd hh:mm:ss(24h) ODBC can.	
SELECT convert(datetime, '2016-10-23 20:44:11.500', 21)	yyyy-mm-dd hh:mm:ss.mmm ODBC	

Date & Time Conversion To / From String

Combine Date & Time String into Datetime

```
DECLARE @DateTimeValue varchar(32), @DateValue char(8), @TimeValue char(6)
 SELECT @DateValue = '20200718',          @TimeValue = '211920'
SELECT           @DateTimeValue =
                 CONCAT(
                 convert(varchar, convert(datetime, @DateValue), 111),
                 ' ', substring(@TimeValue, 1, 2) , ':', substring(@TimeValue, 3, 2) , ':',
substring(@TimeValue, 5, 2)  )

SELECT   DateInput = @DateValue, TimeInput = @TimeValue,  DateTimeOutput = @DateTimeValue;
GO
```

DateInput	TimeInput	DateTimeOutput
20200718	211920	2020/07/18 21:19:20

```
SELECT DATETIMEFROMPARTS (2020, 07, 1, 21, 01, 20, 700)          -- New in SQL Server 2012
```

Date and Time Internal Storage Format

DATETIME 8 bytes internal storage structure:

- 1st 4 bytes: number of days after the base date 1900-01-01
- 2nd 4 bytes: number of clock-ticks (3.33 milliseconds) since midnight

```
SELECT CONVERT(binary(8), CURRENT_TIMESTAMP);
```

Hex
0x0000A09C00F23CE1

DATE 3 bytes internal storage structure:

- 3 bytes integer: number of days after the first date 0001-01-01
- Note: hex byte order reversed

SMALLDATETIME 4 bytes internal storage structure

- 1st 2 bytes: number of days after the base date 1900-01-01
- 2nd 2 bytes: number of minutes since midnight

```
SELECT Hex=CONVERT(binary(4), convert(smalldatetime, getdate()));
```

Hex
0xA09C0375

CHAPTER 13: Basic SELECT Statement Syntax & Examples

Date & Time Operations Using System Operators & Functions

```
-- Conversion from hex (binary) to datetime value
DECLARE @dtHex binary(8)= 0x00009966002d3344;  DECLARE @dt datetime = @dtHex;
SELECT @dt;   -- 2007-07-09 02:44:34.147
```

```
-- SQL convert seconds to HH:MM:SS -
DECLARE  @Seconds INT;  SET @Seconds = 20000 ;
SELECT HH = @Seconds / 3600, MM = (@Seconds%3600) / 60, SS = (@Seconds%60) ;
```

HH	MM	SS
5	33	20

Extract Date Only from DATETIME Data Type

```
DECLARE @Now datetime = CURRENT_TIMESTAMP -- getdate()

SELECT  DateAndTime    = @Now       -- Date portion and Time portion
       ,DateString     = REPLACE(LEFT(CONVERT (varchar, @Now, 112),10),' ','-')
       ,[Date]         = CONVERT(DATE, @Now)  -- SQL Server 2008 and on - date part
       ,Midnight1      = dateadd(day, datediff(day,0, @Now), 0)
       ,Midnight2      = CONVERT(DATETIME,CONVERT(int, @Now))
       ,Midnight3      = CONVERT(DATETIME,CONVERT(BIGINT,@Now) &
(POWER(Convert(bigint,2),32)-1));
```

DateAndTime	DateString	Date	Midnight1	Midnight2	Midnight3
2020-07-28 15:01:51.960	20200728	2020-07-28	2020-07-28 00:00:00.000	2020-07-29 00:00:00.000	2020-07-29 00:00:00.000

```
-- Compare today with database dates
SELECT          TOP (10)  OrderDate = CONVERT(date, OrderDate),
                Today = CONVERT(date, getdate()),
                DeltaDays = DATEDIFF(DD, OrderDate, getdate())
FROM AdventureWorks2012.Sales.SalesOrderHeader  ORDER BY NEWID();  -- random sort
```

OrderDate	Today	DeltaDays
2008-01-15	2012-08-10	1669
2006-07-14	2012-08-10	2219
2008-07-05	2012-08-10	1497
2008-03-01	2012-08-10	1623
2007-10-01	2012-08-10	1775
2007-01-15	2012-08-10	2034
2008-05-27	2012-08-10	1536
2008-04-18	2012-08-10	1575
2008-04-25	2012-08-10	1568
2006-12-17	2012-08-10	2063

Date & Time Conversion To / From String

String Date Formats Without Time

```sql
-- String date format yyyy/mm/dd from datetime
SELECT CONVERT(VARCHAR(10), GETDATE(), 111) AS [YYYY/MM/DD] ;
```

YYYY/MM/DD
2012/07/28

```sql
SELECT CONVERT(VARCHAR(10), GETDATE(), 112) AS [YYYYMMDD];
```

YYYYMMDD
20120728

```sql
SELECT REPLACE(CONVERT(VARCHAR(10), GETDATE(), 111),'/',' ') AS [YYYY MM DD];
```

YYYY MM DD
2020 07 28

```sql
-- Converting to special (non-standard) date formats: DD-MMM-YY
SELECT UPPER(REPLACE(CONVERT(VARCHAR,GETDATE(),6),' ','-')) AS CustomDate;
```

CustomDate
28-JUL-20

```sql
-- SQL convert date string to datetime - time set to 00:00:00.000 or 12:00AM

PRINT CONVERT(datetime,'07-10-2020',110) ;       -- Jul 10 2020 12:00AM
PRINT CONVERT(datetime,'2020/07/10',111) ;       -- Jul 10 2020 12:00AM
PRINT CONVERT(datetime,'20200710', 112);         -- Jul 10 2020 12:00AM
GO
```

```sql
-- SQL Server cast string to date / datetime
DECLARE @DateValue char(8) = '20200718'

SELECT [Date] = CAST (@DateValue AS datetime);
GO
```

Date
2020-07-18 00:00:00.000

CHAPTER 13: Basic SELECT Statement Syntax & Examples

String date to string date conversion with nested CONVERT

```sql
SELECT CONVERT(varchar, CONVERT(datetime, '20140508'), 100) AS StringDate;
```

StringDate
May 8 2014 12:00AM

```sql
-- T-SQL convert date to integer
DECLARE @Date datetime;  SET @Date = getdate();
SELECT DateAsInteger = CAST (CONVERT(varchar,@Date,112) as INT);
GO
```

DateAsInteger
20120728

```sql
-- SQL Server convert integer to datetime
DECLARE @iDate int = 20151225;
SELECT IntegerToDatetime = CAST(convert(varchar,@iDate) as datetime)
GO
```

IntegerToDatetime
2015-12-25 00:00:00.000

```sql
-- Alternates: date-only datetime values

SELECT [DATE-ONLY]=CONVERT(DATETIME, FLOOR(CONVERT(FLOAT, GETDATE())));

SELECT [DATE-ONLY]=CONVERT(DATETIME, FLOOR(CONVERT(MONEY, GETDATE())));

SELECT [DATE-ONLY]=CONVERT(DATETIME, CONVERT(DATE, GETDATE()));
```

```sql
-- CAST string to datetime
-- String date preparation, length is 10 characters
SELECT CONVERT(varchar, GETDATE(), 101), LEN (CONVERT(varchar, GETDATE(), 101))
--        07/28/2018        10

SELECT [DATE-ONLY]=CAST(CONVERT(varchar, GETDATE(), 101) AS DATETIME);
```

DATE-ONLY
2018-07-28 00:00:00.000

CHAPTER 13: Basic SELECT Statement Syntax & Examples

Date & Time Conversion To / From String

DATEADD() and DATEDIFF() Functions

```sql
-- T-SQL strip time from date
SELECT getdate() AS [DateTime], dateadd(dd, datediff(dd, 0, getdate()), 0) [DateOnly];
```

DateTime	DateOnly
2012-07-28 17:24:07.300	2012-07-28 00:00:00.000

```sql
-- First day of current month
SELECT dateadd(month, datediff(month, 0, getdate()), 0)  AS FirstDayOfCurrentMonth;
SELECT dateadd(dd,1, EOMONTH(getdate(),-1));  -- New to SQL Server 2012
```

FirstDayOfCurrentMonth
2020-07-01 00:00:00.000

```sql
-- 15th day of current month
SELECT dateadd(day,14,dateadd(month, datediff(month,0,getdate()),0))
                                                        AS MiddleOfCurrentMonth;
SELECT dateadd(dd,15, EOMONTH(getdate(),-1));  -- New to SQL Server 2012
```

MiddleOfCurrentMonth
2012-07-15 00:00:00.000

```sql
-- First Monday of current month
SELECT   dateadd(day, (9-datepart(weekday,
         dateadd(month, datediff(month, 0, getdate()), 0)))%7,
         dateadd(month, datediff(month, 0, getdate()), 0))  AS [First Monday Of Current Month];
GO
```

First Monday Of Current Month
2012-07-02 00:00:00.000

```sql
-- Next Monday calculation from the reference date which was a Monday
DECLARE @Now datetime = GETDATE();
DECLARE @NextMonday datetime = dateadd(dd, ((datediff(dd, '19000101', @Now)
                / 7) * 7) + 7, '19000101');
SELECT [Now]=@Now, [Next Monday]=@NextMonday;
GO
```

Now	Next Monday
2012-07-28 17:35:29.657	2012-07-30 00:00:00.000

CHAPTER 13: Basic SELECT Statement Syntax & Examples

Last Date & First Date Calculations

-- Last Friday of current month

SELECT   dateadd(day, -7+(6-datepart(weekday,

           dateadd(month, datediff(month, 0, getdate())+1, 0)))%7,

           dateadd(month, datediff(month, 0, getdate())+1, 0)) ;

-- First day of next month

SELECT dateadd(month, datediff(month, 0, getdate())+1, 0) ;

-- 15th of next month

SELECT dateadd(day,14, dateadd(month, datediff(month, 0, getdate())+1, 0));

-- First Monday of next month

SELECT   dateadd(day, (9-datepart(weekday,
           dateadd(month, datediff(month, 0, getdate())+1, 0)))%7,
           dateadd(month, datediff(month, 0, getdate())+1, 0));

-- Next 12 months start & end - EOMONTH is new to SQL Server 2012
SELECT TOP 12
        DATEADD(DD,1, EOMONTH(getdate(),number-1))   AS Start,
        EOMONTH(getdate(),number)   AS [End]
FROM master.dbo.spt_values   -- get integer sequence
WHERE type='P' ORDER BY number;
GO

Start	End
2016-08-01	2016-08-31
2016-09-01	2016-09-30
2016-10-01	2016-10-31
2016-11-01	2016-11-30
2016-12-01	2016-12-31
2017-01-01	2017-01-31
2017-02-01	2017-02-28
2017-03-01	2017-03-31
2017-04-01	2017-04-30
2017-05-01	2017-05-31
2017-06-01	2017-06-30
2017-07-01	2017-07-31

Date & Time Conversion To / From String

BETWEEN Operator for Date Range

Date time range SELECT using the using >= and < operators. Count Sales Orders for date range 2007 OCT-NOV.

```
DECLARE  @StartDate DATETIME,  @EndDate DATETIME
SET @StartDate = convert(DATETIME,'10/01/2007',101)
SET @EndDate   = convert(DATETIME,'11/30/2007',101)
SELECT @StartDate, @EndDate
-- 2007-10-01 00:00:00.000  2007-11-30 00:00:00.000
SELECT dateadd(DAY,1,@EndDate),    dateadd(ms,-3,dateadd(DAY,1,@EndDate))
-- 2007-12-01 00:00:00.000  2007-11-30 23:59:59.997

SELECT [Sales Orders for 2007 OCT-NOV] = COUNT(* )
FROM   AdventureWorks2012.Sales.SalesOrderHeader
WHERE  OrderDate >= @StartDate
       AND OrderDate < dateadd(DAY,1,@EndDate)
```

Sales Orders for 2007 OCT-NOV
3668

Equivalent date range query using BETWEEN comparison. It requires a bit of trick programming. 23.59.59.997 is the last available time in a day.

```
SELECT [Sales Orders for 2007 OCT-NOV] = COUNT(* )
FROM   AdventureWorks2012.Sales.SalesOrderHeader
WHERE  OrderDate BETWEEN @StartDate
       AND dateadd(ms,-3, dateadd(DAY, 1, @EndDate))
GO
```

Sales Orders for 2007 OCT-NOV
3668

The BETWEEN operator can be used with string dates as well. Note: anything after midnight on 2004-02-10 is not included.

```
USE AdventureWorks;
SELECT POs=COUNT(*) FROM Purchasing.PurchaseOrderHeader
WHERE OrderDate BETWEEN '20040201' AND '20040210'
GO
```

POs
108

BETWEEN Dates Without Time: Entire 2004-02-10 Day Included This Fashion

```
SELECT POs=COUNT(*) FROM Purchasing.PurchaseOrderHeader
WHERE datediff(dd,0,OrderDate)
       BETWEEN datediff(dd,0,'20040201 12:11:39') AND datediff(dd,0,'20040210 14:33:19')
```

POs
108

The datetime range BETWEEN is equivalent to >=...AND....<= operators.

```
SELECT POs=COUNT(*) FROM Purchasing.PurchaseOrderHeader
WHERE OrderDate  BETWEEN '2004-02-01 00:00:00.000' AND '2004-02-10  00:00:00.000'
```

POs
108

Orders with datetime OrderDate-s of

'2004-02-10 00:00:01.000'	1 second after midnight (start of day at 12:00AM)
'2004-02-10 00:01:00.000'	1 minute after midnight
'2004-02-10 01:00:00.000'	1 hour after midnight
'2004-02-10 23:00:00.000'	23 hours after midnight

would not included in the preceding two queries. Only datetime OrderDate of '2004-02-10 00:00:00.000' would be included. That would be OK if the time part is not used. But even in that case and order can be entered accidentally with a time part, that would throw off the count.

To include the entire day of 2004-02-10, move the day up by one and use the < operator:

```
SELECT POs=COUNT(*) FROM Purchasing.PurchaseOrderHeader
WHERE OrderDate >= '20040201' AND OrderDate < '20040211';
```

POs
108

The reason we cannot detect a difference is due to lack of data passed midnight on 2004-02-11.

```
SELECT  [PurchaseOrderID], [RevisionNumber], [Status],
        [EmployeeID], [VendorID], [ShipMethodID], [OrderDate]
FROM [AdventureWorks].[Purchasing].[PurchaseOrderHeader] WHERE PurchaseOrderID = 1665;
```

PurchaseOrderID	RevisionNumber	Status	EmployeeID	VendorID	ShipMethodID	OrderDate
1665	0	4	261	43	5	2004-02-10 00:00:00.000

CHAPTER 13: Basic SELECT Statement Syntax & Examples

Date & Time Conversion To / From String 461

Advance the datetime one second from midnight, the BETWEEN datetime query is not going to count it

```
UPDATE [AdventureWorks].[Purchasing].[PurchaseOrderHeader]
    SET OrderDate = '2004-02-10 00:00:01.000'
WHERE PurchaseOrderID = 1665;  -- (1 row(s) affected)
```

This is the current value for OrderDate datetime.

PurchaseOrderID	RevisionNumber	Status	EmployeeID	VendorID	ShipMethodID	OrderDate
1665	0	4	261	43	5	2004-02-10 00:00:01.000

The following queries are not going to count this passed midnight record any more.

```
SELECT POs=COUNT(*) FROM Purchasing.PurchaseOrderHeader
WHERE OrderDate BETWEEN '2004-02-01 00:00:00.000' AND '2004-02-10 00:00:00.000'
```

POs
107

```
USE AdventureWorks; SELECT POs=COUNT(*) FROM Purchasing.PurchaseOrderHeader
WHERE OrderDate BETWEEN '20040201' AND '20040210'
```

POs
107

While the query we designed specifically for a case like this will count it correctly.

```
SELECT POs=COUNT(*) FROM Purchasing.PurchaseOrderHeader
WHERE OrderDate >= '20040201' AND OrderDate < '20040211'
```

POs
108

We restore the data to its original value.

```
UPDATE [AdventureWorks].[Purchasing].[PurchaseOrderHeader]
    SET OrderDate = '2004-02-10 00:00:00.000'
WHERE PurchaseOrderID = 1665;    -- (1 row(s) affected)
```

CHAPTER 13: Basic SELECT Statement Syntax & Examples

Date Validation Function ISDATE()

```
DECLARE @StringDate varchar(32);
SET @StringDate = '2011-03-15 18:50';
IF EXISTS( SELECT * WHERE ISDATE(@StringDate) = 1)
   PRINT 'VALID DATE: ' + @StringDate
ELSE
   PRINT 'INVALID DATE: ' + @StringDate;
```

```
VALID DATE: 2011-03-15 18:50
```

```
DECLARE @StringDate varchar(32) ;
SET @StringDate = '20112-03-15 18:50';
IF EXISTS( SELECT * WHERE ISDATE(@StringDate) = 1)
   PRINT 'VALID DATE: ' + @StringDate
ELSE  PRINT 'INVALID DATE: ' + @StringDate;
GO
```

```
INVALID DATE: 20112-03-15 18:50
```

First and Last Day of Date Periods

Calculating date periods markers is a very important task in T-SQL programming, especially related to reporting queries.

```
DECLARE @Date DATE = '20161023';  SELECT ReferenceDate   = @Date;

SELECT FirstDayOfYear    = CONVERT(DATE, dateadd(yy, datediff(yy,0, @Date),0));

SELECT LastDayOfYear     = CONVERT(DATE, dateadd(yy, datediff(yy,0, @Date)+1,-1));

SELECT FDofSemester      = CONVERT(DATE, dateadd(qq,((datediff(qq,0,@Date)/2)*2),0));

SELECT LastDayOfSemester = CONVERT(DATE, dateadd(qq,((datediff(qq,0,@Date)/2)*2)+2,-1));

SELECT FirstDayOfQuarter = CONVERT(DATE, dateadd(qq, datediff(qq,0, @Date),0));

SELECT LastDayOfQuarter  = CONVERT(DATE, dateadd(qq, datediff(qq,0,@Date)+1,-1));
```

LastDayOfQuarter
2016-12-31

Date & Time Conversion To / From String

The brand-new EOMonth() function simplifies month start/end formulas

```sql
SELECT LastDayOfMonth = EOMonth (@Date);  -- New in SQL Server 2012

SELECT FirstDayOfMonth = CONVERT(DATE, dateadd(mm, datediff(mm,0, @Date),0));

SELECT LastDayOfMonth  = CONVERT(DATE, dateadd(mm, datediff(mm,0, @Date)+1,-1));

SELECT FirstDayOfWeek  = CONVERT(DATE, dateadd(wk, datediff(wk,0, @Date),0));

SELECT LastDayOfWeek   = CONVERT(DATE, dateadd(wk, datediff(wk,0, @Date)+1,-1));
GO
```

Month Sequence Generator

Sometimes date based data may have gaps missing months. For reporting purposes we may want to include all months from start date to end date. To do that we have to generate a continuous sequence of months, and use it to fill in the gaps. Calendar table can also be used for such a task.

```sql
DECLARE @Date date = '2000-01-01'
SELECT MonthStart=dateadd(MM, number, @Date)
FROM  master.dbo.spt_values
WHERE type='P' AND  dateadd(MM, number, @Date) <= CURRENT_TIMESTAMP
ORDER BY MonthStart;    -- (151 row(s) affected) - Partial results.
```

MonthStart
2000-01-01
2000-02-01
2000-03-01
2000-04-01
2000-05-01
2000-06-01
2000-07-01
2000-08-01
2000-09-01
2000-10-01
2000-11-01
2000-12-01
2001-01-01
2001-02-01
2001-03-01
2001-04-01

CHAPTER 13: Basic SELECT Statement Syntax & Examples

Selected U.S. & International Date Styles

The U.S. date style is m/d/y.

```
DECLARE @DateTimeValue varchar(32) = '10/23/2016';

SELECT StringDate=@DateTimeValue,   [SSMS-Style] = CONVERT(datetime, @DatetimeValue);

SELECT @DateTimeValue = '10/23/2016 23:01:05';

SELECT StringDate = @DateTimeValue, [SSMS-Style] = CONVERT(datetime, @DatetimeValue);
GO
```

StringDate	SSMS-Style
10/23/2016	2016-10-23 00:00:00.000

StringDate	SSMS-Style
10/23/2016 23:01:05	2016-10-23 23:01:05.000

The UK or British/French style is dmy.

```
DECLARE @DateTimeValue varchar(32) = '23/10/16 23:01:05';

SELECT StringDate = @DateTimeValue, [SSMS-Style] = CONVERT(datetime, @DatetimeValue, 3);

 SELECT @DateTimeValue = '23/10/2016 04:01 PM';

SELECT StringDate = @DateTimeValue, [SSMS-Style] = CONVERT(datetime, @DatetimeValue, 103);
GO
```

The German style is dmy as well with a new twist to it: period instead of slash.

```
DECLARE @DateTimeValue varchar(32)  = '23.10.16 23:01:05';
SELECT StringDate = @DateTimeValue, [SSMS -Style] = CONVERT(datetime, @DatetimeValue, 4);
 SELECT @DateTimeValue = '23.10.2016 04:01 PM';
SELECT StringDate = @DateTimeValue, [SSMS -Style] = CONVERT(datetime, @DatetimeValue, 104);
GO
```

```
-- Nondeterministic month name (mon)
SET LANGUAGE Spanish; SELECT CONVERT(varchar, getdate(), 100);      -- Ago 10 2018  4:43PM
SET LANGUAGE Turkish; SELECT CONVERT(varchar, getdate(), 100);      -- Agu 10 2018  4:44PM
SET LANGUAGE Polish; SELECT CONVERT(varchar, getdate(), 100);       -- VIII 10 2018  4:46PM
SET LANGUAGE Hungarian; SELECT CONVERT(varchar, getdate(), 100);    -- aug 10 2018  4:46PM
SET LANGUAGE Russian; SELECT CONVERT(nvarchar, getdate(), 100);     -- авг 10 2018  4:47PM
```

Date & Time Conversion To / From String

The DATEPART() Function to Decompose a Date
The DATEPART() function returns a part of a date.

```
DECLARE @dt datetime = getdate();
SELECT DATEPART(YEAR, @dt)       AS YYYY,
       DATEPART(MONTH, @dt)      AS MM,
       DATEPART(DAY, @dt)        AS DD;
```

YYYY	MM	DD
2016	7	29

```
SELECT * FROM Northwind.dbo.Orders
WHERE DATEPART(YEAR, OrderDate)       = '1996'  AND
      DATEPART(MONTH,OrderDate)       = '07'    AND
      DATEPART(DAY, OrderDate)        = '10'
```

```
/*OrderID    CustomerID   EmployeeID   OrderDate                RequiredDate              ShippedDate
   ShipVia   Freight  ShipName        Shipaddress      ShipCity ShipRegion        ShipPostalCode
   ShipCountry
10253   HANAR  3          1996-07-10 00:00:00.000  1996-07-24 00:00:00.000  1996-07-16 00:00:00.000
        2      58.17      Hanari Carnes    Rua do Paço, 67  Rio de Janeiro   RJ       05454-876
   Brazil  */
```

Alternate syntax for DATEPART.

```
SELECT * FROM Northwind.dbo.Orders
WHERE       YEAR(OrderDate)    = 1996    AND
            MONTH(OrderDate)   = 07      AND
            DAY(OrderDate)     = 10
GO
```

```
-- Additional datepart parameters including Julian date
DECLARE @dt datetime = getdate();
SELECT DATEPART(DAY, @dt)            AS DD,
       DATEPART(WEEKDAY, @dt)        AS WD,
       DATEPART(DAYOFYEAR, @dt)      AS JulianDate,
       DATEPART(WEEK, @dt)           AS Week,
       DATEPART(ISO_WEEK, @dt)       AS ISOWeek,
       DATEPART(HOUR, @dt)           AS HH;
```

DD	WD	JulianDate	Week	ISOWeek	HH
10	5	223	33	32	17

CHAPTER 13: Basic SELECT Statement Syntax & Examples

The DATENAME() Function to Get Date Part Names

The DATENAME() function can be used to find out the words for months and weekdays.

```
SELECT DayName=DATENAME(weekday, OrderDate), SalesPerWeekDay = COUNT(*)
FROM AdventureWorks2008.Sales.SalesOrderHeader
GROUP BY DATENAME(weekday, OrderDate), DATEPART(weekday,OrderDate)
ORDER BY DATEPART(weekday,OrderDate);
```

DayName	SalesPerWeekDay
Sunday	4482
Monday	4591
Tuesday	4346
Wednesday	4244
Thursday	4483
Friday	4444
Saturday	4875

DATENAME application for month names

```
SELECT MonthName=DATENAME(month, OrderDate), SalesPerMonth = COUNT(*)
FROM AdventureWorks2008.Sales.SalesOrderHeader
GROUP BY DATENAME(month, OrderDate), MONTH(OrderDate) ORDER BY MONTH(OrderDate);
```

MonthName	SalesPerMonth
January	2483
February	2686
March	2750
April	2740
May	3154
June	3079
July	2094
August	2411
September	2298
October	2282
November	2474
December	3014

```
SELECT DATENAME(MM,dateadd(MM,7,-1))  -- July  - Month name from month number
```

CHAPTER 13: Basic SELECT Statement Syntax & Examples

Date & Time Conversion To / From String

Extract Date from Text with PATINDEX Pattern Matching

```
USE tempdb;
go

CREATE TABLE InsiderTransaction (
    InsiderTransactionID int identity primary key,
    TradeDate datetime,
    TradeMsg varchar(256),
    ModifiedDate datetime default (getdate())  );

-- Populate table with dummy data
INSERT InsiderTransaction (TradeMsg)
VALUES ('INSIDER TRAN QABC Hammer, Bruce D. CSO 09-02-08 Buy 2,000 6.10');
INSERT InsiderTransaction (TradeMsg)
VALUES ('INSIDER TRAN QABC Schmidt, Steven CFO 08-25-08 Buy 2,500 6.70') ;
INSERT InsiderTransaction (TradeMsg)
VALUES ('INSIDER TRAN QABC  Hammer, Bruce D. CSO  08-20-08 Buy 3,000 8.59');
INSERT InsiderTransaction (TradeMsg)
VALUES ('INSIDER TRAN QABC Walters,  Jeff CTO 08-15-08  Sell 5,648 8.49');
INSERT InsiderTransaction (TradeMsg)
VALUES  ('INSIDER TRAN  QABC  Walters, Jeff CTO   08-15-08 Option Exercise 5,648 2.15');
INSERT InsiderTransaction (TradeMsg)
VALUES('INSIDER TRAN QABC Hammer, Bruce D. CSO 07-31-08  Buy 5,000 8.05');
INSERT InsiderTransaction (TradeMsg)
VALUES('INSIDER TRAN QABC Lennot, Mark  Director  08-31-07 Buy 1,500 9.97');
INSERT InsiderTransaction (TradeMsg)
VALUES('INSIDER TRAN QABC  O''Neal, Linda COO  08-01-08 Sell 5,000 6.50');
```

Pattern match for MM-DD-YY using the PATINDEX string function to extract dates from stock trade message text.

```
SELECT  InsiderTransactionID ,     substring(TradeMsg,
        patindex('%[01][0-9]-[0123][0-9]-[0-9][0-9]%', TradeMsg),8) AS TradeDate
FROM InsiderTransaction  WHERE  patindex('%[01][0-9]-[0123][0-9]-[0-9][0-9]%', TradeMsg) > 0;
```

InsiderTransactionID	TradeDate
1	09-02-08
2	08-25-08
3	08-20-08
4	08-15-08
5	08-15-08
6	07-31-08
7	08-31-07
8	08-01-08

Valid Ranges for Date & Time Data Types

- DATE (3 bytes) date range:
- January 1, 1 through December 31, 9999 A.D.

- SMALLDATETIME (4 bytes) date range:
- January 1, 1900 through June 6, 2079

- DATETIME (8 bytes) date range:
- January 1, 1753 through December 31, 9999

- DATETIME2 (6-8 bytes) date range:
- January 1, 1 A.D. through December 31, 9999 A.D.

Smalldatetime has limited range. The statement below will give a date range error.

```
SELECT CONVERT(smalldatetime, '2110-01-01')
/* Msg 242, Level 16, State 3, Line 1
The conversion of a varchar data type to a smalldatetime data type
resulted in an out-of-range value. */
```

```
-- Date Columbus discovers America
SELECT CONVERT(datetime, '14921012');
/* Msg 242, Level 16, State 3, Line 2
The conversion of a varchar data type to a datetime data type resulted in an out-of-range value. */
```

```
SELECT CONVERT(datetime2, '14921012');    -- 1492-10-10 00:00:00.0000000
```

```
SELECT CONVERT(date, '14921012');          -- 1492-10-12
```

CHAPTER 13: Basic SELECT Statement Syntax & Examples

Date & Time Conversion To / From String

Last Week Calculations

```sql
-- SQL last Friday - Implied string to datetime conversions in dateadd & datediff
DECLARE @BaseFriday CHAR(8), @LastFriday datetime, @LastMonday datetime;
SET @BaseFriday = '19000105';
SELECT  @LastFriday = dateadd(dd,
        (datediff (dd, @BaseFriday, CURRENT_TIMESTAMP) / 7) * 7, @BaseFriday) ;
SELECT [Last Friday] = @LastFriday ;
```

Last Friday
2012-07-27 00:00:00.000

```sql
-- Last Monday (last week's Monday)
SELECT  @LastMonday=dateadd(dd,  (datediff (dd, @BaseFriday,
        CURRENT_TIMESTAMP) / 7) * 7 - 4, @BaseFriday)
SELECT [Last Monday]= @LastMonday;
```

Last Monday
2012-07-23 00:00:00.000

```sql
-- Last week - SUN - SAT
SELECT          [Last Week] = CONCAT(CONVERT(varchar,dateadd(day, -1, @LastMonday), 101), ' - ',
                CONVERT(varchar, dateadd(day, 1,  @LastFriday), 101))
```

Last Week
07/22/2012 - 07/28/2012

```sql
-- Next 10 weeks including this one; SUN - SAT
SELECT  TOP 10   [ Week] = CONCAT(CONVERT(varchar,dateadd(day, -1+number*7, @LastMonday), 101),
        ' - ',    CONVERT(varchar, dateadd(day, 1+number*7, @LastFriday), 101))
FROM master.dbo.spt_values  WHERE type = 'P';
```

Week
08/05/2012 - 08/11/2012
08/12/2012 - 08/18/2012
08/19/2012 - 08/25/2012
08/26/2012 - 09/01/2012
09/02/2012 - 09/08/2012
09/09/2012 - 09/15/2012
09/16/2012 - 09/22/2012
09/23/2012 - 09/29/2012
09/30/2012 - 10/06/2012
10/07/2012 - 10/13/2012

Specific Day Calculations

```sql
-- First day of current month
SELECT dateadd(month, datediff(month, 0, getdate()), 0);
```

```sql
 -- 15th day of current month
SELECT dateadd(day,14,dateadd(month,datediff(month,0,getdate()),0));
```

```sql
-- First Monday of current month
SELECT   dateadd(day, (9-datepart(weekday,
         dateadd(month, datediff(month, 0, getdate()), 0)))%7,
         dateadd(month, datediff(month, 0, getdate()), 0)) ;
```

```sql
-- Next Monday calculation from the reference date which was a Monday
DECLARE @Now datetime = GETDATE();
DECLARE @NextMonday datetime = dateadd(dd, ((datediff(dd, '19000101', @Now)  / 7) * 7) + 7, '19000101');
SELECT [Now]=@Now, [Next Monday]=@NextMonday;
```

```sql
-- Last Friday of current month
SELECT   dateadd(day, -7+(6-datepart(weekday,
         dateadd(month, datediff(month, 0, getdate())+1, 0)))%7,
         dateadd(month, datediff(month, 0, getdate())+1, 0)) ;
```

```sql
-- First day of next month
SELECT dateadd(month, datediff(month, 0, getdate())+1, 0);
```

```sql
-- 15th of next month
SELECT dateadd(day,14, dateadd(month, datediff(month, 0, getdate())+1, 0));
```

```sql
-- First Monday of next month
SELECT   dateadd(day, (9-datepart(weekday,
         dateadd(month, datediff(month, 0, getdate())+1, 0)))%7,
          dateadd(month, datediff(month, 0, getdate())+1, 0))  AS NextMonthMonday;
```

NextMonthMonday
2012-08-06 00:00:00.000

CHAPTER 13: Basic SELECT Statement Syntax & Examples

CHAPTER 14: Subqueries in SELECT Statements

Subqueries

Subquery ("inner query") is query within a query which is called the "outer query".

When a subquery involves columns form the outer query, it is called correlated subquery.

When a subquery has a table alias, it is called a derived table.

With SQL Server 2005 a new kind of subquery was introduced: Common Table Expression (CTE). A query can have one or more CTEs. If they are related, they are called nested CTEs. CTEs support recursion.

Correlated subquery is used to retrieve the last freight cost for the customer.

```
-- Correlated subquery - it has reference to an outer query column: A.CustomerID
USE Northwind;

SELECT   A.CustomerID,
    FORMAT(MIN(A.OrderDate), 'd')                          AS FirstOrder,
    FORMAT(MAX(A.OrderDate), 'd')                          AS LastOrder,
    FORMAT( (SELECT   TOP 1 B.Freight
            FROM    Orders B
            WHERE   B.CustomerID = A.CustomerID
            ORDER BY OrderDate DESC),'c','en-US')          AS LastFreight
FROM    Orders A
GROUP BY A.CustomerID ORDER BY A.CustomerID;   -- (89 row(s) affected) - Partial results.
```

CustomerID	FirstOrder	LastOrder	LastFreight
ALFKI	8/25/1997	4/9/1998	$1.21
ANATR	9/18/1996	3/4/1998	$39.92
ANTON	11/27/1996	1/28/1998	$58.43
AROUT	11/15/1996	4/10/1998	$33.80
BERGS	8/12/1996	3/4/1998	$151.52
BLAUS	4/9/1997	4/29/1998	$31.14
BLONP	7/25/1996	1/12/1998	$7.09
BOLID	10/10/1996	3/24/1998	$16.16
BONAP	10/16/1996	5/6/1998	$38.28
BOTTM	12/20/1996	4/24/1998	$24.12
BSBEV	8/26/1996	4/14/1998	$123.83
CACTU	4/29/1997	4/28/1998	$0.33

Non-Correlated Subqueries

In the next query, the inner query is not linked to the outer query at all (no outer column is used in the inner query). The implication is that the inner query can be executed by itself. The inner query needs to return a single value in this instance due to the ">=" operator. If it were to return multiple values, error would result.

```
-- Non-correlated subquery
SELECT          Name,
                FORMAT(ListPrice, 'c','en-US')          AS ListPrice,
                ProductNumber,
                FORMAT(StandardCost, 'c','en-US')       AS StandardCost
FROM AdventureWorks2012.Production.Product
WHERE ListPrice >=
                (SELECT ListPrice
                 FROM AdventureWorks.Production.Product
                 WHERE Name = 'Road-250 Black, 48' )

ORDER BY ListPrice DESC, Name;
GO
```

Name	ListPrice	ProductNumber	StandardCost
Road-150 Red, 44	$3,578.27	BK-R93R-44	$2,171.29
Road-150 Red, 48	$3,578.27	BK-R93R-48	$2,171.29
Road-150 Red, 52	$3,578.27	BK-R93R-52	$2,171.29
Road-150 Red, 56	$3,578.27	BK-R93R-56	$2,171.29
Road-150 Red, 62	$3,578.27	BK-R93R-62	$2,171.29
Mountain-100 Silver, 38	$3,399.99	BK-M82S-38	$1,912.15
Mountain-100 Silver, 42	$3,399.99	BK-M82S-42	$1,912.15
Mountain-100 Silver, 44	$3,399.99	BK-M82S-44	$1,912.15
Mountain-100 Silver, 48	$3,399.99	BK-M82S-48	$1,912.15
Mountain-100 Black, 38	$3,374.99	BK-M82B-38	$1,898.09
Mountain-100 Black, 42	$3,374.99	BK-M82B-42	$1,898.09
Mountain-100 Black, 44	$3,374.99	BK-M82B-44	$1,898.09
Mountain-100 Black, 48	$3,374.99	BK-M82B-48	$1,898.09
Road-250 Black, 44	$2,443.35	BK-R89B-44	$1,554.95
Road-250 Black, 48	$2,443.35	BK-R89B-48	$1,554.95
Road-250 Black, 52	$2,443.35	BK-R89B-52	$1,554.95
Road-250 Black, 58	$2,443.35	BK-R89B-58	$1,554.95
Road-250 Red, 44	$2,443.35	BK-R89R-44	$1,518.79
Road-250 Red, 48	$2,443.35	BK-R89R-48	$1,518.79
Road-250 Red, 52	$2,443.35	BK-R89R-52	$1,518.79
Road-250 Red, 58	$2,443.35	BK-R89R-58	$1,554.95

Subqueries

Subquery returned more than 1 value Error

The following query fails. The reason: the ">=" requires a single value on the right side. The subquery returns 46 values.

```
-- Non-correlated subquery
SELECT        Name,
              FORMAT(ListPrice, 'c','en-US')          AS ListPrice,
              ProductNumber,
              FORMAT(StandardCost, 'c','en-US')       AS StandardCost
FROM AdventureWorks2012.Production.Product
WHERE ListPrice >=
   (SELECT ListPrice
    FROM AdventureWorks.Production.Product
    WHERE Name LIKE 'Road%' )
ORDER BY ListPrice DESC, Name;
GO
/* Msg 512, Level 16, State 1, Line 3
Subquery returned more than 1 value. This is not permitted when the subquery follows =, !=, <, <= , >, >=
or when the subquery is used as an expression. */
```

If we change the WHERE clause predicate operator from ">=" to "IN" then the query will execute correctly since the IN operator works with a set of values on the right side.

```
-- Non-correlated subquery
SELECT    Name,
          FORMAT(ListPrice, 'c','en-US')          AS ListPrice,
          ProductNumber,
          FORMAT(StandardCost, 'c','en-US')       AS StandardCost
FROM AdventureWorks2012.Production.Product
WHERE ListPrice IN
          (SELECT ListPrice
           FROM AdventureWorks.Production.Product  WHERE Name LIKE 'Road%' )
ORDER BY ListPrice DESC, Name;
-- (253 row(s) affected)  -- Partial results.
```

Name	ListPrice	ProductNumber	StandardCost
AWC Logo Cap	$8.99	CA-1098	$6.92
Racing Socks, L	$8.99	SO-R809-L	$3.36
Racing Socks, M	$8.99	SO-R809-M	$3.36
Road Bottle Cage	$8.99	BC-R205	$3.36
Road-650 Black, 44	$782.99	BK-R50B-44	$486.71
Road-650 Black, 48	$782.99	BK-R50B-48	$486.71
Road-650 Black, 52	$782.99	BK-R50B-52	$486.71

CHAPTER 14: Subqueries in SELECT Statements

Correlated Subqueries

In a correlated subquery there is a reference to an outer query column. In other words, the subquery by itself cannot be executed due to the correlation. In the next query, the inner query references soh.SalesOrderID column from the outer query in the WHERE clause predicate which is like an EQUI-JOIN.

```
SELECT          soh.SalesOrderID,
                FORMAT (soh.OrderDate, 'yyyy-MM-dd')                    AS OrderDate,

                ( SELECT FORMAT(MAX(sod.UnitPrice),'c','en-US')
                  FROM   AdventureWorks2012.Sales.SalesOrderDetail AS sod
                  WHERE  soh.SalesOrderID = sod.SalesOrderID )          AS MaxUnitPrice,

                FORMAT(TotalDue, 'c', 'en-US')                          AS TotalDue
FROM    AdventureWorks2012.Sales.SalesOrderHeader AS soh
ORDER BY MaxUnitPrice DESC, SalesOrderID;    -- (31465 row(s) affected) - Partial results.
```

SalesOrderID	OrderDate	MaxUnitPrice	TotalDue
51087	2007-07-01	$953.63	$2,721.27
51099	2007-07-01	$953.63	$5,276.64
51119	2007-07-01	$953.63	$2,040.14
51173	2007-07-01	$953.63	$1,457.54
51701	2007-08-01	$953.63	$2,634.93
51798	2007-08-01	$953.63	$907.09
51805	2007-08-01	$953.63	$907.09
51808	2007-08-01	$953.63	$1,827.45
51861	2007-08-01	$953.63	$11,762.43
53489	2007-09-01	$953.63	$1,814.18

The next query with correlated subquery list sales staff with 0.015 commission rate.

```
SELECT CONCAT(p.LastName,', ', p.FirstName) AS SalesPerson, e.BusinessEntityID AS EmployeeID
FROM AdventureWorks2012.Person.Person AS p
        INNER JOIN AdventureWorks2012.HumanResources.Employee AS e
        ON e.BusinessEntityID = p.BusinessEntityID
WHERE 0.015 IN  (SELECT CommissionPct  FROM AdventureWorks2012.Sales.SalesPerson sp
                WHERE e.BusinessEntityID = sp.BusinessEntityID)  ORDER BY SalesPerson;
```

SalesPerson	EmployeeID
Carson, Jillian	277
Mitchell, Linda	276
Saraiva, José	282

CHAPTER 14: Subqueries in SELECT Statements

Subqueries

Single-Valued Correlated Subqueries

The query syntax determines if we can use a single-valued subquery or multiple-valued. A subquery can be the argument of a function.

```
USE AdventureWorks2012;
```

```
-- Single value subquery in SELECT list
SELECT  SOH.SalesOrderID                          AS SOID,
        CONVERT(DATE,SOH.OrderDate)               AS OrderDate,
        FORMAT(SOH.Subtotal,'c0','en-US')         AS Subtotal,
        (SELECT MAX(SOD.UnitPrice)
         FROM Sales.SalesOrderDetail AS SOD
         WHERE SOH.SalesOrderID=SOD.SalesOrderID) AS MaxUnitPrice
FROM Sales.SalesOrderHeader SOH    ORDER BY SOID;
--(31467 row(s) affected) - Partial results.
```

SOID	OrderDate	Subtotal	MaxUnitPrice
43659	2005-07-01	$20,566	2039.994
43660	2005-07-01	$1,294	874.794

```
-- Make the subquery the argument of the FORMAT function
SELECT  TOP (10)    SOH.SalesOrderID                  AS SOID,
        CONVERT(DATE,SOH.OrderDate)                   AS OrderDate,
        FORMAT(SOH.Subtotal,'c0','en-US')             AS Subtotal,
        FORMAT(
    (SELECT MAX(SOD.UnitPrice)
    FROM Sales.SalesOrderDetail AS SOD
    WHERE SOH.SalesOrderID=SOD.SalesOrderID)
            ,'c2','en-US')                            AS MaxUnitPrice
FROM Sales.SalesOrderHeader SOH    ORDER BY SOID;
```

SOID	OrderDate	Subtotal	MaxUnitPrice
43659	2005-07-01	$20,566	$2,039.99
43660	2005-07-01	$1,294	$874.79
43661	2005-07-01	$32,726	$2,039.99
43662	2005-07-01	$28,833	$2,146.96
43663	2005-07-01	$419	$419.46
43664	2005-07-01	$24,433	$2,039.99
43665	2005-07-01	$14,353	$2,039.99
43666	2005-07-01	$5,056	$2,146.96
43667	2005-07-01	$6,107	$2,039.99
43668	2005-07-01	$35,944	$2,146.96

CHAPTER 14: Subqueries in SELECT Statements

Correlated Subqueries with Same Table

In a correlated subquery, we can use a table from the outer query. In such a case table alias usage is required. In the next query with correlated subquery which lists same part suppliers, the ProductVendor table is referenced by both the outer query and inner query, therefore table alias is required.

```
SELECT       p.Name                        AS ProductName,
             v.Name                        AS Vendor,
             pv1.BusinessEntityID          AS VendorID
FROM AdventureWorks2012.Purchasing.ProductVendor pv1
   INNER JOIN AdventureWorks2012.Production.Product p ON p.ProductID = pv1.ProductID
   INNER JOIN AdventureWorks2012.Purchasing.Vendor v   ON v.BusinessEntityID = pv1.BusinessEntityID
WHERE pv1.ProductID IN    (      SELECT pv2.ProductID
                                 FROM AdventureWorks2012.Purchasing.ProductVendor pv2
                                 WHERE pv1.BusinessEntityID <> pv2.BusinessEntityID)
ORDER  BY ProductName, Vendor;           -- (347 row(s) affected) - Partial results.
```

ProductName	Vendor	VendorID
Internal Lock Washer 7	Aurora Bike Center	1616
Internal Lock Washer 7	Pro Sport Industries	1686
Internal Lock Washer 8	Aurora Bike Center	1616
Internal Lock Washer 8	Pro Sport Industries	1686
Internal Lock Washer 9	Aurora Bike Center	1616
Internal Lock Washer 9	Pro Sport Industries	1686
LL Crankarm	Proseware, Inc.	1678

CROSS APPLY with Correlated Subquery

The CROSS APPLY operator can connect tables with correlated subqueries as demonstrated following, INNER JOIN would not work in this case.

```
USE AdventureWorks;      DECLARE  @Year  INT = 2003, @Month INT = 2;
SELECT   s.Name                                                  AS Customer,
         FORMAT(SalesAmount.OrderTotal,'c','en-US')              AS [Total Sales]
FROM     Sales.Customer AS c   INNER JOIN Sales.Store AS s   ON s.CustomerID = c.CustomerID
    CROSS APPLY (      SELECT  soh.CustomerId,   Sum(sod.LineTotal) AS OrderTotal
                       FROM    Sales.SalesOrderHeader AS soh
              INNER JOIN Sales.SalesOrderDetail AS sod    ON sod.SalesOrderId = soh.SalesOrderId
                       WHERE soh.CustomerId = c.CustomerId
              AND OrderDate > = DATEFROMPARTS(@Year, @Month, 1)
              AND OrderDate <  DATEADD(mm, 1, DATEFROMPARTS(@Year, @Month, 1))
                       GROUP BY soh.CustomerId)             AS SalesAmount
ORDER BY Customer;       -- (132 row(s) affected) - Partial results.
```

Customer	Total Sales
Ace Bicycle Supply	$647.99
Affordable Sports Equipment	$50,953.32
Alpine Ski House	$939.59
Basic Sports Equipment	$159.56

CHAPTER 14: Subqueries in SELECT Statements

Derived Tables: SELECT from SELECT

A non-correlated subquery can be made into a derived table by enclosing it in parenthesis and assigning a table alias, such as "CAT" in the following example. It can then be used like a regular table for example in JOINs.

```
USE Northwind;

SELECT   c.CategoryName  AS Category,
         p.ProductName,   p.UnitPrice,   CAT.NoOfProducts
FROM     Categories c
   INNER JOIN Products p
     ON c.CategoryID = p.CategoryID
   INNER JOIN
                    (SELECT  c.CategoryID,
                             NoOfProducts = count(* )
                     FROM    Categories c
                        INNER JOIN Products p1
                             ON c.CategoryID = p1.CategoryID
                        GROUP BY c.CategoryID)                AS CAT

     ON c.CategoryID = CAT.CategoryID
ORDER BY Category;
-- (77 row(s) affected)  - Partial results.
```

Category	ProductName	UnitPrice
Dairy Products	Raclette Courdavault	55.00
Dairy Products	Camembert Pierrot	34.00
Dairy Products	Gudbrandsdalsost	36.00
Dairy Products	Flotemysost	21.50
Dairy Products	Mozzarella di Giovanni	34.80
Grains/Cereals	Gustaf's Knäckebröd	21.00
Grains/Cereals	Tunnbröd	9.00
Grains/Cereals	Singaporean Hokkien Fried Mee	14.00
Grains/Cereals	Filo Mix	7.00
Grains/Cereals	Gnocchi di nonna Alice	38.00
Grains/Cereals	Ravioli Angelo	19.50

Results from the subquery (derived table).

CategoryID	NoOfProducts
1	12
2	12
3	13
4	10
5	7
6	6
7	5
8	12

CHAPTER 14: Subqueries in SELECT Statements

The UNION & UNION ALL Set Operators

UNION (distinct, duplicates eliminated) and UNION ALL (duplicates allowed) merge two or more sets of data into one set. Important points to remember about UNION:

> First SELECT column list establishes column names and data types; if INTO used it goes here
> Subsequent SELECTs must match the column structure; column names can be any; NULL if no data
> ORDER BY goes at the very end with the last SELECT

T-SQL UNION query merges data from different countries into a single result set.

```
USE NorthWind;
SELECT   ContactName,
         CompanyName,
         City,
         Country,
         Phone
FROM   Customers
WHERE  Country IN ( 'USA', 'Canada' )
-- (16 row(s) affected)
UNION
SELECT   ContactName,
         CompanyName             AS Company,
         City,     Country,
         Phone                   AS Telephone
FROM   Customers
WHERE  Country IN ( 'Germany', 'France' )
-- (22 row(s) affected)
UNION
SELECT   ContactName             AS Contact,
         CompanyName,   City,    Country,
         Phone                   AS Telephone
FROM   Customers
WHERE  Country IN ( 'Brazil', 'Spain' )
-- (14 row(s) affected)
ORDER  BY CompanyName,    ContactName ASC;
-- (52 row(s) affected)   - Partial results.
```

ContactName	CompanyName	City	Country	Phone
Maria Anders	Alfreds Futterkiste	Berlin	Germany	030-0074321
Hanna Moos	Blauer See Delikatessen	Mannheim	Germany	0621-08460
Frédérique Citeaux	Blondesddsl père et fils	Strasbourg	France	88.60.15.31
Martín Sommer	Bólido Comidas preparadas	Madrid	Spain	(91) 555 22 82

CHAPTER 14: Subqueries in SELECT Statements

CTE: Common Table Expression for Structured Coding

Common Table Expression is new in SQL Server 2005. It is similar to derived tables in one aspect with a difference: it is defined at the very beginning of a the query, above the main(outer) query. In addition, CTEs can be nested and defined as recursive.

```
USE AdventureWorks;

WITH CTE(ManagerID, StaffCount)
AS
(
    SELECT ManagerID, COUNT(*)
    FROM HumanResources.Employee AS e
    GROUP BY ManagerID
)

SELECT      CONCAT(LEFT(FirstName,1), '. ', LastName)       AS Manager,
            e.Title, StaffCount
FROM CTE s
        INNER JOIN HumanResources.Employee e
    ON s.ManagerID = e.EmployeeID
        INNER JOIN Person.Contact c
    ON c.ContactID = e.ContactID
ORDER BY Manager;
-- (47 row(s) affected) - Partial results.
```

Manager	Title	StaffCount
A. Alberts	European Sales Manager	3
A. Hill	Production Supervisor - WC10	7
A. Wright	Master Scheduler	4
B. Diaz	Production Supervisor - WC40	12
B. Welcker	Vice President of Sales	3
C. Kleinerman	Maintenance Supervisor	4
C. Petculescu	Production Supervisor - WC10	5
C. Randall	Production Supervisor - WC30	6
D. Bradley	Marketing Manager	8
D. Hamilton	Production Supervisor - WC40	6
D. Liu	Accounts Manager	7
D. Miller	Research and Development Manager	3
E. Gubbels	Production Supervisor - WC20	10
G. Altman	Facilities Manager	2
H. Abolrous	Quality Assurance Manager	2

CHAPTER 14: Subqueries in SELECT Statements

Multiple CTEs Query

A query can have multiple CTEs, they can even be nested (CTE has reference to previous CTE). The two CTEs in the following query are first name and last name frequencies.

```
USE AdventureWorks2012;

WITH cteLastNameFreq

   AS (SELECT    LastName        AS [LastNames],
                 count(*)        AS [LNFrequency]
      FROM    Person.Person
      GROUP BY LastName),

   cteFirstNameFreq
   AS (SELECT    FirstName       AS [FirstNames],
                 count(*)        AS [FNFrequency]
      FROM    Person.Person
      GROUP BY FirstName)

SELECT    CONCAT(rtrim(FirstName), ' ', rtrim(LastName))     AS [Name],
          isnull(Title,'')                                   AS [Title] ,
          f.FNFrequency,
          l.LNFrequency
FROM    Person.Person c
     INNER JOIN cteFirstNameFreq AS f
     ON c.FirstName = f.FirstNames
     INNER JOIN cteLastNameFreq AS l
     ON c.LastName = l.LastNames
WHERE    LastName LIKE 'P%' ORDER BY [Name];
-- (1187 row(s) affected) - Partial results;
```

Name	Title	FNFrequency	LNFrequency
Aaron Patterson		56	117
Aaron Perez		56	170
Aaron Perry		56	122
Aaron Phillips		56	80
Aaron Powell		56	116
Abby Patel		19	86
Abby Perez		19	170
Abigail Patterson		76	117
Abigail Patterson		76	117
Abigail Perry		76	122
Abigail Peterson		76	92
Abigail Powell		76	116

CTE: Common Table Expression for Structured Coding

Testing Common Table Expressions

A CTE can be tested independently of the main query if it does not have nesting (reference to a previous CTE). The following screen snapshot displays the execution of the first CTE SELECT query.

```
WITH cteLastNameFreq
     AS (SELECT    LastName   AS [LastNames],
                   count(*)   AS [LNFrequency]
         FROM      Person.Person
         GROUP BY LastName),

     cteFirstNameFreq
     AS (SELECT    FirstName  AS [FirstNames],
                   count(*)   AS [FNFrequency]
         FROM      Person.Person
         GROUP BY FirstName)

SELECT     CONCAT(rtrim(FirstName), ' ', rtrim(LastName))   AS [Name],
           isnull(Title,'')                                  AS [Title] ,
           f.FNFrequency,
           l.LNFrequency
FROM       Person.Person c
```

	LastNames	LNFrequency
1	Abbas	1
2	Abel	1
3	Abercrombie	3
4	Abolrous	2
5	Acevedo	1
6	Achong	1
7	Ackerman	2
8	Adams	86
9	Adina	1
10	Agbonile	1

CHAPTER 14: Subqueries in SELECT Statements

Nested CTEs Queries
CTEs can be nested by reference to a previous CTE like a table.

```sql
;WITH CTE1
   AS (SELECT 1 AS NUMBER
       UNION ALL
       SELECT 1),
   CTE2
   AS (SELECT 1 AS NUMBER
       FROM   CTE1 x,
              CTE1 y),
   CTE3
   AS (SELECT 1 AS NUMBER
       FROM   CTE2 x,
              CTE2 y),
   CTE4
   AS (SELECT 1 AS NUMBER
       FROM   CTE3 x,
              CTE3 y),
   CTE8BIT
   AS (SELECT ROW_NUMBER()
              OVER(ORDER BY NUMBER) AS INTSequence
       FROM   CTE4)
SELECT *
FROM   CTE8BIT
ORDER BY INTSequence;
-- (256 row(s) affected) - Partial results.
```

INTSequence
241
242
243
244
245
246
247
248
249
250
251
252
253
254
255
256

CTE: Common Table Expression for Structured Coding

CTE nesting: cteLastSalary has a nested reference to cteLastSalaryChange

```
USE AdventureWorks2012;

WITH cteLastSalaryChange
    AS (SELECT    BusinessEntityID        AS EmployeeID,
                  Max(RateChangeDate)     AS ChangeDate
        FROM   HumanResources.EmployeePayHistory   GROUP BY BusinessEntityID),

    cteLastSalary
    AS (SELECT    eph.BusinessEntityID        AS EmployeeID,    Rate
        FROM   HumanResources.EmployeePayHistory eph
           INNER JOIN cteLastSalaryChange lsc
           ON lsc.EmployeeID = eph.BusinessEntityID
           AND lsc.ChangeDate = eph.RateChangeDate)

-- SELECT * FROM cteLastSalary  -- for testing & debugging

SELECT TOP 1 FORMAT( Rate, 'c', 'en-US') AS SecondHighestPayRate
FROM    (SELECT   TOP 2 Rate    FROM    cteLastSalary    ORDER BY Rate DESC) a   -- Derived table
ORDER BY Rate ASC;
```

SecondHighestPayRate
$84.13

Testing Nested CTEs

Nested CTEs can be tested independently of the main query the following way.

```
USE AdventureWorks2012;
WITH cteLastSalaryChange
    AS (SELECT    BusinessEntityID        AS EmployeeID,
                  Max(RateChangeDate)     AS ChangeDate
        FROM   HumanResources.EmployeePayHistory
        GROUP BY BusinessEntityID),
    cteLastSalary
    AS (SELECT    eph.BusinessEntityID        AS EmployeeID,
                  Rate
        FROM   HumanResources.EmployeePayHistory eph
           INNER JOIN cteLastSalaryChange lsc
           ON lsc.EmployeeID = eph.BusinessEntityID
           AND lsc.ChangeDate = eph.RateChangeDate)
SELECT * FROM cteLastSalary  -- for testing & debugging
```

CTE: Common Table Expression for Structured Coding

In Query Editor, uncomment the testing line, select (highlight) the top part of the query and execute it

```sql
USE AdventureWorks2012;

WITH cteLastSalaryChange

    AS (SELECT      BusinessEntityID        AS EmployeeID,
                    Max(RateChangeDate)     AS ChangeDate
        FROM    HumanResources.EmployeePayHistory
        GROUP BY BusinessEntityID),

    cteLastSalary
    AS (SELECT      eph.BusinessEntityID    AS EmployeeID,
                    Rate
        FROM    HumanResources.EmployeePayHistory eph
            INNER JOIN cteLastSalaryChange lsc
                ON lsc.EmployeeID = eph.BusinessEntityID
                AND lsc.ChangeDate = eph.RateChangeDate)

SELECT * FROM cteLastSalary    -- for testing & debugging

SELECT TOP 1 FORMAT( Rate, 'c', 'en-US') AS SecondHighestPayRate
```

	EmployeeID	Rate
1	290	23.0769
2	289	23.0769
3	288	23.0769
4	287	48.101
5	286	23.0769
6	285	48.101
7	284	23.0769
8	283	23.0769

290 rows

Recursive CTEs for Tree Hierarchy Processing

Recursive CTEs are one of the most exciting new features introduced with SQL Server 2005. They allow tree processing, such as organizational charts or bill of materials parts assembly, as well as generating sets of data without tables. The following recursive CTE generates 1 million integers all by itself. The query execution time is 10 seconds as it can be seen in the lower right.

```
-- Recursive CTE
;WITH cteINTSequence ( SeqNo) as
(
    SELECT 1
    UNION ALL
    SELECT SeqNo + 1
    FROM cteINTSequence
    WHERE SeqNo < 1000000
)
SELECT TOP 10 * FROM cteINTSequence
ORDER BY SeqNo DESC
OPTION ( MAXRECURSION 0);
GO
```

	SeqNo
1	1000000
2	999999
3	999998
4	999997
5	999996
6	999995
7	999994
8	999993
9	999992

Recursive Generation of Date & Month Sequences

Date sequence can be generated without a calendar table (Note: generally it is helpful to have a calendar table in the database) using recursive CTE.

```
DECLARE @StartDate date = '20160701', @Range smallint = 1000;

WITH cteSEQ ( SeqNo) as
(
    SELECT 0                                    -- Anchor member
    UNION ALL                                   -- Assemble set
    SELECT SeqNo + 1                            -- Recursive member
    FROM cteSEQ
    WHERE SeqNo < @Range
)
SELECT TOP 10 [DATE]=DATEADD(day, SeqNo, @StartDate)
FROM cteSEQ
OPTION ( MAXRECURSION 0);
GO
```

DATE
2016-07-01
2016-07-02
2016-07-03
2016-07-04
2016-07-05
2016-07-06
2016-07-07
2016-07-08
2016-07-09
2016-07-10

```
-- Month sequence generation
DECLARE @StartDate date = '20160701', @Range smallint = 100;
WITH cteSEQ ( SeqNo) as
(
    SELECT 0                                    -- Anchor member
    UNION ALL                                   -- Assemble set
    SELECT SeqNo + 1                            -- Recursive member
    FROM cteSEQ
    WHERE SeqNo < @Range
)
SELECT TOP 3 [DATE]=DATEADD(month, SeqNo, @StartDate)
FROM cteSEQ  OPTION ( MAXRECURSION 0);
```

Generate Month Names in Different Languages

The following query can be used to generate month names in any of the SQL Server 2012 supported languages.

```sql
SET language Spanish;  -- Se cambió la configuración de idioma a Español.
;WITH CTE AS
(   SELECT    1 MonthNo, CONVERT(DATE, '19000101') MonthFirst
    UNION ALL
    SELECT    MonthNo+1, DATEADD(Month, 1, MonthFirst)
    FROM  CTE
    WHERE Month(MonthFirst) < 12   )
SELECT  MonthNo AS MonthNumber,  DATENAME(MONTH, MonthFirst) AS MonthName
FROM  CTE
ORDER BY MonthNo;
SET language English; -- Changed language setting to us_english.
```

```sql
SET language Hungarian;  -- Nyelvi beállítás átállítva a következőre: magyar.
;WITH CTE AS
(   SELECT    1 MonthNo, CONVERT(DATE, '19000101') MonthFirst
    UNION ALL
    SELECT    MonthNo+1, DATEADD(Month, 1, MonthFirst)
    FROM  CTE
    WHERE Month(MonthFirst) < 12   )
SELECT  MonthNo AS MonthNumber,  DATENAME(MONTH, MonthFirst) AS MonthName
FROM  CTE
ORDER BY MonthNo;
SET language English; -- Changed language setting to us_english.
```

MonthNumber	MonthName	MonthNumber	MonthName
1	Enero	1	január
2	Febrero	2	február
3	Marzo	3	március
4	Abril	4	április
5	Mayo	5	május
6	Junio	6	június
7	Julio	7	július
8	Agosto	8	augusztus
9	Septiembre	9	szeptember
10	Octubre	10	október
11	Noviembre	11	november
12	Diciembre	12	december

CHAPTER 14: Subqueries in SELECT Statements

Graphical Organizational Chart of AdventureWorks Cycles

T-SQL recursive CTE query generates the entire company chart of AdventureWorks Cycles. The anchor term is Ken Sanchez CEO with ManagerID as NULL. Everybody else in the company has a ManagerID which is not NULL.

```sql
USE AdventureWorks;

WITH cteEmployeeTree
   AS (SELECT    Root.EmployeeName, Root.ManagerName,
                 Root.EmployeeId, Root.ManagerId,
                 CONVERT(VARCHAR(MAX),Root.PathSequence) AS PathLabel
       FROM  (SELECT EmployeeName = CONCAT(c.FirstName, SPACE(1), c.LastName),
              ManagerName = convert(VARCHAR(128),''),
              e.EmployeeId,
              e.ManagerId,
              char(64 + ROW_NUMBER() OVER(ORDER BY e.EmployeeId)) AS PathSequence
           FROM   HumanResources.Employee e
              INNER JOIN Person.Contact c
              ON e.ContactID = c.ContactID
           WHERE  e.ManagerId IS NULL) Root           -- Anchor/root term (above)
       UNION ALL                                      -- Build a set
       SELECT    Branch.EmployeeName,                 -- Recursive term (below)
                 Branch.ManagerName,
                 Branch.EmployeeId, Branch.ManagerId,
                 PathLabel = Branch.PathLabel + CONVERT(VARCHAR(MAX), Branch.PathSequence)
       FROM  (SELECT EmployeeName = CONCAT(c.FirstName, SPACE(1), c.LastName),
              ManagerName = CONVERT(VARCHAR(128),CONCAT(cm.FirstName, SPACE(1), cm.LastName)),
              e.EmployeeId,
              e.ManagerId,
              cte.PathLabel,
              PathSequence = char(64 + ROW_NUMBER() OVER(ORDER BY e.EmployeeId))
           FROM   cteEmployeeTree cte
              INNER JOIN HumanResources.Employee e
              ON e.ManagerId = cte.EmployeeId
              INNER JOIN Person.Contact c
              ON e.ContactID = c.ContactID
              INNER JOIN HumanResources.Employee em
              ON em.EmployeeID = e.ManagerID
              INNER JOIN Person.Contact cm
              ON em.ContactID = cm.ContactID) Branch)
-- Outer / main query
SELECT   CONCAT(REPLICATE(CHAR(9), LEN(PathLabel)-1),   -- tabs for indenting
              EmployeeName) AS EmployeeName
FROM     cteEmployeeTree  ORDER BY PathLabel;
```

CHAPTER 14: Subqueries in SELECT Statements

Chain of Command Recursive Query

The resulting organizational chart was generated by Word as tabs (CHAR(9)) were converted to table columns (partial results).

EmployeeName					
Ken Sánchez					
	David Bradley				
		Kevin Brown			
		Sariya Harnpadoungsataya			
		Mary Gibson			
		Jill Williams			
		Terry Eminhizer			
		Wanida Benshoof			
		John Wood			
		Mary Dempsey			
	Terri Duffy				
		Roberto Tamburello			
			Rob Walters		
			Gail Erickson		
			Jossef Goldberg		
			Dylan Miller		
				Diane Margheim	
				Gigi Matthew	
				Michael Raheem	
			Ovidiu Cracium		
				Thierry D'Hers	
				Janice Galvin	
			Michael Sullivan		
			Sharon Salavaria		
	Jean Trenary				
		Janaina Bueno			
		Dan Bacon			
		François Ajenstat			
		Dan Wilson			
		Ramesh Meyyappan			
		Stephanie Conroy			
			Ashvini Sharma		
			Peter Connelly		
		Karen Berg			
	Laura Norman				
		Paula Barreto de Mattos			
			Willis Johnson		
			Mindy Martin		
			Vidur Luthra		
			Hao Chen		
			Grant Culbertson		
		Wendy Kahn			
			Sheela Word		
				Mikael Sandberg	
				Arvind Rao	
				Linda Meisner	
				Fukiko Ogisu	
				Gordon Hee	
				Frank Pellow	
				Eric Kurjan	
				Erin Hagens	
				Ben Miller	
				Annette Hill	
				Reinout Hillmann	
		David Barber			
		David Liu			
			Deborah Poe		
			Candy Spoon		
			Bryan Walton		
			Dragan Tomic		
			Barbara Moreland		
			Janet Sheperdigian		
			Mike Seamans		
	James Hamilton				
		Peter Krebs			
			JoLynn Dobney		
				Simon Rapier	
				James Kramer	
				Nancy Anderson	
				Bryan Baker	
				Eugene Kogan	
				Thomas Michaels	
			Taylor Maxwell		
				Kendall Keil	
				Bob Hohman	
				Pete Male	
				Diane Tibbott	
				Denise Smith	

CHAPTER 14: Subqueries in SELECT Statements

Chain of Command Recursive Query

Find all ancestors (superiors) of a tree node(employee), all the up to the root of the tree (CEO in this instance).

```
USE AdventureWorks; DECLARE @EmployeeID INT = 100;
WITH CTE(Name, EmployeeID, ManagerID, Level)
    AS (SELECT    CONCAT(FirstName,' ', LastName),
                  EmployeeID,   ManagerID,  0 AS Level
        FROM   HumanResources.Employee AS E
            INNER JOIN Person.Contact AS C
                ON C.ContactID = E.ContactID
        WHERE  EmployeeID = @EmployeeID
        UNION ALL
        SELECT    CONCAT(C.FirstName,' ',C.LastName),
                  HRE.EmployeeID,  HRE.ManagerID,  Level + 1
        FROM   HumanResources.Employee AS HRE
            INNER JOIN Person.Contact AS C
                ON C.ContactID = HRE.ContactID
            INNER JOIN CTE AS E
                ON E.ManagerID = HRE.EmployeeID)
SELECT STUFF((SELECT CONCAT(', ', Name)
        FROM   CTE      ORDER  BY Level
        FOR XML path('')), 1, 2, '') AS [Chain of Command];
```

Chain of Command
Lane Sacksteder, Yuhong Li, Peter Krebs, James Hamilton, Ken Sánchez

CHAPTER 14: Subqueries in SELECT Statements

Chain of Command Recursive Query

Graphical Bill of Materials for Mountain-100 Silver, 44 Bike

T-SQL query will generate bill of materials (assembly) listing for Mountain-100 Silver, 44 mountain bike. The AdventureWorks2012 database image for Mountain-100 Silver, 44 in Production.ProductPhoto table.

```
USE AdventureWorks2012;
DECLARE     @StartProductID int     = 773,          -- Mountain-100 Silver, 44
            @CheckDate datetime     = '20080201';

WITH cteBOM(ProductAssemblyID, ComponentID, ComponentName,   RecursionLevel)
AS (
  SELECT b.ProductAssemblyID, b.ComponentID, p.Name,  0
      FROM Production.BillOfMaterials b
        INNER JOIN Production.Product p
          ON b.ComponentID = p.ProductID
    WHERE     b.ProductAssemblyID = @StartProductID
              AND @CheckDate >= b.StartDate
              AND @CheckDate <= ISNULL(b.EndDate, @CheckDate)   -- Anchor/root member (above)
    UNION ALL                                                    -- Build a set
    SELECT    b.ProductAssemblyID, b.ComponentID, p.Name,       -- Recursive member (below)
              RecursionLevel + 1
    FROM cteBOM c
      INNER JOIN Production.BillOfMaterials b
        ON b.ProductAssemblyID = c.ComponentID
      INNER JOIN Production.Product p
        ON b.ComponentID = p.ProductID
    WHERE     @CheckDate >= b.StartDate         AND @CheckDate <= ISNULL(b.EndDate, @CheckDate)   )
-- Outer/main query
  SELECT CONCAT(REPLICATE(CHAR(9), RecursionLevel),   -- Generate indents with tab character
              (SELECT Name FROM Production.Product WHERE ProductID=ProductAssemblyID)) AS PartName,
              ComponentName
      FROM cteBOM   GROUP BY  RecursionLevel,ProductAssemblyID,ComponentName
  ORDER BY    RecursionLevel, ProductAssemblyID,ComponentName   OPTION (MAXRECURSION 10);
-- (87 row(s) affected)
```

CHAPTER 14: Subqueries in SELECT Statements

The resulting graphical bill of materials for the mountain bike.

PartName	ComponentName		
Mountain-100 Silver, 44	Chain		
Mountain-100 Silver, 44	Front Brakes		
Mountain-100 Silver, 44	Front Derailleur		
Mountain-100 Silver, 44	HL Bottom Bracket		
Mountain-100 Silver, 44	HL Crankset		
Mountain-100 Silver, 44	HL Headset		
Mountain-100 Silver, 44	HL Mountain Frame - Silver, 44		
Mountain-100 Silver, 44	HL Mountain Front Wheel		
Mountain-100 Silver, 44	HL Mountain Handlebars		
Mountain-100 Silver, 44	HL Mountain Pedal		
Mountain-100 Silver, 44	HL Mountain Rear Wheel		
Mountain-100 Silver, 44	HL Mountain Seat Assembly		
Mountain-100 Silver, 44	Rear Brakes		
Mountain-100 Silver, 44	Rear Derailleur		
	HL Mountain Seat Assembly	HL Mountain Seat/Saddle	
	HL Mountain Seat Assembly	Pinch Bolt	
	HL Mountain Seat Assembly	Seat Lug	
	HL Mountain Seat Assembly	Seat Post	
	HL Mountain Frame - Silver, 44	Chain Stays	
	HL Mountain Frame - Silver, 44	Decal 1	
	HL Mountain Frame - Silver, 44	Decal 2	
	HL Mountain Frame - Silver, 44	Down Tube	
	HL Mountain Frame - Silver, 44	Head Tube	
	HL Mountain Frame - Silver, 44	HL Fork	
	HL Mountain Frame - Silver, 44	Paint - Silver	
	HL Mountain Frame - Silver, 44	Seat Stays	
	HL Mountain Frame - Silver, 44	Seat Tube	
	HL Mountain Frame - Silver, 44	Top Tube	
	HL Headset	Adjustable Race	
	HL Headset	Crown Race	
	HL Headset	Headset Ball Bearings	
	HL Headset	Keyed Washer	
	HL Headset	Lock Nut 19	
	HL Headset	Lower Head Race	
	HL Mountain Handlebars	Handlebar Tube	
	HL Mountain Handlebars	HL Grip Tape	
	HL Mountain Handlebars	Mountain End Caps	
	HL Mountain Handlebars	Stem	
	HL Mountain Front Wheel	HL Hub	
	HL Mountain Front Wheel	HL Mountain Rim	
	HL Mountain Front Wheel	HL Mountain Tire	
	HL Mountain Front Wheel	HL Nipple	
	HL Mountain Front Wheel	Mountain Tire Tube	
	HL Mountain Front Wheel	Reflector	
	HL Mountain Front Wheel	Spokes	
	HL Mountain Rear Wheel	HL Hub	
	HL Mountain Rear Wheel	HL Mountain Rim	
	HL Mountain Rear Wheel	HL Mountain Tire	
	HL Mountain Rear Wheel	HL Nipple	
	HL Mountain Rear Wheel	Mountain Tire Tube	
	HL Mountain Rear Wheel	Reflector	
	HL Mountain Rear Wheel	Spokes	
	Rear Derailleur	Guide Pulley	
	Rear Derailleur	Rear Derailleur Cage	
	Rear Derailleur	Tension Pulley	
	Front Derailleur	Front Derailleur Cage	
	Front Derailleur	Front Derailleur Linkage	
	HL Crankset	Chainring	
	HL Crankset	Chainring Bolts	

	HL Crankset	Chainring Nut	
	HL Crankset	Freewheel	
	HL Crankset	HL Crankarm	
	HL Bottom Bracket	BB Ball Bearing	
	HL Bottom Bracket	HL Shell	
		BB Ball Bearing	Bearing Ball
		BB Ball Bearing	Cone-Shaped Race
		BB Ball Bearing	Cup-Shaped Race
		BB Ball Bearing	Lock Ring
		Chain Stays	Metal Sheet 5
		Down Tube	Metal Sheet 3
		Mountain End Caps	Metal Sheet 2
		Handlebar Tube	Metal Sheet 6
		Head Tube	Metal Sheet 4
		HL Hub	HL Shell
		HL Hub	HL Spindle/Axle
		Stem	Metal Bar 1
		Seat Stays	Metal Sheet 7
		Seat Tube	Metal Bar 2
		Top Tube	Metal Sheet 2
		HL Fork	Blade
		HL Fork	Fork Crown
		HL Fork	Fork End
		HL Fork	Steerer
			Blade	Metal Sheet 5
			Fork End	Metal Sheet 2
			Fork Crown	Metal Sheet 5
			Steerer	Metal Sheet 6

CHAPTER 14: Subqueries in SELECT Statements

PIVOT Operator to Transform Rows Into Columns

The PIVOT operator, new to SQL Server 2005, can be used to create pivot table also called cross tabulation (crosstab). The data to be PIVOTed is generated by a CTE.

```
USE AdventureWorks2012;
;WITH CTE    AS (SELECT   YEAR       = YEAR(orderDate),
                          QUARTER    = DatePart(qq,OrderDate),
                          Sales      = Sum(TotalDue)
     FROM    Sales.SalesOrderHeader  GROUP BY YEAR(OrderDate), DatePart(qq,OrderDate))
SELECT * FROM CTE;
```

YEAR	QUARTER	Sales
2007	4	14886562.6775
2006	3	11555907.1472
2007	1	7492396.3224
2007	2	9379298.7027
2006	1	6562121.6796
2006	4	9397824.1785
2008	3	56178.9223
2007	3	15413231.8434
2005	3	5203127.8807
2008	1	12744940.3554
2005	4	7490122.7457
2008	2	16087078.2305
2006	2	6947995.43

PIVOT operator takes the data from the CTE source, aggregates it and transforms it to columns.

```
;WITH CTE    AS (SELECT   YEAR       = YEAR(orderDate),
                          QUARTER    = DatePart(qq,OrderDate),
                          Sales      = Sum(TotalDue)
     FROM    Sales.SalesOrderHeader  GROUP BY YEAR(OrderDate), DatePart(qq,OrderDate)   )
SELECT    YEAR
              ,FORMAT ([1], 'c','en-US') AS Q1
              ,FORMAT ([2], 'c','en-US') AS Q2
              ,FORMAT ([3], 'c','en-US') AS Q3
              ,FORMAT ([4], 'c','en-US') AS Q4
FROM    (SELECT * FROM CTE) AS PivotInput
    PIVOT    (SUM(Sales)  FOR QUARTER IN ( [1],[2],[3],[4] ) ) AS PivotOutput  ORDER BY YEAR;
```

YEAR	Q1	Q2	Q3	Q4
2005	NULL	NULL	$5,203,127.88	$7,490,122.75
2006	$6,562,121.68	$6,947,995.43	$11,555,907.15	$9,397,824.18
2007	$7,492,396.32	$9,379,298.70	$15,413,231.84	$14,886,562.68
2008	$12,744,940.36	$16,087,078.23	$56,178.92	NULL

UNPIVOT Crosstab View Results

The vSalesPersonSalesByFiscalYears view is a crosstab listing of sales person (rows) and sales by year (columns). The UNPIVOT operation transforms the year columns into rows.

```sql
SELECT * FROM [Sales].[vSalesPersonSalesByFiscalYears];
GO

SELECT  SalesPersonID, FullName, JobTitle, SalesTerritory
       ,Sales        -- unpivoted
       ,[Year]       -- unpivoted
FROM (SELECT * FROM [Sales].[vSalesPersonSalesByFiscalYears]) p
UNPIVOT
       (Sales FOR Year IN ( [2006],[2007],[2008] ) ) AS unpvt
ORDER BY FullName, Year DESC;
GO
```

Results (top):

#	Sales...	FullName	JobTitle	SalesTerritory	2006	2007	2008
9	283	David R Camp...	Sales Repr...	Northwest	1017402.8563	1139529.5544	1573012.9383
10	284	Tete A Mensa-...	Sales Repr...	Northwest	NULL	735983.4934	1576562.1966
11	286	Lynn N Tsoflias	Sales Repr...	Australia	NULL	NULL	1421810.9242
12	288	Rachel B Valdez	Sales Repr...	Germany	NULL	NULL	1827066.7118

Results (bottom):

#	SalesPersonID	FullName	JobTitle	SalesTerritory	Sales	Year
1	283	David R Campbell	Sales Representative	Northwest	1573012.9383	2008
2	283	David R Campbell	Sales Representative	Northwest	1139529.5544	2007
3	283	David R Campbell	Sales Representative	Northwest	1017402.8563	2006
4	278	Garrett R Vargas	Sales Representative	Canada	1453719.4653	2008
5	278	Garrett R Vargas	Sales Representative	Canada	1225468.2836	2007
6	278	Garrett R Vargas	Sales Representative	Canada	930259.4659	2006
7	289	Jae B Pak	Sales Representative	United King...	4116871.2277	2008
8	289	Jae B Pak	Sales Representative	United King...	4386467.418	2007

Using Subquery in Column List of SELECT

A subquery can be used in the column list of a SELECT statement.

```
USE Northwind;
GO
```

```
;WITH CTE AS
(
 SELECT ShipCity,
        CONVERT(DATE, OrderDate)                                    AS OrderDate,
        (SELECT CONVERT(DATE, MAX(OrderDate))   FROM dbo.Orders)    AS CurrentOrderDate,
        DATEDIFF(dd,OrderDate,(SELECT MAX(OrderDate) FROM dbo.Orders)) AS DeltaDays,
        ROW_NUMBER() OVER (PARTITION BY ShipCity
                           ORDER BY OrderDate DESC)                 AS RN
 FROM dbo.Orders
)

SELECT TOP 20 ShipCity, OrderDate, CurrentOrderDate, DeltaDays
FROM CTE
WHERE RN=1     ORDER BY DeltaDays DESC;
GO
```

ShipCity	OrderDate	CurrentOrderDate	DeltaDays
Walla Walla	1997-05-22	1998-05-06	349
Elgin	1997-09-08	1998-05-06	240
Montréal	1997-10-30	1998-05-06	188
Reims	1997-11-12	1998-05-06	175
Caracas	1997-12-18	1998-05-06	139
Lille	1997-12-22	1998-05-06	135
Vancouver	1998-01-01	1998-05-06	125
Kirkland	1998-01-08	1998-05-06	118
Strasbourg	1998-01-12	1998-05-06	114
Lyon	1998-01-23	1998-05-06	103
San Francisco	1998-02-12	1998-05-06	83
Luleå	1998-03-04	1998-05-06	63
Barcelona	1998-03-05	1998-05-06	62
Cowes	1998-03-06	1998-05-06	61
Resende	1998-03-09	1998-05-06	58
Leipzig	1998-03-12	1998-05-06	55
Bergamo	1998-03-16	1998-05-06	51
Münster	1998-03-23	1998-05-06	44
Nantes	1998-03-24	1998-05-06	43
Versailles	1998-03-24	1998-05-06	43

CHAPTER 15: SELECT INTO Table Creation & Population

Simple SELECT INTO Statement Variations

SELECT INTO is an easy way to create a table for ad-hoc purposes in database development and administration. **An added benefit is minimal logging, therefore good performance**. INSERT SELECT is logged, although with special setup minimal logging can be achieved in some cases.

```sql
-- Create and populate copy of the product table in tempdb
SELECT *
INTO   tempdb.dbo.Product
FROM   AdventureWorks2012.Production.Product;
-- (504 row(s) affected)
```

```sql
SELECT TableRows = count(*)  FROM tempdb.dbo.Product;  -- 504
```

```sql
-- Copy all persons into new table with last name starting with 'A'
SELECT    BusinessEntityID                         AS ID,
          CONCAT(FirstName, ' ', LastName)  AS FullName,
          PersonType
INTO   ListA
FROM   AdventureWorks2012.Person.Person
WHERE  LEFT(LastName, 1) = 'A'
ORDER BY LastName, FirstName;
-- (911 row(s) affected)
```

```sql
SELECT TOP (10) ID, FullName, PersonType FROM ListA ORDER BY ID;
```

ID	FullName	PersonType
38	Kim Abercrombie	EM
43	Nancy Anderson	EM
67	Jay Adams	EM
121	Pilar Ackerman	EM
207	Greg Alderson	EM
211	Hazem Abolrous	EM
216	Sean Alexander	EM
217	Zainal Arifin	EM
227	Gary Altman	EM
270	François Ajenstat	EM

SELECT TOP(0) Creates an Empty Table

```sql
USE AdventureWorks2012;

-- Create a copy of table in a different schema, same name
-- The WHERE clause predicate with >=, < comparison is better performing than the YEAR function
SELECT *
INTO   dbo.SalesOrderHeader
FROM   Sales.SalesOrderHeader
WHERE  OrderDate >= '20080101' AND OrderDate < '20090101';  -- YEAR(OrderDate)=2008
-- (13951 row(s) affected)
```

```sql
-- Create a table without population
SELECT TOP (0)   SalesOrderID,     OrderDate
INTO   SOH
FROM   Sales.SalesOrderHeader;
-- (0 row(s) affected)
```

```sql
-- SELECT INTO cannot be used to target an existing table
SELECT * INTO  SOH FROM   Sales.SalesOrderHeader;
/* Msg 2714, Level 16, State 6, Line 1
There is already an object named 'SOH' in the database.  */
```

> **NOTE**
> IDENTITY column is automatically populated.
> Direct insert into IDENTITY column requires using of SET IDENTITY_INSERT.

```sql
INSERT SOH (SalesOrderID, OrderDate)
SELECT SalesOrderID, OrderDate
FROM   Sales.SalesOrderHeader ORDER BY SalesOrderID;
GO
/* ERROR due to SalesOrderID in SOH inherited the IDENTITY property.
Msg 544, Level 16, State 1, Line 1
Cannot insert explicit value for identity column in table 'SOH' when IDENTITY_INSERT is set to OFF.  */
```

```sql
-- Turn on forced IDENTITY insert
SET IDENTITY_INSERT dbo.SOH ON;
GO
```

```sql
INSERT SOH(SalesOrderID, OrderDate)
SELECT SalesOrderID, OrderDate  FROM   Sales.SalesOrderHeader ORDER BY SalesOrderID;
GO
-- (31465 row(s) affected)
```

```sql
SET IDENTITY_INSERT dbo.SOH OFF;
```

Simple SELECT INTO Statement Variations

Any Kind of SELECT Result Set Can Be Turned into a Table

```
-- Filter on date
SELECT *
INTO   SOH1
FROM   Sales.SalesOrderHeader WHERE  OrderDate >= '20080101' AND OrderDate < '20090101';
-- (13951 row(s) affected)
```

```
-- Descending sort for population
SELECT *
INTO   SOH2
FROM   Sales.SalesOrderHeader
ORDER  BY SalesOrderID DESC
-- (31465 row(s) affected)
```

```
-- 3 columns only
SELECT   SalesOrderID,
         OrderDate,
         SubTotal
INTO   SOH3
FROM   Sales.SalesOrderHeader;
-- (31465 row(s) affected)
```

```
-- SELECT INTO with GROUP BY query source
SELECT   [Year]=YEAR(OrderDate),
         Orders=COUNT(*)
INTO   SOH4
FROM   Sales.SalesOrderHeader
GROUP  BY YEAR(OrderDate)
-- (4 row(s) affected)
```

SELECT * FROM SOH4 ORDER BY Year DESC;

Year	Orders
2008	13951
2007	12443
2006	3692
2005	1379

```
-- All source columns, and a new populated datetime column
SELECT   *,      [CreateDate]=getdate()
INTO   SOH5
FROM   Sales.SalesOrderHeader ;
-- (31465 row(s) affected)
```

CHAPTER 15: SELECT INTO Table Creation & Population

SELECT INTO Can Create Temporary Tables or Tables in tempdb

```sql
-- SELECT INTO temporary table
SELECT TotalOrders = COUNT(*)
INTO   #TotalOrders
FROM   Sales.SalesOrderHeader ;
-- (1 row(s) affected)
```

```sql
SELECT * FROM #TotalOrders;
```

TotalOrders
31465

```sql
-- Empty table create with one NULL row
SELECT   Name=CONVERT(VARCHAR(45), NULL),
         Age=CONVERT(INT, NULL)
INTO   tempdb.dbo.Person;
```

```sql
INSERT tempdb.dbo.Person (Name, Age)
SELECT 'Roger Bond', 45;
-- (1 row(s) affected)
```

```sql
SELECT * FROM tempdb.dbo.Person;
```

Name	Age
NULL	NULL
Roger Bond	45

```sql
DELETE tempdb.dbo.Person WHERE Name is NULL;
-- (1 row(s) affected)
```

```sql
SELECT * FROM tempdb.dbo.Person;
```

Name	Age
Roger Bond	45

```sql
-- Create gaps in ID sequence; increment by 2:  2, 4, 6, 8 instead of 1, 2, 3, 4
SELECT   2 * [BusinessEntityID]           AS BusinessEntityID
        ,[PhoneNumber]
        ,[PhoneNumberTypeID]
        ,[ModifiedDate]
 INTO dbo.Phone
 FROM [AdventureWorks2012].[Person].[PersonPhone] pp    ORDER BY pp.BusinessEntityID;
-- (19972 row(s) affected)
```

CHAPTER 15: SELECT INTO Table Creation & Population

SELECT INTO with IDENTITY Column

The SELECT INTO Created Table is a "Regular" Table

```sql
-- Populate with 100 random rows
SELECT TOP (100) *
INTO   POH
FROM   Purchasing.PurchaseOrderHeader ORDER BY NEWID(); -- (100 row(s) affected)

SELECT      PurchaseOrderID,
            CONVERT(date, OrderDate)         AS OrderDate,
            FORMAT(SubTotal, 'c', 'en-US')   AS SubTotal
FROM POH;
```

PurchaseOrderID	OrderDate	SubTotal
3553	2008-08-03	$9,948.33
1637	2008-02-07	$25,531.28
2796	2008-05-31	$97.97
684	2007-09-26	$270.81
3478	2008-07-28	$28,072.28
1904	2008-03-09	$43,878.45
755	2007-10-01	$50,860.43
2660	2008-05-19	$944.37
2787	2008-05-31	$34,644.23
601	2007-09-19	$146.29

```sql
-- SELECT INTO with data transformation
SELECT   CultureID
        ,UPPER(Name)                  AS Name
        ,CONVERT(date,ModifiedDate)   AS ModifiedDate
INTO dbo.Culture
FROM [AdventureWorks2012].[Production].[Culture]
ORDER BY CultureID;
-- (8 row(s) affected)
```

SELECT * FROM dbo.Culture WHERE CultureID != '' ORDER BY CultureID; -- exclude empty ID

CultureID	Name	ModifiedDate
ar	ARABIC	2002-06-01
en	ENGLISH	2002-06-01
es	SPANISH	2002-06-01
fr	FRENCH	2002-06-01
he	HEBREW	2002-06-01
th	THAI	2002-06-01
zh-cht	CHINESE	2002-06-01

CHAPTER 15: SELECT INTO Table Creation & Population

SELECT INTO with IDENTITY Column

The column data types are inherited in SELECT INTO table create. The IDENTITY property is also inherited in a SELECT INTO unless it is prevented with special coding. No other constraint is inherited.

```sql
-- IDENTITY property of ProductID is inherited
SELECT TOP (0) ProductID, ProductNumber, ListPrice, Color
INTO tempdb.dbo.Product
FROM AdventureWorks2012.Production.Product;  -- (0 row(s) affected)
```

```sql
INSERT tempdb.dbo.Product (ProductID, ProductNumber, ListPrice, Color)
SELECT 20001, 'FERRARI007RED', $400000, 'Red';
GO
/* Msg 544, Level 16, State 1, Line 1
Cannot insert explicit value for identity column in table 'Product'
when IDENTITY_INSERT is set to OFF. */
```

```sql
-- The following is one way to check for IDENTITY property
USE tempdb;
EXEC sp_help 'dbo.Product';
```

Identity	Seed	Increment	Not For Replication
ProductID	1	1	0

```sql
USE AdventureWorks2012;
DROP TABLE tempdb.dbo.Product;
GO
```

```sql
-- The following construct will prevent IDENTITY inheritance
SELECT TOP (0)   CAST(ProductID AS INT) AS ProductID,  -- Cast/Convert the identity column
                 ProductNumber,
                 ListPrice,
                 Color
INTO tempdb.dbo.Product  FROM AdventureWorks2012.Production.Product;
-- (0 row(s) affected)
```

```sql
INSERT tempdb.dbo.Product (ProductID, ProductNumber, ListPrice, Color)
SELECT 20001, 'FERRARI007RED', $400000, 'Firehouse Red';
GO
```

```sql
SELECT * FROM tempdb.dbo.Product;
```

ProductID	ProductNumber	ListPrice	Color
20001	FERRARI007RED	400000.00	Firehouse Red

CHAPTER 15: SELECT INTO Table Creation & Population

SELECT INTO From Multiple-Table Queries

SELECT INTO works with any query with some restrictions such as XML data type columns cannot be included.

```
SELECT   JobCandidateID
        ,BusinessEntityID
        ,Resume
        ,ModifiedDate
 INTO dbo.Resume
 FROM AdventureWorks2012.HumanResources.JobCandidate;
/* ERROR MESSAGE
Msg 458, Level 16, State 0, Line 2
Cannot create the SELECT INTO target table "dbo.Resume" because the xml column "Resume"
is typed with a schema collection "HRResumeSchemaCollection" from database "AdventureWorks2012".
Xml columns cannot refer to schemata across databases.
*/

-- SELECT INTO from joined tables
SELECT          soh.SalesOrderID,
                OrderDate,
                OrderQty,
                ProductID
INTO   SalesOrder
FROM   Sales.SalesOrderHeader soh
    INNER JOIN Sales.SalesOrderDetail sod
        ON soh.SalesOrderID = sod.SalesOrderID ;
-- (121317 row(s) affected)

SELECT TOP(5) * FROM SalesOrder ORDER BY SalesOrderID DESC;
```

SalesOrderID	OrderDate	OrderQty	ProductID
75123	2008-07-31 00:00:00.000	1	878
75123	2008-07-31 00:00:00.000	1	879
75123	2008-07-31 00:00:00.000	1	712
75122	2008-07-31 00:00:00.000	1	878
75122	2008-07-31 00:00:00.000	1	712

```
-- Check column types - partial results
EXEC sp_help SalesOrder;
```

Column_name	Type	Computed	Length	Prec	Scale
SalesOrderID	int	no	4	10	0
OrderDate	datetime	no	8		
OrderQty	smallint	no	2	5	0
ProductID	int	no	4	10	0

SELECT INTO with Sorted Table Population

We can create ordering in a new temporary table by using the IDENTITY function. **There is no guarantee though that the IDENTITY sequence will be the same as the ORDER BY clause specifications**. Unique identity values on the other hand are guaranteed.

```sql
SELECT  ID=IDENTITY(int, 1, 1),
        ProductNumber,
        ProductID=CAST(ProductID AS INT),
        ListPrice,
        COALESCE(Color, 'N/A') AS Color
INTO    #Product
FROM    Production.Product WHERE  ListPrice > 0.0 ORDER BY ProductNumber;
GO -- (304 row(s) affected)
```

```sql
SELECT TOP 10 * FROM #Product  ORDER BY ID;
```

ID	ProductNumber	ProductID	ListPrice	Color
1	BB-7421	994	53.99	N/A
2	BB-8107	995	101.24	N/A
3	BB-9108	996	121.49	N/A
4	BC-M005	871	9.99	N/A
5	BC-R205	872	8.99	N/A
6	BK-M18B-40	989	539.99	Black
7	BK-M18B-42	990	539.99	Black
8	BK-M18B-44	991	539.99	Black
9	BK-M18B-48	992	539.99	Black
10	BK-M18B-52	993	539.99	Black

```sql
-- Permanent table create
SELECT * INTO ProductByProdNo FROM #Product ORDER BY ID;
GO -- (304 row(s) affected)
```

```sql
SELECT TOP (6) * FROM ProductByProdNo ORDER BY ID;
```

ID	ProductNumber	ProductID	ListPrice	Color
1	BB-7421	994	53.99	N/A
2	BB-8107	995	101.24	N/A
3	BB-9108	996	121.49	N/A
4	BC-M005	871	9.99	N/A
5	BC-R205	872	8.99	N/A
6	BK-M18B-40	989	539.99	Black

CHAPTER 15: SELECT INTO Table Creation & Population

SELECT INTO with Random Population

We can create a random population by sorting with the NEWID() function.

```
USE tempdb;

SELECT TOP(5)   ID          = ContactID,
                FullName    = CONCAT(FirstName, ' ', LastName),
                Email       = EmailAddress
INTO  dbo.Person
FROM  AdventureWorks.Person.Contact
WHERE EmailPromotion = 2
ORDER BY NEWID();
-- (5 row(s) affected)

SELECT * FROM dbo.Person;
GO
```

ID	FullName	Email
1075	Diane Glimp	diane0@adventure-works.com
15739	Jesse Mitchell	jesse36@adventure-works.com
5405	Jose Patterson	jose33@adventure-works.com
1029	Wanida Benshoof	wanida0@adventure-works.com
8634	Andrea Collins	andrea26@adventure-works.com

```
-- Rerun the script again after dropping the table
DROP TABLE tempdb.dbo.Person;
GO
-- Command(s) completed successfully.

SELECT TOP(5) ID        = ContactID,
        FullName        = CONCAT(FirstName, ' ', LastName),
        Email           = EmailAddress
INTO  dbo.Person
FROM  AdventureWorks.Person.Contact
WHERE EmailPromotion = 2 ORDER BY NEWID();

SELECT * FROM dbo.Person;
```

ID	FullName	Email
9984	Sydney Clark	sydney81@adventure-works.com
15448	Denise Raman	denise13@adventure-works.com
12442	Carson Jenkins	carson5@adventure-works.com
1082	Mary Baker	mary1@adventure-works.com
18728	Emma Kelly	emma46@adventure-works.com

CHAPTER 15: SELECT INTO Table Creation & Population

Combining SELECT INTO with INSERT SELECT

First we create an empty table with identity property using SELECT INTO, then we populate it with INSERT SELECT.

```
-- Following will fail - only one IDENTITY column per table
SELECT TOP (0)    IDENTITY(int, 1, 1)          AS ID,
        ProductID,
        Name                                    AS ProductName,
        ListPrice,
        COALESCE(Color, 'N/A')                  AS Color
INTO   #Product   FROM   Production.Product;
GO
/* ERROR Msg 8108, Level 16, State 1, Line 1
Cannot add identity column, using the SELECT INTO statement, to table '#Product',
which already has column 'ProductID' that inherits the identity property. */
```

```
SELECT TOP (0)    IDENTITY(int, 1, 1)          AS ID,
        CAST(ProductID AS INT)                  AS ProductID, -- IDENTITY will not be inherited
        Name                                    AS ProductName,
        ListPrice,
        COALESCE(Color, 'N/A')                  AS Color
INTO   #Product   FROM   Production.Product;
GO
-- (0 row(s) affected)
```

```
DECLARE @Rows tinyint = 5;
INSERT INTO #Product   (ProductID, ProductName,  ListPrice,  Color)
SELECT TOP (@Rows)     ProductID,
              Name,
              ListPrice,
              Color
FROM   Production.Product
WHERE  ListPrice > 0.0    AND Color IS NOT NULL  ORDER BY ListPrice DESC;
-- (5 row(s) affected)
```

```
SELECT * FROM #Product;
```

ID	ProductID	ProductName	ListPrice	Color
1	749	Road-150 Red, 62	3578.27	Red
2	750	Road-150 Red, 44	3578.27	Red
3	751	Road-150 Red, 48	3578.27	Red
4	752	Road-150 Red, 52	3578.27	Red
5	753	Road-150 Red, 56	3578.27	Red

Copy Table into Different Database with SELECT INTO

It requires 3-part name referencing to operate between databases (cross database). The current database requires only 2-part object name referencing.

```
USE tempdb;
SELECT *, CopyDate = CONVERT(DATE,GETDATE())
INTO Department
FROM AdventureWorks.HumanResources.Department  ORDER BY DepartmentID;
GO

SELECT TOP (5) DepartmentID, Department=Name, CopyDate  FROM Department ORDER BY DepartmentID;
```

DepartmentID	Department	CopyDate
1	Engineering	2016-07-19
2	Tool Design	2016-07-19
3	Sales	2016-07-19
4	Marketing	2016-07-19
5	Purchasing	2016-07-19

```
-- SQL drop table - full referencing of table for mistake reduction
DROP TABLE tempdb.dbo.Department;
```

Combining SELECT INTO with UPDATE

After creating a populated table with SELECT INTO, we perform UPDATE to change a column.

```
USE tempdb;
SELECT TOP 100 * INTO   PurchaseOrderHeader
FROM   AdventureWorks.Purchasing.PurchaseOrderHeader  ORDER  BY NEWID();
GO

-- The following logic updates dates to different values - multiple value assignment operator
DECLARE @OrderDate DATETIME = CURRENT_TIMESTAMP;
UPDATE PurchaseOrderHeader  SET    @OrderDate = OrderDate = dateadd(day, -1, @OrderDate);
GO

SELECT TOP (5)  PurchaseOrderID,   VendorID,   OrderDate  FROM   PurchaseOrderHeader;
```

PurchaseOrderID	VendorID	OrderDate
631	39	2016-07-18 09:03:18.193
759	32	2016-07-17 09:03:18.193
2652	33	2016-07-16 09:03:18.193
769	80	2016-07-15 09:03:18.193
949	30	2016-07-14 09:03:18.193

```
DROP TABLE tempdb.dbo.PurchaseOrderHeader;
```

CHAPTER 15: SELECT INTO Table Creation & Population

SELECT INTO Table Create from Complex Query

SELECT INTO table create works from simple to very complex queries.

```
USE AdventureWorks;

SELECT      SalesStaff      = CONCAT(C.LastName, ', ', C.FirstName),
            ZipCode         = A.PostalCode,
            TotalSales      = FORMAT(SUM(SOD.LineTotal),'c', 'en-US'),
            PercentOfTotal  = FORMAT( SUM(SOD.LineTotal) /
                              SUM(SUM(SOD.LineTotal))  OVER (PARTITION BY 1, 2 ),'p')
INTO   tempdb.dbo.SalesSummary
FROM   Person.Contact C
   INNER JOIN Person.[Address] A
       ON A.AddressID = C.ContactID
   INNER JOIN Sales.SalesOrderHeader SOH
       ON SOH.SalesPersonID = C.ContactID
   INNER JOIN Sales.SalesOrderDetail SOD
       ON SOD.SalesOrderID = SOH.SalesOrderID
WHERE  TerritoryID IS NOT NULL
GROUP  BY C.FirstName,   C.LastName,   A.PostalCode,   C.ContactID
ORDER  BY SalesStaff,   ZipCode;
-- (17 row(s) affected)


-- SELECT 10 rows random, then sort them by name (SalesStaff) - derived table construct
SELECT * FROM
(
        SELECT TOP (10) *
        FROM   tempdb.dbo.SalesSummary ORDER  BY NEWID()
) x         -- x is called a derived table; also dubbed SELECT FROM SELECT
ORDER BY SalesStaff;
```

SalesStaff	ZipCode	TotalSales	PercentOfTotal
Dusza, Maciej	98027	$9,293,903.00	11.55 %
Dyck, Shelley	98027	$10,367,007.43	12.88 %
Ecoffey, Linda	98027	$10,065,803.54	12.51 %
Eldridge, Carla	98027	$3,609,447.21	4.48 %
Elliott, Carol	98027	$7,171,012.75	8.91 %
Emanuel, Michael	98055	$5,926,418.36	7.36 %
Erickson, Gail	98055	$8,503,338.65	10.56 %
Estes, Julie	98055	$172,524.45	0.21 %
Esteves, Janeth	98055	$1,827,066.71	2.27 %
Evans, Twanna	98055	$1,421,810.92	1.77 %

DROP TABLE tempdb.dbo.SalesSummary ;

SELECT INTO Table Create from System Procedure Execution

Using OPENROWSET and OPENQUERY, we can make the result sets of system procedures and user stored procedures table-like.

```
SELECT * INTO  #spwho
FROM   OPENROWSET ( 'SQLOLEDB',
         'SERVER=.;Trusted_Connection=yes',
         'SET FMTONLY OFF EXEC sp_who');
GO  -- (64 row(s) affected) - it varies, depends on the number server connections
```

```
SELECT TOP (5) *  FROM  #spwho  ORDER BY spid;
```

spid	ecid	status	loginame	hostname	blk	dbname	cmd	request_id
1	0	background	sa		0	NULL	LOG WRITER	0
2	0	background	sa		0	NULL	RECOVERY WRITER	0
3	0	background	sa		0	NULL	LAZY WRITER	0
4	0	background	sa		0	NULL	LOCK MONITOR	0
5	0	background	sa		0	master	SIGNAL HANDLER	0

```
/* Requirement for OPENQUERY operation on current instance.

DATA ACCESS to current SQL Server named instance can be setup the following way:

exec sp_serveroption @server = 'PRODSVR\SQL2008'  -- computer name for default instance
   ,@optname = 'DATA ACCESS'
   ,@optvalue = 'TRUE' ;

This way, OPENQUERY can be used against current instance. Usually OPENQUERY is used to access linked servers.  */
```

```
SELECT   DB_NAME(dbid) AS DB,  *
INTO  #splock FROM   OPENQUERY(HPESTAR, 'EXEC sp_lock');
GO
-- (156 row(s) affected)  - it varies, depends how busy is the system with OLTP activities
```

```
SELECT TOP(2) * FROM  #splock ;
```

DB	spid	dbid	ObjId	IndId	Type	Resource	Mode	Status
ReportServer	52	5	0	0	DB		S	GRANT
msdb	54	4	0	0	DB		S	GRANT

System procedure to list all tables in a database. Corresponding procedure for linked server: sp_tables_ex.

```
EXEC pubs..sp_tables @table_type = "'TABLE'";
```

CHAPTER 15: SELECT INTO Table Creation & Population

SELECT INTO from OPENQUERY Stored Procedure Execution

The following is the only way to make stored procedure results table-like. The bill-of-materials stored procedure is recursive.

```
USE AdventureWorks2012;
GO
SELECT Name FROM Production.Product
WHERE ProductID = 900;   -- LL Touring Frame - Yellow, 50
```

```
-- First we test the query execution
DECLARE @RC int;  DECLARE @StartProductID int; DECLARE @CheckDate datetime;

EXECUTE @RC = [dbo].[uspGetBillOfMaterials]    @StartProductID = 900 , @CheckDate = '20080216';
GO
-- 24 rows returned
```

```
-- Transform query into SELECT INTO table create  - Single quotes (around date literal) must be doubled
SELECT * INTO BOM900
FROM OPENQUERY(HPESTAR, 'EXECUTE [AdventureWorks2012].[dbo].[uspGetBillOfMaterials]
900,''20080216''');
GO
-- (1 row(s) affected)          -- create table
-- (24 row(s) affected)         -- inserts
```

SELECT * FROM BOM900;

ProductAssemblyID	ComponentID	ComponentDesc	TotalQuantity	StandardCost	ListPrice	BOMLevel	RecursionLevel
900	324	Chain Stays	2.00	0.00	0.00	2	0
900	325	Decal 1	2.00	0.00	0.00	2	0
900	326	Decal 2	1.00	0.00	0.00	2	0
900	327	Down Tube	1.00	0.00	0.00	2	0
900	399	Head Tube	1.00	0.00	0.00	2	0
900	496	Paint - Yellow	8.00	0.00	0.00	2	0
900	532	Seat Stays	4.00	0.00	0.00	2	0
900	533	Seat Tube	1.00	0.00	0.00	2	0
900	534	Top Tube	1.00	0.00	0.00	2	0
900	802	LL Fork	1.00	65.8097	148.22	2	0
324	486	Metal Sheet 5	1.00	0.00	0.00	3	1
327	483	Metal Sheet 3	1.00	0.00	0.00	3	1
399	485	Metal Sheet 4	1.00	0.00	0.00	3	1
532	484	Metal Sheet 7	1.00	0.00	0.00	3	1
533	478	Metal Bar 2	1.00	0.00	0.00	3	1
534	482	Metal Sheet 2	1.00	0.00	0.00	3	1
802	316	Blade	2.00	0.00	0.00	3	1
802	331	Fork End	2.00	0.00	0.00	3	1
802	350	Fork Crown	1.00	0.00	0.00	3	1
802	531	Steerer	1.00	0.00	0.00	3	1
316	486	Metal Sheet 5	1.00	0.00	0.00	4	2
331	482	Metal Sheet 2	1.00	0.00	0.00	4	2
350	486	Metal Sheet 5	1.00	0.00	0.00	4	2
531	487	Metal Sheet 6	1.00	0.00	0.00	4	2

Execution of SELECT INTO from Dynamic SQL

T-SQL script demonstrates SELECT INTO execution within a dynamic SQL. Biggest challenge is to get the single quotes right. CHAR(39) use is an option.

```sql
-- SQL Server 2008 new feature: instant assignment to a localvariable
DECLARE @DynamicQuery nvarchar(max) =
   'SELECT *
   INTO BOM400
   FROM OPENQUERY(' + QUOTENAME(CONVERT(sysname, @@SERVERNAME))+ ',
   ''EXECUTE [AdventureWorks2012].[dbo].[uspGetWhereUsedProductID] 400,
   ''''2007-11-21'''''')' ;
```

```sql
PRINT @DynamicQuery;    -- test query; this is the static query which will be executed
/*
SELECT *
   INTO BOM400
   FROM OPENQUERY([HPESTAR],
   'EXECUTE [AdventureWorks2012].[dbo].[uspGetWhereUsedProductID] 400,
   ''2007-11-21''')
*/
```

```sql
EXEC sp_executeSQL @DynamicQuery;
GO -- (64 row(s) affected)
```

```sql
SELECT TOP ( 5 ) * FROM BOM400 ORDER BY NEWID() ;
GO
```

ProductAssemblyID	ComponentID	ComponentDesc	TotalQuantity	StandardCost	ListPrice	BOMLevel	RecursionLevel
761	818	Road-650 Red, 62	1.00	486.7066	782.99	1	1
987	823	Mountain-500 Silver, 48	1.00	308.2179	564.99	1	1
990	823	Mountain-500 Black, 42	1.00	294.5797	539.99	1	1
765	826	Road-650 Black, 58	1.00	486.7066	782.99	1	1
770	818	Road-650 Black, 52	1.00	486.7066	782.99	1	1

```sql
-- Cleanup
DROP TABLE BOM400;
```

CHAPTER 15: SELECT INTO Table Creation & Population

SELECT INTO Table Create from View
Transact-SQL script demonstrates how to import view query results into a table.

```
SELECT [FullName],
    [SalesPersonID]                          AS StaffID,
    [SalesTerritory],
    COALESCE(FORMAT([2006], 'c','en-US'), '')   AS [2006],
    COALESCE(FORMAT([2007], 'c','en-US'), '')   AS [2007],
    COALESCE(FORMAT([2008], 'c','en-US'), '')   AS [2008]
INTO  #Sales
FROM  [AdventureWorks2012].[Sales].[vSalesPersonSalesByFiscalYears]
ORDER BY SalesTerritory, FullName;
GO
```

```
SELECT *
FROM  #Sales
ORDER BY SalesTerritory, FullName;
GO
```

FullName	StaffID	SalesTerritory	2006	2007	2008
Lynn N Tsoflias	286	Australia			$1,421,810.92
Garrett R Vargas	278	Canada	$930,259.47	$1,225,468.28	$1,453,719.47
José Edvaldo Saraiva	282	Canada	$2,088,491.17	$1,233,386.47	$2,604,540.72
Jillian Carson	277	Central	$2,737,537.88	$4,138,847.30	$3,189,418.37
Ranjit R Varkey Chudukatil	290	France		$1,388,272.61	$3,121,616.32
Rachel B Valdez	288	Germany			$1,827,066.71
Michael G Blythe	275	Northeast	$1,602,472.39	$3,928,252.44	$3,763,178.18
David R Campbell	283	Northwest	$1,017,402.86	$1,139,529.55	$1,573,012.94
Pamela O Ansman-Wolfe	280	Northwest	$1,226,461.83	$746,063.63	$1,352,577.13
Tete A Mensa-Annan	284	Northwest		$735,983.49	$1,576,562.20
Tsvi Michael Reiter	279	Southeast	$2,645,436.95	$2,210,390.19	$2,315,185.61
Linda C Mitchell	276	Southwest	$2,260,118.45	$3,855,520.42	$4,251,368.55
Shu K Ito	281	Southwest	$1,593,742.92	$2,374,727.02	$2,458,535.62
Jae B Pak	289	United Kingdom		$4,386,467.42	$4,116,871.23

SELECT INTO Data Import from Excel
T-SQL OPENROWSET query imports data into a temporary table from Excel. Your Excel library maybe different than the one in the example. SQL Server Import and Export Wizard is the best way to exchange date between SS database and Excel.

```
SELECT * INTO ContactList FROM OPENROWSET('Microsoft.Jet.OLEDB.4.0',
     'Excel 8.0;Database=D:\data\excel\Contact.xls', 'SELECT * FROM [Contact$]')
-- (19972 row(s) affected)
```

CHAPTER 15: SELECT INTO Table Creation & Population

CHAPTER 16: Modify Data - INSERT, UPDATE, DELETE & MERGE

INSERT VALUES - Table Value Constructor

T-SQL scripts illustrate the use of INSERT VALUES with Table Value Constructor (a list of values). Because the text columns are defined as nvarchar the string literals are prefixed with "N" indicating UNICODE literal. Since only Latin letters used, the "N" can be omitted.

```
USE tempdb;
SELECT TOP 0 * INTO dbo.Department FROM AdventureWorks2012.HumanResources.Department;
-- This is necessary because IDENTITY property was inherited in the SELECT INTO
SET IDENTITY_INSERT dbo.Department ON;
GO
INSERT dbo.Department (DepartmentID, Name, GroupName, ModifiedDate) VALUES
(1, N'Engineering', N'Research and Development', getdate()),
(2, N'Tool Design', N'Research and Development', getdate()),
(3, N'Sales', N'Sales and Marketing', getdate()),
(4, N'Marketing', N'Sales and Marketing', getdate()),
(5, N'Purchasing', N'Inventory Management', getdate()),
(6, N'Research and Development', N'Research and Development', getdate()),
(7, N'Production', N'Manufacturing', getdate()),
(8, N'Production Control', N'Manufacturing', getdate()),
(9, N'Human Resources', N'Executive General and Administration', getdate()),
(10, N'Finance', N'Executive General and Administration', getdate()),
(11, N'Information Services', N'Executive General and Administration', getdate()),
(12, N'Document Control', N'Quality Assurance', getdate()),
(13, N'Quality Assurance', N'Quality Assurance', getdate()),
(14, N'Facilities and Maintenance', N'Executive General and Administration', getdate()),
(15, N'Shipping and Receiving', N'Inventory Management', getdate()),
(16, N'Executive', N'Executive General and Administration',getdate());
GO
SET IDENTITY_INSERT dbo.Department OFF;
GO
SELECT TOP 4 * FROM dbo.Department ORDER BY DepartmentID;
```

DepartmentID	Name	GroupName	ModifiedDate
1	Engineering	Research and Development	2016-08-02 06:35:44.623
2	Tool Design	Research and Development	2016-08-02 06:35:44.623
3	Sales	Sales and Marketing	2016-08-02 06:35:44.623
4	Marketing	Sales and Marketing	2016-08-02 06:35:44.623

INSERT VALUES - Ye Olde Way

T-SQL scripts illustrate the INSERT VALUES for single row insert, the only available method prior to SQL Server 2008.

```sql
USE AdventureWorks2012;
GO
```

```sql
CREATE TABLE Shift(
        ShiftID tinyint IDENTITY(1,1) NOT NULL,
        Name dbo.Name NOT NULL,
        StartTime time(7) NOT NULL,
        EndTime time(7) NOT NULL,
        ModifiedDate datetime NOT NULL,
        CONSTRAINT PK_Shift_ShiftID PRIMARY KEY CLUSTERED (ShiftID ASC) );
GO
```

```sql
SET IDENTITY_INSERT Shift ON;              -- To force insert into ShiftID
```

```sql
INSERT Shift (ShiftID, Name, StartTime, EndTime, ModifiedDate)
VALUES (1, N'Day', CAST(0x0700D85EAC3A0000 AS Time), CAST(0x07001882BA7D0000 AS Time), CAST(0x0000921E00000000 AS DateTime))
INSERT Shift (ShiftID, Name, StartTime, EndTime, ModifiedDate)
VALUES (2, N'Evening', CAST(0x07001882BA7D0000 AS Time), CAST(0x070058A5C8C00000 AS Time), getdate());
INSERT Shift (ShiftID, Name, StartTime, EndTime, ModifiedDate)
VALUES (3, N'Night', CAST(0x070058A5C8C00000 AS Time), CAST(0x0700D85EAC3A0000 AS Time), CURRENT_TIMESTAMP);
GO
```

```sql
SET IDENTITY_INSERT Shift OFF;
```

```sql
ALTER TABLE Shift ADD  CONSTRAINT DF_Shift_ModifiedDate  DEFAULT (getdate()) FOR ModifiedDate
GO
```

```sql
SELECT * FROM Shift ORDER BY ShiftID;
GO
```

ShiftID	Name	StartTime	EndTime	ModifiedDate
1	Day	07:00:00.0000000	15:00:00.0000000	2002-06-01 00:00:00.000
2	Evening	15:00:00.0000000	23:00:00.0000000	2018-08-20 19:31:02.293
3	Night	23:00:00.0000000	07:00:00.0000000	2018-08-20 19:31:02.293

```sql
DROP TABLE Shift;
GO
```

CHAPTER 16: Modify Data - INSERT, UPDATE, DELETE & MERGE

INSERT SELECT

INSERT SELECT Literal List

T-SQL scripts demonstrate the insertion of literal records (rows) using INSERT SELECT.

```
USE tempdb;
GO
SELECT TOP 0 * INTO dbo.Department FROM AdventureWorks2012.HumanResources.Department;
GO
-- This is necessary because IDENTITY property was inherited in the SELECT INTO
SET IDENTITY_INSERT dbo.Department ON;
GO
INSERT dbo.Department (DepartmentID, Name, GroupName, ModifiedDate)
SELECT 1, N'Engineering', N'Research and Development', CURRENT_TIMESTAMP UNION
SELECT 2, N'Tool Design', N'Research and Development', CURRENT_TIMESTAMP UNION
SELECT 3, N'Sales', N'Sales and Marketing', CURRENT_TIMESTAMP UNION
SELECT 4, N'Marketing', N'Sales and Marketing', CURRENT_TIMESTAMP UNION
SELECT 5, N'Purchasing', N'Inventory Management', CURRENT_TIMESTAMP UNION
SELECT 6, N'Research and Development', N'Research and Development', CURRENT_TIMESTAMP UNION
SELECT 7, N'Production', N'Manufacturing', CURRENT_TIMESTAMP UNION
SELECT 8, N'Production Control', N'Manufacturing', CURRENT_TIMESTAMP UNION
SELECT 9, N'Human Resources', N'Executive General and Administration', CURRENT_TIMESTAMP UNION
SELECT 10, N'Finance', N'Executive General and Administration', CURRENT_TIMESTAMP UNION
SELECT 11, N'Information Services', N'Executive General and Administration', CURRENT_TIMESTAMP UNION
SELECT 12, N'Document Control', N'Quality Assurance', CURRENT_TIMESTAMP UNION
SELECT 13, N'Quality Assurance', N'Quality Assurance', CURRENT_TIMESTAMP UNION
SELECT 14, N'Facilities and Maintenance', N'Executive General and Administration', CURRENT_TIMESTAMP UNION
SELECT 15, N'Shipping and Receiving', N'Inventory Management', CURRENT_TIMESTAMP UNION
SELECT 16, N'Executive', N'Executive General and Administration', CURRENT_TIMESTAMP;
GO
SET IDENTITY_INSERT dbo.Department OFF;
GO
SELECT TOP 4 * FROM dbo.Department ORDER BY DepartmentID;
GO
```

DepartmentID	Name	GroupName	ModifiedDate
1	Engineering	Research and Development	2016-08-02 06:35:44.623
2	Tool Design	Research and Development	2016-08-02 06:35:44.623
3	Sales	Sales and Marketing	2016-08-02 06:35:44.623
4	Marketing	Sales and Marketing	2016-08-02 06:35:44.623

```
-- Cleanup
DROP TABLE tempdb.dbo.Department;
```

INSERT SELECT from Table

T-SQL script demonstrates table population with table SELECT.

```
USE tempdb;
SELECT TOP 0 * INTO dbo.Department FROM AdventureWorks2012.HumanResources.Department;
GO
-- This is necessary because IDENTITY property was inherited in the SELECT INTO
SET IDENTITY_INSERT dbo.Department ON;
GO
INSERT dbo.Department (DepartmentID, Name, GroupName, ModifiedDate)
SELECT TOP 15 DepartmentID, Name, GroupName, ModifiedDate
FROM AdventureWorks2012.HumanResources.Department  ORDER BY DepartmentID;
GO
-- (15 row(s) affected)
SELECT TOP 4 * FROM dbo.Department ORDER BY DepartmentID;
```

DepartmentID	Name	GroupName	ModifiedDate
1	Engineering	Research and Development	2016-08-02 06:35:44.623
2	Tool Design	Research and Development	2016-08-02 06:35:44.623
3	Sales	Sales and Marketing	2016-08-02 06:35:44.623
4	Marketing	Sales and Marketing	2016-08-02 06:35:44.623

SCOPE_IDENTITY() for Last-Inserted IDENTITY Value

The last inserted IDENTITY value can be returned with the SCOPE_IDENTITY() or @@IDENTITY system function (variable). SCOPE_IDENTITY() is better choice since it is within the current connection scope. @@IDENTITY is at server level. The best choice though is the OUTPUT clause.

```
INSERT dbo.Department (DepartmentID, Name, GroupName, ModifiedDate)
SELECT TOP 1 DepartmentID, Name, GroupName, ModifiedDate
FROM AdventureWorks2012.HumanResources.Department  ORDER BY DepartmentID DESC;
GO
-- (1 row(s) affected)
```

Alternate is SELECT @@IDENTITY; @@ variables are system variables.

```
DECLARE @LastID INT = SCOPE_IDENTITY();
SELECT @LastID;   -- 16
```

```
SET IDENTITY_INSERT dbo.Department OFF;
GO
```

```
-- Cleanup
DROP TABLE tempdb.dbo.Department;
```

CHAPTER 16: Modify Data - INSERT, UPDATE, DELETE & MERGE

INSERT with Subset of Columns

Only the required columns must be present in the INSERT column list. A column with default or NULL property can be omitted. In the next T-SQL script, ModifiedDate is filled by default with getdate().

```
USE tempdb;
SELECT TOP 0 * INTO dbo.Department FROM AdventureWorks2012.HumanResources.Department;
GO
ALTER TABLE dbo.Department ADD CONSTRAINT DF_Dept_ModDate
DEFAULT getdate() FOR ModifiedDate;
GO
SET IDENTITY_INSERT dbo.Department ON;
GO
INSERT dbo.Department (DepartmentID, Name, GroupName)
SELECT DepartmentID, Name, GroupName  FROM AdventureWorks2012.HumanResources.Department;
GO  -- (16 row(s) affected)
SELECT TOP 4 * FROM dbo.Department ORDER BY DepartmentID;
```

DepartmentID	Name	GroupName	ModifiedDate
1	Engineering	Research and Development	2016-08-02 06:35:44.623
2	Tool Design	Research and Development	2016-08-02 06:35:44.623
3	Sales	Sales and Marketing	2016-08-02 06:35:44.623
4	Marketing	Sales and Marketing	2016-08-02 06:35:44.623

Capturing Last-Inserted IDENTITY Set Values with OUTPUT

When more than one row is inserted with one statement, the OUTPUT clause can be used to capture the list of just inserted IDENTITY values.

```
DECLARE @LastInserted TABLE (ID INT);
INSERT dbo.Department (DepartmentID, Name, GroupName)
       OUTPUT inserted.DepartmentID INTO @LastInserted
SELECT DepartmentID+1000, Name, GroupName  FROM
AdventureWorks2012.HumanResources.Department;
SELECT TOP 5 * FROM @LastInserted ORDER BY ID;
GO
```

ID
1001
1002
1003
1004
1005

```
SET IDENTITY_INSERT dbo.Department OFF;
DROP TABLE tempdb.dbo.Department;
```

INSERT EXEC Stored Procedure

Data can be directly inserted from the execution of a user-defined stored procedure or system procedure. We create a table and a stored procedure, then perform INSERT EXEC.

```
USE AdventureWorks2012;
IF OBJECT_ID ('dbo.EmployeeSales', 'U') IS NOT NULL   DROP TABLE dbo.EmployeeSales;
IF OBJECT_ID ('dbo.uspGetEmployeeSales', 'P') IS NOT NULL   DROP PROCEDURE uspGetEmployeeSales;
CREATE TABLE dbo.EmployeeSales
 (
   BusinessEntityID     VARCHAR(11) NOT NULL PRIMARY KEY,
   LastName             VARCHAR(40) NOT NULL,
   SalesDollars         MONEY NOT NULL,
   DataSource           VARCHAR(20) NOT NULL
 );
GO

CREATE PROCEDURE dbo.uspGetEmployeeSales AS
 BEGIN
   SELECT       e.BusinessEntityID, c.LastName, sp.SalesYTD, 'PROCEDURE'
   FROM   HumanResources.Employee AS e
      INNER JOIN Sales.SalesPerson AS sp
         ON e.BusinessEntityID = sp.BusinessEntityID
      INNER JOIN Person.Person AS c
         ON e.BusinessEntityID = c.BusinessEntityID
   WHERE  e.BusinessEntityID > 280   ORDER BY   e.BusinessEntityID,  c.LastName;
 END;
GO

--INSERT...EXECUTE user-defined stored procedure
INSERT EmployeeSales EXECUTE uspGetEmployeeSales;

SELECT * FROM  EmployeeSales;
```

BusinessEntityID	LastName	SalesDollars	DataSource
281	Ito	2458535.6169	PROCEDURE
282	Saraiva	2604540.7172	PROCEDURE
283	Campbell	1573012.9383	PROCEDURE
284	Mensa-Annan	1576562.1966	PROCEDURE
285	Abbas	172524.4512	PROCEDURE
286	Tsoflias	1421810.9242	PROCEDURE
287	Alberts	519905.932	PROCEDURE
288	Valdez	1827066.7118	PROCEDURE
289	Pak	4116871.2277	PROCEDURE
290	Varkey Chudukatil	3121616.3202	PROCEDURE

CHAPTER 16: Modify Data - INSERT, UPDATE, DELETE & MERGE

INSERT EXEC Stored Procedure

Insert Into A Table Via The Direct Execution Of An SQL Query With The EXEC Command

```
SELECT Population = count(*)  FROM  dbo.EmployeeSales;
```

Population
10

```
--INSERT...EXECUTE('string') example
INSERT EmployeeSales
EXECUTE ('   SELECT e.BusinessEntityID, c.LastName,    sp.SalesYTD, "EXEC SQL STRING"
             FROM HumanResources.Employee AS e     INNER JOIN Sales.SalesPerson AS sp
             ON e.BusinessEntityID = sp.BusinessEntityID    INNER JOIN Person.Person AS c
             ON e.BusinessEntityID = c.BusinessEntityID
             WHERE e.BusinessEntityID BETWEEN 270 and 280
             ORDER BY e.BusinessEntityID, c.LastName ');
GO
-- (7 row(s) affected)
```

Inserted number of rows can be captured for later use. **Capture must be done immediately after the monitored statement.** Any following statement will change @@ROWCOUNT value.

```
DECLARE @InsertCount int = @@ROWCOUNT;
SELECT @InsertCount;   -- 7
GO
```

```
SELECT * FROM  dbo.EmployeeSales ORDER BY BusinessEntityID ;
```

BusinessEntityID	LastName	SalesDollars	DataSource
274	Jiang	559697.5639	EXEC SQL STRING
275	Blythe	3763178.1787	EXEC SQL STRING
276	Mitchell	4251368.5497	EXEC SQL STRING
277	Carson	3189418.3662	EXEC SQL STRING
278	Vargas	1453719.4653	EXEC SQL STRING
279	Reiter	2315185.611	EXEC SQL STRING
280	Ansman-Wolfe	1352577.1325	EXEC SQL STRING
281	Ito	2458535.6169	PROCEDURE
282	Saraiva	2604540.7172	PROCEDURE
283	Campbell	1573012.9383	PROCEDURE
284	Mensa-Annan	1576562.1966	PROCEDURE
285	Abbas	172524.4512	PROCEDURE
286	Tsoflias	1421810.9242	PROCEDURE
287	Alberts	519905.932	PROCEDURE
288	Valdez	1827066.7118	PROCEDURE
289	Pak	4116871.2277	PROCEDURE
290	Varkey Chudukatil	3121616.3202	PROCEDURE

CHAPTER 16: Modify Data - INSERT, UPDATE, DELETE & MERGE

INSERT EXEC System Procedure

Data can be inserted into a table by the execution of a system procedure. We create a test table with SELECT INTO FROM OPENQUERY. We can also create the table manually if we know the data type of columns.

```
-- DATA ACCESS must be turned on at YOURSERVER SQL Server instance
SELECT TOP(0) * INTO #SPWHO
FROM OPENQUERY(YOURSERVER, 'exec sp_who');        -- will not work with sp_who2 due to duplicate
                                                   column name
```

```
/* Table created
CREATE TABLE [dbo].[#SPWHO](
        [spid] [smallint] NOT NULL,
        [ecid] [smallint] NOT NULL,
        [status] [nchar](30) NOT NULL,
        [loginame] [nvarchar](128) NULL,
        [hostname] [nchar](128) NOT NULL,
        [blk] [char](5) NULL,
        [dbname] [nvarchar](128) NULL,
        [cmd] [nchar](16) NOT NULL,
        [request_id] [int] NOT NULL
); */
```

```
INSERT #SPWHO   EXEC sp_who
```

The blk column contains blocking spid if any. A large update for example may block other queries until it completes. The spid of the current session is @@SPID.

```
SELECT * FROM #SPWHO
GO -- (42 row(s) affected) - Partial results.
```

spid	ecid	status	loginame	hostname	blk	dbname	cmd	request_id
21	0	background	sa		0	master	TASK MANAGER	0
22	0	background	sa		0	master	CHECKPOINT	0
23	0	sleeping	sa		0	master	TASK MANAGER	0
24	0	background	sa		0	master	BRKR TASK	0
25	0	sleeping	sa		0	master	TASK MANAGER	0
26	0	sleeping	sa		0	master	TASK MANAGER	0
27	0	sleeping	sa		0	master	TASK MANAGER	0
28	0	sleeping	sa		0	master	TASK MANAGER	0
29	0	sleeping	sa		0	master	TASK MANAGER	0
30	0	sleeping	sa		0	master	TASK MANAGER	0
40	0	background	sa		0	master	BRKR TASK	0
42	0	background	sa		0	master	BRKR TASK	0
43	0	background	sa		0	master	BRKR TASK	0
51	0	sleeping	YOURSERVER\Owner	YOURSERVER	0	AdventureWorks2012	AWAITING COMMAND	0
52	0	sleeping	NT SERVICE\SQLSERVERAGENT	YOURSERVER	0	msdb	AWAITING COMMAND	0

```
DROP TABLE #SPWHO
GO
```

CHAPTER 16: Modify Data - INSERT, UPDATE, DELETE & MERGE

INSERT Only New Rows Omit the Rest

INSERT only new records. If record exists, do nothing. Note: DELETE will not rollback IDENTITY current value. Therefore with repeated testing, the IDENTITY current value will roll ahead.

```
USE AdventureWorks2012;
SELECT COUNT(*) FROM HumanResources.Department;          -- 16

-- All rows exists, no new row insertion
INSERT HumanResources.Department (Name, GroupName)
SELECT Name, GroupName
FROM AdventureWorks2008.HumanResources.Department D
WHERE NOT EXISTS (      SELECT * FROM HumanResources.Department DD  -- Correlated subquery
                    WHERE D.Name = DD.Name
                        AND D.GroupName = DD.GroupName);
GO -- (0 row(s) affected)

-- Prefix Name with "ZZZ", 16 successful new inserted rows
INSERT HumanResources.Department (Name, GroupName)
SELECT CONCAT('ZZZ', Name), GroupName
FROM AdventureWorks2008.HumanResources.Department D
WHERE NOT EXISTS (      SELECT * FROM HumanResources.Department DD
            WHERE DD.Name = CONCAT('ZZZ', D.Name)    AND DD.GroupName = D.GroupName);
GO -- (16 row(s) affected)

DELETE TOP ( 7 ) HumanResources.Department WHERE Name LIKE ('ZZZ%');     -- (7 row(s) affected)
```

Only 7 rows will be inserted since the rest are duplicates.

```
INSERT HumanResources.Department (Name, GroupName)
SELECT CONCAT('ZZZ', Name), GroupName
FROM AdventureWorks2008.HumanResources.Department D
WHERE NOT EXISTS (      SELECT * FROM HumanResources.Department DD
              WHERE DD.Name = CONCAT('ZZZ', D.Name)    AND DD.GroupName = DD.GroupName);
GO
-- (7  row(s) affected)

SELECT * FROM HumanResources.Department;   -- (32 row(s) affected)  -- Partial results;
```

DepartmentID	Name	GroupName	ModifiedDate
16	Executive	Executive General and Administration	2002-06-01 00:00:00.000
65	ZZZEngineering	Research and Development	2018-08-13 08:32:43.133

```
DELETE HumanResources.Department
WHERE Name LIKE ('ZZZ%');         -- (16 row(s) affected)
SELECT COUNT(*) FROM HumanResources.Department;              -- 16
```

CHAPTER 16: Modify Data - INSERT, UPDATE, DELETE & MERGE

DELETE - A Dangerous Operation

DELETE is a logged operation. DELETE may be slow from large table with indexes due to index reorganization. Warning: **DELETE is a dangerous operation since it removes data. Protection: regular database backup and/or creating a copy of the table prior to DELETE with SELECT INTO.**

```
USE [AdventureWorks2012]
GO
-- Create test table with SELECT INTO
SELECT [SalesOrderID]
    ,CONVERT(INT,[SalesOrderDetailID]) AS SalesOrderDetailID
    ,[CarrierTrackingNumber]
    ,[OrderQty]
    ,[ProductID]
    ,[SpecialOfferID]
    ,[UnitPrice]
    ,[UnitPriceDiscount]
    ,[LineTotal]
    ,[rowguid]
    ,[ModifiedDate]
INTO tempdb.dbo.SOD
FROM [Sales].[SalesOrderDetail];
GO -- (121317 row(s) affected)
```

```
-- Increase table population 64 fold
INSERT  tempdb.dbo.SOD  SELECT * FROM tempdb.dbo.SOD;
GO 6
/* Beginning execution loop
(121317 row(s) affected)
(242634 row(s) affected)
(485268 row(s) affected)
(970536 row(s) affected)
(1941072 row(s) affected)
(3882144 row(s) affected)
Batch execution completed 6 times.
Execution time - 00:01.27  */
```

```
CREATE INDEX idxSOD on tempdb.dbo.SOD (SalesOrderID, ProductID);
-- Command(s) completed successfully. Time: 00:00:06
```

```
SELECT COUNT(*) FROM tempdb.dbo.SOD;  -- 7764288
```

```
-- Delete even SalesOrderID records
DELETE FROM tempdb.dbo.SOD WHERE SalesOrderID % 2 = 0;
-- (3925184 row(s) affected)  - Execution time - 00:01:30
```

CHAPTER 16: Modify Data - INSERT, UPDATE, DELETE & MERGE

TRUNCATE TABLE & DBCC CHECKIDENT

TRUNCATE TABLE command is very fast since it is minimally logged. It also resets IDENTITY column to (1,1). Warning: **TRUNCATE is a dangerous operation since it removes all the data in a table**. Protection: regular database backup and/or creating a copy of the table prior to TRUNCATE with SELECT INTO.

SELECT COUNT(*) FROM tempdb.dbo.SOD; -- 3839104

TRUNCATE TABLE tempdb.dbo.SOD;
-- Command(s) completed successfully. Execution time: 00:00:00

SELECT COUNT(*) FROM tempdb.dbo.SOD;   -- 0
GO

DROP TABLE tempdb.dbo.SOD;
GO
-- Command(s) completed successfully

-- Create new test table with SELECT INTO
USE tempdb;

SELECT * INTO SOD FROM AdventureWorks2012.Sales.SalesOrderDetail;
GO -- (121317 row(s) affected)

-- Next IDENTITY value will be 121318.
DBCC CHECKIDENT ("dbo.SOD");
/* Checking identity information: current identity value '121317', current column value '121317'.
DBCC execution completed. If DBCC printed error messages, contact your system administrator. */

TRUNCATE TABLE SOD;
GO
-- Command(s) completed successfully.

-- IDENTITY is reset
DBCC CHECKIDENT ("dbo.SOD");
/* Checking identity information: current identity value 'NULL', current column value 'NULL'.
DBCC execution completed. If DBCC printed error messages, contact your system administrator. */

EXEC sp_help SOD;
GO
-- Partial results.

Identity	Seed	Increment	Not For Replication
SalesOrderDetailID	1	1	0

CHAPTER 16: Modify Data - INSERT, UPDATE, DELETE & MERGE

Reseeding IDENTITY

```
-- Without this command, it may not start at 1
DBCC CHECKIDENT ("SOD", RESEED, 1);
```

```
-- Populate the table with 5 rows
INSERT INTO SOD
      ([SalesOrderID]
      ,[CarrierTrackingNumber]
      ,[OrderQty]
      ,[ProductID]
      ,[SpecialOfferID]
      ,[UnitPrice]
      ,[UnitPriceDiscount]
      ,[LineTotal]
      ,[rowguid]
      ,[ModifiedDate])
 SELECT  TOP (5)
      [SalesOrderID]
      ,[CarrierTrackingNumber]
      ,[OrderQty]
      ,[ProductID]
      ,[SpecialOfferID]
      ,[UnitPrice]
      ,[UnitPriceDiscount]
      ,[LineTotal]
      ,[rowguid]
      ,[ModifiedDate]
FROM AdventureWorks2012.Sales.SalesOrderDetail;
GO
-- (5 row(s) affected)
```

```
-- Next value assigned is 6
DBCC CHECKIDENT ("dbo.SOD");
/*Checking identity information: current identity value '5', current column value '5'.
DBCC execution completed. If DBCC printed error messages, contact your system administrator. */
```

```
SELECT * FROM SOD;
-- (5 row(s) affected) - Partial results.
```

SalesOrderID	SalesOrderDetailID	CarrierTrackingNumber	OrderQty	ProductID	SpecialOfferID	UnitPrice	UnitPriceDiscount	LineTotal
43659	1	4911-403C-98	1	776	1	2024.994	0.00	2024.994000
43659	2	4911-403C-98	3	777	1	2024.994	0.00	6074.982000
43659	3	4911-403C-98	1	778	1	2024.994	0.00	2024.994000
43659	4	4911-403C-98	1	771	1	2039.994	0.00	2039.994000
43659	5	4911-403C-98	1	772	1	2039.994	0.00	2039.994000

UPDATE - A Complex Operation

UPDATE changes data content at a row and column level (cell). It is a logged operation: deleted row contains previous data, inserted row contains new data. Warning: UPDATE is a dangerous operation since it changes the data in a table. Protection: regular database backup and/or creating a copy of the table prior to UPDATE with SELECT INTO.

Some UPDATEs are reversible, such as some calculated UPDATE, others may be irreversible.

Checking Cardinality & Changes by UPDATE Prior to Execution

Since UPDATE is replaces previous data, it is very important to check prior to execution that is works correctly. It is quite simple to convert UPDATE into a checking SELECT. We intend to UPDATE the SalesYTD column with the last day sales for each salesperson.

```
USE AdventureWorks2012;
SELECT   sp.BusinessEntityID, SalesYTD,
            [NewSalesYTD]=SalesYTD
         + (SELECT SUM(SODa.SubTotal)
           FROM   Sales.SalesOrderHeader AS SODa
           WHERE  CONVERT(date,SODa.OrderDate) = CONVERT(date,(SELECT MAX(OrderDate)
           FROM   Sales.SalesOrderHeader AS SODb
           WHERE
                SODb.SalesPersonID = SODa.SalesPersonID))
                AND sp.BusinessEntityID =   SODa.SalesPersonID
           GROUP  BY SODa.SalesPersonID)
FROM Sales.SalesPerson sp  ORDER BY sp.BusinessEntityID;
GO
```

BusinessEntityID	SalesYTD	NewSalesYTD
274	559697.5639	597350.4859
275	3763178.1787	4133185.161
276	4251368.5497	4534079.5941
277	3189418.3662	3527404.588
278	1453719.4653	1599132.4735
279	2315185.611	2548077.4756
280	1352577.1325	1503691.0098
281	2458535.6169	2678660.7921
282	2604540.7172	3030519.8258
283	1573012.9383	1714964.9067
284	1576562.1966	1719945.1917
285	172524.4512	176721.5652
286	1421810.9242	1649155.9058
287	519905.932	520578.226
288	1827066.7118	1962768.1658
289	4116871.2277	4556655.2802
290	3121616.3202	3240852.6195

UPDATE - A Complex Operation

ANSI Style UPDATE

T-SQL supports ANSI UPDATE, in addition T-SQL supports the FROM clause in UPDATE.

```
USE AdventureWorks2012;
UPDATE Sales.SalesPerson
SET    SalesYTD = SalesYTD
         + (SELECT SUM(SODa.SubTotal)
           FROM   Sales.SalesOrderHeader AS SODa
           WHERE  CONVERT(date,SODa.OrderDate) =
                  CONVERT(date,(SELECT MAX(OrderDate)
            FROM   Sales.SalesOrderHeader AS SODb
            WHERE
               SODb.SalesPersonID = SODa.SalesPersonID))
                AND Sales.SalesPerson.BusinessEntityID =   SODa.SalesPersonID
           GROUP  BY SODa.SalesPersonID);
GO
-- (17 row(s) affected)
```

```
SELECT BusinessEntityID, SalesQuota, SalesYTD, SalesLastYear
FROM Sales.SalesPerson
ORDER BY BusinessEntityID;
GO
```

BusinessEntityID	SalesQuota	SalesYTD	SalesLastYear
274	NULL	597350.4859	0.00
275	300000.00	4133185.161	1750406.4785
276	250000.00	4534079.5941	1439156.0291
277	250000.00	3527404.588	1997186.2037
278	250000.00	1599132.4735	1620276.8966
279	300000.00	2548077.4756	1849640.9418
280	250000.00	1503691.0098	1927059.178
281	250000.00	2678660.7921	2073505.9999
282	250000.00	3030519.8258	2038234.6549
283	250000.00	1714964.9067	1371635.3158
284	300000.00	1719945.1917	0.00
285	NULL	176721.5652	0.00
286	250000.00	1649155.9058	2278548.9776
287	NULL	520578.226	0.00
288	250000.00	1962768.1658	1307949.7917
289	250000.00	4556655.2802	1635823.3967
290	250000.00	3240852.6195	2396539.7601

CHAPTER 16: Modify Data - INSERT, UPDATE, DELETE & MERGE

UPDATE - A Complex Operation

UPDATE from Table in Another Database

UPDATE can be performed with data from a second database. ZorigAdventureWorks2012 is an original read-only copy of the AdventureWorks2012 database. The "Z" prefix is to force it to the end of alphabetical database list in SSMS Object Explorer.

```
UPDATE Sales.SalesPerson
     SET SalesYTD = (
                     SELECT SalesYTD
                     FROM ZorigAdventureWorks2012.Sales.SalesPerson sp
                     WHERE sp.BusinessEntityID =
Sales.SalesPerson.BusinessEntityID
                    );
GO


SELECT BusinessEntityID,
       SalesQuota,
       SalesYTD,
       SalesLastYear
FROM Sales.SalesPerson
ORDER BY BusinessEntityID;
GO
```

BusinessEntityID	SalesQuota	SalesYTD	SalesLastYear
274	NULL	559697.5639	0.00
275	300000.00	3763178.1787	1750406.4785
276	250000.00	4251368.5497	1439156.0291
277	250000.00	3189418.3662	1997186.2037
278	250000.00	1453719.4653	1620276.8966
279	300000.00	2315185.611	1849640.9418
280	250000.00	1352577.1325	1927059.178
281	250000.00	2458535.6169	2073505.9999
282	250000.00	2604540.7172	2038234.6549
283	250000.00	1573012.9383	1371635.3158
284	300000.00	1576562.1966	0.00
285	NULL	172524.4512	0.00
286	250000.00	1421810.9242	2278548.9776
287	NULL	519905.932	0.00
288	250000.00	1827066.7118	1307949.7917
289	250000.00	4116871.2277	1635823.3967
290	250000.00	3121616.3202	2396539.7601

UPDATE Syntax Challenges

The UPDATE statement in SQL has perplexing and potentially confusing syntax. Typically mastered by expert DBA-s and SQL developers, and the rest of the database community uses it in an insecure manner: never sure if it works as intended. Simple T-SQL examples demonstrate some of the issues with the UPDATE syntax and offer solutions.

First we create a new table for experimentation from the AdventureWorks2012 database and perform a demo inner join UPDATE on the new table.

```
USE tempdb;

SELECT ProductID,
    ProductName = Name,
    StandardCost AS Cost,
    ListPrice,
    Color,
    CONVERT(date, ModifiedDate) AS ModifiedDate
INTO   Product
FROM   AdventureWorks2012.Production.Product
WHERE  ListPrice > 0.0
       AND Color IS NOT NULL;
GO
-- (245 row(s) affected)
```

```
SELECT TOP 5 * FROM Product
ORDER BY ProductID DESC;
GO
```

ProductID	ProductName	Cost	ListPrice	Color	ModifiedDate
999	Road-750 Black, 52	343.6496	539.99	Black	2008-03-11
998	Road-750 Black, 48	343.6496	539.99	Black	2008-03-11
997	Road-750 Black, 44	343.6496	539.99	Black	2008-03-11
993	Mountain-500 Black, 52	294.5797	539.99	Black	2008-03-11
992	Mountain-500 Black, 48	294.5797	539.99	Black	2008-03-11

We shall proceed and update ALL (no WHERE clause) the rows in the Product table. We increase the ListPrice by 5%.

```
UPDATE Product    SET ListPrice = ListPrice * 1.05; -- (245 row(s) affected)
```

In this instance a reversible UPDATE. But not always.

```
UPDATE Product    SET ListPrice = ListPrice / 1.05;
-- (245 row(s) affected)
```

CHAPTER 16: Modify Data - INSERT, UPDATE, DELETE & MERGE

UPDATE - A Complex Operation

UPDATE with INNER JOIN

The UPDATE uses a table alias from the FROM clause.

SELECT TOP 2 * FROM Product WHERE Color = 'Yellow' ORDER BY ProductID DESC;

ProductID	ProductName	Cost	ListPrice	Color	ModifiedDate
976	Road-350-W Yellow, 48	1082.51	1700.99	Yellow	2008-03-11
975	Road-350-W Yellow, 44	1082.51	1700.99	Yellow	2008-03-11

UPDATE p SET   p.ModifiedDate = DATEADD(HH,1,awp.ModifiedDate)
FROM   Product p   INNER JOIN AdventureWorks2012.Production.Product awp
                ON p.ProductID = awp.ProductID AND p.Size LIKE '4%' ;
-- (91 row(s) affected)

Capturing Affected Rows with @@ROWCOUNT

When we have to know the number of updated rows, it is best to capture it into local variable and use it from there in the program logic.

DECLARE @UpdatedRows int;   -- capture @@ROWCOUNT for subsequent use in the program

UPDATE p SET   p.ModifiedDate = DATEADD(mm,1,awp.ModifiedDate)
FROM   Product p
     INNER JOIN AdventureWorks2012.Production.Product awp   ON p.ProductID = awp.ProductID
WHERE p.Color = 'Yellow' ;
-- (36 row(s) affected)

SET @UpdatedRows = @@ROWCOUNT;

SELECT @@ROWCOUNT;   -- @@ROWCOUNT already changed
-- 1
SELECT TOP 5 * FROM Product WHERE Color = 'Yellow' ORDER BY ProductID DESC;

SELECT @@ROWCOUNT;   -- @@ROWCOUNT changed again
-- 5
SELECT @UpdatedRows;   -- local variable kept the UPDATE count
-- 36

ProductID	ProductName	Cost	ListPrice	Color	ModifiedDate
976	Road-350-W Yellow, 48	1082.51	1700.99	Yellow	2008-04-11
975	Road-350-W Yellow, 44	1082.51	1700.99	Yellow	2008-04-11
974	Road-350-W Yellow, 42	1082.51	1700.99	Yellow	2008-04-11
973	Road-350-W Yellow, 40	1082.51	1700.99	Yellow	2008-04-11
965	Touring-3000 Yellow, 62	461.4448	742.35	Yellow	2008-04-11

CHAPTER 16: Modify Data - INSERT, UPDATE, DELETE & MERGE

UPDATE with Common Table Expression

UPDATE can be issued through a CTE to UPDATE the underlying table, Product in this case. Prices are increased 5% for products with over $1,000.00 list price.

```
SELECT TOP 5 * FROM Product  WHERE ListPrice > 1000.0 ORDER BY ProductID DESC;
GO
```

ProductID	ProductName	Cost	ListPrice	Color	ModifiedDate
976	Road-350-W Yellow, 48	1082.51	1700.99	Yellow	2008-04-11
975	Road-350-W Yellow, 44	1082.51	1700.99	Yellow	2008-04-11
974	Road-350-W Yellow, 42	1082.51	1700.99	Yellow	2008-04-11
973	Road-350-W Yellow, 40	1082.51	1700.99	Yellow	2008-04-11
972	Touring-2000 Blue, 54	755.1508	1214.85	Blue	2008-03-11

```
;WITH CTE
   AS (SELECT Price = ListPrice
      FROM   Product
      WHERE  ListPrice > 1000.0)
UPDATE CTE
SET    Price = Price * 1.05
GO
-- (86 row(s) affected)
```

```
SELECT TOP 5 * FROM Product  WHERE ListPrice > 1000.0 ORDER BY ProductID DESC;
```

ProductID	ProductName	Cost	ListPrice	Color	ModifiedDate
976	Road-350-W Yellow, 48	1082.51	1786.0395	Yellow	2008-04-11
975	Road-350-W Yellow, 44	1082.51	1786.0395	Yellow	2008-04-11
974	Road-350-W Yellow, 42	1082.51	1786.0395	Yellow	2008-04-11
973	Road-350-W Yellow, 40	1082.51	1786.0395	Yellow	2008-04-11
972	Touring-2000 Blue, 54	755.1508	1275.5925	Blue	2008-03-11

Similar data modification with ANSI SQL UPDATE.

```
UPDATE Product
SET   ListPrice = (SELECT p8.ListPrice * 1.05
         FROM   AdventureWorks2012.Production.Product p8   WHERE  Product.ProductID = p8.ProductID)
WHERE  EXISTS (SELECT * FROM  AdventureWorks2012.Production.Product p8
      WHERE  Product.ProductID = p8.ProductID   AND Product.ListPrice > 1000.0);
```

Four Methods of UPDATE with GROUP BY Query

UPDATE can be done a few ways with GROUP BY aggregates.

```
USE tempdb;
SELECT Color=ISNULL(Color,'N/A'), ItemCount=0 INTO ProductColor
FROM AdventureWorks2008.Production.Product
GROUP BY Color
GO
-- (10 row(s) affected)
```

```
SELECT * FROM ProductColor
GO
```

Color	ItemCount
N/A	0
Black	0
Blue	0
Grey	0
Multi	0
Red	0
Silver	0
Silver/Black	0
White	0
Yellow	0

ANSI UPDATE

```
UPDATE ProductColor
SET ItemCount = (SELECT ProductColorCount FROM  (SELECT Color=ISNULL(Color, 'N/A'),
             ProductColorCount=COUNT(*)
              FROM AdventureWorks2008.Production.Product
              GROUP BY Color) cg WHERE  ProductColor.Color = cg.Color)
GO -- (10 row(s) affected)
```

FROM Clause UPDATE with Derived Table

```
UPDATE pc   SET pc.ItemCount = cg.ProductColorCount
FROM ProductColor pc
INNER JOIN (SELECT Color=ISNULL(Color, 'N/A'), ProductColorCount=COUNT(*)
       FROM AdventureWorks2008.Production.Product GROUP BY Color) cg
ON pc.Color = cg.Color;
-- (10 row(s) affected)
```

FROM Clause UPDATE with CTE

```
;WITH CTE AS (SELECT Color=ISNULL(Color, 'N/A'), ProductColorCount=COUNT(*)
    FROM AdventureWorks2008.Production.Product
    GROUP BY Color)
UPDATE pc
SET pc.ItemCount = CTE.ProductColorCount
FROM ProductColor pc
INNER JOIN CTE
ON pc.Color = CTE.Color;
GO
-- (10 row(s) affected)
```

CTE UPDATE

```
;WITH CTE AS (SELECT * FROM ProductColor pc
    INNER JOIN (SELECT ColorPrd=ISNULL(Color, 'N/A'), ProductColorCount=COUNT(*)
    FROM AdventureWorks2008.Production.Product
    GROUP BY Color) cg
            ON pc.Color = cg.ColorPrd)
UPDATE CTE SET CTE.ItemCount = CTE.ProductColorCount;
GO
-- (10 row(s) affected)
```

```
SELECT * FROM ProductColor;
GO
```

Color	ItemCount
N/A	248
Black	93
Blue	26
Grey	1
Multi	8
Red	38
Silver	43
Silver/Black	7
White	4
Yellow	36

```
DROP TABLE tempdb.dbo.ProductColor;
```

CHAPTER 16: Modify Data - INSERT, UPDATE, DELETE & MERGE

MERGE for Combination INSERT, UPDATE or DELETE

The MERGE statement can be used to INSERT, UPDATE and/or DELETE all in one statement.

```
USE tempdb;
go

-- Setup 2 test tables
SELECT TOP (5000) ResellerKey,
        OrderDateKey,
        ProductKey,
        OrderQuantity,
        SalesAmount
INTO   FactResellerSales
FROM   AdventureWorksDW2012.dbo.FactResellerSales
ORDER BY OrderDateKey ;
go
-- (5000 row(s) affected)

SELECT TOP (8000) ResellerKey,
        OrderDateKey,
        ProductKey,
        OrderQuantity,
        SalesAmount
INTO   ResellerSalesTransaction
FROM   AdventureWorksDW2012.dbo.FactResellerSales ;
go
-- (8000 row(s) affected)

DELETE rsc
FROM   ResellerSalesTransaction rsc
    JOIN (SELECT TOP 1000 *
        FROM   ResellerSalesTransaction
        ORDER  BY ResellerKey DESC) x
    ON x.ResellerKey = rsc.ResellerKey ;
go
-- (1010 row(s) affected)

UPDATE TOP (6000) ResellerSalesTransaction
SET    SalesAmount = SalesAmount * 1.1 ;
go
-- (6000 row(s) affected)
```

CHAPTER 16: Modify Data - INSERT, UPDATE, DELETE & MERGE

MERGE is a very powerful statement

```sql
SELECT TOP (10) *
FROM   FactResellerSales
ORDER  BY ResellerKey,        OrderDateKey,        ProductKey ;
go
```

ResellerKey	OrderDateKey	ProductKey	OrderQuantity	SalesAmount
1	20050801	270	1	183.9382
1	20050801	275	1	356.898
1	20050801	285	1	178.5808
1	20050801	314	2	4293.924
1	20050801	317	1	874.794
1	20050801	319	2	1749.588
1	20050801	324	2	838.9178
1	20050801	326	1	419.4589
1	20050801	328	1	419.4589
1	20050801	332	2	838.9178

```sql
SELECT BeforeFactCount=COUNT(*)
FROM   FactResellerSales ;
-- 5000


-- Ready for the MERGE (update if exists, insert otherwise)
MERGE FactResellerSales AS fact
USING (SELECT *
    FROM   ResellerSalesTransaction) AS feed
ON ( fact.ProductKey = feed.ProductKey
   AND fact.ResellerKey = feed.ResellerKey
   AND fact.OrderDateKey = feed.OrderDateKey )
WHEN MATCHED THEN
 UPDATE SET fact.OrderQuantity += feed.OrderQuantity,
       fact.SalesAmount += feed.SalesAmount
WHEN NOT MATCHED THEN
 INSERT (ResellerKey,
     OrderDateKey,
     ProductKey,
     OrderQuantity,
     SalesAmount)
 VALUES (feed.ResellerKey,
     feed.OrderDateKey,
     feed.ProductKey,
     feed.OrderQuantity,
     feed.SalesAmount);
go  -- (6990 row(s) affected)
```

Using MERGE Instead of UPDATE

Checking results after MERGE

```
SELECT TOP (10) *
FROM   FactResellerSales ORDER BY        ResellerKey,    OrderDateKey,    ProductKey;
```

ResellerKey	OrderDateKey	ProductKey	OrderQuantity	SalesAmount
1	20050801	270	2	386.2702
1	20050801	275	2	749.4858
1	20050801	285	2	375.0197
1	20050801	314	4	9017.2404
1	20050801	317	2	1837.0674
1	20050801	319	4	3674.1348
1	20050801	324	4	1761.7274
1	20050801	326	2	880.8637
1	20050801	328	2	880.8637
1	20050801	332	4	1761.7274

```
SELECT AfterFactCount=COUNT(*)  FROM   FactResellerSales ;
go
-- 7658

DROP TABLE ResellerSalesTransaction;  DROP TABLE FactResellerSales;
go
```

CHAPTER 16: Modify Data - INSERT, UPDATE, DELETE & MERGE

Using MERGE Instead of UPDATE

MERGE statement can be used in the UPDATE only mode to replace UPDATE.

```sql
-- Prepare 2 test tables
USE tempdb;
SELECT TOP (5000) ResellerKey, OrderDateKey, ProductKey, OrderQuantity, SalesAmount
INTO  FactResellerSales FROM  AdventureWorksDW2012.dbo.FactResellerSales;
GO -- (5000 row(s) affected)
SELECT TOP (8000) ResellerKey, OrderDateKey, ProductKey, OrderQuantity, SalesAmount
INTO  ResellerSalesTransaction FROM  AdventureWorksDW2012.dbo.FactResellerSales;
GO -- (8000 row(s) affected)
```

```sql
-- Alter the test data
DELETE rsc
FROM  ResellerSalesTransaction rsc
    INNER JOIN (SELECT TOP 1000 * FROM  ResellerSalesTransaction
        ORDER BY ResellerKey DESC) x  -- subquery inner join
      ON x.ResellerKey = rsc.ResellerKey;
GO --(1010 row(s) affected)
UPDATE TOP (6000) ResellerSalesTransaction SET SalesAmount = SalesAmount * 1.1;
GO -- (6000 row(s) affected)
```

```sql
SELECT BeforeFactCount=COUNT(*) FROM  FactResellerSales;
GO -- 5000
```

```sql
-- Ready for the MERGE UPDATE only mode
MERGE FactResellerSales AS fact
USING (SELECT * FROM  ResellerSalesTransaction) AS feed
ON ( fact.ProductKey = feed.ProductKey
    AND fact.ResellerKey = feed.ResellerKey
    AND fact.OrderDateKey = feed.OrderDateKey )
WHEN MATCHED THEN
  UPDATE SET fact.OrderQuantity = fact.OrderQuantity + feed.OrderQuantity,
        fact.SalesAmount = fact.SalesAmount + feed.SalesAmount;
GO -- 4332 row(s) affected
```

```sql
SELECT AfterFactCount=COUNT(*) FROM  FactResellerSales;
GO -- 5000

DROP TABLE ResellerSalesTransaction;  DROP TABLE FactResellerSales;
```

CHAPTER 17: The Magic of Transact-SQL Programming

IF...ELSE Conditional

IF... ELSE is a step toward a bona fide programming language.

```
DECLARE @StringNumber varchar(32) ;
SET @StringNumber = '12,000,000';
IF EXISTS( SELECT * WHERE ISNUMERIC(@StringNumber) = 1)
        PRINT 'VALID NUMBER: ' + @StringNumber
ELSE    PRINT 'INVALID NUMBER: ' + @StringNumber;
GO
-- VALID NUMBER: 12,000,000
```

```
DECLARE @StringNumber varchar(32) = '12,000:000';

IF EXISTS( SELECT * WHERE ISNUMERIC(@StringNumber) = 1)
        PRINT CONCAT('VALID NUMBER: ' , @StringNumber)
ELSE    PRINT CONCAT('INVALID NUMBER: ', @StringNumber);
GO
-- INVALID NUMBER: 12,000:000
```

```
DECLARE @StringDate varchar(32);

SET @StringDate = '2017-03-15 18:50';

IF EXISTS( SELECT * WHERE ISDATE(@StringDate) = 1)
        PRINT 'VALID DATE: ' + @StringDate
ELSE    PRINT 'INVALID DATE: ' + @StringDate;
GO
-- Result: VALID DATE: 2017-03-15 18:50
```

```
DECLARE @StringDate varchar(32) = '20116-03-15 18:50';
IF EXISTS( SELECT * WHERE ISDATE(@StringDate) = 1)
        PRINT CONCAT('VALID DATE: ', @StringDate)
ELSE    PRINT CONCAT('INVALID DATE: ', @StringDate);
-- Result: INVALID DATE: 20116-03-15 18:50
```

WHILE Looping - UPDATE in Batches

WHILE looping can be used to break down large transaction to small batches. Executing in small batches is safer and does not block other OLTP transactions for a long time. Blocking can be seen by running sp_who system stored procedure

```
EXEC sp_who;
```

UPDATE of 121,317 rows is batched to 13 batches of 10,000 or less.

```
USE tempdb;
SELECT * INTO SOD
FROM AdventureWorks2012.Sales.SalesOrderDetail ORDER BY SalesOrderDetailID;
GO
--(121317 row(s) affected)
```

```
WHILE (2 > 1)   -- Infinite loop until BREAK is issued
 BEGIN
  UPDATE TOP ( 10000 ) SOD
  SET   UnitPriceDiscount = 0.08,  ModifiedDate = CONVERT(DATE, getdate())
  WHERE  ModifiedDate < CONVERT(DATE, getdate());

  IF @@ROWCOUNT = 0
   BEGIN
    BREAK;
   END
  -- 1 second delay - Very important for other OLTP transactions execution
  WAITFOR DELAY '00:00:01'
 END; -- WHILE
GO
```

(10000 row(s) affected)
(10000 row(s) affected)
(10000 row(s) affected)
(10000 row(s) affected)
(10000 row(s) affected)
(10000 row(s) affected)
(10000 row(s) affected)
(10000 row(s) affected)
(10000 row(s) affected)
(10000 row(s) affected)
(10000 row(s) affected)
(10000 row(s) affected)
(1317 row(s) affected)
(0 row(s) affected)

```
DROP TABLE tempdb.dbo.SOD
```

WHILE Loop Usage in Cursors

Transact-SQL logic will visit all databases on the current SQL Server instance using a cursor.
NOTE: **cursor solutions do not scale well, first choice is set-based logic if appropriate.**

```
DECLARE @CurrentDB sysname;
DECLARE AllDBCursor CURSOR  STATIC LOCAL FOR
        SELECT   name FROM    MASTER.dbo.sysdatabases
        WHERE    name NOT IN ('master','tempdb','model','msdb') ORDER BY name;
OPEN AllDBCursor;
FETCH AllDBCursor INTO @CurrentDB;
WHILE (@@FETCH_STATUS = 0) -- loop through all db-s
 BEGIN
/***** PROCESSING (like BACKUP database)   *****/
        PRINT @CurrentDB;
        FETCH AllDBCursor  INTO @CurrentDB;
 END; -- while
CLOSE AllDBCursor; DEALLOCATE AllDBCursor;

/*.... AdventureWorks
AdventureWorks2008
AdventureWorks2012
AdventureWorksDW2012  .... */
```

Transact-SQL script demonstrates a subcategory cursor.

```
USE AdventureWorks2012;
DECLARE curSubcategory CURSOR STATIC LOCAL  FOR          -- declare cursor
        SELECT ProductSubcategoryID, Subcategory=Name
        FROM Production.ProductSubcategory ORDER BY Subcategory;
DECLARE @Subcategory varchar(40), @PSID int
OPEN curSubcategory
FETCH NEXT FROM curSubcategory INTO @PSID, @Subcategory  -- fetch cursor
WHILE (@@fetch_status = 0)            -- cursor fetch_status
BEGIN -- begin cursor loop
/***** USER DEFINED PROCESSING CODE HERE  *****/
        DECLARE @Msg varchar(128);
  SELECT @Msg = CONCAT('ProductSubcategory info: ', @Subcategory,' ',CONVERT(varchar, @PSID));
        PRINT @Msg;
FETCH NEXT FROM curSubcategory INTO @PSID, @Subcategory;   -- fetch cursor
END; -- end cursor loop
CLOSE curSubcategory;   DEALLOCATE curSubcategory;

/* ... ProductSubcategory info: Bike Stands 27
ProductSubcategory info: Bottles and Cages 28
ProductSubcategory info: Bottom Brackets 5   ... */
```

CHAPTER 17: The Magic of Transact-SQL Programming

WHILE Loop with Table Variable (@tablevariable)

WHILE loop with table variable is similar to cursor WHILE loop. SELECT is used to return query results. RAISERROR or PRINT can be used to return debugging or informational messages. **RAISERROR returns message immediately.** PRINT output maybe delayed.

```sql
USE Northwind;
GO
CREATE PROC SupplierStats AS
 BEGIN
 SET nocount ON;
   DECLARE @imax INT, @i INT;
   DECLARE @Contact VARCHAR(100), @Company VARCHAR(50), @Msg nvarchar(255) ;
   DECLARE @CompanyInfo TABLE(
               RowID    INT   IDENTITY ( 1 , 1 ) PRIMARY KEY,
               CompanyName VARCHAR(100),
               ContactName VARCHAR(50)                    );
   INSERT @CompanyInfo
   SELECT CompanyName,  ContactName   FROM    Suppliers
   WHERE   ContactName LIKE '[a-k]%'    ORDER BY CompanyName;
   SET @imax = @@ROWCOUNT;   SET @i = 1;
   WHILE (@i <= @imax)      BEGIN
     SELECT @Contact = ContactName,   @Company = CompanyName
     FROM @CompanyInfo   WHERE RowID = @i;
       -------------------------------------------------------
       -- INSERT PROCESSING HERE
       -------------------------------------------------------
     SET @Msg = CONCAT(CONVERT(varchar,@i), ' Contact: ', @Contact ,' at ', @Company);
       RAISERROR (@Msg,-1,-1, '');     --    PRINT @Msg;
     SET @i = @i + 1;      END; -- WHILE
 END; -- SPROC
GO
-- Stored procedure execution - test stored procedure
EXEC SupplierStats;
```

Partial results.

1 Contact: Guylène Nodier at Aux joyeux ecclésiastiques
2 Contact: Cheryl Saylor at Bigfoot Breweries
3 Contact: Antonio del Valle Saavedra at Cooperativa de Quesos 'Las Cabras'
4 Contact: Charlotte Cooper at Exotic Liquids
5 Contact: Chantal Goulet at Forêts d'érables

CHAPTER 17: The Magic of Transact-SQL Programming

T-SQL Transaction

Transact-SQL language has been extended with features beyond ANSI SQL such as variables, IF...ELSE and WHILE. **"Transact" refers to the capability to execute business transactions which require the synchronized update of tables as one or none at all.**

DELETE from 2 Tables with TRANSACTION Control

DELETE PRIMARY KEY rows from PK table and related FOREIGN KEY rows from FK table in a single transaction. NOTE: Deleting lots of rows may interfere with online access in an ecommerce database.

Alternate method: define tables with CASCADE ON DELETE action.

```
BEGIN TRANSACTION

-- First delete from FOREIGN KEY table
DELETE OmegaFK
FROM Omega AS OmegaFK
  INNER JOIN Delta AS DeltaPK
    ON DeltaPK.ColApk = OmegaFK.ColBfk
WHERE DeltaPK.ColApk = {single value A} ;


IF @@ERROR <> 0
BEGIN
        ROLLBACK TRANSACTION;
        RAISERROR('FK delete failed.', 10, 1);
END
-- if no error, delete from PRIMARY KEY table
ELSE
        DELETE
        FROM Delta
        WHERE ColApk = = {single value A};


-- Commit transaction only if both DELETE-s succeeded
IF @@ERROR <> 0
BEGIN
        ROLLBACK TRANSACTION;
        RAISERROR('PK delete failed.', 10, 1);
ELSE
        COMMIT TRANSACTION;
```

CHAPTER 17: The Magic of Transact-SQL Programming

Stored Procedure with Input & Output Parameters

A stored procedure usually returns a table-like result set from the SELECT(s) in the stored procedure. Scalar value can also be returned with the OUTPUT option.

```sql
USE AdventureWorks2012;
GO
CREATE PROCEDURE uspQuarterSales     @StartYear  INT,      @TotalSales MONEY  OUTPUT
AS
 BEGIN -- sproc definition
   SET NOCOUNT  ON -- turn off rows affected messages
   SELECT @TotalSales = SUM(SubTotal)
   FROM   Sales.SalesOrderHeader    WHERE  OrderDate >= DATEADD(YY,@StartYear-1900,'19000101')

  SELECT  YEAR = YEAR(OrderDate),
        COALESCE(FORMAT(SUM(CASE
             WHEN DATEPART(QQ,OrderDate) = 1 THEN SubTotal
                   END),'c','en-US'),'') AS 'Q1',
        COALESCE(FORMAT(SUM(CASE
             WHEN DATEPART(QQ,OrderDate) = 2 THEN SubTotal
                   END),'c','en-US'),'') AS 'Q2',
        COALESCE(FORMAT(SUM(CASE
             WHEN DATEPART(QQ,OrderDate) = 3 THEN SubTotal
                   END),'c','en-US'),'') AS 'Q3',
        COALESCE(FORMAT(SUM(CASE
             WHEN DATEPART(QQ,OrderDate) = 4 THEN SubTotal
                   END),'c','en-US'),'') AS 'Q4'
  FROM    Sales.SalesOrderHeader soh
  WHERE   OrderDate >= DATEADD(YY,@StartYear-1900,'19000101')
   GROUP BY YEAR(OrderDate)    ORDER BY YEAR(OrderDate);
 END; -- sproc definition
GO
```

```sql
-- Execute stored procedure with INPUT/OUTPUT parameters
DECLARE @TotSales money
EXEC uspQuarterSales  2007, @TotSales OUTPUT;
SELECT TotalSales = @TotSales;
```

YEAR	Q1	Q2	Q3	Q4
2007	$6,679,873.80	$8,357,874.88	$13,681,907.05	$13,291,381.43
2008	$11,398,376.28	$14,379,545.19	$50,840.63	

TotalSales
67839799.2669

CHAPTER 17: The Magic of Transact-SQL Programming

Dynamic SQL Stored Procedure to REBUILD Indexes

The following dynamic SQL stored procedure uses database metadata to loop through all tables in the database, assemble and execute the index REBUILD command.

```sql
USE AdventureWorks2012;
GO

CREATE PROC sprocAllTablesIndexREBUILD @FILLFACTOR INT = 90
AS
 BEGIN
   DECLARE @DatabaseName SYSNAME = DB_NAME(),
       @TableName   VARCHAR(256);
   DECLARE @DynamicSQL NVARCHAR(max) = CONCAT('DECLARE cursorForAllTables CURSOR FOR
            SELECT CONCAT(TABLE_SCHEMA,''.'', TABLE_NAME) AS TABLENAME    FROM ',
@DatabaseName,
        '.INFORMATION_SCHEMA.TABLES WHERE   TABLE_TYPE = ''BASE TABLE''');
   BEGIN
     EXEC sp_executeSQL
      @DynamicSQL; -- create tables cursor
     OPEN cursorForAllTables;

     FETCH NEXT FROM cursorForAllTables INTO @TableName;
     WHILE ( @@FETCH_STATUS = 0 )
      BEGIN
        SET @DynamicSQL = CONCAT('ALTER INDEX ALL ON ', @TableName,
             ' REBUILD WITH ( FILLFACTOR = ',
                      CONVERT(VARCHAR, @FILLFACTOR), ')'  );
        PRINT @DynamicSQL;  -- test & debug
        EXEC sp_executeSQL
          @DynamicSQL;
        FETCH NEXT FROM cursorForAllTables INTO @TableName;
      END; -- cursor WHILE
     CLOSE cursorForAllTables;   DEALLOCATE cursorForAllTables;
   END;
 END; -- sproc
GO
-- Command(s) completed successfully.

-- Reindex tables with 85% fill factor leaving 15% free space for growth
EXEC sprocAllTablesIndexREBUILD 85;
/*
ALTER INDEX ALL ON Production.ScrapReason REBUILD WITH ( FILLFACTOR = 85)
ALTER INDEX ALL ON HumanResources.Shift REBUILD WITH ( FILLFACTOR = 85)
....  */
```

User-Defined Functions

Table-Valued Functions

A table-valued function returns a table variable, therefore, it has to be invoked like it were a table in a query. T-SQL table-valued function creates a table from a delimited string of values.

```sql
CREATE FUNCTION dbo.ufnSplitDelimitedString (  @StringList VARCHAR(MAX),    @Delimiter CHAR(1))
RETURNS @TableList TABLE(ID int identity(1,1), StringLiteral VARCHAR(128))
BEGIN
   IF @StringList = '' RETURN;
   IF @Delimiter = ''
   BEGIN
     WITH Split AS                             -- Recursive CTE
        ( SELECT CharOne=LEFT(@StringList,1),R=RIGHT(@StringList,len(@StringList)-1)
          UNION ALL
          SELECT LEFT(R,1), R=RIGHT(R, len(R)-1)
          FROM Split   WHERE LEN(R)>0  )        -- End of CTE
     INSERT @TableList
     SELECT CharOne FROM Split    OPTION ( MAXRECURSION 0);
     RETURN;
   END; -- IF
   DECLARE @XML xml=CONCAT('<root><csv>',replace(@StringList,@Delimiter,'</csv><csv>'),
                           '</csv></root>');
   INSERT @TableList
   SELECT rtrim(ltrim(replace(Word.value('.','nvarchar(128)'),char(10),'')))    AS ListMember
   FROM @XML.nodes('/root/csv') AS WordList(Word);
RETURN;
END; -- FUNCTION
GO
```

```sql
SELECT * FROM dbo.ufnSplitDelimitedString ('New York, California, Arizona, Texas, Toronto, Grand Canyon, Yosemite,  Yellowstone, Niagara Falls, Belgium, Denmark, South Africa, Sweden', ',');
```

ID	StringLiteral
1	New York
2	California
3	Arizona
4	Texas
5	Toronto
6	Grand Canyon
7	Yosemite
8	Yellowstone
9	Niagara Falls
10	Belgium
11	Denmark
12	South Africa
13	Sweden

CHAPTER 17: The Magic of Transact-SQL Programming

User-Defined Functions

Table-Valued Function for PRIME Numbers Generation

Transact-SQL table-valued function generates prime numbers up to the input parameter limit.

```
USE AdventureWorks2012;
GO

CREATE FUNCTION ufnPrimeNumbers ( @Stop INT)
RETURNS @Result TABLE  (Prime INT)
BEGIN
WITH CTE ( SeqNo)
   AS (SELECT 0
      UNION ALL
      SELECT SeqNo + 1
      FROM   CTE
      WHERE  SeqNo < @Stop)
INSERT @Result
SELECT PrimeNo = N2.SeqNo
FROM   CTE N1
    INNER JOIN CTE N2
  ON  N2.SeqNo % N1.SeqNo > 0
     AND N2.SeqNo % 2 > 0
     AND N1.SeqNo < N2.SeqNo
     AND N2.SeqNo > 1
     AND N1.SeqNo >= 1
GROUP  BY N2.SeqNo
HAVING ( N2.SeqNo - COUNT(*) ) = 2
OPTION ( MAXRECURSION 0);
RETURN ;
END;
GO

SELECT * FROM dbo.ufnPrimeNumbers (1000);
GO
-- (167 row(s) affected) - Partial results.
```

Prime
3
5
7
11
13
17
19
23
29
31

CHAPTER 17: The Magic of Transact-SQL Programming

Inline Functions

An inline user-defined function, returns table, can be used as a parameterized view.

```
USE AdventureWorks2012
GO

CREATE FUNCTION Sales.ufnStaffSalesByFiscalYear (@OrderYear INT)
RETURNS TABLE AS
RETURN
SELECT
     CONVERT(date, soh.OrderDate)                                             AS OrderDate
    ,CONCAT(p.FirstName, ' ', COALESCE(p.MiddleName, ''), ' ', p.LastName)    AS FullName
    ,e.JobTitle
    ,st.Name                                                                  AS SalesTerritory
    ,FORMAT(soh.SubTotal, 'c', 'en-US')                                       AS SalesAmount
    ,YEAR(DATEADD(mm, 6, soh.OrderDate))                                      AS FiscalYear
FROM Sales.SalesPerson sp
    INNER JOIN Sales.SalesOrderHeader soh
        ON sp.BusinessEntityID = soh.SalesPersonID
    INNER JOIN Sales.SalesTerritory st
        ON sp.TerritoryID = st.TerritoryID
    INNER JOIN HumanResources.Employee e
        ON soh.SalesPersonID = e.BusinessEntityID
    INNER JOIN Person.Person p
        ON p.BusinessEntityID = sp.BusinessEntityID
WHERE         soh.OrderDate >= datefromparts(@OrderYear, 1, 1)
          AND soh.OrderDate < dateadd(yy,1, datefromparts(@OrderYear, 1, 1));
GO
-- Command(s) completed successfully.
```

```
SELECT * FROM Sales.ufnStaffSalesByFiscalYear (2007)
ORDER BY FullName, CONVERT(money, SalesAmount) DESC;   --  SalesAmount (string) does not sort correctly
--( 1476  row(s) affected)  -- Partial results.
```

OrderDate	FullName	JobTitle	SalesTerritory	SalesAmount	FiscalYear
2007-08-01	David R Campbell	Sales Representative	Northwest	$101,609.29	2008
2007-07-01	David R Campbell	Sales Representative	Northwest	$93,397.64	2008
2007-04-01	David R Campbell	Sales Representative	Northwest	$75,104.65	2007
2007-07-01	David R Campbell	Sales Representative	Northwest	$74,149.95	2008
2007-04-01	David R Campbell	Sales Representative	Northwest	$73,963.26	2007
2007-08-01	David R Campbell	Sales Representative	Northwest	$71,283.24	2008
2007-09-01	David R Campbell	Sales Representative	Northwest	$66,871.84	2008
2007-01-01	David R Campbell	Sales Representative	Northwest	$63,864.71	2007
2007-11-01	David R Campbell	Sales Representative	Northwest	$63,339.26	2008
2007-10-01	David R Campbell	Sales Representative	Northwest	$60,519.95	2008

Dynamic PIVOT Script

Scalar Functions

A scalar user-defined function returns a scalar value. It can be used in a query wherever a single value is required.

```sql
USE AdventureWorks2012;
GO
CREATE FUNCTION dbo.ufnNumberToEnglish (@Number INT)
RETURNS VARCHAR(1024)  AS
 BEGIN
   DECLARE @Below20 TABLE    ( ID  INT IDENTITY ( 0, 1 ),   Word VARCHAR(32) );
   DECLARE @Tens TABLE  ( ID  INT IDENTITY ( 2, 1 ),    Word VARCHAR(32) );
   INSERT @Below20  (Word)
   VALUES('Zero'), ('One'),('Two'),  ('Three'), ('Four'), ('Five'), ('Six'), ('Seven'), ('Eight'),
        ('Nine'), ('Ten'), ('Eleven'), ('Twelve'), ('Thirteen'), ('Fourteen'), ('Fifteen'),
        ('Sixteen'), ('Seventeen'), ('Eighteen'), ('Nineteen');
   INSERT @Tens
   VALUES('Twenty'),   ('Thirty'), ('Forty'), ('Fifty'), ('Sixty'), ('Seventy'), ('Eighty'), ('Ninety');
   DECLARE @English VARCHAR(1024) = (SELECT CASE
         WHEN @Number = 0 THEN ''
         WHEN @Number BETWEEN 1 AND 19
             THEN (SELECT Word FROM   @Below20 WHERE  ID = @Number)
         WHEN @Number BETWEEN 20 AND 99 THEN
      CONCAT((SELECT Word FROM   @Tens
WHERE  ID = @Number / 10), '-', dbo.ufnNumberToEnglish(@Number%10))
      WHEN @Number BETWEEN 100 AND 999 THEN CONCAT((
          dbo.ufnNumberToEnglish(@Number / 100) ), ' Hundred ',
dbo.ufnNumberToEnglish(@Number%100))
      WHEN @Number BETWEEN 1000 AND 999999 THEN CONCAT((
          dbo.ufnNumberToEnglish(@Number / 1000) ), ' Thousand ',
dbo.ufnNumberToEnglish(@Number%1000))
      WHEN @Number BETWEEN 1000000 AND 999999999 THEN CONCAT((
          dbo.ufnNumberToEnglish(@Number / 1000000) ), ' Million ',
dbo.ufnNumberToEnglish(@Number%1000000))
    ELSE ' INVALID INPUT'  END);
   SELECT @English = RTRIM(@English);
   SELECT @English = RTRIM(LEFT(@English, len(@English) - 1))    WHERE  RIGHT(@English, 1) = '-';
   RETURN ( @English );                         END;
GO  -- Command(s) completed successfully.

SELECT dbo.ufnNumberToEnglish (9999);   -- Nine Thousand Nine Hundred Ninety-Nine

SELECT dbo.ufnNumberToEnglish (1000001);  -- One Million One

SELECT dbo.ufnNumberToEnglish (7777777);
-- Seven Million Seven Hundred Seventy-Seven Thousand Seven Hundred Seventy-Seven
```

CHAPTER 17: The Magic of Transact-SQL Programming

Dynamic PIVOT Script

Static PIVOT has pretty limited role since it has to be changed when data changes effects the PIVOT range. Dynamic SQL makes PIVOT data driven. Instead of hard-wired columns, dynamic PIVOT builds the columns from the data dynamically.

```sql
USE AdventureWorks;
GO

DECLARE @OrderYear AS TABLE
 (
   YYYY INT NOT NULL PRIMARY KEY
 );
DECLARE @DynamicSQL AS NVARCHAR(4000) ;

INSERT INTO @OrderYear
SELECT DISTINCT YEAR(OrderDate)
FROM   Sales.SalesOrderHeader;

DECLARE @ReportColumnNames AS NVARCHAR(MAX), @IterationYear   AS INT;

SET @IterationYear = (SELECT MIN(YYYY)    FROM  @OrderYear);
SET @ReportColumnNames = N'';

-- Assemble pivot list dynamically
WHILE ( @IterationYear IS NOT NULL )
 BEGIN
   SET @ReportColumnNames = @ReportColumnNames + N','
            + QUOTENAME(CAST(@IterationYear AS NVARCHAR(10)));
   SET @IterationYear = (SELECT MIN(YYYY)
            FROM   @OrderYear
            WHERE  YYYY > @IterationYear);
 END;

SET @ReportColumnNames = SUBSTRING(@ReportColumnNames, 2,
          LEN(@ReportColumnNames));

PRINT @ReportColumnNames; -- [2001],[2002],[2003],[2004]

SET @DynamicSQL = CONCAT(N'SELECT * FROM (SELECT [Store (Freight Summary)]=s.Name,
      YEAR(OrderDate) AS OrderYear,  Freight = convert(money, convert(varchar, Freight))
      FROM Sales.SalesOrderHeader soh
      INNER JOIN Sales.Store s
      ON soh.CustomerID = s.CustomerID) as Header
      PIVOT (SUM(Freight)   FOR OrderYear IN(', @ReportColumnNames,N')) AS Pvt ORDER BY 1;');
-- T-SQL script continued
```

INSERT, UPDATE & DELETE through a View

```
PRINT @DynamicSQL; -- Testing & debugging
/* SELECT * FROM (SELECT [Store (Freight Summary)]=s.Name,
      YEAR(OrderDate) AS OrderYear, Freight = convert(money, convert(varchar, Freight))
      FROM Sales.SalesOrderHeader soh
      INNER JOIN Sales.Store s    ON soh.CustomerID = s.CustomerID) as Header
      PIVOT (SUM(Freight)   FOR OrderYear IN([2001],[2002],[2003],[2004]))  AS Pvt ORDER BY 1;*/

-- Execute dynamic sql
EXEC sp_executesql  @DynamicSQL;
GO  -- (633 row(s) affected) - Partial results.
```

Store (Freight Summary)	2001	2002	2003	2004
A Bike Store	921.55	1637.24	NULL	NULL
A Great Bicycle Company	142.08	114.34	15.24	NULL
A Typical Bike Shop	976.61	1529.08	NULL	NULL
Acceptable Sales & Service	12.58	25.17	NULL	NULL

INSERT, UPDATE & DELETE through a View

Underlying table can be modified through a view, thus adding flexibility to security access since a view can be permissioned independently of the table.

```
USE tempdb;
SELECT CONVERT(INT, ProductID) AS ID, Name AS ProductName, ListPrice, ModifiedDate INTO Product
FROM AdventureWorks2012.Production.Product;
GO -- (504 row(s) affected)
CREATE VIEW vProduct AS SELECT * FROM Product;
GO
UPDATE vProduct SET ModifiedDate = '2018-01-01';
GO -- (504 row(s) affected)
INSERT vProduct VALUES (2000, 'Three-Wheeler Bike', $999.99, getdate());
GO -- (1 row(s) affected)
DELETE TOP (10) FROM vProduct;
GO -- (1 row(s) affected)
SELECT TOP (1) * FROM Product;  -- 322 Chainring      0.00    2018-01-01 00:00:00.000
GO
DROP VIEW dbo.vProduct;
DROP TABLE tempdb.dbo.Product;
GO
```

Sensitive Data Audit Trigger

Triggers can be used to track sensitive data changes into an audit table. The OUTPUT clause is an alternative, but not exactly equivalent.

```
USE Payroll;
GO
```

```
CREATE TRIGGER uTrgEmployeeUpdate
ON Employee
AFTER UPDATE
AS
  IF ( Update(Salary)
       OR Update(SSN) )
    BEGIN
      INSERT INTO CorpSecurityEmployeeAudit
            (auditlogtype,
             auditEmployeeDeptID,
             auditEmployeeID,
             auditEmployeeSalary,
             auditEmployeeSSN,
             auditUpdatedBy)
      SELECT 'PREVIOUSDATA',
          DeptID,
          EmployeeID,
          Salary,
          SSN,
          User_name()
      FROM   DELETED

      INSERT INTO CorpSecurityEmployeeAudit
            (auditlogtype,
             auditEmployeeDeptID,
             auditEmployeeID,
             auditEmployeeSalary,
             auditEmployeeSSN,
             auditUpdatedBy)
      SELECT 'NEWDATA',
          DeptID,
          EmployeeID,
          Salary,
          SSN,
          User_name()
      FROM   INSERTED
    END;
GO
```

Automatic Timestamp Trigger

Whenever the Person.Contact is updated, the ModifiedDate will be updated to current time by the update after trigger. NOTE: disable/drop other update triggers on this table, if any, for the test.

```sql
USE AdventureWorks;
GO

CREATE TRIGGER uTrgContactTimestamp
ON Person.Contact
FOR UPDATE
AS
  BEGIN
   IF TRIGGER_NESTLEVEL() > 1    RETURN;
    UPDATE Person.Contact  SET    Person.Contact.ModifiedDate = CURRENT_TIMESTAMP
    FROM   Person.Contact c
        INNER JOIN INSERTED i
         ON c.ContactID = i.ContactID
  END
GO
-- (1 row(s) affected)

SELECT *
FROM  Person.Contact
WHERE  FirstName = 'Kim'   AND MiddleName = 'B'    AND LastName = 'Abercrombie'
GO
-- ModifiedDate: 2000-02-10 00:00:00.000

-- Updating a column will automatically update the ModifiedDate
UPDATE Person.Contact         SET    Phone = '299 484-3924'
WHERE  FirstName = 'Kim'   AND MiddleName = 'B'    AND LastName = 'Abercrombie'
GO

SELECT *
FROM   Person.Contact WHERE  FirstName = 'Kim'   AND MiddleName = 'B'   AND LastName = 'Abercrombie'
GO
-- ModifiedDate: 2018-08-11 07:22:01.157

-- Cleanup
DROP TRIGGER Person.uTrgContactTimestamp
```

CHAPTER 17: The Magic of Transact-SQL Programming

Recursive Product Assembly

Recursive Common Table Expression (CTE) is used to assemble a bike frame based on the BillOfMaterials table.

```
USE AdventureWorks2012;

DECLARE @ProductID int = 831;
WITH CTE(AssemblyID, ComponentID, PerAssemblyQty, AssemblyLevel) AS
(       SELECT bom0.ProductAssemblyID, bom0.ComponentID, bom0.PerAssemblyQty,
                0 AS AssemblyLevel
        FROM Production.BillOfMaterials AS bom0
        WHERE bom0.ProductAssemblyID = @ProductID
                AND bom0.EndDate is null
        UNION ALL
        SELECT bom.ProductAssemblyID, bom.ComponentID, p.PerAssemblyQty,
                AssemblyLevel + 1
        FROM Production.BillOfMaterials AS bom
                INNER JOIN CTE AS p
                        ON bom.ProductAssemblyID = p.ComponentID   AND bom.EndDate is null   )
SELECT pp.Name AS ProductName, AssemblyID, ComponentID,
        p.Name AS AssemblyName, PerAssemblyQty, AssemblyLevel
FROM CTE
        INNER JOIN Production.Product AS p
                ON CTE.ComponentID = p.ProductID
        INNER JOIN Production.Product AS pp
                ON CTE.AssemblyID = pp.ProductID
ORDER BY AssemblyLevel, AssemblyID, ComponentID;
```

ProductName	AssemblyID	ComponentID	AssemblyName	PerAssemblyQty	AssemblyLevel
ML Mountain Frame - Black, 44	831	324	Chain Stays	2.00	0
ML Mountain Frame - Black, 44	831	325	Decal 1	2.00	0
ML Mountain Frame - Black, 44	831	326	Decal 2	1.00	0
ML Mountain Frame - Black, 44	831	327	Down Tube	1.00	0
ML Mountain Frame - Black, 44	831	399	Head Tube	1.00	0
ML Mountain Frame - Black, 44	831	492	Paint - Black	8.00	0
ML Mountain Frame - Black, 44	831	532	Seat Stays	4.00	0
ML Mountain Frame - Black, 44	831	533	Seat Tube	1.00	0
ML Mountain Frame - Black, 44	831	534	Top Tube	1.00	0
ML Mountain Frame - Black, 44	831	803	ML Fork	1.00	0
Chain Stays	324	486	Metal Sheet 5	2.00	1
Down Tube	327	483	Metal Sheet 3	1.00	1
Head Tube	399	485	Metal Sheet 4	1.00	1
Seat Stays	532	484	Metal Sheet 7	4.00	1
Seat Tube	533	478	Metal Bar 2	1.00	1
Top Tube	534	482	Metal Sheet 2	1.00	1
ML Fork	803	316	Blade	1.00	1
ML Fork	803	331	Fork End	1.00	1
ML Fork	803	350	Fork Crown	1.00	1
ML Fork	803	531	Steerer	1.00	1
Blade	316	486	Metal Sheet 5	1.00	2
Fork End	331	482	Metal Sheet 2	1.00	2
Fork Crown	350	486	Metal Sheet 5	1.00	2
Steerer	531	487	Metal Sheet 6	1.00	2

Percent on Base Calculation

When deriving percent on base, we need to calculate the overall total in a single value subquery to use it as denominator in the percentile calculation.

```
USE AdventureWorks2012;

SELECT YEAR(OrderDate) AS [Year],
    FORMAT(SUM(TotalDue),'c0','en-US') AS YearTotal,
    FORMAT(SUM(TotalDue) /
        (SELECT SUM(TotalDue) FROM Sales.SalesOrderHeader),'p0') AS Percentile
FROM Sales.SalesOrderHeader
GROUP BY YEAR(OrderDate)
ORDER BY YEAR ASC;
```

Year	YearTotal	Percentage
2005	$12,693,251	10 %
2006	$34,463,848	28 %
2007	$47,171,490	38 %
2008	$28,888,198	23 %

Adding a Grand Total line with ROLLUP.

```
SELECT COALESCE(CONVERT(varchar,YEAR(OrderDate)), 'Grand Total') AS [Year],
    FORMAT(SUM(TotalDue),'c0','en-US') AS [SalesTotal],
    FORMAT(SUM(TotalDue) /
        (SELECT SUM(TotalDue) FROM Sales.SalesOrderHeader),'p0') AS Percentage
FROM Sales.SalesOrderHeader
GROUP BY YEAR(OrderDate)
    WITH ROLLUP
ORDER BY YEAR ASC;
```

Year	SalesTotal	Percentage
2005	$12,693,251	10 %
2006	$34,463,848	28 %
2007	$47,171,490	38 %
2008	$28,888,198	23 %
Grand Total	$123,216,786	100 %

CHAPTER 18: Exporting & Importing Data

Saving a T-SQL Script as .sql File

Any T-SQL script can be saved as .sql file. One easy way is saving from Management Studio Query Editor. Here is the script we will save.

```sql
CREATE TABLE #Order (
    OrderID INT IDENTITY(1,1) PRIMARY KEY,
    ProductID INT NOT NULL,
    StringDate varchar(32) NOT NULL,
    OrderDate AS TRY_PARSE(StringDate AS DATE)); -- new in SS 2012

INSERT #Order VALUES (100, '10/23/2016');
INSERT #Order VALUES (101, 'OCT 23 2016');
INSERT #Order VALUES (102, '23 OCT 2016');
INSERT #Order VALUES (1022, '10/32/2016');   -- Invalid date
INSERT #Order VALUES (112, '23 october 2016');
INSERT #Order VALUES (112, '2016 OCT 23');

SELECT * FROM #Order;
DROP TABLE #Order;
```

	Order...	Produc...	StringDate	OrderDate
1	1	100	10/23/2016	2016-10-23
2	2	101	OCT 23 2016	2016-10-23
3	3	102	23 OCT 2016	2016-10-23
4	4	1022	10/32/2016	NULL
5	5	112	23 october 2016	2016-10-23
6	6	112	2016 OCT 23	2016-10-23

Click on File, click on Save .. As, choose a path and enter the file name for the script.

To load it back: click on File, click on Open File, locate file in Open File dialog pop-up.

Executing a .sql Script File Using SQLCMD

The SQLCMD command line utility can be used to execute a .sql script file typically with the -i (input) and -o (output) options. **Note: with any of the Command Prompt utilities the command line should not be broken with carriage return or line feed (CR/LF), it has to be one long line.**

SQLCMD -S"HPESTAR" -Uyourlogin -Psecret007 -i "f:\data\sql\tryparsedemo.sql" -o"f:\data\result\tryparsedemo.txt"

"HPESTAR" is the name of the SQL Server. With Windows authentication:

SQLCMD -S"HPESTAR" -i "f:\data\sql\tryparsedemo.sql" -o"f:\data\result\tryparsedemo.txt"

```
Microsoft Windows [Version 6.1.7601]
Copyright (c) 2009 Microsoft Corporation.  All rights reserved.

C:\Users\Owner>SQLCMD -S"HPESTAR"  -i "f:\data\sql\tryparsedemo.sql" -o"f:\data\result\tryparsedemo.txt"

C:\Users\Owner>
```

The output file collects warnings, messages, errors and results.

```
(1 rows affected)

(1 rows affected)

(1 rows affected)

(1 rows affected)

(1 rows affected)

(1 rows affected)
OrderID    ProductID  StringDate           OrderDate
---------- ---------- -------------------- ----------
         1        100 10/23/2016           2016-10-23
         2        101 OCT 23 2016          2016-10-23
         3        102 23 OCT 2016          2016-10-23
         4       1022 10/32/2016           NULL
         5        112 23 october 2016      2016-10-23
         6        112 2016 OCT 23          2016-10-23

(6 rows affected)
```

CHAPTER 18: Exporting & Importing Data

Making a T-SQL Script Rerunnable

It takes special attention to make a T-SQL script re-executable as many times as desired. A CREATE VIEW script can only be executed once.

```
CREATE VIEW vSalesOrder
AS
SELECT soh.*, sod.OrderQty, sod.ProductID
FROM AdventureWorks2012.Sales.SalesOrderHeader AS soh
INNER JOIN AdventureWorks2012.Sales.SalesOrderDetail AS sod
    ON soh.SalesOrderID = sod.SalesOrderID
GO
```

Command(s) completed successfully.

Repeat execution gives an error.

```
CREATE VIEW vSalesOrder
AS
SELECT soh.*, sod.OrderQty, sod.ProductID
FROM AdventureWorks2012.Sales.SalesOrderHeader AS soh
INNER JOIN AdventureWorks2012.Sales.SalesOrderDetail AS sod
    ON soh.SalesOrderID = sod.SalesOrderID
GO
```

Msg 2714, Level 16, State 3, Procedure vSalesOrder, Line 1
There is already an object named 'vSalesOrder' in the database.

CHAPTER 18: Exporting & Importing Data

Making a T-SQL Script Rerunnable

IF...ELSE Conditional Way to Make a Script Rerunnable

IF...ELSE is frequently the solution to prepare a rerunnable script. In this instance, first we check if the view exists. If it doesn't exist, we just go ahead and create it. If indeed it exists, we drop it first, then create it again.

```sql
-- T-SQL rerunnable script
USE AdventureWorks2012;
IF EXISTS (SELECT TABLE_NAME FROM INFORMATION_SCHEMA.VIEWS
        WHERE TABLE_NAME = 'vSalesOrder')
    DROP VIEW [dbo].[vSalesOrder];
GO

CREATE VIEW vSalesOrder AS
    SELECT soh.*, sod.OrderQty, sod.ProductID
    FROM Sales.SalesOrderHeader AS soh
        INNER JOIN Sales.SalesOrderDetail AS sod
            ON soh.SalesOrderID = sod.SalesOrderID;
GO

SELECT * FROM vSalesOrder ORDER BY SalesOrderID DESC;
-- (121317 row(s) affected)
```

	SalesOrde...	RevisionNum...	OrderDate	DueDate
1	75123	3	2008-07-31 00:00:00.000	2008-08-12 00:00:00.000
2	75123	3	2008-07-31 00:00:00.000	2008-08-12 00:00:00.000
3	75123	3	2008-07-31 00:00:00.000	2008-08-12 00:00:00.000
4	75122	3	2008-07-31 00:00:00.000	2008-08-12 00:00:00.000

CHAPTER 18: Exporting & Importing Data

bcp Usage for Exporting & Importing Data

bcp (Bulk Copy Program) is a command line utility for moving data. The Production.Product table is exported to a flat file with bcp using Windows authentication.

For SQL Server authentication, add the "-Uyourlogin -Pyourpasswrd" parameters. **Note: the command must be one long line without breaks.**

```
Command Prompt
Microsoft Windows [Version 6.1.7601]
Copyright (c) 2009 Microsoft Corporation.  All rights reserved.

C:\Users\Owner>bcp AdventureWorks2012.Production.Product out F:\data\export\prod
uctz.txt -w -T -S"HPESTAR"

Starting copy...
SQLState = S1000, NativeError = 0
Error = [Microsoft][SQL Server Native Client 11.0]Warning: BCP import with a for
mat file will convert empty strings in delimited columns to NULL.

504 rows copied.
Network packet size (bytes): 4096
Clock Time (ms.) Total     : 125    Average : (4032.00 rows per sec.)

C:\Users\Owner>
```

The **results of a query execution** can be exported with bcp as well using the queryout option. Rule is the same, no carriage return or line feed in the command no matter how long is it. The command can be edited in SSMS Query Editor and pasted into Command Prompt with Right Mouse Click Paste. CTRL-V does not work.

```
Command Prompt
C:\Users\Owner>bcp "SELECT * from AdventureWorks2012.HumanResources.Department"
queryout F:\data\export\departmentz.txt -w -T -S"HPESTAR"

Starting copy...

16 rows copied.
Network packet size (bytes): 4096
Clock Time (ms.) Total     : 453    Average : (35.32 rows per sec.)

C:\Users\Owner>
```

CHAPTER 18: Exporting & Importing Data

bcp Usage for Exporting & Importing Data

Importing Data with the bcp Utility

Importing is very similar to exporting. For better control though it is necessary to use a format file. First we create an empty table for the data.

```
use tempdb;
select TOP 0 * into product1 from AdventureWorks2012.Production.Product;
go
```

We are ready to execute the bcp import command.

```
C:\Users\Owner>bcp tempdb.dbo.product1 in F:\data\export\productz.txt -w -T -S"H
PESTAR"

Starting copy...

504 rows copied.
Network packet size (bytes): 4096
Clock Time (ms.) Total     : 312     Average : (1615.38 rows per sec.)

C:\Users\Owner>
```

Checking the results.

```
SELECT * FROM tempdb.dbo.product1 ORDER BY ProductID;
-- (504 row(s) affected)
```

	Product...	Name	ProductNum...	MakeFl...	FinishedGoodsF...	Colo
1	1	Adjustable Race	AR-5381	0	0	NUL
2	2	Bearing Ball	BA-8327	0	0	NUL
3	3	BB Ball Bearing	BE-2349	1	0	NUL
4	4	Headset Ball Bearings	BE-2908	0	0	NUL
5	5	Blade	BL-2036	1	0	NUL
6	6	LL Crankarm	CA-5965	0	0	Blac
7	7	ML Crankarm	CA-6738	0	0	Blac
8	8	HL Crankarm	CA-7457	0	0	Blac

CHAPTER 18: Exporting & Importing Data

Exporting Data with SQL Server Import and Export Wizard

We will export a view query results to a new Excel worksheet. The SELECT query returns 8,914 rows from the vPersonDemographics view.

```
SELECT BusinessEntityID
      ,TotalPurchaseYTD
      ,DateFirstPurchase
      ,BirthDate
      ,MaritalStatus
      ,YearlyIncome
      ,Gender
      ,TotalChildren
      ,NumberChildrenAtHome
      ,Education
      ,Occupation
      ,HomeOwnerFlag
      ,NumberCarsOwned
FROM AdventureWorks2012.Sales.vPersonDemographics
WHERE YearlyIncome is not null AND TotalPurchaseYTD > 100.0
ORDER BY DateFirstPurchase DESC;
```

	BusinessEntit...	TotalPurchaseY...	DateFirstPurchase	BirthDate
1	6615	123.98	2004-07-29 00:00:00.000	1976-06-19 00:00:0
2	16467	117.96	2004-07-26 00:00:00.000	1973-03-22 00:00:0
3	19475	119.98	2004-07-24 00:00:00.000	1929-07-03 00:00:0
4	14319	119.98	2004-07-23 00:00:00.000	1963-05-09 00:00:0

HPESTAR (11.0 RTM)   HPESTAR\Owner (52)   AdventureWorks2012   00:00:02   8914 rows

CHAPTER 18: Exporting & Importing Data

Exporting Data with SQL Server Import and Export Wizard

Starting the SSIS Import and Export Wizard

We start the SSIS Import/Export Wizard by a Right Click on the database in Object Explorer. It does not matter much if we choose Import Data or Export data since it only presets the destination or source pages respectively.

CHAPTER 18: Exporting & Importing Data

Optional Wizard Starting Welcome Screen
There is a checkmark option on the bottom to turn it off.

Exporting Data with SQL Server Import and Export Wizard

Configuring the Data Source Page
The data source is a database, therefore the server and database must be set up on this page.

Configuring the Destination Page

The destination is a new Excel worksheet. Path & name must be given.

SQL Server Import and Export Wizard

Choose a Destination
Specify where to copy data to.

Destination: Microsoft Excel

Excel connection settings

Excel file path:
C:\data\export\AW12Demographics.xls   Browse...

Excel version:
Microsoft Excel 2007

☑ First row has column names

[Help]   [< Back]   [Next >]   [Finish >>|]   [Cancel]

Exporting Data with SQL Server Import and Export Wizard

Specifying Table/View or Query Source

The Wizard logic branches based on what radio button we choose. If the choose table/view source, the next dialog box offers the entire list of tables/views in the database for checkmark selection.

Entering the Query Source

We should use a tested query in order to avoid a failure in the execution of the generated SSIS package. Parse option is available for syntax checking.

```
SELECT BusinessEntityID
    ,TotalPurchaseYTD
    ,DateFirstPurchase
    ,BirthDate
    ,MaritalStatus
    ,YearlyIncome
    ,Gender
    ,TotalChildren
    ,NumberChildrenAtHome
    ,Education
    ,Occupation
    ,HomeOwnerFlag
    ,NumberCarsOwned
FROM AdventureWorks2012.Sales.vPersonDemographics
WHERE YearlyIncome is not null AND TotalPurchaseYTD > 100.0
ORDER BY DateFirstPurchase DESC;
```

Option to Edit Mappings & Review Data

If you trust the Wizard, you can just click "Next". Otherwise, you can edit column mappings and review the data.

Edit Mappings & Preview

The next Wizard screen offers popup windows for editing the column mappings, changing the CREATE TABLE SQL and preview the data. We don't perform any change.

Column Mappings

Source: [Query]
Destination: `Query`

(•) Create destination table   Edit SQL...
( ) Delete rows in destination table   [ ] Drop and re-create destination table
( ) Append rows to the destination table

Mappings:

Source	Destination	Type	Nullable	Size	Precision	Scale
BusinessEntityID	BusinessEntityID	Long	☐			
TotalPurchaseYTD	TotalPurchaseYTD	Currency	☑			
DateFirstPurchase	DateFirstPurchase	VarChar	☑	29		
BirthDate	BirthDate	VarChar	☑	29		
MaritalStatus	MaritalStatus	LongText	☑			
YearlyIncome	YearlyIncome	LongText	☑			
Gender	Gender	LongText	☑			
TotalChildren	TotalChildren	Long	☑			
NumberChildrenA...	NumberChildrenA...	Long	☑			

Source column: BusinessEntityID int (4) (10, 255) NOT NULL

[OK] [Cancel]

Preview Data

Source: SELECT BusinessEntityID
         ,TotalPurchaseYTD

BusinessEntityID	TotalPurchaseYTD	DateFirstPurchase	BirthDate
6615	123.98	7/29/2004 12:00:00 AM	6/19/1976 12:00:00 AM
16467	117.96	7/26/2004 12:00:00 AM	3/22/1973 12:00:00 AM
19475	119.98	7/24/2004 12:00:00 AM	7/3/1929 12:00:00 AM
14319	119.98	7/23/2004 12:00:00 AM	5/9/1963 12:00:00 AM
8213	106.93	7/23/2004 12:00:00 AM	2/26/1976 12:00:00 AM
12168	106.95	7/17/2004 12:00:00 AM	10/26/1962 12:00:00 AM
20478	124.97	7/9/2004 12:00:00 AM	10/12/1946 12:00:00 AM
7592	119.98	7/6/2004 12:00:00 AM	2/5/1947 12:00:00 AM
6488	539.99	6/30/2004 12:00:00 AM	3/23/1969 12:00:00 AM

[OK]

Exporting Data with SQL Server Import and Export Wizard

Review Data Type Mappings
Column data mappings can be reviewed in detail on this dialog box.

SQL Server Import and Export Wizard					
Review Data Type Mapping Select a table to review how its data types map to those in the destination and how it handles conversion issues.					

Table:

Source	Destination
⚠ [Query]	🔲 `Query`

Data type mapping:

Source Column	Source Type	Destination Col...	Destination Type	Convert	On Er
⊘ BusinessEntityID	int	BusinessEntityID	Long		
⊘ TotalPurchase...	money	TotalPurchase...	Currency		
⚠ DateFirstPurch...	datetime2	DateFirstPurch...	VarChar	✓	Use C
⚠ BirthDate	datetime2	BirthDate	VarChar	✓	Use C
⊘ MaritalStatus	nvarchar	MaritalStatus	LongText		
⊘ YearlyIncome	nvarchar	YearlyIncome	LongText		
⊘ Gender	nvarchar	Gender	LongText		
⊘ TotalChildren	int	TotalChildren	Long		

To view conversion details, double-click the row that contains the column source type to be converted.

On Error (global):   Fail
On Truncation (global):   Fail

[Help]   [< Back] [Next >] [Finish >>|]   [Cancel]

CHAPTER 18: Exporting & Importing Data

Save and/or Run Package

The Wizard generated SSIS package can be saved for future use or enhancements. If we run it immediately without saving, it will just go away after execution.

Exporting Data with SQL Server Import and Export Wizard

Verification Screen before Execution

At this point we still can go back and make changes should it be necessary. Once we click on Finish and we did not checkmark Save, the package will execute and goes away on success or failure.

```
SQL Server Import and Export Wizard

Complete the Wizard
    Verify the choices made in the wizard and click Finish.

Click Finish to perform the following actions:

Source Location : HPESTAR
Source Provider : SQLNCLI11
Destination Location : C:\data\export\AW12Demographics.xls
Destination Provider : Microsoft.ACE.OLEDB.12.0

•   Copy rows from [Query] to `Query`
    The new target table will be created.

•   The package will not be saved.
•   The package will be run immediately.

Provider mapping file : C:\Program Files (x86)\Microsoft SQL Server\110\DTS\MappingFiles\MSSqlToJet4.XML
```

Execution Results Screen

If there are errors in the execution of the package, they will show in this window. The current Wizard generated SSIS package executed successfully.

Action	Status	Message
Initializing Data Flow Task	Success	
Initializing Connections	Success	
Setting SQL Command	Success	
Setting Source Connection	Success	
Setting Destination Connection	Success	
Validating	Success	
Prepare for Execute	Success	
Pre-execute	Success	
Executing	Success	
Copying to `Query`	Success	8914 rows transferred
Post-execute	Success	

The execution was successful

Success — 11 Total, 11 Success, 0 Error, 0 Warning

Exporting Data with SQL Server Import and Export Wizard

Checking Results in Excel
If the double click on the destination filename, the transferred data is displayed by Excel.

	A	B	C	D	E	F	G	H
1	BusinessEr	TotalPurcl	DateFirstP	BirthDate	MaritalSta	YearlyInco	Gender	TotalChild
2	6615	123.98	2004-07-2	1976-06-1	S	50001-75C	M	0
3	16467	117.96	2004-07-2	1973-03-2	S	25001-50C	M	1
4	19475	119.98	2004-07-2	1929-07-0	M	0-25000	F	2
5	14319	119.98	2004-07-2	1963-05-0	S	75001-10C	F	0
6	8213	106.93	2004-07-2	1976-02-2	S	25001-50C	M	0
7	12168	106.95	2004-07-1	1962-10-2	M	0-25000	F	1
8	20478	124.97	2004-07-0	1946-10-1	S	75001-10C	M	5
9	7592	119.98	2004-07-0	1947-02-0	S	25001-50C	F	4
10	6488	539.99	2004-06-3	1969-03-2	M	75001-10C	M	3
11	3069	1,120.49	2004-06-3	1970-02-0	M	50001-75C	F	2
12	3996	2,374.96	2004-06-3	1962-06-2	S	greater tha	M	1
13	12177	2,319.99	2004-06-3	1960-12-2	S	greater tha	F	3
14	13121	756.33	2004-06-3	1967-04-2	S	0-25000	M	1
15	15825	553.97	2004-06-3	1969-07-2	S	0-25000	M	0
16	15556	110.97	2004-06-2	1960-03-0	M	50001-75C	F	5
17	15404	1,729.97	2004-06-2	1948-09-0	M	50001-75C	M	2
18	16256	1,144.98	2004-06-2	1970-03-0	M	25001-50C	M	1
19	14945	539.99	2004-06-2	1942-02-2	S	25001-50C	M	2
20	15071	1,120.49	2004-06-2	1970-11-1	M	25001-50C	M	1

Cell C5: 2004-07-23 00:00:00

CHAPTER 18: Exporting & Importing Data

Importing Data with SQL Server Import and Export Wizard

Importing with the Wizard is very similar to the exporting process. We are going to import the just created AW12Demographics.xls Excel worksheet into a new database table. We start the Wizard the same as for export. First we configure the source as Excel worksheet.

Specify Data Source

Importing Data with SQL Server Import and Export Wizard

Specify Data Destination as Database
AdventureWorks2012 is the destination for the data movement.

CHAPTER 18: Exporting & Importing Data

Excel Worksheet Source Is Considered a Table

Select Excel Sheet and Assign Database Table Name

Column Mappings & CREATE TABLE Edit Panels

Column Mappings

Source: `Query`
Destination: [dbo].[Demographics]

● Create destination table   Edit SQL...
○ Delete rows in destination table   ☑ Drop and re-create destination table
○ Append rows to the destination table   ☐ Enable identity insert

Mappings:

Source	Destination	Type	Nullable	Size	Precision	Scale
BusinessEntityID	BusinessEntityID	float	☑			
TotalPurchaseYTD	TotalPurchaseYTD	float	☑			
DateFirstPurchase	DateFirstPurchase	nvarchar	☑	255		
BirthDate	BirthDate	nvarchar	☑	255		
MaritalStatus	MaritalStatus	nvarchar	☑	255		
YearlyIncome	YearlyIncome	nvarchar	☑	255		
Gender	Gender	nvarchar	☑	255		
TotalChildren	TotalChildren	float	☑			
NumberChildrenA...	NumberChildrenA...	float	☑			
Education	Education	nvarchar	☑	255		
Occupation	Occupation	nvarchar	☑	255		
HomeOwnerFlag	HomeOwnerFlag	float	☑			
NumberCarsOwned	NumberCarsOwned	float	☐			

Source column: TotalChildren Double (15)

Create Table SQL Statement

You can customize the default CREATE TABLE statement. However, after you have customized the statement, you must manually maintain any subsequent changes to the column mappings by editing the statement.

SQL statement:

```
CREATE TABLE [dbo].[Demographics] (
[BusinessEntityID] float,
[TotalPurchaseYTD] float,
[DateFirstPurchase] nvarchar(255),
[BirthDate] nvarchar(255),
[MaritalStatus] nvarchar(255),
[YearlyIncome] nvarchar(255),
[Gender] nvarchar(255),
[TotalChildren] float,
[NumberChildrenAtHome] float,
[Education] nvarchar(255),
[Occupation] nvarchar(255),
[HomeOwnerFlag] float,
[NumberCarsOwned] float
)
```

Auto Generate   OK   Cancel

Source Data Inspection with Preview Data

This is a very important step. If the data does not look correct here, it will not be correct in the database table either.

is	YearlyIncome	Gender	TotalChildren	NumberChildrenAtHome	Education	O
	50001-75000	M	0	0	Partial College	S
	25001-50000	M	1	0	Graduate Degree	S
	0-25000	F	2	0	Partial College	C
	75001-100000	F	0	0	Partial College	P
	25001-50000	M	0	0	Partial College	C
	0-25000	F	1	0	Graduate Degree	C
	75001-100000	M	5	0	Partial College	P
	25001-50000	F	4	0	High School	P
	75001-100000	M	3	0	Graduate Degree	P
	50001-75000	F	2	0	Graduate Degree	P
	greater than ...	M	1	3	High School	P
	greater than ...	F	3	3	Partial College	P
	0-25000	M	1	1	Partial College	M
	0-25000	M	0	0	Partial College	M
	50001-75000	F	5	4	Partial College	S
	50001-75000	M	2	1	Bachelors	M
	25001-50000	M	1	1	Bachelors	S
	25001-50000	M	2	0	Bachelors	M
	25001-50000	M	1	1	Bachelors	S
	25001-50000	F	1	1	Bachelors	S
	25001-50000	F	1	0	Bachelors	S
	25001-50000	F	1	1	Bachelors	S
	75001-100000	F	5	4	Partial College	P
	50001-75000	F	2	0	Graduate Degree	P
	0-25000	M	4	0	High School	S
	25001-50000	F	2	1	Partial High Sc...	S
	25001-50000	F	0	0	Partial College	S
	greater than ...	F	1	2	Graduate Degree	M
	25001-50000	F	0	0	Partial College	C

Importing Data with SQL Server Import and Export Wizard

Indicate Saving and/or Run the SSIS Package

The Final Release Screen for Execution

SQL Server Import and Export Wizard

Complete the Wizard
Verify the choices made in the wizard and click Finish.

Click Finish to perform the following actions:

Source Location : C:\data\export\AW12Demographics.xls
Source Provider : Microsoft.ACE.OLEDB.12.0
Destination Location : HPESTAR
Destination Provider : SQLNCLI11

- Copy rows from `Query` to [dbo].[Demographics]
  The new target table will be created.

- The package will not be saved.
- The package will be run immediately.

Provider mapping file : C:\Program Files (x86)\Microsoft SQL Server\110\DTS\MappingFiles\JetToMSSql9.xml

Help   < Back   Next >   Finish   Cancel

Importing Data with SQL Server Import and Export Wizard

Successful Execution Screen
In case of errors, hyperlink to errors will display.

SQL Server Import and Export Wizard

The execution was successful

Success — 11 Total, 11 Success, 0 Error, 0 Warning

Details:

Action	Status	Message
Initializing Data Flow Task	Success	
Initializing Connections	Success	
Setting SQL Command	Success	
Setting Source Connection	Success	
Setting Destination Connection	Success	
Validating	Success	
Prepare for Execute	Success	
Pre-execute	Success	
Executing	Success	
Copying to [dbo].[Query]	Success	8914 rows transferred
Post-execute	Success	

CHAPTER 18: Exporting & Importing Data

Check New Table in Database

Exporting Database Table to Excel

The Wizard sequence is very similar to exporting query results. We shall export Sales.SalesOrderHeader table.

Specify Destination

Choose Table Copy or Query

SQL Server Import and Export Wizard

Specify Table Copy or Query
Specify whether to copy one or more tables and views or to copy the results of a query from the data source.

⦿ **Copy data from one or more tables or views**
Use this option to copy all the data from the existing tables or views in the source database.

○ **Write a query to specify the data to transfer**
Use this option to write an SQL query to manipulate or to restrict the source data for the copy operation.

[Help]   [< Back]   [Next >]   [Finish >>|]   [Cancel]

Checkmark Source Table

SQL Server Import and Export Wizard

Select Source Tables and Views
Choose one or more tables and views to copy.

Tables and views:

☑ Source: HPESTAR	Destination: C:\data\export\SalesOrderHeade...
☐ [Purchasing].[Vendor]	
☐ [Sales].[CountryRegionCurrency]	
☐ [Sales].[CreditCard]	
☐ [Sales].[Currency]	
☐ [Sales].[CurrencyRate]	
☐ [Sales].[Customer]	
☐ [Sales].[PersonCreditCard]	
☐ [Sales].[SalesOrderDetail]	
☑ [Sales].[SalesOrderHeader]	`SalesOrderHeader`
☐ [Sales].[SalesOrderHeaderSalesReason]	
☐ [Sales].[SalesPerson]	
☐ [Sales].[SalesPersonQuotaHistory]	
☐ [Sales].[SalesReason]	
☐ [Sales].[SalesTaxRate]	
☐ [Sales].[SalesTerritory]	
☐ [Sales].[SalesTerritoryHistory]	
☐ [Sales].[ShoppingCartItem]	
☐ [Sales].[SpecialOffer]	
☐ [Sales].[SpecialOfferProduct]	

Edit Mappings...   Preview...

Help   < Back   Next >   Finish >>| Cancel

Exporting Database Table to Excel

Check Data Type Mapping

SQL Server Import and Export Wizard

Review Data Type Mapping
Select a table to review how its data types map to those in the destination and how it handles conversion issues.

Table:

Source	Destination
⚠ [Sales].[SalesOrderHeader]	`SalesOrderHeader`

Data type mapping:

Source Column	Source Type	Destination Col...	Destination Type	Convert	On Er
SalesOrderID	int	SalesOrderID	Long		
RevisionNumber	tinyint	RevisionNumber	Byte		
OrderDate	datetime	OrderDate	DateTime		
DueDate	datetime	DueDate	DateTime		
ShipDate	datetime	ShipDate	DateTime		
Status	tinyint	Status	Byte		
OnlineOrderFlag	bit	OnlineOrderFlag	Short	☑	Use C
SalesOrderNu...	nvarchar	SalesOrderNu...	LongText	☑	Use C

To view conversion details, double-click the row that contains the column source type to be converted.

On Error (global): Fail
On Truncation (global): Fail

[Help]   [< Back]   [Next >]   [Finish >>|]   [Cancel]

CHAPTER 18: Exporting & Importing Data

Save and/or Run Package

SQL Server Import and Export Wizard

Save and Run Package
Indicate whether to save the SSIS package.

☑ Run immediately

☐ Save SSIS Package
  ○ SQL Server
  ○ File system

Package protection level:
[Encrypt sensitive data with user key]

Password:
Retype password:

[Help] [< Back] [Next >] [Finish >>|] [Cancel]

Complete the Wizard

```
SQL Server Import and Export Wizard

Complete the Wizard
    Verify the choices made in the wizard and click Finish.

Click Finish to perform the following actions:

Source Location : HPESTAR
Source Provider : SQLNCLI11
Destination Location : C:\data\export\SalesOrderHeader.xls
Destination Provider : Microsoft.Jet.OLEDB.4.0

 • Copy rows from [Sales].[SalesOrderHeader] to `SalesOrderHeader`
   The new target table will be created.

 • The package will not be saved.
 • The package will be run immediately.

Provider mapping file : C:\Program Files (x86)\Microsoft SQL Server\110\DTS\MappingFiles\MSSqlToJet4.XML
```

Successful Execution Screen

SQL Server Import and Export Wizard		

The execution was successful ✓

Success   11 Total   0 Error
             11 Success   0 Warning

Details:

Action	Status	Message
Initializing Data Flow Task	Success	
Initializing Connections	Success	
Setting SQL Command	Success	
Setting Source Connection	Success	
Setting Destination Connection	Success	
Validating	Success	
Prepare for Execute	Success	
Pre-execute	Success	
Executing	Success	
Copying to `SalesOrderHeader`	Success	31465 rows transferr...
Post-execute	Success	

Stop   Report ▼

Close

Exporting Database Table to Excel

Check File in Folder and Data in Excel

CHAPTER 18: Exporting & Importing Data

Exporting Data Directly into a Flat File

There is no equivalent of BULK INSERT, however, with xp_cmdshell & ECHO commands we can export data directly into a flat file.

> Security blog on xp_cmdshell (usually disabled on production server):
> http://blogs.msdn.com/b/sqlsecurity/archive/2008/01/10/xp-cmdshell.aspx .

```sql
USE AdventureWorks;
GO
CREATE PROC uspWeeklySupplierSummary  @FilePath VARCHAR(100) AS  BEGIN
   DECLARE  @Line NVARCHAR(1000), @Command NVARCHAR(2000) ,@Return INT;
   DECLARE  @VendorID   INT,   @VendorName NVARCHAR(50), @ProductName NVARCHAR(50);
   SET @Line = '******** SUPPLIERS PRODUCTS REPORT ********';
   SET @Command = CONCAT('echo ', @Line , ' >>', @FilePath);
   EXEC @Return = master..xp_cmdshell  @Command, no_output;
   DECLARE curVendor CURSOR FAST_FORWARD FOR
   SELECT   VendorID, Name  FROM  Purchasing.Vendor  WHERE   CreditRating = 1   ORDER BY VendorID;
   OPEN curVendor  FETCH NEXT FROM curVendor  INTO @VendorID,  @VendorName;
   WHILE @@FETCH_STATUS = 0      BEGIN
      SET @Line = '. '; SET @Command = CONCAT('echo ', @Line,' >>', @FilePath);
      EXEC @Return = master..xp_cmdshell  @Command, no_output;
      SET @Line = '***** Products From Supplier: ' + @VendorName;
      SET @Command = CONCAT('echo ', @Line, ' >>', @FilePath);
      EXEC @Return = master..xp_cmdshell  @Command, no_output
      DECLARE curProduct CURSOR FAST_FORWARD FOR
      SELECT v.Name  FROM   Purchasing.ProductVendor pv INNER JOIN Production.Product v
      ON  pv.ProductID = v.ProductID   AND pv.VendorID = @VendorID;
      OPEN curProduct; FETCH NEXT FROM curProduct INTO @ProductName;
      IF @@FETCH_STATUS <> 0    BEGIN
         SET @Line = '*** NO PRODUCTS AVAILABLE AT THIS TIME *** ';
         SET @Command = CONCAT('echo ', @Line,' >>', @FilePath);
         EXEC @Return = master..xp_cmdshell  @Command,  no_output;
      END;
      WHILE @@FETCH_STATUS = 0  BEGIN
         SET @Line = CONCAT( SPACE(1), @ProductName );
         SET @Command = CONCAT('echo ', @Line,' >>',@FilePath);
         EXEC @Return = master..xp_cmdshell  @Command,  no_output;
         FETCH NEXT FROM curProduct   INTO @ProductName;
      END;   CLOSE curProduct;  DEALLOCATE curProduct;
      FETCH NEXT FROM curVendor  INTO @VendorID, @VendorName;
   END ;   CLOSE curVendor;   DEALLOCATE curVendor;
END
GO

EXEC uspWeeklySupplierSummary    'F:\data\export\SUPPWeek31.txt' ;
```

Command Prompt Commands List by HELP

Command Prompt commands can be used for data transport as well including COPY & XCOPY. We can get the entire command list by typing the "HELP" command. It is like a time machine back to the programming style of 1960-s.

```
EXEC xp_cmdshell 'HELP';
```

output	
For more information on a specific command, type HELP command-name	
ASSOC	Displays or modifies file extension associations.
ATTRIB	Displays or changes file attributes.
BREAK	Sets or clears extended CTRL+C checking.

Command List

ASSOC	Displays or modifies file extension associations.
ATTRIB	Displays or changes file attributes.
BREAK	Sets or clears extended CTRL+C checking.
BCDEDIT	Sets properties in boot database to control boot loading.
CACLS	Displays or modifies access control lists (ACLs) of files.
CALL	Calls one batch program from another.
CD	Displays the name of or changes the current directory.
CHCP	Displays or sets the active code page number.
CHDIR	Displays the name of or changes the current directory.
CHKDSK	Checks a disk and displays a status report.
CHKNTFS	Displays or modifies the checking of disk at boot time.
CLS	Clears the screen.
CMD	Starts a new instance of the Windows command interpreter.
COLOR	Sets the default console foreground and background colors.
COMP	Compares the contents of two files or sets of files.
COMPACT	Displays or alters the compression of files on NTFS partitions.
CONVERT	Converts FAT volumes to NTFS. You cannot convert the current drive.
COPY	Copies one or more files to another location.
DATE	Displays or sets the date.
DEL	Deletes one or more files.
DIR	Displays a list of files and subdirectories in a directory.
DISKCOMP	Compares the contents of two floppy disks.
DISKCOPY	Copies the contents of one floppy disk to another.
DISKPART	Displays or configures Disk Partition properties.
DOSKEY	Edits command lines, recalls Windows commands, and creates macros.
DRIVERQUERY	Displays current device driver status and properties.
ECHO	Displays messages, or turns command echoing on or off.
ENDLOCAL	Ends localization of environment changes in a batch file.
ERASE	Deletes one or more files.
EXIT	Quits the CMD.EXE program (command interpreter).
FC	Compares two files or sets of files, and displays the differences between them.
FIND	Searches for a text string in a file or files.

CHAPTER 18: Exporting & Importing Data

Command	Description
FINDSTR	Searches for strings in files.
FOR	Runs a specified command for each file in a set of files.
FORMAT	Formats a disk for use with Windows.
FSUTIL	Displays or configures the file system properties.
FTYPE	Displays or modifies file types used in file extension associations.
GOTO	Directs the Windows command interpreter to a labeled line in a batch program.
GPRESULT	Displays Group Policy information for machine or user.
GRAFTABL	Enables Windows to display an extended character set in graphics mode.
HELP	Provides Help information for Windows commands.
ICACLS	Display, modify, backup, or restore ACLs for files and directories.
IF	Performs conditional processing in batch programs.
LABEL	Creates, changes, or deletes the volume label of a disk.
MD	Creates a directory.
MKDIR	Creates a directory.
MKLINK	Creates Symbolic Links and Hard Links
MODE	Configures a system device.
MORE	Displays output one screen at a time.
MOVE	Moves one or more files from one directory to another directory.
OPENFILES	Displays files opened by remote users for a file share.
PATH	Displays or sets a search path for executable files.
PAUSE	Suspends processing of a batch file and displays a message.
POPD	Restores the previous value of the current directory saved by PUSHD.
PRINT	Prints a text file.
PROMPT	Changes the Windows command prompt.
PUSHD	Saves the current directory then changes it.
RD	Removes a directory.
RECOVER	Recovers readable information from a bad or defective disk.
REM	Records comments (remarks) in batch files or CONFIG.SYS.
REN	Renames a file or files.
RENAME	Renames a file or files.
REPLACE	Replaces files.
RMDIR	Removes a directory.
ROBOCOPY	Advanced utility to copy files and directory trees
SET	Displays, sets, or removes Windows environment variables.
SETLOCAL	Begins localization of environment changes in a batch file.
SC	Displays or configures services (background processes).
SCHTASKS	Schedules commands and programs to run on a computer.
SHIFT	Shifts the position of replaceable parameters in batch files.
SHUTDOWN	Allows proper local or remote shutdown of machine.
SORT	Sorts input.
START	Starts a separate window to run a specified program or command.
SUBST	Associates a path with a drive letter.
SYSTEMINFO	Displays machine specific properties and configuration.
TASKLIST	Displays all currently running tasks including services.
TASKKILL	Kill or stop a running process or application.
TIME	Displays or sets the system time.
TITLE	Sets the window title for a CMD.EXE session.
TREE	Graphically displays the directory structure of a drive or path.
TYPE	Displays the contents of a text file.
VER	Displays the Windows version.
VERIFY	Tells Windows whether to verify that your files are written correctly to a disk.
VOL	Displays a disk volume label and serial number.
XCOPY	Copies files and directory trees.
WMIC	Displays WMI information inside interactive command shell.

BULK INSERT Command

BULK INSERT is a T-SQL command which corresponds to bcp "in" action for uploading a file into a database table. The command includes an optional format file. Generally it is a good idea to use format file with BULK INSERT and bcp for more reliable and successful data transfer.

Format File Generation with bcp

Format file can be created manually by an editor or automatically by bcp. Execute at Command Prompt as one line with no breaks to create a non-XML format file:

```
bcp AdventureWorks2012.HumanResources.Department format nul -T -n -f
f:\data\bcpdemo\hrdept.fmt
```

The generated format file:

```
11.0
4
1       SQLSMALLINT     0    2    ""    1    DepartmentID                 ""
2       SQLNCHAR        2    100  ""    2    Name            SQL_Latin1_General_CP1_CI_AS
3       SQLNCHAR        2    100  ""    3    GroupName       SQL_Latin1_General_CP1_CI_AS
4       SQLDATETIME     0    8    ""    4    ModifiedDate                 ""
```

11.0 refers to SQL Server 2012 internal version number.

Export Data with bcp Format File Option

We use the format file for exporting the data at Command Prompt.

```
bcp AdventureWorks2012.HumanResources.Department out  f:\data\bcpdemo\hrdept.txt  -f
f:\data\bcpdemo\hrdept.fmt  -T
```

This is how the exported data looks in Notepad:

CHAPTER 18: Exporting & Importing Data

Import Data with BULK INSERT Format File Option

The same format file can be used to import the data into the database with BULK INSERT. First we create an empty table for the data import.

```
USE tempdb;
SELECT TOP(0)
        [DepartmentID] = CONVERT(INT, DepartmentID) --prevent IDENTITY inheritance
        ,[Name]
        ,[GroupName]
        ,[ModifiedDate]
INTO Department
FROM [AdventureWorks2012].[HumanResources].[Department];
GO
-- (0 row(s) affected)
```

```
BULK INSERT Department
        FROM 'f:\data\bcpdemo\hrdept.txt'
        WITH (FORMATFILE = 'f:\data\bcpdemo\hrdept.fmt');
GO
-- (16 row(s) affected)
```

```
SELECT TOP (3) * FROM Department ORDER BY NEWID();
GO
```

DepartmentID	Name	GroupName	ModifiedDate
14	Facilities and Maintenance	Executive General and Administration	2002-06-01 00:00:00.000
15	Shipping and Receiving	Inventory Management	2002-06-01 00:00:00.000
3	Sales	Sales and Marketing	2002-06-01 00:00:00.000

We can use the -n native mode for exporting data and DATAFILETYPE for importing.

```
bcp AdventureWorks2012.HumanResources.Shift out f:\temp\shift.txt -n -T
```

```
CREATE TABLE [Shift](
        [ShiftID] [tinyint]  NOT NULL,
        [Name] [dbo].[Name] NOT NULL,
        [StartTime] [time](7) NOT NULL,
        [EndTime] [time](7) NOT NULL,
        [ModifiedDate] [datetime] NOT NULL,
);
```

```
BULK INSERT Shift    FROM 'f:\temp\shift.txt'    WITH (DATAFILETYPE='native');
```

Importing & Exporting Images

Importing & exporting images and other binary large objects (BLOB) requires special techniques. We use OPENROWSET BULK method to import an image.

```sql
USE AdventureWorks2012;
GO
-- Create image warehouse for storing images in database
CREATE TABLE dbo.PhotoLand (
  PhotoLandID      INT      IDENTITY ( 1 , 1 )    PRIMARY KEY,
  ImageName        VARCHAR(100) UNIQUE,
  Photo            VARBINARY(MAX),
  ModifiedDate datetime default (CURRENT_TIMESTAMP));
GO
-- Insert image name
INSERT INTO dbo.PhotoLand ([ImageName]) VALUES   ('ALASKALODGE.JPG');
-- (1 row(s) affected)

DECLARE @ID INT = SCOPE_IDENTITY();   -- get last identity inserted

UPDATE dbo.PhotoLand
SET    Photo = (SELECT *
               FROM   OPENROWSET(BULK 'f:\data\images\ALASKALODGE.JPG',
                     SINGLE_BLOB) AS x)
WHERE  PhotoLandID = @ID;
GO
--(1 row(s) affected)

-- Check table population
SELECT * FROM   dbo.PhotoLand;
GO
```

PhotoLand...	ImageName	Photo	ModifiedDate
1	1	ALASKALODGE.JPG	0xFFD8FFE000104A464946000102000...	2012-11-12 16:52:03.727

Exporting Image with bcp

The bcp command can be used to export an image. In the following demo, it is executed from xp_cmdshell. **NOTE: on most production servers the xp_cmdshell option is disabled due to security concerns.**

```
DECLARE  @Command NVARCHAR(4000);

-- Keep the command on ONE LINE - here it wraps around
SET @Command = 'bcp "SELECT Photo FROM AdventureWorks2012.dbo.PhotoLand WHERE PhotoLandID=1"  queryout "F:\temp\ALASKALODGE.jpg" -T -n' ;

PRINT @Command -- debugging

EXEC xp_cmdshell   @Command;
GO
/*NULL
Starting copy...
NULL
1 rows copied.
Network packet size (bytes): 4096
Clock Time (ms.) Total     : 203    Average : (4.93 rows per sec.)
NULL */
```

Building a bcp Format File Interactively for Image Export

```
C:\Users\Owner>bcp "SELECT LargePhoto FROM AdventureWorks2012.Production.Product
Photo WHERE ProductPhotoID = 78" queryout "f:\data\images\productphoto\hotrodbik
e_black_large.gif" -T

Enter the file storage type of field LargePhoto [varbinary(max)]:
Enter prefix-length of field LargePhoto [8]: 0
Enter length of field LargePhoto [0]:
Enter field terminator [none]:

Do you want to save this format information in a file? [Y/n] Y
Host filename [bcp.fmt]: bcpimage.fmt

Starting copy...

1 rows copied.
Network packet size (bytes): 4096
Clock Time (ms.) Total     : 1      Average : (1000.00 rows per sec.)

C:\Users\Owner>
```

CHAPTER 18: Exporting & Importing Data

BULK INSERT Command

Exporting All Images from Table

The content of the previously created bcp format file.

```
11.0
1
1       SQLBINARY       0       0       ""      1       LargePhoto              ""
```

T-SQL script for exporting all images to the file system from Production.ProductPhoto table LargePhoto column.

```sql
USE AdventureWorks2012;
GO


DECLARE @Command   VARCHAR(4000),  @PhotoID  INT,  @ImageFileName VARCHAR(128) ;
DECLARE PHOTOcursor CURSOR  FOR
        SELECT ProductPhotoID,   LargePhotoFileName  FROM   Production.ProductPhoto
          WHERE  LargePhotoFileName != 'no_image_available_large.gif';

OPEN PHOTOcursor FETCH NEXT FROM PHOTOcursor INTO @PhotoID,  @ImageFileName;

WHILE (@@FETCH_STATUS = 0) -- Cursor loop
  BEGIN
-- No carriage return or new line in bcp command string!
   SET @Command = CONCAT('bcp "SELECT LargePhoto FROM
AdventureWorks2012.Production.ProductPhoto WHERE ProductPhotoID = ',
   convert(VARCHAR,@PhotoID) + '" queryout "f:\data\images\productphoto\',
   @ImageFileName,'" -T -f "f:\data\images\bcpimage.fmt" ');

   PRINT @Command -- debugging
   EXEC xp_cmdshell @Command, no_output;

   FETCH NEXT FROM PHOTOcursor  INTO @PhotoID,    @ImageFileName;
  END;  -- cursor loop

CLOSE PHOTOcursor; DEALLOCATE PHOTOcursor;
GO
```

Product Photo Icons in the ProductPhoto Folder

The folder contains 100 exported product photos. The photos cannot be visualized in SSMS, but in the file system or SSRS reports. The following is a partial list of image icons.

awc_jersey_female_large	awc_jersey_male_large	awc_tee_female_large	awc_tee_male_large	awc_tee_male_yellow_large
bike_lock_large	bike_shoes_large	bike_shorts_female_large	bike_shorts_male_large	bikepump_large
chain_large	chain_lube_large	clipless_pedals_large	co2_4tire_large	double_headlight_large
fork_large	frame_black_large	frame_blue_large	frame_large	frame_red_large
frame_silver_large	frame_yellow_large	handlebar_large	handpump_large	hotrodbike_black_large
hotrodbike_blue_	hotrodbike_f_larg	hotrodbike_f_silv	hotrodbike_large	hotrodbike_red_l

In SSIS the Export Column & Import Column Transformations can be used for exporting and importing a set of images to and from folders.

CHAPTER 18: Exporting & Importing Data

CHAPTER 19: Maintaining Data Integrity in the Enterprise

Why is Data Integrity Paramount

A business or organization can only operate efficiently with good quality data. Computers were the real engine of economic progress since the 1950-s. Without computers, we would pretty much be at post Second World War level. Computers work with data and produce data. As the saying goes: garbage in, garbage out. Therefore it is our job as database designers, database developers and database administrators to ensure the data integrity in a database. What are the sources of the bad data? They can be data feeds received from various sources, data entry by people, and bugs in database or application programming. The best way to minimize bugs is putting each piece of new software through rigorous quality assurance (QA) process. To prevent bad data getting into the database there are a number of possibilities: table design, constraints, stored procedures, triggers and application software.

At the lowest level, constraints make up the guarding force over data integrity. The default constraint is different from the rest: it provides predefined default value if no value is provided for a cell (a column in a row), it does not give an error message.

```
USE AdventureWorks2012;
SELECT          ConstraintType = type_desc,  [Count] = COUNT(*)
FROM sys.objects
WHERE type_desc in       (
                'CHECK_CONSTRAINT',
                'DEFAULT_CONSTRAINT',
                'FOREIGN_KEY_CONSTRAINT',
                'PRIMARY_KEY_CONSTRAINT',
                'UNIQUE_CONSTRAINT'
                )
GROUP BY type_desc ORDER BY type_desc;
```

ConstraintType	Count
CHECK_CONSTRAINT	89
DEFAULT_CONSTRAINT	152
FOREIGN_KEY_CONSTRAINT	90
PRIMARY_KEY_CONSTRAINT	71
UNIQUE_CONSTRAINT	1

Entity Integrity

Entity Integrity defines a row as a unique entity for a particular table. The main enforcing mechanisms are: NOT NULL constraint and unique index. PRIMARY KEY implies not null, and unique index automatically created. In the Production.Product table ProductID is the INT IDENTITY PRIMARY KEY, Name & ProductNumber are NATURAL KEYs and rowguid is a system generated unique key. All four keys are not null and all have unique index defined. The implication is that we can use any of 4 columns for row identification. However, ProductID INT (4 bytes) column is the most efficient row (record) identifier.

```
Solution1 - Microsoft SQL Server Management Studio
File  Edit  View  Project  Debug  Tools  Window  Help

Object Explorer
Connect ▼

⊟ ☐ Production.Product
  ⊟ ☐ Columns
    ♀ ProductID (PK, int, not null)
    ▦ Name (Name(nvarchar(50)), not null)
    ▦ ProductNumber (nvarchar(25), not null)
    ▦ MakeFlag (Flag(bit), not null)
    ▦ FinishedGoodsFlag (Flag(bit), not null)
    ▦ Color (nvarchar(15), null)
    ▦ SafetyStockLevel (smallint, not null)
    ▦ ReorderPoint (smallint, not null)
    ▦ StandardCost (money, not null)
    ▦ ListPrice (money, not null)
    ▦ Size (nvarchar(5), null)
    ♀ SizeUnitMeasureCode (FK, nchar(3), null)
    ♀ WeightUnitMeasureCode (FK, nchar(3), null)
    ▦ Weight (decimal(8,2), null)
    ▦ DaysToManufacture (int, not null)
    ▦ ProductLine (nchar(2), null)
    ▦ Class (nchar(2), null)
    ▦ Style (nchar(2), null)
    ♀ ProductSubcategoryID (FK, int, null)
    ♀ ProductModelID (FK, int, null)
    ▦ SellStartDate (datetime, not null)
    ▦ SellEndDate (datetime, null)
    ▦ DiscontinuedDate (datetime, null)
    ▦ rowguid (uniqueidentifier, not null)
    ▦ ModifiedDate (datetime, not null)
  ⊞ ☐ Keys
  ⊞ ☐ Constraints
  ⊞ ☐ Triggers
  ⊞ ☐ Indexes
  ⊞ ☐ Statistics
⊞ ☐ Production.ProductCategory
```

```
⊟ ☐ Indexes
   ⛓ AK_Product_Name (Unique, Non-Clustered)
   ⛓ AK_Product_ProductNumber (Unique, Non-Clustered)
   ⛓ AK_Product_rowguid (Unique, Non-Clustered)
   ♀ PK_Product_ProductID (Clustered)
```

CHAPTER 19: Maintaining Data Integrity in the Enterprise

How to Remove Duplicates in a Table

The best way to prevent duplicates is by placing a UNIQUE KEY or unique index on the unique column(s). PRIMARY KEY & UNIQUE KEY constraints automatically create a unique index on the key column(s). If the entire row is a duplicate, removal is real simple with the DISTINCT clause.

```
SELECT DISTINCT * INTO T2 FROM T1;
GO
```

If duplicates are only in one or more columns, then duplicates removal is fairly easy with the ROW_NUMBER method, it is more involved with the GROUP BY method (prior to SQL Server 2005).

```
-- Create test table
USE tempdb;
SELECT      ProductID=CONVERT(int, ProductID),
            ProductName = Name,  ProductNumber,
            ListPrice = ListPrice + 1.00
INTO Product
FROM AdventureWorks2012.Production.Product   WHERE ListPrice > 0.0;
GO  -- (304 row(s) affected)
```

```
-- Unique index prevents duplicates
CREATE UNIQUE INDEX idxProd ON Product(ProductName, ProductNumber);
GO
```

```
 -- Try to insert  duplicates on ProductName & ProductNumber
INSERT INTO Product
SELECT          TOP (100) ProductID=CONVERT(int, ProductID) + 1000,
                ProductName = Name, ProductNumber,
                ListPrice = ListPrice + 2.00
FROM AdventureWorks2008.Production.Product
WHERE ListPrice > 0.0 ORDER BY NEWID();
GO
/*  Msg 2601, Level 14, State 1, Line 2
Cannot insert duplicate key row in object 'dbo.Product' with unique index 'idxProd'.
The duplicate key value is (Fender Set - Mountain, FE-6654).
The statement has been terminated.  */
```

```
DROP INDEX Product.idxProd;
GO
```

CHAPTER 19: Maintaining Data Integrity in the Enterprise

Rows with Duplicates Can Be Numbered in Ordered or Random Manner

```
-- Insert 100 duplicates on ProductName & ProductNumber
INSERT INTO Product
SELECT          TOP (100) ProductID=CONVERT(int, ProductID) + 1000,
                ProductName = Name, ProductNumber,   ListPrice = ListPrice + 2.00
FROM AdventureWorks2008.Production.Product
WHERE ListPrice > 0.0
ORDER BY NEWID();
GO
```

```
-- Quantify duplicates with GROUP BY query
SELECT ProductName, ProductNumber, [Count] = count(*)
FROM Product
GROUP BY ProductName, ProductNumber
        HAVING count(*) > 1
ORDER BY ProductName, ProductNumber;
GO -- (100 row(s) affected) - Partial results.
```

ProductName	ProductNumber	Count
Bike Wash - Dissolver	CL-9009	2
Classic Vest, L	VE-C304-L	2
Classic Vest, S	VE-C304-S	2
Front Brakes	FB-9873	2
Full-Finger Gloves, M	GL-F110-M	2

```
-- Quantify duplicates with ROW_NUMBER OVER - we don't care about duplicates ordering
;WITH CTE AS (
    SELECT RN=ROW_NUMBER() OVER (PARTITION BY ProductName, ProductNumber
    ORDER BY NEWID() ),  ProductName, ProductNumber
    FROM Product)
SELECT * FROM CTE WHERE RN > 1
ORDER BY ProductName, ProductNumber;
GO -- (100 row(s) affected) - Partial results.
```

RN	ProductName	ProductNumber
2	Bike Wash - Dissolver	CL-9009
2	Classic Vest, L	VE-C304-L
2	Classic Vest, S	VE-C304-S
2	Front Brakes	FB-9873
2	Full-Finger Gloves, M	GL-F110-M

Domain Integrity

Remove Duplicates with CTE & ROW_NUMBER OVER PARTITION BY

```
-- To removal of duplicates is real easy with CTE & ROW_NUMBER
;WITH CTE AS (
    SELECT RN=ROW_NUMBER() OVER (PARTITION BY ProductName, ProductNumber
    ORDER BY NEWID()),  ProductName, ProductNumber    FROM Product)
DELETE CTE  WHERE RN > 1;
GO -- (100 row(s) affected)
```

```
-- Test for duplicates again
SELECT ProductName, ProductNumber, [Count] = count(*)
FROM Product  GROUP BY ProductName, ProductNumber  HAVING count(*) > 1
ORDER BY ProductName, ProductNumber;
GO -- (0 row(s) affected)
```

```
SELECT COUNT(*) FROM Product;  -- 304
GO
```

Remove Duplicates with GROUP BY

```
-- Insert  duplicates on ProductName & ProductNumber
INSERT INTO Product    SELECT    TOP (100) ProductID=CONVERT(int, ProductID) + 1000,
              ProductName = Name, ProductNumber,    ListPrice = ListPrice + 2.00
FROM AdventureWorks2008.Production.Product  WHERE ListPrice > 0.0  ORDER BY NEWID();
GO
```

```
-- Sample of conflicting data - It is a business decision what to keep
SELECT TOP (4) * FROM Product WHERE ProductNumber IN
   ( SELECT ProductNumber FROM Product   GROUP BY ProductNumber HAVING count(*) > 1   )
ORDER BY ProductNumber;
```

ProductID	ProductName	ProductNumber	ListPrice
992	Mountain-500 Black, 48	BK-M18B-48	540.9900
1992	Mountain-500 Black, 48	BK-M18B-48	541.9900
993	Mountain-500 Black, 52	BK-M18B-52	540.9900
1993	Mountain-500 Black, 52	BK-M18B-52	541.9900

```
-- Assume it does not matter which duplicate to keep: any ProductID and any ListPrice OK
SELECT ProductID=MIN(ProductID), ProductName, ProductNumber, ListPrice=MIN(ListPrice)
INTO Product1 FROM Product GROUP BY ProductName, ProductNumber ORDER BY ProductID;
GO  -- (304 row(s) affected)
```

CHAPTER 19: Maintaining Data Integrity in the Enterprise

Domain Integrity

A domain defines the possible values for a column. Domain Integrity rules enforce the validity data in a column:

Data type	table design
Data length	table design
Nullability	table design
Collation	table design
Allowable values	check constraints - table design
Default value	default constraints - table design

CHECK constraint is used for simple rules such as OrderQty > 0. UDF CHECK constraints can be used for complex rules. In addition, at the development phase, triggers, stored procedures and client-side application software can be developed to enforce Domain Integrity.

Server-side CHECK constraints are the most desirable. Client-side Domain Integrity enforcement is the least desirable. However, it may happen that there is no database expert on the project and developers feel more confident programming data validity rules in the application software. Ultimately what counts is valid data in the database. Usually big-budget projects can do everything the right way due to the availability of expert-level resources in all areas of the software development project. Basic table definition data from INFORMATION_SCHEMA views.

```
SELECT      COLUMN_NAME, ORDINAL_POSITION, DATA_TYPE, IS_NULLABLE,
            CHARACTER_MAXIMUM_LENGTH, COLLATION_NAME, COLUMN_DEFAULT
FROM INFORMATION_SCHEMA.COLUMNS WHERE TABLE_NAME = 'SalesOrderHeader';
```

COLUMN_NAME	ORDINAL_POSITION	DATA_TYPE	IS_NULLABLE	CHARACTER_MAXIMUM_LENGTH	COLLATION_NAME	COLUMN_DEFAULT
SalesOrderID	1	int	NO	NULL	NULL	NULL
RevisionNumber	2	tinyint	NO	NULL	NULL	((0))
OrderDate	3	datetime	NO	NULL	NULL	(getdate())
DueDate	4	datetime	NO	NULL	NULL	NULL
ShipDate	5	datetime	YES	NULL	NULL	NULL
tatus	6	tinyint	NO	NULL	NULL	((1))
OnlineOrderFlag	7	bit	NO	NULL	NULL	((1))
SalesOrderNumber	8	nvarchar	NO	25	SQL_Latin1_General_CP1_CI_AS	NULL
PurchaseOrderNumber	9	nvarchar	YES	25	SQL_Latin1_General_CP1_CI_AS	NULL
AccountNumber	10	nvarchar	YES	15	SQL_Latin1_General_CP1_CI_AS	NULL
CustomerID	11	int	NO	NULL	NULL	NULL
SalesPersonID	12	int	YES	NULL	NULL	NULL
TerritoryID	13	int	YES	NULL	NULL	NULL
BillToAddressID	14	int	NO	NULL	NULL	NULL
ShipToAddressID	15	int	NO	NULL	NULL	NULL
ShipMethodID	16	int	NO	NULL	NULL	NULL
CreditCardID	17	int	YES	NULL	NULL	NULL
CreditCardApprovalCode	18	varchar	YES	15	SQL_Latin1_General_CP1_CI_AS	NULL
CurrencyRateID	19	int	YES	NULL	NULL	NULL
SubTotal	20	money	NO	NULL	NULL	((0.00))
TaxAmt	21	money	NO	NULL	NULL	((0.00))
Freight	22	money	NO	NULL	NULL	((0.00))
TotalDue	23	money	NO	NULL	NULL	NULL
Comment	24	nvarchar	YES	128	SQL_Latin1_General_CP1_CI_AS	NULL
rowguid	25	uniqueidentifier	NO	NULL	NULL	(newid())
ModifiedDate	26	datetime	NO	NULL	NULL	(getdate())

CHAPTER 19: Maintaining Data Integrity in the Enterprise

Domain Integrity

Domain Integrity Summary Display with sp_help

The sp_help system procedure provides a convenient way to display a summary of Domain Integrity definitions for a table.

```
exec sp_help 'Sales.SalesOrderDetail';
```

Column_name	Type	Computed	Length	Prec	Scale	Nullable	Tri...	Fix...	Collation
SalesOrderID	int	no	4	10	0	no	(n/a)	(n...	NULL
SalesOrderDetailID	int	no	4	10	0	no	(n/a)	(n...	NULL
CarrierTrackingNumber	nvarchar	no	50			yes	(n/a)	(n...	SQL_Latin1_General_CP1_CI_AS
OrderQty	smallint	no	2	5	0	no	(n/a)	(n...	NULL
ProductID	int	no	4	10	0	no	(n/a)	(n...	NULL
SpecialOfferID	int	no	4	10	0	no	(n/a)	(n...	NULL
UnitPrice	money	no	8	19	4	no	(n/a)	(n...	NULL
UnitPriceDiscount	money	no	8	19	4	no	(n/a)	(n...	NULL

Identity	Seed	Increment	Not For Replication
SalesOrderDetailID	1	1	0

RowGuidCol
rowguid

Data_located_on_filegroup
PRIMARY

index_name	index_description	index_keys
AK_SalesOrderDetail_rowguid	nonclustered, unique located on PRIMARY	rowguid

	constraint_type	constraint_name	delete_a...	update_a...	stat...	statu...	constraint_keys
1	CHECK on column OrderQty	CK_SalesOrderDet...	(n/a)	(n/a)	En...	Is_F...	([OrderQty]>(0))
2	CHECK on column UnitPrice	CK_SalesOrderDet...	(n/a)	(n/a)	En...	Is_F...	([UnitPrice]>=(0.00))
3	CHECK on column UnitPri...	CK_SalesOrderDet...	(n/a)	(n/a)	En...	Is_F...	([UnitPriceDiscount]>=(0.00))
4	DEFAULT on column Modi...	DF_SalesOrderDet...	(n/a)	(n/a)	(n/a)	(n/a)	(getdate())
5	DEFAULT on column rowg...	DF_SalesOrderDet...	(n/a)	(n/a)	(n/a)	(n/a)	(newid())
6	DEFAULT on column Unit...	DF_SalesOrderDet...	(n/a)	(n/a)	(n/a)	(n/a)	((0.0))
7	FOREIGN KEY	FK_SalesOrderDet...	Cascade	No Action	En...	Is_F...	SalesOrderID

We can query "sys" system views metadata for column definition as well.

```
SELECT * FROM sys.columns
WHERE object_name(object_id) = 'PurchaseOrderHeader'  ORDER BY column_id;
-- (13 row(s) affected) - Partial results.
```

object_id	name	column_id	system_type_id	user_type_id	max_length	precision	scale	collation_name
946102411	PurchaseOrderID	1	56	56	4	10	0	NULL

CHAPTER 19: Maintaining Data Integrity in the Enterprise

THE COLUMNPROPERTY() Function

The COLUMNPROPERTY() function can be used for programmatic discovery of column properties. Script to generate SELECT queries for all properties.

```
USE AdventureWorks2012;
GO
```

```
DECLARE @Parms TABLE (Property varchar(32))
INSERT  @Parms VALUES
('AllowsNull'), ('ColumnId'),
('FullTextTypeColumn'), ('IsComputed'),
('IsCursorType'), ('IsDeterministic'),
('IsFulltextIndexed'), ('IsIdentity'),
('IsIdNotForRepl'), ('IsIndexable'),
('IsOutParam'), ('IsPrecise'),
('IsRowGuidCol'), ('IsSystemVerified'),
('IsXmlIndexable'), ('Precision'),
('Scale'), ('StatisticalSemantics'),
('SystemDataAccess'), ('UserDataAccess'),
('UsesAnsiTrim'), ('IsSparse'),
('IsColumnSet')
SELECT CONCAT('SELECT COLUMNPROPERTY( OBJECT_ID(''Person.Person''), ''LastName'', ''',
              Property, ''') AS [', Property, '];')
FROM @Parms
GO  -- Partial results.
```

```
SELECT COLUMNPROPERTY( OBJECT_ID('Person.Person'), 'LastName', 'AllowsNull') AS [AllowsNull];
SELECT COLUMNPROPERTY( OBJECT_ID('Person.Person'), 'LastName', 'ColumnId') AS [ColumnId];
SELECT COLUMNPROPERTY( OBJECT_ID('Person.Person'), 'LastName', 'FullTextTypeColumn') AS [FullTextTypeColumn];
SELECT COLUMNPROPERTY( OBJECT_ID('Person.Person'), 'LastName', 'IsComputed') AS [IsComputed];
SELECT COLUMNPROPERTY( OBJECT_ID('Person.Person'), 'LastName', 'IsCursorType') AS [IsCursorType];
```

Executing the queries, the column properties are returned one by one.

	AllowsNull
1	0

	ColumnId
1	7

	FullTextTypeColumn
1	0

	IsComputed
1	0

	IsCursorType
1	0

Column List Using System Views & Data Dictionary

We can combine sys. system views with data dictionary description to get a valuable list when working with domain integrity.

```
USE AdventureWorks2012;
SELECT SCHEMA_NAME(T.schema_id)     AS SchemaName,
    T.name                          AS TableName,
    C.name                          AS ColumnName,
    TP.name                         AS ColumnType,
    C.max_length                    AS ColumnLength,
    COALESCE(EP.value, Space(1))    AS ColumnDesc
FROM  sys.tables AS T
    INNER JOIN sys.columns AS C
        ON T.object_id = C.object_id
    INNER JOIN sys.types AS TP
        ON  C.system_type_id = TP.user_type_id
    LEFT JOIN sys.extended_properties AS EP
        ON EP.major_id = T.object_id
            AND EP.minor_id = C.column_id
ORDER BY SchemaName, TableName, ColumnName;
GO  -- (643 row(s) affected) - Partial Results.
```

Purchasing	PurchaseOrderHeader	EmployeeID	int	4	Employee who created the purchase order. Foreign key to Employee.BusinessEntityID.
Purchasing	PurchaseOrderHeader	Freight	money	8	Shipping cost.
Purchasing	PurchaseOrderHeader	ModifiedDate	datetime	8	Date and time the record was last updated.
Purchasing	PurchaseOrderHeader	OrderDate	datetime	8	Purchase order creation date.
Purchasing	PurchaseOrderHeader	PurchaseOrderID	int	4	Primary key.
Purchasing	PurchaseOrderHeader	PurchaseOrderID	int	4	Clustered index created by a primary key constraint.
Purchasing	PurchaseOrderHeader	RevisionNumber	tinyint	1	Incremental number to track changes to the purchase order over time.
Purchasing	PurchaseOrderHeader	RevisionNumber	tinyint	1	Nonclustered index.
Purchasing	PurchaseOrderHeader	ShipDate	datetime	8	Estimated shipment date from the vendor.
Purchasing	PurchaseOrderHeader	ShipMethodID	int	4	Shipping method. Foreign key to ShipMethod.ShipMethodID.
Purchasing	PurchaseOrderHeader	Status	tinyint	1	Order current status. 1 = Pending; 2 = Approved; 3 = Rejected; 4 = Complete
Purchasing	PurchaseOrderHeader	Status	tinyint	1	Nonclustered index.
Purchasing	PurchaseOrderHeader	SubTotal	money	8	Purchase order subtotal. Computed as SUM(PurchaseOrderDetail.LineTotal)for the appropriate PurchaseOrderID.
Purchasing	PurchaseOrderHeader	TaxAmt	money	8	Tax amount.
Purchasing	PurchaseOrderHeader	TotalDue	money	8	Total due to vendor. Computed as Subtotal + TaxAmt + Freight.
Purchasing	PurchaseOrderHeader	VendorID	int	4	Vendor with whom the purchase order is placed. Foreign key to Vendor.BusinessEntityID.

Declarative Referential Integrity

Referential Integrity refers to ensuring that relationships between tables remain consistent. Declarative means it is part of table setup, not in programming objects like stored procedure. When one table attempts to create a FOREIGN KEY to another (PK) table, Referential Integrity requires that the primary key value exists in the referenced (PK) table. The optional cascading update & cascading delete ensure that changes made to the primary table are reflected in the linked referencing (FK) table. For example, if a row is deleted in the primary table, then all referencing rows are automatically deleted in the linked (FK) table when ON DELETE CASCADE is set. All three Referential Integrity constraint actions are demonstrated by the following script.

```
USE tempdb;

-- Create 2 test tables with PK-FK relationship
CREATE TABLE Product (
        ProductID INT PRIMARY KEY,
        ProductName varchar(50) UNIQUE,
        ProductNumber varchar(20) UNIQUE,
        ListPrice MONEY);
GO
```

```
-- First we test without the DELETE CASCADE action
CREATE TABLE OrderDetail (
        SalesOrderID INT,
        SalesOrderDetailID INT,
        PRIMARY KEY (SalesOrderID, SalesOrderDetailID),
        OrderQty INT ,
        ProductID INT REFERENCES Product(ProductID)  -- ON DELETE CASCADE  );
GO
```

Product
- 🔑 ProductID
- ProductName
- ProductNumber
- ListPrice

OrderDetail
- 🔑 SalesOrderID
- 🔑 SalesOrderDetailID
- OrderQty
- ProductID

Declarative Referential Integrity

FOREIGN KEY Constraint Protects Two Ways

```
-- Populate test tables
INSERT Product
SELECT ProductID, Name, ProductNumber, ListPrice
FROM AdventureWorks2012.Production.Product
ORDER BY ProductID;
GO
--(504 row(s) affected)
```

```
INSERT OrderDetail
SELECT      SalesOrderID,
            SalesOrderDetailID,
            OrderQty,
            ProductID
FROM AdventureWorks2012.Sales.SalesOrderDetail
ORDER BY SalesOrderID, SalesOrderDetailID;
GO
-- (121317 row(s) affected)
```

```
-- Attempting to insert into FK table a reference to a non-existing (PK) ProductID
INSERT OrderDetail
SELECT      SalesOrderID = 100000,
            SalesOrderDetailID = 1000000,
            OrderQty = 5,
            ProductID = 2000
GO
/* Msg 547, Level 16, State 0, Line 1
The INSERT statement conflicted with the FOREIGN KEY constraint
"FK__OrderDeta__Produ__59FA5E80". The conflict occurred in database "tempdb", table
"dbo.Product", column 'ProductID'.
The statement has been terminated.   */
```

```
-- Attempting to delete from  PK table a ProductID which is referenced from the FK table
DELETE Product WHERE ProductID = 800;
GO
/* Msg 547, Level 16, State 0, Line 1
The DELETE statement conflicted with the REFERENCE constraint
"FK__OrderDeta__Produ__59FA5E80". The conflict occurred in database "tempdb", table
"dbo.OrderDetail", column 'ProductID'.
The statement has been terminated.   */
```

CHAPTER 19: Maintaining Data Integrity in the Enterprise

ON DELETE CASCADE Action Causes DELETE Chain Reaction

```
-- Change FOREIGN KEY: specify ON DELETE CASCADE option
-- Lookup FK constraints name
SELECT * FROM INFORMATION_SCHEMA.REFERENTIAL_CONSTRAINTS;
```

CONSTRAINT_ CATALOG	CONSTRAINT _SCHEMA	CONSTRAINT_NAME	UNIQUE_CONSTRAI NT_CATALOG	UNIQUE_CONSTRAI NT_SCHEMA	UNIQUE_CONSTRAIN T_NAME	MATCH_ OPTION	UPDATE _RULE	DELETE _RULE
tempdb	dbo	FK__OrderDeta__Produ__0A9D95DB	tempdb	dbo	PK__Product__B40CC6ED66641298	SIMPLE	NO ACTION	NO ACTION

```
BEGIN TRANSACTION
GO
ALTER TABLE dbo.OrderDetail DROP CONSTRAINT FK__OrderDeta__Produ__0A9D95DB;
GO
ALTER TABLE dbo.Product SET (LOCK_ESCALATION = TABLE)
GO
COMMIT TRANSACTION -- Command(s) completed successfully.
```

```
BEGIN TRANSACTION;
GO
ALTER TABLE dbo.OrderDetail ADD CONSTRAINT FK__OrderDeta__Produ__0A9D95DB
FOREIGN KEY (ProductID) REFERENCES dbo.Product (ProductID) ON DELETE CASCADE;
GO
ALTER TABLE dbo.OrderDetail SET (LOCK_ESCALATION = TABLE);
GO
COMMIT TRANSACTION; -- Command(s) completed successfully.
```

```
SELECT * FROM INFORMATION_SCHEMA.REFERENTIAL_CONSTRAINTS;
```

CONSTRAINT_ CATALOG	CONSTRAINT _SCHEMA	CONSTRAINT_NAME	UNIQUE_CONSTRAI NT_CATALOG	UNIQUE_CONSTRAI NT_SCHEMA	UNIQUE_CONSTRAIN T_NAME	MATCH_ OPTION	UPDATE _RULE	DELETE _RULE
tempdb	dbo	FK__OrderDeta__Produ__0A9D95DB	tempdb	dbo	PK__Product__B40CC6ED66641298	SIMPLE	NO ACTION	CASCADE

```
SELECT COUNT(*) FROM OrderDetail;
GO  -- 121317
```

```
-- Cascading DELETE: first DELETE all referencing FK records, then DELETE PK record
DELETE Product WHERE ProductID = 800;
GO
-- (1 row(s) affected)
```

```
SELECT COUNT(*) FROM OrderDetail;
GO  -- 120822
```

CHAPTER 19: Maintaining Data Integrity in the Enterprise

Declarative Referential Integrity

FOREIGN KEY Constraints Represent the Only Connections Among Tables

While we talk about linked tables in functional terms such as master/header-detail, parent-child, dimension-fact, junction, etc., **there is only a single way to connect tables: FOREIGN KEY references PRIMARY KEY in another table**. We are going to demonstrate it in a grand manner: we will create 290 tables with the names of all the employees of AdventureWorks Cycles (fictional) company in a new test database. We shall connect all of them with FOREIGN KEY constraints: employee (FK table) references manager (PK table).

```
USE master;
GO
CREATE DATABASE AWOrgChart;
GO
USE AWOrgChart;
GO

DECLARE @SQL NVARCHAR(max) = '';

WITH CTE (ID, Emp, Mgr, MgrNode)  -- CTE with column names
    AS
(    SELECT E.BusinessEntityID,
           Emp=CONCAT(P.FirstName, SPACE(1), P.LastName),
           NULL,
           NULL
     FROM   AdventureWorks2012.HumanResources.Employee E
           INNER JOIN AdventureWorks2012.Person.Person P
              ON E.BusinessEntityID = P.BusinessEntityID
     WHERE  E.OrganizationNode = 0x                        -- Root node
     UNION
     SELECT E.BusinessEntityID,
         CONCAT(P.FirstName, SPACE(1), P.LastName)         AS Emp,
         CONCAT(PP.FirstName, SPACE(1), PP.LastName)       AS Mgr,
         E.OrganizationNode.GetAncestor(1)                 AS SuperNode
     FROM   AdventureWorks2012.HumanResources.Employee E
           INNER JOIN AdventureWorks2012.Person.Person P
              ON E.BusinessEntityID = P.BusinessEntityID
           INNER JOIN AdventureWorks2012.HumanResources.Employee EE
              ON ( EE.OrganizationNode =  E.OrganizationNode.GetAncestor(1) )
           INNER JOIN AdventureWorks2012.Person.Person PP
              ON EE.BusinessEntityID = PP.BusinessEntityID)
```

```sql
SELECT @SQL = CONCAT(@SQL, CONCAT('CREATE TABLE ', QUOTENAME(Emp),
            '( ID INT PRIMARY KEY ,',
                ' MgrID INT ',
                    CASE
                WHEN Mgr IS NOT NULL THEN CONCAT(' REFERENCES ',
                        QUOTENAME(Mgr),   '(ID)')
                ELSE ''   END, '); '))
FROM   CTE;

PRINT @SQL;  -- Partial text.
```

CREATE TABLE [Ken Sánchez](ID INT PRIMARY KEY , MgrID INT);
CREATE TABLE [Terri Duffy](ID INT PRIMARY KEY , MgrID INT REFERENCES [Ken Sánchez](ID));
CREATE TABLE [Roberto Tamburello](ID INT PRIMARY KEY , MgrID INT REFERENCES [Terri Duffy](ID));
CREATE TABLE [Rob Walters](ID INT PRIMARY KEY , MgrID INT REFERENCES [Roberto Tamburello](ID));
CREATE TABLE [Gail Erickson](ID INT PRIMARY KEY , MgrID INT REFERENCES [Roberto Tamburello](ID));
CREATE TABLE [Jossef Goldberg](ID INT PRIMARY KEY , MgrID INT REFERENCES [Roberto Tamburello](ID));
CREATE TABLE [Dylan Miller](ID INT PRIMARY KEY , MgrID INT REFERENCES [Roberto Tamburello](ID));
CREATE TABLE [Diane Margheim](ID INT PRIMARY KEY , MgrID INT REFERENCES [Dylan Miller](ID));
CREATE TABLE [Gigi Matthew](ID INT PRIMARY KEY , MgrID INT REFERENCES [Dylan Miller](ID));
CREATE TABLE [Michael Raheem](ID INT PRIMARY KEY , MgrID INT REFERENCES [Dylan Miller](ID));
CREATE TABLE [Ovidiu Cracium](ID INT PRIMARY KEY , MgrID INT REFERENCES [Roberto Tamburello](ID));
CREATE TABLE [Thierry D'Hers](ID INT PRIMARY KEY , MgrID INT REFERENCES [Ovidiu Cracium](ID));

The functional meaning of Terry Duffy "references" Ken Sanchez: Duffy reports to Sanchez.

```sql
EXEC sp_executeSQL @SQL;  -- Dynamic SQL execution: create 290 linked tables
GO

-- USE master;
DROP DATABASE AWOrgChart;
```

CHAPTER 19: Maintaining Data Integrity in the Enterprise

Enterprise-Level Business Rules Enforcement

Diagram Tool Can Be Used for Organizational Charts

We can use the diagram tool in the AWOrgChart database as an orgchart tool. We add a chosen table to the diagram, for example, [Ken Sanchez]. With the right click menu, we add related tables, set view to table name only & arrange selection. The result is orgchart with the CEO and executive managers.

Orgchart starting with [David Hamilton]. Hamilton reports to Krebs (Gold Key).

CHAPTER 19: Maintaining Data Integrity in the Enterprise

Enterprise-Level Business Rules Enforcement

Enterprise-Level Business Rules can be enforced by stored procedures & triggers on the server-side and application programs on the client-side. While stored procedures & application programs can be used to implement a complex set of business rules, they can only effect the current application. Stored procedure or application cannot catch an UPDATE transaction, for example, coming from a legacy application nobody dares to touch at the IT department. In a way stored procedure can be configured to perform after-the-fact near-real-time updates for recently posted data: configure the stored procedure as SQL Server Agent job and schedule it to run each minute.

Special Role of Triggers

Triggers, on the other hand, can catch, for example, an INSERT to the ProductPrice table, wherever it is coming from; current in-house application software, old in-house application, another profit-center of the enterprise application or 3rd party software package. An example for an enterprise business rule: convert foreign currency pricing to USD in the INSERT record to ProductPrice using the latest conversion rates from the ForeignExchange table. A constraint cannot be used to implement such a rule, a trigger can. Trigger code almost as flexible as stored procedure code. Triggers can also be used for cross-database referential integrity enforcement. While triggers are compiled into one database, they can access tables in another database. Because of their omnipotent nature, triggers are frequently misapplied as fix-it-all tools.

> **WARNING**
> Triggers are high maintenance database objects. Triggers are not for junior staff.
> Dropped/disabled triggers do not "COMPLAIN": stealth behavior.

Triggers are just like silent workhorses. They can be forgotten after months of operation since they don't have to be called explicitly from the client-side application programs, they are event launched on the server-side. DDL trigger can be applied to guard DML triggers, but then someone or something has to guard the DDL trigger as well. On the other hand, a dropped stored procedure causes user error ("complains"). Dropped trigger can cause user error also, but the error cannot easily be traced back the trigger.

The following update trigger will prevent last name update from new software, old software, other department's software or even 3rd party software package.

```
CREATE TRIGGER trgEmployee  ON Employee FOR UPDATE AS
    IF (UPDATE(LastName))                    BEGIN
       RAISERROR ('Last name cannot be changed', 16, 1);   ROLLBACK TRAN;   RETURN;    END
GO
```

CHAPTER 19: Maintaining Data Integrity in the Enterprise

Enterprise-Level Business Rules Enforcement

Product Reorder Trigger

The UPDATE trigger is attached to the Products table. It fires whenever there is an UPDATE for the table, no matter what kind of software application from what part of the world executed the UPDATE statement. **A trigger should never return a result set**. However, there is no error if we try to return a result set with a SELECT statement just like in a stored procedure. For testing & debugging purposes we can return results.

```sql
USE Northwind
GO


-- Logging table for product reorder notices
CREATE TABLE Reorder (
        ID INT IDENTITY(1,1) PRIMARY KEY,
        Message varchar(256),
        CreateDate datetime default (CURRENT_TIMESTAMP));
GO


IF EXISTS (select * from sys.objects where type='TR' and name = 'trgProductReorder')
        DROP TRIGGER trgProductReorder
GO


CREATE TRIGGER trgProductReorder
ON Products FOR UPDATE
AS
 BEGIN
   SET NOCOUNT ON;
   DECLARE @MsgText    varchar(128),   @QtyOnHand  int, @ReorderLevel int;
   SELECT @MsgText = CONCAT('Please place a reorder for ', Rtrim(ProductName))
   FROM  inserted;

   SELECT @QtyOnHand = UnitsInStock,  @ReorderLevel = ReorderLevel  FROM  inserted;

   IF @QtyOnHand < @ReorderLevel
       INSERT Reorder (Message)     SELECT @MsgText;

 --select * from deleted -- for testing &debugging only
 --select * from inserted
 --select @MsgText
  END
GO
```

CHAPTER 19: Maintaining Data Integrity in the Enterprise

A Trigger Should Never Return A Result Set Like A Stored Procedure

Check Data Manipulation Language (DML) trigger existence with sp_helptrigger system procedure.

```
EXEC sp_helptrigger Products ;
GO
```

trigger_name	trigger_owner	isupdate	isdelete	isinsert	isafter	isinsteadof	trigger_schema
trgProductReorder	dbo	1	0	0	1	0	dbo

```
-- Test trigger
/* For demonstration purposes, the debugging statements in trigger were uncommented */
UPDATE Products
    SET   UnitsInStock = 10
    WHERE  ProductID = 77;
GO
```

SQL Server UPDATE is implemented as complete deleted (old) and inserted (new) rows. Even if 1 byte updated, a complete row deleted and complete row inserted generated for logging.

deleted table row:

ProductID	ProductName	SupplierID	CategoryID	QuantityPerUnit	UnitPrice	**UnitsInStock**	UnitsOnOrder	ReorderLevel	Discontinued
77	Original Frankfurter grüne Soße	12	2	12 boxes	13.00	**50**	0	15	0

inserted table row:

ProductID	ProductName	SupplierID	CategoryID	QuantityPerUnit	UnitPrice	**UnitsInStock**	UnitsOnOrder	ReorderLevel	Discontinued
77	Original Frankfurter grüne Soße	12	2	12 boxes	13.00	**10**	0	15	0

```
SELECT * FROM   Reorder;
GO
```

ID	Message	CreateDate
1	Please place a reorder for Original Frankfurter grüne Soße	2016-11-25 06:06:45.043

```
DROP TRIGGER trgProductReorder;
DROP TABLE Reorder;
```

CHAPTER 19: Maintaining Data Integrity in the Enterprise

Trigger Examples In AdventureWorks2012

List of triggers in the sample database. parent_object_id is the object_id of the trigger parent table. SELF-JOIN is required to get the parent information.

```
USE AdventureWorks2012;
SELECT
    o.name                                                       AS TriggerName,
    SCHEMA_NAME(po.schema_id)                                    AS TableSchema,
    OBJECT_NAME(o.parent_object_id)                              AS TableName,
    OBJECTPROPERTY( o.object_id, 'ExecIsUpdateTrigger')          AS [isupdate],
    OBJECTPROPERTY( o.object_id, 'ExecIsDeleteTrigger')          AS [isdelete],
    OBJECTPROPERTY( o.object_id, 'ExecIsInsertTrigger')          AS [isinsert],
    OBJECTPROPERTY( o.object_id, 'ExecIsAfterTrigger')           AS [isafter],
    OBJECTPROPERTY( o.object_id, 'ExecIsInsteadOfTrigger')       AS [isinsteadof],
    OBJECTPROPERTY( o.object_id, 'ExecIsTriggerDisabled')        AS [disabled]
FROM sys.objects AS o
    INNER JOIN sys.objects AS po    ON o.parent_object_id = po.object_id
WHERE o.[type] = 'TR'  ORDER BY TableSchema, TableName, TriggerName;
```

TriggerName	TableSchema	TableName	isupdate	isdelete	isinsert	isafter	isinsteadof	disabled
dEmployee	HumanResources	Employee	0	1	0	0	1	0
iuPerson	Person	Person	1	0	1	1	0	0
iWorkOrder	Production	WorkOrder	0	0	1	1	0	0
uWorkOrder	Production	WorkOrder	1	0	0	1	0	0
iPurchaseOrderDetail	Purchasing	PurchaseOrderDetail	0	0	1	1	0	0
uPurchaseOrderDetail	Purchasing	PurchaseOrderDetail	1	0	0	1	0	0
uPurchaseOrderHeader	Purchasing	PurchaseOrderHeader	1	0	0	1	0	0
dVendor	Purchasing	Vendor	0	1	0	0	1	0
iduSalesOrderDetail	Sales	SalesOrderDetail	1	1	1	1	0	0
uSalesOrderHeader	Sales	SalesOrderHeader	1	0	0	1	0	0

Alternate method of obtaining all triggers information.

```
SELECT * FROM sys.triggers ORDER BY name;  -- Partial results.
```

name	object_id	parent_class	parent_class_desc	parent_id	type	type_desc
ddlDatabaseTriggerLog	261575970	0	DATABASE	0	TR	SQL_TRIGGER
dEmployee	1739153241	1	OBJECT_OR_COLUMN	1237579447	TR	SQL_TRIGGER
dVendor	1851153640	1	OBJECT_OR_COLUMN	766625774	TR	SQL_TRIGGER
iduSalesOrderDetail	1819153526	1	OBJECT_OR_COLUMN	1154103152	TR	SQL_TRIGGER
iPurchaseOrderDetail	1771153355	1	OBJECT_OR_COLUMN	850102069	TR	SQL_TRIGGER
iuPerson	1755153298	1	OBJECT_OR_COLUMN	1765581328	TR	SQL_TRIGGER
iWorkOrder	1867153697	1	OBJECT_OR_COLUMN	846626059	TR	SQL_TRIGGER
uPurchaseOrderDetail	1787153412	1	OBJECT_OR_COLUMN	850102069	TR	SQL_TRIGGER
uPurchaseOrderHeader	1803153469	1	OBJECT_OR_COLUMN	946102411	TR	SQL_TRIGGER
uSalesOrderHeader	1835153583	1	OBJECT_OR_COLUMN	1266103551	TR	SQL_TRIGGER
uWorkOrder	1883153754	1	OBJECT_OR_COLUMN	846626059	TR	SQL_TRIGGER

Trigger Can Be Modified in Object Explorer

When the Modify Trigger option is picked, Object Explorer loads it as ALTER TRIGGER script.

Programmatic way to get trigger definition.

```
SELECT OBJECT_DEFINITION( object_id('Person.iuPerson'));
```

CREATE TRIGGER [Person].[iuPerson] ON [Person].[Person]
AFTER INSERT, UPDATE NOT FOR REPLICATION AS
BEGIN
DECLARE @Count int;
SET @Count = @@ROWCOUNT;
IF @Count = 0   RETURN;
SET NOCOUNT ON;
IF UPDATE([BusinessEntityID]) OR UPDATE([Demographics])

Business Intelligence in the Enterprise

SQL Server Analysis Services (SSAS), SQL Server Integration Services (SSIS) & SQL Server Reporting Services (SSRS) are the server side Business Intelligence software components. Easy to remember associations: SSAS: OLAP cubes and more, SSIS: ETL (extract, transform, load) data transfer system & SSRS: traditional reports, interactive & OLAP reports. SQL Server Data Tools (SSDT) provides 3 customized templates as design environments.

SSRS: Designing Complex Interactive Reports

SSDT report design environment: product catalog in the report design editor.

CHAPTER 19: Maintaining Data Integrity in the Enterprise

Previewing the Report Design

The product catalog is interactive with a drill down directory on the left which is based on the Production.ProductCategory and Production.ProductSubcategory tables. The Product, ProductSubcategory & ProductCategory tables form a hierarchy which is neatly exploited in the product catalog report. What makes the report design environment extremely powerful that you can try the look & feel of a report just by clicking a tab and staying in the studio environment. The product images are from the ProductPhoto table(in Management Studio we cannot see the images, only the binary code).

Business Intelligence in the Enterprise

Detailed Preview of AWC Product Catalog

Mountain-200

Serious back-country riding. Perfect for all levels of competition. Uses the same HL Frame as the Mountain-100.

Product No.	Product	Color	Size	Weight	Dealer	List Price
BK-M68B-46	Mountain-200 Black, 46	Black	46	24	$1,251.98	$2,294.99
BK-M68B-42	Mountain-200 Black, 42	Black	42	24	$1,251.98	$2,294.99
BK-M68B-38	Mountain-200 Black, 38	Black	38	23	$1,251.98	$2,294.99
BK-M68S-46	Mountain-200 Silver, 46	Silver	46	24	$1,265.62	$2,319.99
BK-M68S-42	Mountain-200 Silver, 42	Silver	42	24	$1,265.62	$2,319.99
BK-M68S-38	Mountain-200 Silver, 38	Silver	38	23	$1,265.62	$2,319.99

Mountain-300

For true trail addicts. An extremely durable bike that will go anywhere and keep you in control on challenging terrain - without breaking your budget.

Product No.	Product	Color	Size	Weight	Dealer	List Price
BK-M47B-48	Mountain-300 Black, 48	Black	48	26	$598.44	$1,079.99
BK-M47B-44	Mountain-300 Black, 44	Black	44	26	$598.44	$1,079.99
BK-M47B-40	Mountain-300 Black, 40	Black	40	26	$598.44	$1,079.99
BK-M47B-38	Mountain-300 Black, 38	Black	38	25	$598.44	$1,079.99

CHAPTER 19: Maintaining Data Integrity in the Enterprise

SSAS: Designing Multi-Dimensional Cubes

SSAS cubes contain millions of pre-calculated answers just waiting for the question like: what was the net revenue in Florida for the 3rd Quarter of 2016? Since the answer is ready, the response time is sub-second. AS cubes are derived from dimension tables and fact tables in a data warehouse database.

Test OLAP Analysis Services Cube Design with Browser

Dimension Usage Display

CHAPTER 19: Maintaining Data Integrity in the Enterprise

Browsing Multidimensional Cube in Management Explorer

In Object Explorer we can connect to Analysis Server and browse the available multidimensional cubes.

```
USE AdventureWorksDW2012;
-- Searching data warehouse database metadata for table objects
SELECT  CONCAT(schema_name(O.schema_id),'.', O.NAME) AS ObjectName,
        O.TYPE AS ObjectType,     C.NAME AS ColumnName
FROM sys.objects O INNER JOIN sys.columns C ON O.OBJECT_ID = C.OBJECT_ID
WHERE  O.type='U' AND O.NAME LIKE '%sales%' AND C.NAME LIKE '%price%'
ORDER BY ObjectName, ColumnName;   -- Partial results.
-- dbo.FactInternetSales     U          UnitPrice
```

CHAPTER 19: Maintaining Data Integrity in the Enterprise

Excel PivotTable Report Using AS Cube Datasource

Excel can use as datasource SQL Server database and Analysis Services database(bottom image). Actually PivotTable is a very good match for browsing multidimensional cubes since the underlying concepts are very similar: summary data tabulations by dimensions.

Sales Reason Comparison Report Based on AS Cube

The Sales Reason Comparison report (converted to 2012) is based on the multidimensional AdventureWorksAS AS cube. Design mode and report segment in preview mode.

Sales Reason	Europe			North America		
	Internet Orders	Internet Sales Amount	Internet Total Product Cost	Internet Orders	Internet Sales Amount	Inter Prod
Manufacturer	$352	$1,206,594	$733,050	$803	$2,765,552	$
On Promotion	$1,118	$2,009,804	$1,182,740	$1,298	$2,217,191	$
Other	$111	$65,666	$39,932	$109	$62,743	
Price	$2,275	$3,586,028	$2,120,140	$2,630	$4,158,322	$
Quality	$316	$1,130,733	$686,129	$718	$2,569,198	$
Review	$226	$436,477	$250,168	$319	$578,245	

CHAPTER 19: Maintaining Data Integrity in the Enterprise

Business Intelligence in the Enterprise

SSIS: Enterprise Level Data Integration

SSIS is an enterprise level data integration and data transformation software tool. Transmit (clean, transformed) data from different data sources to the database and vice versa. The Data Flow editor in SSDT for an SSIS sample project.

CHAPTER 19: Maintaining Data Integrity in the Enterprise

SSAS, SSIS, SSRS in Configuration Manager

SSIS is shared for all instances. SSAS & SSRS are per instance. MSSQLSERVER means the default instance, HPESTAR. SQL12 means the names instance HPESTAR\SQL12.

ReportServer & ReportServerTempDB Databases

Each Reporting Services instance is supported by two databases.

CHAPTER 19: Maintaining Data Integrity in the Enterprise

Full-Text Index & Full-Text Search

Full-Text Search in SQL Server 2012 allows users and application programs, such as C#, to execute Full-Text Search queries against text-based data in SQL Server 2012 tables. Prior to running full-text search queries on a table, full-text catalog and full-text indexes on table text column(s) must be created.

```
USE AdventureWorks2012;
SELECT * INTO dbo.JobCandidate FROM HumanResources.JobCandidate; ; -- (13 row(s) affected)
GO
CREATE UNIQUE INDEX idxHRJC ON JobCandidate(JobCandidateID);
CREATE FULLTEXT CATALOG HRFullText AS DEFAULT;
CREATE FULLTEXT INDEX ON JobCandidate(Resume) KEY INDEX idxHRJC WITH STOPLIST = SYSTEM;
GO
```

```
SELECT JobCandidateID FROM JobCandidate WHERE CONTAINS(Resume, ' "production line" ');    -- 2

SELECT JobCandidateID FROM JobCandidate WHERE CONTAINS(Resume, ' "C#" ');    -- 3

SELECT JobCandidateID FROM JobCandidate WHERE CONTAINS (Resume, ' "machin*" ' );    -- 1, 7

SELECT * FROM CONTAINSTABLE(JobCandidate, Resume, 'ISABOUT ("mach*",
    tool WEIGHT(0.9),  automatic WEIGHT(0.1)   )' );
```

KEY	RANK
1	51
7	22

```
SELECT jc.JobCandidateID, x.* FROM JobCandidate jc
        INNER JOIN  CONTAINSTABLE(JobCandidate, Resume, 'ISABOUT ("mach*",
               tool WEIGHT(0.9),  automatic WEIGHT(0.1)  )' ) x  ON x.[KEY] = jc.JobCandidateID;
```

JobCandidateID	KEY	RANK
1	1	51
7	7	22

```
SELECT JobCandidateID FROM JobCandidate WHERE CONTAINS(Resume, '(ingénierie NEAR expérimenté)');  -- 7

SELECT JobCandidateID FROM JobCandidate WHERE CONTAINS(Resume, '(visual and basic)');  -- 3

SELECT JobCandidateID FROM JobCandidate WHERE CONTAINS(Resume, '(visual or basic)'); -- 2, 3

SELECT JobCandidateID FROM JobCandidate WHERE CONTAINS (Resume,'FORMSOF(INFLECTIONAL,"computer")'); -- 1
GO

DROP TABLE dbo.JobCandidate;
DROP FULLTEXT CATALOG HRFullText;
GO
```

CHAPTER 19: Maintaining Data Integrity in the Enterprise

SQL Azure - Enterprise in the Clouds

Microsoft Windows Azure account is available at:

http://www.windowsazure.com/en-us/ .

There is a 90-day free trial package available which includes an SQL database. Credit card is required for an Azure account. One form of verification: a code is sent to your mobile phone.

Creating an SQL database in the "clouds".

CHAPTER 19: Maintaining Data Integrity in the Enterprise

SQL Azure - Enterprise in the Clouds 633

Getting Started with SQL Azure Database

Basic configuration has to be done online such as setting SQL Azure server login & password, and setting up firewall rules so you can use Management Studio and other client software from your computer. The configuration processes are automated to a large degree and user-friendly. The best part: once you are finished with configuration, you can continue with the "friendly skies" from the friendly Management Studio environment.

CHAPTER 19: Maintaining Data Integrity in the Enterprise

Connecting Azure SQL Server from Management Studio

You can connect to the Azure SQL Server after setting up a firewall rule for your computer IP using the regular dialog box with SQL Server authentication. The server name is: yourazureserver.database.windows.net. The login & password is what you configured on Azure. Some server & login information has been blanked out on the following screenshot. The Azure T-SQL is different from SQL Server 2012 T-SQL

We can get SQL Azure version information by a SELECT:

select @@version -- Microsoft SQL Azure (RTM) - 11.0.2065.0 Aug 29 2012 18:41:07

CHAPTER 19: Maintaining Data Integrity in the Enterprise

CHAPTER 20: Query & Stored Procedure Optimization

Optimization Basics

Optimization revolves around techniques for the reduction of the resource requirements to carry out an operation such as a SELECT query. There are two ways to do optimization:

- Engineering the query / script the optimal way
- Creating indexes on the tables

In both instances the usual objective is "reads" (logical 8K page reads) reduction. While the final objective is the "duration" reduction, that measure involves blocking as well so it is not as reliable as the "reads" measure. Using the first software engineering technique, we aim to eliminate unneeded operations or find a replacement which is less resource intensive. The second indexing technique is purely "reads" reduction in focus, we are not changing the query or the script. T-SQL has 2 statistics commands for taking basic performance measures. For even tests, we don't want to use cache memory (fast), but only disk (slow). A "cold" execute of a query may take 8 seconds, while the next (using cache) 1 second only.

```
USE AdventureWorks2012;
DBCC DROPCLEANBUFFERS;  -- Forces reload of data pages (forces disk io) in cache buffer memory
SET STATISTICS IO ON; SET STATISTICS TIME ON;
       EXEC uspGetBillOfMaterials 801, '2008-01-05';
SET STATISTICS TIME OFF; SET STATISTICS IO OFF;  -- Messages
```

```
DBCC execution completed. If DBCC printed error messages, contact your system administrator.
SQL Server parse and compile time:
  CPU time = 0 ms, elapsed time = 0 ms.

SQL Server Execution Times:
  CPU time = 0 ms,  elapsed time = 0 ms.
Table 'Product'. Scan count 0, logical reads 178, physical reads 3, read-ahead reads 0, lob logical reads 0, lob physical reads 0, lob read-ahead reads 0.
Table 'BillOfMaterials'. Scan count 90, logical reads 181, physical reads 4, read-ahead reads 0, lob logical reads 0, lob physical reads 0, lob read-ahead reads 0.
Table 'Worktable'. Scan count 2, logical reads 510, physical reads 0, read-ahead reads 0, lob logical reads 0, lob physical reads 0, lob read-ahead reads 0.

SQL Server Execution Times:
  CPU time = 16 ms,  elapsed time = 6 ms.

SQL Server Execution Times:
  CPU time = 16 ms,  elapsed time = 6 ms.
```

CHAPTER 20: Query & Stored Procedure Optimization

No Disk IO Needed When All Pages for a Query Are in Buffer Cache
When we execute a query shortly after the previous execution, most pages may still be on cache memory, thus reduction in the need for (slow) disk io.

```
USE AdventureWorks2012;
SET STATISTICS IO ON;
SET STATISTICS TIME ON;
        EXEC uspGetBillOfMaterials 801, '2008-01-05';
SET STATISTICS TIME OFF;  SET STATISTICS IO OFF;
GO -- Messages
```

SQL Server parse and compile time:
  CPU time = 0 ms, elapsed time = 0 ms.

SQL Server Execution Times:
  CPU time = 0 ms, elapsed time = 0 ms.
Table 'Product'. Scan count 0, logical reads 178, **physical reads 0**, read-ahead reads 0, lob logical reads 0, lob physical reads 0, lob read-ahead reads 0.
Table 'BillOfMaterials'. Scan count 90, logical reads 181, **physical reads 0,** read-ahead reads 0, lob logical reads 0, lob physical reads 0, lob read-ahead reads 0.
Table 'Worktable'. Scan count 2, logical reads 510, physical reads 0, read-ahead reads 0, lob logical reads 0, lob physical reads 0, lob read-ahead reads 0.

SQL Server Execution Times:
  CPU time = 0 ms, elapsed time = 2 ms.

SQL Server Execution Times:
  CPU time = 0 ms, elapsed time = 2 ms.

We can see that physical reads have been eliminated, hence the faster execution. Note, however, timing will vary due to server activities. Therefore, to obtain good measurements we should average over multiple executions, for example 3, 11 or 31. When we monitor a similar execution sequence in SQL Server Profiler, we can see that the logical reads (Reads) were the same but the execution was faster (2 milliseconds) the second time due to the lack of disk io (physical reads). Note: STATISTICS IO and Profiler are 2 different piece of software, hence the difference in figures.

CPU	Reads	Writes	Duration
0	1096	0	7
0	1096	0	2

CHAPTER 20: *Query & Stored Procedure Optimization*

Optimizing a Query by Reengineering

Less fancy way of saying is rewriting the query. Consider an INNER JOIN query with a view which may look simple until we look at the view underlying code. The database engine has to expand the view definition "on the fly" and develop a plan for the more complex query.

```
USE [AdventureWorks2012]
GO
DBCC DROPCLEANBUFFERS;
SET STATISTICS IO ON;
SET STATISTICS TIME ON;
SELECT  LTRIM(CONCAT(ISNULL(Title,''),SPACE(1), FullName))           AS SalesPerson,
        JobTitle, SalesTerritory, FORMAT([2008],'c0','en-US')        AS [2008]
FROM [Sales].[vSalesPersonSalesByFiscalYears] VSP
  INNER JOIN Person.Person P
    ON CONCAT(FirstName, ' ', MiddleName, ' ', LastName) = VSP.FullName
ORDER BY [2008] DESC;
SET STATISTICS TIME OFF;  SET STATISTICS IO OFF;
```

SalesPerson	JobTitle	SalesTerritory	2008
Linda C Mitchell	Sales Representative	Southwest	$4,251,369
Jae B Pak	Sales Representative	United Kingdom	$4,116,871
Michael G Blythe	Sales Representative	Northeast	$3,763,178
Jillian Carson	Sales Representative	Central	$3,189,418
Ranjit R Varkey Chudukatil	Sales Representative	France	$3,121,616
José Edvaldo Saraiva	Sales Representative	Canada	$2,604,541
Shu K Ito	Sales Representative	Southwest	$2,458,536
Tsvi Michael Reiter	Sales Representative	Southeast	$2,315,186
Rachel B Valdez	Sales Representative	Germany	$1,827,067
Mr. Tete A Mensa-Annan	Sales Representative	Northwest	$1,576,562
David R Campbell	Sales Representative	Northwest	$1,573,013
Garrett R Vargas	Sales Representative	Canada	$1,453,719
Lynn N Tsoflias	Sales Representative	Australia	$1,421,811
Pamela O Ansman-Wolfe	Sales Representative	Northwest	$1,352,577

DBCC execution completed. If DBCC printed error messages, contact your system administrator.

(14 row(s) affected)
Table 'Worktable'. Scan count 0, logical reads 0, physical reads 0, read-ahead reads 0, lob logical reads 0, lob physical reads 0, lob read-ahead reads 0.
Table 'SalesOrderHeader'. Scan count 5, logical reads 865, physical reads 2, read-ahead reads 784, lob logical reads 0, lob physical reads 0, lob read-ahead reads 0.
Table 'Employee'. Scan count 0, logical reads 28, physical reads 1, read-ahead reads 0, lob logical reads 0, lob physical reads 0, lob read-ahead reads 0.
Table 'Person'. Scan count 5, logical reads 4240, physical reads 2, read-ahead reads 3817, lob logical reads 0, lob physical reads 0, lob read-ahead reads 0.
Table 'SalesTerritory'. Scan count 0, logical reads 28, physical reads 1, read-ahead reads 0, lob logical reads 0, lob physical reads 0, lob read-ahead reads 0.
Table 'SalesPerson'. Scan count 0, logical reads 34, physical reads 1, read-ahead reads 0, lob logical reads 0, lob physical reads 0, lob read-ahead reads 0.
Table 'Worktable'. Scan count 0, logical reads 0, physical reads 0, read-ahead reads 0, lob logical reads 0, lob physical reads 0, lob read-ahead reads 0.
SQL Server Execution Times:
   CPU time = 172 ms, elapsed time = 1162 ms.

JOIN on INT Columns Faster Than on nvarchar Strings

Our suspicion is that JOINing on nvarchar fields may be improved if we replace it with JOIN on INT columns (4 bytes). Actually, we are in luck, it is just an easy rewrite of the query.

```
USE [AdventureWorks2012]
GO
DBCC DROPCLEANBUFFERS;
SET STATISTICS IO ON;
SET STATISTICS TIME ON;
SELECT  LTRIM(CONCAT(ISNULL(Title,''),SPACE(1), FullName))       AS SalesPerson,
        JobTitle, SalesTerritory, FORMAT([2008],'c0','en-US')    AS [2008]
FROM [Sales].[vSalesPersonSalesByFiscalYears] VSP
  INNER JOIN Person.Person P
    ON P.BusinessEntityID = VSP.SalesPersonID  ORDER BY [2008] DESC;
SET STATISTICS TIME OFF;  SET STATISTICS IO OFF;
GO
```

DBCC execution completed. If DBCC printed error messages, contact your system administrator.

(14 row(s) affected)
Table 'Person'. Scan count 0, logical reads 90, physical reads 2, read-ahead reads 0, lob logical reads 0, lob physical reads 0, lob read-ahead reads 0.
Table 'SalesOrderHeader'. Scan count 14, logical reads 12333, physical reads 9, read-ahead reads 352, lob logical reads 0, lob physical reads 0, lob read-ahead reads 0.
Table 'Employee'. Scan count 0, logical reads 28, physical reads 2, read-ahead reads 0, lob logical reads 0, lob physical reads 0, lob read-ahead reads 0.
Table 'SalesTerritory'. Scan count 0, logical reads 28, physical reads 1, read-ahead reads 0, lob logical reads 0, lob physical reads 0, lob read-ahead reads 0.
Table 'SalesPerson'. Scan count 1, logical reads 2, physical reads 1, read-ahead reads 0, lob logical reads 0, lob physical reads 0, lob read-ahead reads 0.

SQL Server Execution Times:
  CPU time = 16 ms, elapsed time = 68 ms.

When we compare the statistics we observe the elimination of 2 worktables and we reduced the "reads" on the Person table by the more efficient JOIN. The low CPU in the Profiler comparison screenshot indicative of the simpler JOIN. Even though the total "reads" are higher, the indexed INT JOIN proves to be quite advantageous over varchar JOIN as reflected in the lower CPU figure.

CPU	Reads	Writes	Duration
0	0	0	0
236	5314	0	1144
0	0	0	0
78	14194	0	302

Optimizing a Query by Reengineering

Examining the Actual Execution Plan

There are two execution plan which can be turned by clicking on the corresponding icons: estimated and actual. The execution plan can be helpful with missing indexes and improvement considerations. Understanding a complex execution plan requires extensive studying and experience.

CHAPTER 20: Query & Stored Procedure Optimization

Comparing Execution Plan Cost Summary Pop-ups

When hovering with the mouse over the SELECT on the left side of the execution plan, a cost summary panel pops up.

SELECT	
Cached plan size	120 KB
Degree of Parallelism	4
Estimated Operator Cost	0 (0%)
Memory Grant	1018816
Estimated Subtree Cost	15132.9
Estimated Number of Rows	2608890

Statement
SELECT LTRIM(CONCAT(ISNULL
(Title,''),SPACE(1), FullName)) AS
SalesPerson,
JobTitle, SalesTerritory, FORMAT
([2008],'c0','en-US') AS [2008]
FROM [Sales].
[vSalesPersonSalesByFiscalYears] VSP
  INNER JOIN Person.Person P
    ON CONCAT(FirstName, ' ',
MiddleName, ' ', LastName) =
VSP.FullName
ORDER BY [2008] DESC;

SELECT	
Cached plan size	96 KB
Degree of Parallelism	1
Estimated Operator Cost	0 (0%)
Estimated Subtree Cost	1.60204
Memory Grant	7352
Estimated Number of Rows	1306.27

Statement
SELECT LTRIM(CONCAT(ISNULL
(Title,''),SPACE(1), FullName)) AS
SalesPerson,
JobTitle, SalesTerritory, FORMAT
([2008],'c0','en-US') AS [2008]
FROM [Sales].
[vSalesPersonSalesByFiscalYears] VSP
  INNER JOIN Person.Person P
    ON P.BusinessEntityID =
VSP.SalesPersonID
ORDER BY [2008] DESC;

Side by side comparison of the cost panels shows dramatic differences. Cost of 15,132 versus 1.6 are simply shocking. The example powerfully illustrates the challenges in query optimization whereby relatively simple rewrite may result in huge performance improvement. We cannot say much about the optimization state of a query just by looking at cost. Only when we compare it to a different version of the query we can say if worsened, improved or much improved. We can also notice the huge difference in rows: 2.6 million vs. 1,300. Memory requirement for the nvarchar JOIN is over a million grants, while only 7 thousands for the INT JOIN.

Poorly written query not only slow in execution but very resource intensive as well, therefore it slows down other queries executing simultaneously. Hence the need to optimize queries especially frequently executed ones.

An extreme bad query can bring down the mightiest server to its "knees". We can see why just by looking at this very simple example with bad and good INNER JOINs.

Optimizing a Query by Reengineering

Optimizing with Multi Statements Query Using Temporary Tables

Assume that the fast INT JOIN is not available. Another technique: instead of a single statement query multi statements since we have more control over the execution plan. In the current example we are forcing the optimizer to evaluate the view query first and store the results into a temporary table. Note: messages shows the long (real) name of #VSP temporary table, personalized to this connection.

```
DBCC DROPCLEANBUFFERS;
SET STATISTICS IO ON;
SET STATISTICS TIME ON;
SELECT * INTO #VSP FROM [Sales].[vSalesPersonSalesByFiscalYears];

SELECT  LTRIM(CONCAT(ISNULL(Title,''),SPACE(1), FullName))      AS SalesPerson,
        JobTitle, SalesTerritory, FORMAT([2008],'c0','en-US')   AS [2008]
FROM #VSP
  INNER JOIN Person.Person P
    ON CONCAT(FirstName, ' ', MiddleName, ' ', LastName) = #VSP.FullName
ORDER BY [2008] DESC;
SET STATISTICS TIME OFF;
SET STATISTICS IO OFF;
GO
DROP TABLE #VSP
```

Messages

```
DBCC execution completed. If DBCC printed error messages, contact your system administrator.
Table 'SalesOrderHeader'. Scan count 14, logical reads 12452, physical reads 9, read-ahead reads 352, lob logical reads 0, lob physical reads 0, lob read-ahead reads 0.
Table 'Person'. Scan count 0, logical reads 42, physical reads 2, read-ahead reads 0, lob logical reads 0, lob physical reads 0, lob read-ahead reads 0.
Table 'Employee'. Scan count 0, logical reads 28, physical reads 2, read-ahead reads 0, lob logical reads 0, lob physical reads 0, lob read-ahead reads 0.
Table 'SalesTerritory'. Scan count 0, logical reads 28, physical reads 1, read-ahead reads 0, lob logical reads 0, lob physical reads 0, lob read-ahead reads 0.
Table 'SalesPerson'. Scan count 1, logical reads 2, physical reads 1, read-ahead reads 0, lob logical reads 0, lob physical reads 0, lob read-ahead reads 0.

(14 row(s) affected)

(1 row(s) affected)

SQL Server Execution Times:
   CPU time = 94 ms,  elapsed time = 362 ms.
SQL Server parse and compile time:
   CPU time = 0 ms, elapsed time = 70 ms.
SQL Server parse and compile time:
   CPU time = 0 ms, elapsed time = 236 ms.

(14 row(s) affected)
Table 'Person'. Scan count 1, logical reads 3826, physical reads 0, read-ahead reads 3817, lob logical reads 0, lob physical reads 0, lob read-ahead reads 0.
Table 'Worktable'. Scan count 1, logical reads 42166, physical reads 0, read-ahead reads 0, lob logical reads 0, lob physical reads 0, lob read-ahead reads 0.
Table '#VSP_____000000000074'. Scan count 1, logical reads 1, physical reads 0, read-ahead reads 0, lob logical reads 0, lob physical reads 0, lob read-ahead reads 0.

(1 row(s) affected)

SQL Server Execution Times:
   CPU time = 266 ms,  elapsed time = 832 ms.
```

CHAPTER 20: Query & Stored Procedure Optimization

Obstacle: Worktable 42K "reads" Cannot Be Decreased

This course of action is not as good as the JOIN on the INT (integer) keys. Yet the combination of costs came down to 6, a reasonable figure relatively speaking. The Estimated Number of Rows are "reasonable" as well, just like the Memory Grants.

CPU	Reads	Writes	Duration
125	15849	3	1155
203	42536	123	356

SELECT INTO		SELECT	
Cached plan size	120 KB	Cached plan size	32 KB
Degree of Parallelism	1	Degree of Parallelism	1
Estimated Operator Cost	0 (0%)	Estimated Operator Cost	0 (0%)
Estimated Subtree Cost	1.6378	Memory Grant	1024
Estimated Number of Rows	1306.27	Estimated Subtree Cost	4.18429
		Estimated Number of Rows	19972

Statement
SELECT * INTO #VSP FROM [Sales].[vSalesPersonSalesByFiscalYears];

Statement
SELECT LTRIM(CONCAT(ISNULL(Title,''),SPACE(1), FullName)) AS SalesPerson,
JobTitle, SalesTerritory, FORMAT([2008],'c0','en-US') AS [2008]
FROM #VSP
  INNER JOIN Person.Person P
    ON #VSP.FullName = CONCAT(FirstName,' ', MiddleName,' ', LastName)
ORDER BY [2008] DESC;

The 42K "reads" is huge, in this case on an internal work table which is outside our direct control, however, indirectly we may be able to influence it. The common goal of optimization is "reads" reduction usually with indexing if the query is engineered correctly. With indexing we may be able to bring down the reads to 500 or even 50.

Optimizing with Covering Index

We can achieve miracles in query optimization with indexing but at a cost: index represents an overhead since it slows down some operations such as INSERT or DELETE and it has to be maintained. First we add a computed column to the Person.Person table, them create a "covering" index on it which includes the Title used in the SELECT clause. Note: computed column and covering index are "luxury" items which are used to support **business critical queries** only. In a covering index all columns are present in the index for the query as keys or included column. **Note: there is no "free lunch" with indexing only tradeoff**. Covering index tends to be wide and may slow down other than the target queries.

```
ALTER TABLE Person.Person ADD FullName
        AS CONCAT(FirstName, ' ', MiddleName, ' ', LastName)        PERSISTED;
GO
--Command(s) completed successfully.
```

```
CREATE INDEX idxFullName
            on Person.Person(FullName) INCLUDE (Title);
GO
-- Command(s) completed successfully.
```

```
-- DROP INDEX Person.Person.idxFullName;
```

The new query using the new column in the INNER JOIN:

```
SELECT  LTRIM(CONCAT(ISNULL(Title,''),SPACE(1), #VSP.FullName))      AS SalesPerson,
        JobTitle, SalesTerritory, FORMAT([2008],'c0','en-US')        AS [2008]
FROM #VSP
 INNER JOIN Person.Person P
  ON P.FullName = #VSP.FullName
```

The result is simply amazing: the 42K "reads" on the work table is gone. The 123 "writes" are gone as well. Duration is not a stable measure because it includes blocking as well. If there is no blocking duration is proportionally higher with higher CPU, Reads & Writes.

CPU	Reads	Writes	Duration
140	15802	1	551
16	81	0	117

CHAPTER 20: Query & Stored Procedure Optimization

Optimizing with Indexing

The general rule is that all JOIN keys and WHERE condition columns should be indexed. Since PRIMARY KEY is automatically indexed, the rule means that all FOREIGN KEYs should be indexed since that is not automatic.

```
USE tempdb;
SELECT [SalesOrderID]
    ,CONVERT(INT,[SalesOrderDetailID]) AS [SalesOrderDetailID] -- inhibit identity inheritence
    ,[CarrierTrackingNumber], [OrderQty], [ProductID], [SpecialOfferID] ,[UnitPrice]
    ,[UnitPriceDiscount],[LineTotal],[rowguid],[ModifiedDate]
INTO SOD FROM [AdventureWorks2012].[Sales].[SalesOrderDetail];
GO -- (121317 row(s) affected)
INSERT SOD SELECT * FROM SOD;   -- increase size of table by duplicating itself
GO 5    /* Beginning execution loop  (121317 row(s) affected) (242634 row(s) affected)
(485268 row(s) affected)  (970536 row(s) affected)
(1941072 row(s) affected)  Batch execution completed 5 times. */
SELECT FORMAT(COUNT(*), '###,###,###') FROM SOD;  -- 3,882,144
SELECT * INTO Product FROM AdventureWorks2012.Production.Product;
```

The Larger the Table the More Benefits of Indexing

```
DBCC DROPCLEANBUFFERS;  SET STATISTICS IO ON; SET STATISTICS TIME ON;
    SELECT * FROM SOD INNER JOIN Product P
        ON SOD.ProductID = P.ProductID    WHERE P.ProductID = 800;
SET STATISTICS TIME OFF;    SET STATISTICS IO OFF;
```

DBCC execution completed. If DBCC printed error messages, contact your system administrator.
(15840 row(s) affected)
Table 'SOD'. Scan count 5, logical reads 54796, physical reads 0, read-ahead reads 1719, lob logical reads 0, lob physical reads 0, lob read-ahead reads 0.
Table 'Product'. Scan count 1, logical reads 14, physical reads 0, read-ahead reads 0, lob logical reads 0, lob physical reads 0, lob read-ahead reads 0.
Table 'Worktable'. Scan count 0, logical reads 0, physical reads 0, read-ahead reads 0, lob logical reads 0, lob physical reads 0, lob read-ahead reads 0.
SQL Server Execution Times:
CPU time = 483 ms, elapsed time = 845 ms.

> MSDN Article: **Clustered and Nonclustered Indexes Described**
> http://msdn.microsoft.com/en-us/library/ms190457.aspx

Optimizing with Indexing 645

Create Unique Nonclustered & Clustered Indexes

```
CREATE CLUSTERED INDEX idxPrd ON SOD(ProductID);
CREATE UNIQUE INDEX idxPrd ON Product(ProductID);
GO
```

```
DBCC DROPCLEANBUFFERS; SET STATISTICS IO ON;  SET STATISTICS TIME ON;
        SELECT * FROM SOD INNER JOIN Product P
                ON SOD.ProductID = P.ProductID     WHERE P.ProductID = 800;
SET STATISTICS TIME OFF;   SET STATISTICS IO OFF;
GO
```

DBCC execution completed. If DBCC printed error messages, contact your system administrator.
SQL Server parse and compile time:
CPU time = 0 ms, elapsed time = 2 ms.
(15840 row(s) affected)
Table 'SOD'. Scan count 1, logical reads 210, physical reads 0, read-ahead reads 206, lob logical reads 0, lob physical reads 0, lob read-ahead reads 0.
Table 'Product'. Scan count 0, logical reads 3, physical reads 0, read-ahead reads 0, lob logical reads 0, lob physical reads 0, lob read-ahead reads 0.
(1 row(s) affected)
SQL Server Execution Times:
CPU time = 47 ms, elapsed time = 517 ms.

Check Data & Indexes Fragmentation on a Table

The sys.dm_db_index_physical_stats Dynamic Management Function (DMF) can be used to obtain index fragmentation information(Ye Olde Way: DBCC SHOWCONTIG). The clustered index line represents the data fragmentation. 20% fragmentation is considered low, 80% considered high.

```
SELECT object_NAME(object_id) AS TableName, i ndex_id,
        index_type_desc, FORMAT(avg_fragmentation_in_percent, 'p0') AS PcntFrag
    FROM sys.dm_db_index_physical_stats(DB_ID(N'AdventureWorks2012'),
       OBJECT_ID(N'AdventureWorks2012.Sales.SalesOrderDetail'), NULL, NULL , 'LIMITED');
```

TableName	index_id	index_type_desc	PcntFrag
SalesOrderDetail	1	CLUSTERED INDEX	21 %
SalesOrderDetail	2	NONCLUSTERED INDEX	0 %
SalesOrderDetail	3	NONCLUSTERED INDEX	11 %
SalesOrderDetail	10	NONCLUSTERED INDEX	0 %
SalesOrderDetail	13	NONCLUSTERED INDEX	90 %

MSDN Article: **Reorganize and Rebuild Indexes**
http://msdn.microsoft.com/en-us/library/ms189858.aspx

CHAPTER 20: Query & Stored Procedure Optimization

Clustered Index for Business Critical Query Support

Clustered index is another "luxury" item in optimization since there can only be one on a table and 0 to many nonclustered indexes. In this example nonclustered index does some improvement, but not significant. Cleanup commands for the indexing example script.

```
-- DROP INDEX SOD.idxPrd; DROP INDEX Product.idxPrd;
DROP TABLE SOD;  DROP TABLE Product;
```

SQL Profiler statistics on the sequence of batches we sent to the server from SSMS Query Editor.

TextData	CPU	Reads	Writes	Duration	SPID	EventClass
USE tempdb;	0	0	0	0	53	SQL:BatchCompleted
SELECT [SalesOrderID] ,CONVE...	218	3327	672	782	53	SQL:BatchCompleted
INSERT SOD SELECT * FROM SOD; -...	796	496577	2968	832	53	SQL:BatchCompleted
INSERT SOD SELECT * FROM SOD; -...	1685	1026720	3103	1700	53	SQL:BatchCompleted
INSERT SOD SELECT * FROM SOD; -...	3354	2086787	6433	3505	53	SQL:BatchCompleted
INSERT SOD SELECT * FROM SOD; -...	6645	4207017	12832	6709	53	SQL:BatchCompleted
INSERT SOD SELECT * FROM SOD; -...	13229	8447507	25504	13339	53	SQL:BatchCompleted
/* Beginning execution loop (121...	719	55189	9	249	53	SQL:BatchCompleted
DBCC DROPCLEANBUFFERS; SET STATI...	732	57035	1	1182	53	SQL:BatchCompleted
CREATE CLUSTERED INDEX idxPrd ON ...	15398	133236	51211	13607	53	SQL:BatchCompleted
DBCC DROPCLEANBUFFERS; SET STATI...	109	225	0	497	53	SQL:BatchCompleted
-- DROP INDEX SOD.idxPrd -- DROP...	16	480	0	147	53	SQL:BatchCompleted

We can see the reads of 57,035 decreased to 225 after creating the indexes. Not only we speeded up this query but other queries as well by decreasing the load on the server. The execution plan displays **table scan** prior to index creation.

```
Query 9: Query cost (relative to the batch): 4%
SELECT * FROM SOD INNER JOIN Product P ON SOD.ProductID = P.ProductID WH...
Missing Index (Impact 95.6546): CREATE NONCLUSTERED INDEX [<Name of Miss...
```

SELECT
Cost: 0 %

Nested Loops
(Inner Join)
Cost: 0 %

Parallelism
(Gather Streams)
Cost: 2 %

Table Scan
[SOD]
Cost: 94 %

Table Spool
(Lazy Spool)
Cost: 3 %

Table Scan
[Product] [P]
Cost: 0 %

CHAPTER 20: Query & Stored Procedure Optimization

Optimizing with Indexing

Execution Plan after Index Creation & Cost Comparison

The execution plan shows clustered index seek instead of table scan after index creation. Generally our aim with indexing is to replace table scan or index scan with index seek.

```
Results | Messages | Execution plan
Query 1: Query cost (relative to the batch): 100%
SELECT * FROM SOD INNER JOIN Product P ON SOD.ProductID = P.ProductID WHERE P.P:

  SELECT          Nested Loops          Nested Loops          Index Seek (NonClustered)
  Cost: 0 %       (Inner Join)          (Inner Join)          [Product].[idxPrd] [P]
                  Cost: 27 %            Cost: 0 %             Cost: 1 %

                                                              RID Lookup (Heap)
                                                              [Product] [P]
                                                              Cost: 1 %

                                        Clustered Index Seek (Clustered)
                                        [SOD].[idxPrd]
                                        Cost: 71 %
```

Cost comparison before and after index create reflects a very significant improvement in cost, roughly 200 fold.

SELECT			SELECT	
Cached plan size	56 KB		Cached plan size	56 KB
Degree of Parallelism	4		Degree of Parallelism	1
Estimated Operator Cost	0 (0%)		Estimated Operator Cost	0 (0%)
Estimated Subtree Cost	45.4362		Estimated Subtree Cost	0.247049
Memory Grant	72		Estimated Number of Rows	15840
Estimated Number of Rows	15513.1			

Statement

SELECT * FROM SOD INNER JOIN
Product P
    ON SOD.ProductID = P.ProductID
    WHERE P.ProductID = 800;

Statement

SELECT * FROM SOD INNER JOIN Product P
    ON SOD.ProductID = P.ProductID
    WHERE P.ProductID = 800;

CHAPTER 20: Query & Stored Procedure Optimization

Non-SARGable Predicates Force Index Scan

The term SARGable stands for Search ARGument ABLE. It means the WHERE clause OR join ON clause predicate written such a way that the database engine can use the index on the column. Basically means if we form an expression with the indexed column, index scan will be performed instead of index seek, in other words, index will not be used to speed up the query. The (SOD.ProductID +1 - 1) expression in the ON clause causes clustered index scan. The relative query costs are 1% (SARGable) and 99% (non-SARGable) in the batch of 2 queries.

Optimizing with Indexing

SARGable Predicate Construction

It is a challenge to remember all the time to make the predicate SARGable. Frequently, so much easier to make it non-SARGable.

```
YEAR(OrderDate) = 2016 AND MONTH(OrderDate) = 10                          -- non-SARGable
OrderDate >= '2016-10-01' AND OrderDate < DATEADD(MM,1, '2016-10-01') -- SARGable
```

The payoff can be great as shown by the previous SARGable & non-SARGable examples, duration in msec.

CPU	Reads	Writes	Duration
125	223	0	668
1527	51451	0	11497

Clustered Index Seek (Clustered)	
Scanning a particular range of rows from a clustered index.	
Physical Operation	Clustered Index Seek
Logical Operation	Clustered Index Seek
Actual Execution Mode	Row
Estimated Execution Mode	Row
Storage	RowStore
Actual Number of Rows	15840
Actual Number of Batches	0
Estimated Operator Cost	0.174279 (71%)
Estimated I/O Cost	0.156698
Estimated CPU Cost	0.017581
Estimated Subtree Cost	0.174279
Number of Executions	1
Estimated Number of Executions	1
Estimated Number of Rows	15840
Estimated Row Size	112 B
Actual Rebinds	0
Actual Rewinds	0
Ordered	True
Node ID	54

Object
[tempdb].[dbo].[SOD].[idxPrd]
Output List
[tempdb].[dbo].[SOD].SalesOrderID, [tempdb].[dbo].[SOD].SalesOrderDetailID, [tempdb].[dbo].[SOD].CarrierTrackingNumber, [tempdb].[dbo].[SOD].OrderQty, [tempdb].[dbo].[SOD].ProductID, [tempdb].[dbo].[SOD].SpecialOfferID, [tempdb].[dbo].[SOD].UnitPrice, [tempdb].[dbo].[SOD].UnitPriceDiscount, [tempdb].[dbo].[SOD].LineTotal, [tempdb].[dbo].[SOD].rowguid, [tempdb].[dbo].[SOD].ModifiedDate
Seek Predicates
Seek Keys[1]: Prefix: [tempdb].[dbo].[SOD].ProductID = Scalar Operator((800))

Clustered Index Scan (Clustered)	
Scanning a clustered index, entirely or only a range.	
Physical Operation	Clustered Index Scan
Logical Operation	Clustered Index Scan
Actual Execution Mode	Row
Estimated Execution Mode	Row
Actual Number of Rows	15840
Actual Number of Batches	0
Estimated I/O Cost	37.8224
Estimated Operator Cost	39.9576 (97%)
Estimated CPU Cost	2.13526
Estimated Subtree Cost	39.9576
Number of Executions	4
Estimated Number of Executions	1
Estimated Number of Rows	15840
Estimated Row Size	112 B
Actual Rebinds	0
Actual Rewinds	0
Ordered	False
Node ID	58

Predicate
([tempdb].[dbo].[SOD].[ProductID]+(1)-(1))=(800)
Object
[tempdb].[dbo].[SOD].[idxPrd]
Output List
[tempdb].[dbo].[SOD].SalesOrderID, [tempdb].[dbo].[SOD].SalesOrderDetailID, [tempdb].[dbo].[SOD].CarrierTrackingNumber, [tempdb].[dbo].[SOD].OrderQty, [tempdb].[dbo].[SOD].ProductID, [tempdb].[dbo].[SOD].SpecialOfferID, [tempdb].[dbo].[SOD].UnitPrice, [tempdb].[dbo].[SOD].UnitPriceDiscount, [tempdb].[dbo].[SOD].LineTotal, [tempdb].[dbo].[SOD].rowguid, [tempdb].[dbo].[SOD].ModifiedDate

Stored Procedure Parameter Sniffing & Prevention

When SQL Server database engine compiles a stored procedure, it may use the actual parameters supplied to prepare an execution plan. If the parameters are atypical, the plan may be slow for typical parameters. For consistent stored procedure performance parameter sniffing should be eliminated. A telltale sign of parameter sniffing when suddenly a stored procedure executes in 2 minutes, as an example, instead of the usual 10 seconds. *This is different when the first (cold from disk) execution of a stored procedure is much longer than the second & on (warm since pages in buffer memory) execution.* Parameter sniffing may show up also as 5 minutes execution in one environment (like application) and 2 seconds in another (like SSMS).

> Technet Article
> Batch Compilation, Recompilation, and Plan Caching Issues in SQL Server 2005
> http://technet.microsoft.com/en-us/library/cc966425.aspx

First prevention method: remap parameters to local variables and use those only.

```
USE AdventureWorks2012;
GO
CREATE PROCEDURE uspProductByColor @pcolor varchar(20)   AS BEGIN
      DECLARE @color varchar(20) = @pcolor;          -- remapping
      SET NOCOUNT ON;
      SELECT * FROM Production.Product WHERE Color = @color  ORDER BY name;   END
```

```
EXEC uspProductByColor 'Red';  -- 38 rows returned
```

Second prevention method: RECOMPILE stored procedure at each execution (for large procedure compilation time may be significant).

```
CREATE PROCEDURE uspProductByColor @pcolor varchar(20)
WITH RECOMPILE AS BEGIN  SET NOCOUNT ON;
   SELECT * FROM Production.Product WHERE Color = @pcolor    ORDER BY name;    END
```

Optimizing with MERGE

Single statement MERGE can perform better than multi statements INSERT/UPDATE/DELETE.

> Technet Article: **Optimizing MERGE Statement Performance**
> http://technet.microsoft.com/en-us/library/cc879317(v=sql.105).aspx

Stress Testing a View with Include Client Statistics Feature

Client Statistics feature can be turned by icon or right click drop-down menu option. It calculates averages for up to 10 trials. DBCC DROPCLEANBUFFERS equalizes the tests by purging the cached data pages from buffer memory. Note: server load will influence timings. Query drop-down has option to Reset Client Statistics.

```sql
DECLARE @i tinyint = 1, @limit tinyint = 100;
SELECT TOP (0) * INTO #Y FROM Sales.vSalesPersonSalesByFiscalYears;
WHILE ( @i <= @limit)
BEGIN
   DBCC DROPCLEANBUFFERS;
   INSERT #Y SELECT * FROM Sales.vSalesPersonSalesByFiscalYears ORDER BY FullName;
   SET @i += 1;
END; DROP TABLE #Y;
GO
```

	Trial 3	Trial 2	Trial 1	Average
Client Execution Time	19:13:04	19:12:40	19:10:13	
Query Profile Statistics				
Number of INSERT, DELETE and UPDATE statements	100	→ 100	→ 100	→ 100.0000
Rows affected by INSERT, DELETE, or UPDATE statem...	1400	→ 1400	→ 1400	→ 1400.0000
Number of SELECT statements	101	→ 101	→ 101	→ 101.0000
Rows returned by SELECT statements	101	→ 101	→ 101	→ 101.0000
Number of transactions	100	→ 100	→ 100	→ 100.0000
Network Statistics				
Number of server roundtrips	1	→ 1	→ 1	→ 1.0000
TDS packets sent from client	1	→ 1	→ 1	→ 1.0000
TDS packets received from server	7	→ 7	→ 7	→ 7.0000
Bytes sent from client	614	→ 614	→ 614	→ 614.0000
Bytes received from server	26808	→ 26808	→ 26808	→ 26808.0000
Time Statistics				
Client processing time	3880	↓ 4093	↓ 4509	→ 4160.6670
Total execution time	5250	↓ 5453	↓ 6708	→ 5803.6670
Wait time on server replies	1370	↑ 1360	↓ 2199	→ 1643.0000

Maximum Capacity Specifications for SQL Server
http://msdn.microsoft.com/en-us/library/ms143432.aspx

CHAPTER 20: Query & Stored Procedure Optimization

10 Point Optimization Guide

Performance tuning and optimization are a huge topic. We only touch the tip of the iceberg. Nonetheless, the important elements of optimization can be summarized quite easily. It starts with prioritizing what is business critical, what is not. If 500 users are unhappy with a stored procedure, that is business critical. If one user is unhappy with a slow report, that is not business critical, unless that user is the CEO.

1. REBUILD indexes every weekend. Use FILLFACTOR for dynamic tables with lots of INSERTs. FILLFACTOR 70 means 70% data and 30% empty space. Free database maintenance scripts at http://ola.hallengren.com/ - SQL Server Backup, Integrity Check, and Index and Statistics Maintenance.

2. UPDATE STATISTICS every night. The database engine query optimizer uses the statistics to prepare efficient execution plans. Consider setting on Auto Update Statistics / Asynchronously (2 settings) options.

3. Eliminate missing indexes. All FOREIGN KEY & WHERE condition columns should be considered for indexing.

4. Optimize all business critical queries. WHERE & ON clause predicates should be SARGable.

5. Examine execution plan for business critical queries to make sure they are efficient.

6. Optimize all business critical stored procedures. In a sproc all queries should be optimized and looping should be kept at an absolute minimum. Non-scalable cursors should be avoided.

7. Server memory max should be set in server properties. That is quite a challenge with 32-bit OS. For 64 bit OS with 65GB of memory, max memory should be set to 55GB, as a general guideline, to leave enough room for SS and other program operations.

8. Disk configuration should be optimized. Article: http://technet.microsoft.com/en-us/library/cc966412.aspx .

9. Operational solutions for performance problems which cannot be readily resolved due to lack of resources. For example, external feed arrives 11AM every day and promptly uploaded in 1/2 hour thus slowing down the system and annoying users. Instead schedule uploading with SQL Server Agent to low use time like 11pm.

10. Database design should be efficient. Narrow and fixed row size tables are the best performant. Note: frequently database design is frozen, "as is" , for budget reasons or a 3rd party package. Even in a such a case, index & statistics maintenance can improve performance.

10 Point Optimization Guide

Object Explorer GUI REBUILD Indexes

The indexes can be rebuilt in SSMS Object Explorer using Graphical User Interface. REBUILD indexes updates statistics as well. T-SQL command syntax example:

ALTER INDEX ALL ON [Sales].[SalesOrderDetail] REBUILD WITH (FILLFACTOR = 90);

CHAPTER 20: Query & Stored Procedure Optimization

UPDATE STATISTICS on All Tables Stored Procedure

The UPDATE STATISTICS on all tables stored procedure has one parameter: the sample percent for scanning. Lower the number, faster the update. WITH FULLSCAN option does 100% sampling, it may be slow for large tables. Create & execute stored procedure script.

```sql
CREATE PROCEDURE sprocUpdateAllStats (@Sample int)  AS
BEGIN
DECLARE @SQL AS NVARCHAR(1024), @Table sysname, @Schema sysname;
DECLARE curAllTables CURSOR FOR
        SELECT TABLE_SCHEMA, TABLE_NAME
        FROM INFORMATION_SCHEMA.TABLES
        WHERE TABLE_TYPE='BASE TABLE'
        ORDER BY TABLE_SCHEMA, TABLE_NAME;
OPEN curAllTables;
FETCH NEXT FROM curAllTables
        INTO @Schema, @Table;

WHILE (@@FETCH_STATUS = 0)
BEGIN
 SET @SQL =     CONCAT('UPDATE STATISTICS ',
                QUOTENAME( @Schema),'.', QUOTENAME( @Table),
                ' WITH SAMPLE ', CONVERT(char(3), @sample), ' PERCENT;');
--              ' WITH FULLSCAN; ');
 PRINT @SQL;
-- UPDATE STATISTICS [Sales].[Store] WITH SAMPLE 10 PERCENT;

 EXEC sp_executesql @SQL;

 FETCH NEXT FROM curAllTables
        INTO @Schema, @Table;
END -- while
 CLOSE curAllTables;  DEALLOCATE curAllTables;
END
GO
```

```sql
EXEC sprocUpdateAllStats 10;
```

Blocking of a Query by Another Query

SQL Server applies locks at the row, page and table level in order to maintain data integrity. If another query tries to operate on the locked part, it may get blocked. It is easy to see how blocking can degrade the performance of the server. We can simulate blocking. In connection 1 we execute and leave open a transaction. In connection 2 we execute a query which intends to operate on the locked table. The result is blocking of connection 2 query by connection 1 query.

```
-- Connection 1
BEGIN TRAN;
UPDATE HumanResources.Shift SET ModifiedDate = convert(datetime, ModifiedDate);
-- ROLLBACK TRAN;
```

```
-- Connection 2
BEGIN TRAN;
UPDATE HumanResources.Shift SET ModifiedDate = convert(datetime, ModifiedDate);
COMMIT TRAN;
```

Checking blocking by **sp_who** system procedure (exec sp_who in a 3rd connection) and **Activity Monitor** (right click on server menu). The Activity Monitor chart even shows the Head Blocker which is very helpful to trace the source of a blocking chain. A quick resolution is killing the head blocker (kill 55). Long term fix is making the blocking query efficient.

	spid	ecid	status	loginame	hostname	blk	dbname	cmd
36	52	0	runnable	HPES...	HPEST...	0	master	SELECT
37	53	0	sleeping	NT SE...	HPEST...	0	ReportServer	AWAITING COMMAND
38	54	0	sleeping	HPES...	HPEST...	0	master	AWAITING COMMAND
39	55	0	sleeping	HPES...	HPEST...	0	AdventureWorks2012	AWAITING COMMAND
40	56	0	sleeping	NT SE...	HPEST...	0	ReportServer	AWAITING COMMAND
41	57	0	suspended	HPES...	HPEST...	55	AdventureWorks2012	UPDATE

S.	U.	Login	Dat...	Tas...	Com...	Appl...	Wait Tim...	Wait...	Wait...	Blocked By	Head Blocker	Me...
51	1	HPESTA...	master			Microsoft..	0					
52	1	HPESTA...	master			Microsoft..	0					
53	1	NT SER...	ReportS...			Report S...	0					
54	1	HPESTA...	master	RUNNING	SELECT	Microsoft..	0					
55	1	HPESTA...	Adventur..			Microsoft..	0					1
56	1	NT SER...	ReportS...			Report S...	0					
57	1	HPESTA...	Adventur..	SUSPEN...	UPDATE	Microsoft..	172568	LCK_M_U	keylock..		55	

CHAPTER 20: Query & Stored Procedure Optimization

Activity Monitor

The Activity Monitor provides real time operational information in list and graphical chart formats based on operational DMV-s.

Operational Solutions for Performance Problems

Frequently real fix cannot be carried out quickly or at all for a performance issue due to software complexities and limited expert-level resources. In such a case we have to think about implementing operational solutions:

> ➢ Users complain about slow online reports. Setup reports as night jobs with automatic email distribution.
> ➢ Reports slow OLTP activities. Restore last night DB backup under new name as reporting DB. Usually, only a small fraction of reports need to be real-time.

Server & Database Standard Reports

The Server Standard Reports can be accessed via the right click on server drop-down menu in SSMS Object Explorer (top left). The Database Standard Reports can be accessed via the right click on database drop down menu (top right). The reports are based on Dynamic Management Views (DMV-s). They represent operational data since the last restart of the server. At the bottom, partial display of the Index Usage Statistics report.

Server Dashboard	Disk Usage
Configuration Changes History	Disk Usage by Top Tables
Schema Changes History	Disk Usage by Table
Scheduler Health	Disk Usage by Partition
Memory Consumption	Backup and Restore Events
Activity - All Blocking Transactions	All Transactions
Activity - All Cursors	All Blocking Transactions
Activity - Top Cursors	Top Transactions by Age
Activity - All Sessions	Top Transactions by Blocked Transactions Count
Activity - Top Sessions	Top Transactions by Locks Count
Activity - Dormant Sessions	Resource Locking Statistics by Objects
Activity - Top Connections	Object Execution Statistics
Top Transactions by Age	Database Consistency History
Top Transactions by Blocked Transactions Count	Index Usage Statistics
Top Transactions by Locks Count	Index Physical Statistics
Performance - Batch Execution Statistics	Schema Changes History
Performance - Object Execution Statistics	User Statistics
Performance - Top Queries by Average CPU Time	
Performance - Top Queries by Average IO	
Performance - Top Queries by Total CPU Time	
Performance - Top Queries by Total IO	
Service Broker Statistics	
Transaction Log Shipping Status	

HumanResources.Employee

Index Name	Index Type	# User Seeks	# User Scans	# User Updates
PK_Employee_BusinessEntityID	CLUSTERED	697	0	0

HumanResources.Shift

Index Name	Index Type	# User Seeks	# User Scans	# User Updates
PK_Shift_ShiftID	CLUSTERED	0	5	5

Person.Person

CHAPTER 20: Query & Stored Procedure Optimization

Server Dashboard

The Server Dashboard contains important high-level information about the server.

Segment from Performance - Top Queries by Total CPU Time report.

Batching Large INSERT, UPDATE & DELETE

Batch processing jobs best executed at low use time like night or weekend. Frequently, however, we may not have a choice, we have to run them during transactional activities. We can minimize conflict by breaking down a large job to small batches and providing 1 second or so wait time for other queries to execute. During that 1 second hundreds of short transactions may execute. DELETE from large tables may prove to be very slow due to restructuring of the index pages.

```
USE tempdb;
SELECT  ProductID=CONVERT(int, ProductID), ProductName=Name,
        ProductNumber, ListPrice, Color, Size
INTO Product FROM AdventureWorks2008.Production.Product;
```

```
INSERT Product SELECT * FROM Product;  -- Double table rows at each execution
GO 16
/* .....   (16515072 row(s) affected)
Batch execution completed 16 times.   */
SELECT FORMAT(COUNT(*),'###,###,###') FROM Product;   -- 33,030,144
GO
CREATE CLUSTERED INDEX idxProductID
            on Product(ProductID);
GO -- 12 minutes 44 seconds
```

```
DECLARE @BatchSize int = 10000;
WHILE (@@ROWCOUNT > 0)   BEGIN     WAITFOR DELAY '00:00:01';
        DELETE TOP (@BatchSize) FROM Product    WHERE ProductNumber = 'CA-5965';
END
GO   -- 3 minutes 8 seconds
/*(10000 row(s) affected)
(10000 row(s) affected)
(10000 row(s) affected)
(10000 row(s) affected)
(10000 row(s) affected)
(10000 row(s) affected)
(5536 row(s) affected)
(0 row(s) affected)*/
```

```
SELECT FORMAT(COUNT(*),'###,###,###') FROM Product;   -- 32,964,608  -- 5 seconds
GO
DROP TABLE tempdb.dbo.Product;
```

CHAPTER 20: Query & Stored Procedure Optimization

Database Engine Tuning Advisor

The Database Engine Tuning Advisor (DETA or DTA) provides indexing & statistics recommendations based on the supplied workload. A single query can be analyzed as well, right click Query drop-down menu.

DBCC HELP Command

Withe the DBCC HELP command you can get syntax assistance with any of the DBCC commands.

DBCC HELP (checkdb);

CHAPTER 20: Query & Stored Procedure Optimization

CHAPTER 21: Advanced T-SQL Programming Topics

String Pattern Matching & Parsing
The CHARINDEX() function, PATINDEX() function and LIKE operator offer substring search in string functionality with some differences. Frequently, all 3 can be used for the same result.

The LIKE Operator
LIKE operator usage for numeric and alphanumeric differentiation.

USE AdventureWorks2012;
SELECT AddressID, City, StateProvinceID, PostalCode
FROM Person.Address WHERE PostalCode **LIKE** '%[^0-9]%';
-- (3644 row(s) affected) - Partial results.

AddressID	City	StateProvinceID	PostalCode
532	Ottawa	57	K4B 1S2
497	Burnaby	7	V5A 4X1
15272	Haney	7	V2W 1W2
14068	Cambridge	14	CB4 4BZ

SELECT AddressID, City, StateProvinceID, PostalCode
FROM Person.Address WHERE PostalCode **NOT LIKE** '%[^0-9]%';
-- (15970 row(s) affected) - Partial results.

AddressID	City	StateProvinceID	PostalCode
26916	Dunkerque	145	59140
28885	Lille	145	59000
708	Paris	161	75017
23902	Lieusaint	163	77127

Elaborate patterns can be formed from regular characters and wildcard characters. Underscore (_) matches any character.

DECLARE @Pattern varchar(20) = '[CFPS]___[eo]n'
SELECT DISTINCT LastName FROM Person.Person WHERE LastName LIKE @Pattern;
-- Campen, Cannon, Carson, Fulton, Patten, Slaven, Sutton

The CHARINDEX() Function

The CHARINDEX() function locates a substring within a string. A string with 2 hyphens (-) is split into 3 parts.

```
SELECT      ProductNumber,
            [Part1] = LEFT(ProductNumber,CHARINDEX('-',ProductNumber) - 1),
            [Part2] = SUBSTRING(ProductNumber,CHARINDEX('-',ProductNumber) + 1,
                        CHARINDEX('-',ProductNumber,CHARINDEX('-',
                        ProductNumber) + 1) - (CHARINDEX('-',ProductNumber) + 1)),
            [Part3] = RIGHT(ProductNumber,CHARINDEX('-',REVERSE(ProductNumber)) - 1)
FROM AdventureWorks2012.Production.Product
WHERE LEN(ProductNumber) - LEN(REPLACE(ProductNumber, '-','')) = 2;  -- 2 hyphens in string
-- (213 row(s) affected) - Partial results.
```

ProductNumber	Part1	Part2	Part3
BK-M18B-40	BK	M18B	40
BK-M18B-42	BK	M18B	42
BK-M18B-44	BK	M18B	44
BK-M18B-48	BK	M18B	48
BK-M18B-52	BK	M18B	52

Find the left part of a string before the comma. We get an error without the NULLIF function due to subtracting 1 from the LEN() result which may be 0 (zero).

```
SELECT Name, LEFT(Name,CHARINDEX(',',Name)-1) AS NamePrefix
FROM AdventureWorks2012.Production.Product ORDER BY Name;
/* Msg 537, Level 16, State 3, Line 1
Invalid length parameter passed to the LEFT or SUBSTRING function. */
```

```
SELECT  ProductNumber,
        NamePrefix=LEFT(Name,COALESCE(NULLIF(CHARINDEX(',',Name)-1,-1),LEN(Name))),
        ProductName=Name
FROM AdventureWorks2012.Production.Product ORDER BY ProductName;
-- (504 row(s) affected) - Partial results;
```

ProductNumber	NamePrefix	ProductName
FR-T67Y-58	LL Touring Frame - Yellow	LL Touring Frame - Yellow, 58
FR-T67Y-62	LL Touring Frame - Yellow	LL Touring Frame - Yellow, 62
HB-T721	LL Touring Handlebars	LL Touring Handlebars
SA-T467	LL Touring Seat Assembly	LL Touring Seat Assembly

CHAPTER 21: Advanced T-SQL Programming Topics

String Pattern Matching & Parsing

The PATINDEX() Function

The PATINDEX() function can be used for complex pattern searches.

```
use AdventureWorks2012;

select         [Name]                         AS ProductName,
               ProductNumber,
               [Description],
               ListPrice
from [Production].[Product] p
  inner join [Production].[ProductModelProductDescriptionCulture] pmpdc
    on p.ProductModelID = pmpdc.ProductModelID
  inner join [Production].[ProductDescription] pd
    on pmpdc.ProductDescriptionID = pd.ProductDescriptionID
where patindex( '%mountain%innovative%', pd.[Description]) > 0
order by ProductNumber DESC;
-- (8 row(s) affected) - Partial results.
```

ProductName	ProductNumber	Description	ListPrice
Mountain-100 Silver, 48	BK-M82S-48	Top-of-the-line competition mountain bike. Performance-enhancing options include the innovative HL Frame, super-smooth front suspension, and traction for all terrain.	3399.99

Searching UNICODE Chinese text.

```
select [Name] AS ProductName, ProductNumber, [Description], ListPrice
from [Production].[Product] p
  inner join [Production].[ProductModelProductDescriptionCulture] pmpdc
    on p.ProductModelID = pmpdc.ProductModelID
  inner join [Production].[ProductDescription] pd
    on pmpdc.ProductDescriptionID = pd.ProductDescriptionID
where patindex( N'%量的%快速%', pd.[Description]) > 0
order by ProductNumber DESC;
```

ProductName	ProductNumber	Description	ListPrice
HL Headset	HS-3479	高质量的一英寸无螺纹车头碗组具有油口，可确保快速润滑。	124.73

Complex pattern match with wildcards.

```
SELECT PATINDEX('%[A-T,0-9]%[Q,0-9]%[0-9]%','ZQZQXYZABC123');  --2
```

CHAPTER 21: Advanced T-SQL Programming Topics

Composable DML - INSERT into 2 Tables with One Statement

Composable DML is new to SQL Server 2012. It expands the concept of SELECT subquery to INSERT/UPDATE/DELETE/MERGE operation using the OUTPUT clause with some restrictions.

```sql
USE tempdb;
CREATE TABLE PurchaseOrderDetail(            -- Create 2 empty tables for testing
        PurchaseOrderID int NOT NULL,
        PurchaseOrderDetailID int NOT NULL,
        DueDate datetime NOT NULL,
        OrderQty smallint NOT NULL,
        ProductID int NOT NULL,
        UnitPrice money NOT NULL,
        LineTotal  money,
        ReceivedQty decimal(8, 2) NOT NULL,
        RejectedQty decimal(8, 2) NOT NULL,
        StockedQty  int,
        ModifiedDate datetime NOT NULL);
```

```sql
SELECT * INTO POD FROM PurchaseOrderDetail;
```

```sql
INSERT PurchaseOrderDetail  OUTPUT inserted.*        -- Test query with OUTPUT
SELECT * FROM AdventureWorks2012.Purchasing.PurchaseOrderDetail
GO
-- (8845 row(s) affected)
```

```sql
TRUNCATE TABLE PurchaseOrderDetail;
GO
-- Command(s) completed successfully.
```

```sql
INSERT POD                                           -- Composable DML
SELECT *  FROM (
        INSERT PurchaseOrderDetail     OUTPUT inserted.*
        SELECT * FROM AdventureWorks2012.Purchasing.PurchaseOrderDetail ) X ;
GO
```

```sql
SELECT COUNT(*) FROM POD;                            -- 8845
SELECT COUNT(*) FROM PurchaseOrderDetail;            -- 8845
GO
```

```sql
DROP TABLE POD;  DROP TABLE PurchaseOrderDetail;
```

CHAPTER 21: Advanced T-SQL Programming Topics

Double Assignment Operator

The multiple value assignment operator allows more than one assignment for the same value.

```
USE tempdb;

SELECT      CONVERT(int, SalesOrderID)              AS ID,
            CONVERT(date, ModifiedDate)             AS TestDate
INTO  DateSequence
FROM  AdventureWorks2012.Sales.SalesOrderHeader ;
go
--(31465 row(s) affected)

SELECT TOP 5 *
FROM   DateSequence ;
go
```

ID	TestDate
43659	2005-07-08
43660	2005-07-08
43661	2005-07-08
43662	2005-07-08
43663	2005-07-08

```
-- Multiple assignment UPDATE
DECLARE @Date date = dateadd(day, 1, CURRENT_TIMESTAMP),
        @id   int = 0 ;

UPDATE DateSequence
       SET    @id = ID = @id + 1,
              @Date = TestDate = dateadd (Day, -1, @Date);
go

SELECT TOP 5 * FROM   DateSequence ORDER BY TestDate DESC;
go
```

ID	TestDate
1	2012-10-21
2	2012-10-20
3	2012-10-19
4	2012-10-18
5	2012-10-17

Running Total & Average Calculation with the OVER Clause

Running total support is a new feature of SQL Server 2012. OVER clause makes the RT calculation a breeze.

```
USE AdventureWorks2012;
GO

SELECT SalesOrderID,
    FORMAT(TotalDue,'c0','en-US')                                    AS TotalDue,
    FORMAT(COUNT(TotalDue) OVER( ORDER BY SalesOrderID), '###,###') AS RunningCount,
    FORMAT(SUM(TotalDue) OVER( ORDER BY SalesOrderID), 'c0','en-US') AS RunningTotal,
    FORMAT(AVG(TotalDue) OVER( ORDER BY SalesOrderID), 'c0','en-US') AS RunningAvg
FROM Sales.SalesOrderHeader
WHERE OrderDate >='20080201'
      AND OrderDate < DATEADD(mm,1,'20080201')
ORDER BY SalesOrderID;
GO
-- (2032 row(s) affected) - Partial results.
```

SalesOrderID	TotalDue	RunningCount	RunningTotal	RunningAvg
63119	$247	1	$247	$247
63120	$234	2	$481	$240
63121	$187	3	$668	$223
63122	$213	4	$881	$220
63123	$16,320	5	$17,201	$3,440
63124	$36,462	6	$53,663	$8,944
63125	$9,603	7	$63,266	$9,038
63126	$2,298	8	$65,564	$8,196
63127	$8,870	9	$74,435	$8,271
63128	$21,805	10	$96,240	$9,624
63129	$1,691	11	$97,930	$8,903
63130	$4,355	12	$102,285	$8,524
63131	$97,929	13	$200,214	$15,401
63132	$38,158	14	$238,372	$17,027
63133	$36,926	15	$275,298	$18,353
63134	$8,597	16	$283,896	$17,743
63135	$1,872	17	$285,768	$16,810
63136	$41,760	18	$327,528	$18,196
63137	$987	19	$328,515	$17,290
63138	$5,344	20	$333,859	$16,693

Running Total with Subquery - Ye Olde Way
Calculating cumulative totals with subquery is quite inefficient, but it works.

```
USE AdventureWorks2012;
GO

DECLARE @Year INT = 2005, @Month INT = 7;
SELECT   RN = ROW_NUMBER()
             OVER(ORDER BY SalesOrderID),
    OrderDate = convert(CHAR(10),OrderDate,111), -- date formatting
    SalesOrderId,
    TotalDue = '$' + convert(VARCHAR,TotalDue,1), -- Currency formatting
    [Running Total] = '$' + convert(VARCHAR,
    (SELECT sum(TotalDue)
     FROM  Sales.SalesOrderHeader
     WHERE  SalesOrderID <= soh.SalesOrderID    -- Key predicate in the process
       AND year(OrderDate) = @Year
       AND month(OrderDate) = @Month),
              1)
FROM    Sales.SalesOrderHeader soh
WHERE   year(OrderDate) = @Year
    AND month(OrderDate) = @Month
ORDER BY RN;
GO
-- (184 row(s) affected) - Partial results.
```

RN	OrderDate	SalesOrderId	TotalDue	Running Total
1	2005/07/01	43659	$23,153.23	$23,153.23
2	2005/07/01	43660	$1,457.33	$24,610.56
3	2005/07/01	43661	$36,865.80	$61,476.36
4	2005/07/01	43662	$32,474.93	$93,951.30
5	2005/07/01	43663	$472.31	$94,423.61
6	2005/07/01	43664	$27,510.41	$121,934.02
7	2005/07/01	43665	$16,158.70	$138,092.71
8	2005/07/01	43666	$5,694.86	$143,787.57
9	2005/07/01	43667	$6,876.36	$150,663.94
10	2005/07/01	43668	$40,487.72	$191,151.66
11	2005/07/01	43669	$807.26	$191,958.92
12	2005/07/01	43670	$6,893.25	$198,852.17
13	2005/07/01	43671	$9,153.61	$208,005.78
14	2005/07/01	43672	$6,895.41	$214,901.19
15	2005/07/01	43673	$4,216.03	$219,117.21

Running Total with Multiple Assignment UPDATE

Cumulative total can be generated a fast way using double assignment SET in UPDATE command. There are some restrictions such as no table partitioning. It should not be used in production unless there is a serious performance problem.

```
USE AdventureWorks2012;

DECLARE  @RunningTotal MONEY;
DECLARE  @Result  TABLE(
            SalesOrderID INT   NOT NULL   PRIMARY KEY,
            TotalDue   MONEY,
            RunningTotal MONEY
            );
SET @RunningTotal = 0.0;
INSERT INTO @Result
     (SalesOrderID,
      TotalDue)
SELECT   SalesOrderID,     TotalDue
FROM     Sales.SalesOrderHeader
ORDER BY SalesOrderID
-- (31465 row(s) affected)

UPDATE @Result
SET   @RunningTotal = RunningTotal = @RunningTotal + TotalDue;
-- (31465 row(s) affected)

SELECT   SalesOrderId,
         FORMAT(TotalDue,'c0','en-US')       AS TotalDue,
         FORMAT(RunningTotal, 'c0','en-US')  AS RunningTotal
FROM   @Result ORDER BY SalesOrderID;
GO
-- (31465 row(s) affected) -- Partial results.
```

SalesOrderId	TotalDue	RunningTotal
43659	$23,153	$23,153
43660	$1,457	$24,611
43661	$36,866	$61,476
43662	$32,475	$93,951
43663	$472	$94,424
43664	$27,510	$121,934
43665	$16,159	$138,093

Subtotal, Total & Grand Total GROUPING Function

It is a challenge to generate multi-level totals in T-SQL. The GROUPING() function tells us what level we are on in the GROUP BY summary.

```
USE AdventureWorks2012;

SELECT *
FROM  (SELECT COALESCE(CONVERT(VARCHAR, YEAR(OrderDate)), '')         AS YYYY,
             COALESCE(LEFT(CONVERT(VARCHAR, OrderDate, 111), 7), '')  AS MM,
             FORMAT(COUNT(*), '###,###')                              AS ORDERS,
             FORMAT(SUM(TotalDue), 'c0', 'en-US')                     AS SALES,
             CASE    WHEN GROUPING(LEFT(CONVERT(VARCHAR, OrderDate, 111), 7)) = 0
                 AND GROUPING(YEAR(OrderDate)) = 1 THEN 'SUBTOTAL'
               ELSE ''
             END                                                      AS GRPMM,
              CASE   WHEN GROUPING(YEAR(OrderDate)) = 0
                 AND GROUPING(LEFT(CONVERT(VARCHAR, OrderDate, 111), 7)) = 1 THEN 'TOTAL'
               ELSE ''
             END                                                      AS GRPYY,
              CASE   WHEN GROUPING(LEFT(CONVERT(VARCHAR, OrderDate, 111), 7)) = 1
                 AND GROUPING(YEAR(OrderDate)) = 1 THEN 'GRAND TOTAL'
               ELSE ''
             END                                                      AS GRPALL
        FROM   Sales.SalesOrderHeader
      GROUP  BY YEAR(OrderDate), LEFT(CONVERT(VARCHAR, OrderDate, 111), 7) WITH CUBE) rpt
WHERE  GRPMM != '' OR GRPYY != ''  OR GRPALL != ''
ORDER BY CASE  WHEN GRPALL != '' THEN 3  WHEN GRPYY != '' THEN 2   ELSE 1 END,
     YYYY,  MM ;
```

YYYY	MM	ORDERS	SALES	GRPMM	GRPYY	GRPALL
	2008/01	1,946	$3,359,927	SUBTOTAL		
	2008/02	2,032	$4,662,656	SUBTOTAL		
	2008/03	2,109	$4,722,358	SUBTOTAL		
	2008/04	2,128	$4,269,365	SUBTOTAL		
	2008/05	2,386	$5,813,557	SUBTOTAL		
	2008/06	2,374	$6,004,156	SUBTOTAL		
	2008/07	976	$56,179	SUBTOTAL		
2005		1,379	$12,693,251		TOTAL	
2006		3,692	$34,463,848		TOTAL	
2007		12,443	$47,171,490		TOTAL	
2008		13,951	$28,888,198		TOTAL	
		31,465	$123,216,786			GRAND TOTAL

CHAPTER 21: Advanced T-SQL Programming Topics

The GROUP BY Clause with GROUPING SETS

A GROUP BY clause that uses GROUPING SETS is equivalent to multiple GROUP BY queries combined with UNION ALL operator.

```sql
USE AdventureWorks2012;

SELECT T."Group"                        AS N'Continent',
       T.CountryRegionCode              AS N'Country',
       S.Name                           AS N'Dealer',
       CN.LastName                      AS N'SalesStaff',
       FORMAT(SUM(TotalDue), 'c0','en-US')  AS N'TotalSales'
FROM   AdventureWorks.Sales.Customer C
    INNER JOIN AdventureWorks.Sales.Store S
        ON C.CustomerID = S.CustomerID
    INNER JOIN AdventureWorks.Sales.SalesTerritory T
        ON C.TerritoryID = T.TerritoryID
    INNER JOIN AdventureWorks.Sales.SalesOrderHeader H
        ON S.CustomerID = H.CustomerID
    INNER JOIN AdventureWorks.Person.Contact CN
        ON H.SalesPersonID = CN.ContactID
GROUP  BY GROUPING SETS( CUBE(T."Group", T.CountryRegionCode), S.Name, CN.LastName )
ORDER  BY Continent, Country, Dealer, SalesStaff;
-- (664 row(s) affected) - Partial results.
```

Continent	Country	Dealer	SalesStaff	TotalSales
NULL	NULL	Year-Round Sports	NULL	$197,777
NULL	NULL	Yellow Bicycle Company	NULL	$102,699
NULL	AU	NULL	NULL	$2,185,110
NULL	CA	NULL	NULL	$19,316,294
NULL	DE	NULL	NULL	$2,741,548
NULL	FR	NULL	NULL	$6,215,065
NULL	GB	NULL	NULL	$5,758,606
NULL	US	NULL	NULL	$72,049,624
Europe	NULL	NULL	NULL	$14,715,219
Europe	DE	NULL	NULL	$2,741,548
Europe	FR	NULL	NULL	$6,215,065
Europe	GB	NULL	NULL	$5,758,606
North America	NULL	NULL	NULL	$91,365,917
North America	CA	NULL	NULL	$19,316,294
North America	US	NULL	NULL	$72,049,624
Pacific	NULL	NULL	NULL	$2,185,110
Pacific	AU	NULL	NULL	$2,185,110

CHAPTER 21: Advanced T-SQL Programming Topics

SELECT Top N from Each Group

Top 3 in each group is a very popular interview question.

```sql
USE AdventureWorks2012;

DECLARE @TopN tinyint = 3;
WITH cteBestSalesByProduct
    AS (SELECT ROW_NUMBER() OVER( PARTITION BY sod.ProductID
                ORDER BY Sum(sod.LineTotal) DESC)             AS   SeqNo,
            CONCAT(FirstName, SPACE(1), LastName)             AS   [Name],
            p.Name                                            AS ProductName,
            FORMAT(CONVERT(MONEY, Sum(sod.LineTotal)), 'c', 'en-US')  AS TotalBySalesPerson,
            p.ProductNumber,
            sod.ProductID
        FROM   Sales.SalesOrderDetail AS sod
        INNER JOIN Production.Product AS p
            ON sod.ProductID = p.ProductID
        INNER JOIN Sales.SalesOrderHeader AS soh
            ON sod.SalesOrderID = soh.SalesOrderID
        INNER JOIN Person.Person AS pe
            ON soh.SalesPersonID = pe.BusinessEntityID
        WHERE  soh.SalesPersonID IS NOT NULL
        GROUP BY     CONCAT(FirstName, SPACE(1), LastName),
                     sod.ProductID,
                     p.ProductNumber,
                     p.Name )
SELECT *
FROM   cteBestSalesByProduct cte
WHERE  SeqNo <= @TopN
ORDER BY     ProductID,
             SeqNo;
-- (749 row(s) affected) - Partial results.
```

SeqNo	Name	ProductName	TotalBySalesPerson	ProductNumber	ProductID
1	Jae Pak	Women's Mountain Shorts, L	$19,385.51	SH-W890-L	869
2	Linda Mitchell	Women's Mountain Shorts, L	$15,371.85	SH-W890-L	869
3	Michael Blythe	Women's Mountain Shorts, L	$11,411.44	SH-W890-L	869
1	Jillian Carson	Water Bottle - 30 oz.	$936.04	WB-H098	870
2	Linda Mitchell	Water Bottle - 30 oz.	$833.59	WB-H098	870
3	Rachel Valdez	Water Bottle - 30 oz.	$758.01	WB-H098	870
1	Jillian Carson	Patch Kit/8 Patches	$163.51	PK-7098	873
2	Jae Pak	Patch Kit/8 Patches	$120.91	PK-7098	873
3	Ranjit Varkey Chudukatil	Patch Kit/8 Patches	$104.42	PK-7098	873

CHAPTER 21: Advanced T-SQL Programming Topics

SELECT Top N from Each Group Ye Olde Way
SQL Server 2005 has introduced revolutionary enhancements including the OVER clause and recursive CTE-s. It was a bit cumbersome to program certain tasks prior to SS 2005.

```sql
USE AdventureWorks2012;   DECLARE @Top TINYINT = 3;              -- TOP N products in each subcategory
SELECT Subcategory,     ProductName,    ProductID
FROM (   SELECT PSC.Name                                  AS SubCategory,
         P1.Name                                          AS ProductName,    P1.ProductID,
        (SELECT COUNT(*)
        FROM   Production.ProductSubcategory PSC     LEFT JOIN Production.Product P2
        ON P2.ProductSubcategoryID =       PSC.ProductSubcategoryID
        WHERE  P2.ProductSubcategoryID = P1.ProductSubcategoryID AND P2.ProductID <= P1.ProductID) AS RN
   FROM   Production.ProductSubcategory PSC    LEFT JOIN Production.Product P1
          ON P1.ProductSubcategoryID = PSC.ProductSubcategoryID   ) AS    X -- derived table
WHERE RN <= @Top  ORDER BY Subcategory,    ProductID; -- (90 row(s) affected) - Partial results.
```

UPDATE PRIMARY KEY & Connecting FK in a Transaction
Disable & Enable FOREIGN KEY Constraint
The update PRIMARY KEY task (with disable constraint & enable constraint) demonstrates the importance of transaction to protect the integrity of the database: it prevents the database left in a disarray if something goes wrong. Demo only! No reason to change surrogate PK ever!

```sql
USE tempdb;
SELECT CONVERT(INT,ProductSubcategoryID) AS ProductSubcategoryID, ProductCategoryID, Name
INTO Subcategory FROM AdventureWorks2012.Production.ProductSubcategory;   -- (37 row(s) affected)
SELECT * INTO Product FROM AdventureWorks2012.Production.Product;         --(504 row(s) affected)
ALTER TABLE Subcategory ALTER COLUMN ProductSubcategoryID INT NOT NULL;
ALTER TABLE Subcategory ADD CONSTRAINT pkSubcat PRIMARY KEY(ProductSubcategoryID);
ALTER TABLE Product ADD CONSTRAINT pkProd PRIMARY KEY(ProductID);
ALTER TABLE Product ADD CONSTRAINT fkSubcat FOREIGN KEY (ProductSubcategoryID)
REFERENCES Subcategory(ProductSubcategoryID);
GO

SET XACT_ABORT ON;      -- Automatic rollback in case of error
GO
BEGIN TRAN
ALTER TABLE Product NOCHECK CONSTRAINT fkSubcat;           -- Disable constraint
UPDATE Subcategory SET ProductSubcategoryID = 999 WHERE ProductSubcategoryID = 8; --(1 row(s) affected)
UPDATE Product SET ProductSubcategoryID = 999 WHERE ProductSubcategoryID = 8;     -- (3 row(s) affected)
ALTER TABLE Product CHECK CONSTRAINT fkSubcat;             -- Enable constraint
COMMIT TRAN
GO

DROP TABLE tempdb.dbo.Product; DROP TABLE tempdb.dbo.Subcategory;
```

CHAPTER 21: Advanced T-SQL Programming Topics

Table-Valued Parameters

Table-valued parameters were introduced with SQL Server 2008. They can be used to send parameters to SQL statement, stored procedure or function as next demonstrated.

```
USE AdventureWorks2012;
GO
```

```
-- Create new user-defined table data type
CREATE TYPE dbo.utpProdInfo AS TABLE(
        ProdID          int,
        ProdNbr         char(12),
        StandardCost    money,
        ListPrice       money,
        Color   char(16));
GO
```

```
-- Create user- defined table-valued function(UDF) with table-valued parameter
CREATE FUNCTION ufnColorGrouping (@Input dbo.utpProdInfo READONLY)
        RETURNS @Result TABLE (Color char(16), AvgListPrice money)
AS
BEGIN
 INSERT @Result
 SELECT Color, avg(ListPrice) FROM @Input
 GROUP BY Color
 RETURN
END;
GO
```

```
-- Create stored procedure with table-valued parameter
CREATE PROCEDURE uspPriceRange
                    @Input dbo.utpProdInfo READONLY
AS
BEGIN
 SELECT Color,  MinPrice=format(min(ListPrice), 'c0','en-US'),
             MaxPrice=format(max(ListPrice), 'c0','en-US')
 FROM @Input
 GROUP BY Color
 ORDER BY MAX(ListPrice)  DESC
END;
GO
```

CHAPTER 21: Advanced T-SQL Programming Topics

Among the TVP's Benefits: Simple but Powerful Modular Programming

```
-- Test TVF with table-valued parameter
DECLARE @PriceDetail dbo.utpProdInfo
INSERT @PriceDetail SELECT ProductID, ProductNumber, StandardCost, ListPrice, Color
        FROM Production.Product WHERE Color is not null;
```

```
SELECT * FROM ufnColorGrouping (@PriceDetail)
ORDER BY AvgListPrice DESC
```

Color	AvgListPrice
Red	1401.95
Yellow	959.0913
Blue	923.6792
Silver	850.3053
Black	725.121
Grey	125.00
Silver/Black	64.0185
Multi	59.865
White	9.245

```
-- Test stored procedure with table-valued parameter
DECLARE @PriceDetail dbo.utpProdInfo;
INSERT @PriceDetail SELECT ProductID, ProductNumber, StandardCost, ListPrice, Color
        FROM Production.Product WHERE Color is not null;
```

```
EXEC uspPriceRange @PriceDetail;
GO
```

Color	MinPrice	MaxPrice
Red	$35	$3,578
Silver	$0	$3,400
Black	$0	$3,375
Blue	$35	$2,384
Yellow	$54	$2,384
Grey	$125	$125
Multi	$9	$90
Silver/Black	$40	$81
White	$9	$10

```
-- Cleanup
DROP FUNCTION ufnColorGrouping;
DROP PROC uspPriceRange;
DROP TYPE dbo.utpProdInfo;
```

CHAPTER 21: Advanced T-SQL Programming Topics

Creating Comma Delimited String from a Column

XML PATH is the most popular way of accomplishing it, but other methods available as well.

```
;WITH CTE AS (
SELECT   ps.[Name]                                              AS Subcategory,
      Stuff((SELECT ', ' + Color AS [text()]
            FROM AdventureWorks2012.Production.Product p
            WHERE p.ProductSubcategoryID = ps.ProductSubcategoryID
                  AND Color is not null
            GROUP BY Color ORDER BY Color
            FOR XML PATH ('')),1,1,'')                          AS ColorList,
      Stuff((SELECT ', ' + Size AS [text()]
            FROM AdventureWorks2012.Production.Product p
            WHERE p.ProductSubcategoryID = ps.ProductSubcategoryID
                  AND Size is not null
            GROUP BY Size ORDER BY Size
            FOR XML PATH ('')),1,1,'')                          AS SizeList
FROM    AdventureWorks2012.Production.ProductSubcategory ps  )
SELECT * FROM CTE WHERE ColorList is not null AND SizeList is not null  ORDER BY Subcategory;
```

Subcategory	ColorList	SizeList
Bib-Shorts	Multi	L, M, S
Gloves	Black	L, M, S
Hydration Packs	Silver	70
Jerseys	Multi, Yellow	L, M, S, XL
Mountain Bikes	Black, Silver	38, 40, 42, 44, 46, 48, 52
Mountain Frames	Black, Silver	38, 40, 42, 44, 46, 48, 52
Road Bikes	Black, Red, Yellow	38, 40, 42, 44, 48, 52, 56, 58, 60, 62
Road Frames	Black, Red, Yellow	38, 40, 42, 44, 48, 52, 56, 58, 60, 62
Shorts	Black	L, M, S, XL
Socks	White	L, M
Tights	Black	L, M, S
Touring Bikes	Blue, Yellow	44, 46, 50, 54, 58, 60, 62
Touring Frames	Blue, Yellow	44, 46, 50, 54, 58, 60, 62
Vests	Blue	L, M, S

```
DECLARE @CSVList VARCHAR(MAX) = '';      -- Multiple variable assignment method
SELECT @CSVList = CONCAT(Color, ', ', @CSVList)
FROM (SELECT DISTINCT Color FROM AdventureWorks2012.Production.Product
                        WHERE Color is not null) x;
SELECT CommaDelimitedList=@CSVList;
-- Yellow, White, Silver/Black, Silver, Red, Multi, Grey, Blue, Black,
```

Configuring Comma Delimited Result Sets in SSMS

It requires special setup for CSV result sets when using Management Studio. This feature is applicable for the Results to Text mode.

[Options dialog screenshot showing Query Results > SQL Server > Results to Text, with Output format dropdown showing: Column aligned, Comma delimited, Tab delimited, Space delimited, Custom delimiter. Checkboxes include: Include column headers in the result set (checked), Include the query in the result set, Scroll as results are received (checked), Right align numeric values, Discard results after query executes, Display status messages in a separate tab, Display results in a separate tab, Switch to results tab after the query executes. Maximum number of characters displayed in each column: 256.]

[SSMS query window screenshot:]
```
SELECT h.*, d.*
FROM Purchasing.PurchaseOrderHeader h
INNER JOIN Purchasing.PurchaseOrderDetail d
    ON h.PurchaseOrderID = d.PurchaseOrderID
```

Results:
```
4011,7,2,254,1546,3,2008-07-25 00:00:00.000,2008-08-19 00:00:00.000,54492.50,4359.40,1089
4011,7,2,254,1546,3,2008-07-25 00:00:00.000,2008-08-19 00:00:00.000,54492.50,4359.40,1089
4011,7,2,254,1546,3,2008-07-25 00:00:00.000,2008-08-19 00:00:00.000,54492.50,4359.40,1089
4011,7,2,254,1546,3,2008-07-25 00:00:00.000,2008-08-19 00:00:00.000,54492.50,4359.40,1089
4012,6,2,254,1636,3,2008-07-25 00:00:00.000,2008-08-19 00:00:00.000,997680.00,79814.40,19
4012,6,2,254,1636,3,2008-07-25 00:00:00.000,2008-08-19 00:00:00.000,997680.00,79814.40,19
4012,6,2,254,1636,3,2008-07-25 00:00:00.000,2008-08-19 00:00:00.000,997680.00,79814.40,19
4012,6,2,254,1636,3,2008-07-25 00:00:00.000,2008-08-19 00:00:00.000,997680.00,79814.40,19
```

Query execut... | HPESTAR (11.0 RTM) | HPESTAR\Owner (54) | AdventureWorks2012 | 00:00:00 | 8845 rows

Nesting Cursors

Cursors should be avoided with a few exceptions: better performance (rare but happens) or cannot be done by set-based statements. Being new to set-based logic is not a good excuse for using cursors because they do not scale well. Single-level cursor example.

```sql
USE master;

DECLARE @dbName sysname;

DECLARE AllDatabases CURSOR  STATIC LOCAL FOR
      SELECT    name FROM    MASTER.dbo.sysdatabases
      WHERE     name NOT IN ('master','tempdb','model','msdb') -- exclude
      ORDER BY name;

OPEN AllDatabases; FETCH  AllDatabases INTO @dbName;
WHILE (@@FETCH_STATUS = 0) -- loop through all db-s
  BEGIN

/***** PROCESSING STARTS HERE   *****/

    PRINT @dbName;

/***** PROCESSING ENDS HERE   *****/

    FETCH  AllDatabases    INTO @dbName
  END; -- while
CLOSE AllDatabases; DEALLOCATE AllDatabases;
```

Messages:
Accounting
AdventureWorks
AdventureWorks2008
AdventureWorks2012
AdventureWorksDW2012

Nested Cursors

Outer cursor over period Purchase Orders. Inner cursor over products ordered for each PO.

```sql
USE AdventureWorks2012;
DBCC DROPCLEANBUFFERS;  -- Preparation for performance timing - empty memory buffers
DECLARE @StartTime datetime = Getdate();
DECLARE @IterationID INT,  @OrderDetail VARCHAR(max),  @ProductName VARCHAR(10);
DECLARE @Result TABLE ( PurchaseOrderID INT, ProductList VARCHAR(max) ) ;

DECLARE PurchaseOrdersInPeriod CURSOR STATIC LOCAL FOR     -- OUTER CURSOR declaration
  SELECT PurchaseOrderID  FROM  Purchasing.PurchaseOrderHeader
   WHERE  Year(OrderDate) = 2008  AND Month(OrderDate) = 2  ORDER  BY PurchaseOrderID;

OPEN PurchaseOrdersInPeriod; FETCH NEXT FROM PurchaseOrdersInPeriod INTO @IterationID;
PRINT 'OUTER LOOP START';
WHILE ( @@FETCH_STATUS = 0 ) -- sql cursor fetch_status
  BEGIN     SET @OrderDetail = SPACE(0);

    DECLARE POLineItems CURSOR STATIC LOCAL FOR               -- INNER CURSOR declaration
      SELECT p.productNumber   FROM  Purchasing.PurchaseOrderDetail pd
         INNER JOIN Production.Product p  ON pd.ProductID = p.ProductID
      WHERE  pd.PurchaseOrderID = @IterationID ORDER  BY PurchaseOrderDetailID;

    OPEN POLineItems;  FETCH NEXT FROM POLineItems INTO @ProductName;
    PRINT 'INNER LOOP START';
    WHILE ( @@FETCH_STATUS = 0 )
      BEGIN         SET @OrderDetail = CONCAT(@OrderDetail, @ProductName,', ');
         FETCH NEXT FROM POLineItems INTO @ProductName;     PRINT 'INNER LOOP' ;
      END -- inner while
    CLOSE POLineItems;   DEALLOCATE POLineItems;

    SET @OrderDetail = LEFT(@OrderDetail, Len(@OrderDetail) - 1); -- Truncate trailing comma
    INSERT INTO @Result   VALUES     (@IterationID,@OrderDetail);
    FETCH NEXT FROM PurchaseOrdersInPeriod INTO @IterationID ;   PRINT 'OUTER LOOP';
  END -- outer while
CLOSE PurchaseOrdersInPeriod; DEALLOCATE PurchaseOrdersInPeriod;

SELECT * FROM   @Result ORDER  BY PurchaseOrderID;   -- Results  (268 row(s) affected)

SELECT ExecutionMsec = Datediff(millisecond, @StartTime, Getdate());  -- Timing  653 msec
GO
```

CHAPTER 21: Advanced T-SQL Programming Topics

Advanced Graphical Query Designer

Nested Cursor Loops Processing Partial Results

PurchaseOrderID	ProductList
1573	CR-7833
1574	RA-2345
1575	PB-6109
1576	CR-9981
1577	SD-2342, SD-9872
1578	PA-187B, PA-361R, PA-529S, PA-632U, PA-823Y
1579	SE-R581, SE-R908, SE-R995, SE-T312, SE-T762
1580	RF-9198
1581	RC-0291
1582	RM-M464, RM-M692
1583	TP-0923
1584	FC-3982, FL-2301
1585	RM-M464, RM-M692
1586	NI-9522
1587	FW-5160, FW-5800, FW-7160, FW-9160
1588	PD-M282, PD-M340
1589	HN-5400, HN-5811, HN-5818, HN-6320, HN-7161
1590	MS-2348, MS-6061, MT-1000
1591	KW-4091
1592	RM-R436, RM-R600

Set Based Operations Equivalent Code

```
DBCC DROPCLEANBUFFERS;
DECLARE @StartTime datetime = CURRENT_TIMESTAMP;
SELECT poh.PurchaseOrderID,OrderDetail = Stuff((
                -- correlated subquery
                SELECT CONCAT(', ', ProductNumber) AS [text()]
                FROM  Purchasing.PurchaseOrderDetail pod
                    INNER JOIN Production.Product p
                    ON pod.ProductID = p.ProductID
                WHERE  pod.PurchaseOrderID = poh.PurchaseOrderID
                ORDER  BY PurchaseOrderDetailID
                FOR XML PATH ('')), 1, 1, '')
FROM   Purchasing.PurchaseOrderHeader poh
WHERE  Year(OrderDate) = 2004 AND Month(OrderDate) = 2
ORDER  BY PurchaseOrderID;
SELECT ExecutionMsec = Datediff(millisecond, @StartTime, Getdate()) -- Timing: 33 msec
```

CHAPTER 21: Advanced T-SQL Programming Topics

Advanced Graphical Query Designer

While SSMS GUI query / view designer cannot handle very complex queries, it does a pretty good job with "normal" relational database queries.

Aliasing Tables in the Diagram Pane

We start with right click on the top table frame in the Diagram Pane.

In the pop-up dialog box we enter the alias for the table.

CHAPTER 21: Advanced T-SQL Programming Topics

Advanced Graphical Query Designer

Specifying OUTER JOIN in Diagram Pane

To change the INNER JOIN to RIGHT JOIN, right click on the connection square in the middle and click on Properties.

With checkmark selection we can specify LEFT JOIN, RIGHT JOIN or FULL JOIN.

CHAPTER 21: Advanced T-SQL Programming Topics

Query Designer Generated Query

This is the final graphical image in Query Designer prior to the exiting to Query Editor.

```
SELECT PC.Name AS Category, PSC.Name AS Subcategory, P.Name AS Product,
       P.ProductNumber, P.ListPrice
FROM   Production.ProductCategory AS PC
       INNER JOIN Production.ProductSubcategory AS PSC
           ON PC.ProductCategoryID = PSC.ProductCategoryID
       RIGHT OUTER JOIN Production.Product AS P
           ON PSC.ProductSubcategoryID = P.ProductSubcategoryID
WHERE  (P.ProductNumber LIKE N'BK%42') ORDER BY Product, Subcategory, Category;
-- (9 row(s) affected) - Partial results.
```

Category	Subcategory	Product	ProductNumber	ListPrice
Bikes	Mountain Bikes	Mountain-500 Silver, 42	BK-M18S-42	564.99
Bikes	Road Bikes	Road-350-W Yellow, 42	BK-R79Y-42	1700.99

CHAPTER 21: Advanced T-SQL Programming Topics

Template Explorer & Browser

The Template Explorer & Browser helps to start coding by providing a framework code with optional parameter replacements.

CHAPTER 21: Advanced T-SQL Programming Topics

Create Inline Function Template

Double on the template name to get the starter code in a new Query Editor window.

CHAPTER 21: Advanced T-SQL Programming Topics

Template Explorer & Browser

Template Parameters Specifications

The values must be filled in for the parameter in the dialog box.

CHAPTER 21: Advanced T-SQL Programming Topics

Completion of the Function by Entering the SELECT Query with Parameter

Inline user-defined function can be used as a make over for a view with accepting parameters feature.

```sql
CREATE FUNCTION ufnSalesByYear (@year int)
RETURNS TABLE AS
RETURN
(
SELECT   COALESCE(Color, 'N/A')                    AS Color,
         FORMAT(COUNT(*),'###,###')                AS ItemsSold,
         FORMAT(SUM(LineTotal), 'c0','en-US')      AS TotalSale
FROM Sales.SalesOrderHeader H
    INNER JOIN Sales.SalesOrderDetail D
        ON H.SalesOrderID = D.SalesOrderID
    INNER JOIN Production.Product P
        ON P.ProductID = D.ProductID
WHERE   OrderDate >= CONVERT(date, convert(varchar,@year)+'0101')
    AND OrderDate < CONVERT(date, convert(varchar,@year+1)+'0101')
GROUP BY COALESCE(Color, 'N/A')
);
GO
SELECT * FROM ufnSalesByYear(2008) ORDER BY Color;
```

#	Color	ItemsS...	TotalSale
1	Black	7,654	$7,277,726
2	Blue	4,495	$4,676,256
3	Multi	2,953	$128,220
4	N/A	18,205	$405,086
5	Red	1,634	$524,594
6	Silver	3,784	$4,588,420
7	Silver/Black	578	$53,423
8	White	600	$10,148
9	Yellow	5,673	$8,164,889

CHAPTER 21: Advanced T-SQL Programming Topics

Entering PowerShell from Object Explorer

In addition to executing sqlps in Command Prompt, we can enter PowerShell from SSMS Object Explorer via the right click drop-down menu. Entering the get-childitem command will list all the views in the path (directory).

CHAPTER 21: Advanced T-SQL Programming Topics

PowerShell Command List

The following command will list all the PowerShell commands. Partial list presented.

`get-command | out-file 'f:\temp\command.txt'`

CommandType	Name	Definition
Alias	%	ForEach-Object
Alias	?	Where-Object
Function	A:	Set-Location A:
Alias	ac	Add-Content
Cmdlet	Add-Computer	Add-Computer [-DomainName] <...
Cmdlet	Add-Content	Add-Content [-Path] <String[...
Cmdlet	Add-History	Add-History [[-InputObject] ...
Cmdlet	Add-Member	Add-Member [-MemberType] <PS...
Cmdlet	Add-PSSnapin	Add-PSSnapin [-Name] <String...
Cmdlet	Add-RoleMember	Add-RoleMember [-MemberName]...
Cmdlet	Add-SqlAvailabilityDatabase	Add-SqlAvailabilityDatabase ...
Cmdlet	Add-SqlAvailabilityGroupList...	Add-SqlAvailabilityGroupList...
Cmdlet	Add-Type	Add-Type [-TypeDefinition] <...
Alias	asnp	Add-PSSnapIn
Function	B:	Set-Location B:
Cmdlet	Backup-ASDatabase	Backup-ASDatabase [-BackupFi...
Cmdlet	Backup-SqlDatabase	Backup-SqlDatabase [-Databas...
Function	C:	Set-Location C:

We can access help for a command just by typing "help" and the command name. "help" example for format-list.

`help format-list`

```
SQL Server Powershell
PS SQLSERVER:\SQL\HPESTAR\DEFAULT\Databases\AdventureWorks2012\Views> help format-list

NAME
    Format-List

SYNOPSIS
    Formats the output as a list of properties in which each property appears on a new line.

SYNTAX
    Format-List [[-Property] <Object[]>] [-DisplayError] [-Expand <string>] [-Force] [-GroupBy <Object>] [-InputObject <psobject>] [-ShowError] [-View <string>] [<CommonParameters>]

DESCRIPTION
    The Format-List cmdlet formats the output of a command as a list of properties in which each property is displayed on a separate line. You can use Format-List to format and display all or selected properties of an object as a list (format-list *).

    Because more space is available for each item in a list than in a table, Windows PowerShell displays more properties of the object in the list, and th
```

CHAPTER 21: Advanced T-SQL Programming Topics

TRY...CATCH Block With TRANSACTION

If the TRY is successful the transaction is committed, otherwise the transaction (previous statements if any) is rolled back and the error is logged into an errorlog table.

```sql
USE tempdb;  -- Create & configure table for testing
IF OBJECT_ID ('dbo.Product', 'U') IS NOT NULL DROP TABLE dbo.Product ;
SELECT ID=CONVERT(INT,ProductID), ProductName=Name, ListPrice, ModifiedDate
INTO Product FROM AdventureWorks2012.Production.Product WHERE ListPrice > 0;  -- (304 row(s) affected)
ALTER TABLE PRODUCT ADD CONSTRAINT uqProd UNIQUE (ProductName);
ALTER TABLE PRODUCT ADD CONSTRAINT dfProd DEFAULT (CURRENT_TIMESTAMP) FOR ModifiedDate;
ALTER TABLE PRODUCT ADD rowguid UNIQUEIDENTIFIER default(newsequentialid());
GO  -- Command(s) completed successfully.

IF OBJECT_ID ('dbo.ErrorLogForTransactions', 'U') IS NOT NULL  DROP TABLE dbo.ErrorLogForTransactions ;
CREATE TABLE ErrorLogForTransactions(  ID INT IDENTITY(1,1) PRIMARY KEY,
     UserName sysname, TableName sysname, ErrorNumber sysname, ErrorSeverity sysname,
     ErrorState sysname, ErrorMessage nvarchar(1024),  rowguid UNIQUEIDENTIFIER default(newid()),
     ModifiedDate datetime default (getdate()));
GO -- Command(s) completed successfully.

IF OBJECT_ID ('dbo.uspInsertNewProduct', 'P') IS NOT NULL DROP PROC dbo.uspInsertNewProduct ;
GO
CREATE PROCEDURE uspInsertNewProduct ( @NewProduct NVARCHAR(64), @Price  SMALLMONEY) AS
BEGIN    DECLARE @TableName   SYSNAME, @ErrorMessage NVARCHAR(1024);
  BEGIN TRY;   BEGIN TRANSACTION;
   SELECT @ErrorMessage = 'Duplicate insert failed', @TableName = 'Product';
   INSERT dbo.Product (ID, ProductName, ListPrice)
         SELECT max(ID)+1, @NewProduct,  @Price FROM Product;     COMMIT TRANSACTION;
  END TRY
  BEGIN CATCH    ROLLBACK TRANSACTION;     INSERT dbo.ErrorLogForTransactions
          (UserName, TableName, ErrorNumber, errorSeverity, errorState, ErrorMessage)
            VALUES(suser_sname(),@TableName,ERROR_NUMBER(),ERROR_SEVERITY(),
              ERROR_STATE(),ERROR_MESSAGE());    RAISERROR (@ErrorMessage,16,1);   END CATCH
END
GO

EXEC uspInsertNewProduct  'xDelta SmartPhone', 999.99;           -- Valid INSERT
DECLARE @NewProduct varchar(64) = (SELECT TOP(1) ProductName FROM Product), @Price SMALLMONEY = 999.99;
EXEC uspInsertNewProduct  @NewProduct, @Price;               -- Invalid INSERT - duplicate name
GO

SELECT * FROM ErrorLogForTransactions;
```

ID	UserName	TableName	ErrorNumber	ErrorSeverity	ErrorState	ErrorMessage	ModifiedDate
1	HPESTAR\Owner	Product	2627	14	1	Violation of UNIQUE KEY constraint 'uqProd'. Cannot insert duplicate key in object 'dbo.Product'. The duplicate key value is (All-Purpose Bike Stand).	2016-12-09 13:35:23.687

CHAPTER 21: Advanced T-SQL Programming Topics

SET TRANSACTION ISOLATION LEVEL Command

The syntax for the command:

SET TRANSACTION ISOLATION LEVEL

   { READ UNCOMMITTED

   | READ COMMITTED

   | REPEATABLE READ

   | SNAPSHOT

   | SERIALIZABLE

   } [;]

Preparation for demonstrating levels. We have to use 2 connections to represent 2 users of the database. First we create a test table.

```
USE tempdb;
SELECT * INTO Product FROM AdventureWorks2012.Production.Product;
-- (504 row(s) affected)
```

In connection 1 we simulate a large (slow) transaction on the Product table.

```
BEGIN TRAN;
SELECT StartTime = CURRENT_TIMESTAMP;
UPDATE Product SET ListPrice=ListPrice * 1.05;
WAITFOR DELAY '00:00:20'; -- 20 sec delay to keep transaction pending
ROLLBACK TRAN;
SELECT FinishTime = CURRENT_TIMESTAMP;
```

In connection 2 we test the isolation levels. We start execution after connection 1 started. Code for the first test.

```
SET TRANSACTION ISOLATION LEVEL READ UNCOMMITTED
SELECT StartTime = CURRENT_TIMESTAMP;
SELECT TOP (2) * FROM Product ORDER BY ListPrice DESC;
SELECT FinishTime = CURRENT_TIMESTAMP;
```

SET TRANSACTION ISOLATION LEVEL Command

READ UNCOMMITTED Isolation Level - Dirty Reads

The SELECT with TOP started 4 seconds later after the UPDATE, yet it finished immediately without waiting for the UPDATE transaction to come to a conclusion (ROLLBACK or COMMIT).

SQLQuery57.sql:
```
SET TRANSACTION ISOLATION LEVEL READ UNCOMMITTED
SELECT StartTime = CURRENT_TIMESTAMP;
SELECT TOP (2) * FROM Product ORDER BY ListPrice DESC;
SELECT FinishTime = CURRENT_TIMESTAMP;
```

Results:

	StartTime
1	2012-10-26 19:22:42.103

	Product...	Name	ProductNum...	MakeFl...	FinishedGoodsF...	Color	SafetyStockLe...
1	749	Road-150 Red, 62	BK-R93R-62	1	1	Red	100
2	750	Road-150 Red, 44	BK-R93R-44	1	1	Red	100

	FinishTime
1	2012-10-26 19:22:42.127

Query executed successfully. HPESTAR (11.0 RTM) HPESTAR\Owner (53) tempdb 00:00:00 4 rows

SQLQuery56.sql:
```
BEGIN TRAN;
SELECT StartTime = CURRENT_TIMESTAMP;
UPDATE Product SET ListPrice=ListPrice * 1.05;
WAITFOR DELAY '00:00:20'; -- 20 sec delay to keep transaction pending
ROLLBACK TRAN;
SELECT FinishTime = CURRENT_TIMESTAMP;
```

Results:

	StartTime
1	2012-10-26 19:22:38.077

	FinishTime
1	2012-10-26 19:22:58.090

Query executed successfully. HPESTAR (11.0 RTM) HPESTAR\Owner (55) tempdb 00:00:20 2 rows

CHAPTER 21: Advanced T-SQL Programming Topics

READ COMMITTED Isolation Level - Default for SQL Server

The SELECT query waits until the exclusive lock is removed by the UPDATE transaction. To prevent such a wait, frequently the NOLOCK hint (dirty reads) is used.

```sql
SET TRANSACTION ISOLATION LEVEL READ COMMITTED
SELECT StartTime = CURRENT_TIMESTAMP;
SELECT TOP (2) * FROM Product ORDER BY ListPrice DESC;
SELECT FinishTime = CURRENT_TIMESTAMP;
```

	StartTime
1	2012-10-26 19:35:08.990

	Product...	Name	ProductNum...	MakeFl...	FinishedGoodsF...	Color	SafetyStockLe...
1	749	Road-150 Red, 62	BK-R93R-62	1	1	Red	100
2	750	Road-150 Red, 44	BK-R93R-44	1	1	Red	100

	FinishTime
1	2012-10-26 19:35:25.103

Query executed successfully. | HPESTAR (11.0 RTM) | HPESTAR\Owner (53) | tempdb | 00:00:16 | 4 rows

```sql
BEGIN TRAN;
SELECT StartTime = CURRENT_TIMESTAMP;
UPDATE Product SET ListPrice=ListPrice * 1.05;
WAITFOR DELAY '00:00:20'; -- 20 sec delay to keep transaction pending
ROLLBACK TRAN;
SELECT FinishTime = CURRENT_TIMESTAMP;
```

	StartTime
1	2012-10-26 19:35:05.093

	FinishTime
1	2012-10-26 19:35:25.103

Query executed successfully. | HPESTAR (11.0 RTM) | HPESTAR\Owner (55) | tempdb | 00:00:20 | 2 rows

SET TRANSACTION ISOLATION LEVEL Command

REPEATABLE READ Isolation Level

The UPDATE (transaction by itself) must wait until the exclusive lock is released by the 2 SELECT statements transaction. The ListPrice changed after the COMMIT transaction.

```sql
SELECT StartTime = CURRENT_TIMESTAMP;
UPDATE Product SET ListPrice=ListPrice * 1.05;
SELECT FinishTime = CURRENT_TIMESTAMP;
```

StartTime
1 | 2012-10-26 20:09:56.677

FinishTime
1 | 2012-10-26 20:10:08.833

```sql
SET TRANSACTION ISOLATION LEVEL REPEATABLE READ
BEGIN TRAN;
SELECT StartTime = CURRENT_TIMESTAMP;
SELECT TOP (1) ProductNumber, ListPrice FROM Product ORDER BY Name DESC;
WAITFOR DELAY '00:00:20'; -- 20 sec delay to keep transaction pending
SELECT TOP (1) ProductNumber, ListPrice FROM Product ORDER BY Name DESC;
COMMIT TRAN;
SELECT FinishTime = CURRENT_TIMESTAMP;
```

StartTime
1 | 2012-10-26 20:09:48.803

ProductNum... | ListPrice
1 | TG-W091-S | 78.3463

ProductNum... | ListPrice
1 | TG-W091-S | 78.3463

FinishTime
1 | 2012-10-26 20:10:08.830

CHAPTER 21: Advanced T-SQL Programming Topics

SET TRANSACTION ISOLATION LEVEL Command

Redefining the Product table without IDENTITIY & testing it

```
DROP TABLE tempdb.dbo.Product;
SELECT ID = CONVERT(INT, ProductID), Name, ProductNumber, ListPrice, Color
INTO tempdb.dbo.Product FROM AdventureWorks2012.Production.Product;
```

REPEATABLE READ blocks UPDATE & DELETE, but not INSERT. The row counts differ.

Session 1 (SQLQuery57.sql):
```
SELECT StartTime = CURRENT_TIMESTAMP;
INSERT Product VALUES(1000,'Tandem Bike', 'TND-BK-48',1195.00,'Blue');
SELECT FinishTime = CURRENT_TIMESTAMP;
```

Results:
- StartTime: 2012-10-27 11:03:43.310
- FinishTime: 2012-10-27 11:03:43.310

(2 rows, 00:00:00)

Session 2 (SQLQuery56.sql):
```
SET TRANSACTION ISOLATION LEVEL REPEATABLE READ
BEGIN TRAN;
SELECT StartTime = CURRENT_TIMESTAMP;
SELECT ProdCount=COUNT(*) FROM Product;
WAITFOR DELAY '00:00:20';  -- 20 sec delay to keep transaction pending
SELECT ProdCount=COUNT(*) FROM Product;
COMMIT TRAN;
SELECT FinishTime = CURRENT_TIMESTAMP;
```

Results:
- StartTime: 2012-10-27 11:03:38.787
- ProdCount: 504
- ProdCount: 505
- FinishTime: 2012-10-27 11:03:58.790

(4 rows, 00:00:20)

CHAPTER 21: Advanced T-SQL Programming Topics

SET TRANSACTION ISOLATION LEVEL Command

SERIALIZABLE Isolation Level

SERIALIZABLE isolation level blocks INSERT as well in addition to blocking UPDATE & DELETE. The row counts are the same.

```
SELECT StartTime = CURRENT_TIMESTAMP;
INSERT Product VALUES(1000,'Tandem Bike', 'TND-BK-48',1195.00,'Blue');
SELECT FinishTime = CURRENT_TIMESTAMP;
```

StartTime: 2012-10-27 11:09:41.010
FinishTime: 2012-10-27 11:09:55.230

```
SET TRANSACTION ISOLATION LEVEL SERIALIZABLE
BEGIN TRAN;
SELECT StartTime = CURRENT_TIMESTAMP;
SELECT ProdCount=COUNT(*) FROM Product;
WAITFOR DELAY '00:00:20'; -- 20 sec delay to keep transaction pending
SELECT ProdCount=COUNT(*) FROM Product;
COMMIT TRAN;
SELECT FinishTime = CURRENT_TIMESTAMP;
```

StartTime: 2012-10-27 11:09:35.207
ProdCount: 505
ProdCount: 505
FinishTime: 2012-10-27 11:09:55.230

CHAPTER 21: Advanced T-SQL Programming Topics

SNAPSHOT Isolation Level

SNAPSHOT isolation produces the same results as SERIALIZABLE without blocking INSERT (same for UPDATE &DELETE).

```
SELECT StartTime = CURRENT_TIMESTAMP;
INSERT Product VALUES(1000,'Tandem Bike', 'TND-BK-48',1195.00,'Blue');
SELECT FinishTime = CURRENT_TIMESTAMP;
```

Results:

	StartTime
1	2012-10-27 11:48:10.167

	FinishTime
1	2012-10-27 11:48:10.167

Query executed successfully. HPESTAR (11.0 RTM) HPESTAR\Owner (54) tempdb 00:00:00 2 rows

```
ALTER DATABASE tempdb SET ALLOW_SNAPSHOT_ISOLATION ON;
SET TRANSACTION ISOLATION LEVEL SNAPSHOT;
BEGIN TRAN;
SELECT StartTime = CURRENT_TIMESTAMP;
SELECT ProdCount=COUNT(*) FROM Product;
WAITFOR DELAY '00:00:20'; -- 20 sec delay to keep transaction pending
SELECT ProdCount=COUNT(*) FROM Product;
COMMIT TRAN;
SELECT FinishTime = CURRENT_TIMESTAMP;
```

Results:

	StartTime
1	2012-10-27 11:48:05.517

	ProdCount
1	507

	ProdCount
1	507

	FinishTime
1	2012-10-27 11:48:25.583

Query executed successfully. HPESTAR (11.0 RTM) HPESTAR\Owner (51) tempdb 00:00:20 4 rows

CHAPTER 21: Advanced T-SQL Programming Topics

INSERT Data Into Parent-Child Tables in One Transaction

Tabular Summary of Isolation Levels

DBCC command returns the isolation level property for the database among other database options.

```
USE tempdb;
DBCC USEROPTIONS;
/* (13 row(s) affected)
DBCC execution completed. If DBCC printed error messages,
contact your system administrator. */
```

Set Option	Value
textsize	2147483647
language	us_english
dateformat	mdy
datefirst	7
lock_timeout	-1
quoted_identifier	SET
arithabort	SET
ansi_null_dflt_on	SET
ansi_warnings	SET
ansi_padding	SET
ansi_nulls	SET
concat_null_yields_null	SET
isolation level	read committed

Dirty Reads & Phantom Reads

Dirty Reads: reading uncommitted data; there is no guarantee that data read will ever be committed.

Phantom Reads: data working with in the first connection changed by another transaction in the second connection since first read. Subsequent reads of the data in the first connection same transaction could be different.

Isolation level	Dirty read	Nonrepeatable read	Phantom read
Read uncommitted	Yes	Yes	Yes
Read committed	No	Yes	Yes
Repeatable read	No	No	Yes
Serializable	No	No	No
Snapshot	No	No	No

CHAPTER 21: Advanced T-SQL Programming Topics

INSERT Data Into Parent-Child Tables in One Transaction

The business meaning of transaction: either insert successfully to both tables or do nothing, return an error. First we prepare the test data to be inserted in two temporary tables by SELECT INTO table create and populate.

```
USE AdventureWorks2012
GO
```

```
DECLARE @SourceSOID int = 50701;
SELECT  OrderDate
        ,DueDate ,ShipDate,Status,OnlineOrderFlag,PurchaseOrderNumber
        ,AccountNumber,CustomerID,SalesPersonID,TerritoryID,BillToAddressID
        ,ShipToAddressID,ShipMethodID,CreditCardID,CreditCardApprovalCode
        ,CurrencyRateID,SubTotal,TaxAmt,Freight,Comment
INTO #SOH
FROM Sales.SalesOrderHeader
WHERE SalesOrderID = @SourceSOID;   -- (1 row(s) affected)
```

```
SELECT  SalesOrderID,
        CarrierTrackingNumber,OrderQty,ProductID,SpecialOfferID,UnitPrice,UnitPriceDiscount
INTO #SOD
FROM Sales.SalesOrderDetail
WHERE SalesOrderID = @SourceSOID;
GO   -- (6 row(s) affected)
```

```
SELECT * FROM #SOH;
```

OrderDate	DueDate	ShipDate	Status	OnlineOrderFlag	PurchaseOrderNumber	AccountNumber	CustomerID	SalesPersonID	TerritoryID	BillToAddressID	ShipToAddressID	ShipMethodID	CreditCardID	CreditCardApprovalCode	CurrencyRateID	SubTotal	TaxAmt	Freight	Comment
2007-06-01 00:00:00.000	2007-06-13 00:00:00.000	2007-06-08 00:00:00.000	5	0	PO2407199018	10-4020-000225	298	279	5	933	933	5	12808	56789Vi66226	NULL	777.2902	73.4748	22.9609	NULL

```
SELECT * FROM #SOD;
GO
```

CarrierTrackingNumber	OrderQty	ProductID	SpecialOfferID	UnitPrice	UnitPriceDiscount
B67A-4C0A-B3	1	843	1	15.00	0.00
B67A-4C0A-B3	1	726	1	202.332	0.00
B67A-4C0A-B3	1	722	1	183.9382	0.00
B67A-4C0A-B3	4	855	1	53.994	0.00
B67A-4C0A-B3	2	813	1	65.6018	0.00
B67A-4C0A-B3	1	716	1	28.8404	0.00

INSERT Data Into Parent-Child Tables in One Transaction

ROLLBACK Does Not Roll Back Everything
ROLLBACK has no effect on IDENTITY seed, table variable or writing to a flat file. The implication is that IDENTITY column will have gaps where ROLLBACKs happened. With RAISERROR we return an error flag to the calling application program.

```
BEGIN TRANSACTION

DECLARE @Insert TABLE(ID INT); DECLARE @Error INT; DECLARE @ID INT;

INSERT INTO Sales.SalesOrderHeader(OrderDate
        ,DueDate ,ShipDate,Status,OnlineOrderFlag,PurchaseOrderNumber
        ,AccountNumber,CustomerID,SalesPersonID,TerritoryID,BillToAddressID
        ,ShipToAddressID,ShipMethodID,CreditCardID,CreditCardApprovalCode
        ,CurrencyRateID,SubTotal,TaxAmt,Freight,Comment )
OUTPUT inserted.SalesOrderID INTO @Insert(ID)  -- This is the PRIMARY KEY value
SELECT * FROM #SOH; -- (1 row(s) affected)

SET @Error = @@ERROR;
IF @Error <>0 BEGIN
        ROLLBACK TRANSACTION;
        RAISERROR ('An error occured inserting Sales.SalesOrderHeader',12,1);   END
ELSE BEGIN

SELECT * FROM @Insert; -- debugging   -- 75124

SELECT @ID = ID FROM @Insert;  -- FOREIGN KEY value

INSERT Sales.SalesOrderDetail ( SalesOrderID,
        CarrierTrackingNumber, OrderQty, ProductID, SpecialOfferID,
        UnitPrice, UnitPriceDiscount)
SELECT @ID, * FROM #SOD;  -- (6 row(s) affected)

SET @Error = @@ERROR;
IF @Error <>0 BEGIN
 ROLLBACK TRANSACTION;
 RAISERROR ('An error occured inserting Sales.SalesOrderDetail',12,1);
 END
ELSE
        COMMIT TRAN;
END
GO
```

Optimistic Concurrency Control

A table can have only one rowversion(formerly timestamp) column which is used for version-stamping rows. The value in the rowversion column is updated automatically every time a row in the table inserted or updated. Of course this means we cannot use it as a PRIMARY KEY, because we may get many FK orphans quickly if updates are performed on other columns. When a row is modified in a table, the timestamp is updated with the current database timestamp value obtained from the @@DBTS function.

Rowversion is the synonym for timestamp starting with SQL Server 2005. It is an 8 bytes unique binary key within the database. A quick demo of rowversion data type follows. **Rowversion values may not be consecutive.** Since all the columns in the demo table have default values, we can use the DEFAULT VALUES clause for INSERT.

```
USE tempdb;
GO
```

```
CREATE TABLE Alpha ( ID int IDENTITY(1,1) PRIMARY KEY,
        Number int default(datepart(ss,CURRENT_TIMESTAMP)),
        String varchar(16) default(datename(dw, CURRENT_TIMESTAMP)),
        ModifiedDate date default(CURRENT_TIMESTAMP),
        RowStamp rowversion);
GO
```

```
INSERT Alpha DEFAULT VALUES;
GO 100
```

```
SELECT TOP(5) * FROM Alpha ORDER BY ID;
GO
```

ID	Number	String	ModifiedDate	RowStamp
1	43	Sunday	2012-10-28	0x0000000000000840
2	43	Sunday	2012-10-28	0x0000000000000841
3	43	Sunday	2012-10-28	0x0000000000000842
4	43	Sunday	2012-10-28	0x0000000000000843
5	43	Sunday	2012-10-28	0x0000000000000844

The rowversion (timestamp) starts changing as soon as the transaction begins. If the transaction is rolled back, it returns to the original value.

The main purpose is row versioning in multi user environment, in other words concurrency checking. The users may be humans or computer programs.

Pessimistic Concurrency Control vs. Optimistic

Pessimistic concurrency means locking the data at the row, page, or table level and don't allow anyone to modify it until the target user is done modifying the data and saving it back into the database. Trouble with this method: it may take a few minutes for the target user to update a record during which period other users may be prevented from doing their work (locked out from the table by blocking). If the target user called away for a meeting for example in the middle of data entry, you need to unlock the table by a timeout mechanism in order to prevent damaging disruption to data access by other users.

Optimistic concurrency means reading a record in a table and displaying it for the target user, but not locking it. Other users can read and modify the record at anytime while the target user is performing the manual update on the computer screen. When the target user releases the record for database update you need to check if someone changed it in between the initial read and the release (like 1-5 minutes). Usually this is not a problem due to the work distribution among staff (business process organization), nevertheless you have to program for it to avoid conflicting updates and damage to database integrity.

Assume you are a developer and developing a program in Visual Basic to update the name and address table of customers. There will be 100 staff member who can perform this application function. How can you be sure that while target staff Alpha typing in the change, staff Beta is not changing the same row?

Here is what you can do:

- Read the name and address table including the rowversion. You display the info to the user for update and save the rowversion.
- Certain amount of time later, like 2 minutes, the user presses the submit button after changes were typed in.
- You open a transaction with Begin Transaction.
- You read the rowversion of the name and address row.
- You compare the current rowversion to the saved rowversion.
- If the rowversions are same, you update the row and commit the transaction.
- If rowversions are different, you roll back the transaction and notify the user about the fact that the data was changed by someone else. You can let then the user decide what to do or follow the appropriate company business rule for data entry conflict resolution.

This is pretty common practice in multi-user environment. The alternate would be to examine a datetime column, or the entire row which is more processing intensive and less reliable as well due to potential blocking.

Example Showing rowversion (formerly timestamp) in Action

```
USE tempdb;

CREATE TABLE Star
(
        StarID              INT IDENTITY PRIMARY KEY,            -- SURROGATE PK
        FirstName           VARCHAR(25),
        LastName            VARCHAR(30),
        UNIQUE (LastName, FirstName),                             -- NATURAL KEY
        ModifiedDate        DATE default( CURRENT_TIMESTAMP),
        VERSIONSTAMP        ROWVERSION
);
go

-- Populate table
INSERT Star     (FirstName, LastName)
VALUES          ('Tom', 'Jones'),
                ('Jessica', 'Simpson'),
                ('Luciano', 'Pavarotti'),
                ('Stevie',  'Brock'),
                ('Christina', 'Aguilera'),
                ('Frank', 'Sinatra'),
                ('Doris', 'Day'),
                ('Elvis', 'Presley');
go

SELECT * FROM   Star ORDER BY StarID;
go
```

StarID	FirstName	LastName	ModifiedDate	VERSIONSTAMP
1	Tom	Jones	2018-11-07	0x00000000000007E0
2	Jessica	Simpson	2018-11-07	0x00000000000007E1
3	Luciano	Pavarotti	2018-11-07	0x00000000000007E2
4	Stevie	Brock	2018-11-07	0x00000000000007E3
5	Christina	Aguilera	2018-11-07	0x00000000000007E4
6	Frank	Sinatra	2018-11-07	0x00000000000007E5
7	Doris	Day	2018-11-07	0x00000000000007E6
8	Elvis	Presley	2018-11-07	0x00000000000007E7

CHAPTER 21: Advanced T-SQL Programming Topics

Optimistic Concurrency Control

Simulation of Conflicting Updates of the Same Record

```sql
-- Temporary table to store current record version
CREATE TABLE #semaphore
(
  ID              INT IDENTITY(1, 1) PRIMARY KEY,
  StartVersion    BIGINT,
  PK              INT
);
```

```sql
INSERT INTO #semaphore (StartVersion, PK)
SELECT VERSIONSTAMP, StarID
FROM   Star
WHERE  StarID = 1;
```

```sql
SELECT * FROM #semaphore;
```

ID	StartVersion	PK
1	2016	1

```sql
-- We send the info to "our" application user;  user is making changes on the app form;
SELECT StarID, FirstName, LastName
FROM Star
WHERE StarID = 1;
```

```sql
-- SIMULATION: somebody else updating the same record meanwhile
-- Execute the following UPDATE statement in a different SSMS connection
/*********************************************************
UPDATE Star
SET    FirstName = 'Celine',
       LastName = 'Dion'
WHERE  StarID = 1
*********************************************************/
```

```sql
SELECT StarID, FirstName, LastName FROM Star WHERE StarID = 1;
```

StarID	FirstName	LastName
1	Celine	Dion

CHAPTER 21: Advanced T-SQL Programming Topics

We Envelope the UPDATE Attempt into a Transaction

```sql
-- We are attempting to update, but cannot because current version is different
BEGIN TRANSACTION

IF (SELECT StartVersion
    FROM   #semaphore
    WHERE  PK=1 )
      =
   (SELECT VERSIONSTAMP
    FROM   Star
    WHERE  StarID = 1)
  BEGIN
     UPDATE Star
     SET    FirstName = 'Julia',
            LastName  = 'Roberts'
     WHERE  StarID = 1
     COMMIT TRANSACTION
  END
ELSE
  BEGIN
     ROLLBACK TRANSACTION
     PRINT 'ROLLBACK - UPDATE CONFLICT'
     RAISERROR ('Star update conflict.',10,0)
  END;
```

```
/* Messages
ROLLBACK - UPDATE CONFLICT
Star update conflict.    */
```

RAISERROR returns error flag to application. The application will follow a business rule to handle the exception.

CHAPTER 21: Advanced T-SQL Programming Topics

Xquery Examples

The XML data type has the following methods for exposing the data: Query, Value, Exist, Modify, and Nodes.

The query() Method

The query() method takes an XQuery expression that evaluates to a list of XML nodes and allows the extraction of fragments of an XML document. The result is an instance of untyped XML. First we create xml data with the FOR XML AUTO clause, then query it.

```
DECLARE @xml xml = CONCAT('<Root>',
                           (select ProductName=Name, ListPrice
                            from Production.Product
                            where Color is not null
                            and ListPrice > 0.0
                            order by ProductName    for XML AUTO),
                           '</Root>');
SELECT @xml.query('/Root/Production.Product') AS ProdList;
GO
```

ProdList
1 <Production.Product ProductName="AWC Logo Cap" L...

```
<Production.Product ProductName="AWC Logo Cap" ListPrice="8.9900" />
<Production.Product ProductName="Chain" ListPrice="20.2400" />
<Production.Product ProductName="Classic Vest, L" ListPrice="63.5000" />
<Production.Product ProductName="Classic Vest, M" ListPrice="63.5000" />
<Production.Product ProductName="Classic Vest, S" ListPrice="63.5000" />
<Production.Product ProductName="Front Brakes" ListPrice="106.5000" />
<Production.Product ProductName="Front Derailleur" ListPrice="91.4900" /
<Production.Product ProductName="Full-Finger Gloves, L" ListPrice="37.99
<Production.Product ProductName="Full-Finger Gloves, M" ListPrice="37.99
```

The query() Method Retrieves Assembly Instructions from XML Column

inst is a derived table representing the inner query which retrieves information from the ProductModel table XML column. The outer query formats and filters the data to return the final result set.

```sql
USE AdventureWorks2012;
SELECT  ProductModelID,
        rtrim(ltrim(convert(nvarchar(max),[Procedure]))) AS [Procedure]
FROM
(SELECT ProductModelID,Instructions.query(
' declare namespace AWPMMI="http://schemas.microsoft.com/sqlserver/2004/07/adventure-works/ProductModelManuInstructions";
  for $Step in /AWPMMI:root/AWPMMI:Location[1]/AWPMMI:step
    return string($Step)'
) AS [Procedure]
FROM Production.ProductModel WHERE Instructions is not null) inst
WHERE ProductModelID = 53;
GO
```

ProductModelID	Procedure
53	
	Visually examine the pedal spindles to determine left and right pedals. The left and right pedals have different threading directions. It is important you identify them correctly.
	Apply a small amount of grease to the left pedal and thread the pedal onto the left crank arm by hand.
	If the threads do not turn easily, back the spindle out and re-start.
	Securely tighten the spindle against the crank arm using a small wrench.
	Apply a small amount of grease to the right pedal and thread the pedal onto the right crank arm by hand. If the threads do not turn easily, back the spindle out and re-start. Securely tighten the spindle against the crank arm using a small wrench.
	Inspect per specification FI-520.

When we examine the Procedure string with convert(varbinary(max), ...), we can see that it has next line (hex 0A) an leading spaces (hex 20) imbedded for formatting purposes. We can check the size of XML data with the DATALENGTH() function:

```sql
select   MinLen = min(datalength(resume)),  MaxLen = max(datalength(resume)),
         AvgLen = avg(datalength(resume))
from AdventureWorks2012.HumanResources.JobCandidate;
--  3931           9080            6241
```

Xquery Examples

value() Method

The value() method performs an XQuery against the XML and returns a scalar value.

DECLARE @xmlDoc xml =' <root><MP3List><MP3ListID>99</MP3ListID></MP3List> </root>';
SELECT @xmlDoc.value('(/root//MP3List/MP3ListID/text())[1]','nvarchar(32)');   -- 99

nodes() Method

The nodes() method shreds an XML data type instance into relational data. It returns a rowset. In the XML resume example, each column returned as scalar value.

```
SELECT Resume.res.value(N'declare default element namespace
        "http://schemas.microsoft.com/sqlserver/2004/07/adventure-works/Resume";
        (/Resume/Name/Name.First)[1]', 'nvarchar(30)') AS FirstName
      ,Resume.res.value(N'declare default element namespace
        "http://schemas.microsoft.com/sqlserver/2004/07/adventure-works/Resume";
        (/Resume/Name/Name.Last)[1]', 'nvarchar(30)') AS LastName
      ,Resume.res.value(N'declare default element namespace
        "http://schemas.microsoft.com/sqlserver/2004/07/adventure-works/Resume";
        (Address/Addr.Location/Location/Loc.State)[1]', 'nvarchar(100)') AS State
      ,Resume.res.value(N'declare default element namespace
        "http://schemas.microsoft.com/sqlserver/2004/07/adventure-works/Resume";
        (Address/Addr.Location/Location/Loc.City)[1]', 'nvarchar(100)') AS City
      ,LEFT( Resume.res.value(N'declare default element namespace
        "http://schemas.microsoft.com/sqlserver/2004/07/adventure-works/Resume";
        (/Resume/Skills)[1]', 'nvarchar(max)'), 80 ) AS Skills
FROM AdventureWorks2012.HumanResources.JobCandidate jc
CROSS APPLY jc.Resume.nodes(N'declare default element namespace
        "http://schemas.microsoft.com/sqlserver/2004/07/adventure-works/Resume";
        /Resume') AS Resume(res) ORDER BY jc.JobCandidateID;
```

	FirstName	LastName	State	City	Skills
1	Shai	Bassli	MI	Saginaw	I am an experienced and versatile machinist who ca
2	Max	Benson	FL	Orlando	3 years recent experience as a go-cart production li
3	Krishna	Sunkammurali	WA	Issaquah	Expert in C# and Visual Basic 6.0. 7 years experien
4	Stephen	Jiang	WA	Redmond	Considerable expertise in all areas of the sales cycl
5	Thierry	D'Hers	Bouches-du-Rhône	Marseille	Connaissances approfondies de tous les secteurs d
6	Christian	Kleinerman	Pyrénées-Orientales	Perpignan	3 années d'expérience récente en tant que respons
7	Lionel	Penuchot	Var	Bandol	Mécanicien expérimenté et polyvalent qui peut utilise
8	Peng	Wu	WA	Federal Way	熟悉所有销售环节，专业知识丰富。13 年来，为提高公
9	Shengda	Yang	FL	Orlando	最近三年任职婴儿车生产线经理。负责计划生产线预算
10	Tai	Yee	CO	Denver	我是一名经验丰富的机械师，技术全面，不仅单独操作

CHAPTER 21: Advanced T-SQL Programming Topics

exist() Method

The exist() method returns bit 1 (true) if the XQuery expression returns at least one XML node.

Bike models are listed if <Summary> element is included in XML ProductDescription.

```
SELECT          Name                                   AS ModelName,
                CatalogDescription.query('
declare namespace pd="http://schemas.microsoft.com/sqlserver/2004/07/adventure-
works/ProductModelDescription";
  <Product
    ProductModelID= "{ sql:column("ProductModelID") }"
    />
')                                                     AS ProductModelID
FROM AdventureWorks2012.Production.ProductModel
WHERE CatalogDescription.exist('
  declare namespace  pd="http://schemas.microsoft.com/sqlserver/2004/07/adventure-
works/ProductModelDescription";
  /pd:ProductDescription[(pd:Summary)]'
  ) = 1
ORDER BY ModelName;
GO
```

ModelName	ProductModelID
Mountain-100	<Product ProductModelID="19" />
Mountain-500	<Product ProductModelID="23" />
Road-150	<Product ProductModelID="25" />
Road-450	<Product ProductModelID="28" />
Touring-1000	<Product ProductModelID="34" />
Touring-2000	<Product ProductModelID="35" />

The CatalogDescription XML data for ProductModelID 23

```
<?xml-stylesheet href="ProductDescription.xsl" type="text/xsl"?>
<p1:ProductDescription
xmlns:p1="http://schemas.microsoft.com/sqlserver/2004/07/adventure-
works/ProductModelDescription"
xmlns:wm="http://schemas.microsoft.com/sqlserver/2004/07/adventure-
works/ProductModelWarrAndMain" xmlns:wf="http://www.adventure-
```

CHAPTER 21: Advanced T-SQL Programming Topics

works.com/schemas/OtherFeatures" xmlns:html="http://www.w3.org/1999/xhtml" ProductModelID="23" ProductModelName="Mountain-500">
 <p1:Summary>
  <html:p>Suitable for any type of riding, on or off-road.
                Fits any budget. Smooth-shifting with a comfortable ride.
        </html:p>
 </p1:Summary>
 <p1:Manufacturer>
  <p1:Name>AdventureWorks</p1:Name>
  <p1:Copyright>2002</p1:Copyright>
  <p1:ProductURL>HTTP://www.Adventure-works.com</p1:ProductURL>
 </p1:Manufacturer>
 <p1:Features>Product highlights include:
       <wm:Warranty><wm:WarrantyPeriod>1 year</wm:WarrantyPeriod><wm:Description>parts and labor</wm:Description></wm:Warranty><wm:Maintenance><wm:NoOfYears>3 years</wm:NoOfYears><wm:Description>maintenance contact available through dealer</wm:Description></wm:Maintenance><wf:wheel>Stable, durable wheels suitable for novice riders.</wf:wheel><wf:saddle>Made from synthetic leather and features gel padding for increased comfort.</wf:saddle><wf:pedal><html:b>Expanded platform</html:b> so you can ride in any shoes; great for all-around riding.</wf:pedal><wf:crankset> Super rigid spindle.
</wf:crankset><wf:BikeFrame>Our best value frame utilizing the same, ground-breaking technology as the ML aluminum frame.</wf:BikeFrame></p1:Features>
 <!-- add one or more of these elements... one for each specific product in this product model -->
 <p1:Picture>
  <p1:Angle>front</p1:Angle>
  <p1:Size>small</p1:Size>
  <p1:ProductPhotoID>1</p1:ProductPhotoID>
 </p1:Picture>
 <!-- add any tags in <specifications> -->
 <p1:Specifications> These are the product specifications.
        <Height>Varies</Height> Centimeters.
        <Material>Aluminum Alloy</Material><Color>Available in all colors.</Color><ProductLine>Mountain bike</ProductLine><Style>Unisex</Style><RiderExperience>Novice to Intermediate riders</RiderExperience></p1:Specifications>
</p1:ProductDescription>

modify() Method

The modify() method modifies the contents of an XML document. It can only be used in the SET statement or the SET clause of an UPDATE statement for tables with XML columns.

```
DECLARE @XML xml = '<Root>
 <Picture>
  <Angle>front</Angle>
  <Size>small</Size>
  <ProductPhotoID>1</ProductPhotoID>
 </Picture>    </Root>';      SELECT @XML;
```

```
<Root><Picture><Angle>front</Angle><Size>small</Size><ProductPhotoID>1</ProductPhotoID></Picture></Root>
```

```
-- update angle
SET @XML.modify('
 replace value of (/Root/Picture/Angle[1]/text())[1]
 with   "side" ');        SELECT @XML;
```

```
<Root><Picture><Angle>side</Angle><Size>small</Size><ProductPhotoID>1</ProductPhotoID></Picture></Root>
```

```
-- update size
SET @XML.modify('
 replace value of (/Root/Picture/Size[1]/text())[1]
 with   "medium" ');    SELECT @XML;
```

```
<Root><Picture><Angle>side</Angle><Size>medium</Size><ProductPhotoID>1</ProductPhotoID></Picture></Root>
```

```
-- update productphotoid
SET @XML.modify('
 replace value of (/Root/Picture/ProductPhotoID[1]/text())[1]
 with   "99" ');         SELECT @XML;
```

```
<Root><Picture><Angle>side</Angle><Size>medium</Size><ProductPhotoID>99</ProductPhotoID></Picture></Root>
```

CHAPTER 21: Advanced T-SQL Programming Topics

Insert (XML DML)

Insert(XML DML) inserts one or more nodes as child nodes or siblings of the target node.

```
DECLARE @XML xml = '<Root>
 <Picture ID = "4">
  <Angle>front</Angle>
  <Size>small</Size>
  <ProductPhotoID>1</ProductPhotoID>
 </Picture>     </Root>';
SELECT @XML;
```

```
<Root>
 <Picture ID="4">
  <Angle>front</Angle>
  <Size>small</Size>
  <ProductPhotoID>1</ProductPhotoID>
 </Picture>
</Root>
```

```
SET @XML.modify('insert  <Picture ID = "1">
  <Angle>front</Angle>
  <Size>large</Size>
  <ProductPhotoID>45</ProductPhotoID>
 </Picture> as first    into  (/Root)[1] ');
SELECT @XML;
```

```
<Root>
 <Picture ID="1">
  <Angle>front</Angle>
  <Size>large</Size>
  <ProductPhotoID>45</ProductPhotoID>
 </Picture>
 <Picture ID="4">
  <Angle>front</Angle>
  <Size>small</Size>
  <ProductPhotoID>1</ProductPhotoID>
 </Picture>
</Root>
```

CHAPTER 21: Advanced T-SQL Programming Topics

Delete (XML DML)
The delete(XML DML) deletes nodes from an XML instance.

```
DECLARE @XML xml = '<Root>
<Picture ID = "1">
  <Angle>front</Angle>
  <Size>large</Size>
  <ProductPhotoID>45</ProductPhotoID>
</Picture>
<Picture ID = "4">
  <Angle>front</Angle>
  <Size>small</Size>
  <ProductPhotoID>1</ProductPhotoID>
</Picture>
<Picture ID = "8">
  <Angle>above</Angle>
  <Size>small</Size>
  <ProductPhotoID>12</ProductPhotoID>
</Picture>      </Root>';
```

```
SET @XML.modify('
 delete /Root/Picture[@ID=4]  ');
```

```
SELECT @XML;
```

```
    <Root>
     <Picture ID="1">
       <Angle>front</Angle>
       <Size>large</Size>
       <ProductPhotoID>45</ProductPhotoID>
     </Picture>
     <Picture ID="8">
       <Angle>above</Angle>
       <Size>small</Size>
       <ProductPhotoID>12</ProductPhotoID>
     </Picture>
    </Root>
```

CHAPTER 21: Advanced T-SQL Programming Topics

Working with hierarchyid Data Type

Orgchart Based on AdventureWorks2012

Let's take a look at the hierarchyid and related data in the Employee table first.

```
USE AdventureWorks2012;
```

```
SELECT TOP(20) BusinessEntityID, NationalIdNumber, OrganizationNode, OrganizationLevel,
        OrgNodeText=CONVERT(varchar, OrganizationNode),  JobTitle
FROM HumanResources.Employee  ORDER BY OrganizationNode;
```

BusinessEntityID	NationalIdNumber	OrganizationNode	OrganizationLevel	OrgNodeText	JobTitle
1	295847284	0x	0	/	Chief Executive Officer
2	245797967	0x58	1	/1/	Vice President of Engineering
3	509647174	0x5AC0	2	/1/1/	Engineering Manager
4	112457891	0x5AD6	3	/1/1/1/	Senior Tool Designer
5	695256908	0x5ADA	3	/1/1/2/	Design Engineer
6	998320692	0x5ADE	3	/1/1/3/	Design Engineer
7	134969118	0x5AE1	3	/1/1/4/	Research and Development Manager
8	811994146	0x5AE158	4	/1/1/4/1/	Research and Development Engineer
9	658797903	0x5AE168	4	/1/1/4/2/	Research and Development Engineer
10	879342154	0x5AE178	4	/1/1/4/3/	Research and Development Manager
11	974026903	0x5AE3	3	/1/1/5/	Senior Tool Designer
12	480168528	0x5AE358	4	/1/1/5/1/	Tool Designer
13	486228782	0x5AE368	4	/1/1/5/2/	Tool Designer
14	42487730	0x5AE5	3	/1/1/6/	Senior Design Engineer
15	56920285	0x5AE7	3	/1/1/7/	Design Engineer
16	24756624	0x68	1	/2/	Marketing Manager
17	253022876	0x6AC0	2	/2/1/	Marketing Assistant
18	222969461	0x6B40	2	/2/2/	Marketing Specialist
19	52541318	0x6BC0	2	/2/3/	Marketing Assistant
20	323403273	0x6C20	2	/2/4/	Marketing Assistant

```
-- Convert text node to hierarchyid
SELECT CONVERT(hierarchyid, '/3/1/22/4/');   -- 0x7AF07610
```

hierarchyid Based Organizational Chart with Recursive CTE

TAB (CHAR(9)) is used to create the indentation using OrganizationLevel.

```
;WITH cteOrgChart(ManagerID, EmployeeID, EmployeeLevel)
   AS (SELECT    OrganizationNode,                          -- anchor member
                 OrganizationNode,  OrganizationLevel
      FROM   HumanResources.Employee
      WHERE  OrganizationLevel = 0
      UNION ALL
      SELECT     e.OrganizationNode.GetAncestor(1),         -- recursive member
                 e.OrganizationNode, OrganizationLevel
      FROM   HumanResources.Employee e
         INNER JOIN cteOrgChart d
            ON e.OrganizationNode.GetAncestor(1) = d.EmployeeID)

-- SELECT * FROM    cteOrgChart  -- for testing & debugging

SELECT   Employee = CONCAT(replicate(CHAR(9),(EmployeeLevel)), P.LastName, ', ',
P.FirstName)
FROM    cteOrgChart OC
     INNER JOIN HumanResources.Employee E
       ON OC.EmployeeID = E.OrganizationNode
     INNER JOIN Person.Person P
       ON E.BusinessEntityID = P.BusinessEntityID
ORDER BY E.OrganizationNode;
-- (290 row(s) affected)  - Partial Results.
```

Employee					
Sánchez, Ken					
	Duffy, Terri				
		Tamburello, Roberto			
			Walters, Rob		
			Erickson, Gail		
			Goldberg, Jossef		
			Miller, Dylan		
					Margheim, Diane
					Matthew, Gigi
					Raheem, Michael
			Cracium, Ovidiu		
					D'Hers, Thierry
					Galvin, Janice
			Sullivan, Michael		
			Salavaria, Sharon		
	Bradley, David				

CHAPTER 21: Advanced T-SQL Programming Topics

Working with hierarchyid Data Type

Inline User-Defined Function OrgChart at Any Level

We can easily wrap the company orgchart logic into a parameterized function to get the orgchart for any executive or manager in the company.

```
CREATE FUNCTION ufnOrgChart ( @OrganizationNode hierarchyid )
RETURNS TABLE AS RETURN
(WITH cteOrgChart(ManagerID, EmployeeID, EmployeeLevel)
    AS (SELECT OrganizationNode,
         OrganizationNode,
         0
    FROM   HumanResources.Employee
    WHERE  OrganizationNode = @OrganizationNode
    UNION ALL
    SELECT e.OrganizationNode.GetAncestor(1),
         e.OrganizationNode,
         EmployeeLevel+1
    FROM   HumanResources.Employee e
       INNER JOIN cteOrgChart d
         ON e.OrganizationNode.GetAncestor(1) = d.EmployeeID)
SELECT   Employee = CONCAT(replicate(CHAR(9),(EmployeeLevel)), P.LastName, ', ',
                    P.FirstName)
FROM    cteOrgChart OC
     INNER JOIN HumanResources.Employee E
       ON OC.EmployeeID = E.OrganizationNode
     INNER JOIN Person.Person P
       ON E.BusinessEntityID = P.BusinessEntityID  );
GO

SELECT * FROM ufnOrgChart (0x84);   -- (29 row(s) affected) - Partial Results.
```

Employee			
Norman, Laura			
	Barreto de Mattos, Paula		
	Liu, David		
	Kahn, Wendy		
	Barber, David		
		Word, Sheela	
			Sandberg, Mikael
			Rao, Arvind
			Meisner, Linda
			Ogisu, Fukiko

CHAPTER 21: Advanced T-SQL Programming Topics

hierarchyid System Functions

Specialized system hierarchyid functions available to deal with hierarchyid data.

```
SELECT          BusinessEntityID, JobTitle, OrganizationNode, OrganizationLevel,
                OrganizationNode.ToString()            AS TextOrgNode,
                OrganizationNode.GetLevel()            AS NodeLevel,
                OrganizationNode.GetAncestor(1)        AS Ancestor,
                OrganizationNode.IsDescendantOf(0x58)  AS [0x58 Descendant]
FROM HumanResources.Employee   ORDER BY TextOrgNode;
-- (290 row(s) affected) - Partial results.
```

Business EntityID	JobTitle	OrganizationNode	OrganizationLevel	TextOrgNode	NodeLevel	Ancestor	0x58 Descendant
1	Chief Executive Officer	0x	0	/	0	NULL	0
2	Vice President of Engineering	0x58	1	/1/	1	0x	1
3	Engineering Manager	0x5AC0	2	/1/1/	2	0x58	1
4	Senior Tool Designer	0x5AD6	3	/1/1/1/	3	0x5AC0	1
5	Design Engineer	0x5ADA	3	/1/1/2/	3	0x5AC0	1
6	Design Engineer	0x5ADE	3	/1/1/3/	3	0x5AC0	1
7	Research and Development Manager	0x5AE1	3	/1/1/4/	3	0x5AC0	1
8	Research and Development Engineer	0x5AE158	4	/1/1/4/1/	4	0x5AE1	1

Sorting Outline Numbers with hierarchyid

Certain sorts which are obvious to us, due to our Human Intelligence, are a challenge in traditional SQL programming due to lack of tree/hierarchy structure processing. Such a case is outline numbers which are easily convertible to hierarchyid, hence the simple solution.

```
CREATE TABLE #OutlineNumber  (Nbr Varchar(64));   INSERT #OutlineNumber Values
('1'), ('1.1'), ('1.1.1'), ('1.1.9'), ('1.1.10'), ('1.1.11'), ('2'), ('2.1'), ('2.1.1'), ('10.1.2'), ('11.1.9');
SELECT * FROM #OutlineNumber ORDER BY Nbr;
```

Nbr	
1	
1.1	
1.1.1	
1.1.10	
1.1.11	
1.1.9	out of order
10.1.2	out of order
11.1.9	out of order
2	
2.1	
2.1.1	

CHAPTER 21: Advanced T-SQL Programming Topics

Sort Outline Numbering continued

```
-- Sorting on hierarchyid by converting outline string with "/" replaces "." & "/" prefix, suffix
SELECT *, [HierarchyID].ToString() AS TextHierarchyID FROM
  (SELECT *, CONVERT(hierarchyid, CONCAT('/',REPLACE(Nbr, '.', '/') ,'/')) AS [HierarchyID]
    FROM #OutlineNumber) x /* derived table */ ORDER BY HierarchyID;
```

Nbr	HierarchyID	TextHierarchyID
1	0x58	/1/
1.1	0x5AC0	/1/1/
1.1.1	0x5AD6	/1/1/1/
1.1.9	0x5AE980	/1/1/9/
1.1.10	0x5AEA80	/1/1/10/
1.1.11	0x5AEB80	/1/1/11/
2	0x68	/2/
2.1	0x6AC0	/2/1/
2.1.1	0x6AD6	/2/1/1/
10.1.2	0xAAB680	/10/1/2/
11.1.9	0xAEBA60	/11/1/9/

Calculate Percent Ratios by Groups

Ratio calculation is important in Business Intelligence. It can be done in various or all levels of a hierarchical relationship, in this example Product --> Subcategory hierarchy.

```
USE AdventureWorks2012;
SELECT  S.Name                                                          AS Subcategory,
   FORMAT(1.0 * SUM(CASE WHEN Color in ( 'Black', 'Yellow', 'Silver')
   THEN 1 ELSE 0 END) / COUNT(*), 'p')                                  AS RatioOfBlkYlwSlv
FROM Production.Product P
        INNER JOIN Production.ProductSubcategory S
            ON P.ProductSubcategoryID= S.ProductSubcategoryID
WHERE Color is not null and P.ProductSubcategoryID is not null
GROUP BY S.Name  ORDER BY S.Name;
-- (23 row(s) affected) - Partial results.
```

Subcategory	RatioOfBlkYlwSlv
Pedals	0.00 %
Road Bikes	53.49 %
Road Frames	48.48 %
Shorts	100.00 %
Socks	0.00 %

CHAPTER 21: Advanced T-SQL Programming Topics

Dynamic SQL PIVOT

Dynamic SQL PIVOT transposes rows into columns based on dynamic data. Dynamic PIVOT contrasts hard-wired PIVOT. Prior to coding the dynamic SQL, write out & test the static query.

> Database security article: Dynamic SQL & SQL Injection:
> http://blogs.msdn.com/b/raulga/archive/2007/01/04/dynamic-sql-sql-injection.aspx

We need the following data-driven column header list of years:

[2005], [2006], [2007], [2008]

We need the following static PIVOT query to be generated dynamically:

```
SELECT * FROM (SELECT [Store (Freight Summary)] = S.Name,
        YEAR(OrderDate) AS OrderYear,  Freight
FROM    Sales.SalesOrderHeader SOH
INNER JOIN Sales.Customer C ON SOH.CustomerID = C.CustomerID
INNER JOIN Sales.Store S ON C.StoreID = S.BusinessEntityID) as Header
PIVOT (SUM(Freight) FOR OrderYear IN( [2005], [2006], [2007], [2008])) AS Pvt ORDER BY 1;
-- (633 row(s) affected) - Partial results.
```

Store (Freight Summary)	2005	2006	2007	2008
Sensible Sports	NULL	NULL	364.2076	472.8672
Separate Parts Corporation	1243.1035	4883.5698	2493.3725	NULL
Serious Cycles	4868.9888	3511.0184	354.9403	NULL
Seventh Bike Store	831.2495	4329.8166	4866.4755	2024.7107
Sharp Bikes	912.9061	549.7834	NULL	NULL
Sheet Metal Manufacturing	NULL	6050.2523	9169.2709	3328.5167
Shipping Specialists	NULL	NULL	NULL	12.9692
Showcase for Cycles	NULL	NULL	35.2509	6.2386
Simple Bike Parts	87.9217	100.5808	31.1732	29.8886
Sixth Bike Store	426.1619	1346.1144	79.9409	NULL
Sleek Bikes	NULL	NULL	3407.692	2364.0185
Small Bike Accessories Shop	NULL	NULL	1116.6658	992.0197
Small Bike Shop	2359.1319	5277.5806	3681.3405	2216.5242
Small Cycle Store	152.3481	989.9408	801.0264	553.2965
Social Activities Club	177.3895	52.9214	9.7198	29.8886
Solid Bike Parts	1134.6482	1535.374	372.4571	NULL
Some Discount Store	2499.3443	733.0964	38.0211	1.1373
South Bike Company	NULL	NULL	1043.9713	837.2011
Spa and Exercise Outfitters	NULL	94.3411	3777.5336	2441.4004

CHAPTER 21: Advanced T-SQL Programming Topics

Dynamic SQL PIVOT: Dealer Freight Cost by Year

```sql
USE AdventureWorks2012;

DECLARE @OrderYear AS TABLE( YYYY INT  NOT NULL   PRIMARY KEY )
DECLARE @DynamicSQL AS NVARCHAR(MAX)

INSERT INTO @OrderYear
SELECT DISTINCT YEAR(OrderDate) FROM  Sales.SalesOrderHeader

DECLARE @ReportColumnNames AS NVARCHAR(MAX),   @IterationYear   AS INT
SET @IterationYear = (SELECT MIN(YYYY) FROM  @OrderYear)
SET @ReportColumnNames = N''

-- Assemble pivot list dynamically
WHILE (@IterationYear IS NOT NULL)
 BEGIN
  SET @ReportColumnNames = CONCAT(@ReportColumnNames, N', ',
   QUOTENAME(CAST(@IterationYear AS NVARCHAR(10))))
  SET @IterationYear = (SELECT MIN(YYYY)
           FROM  @OrderYear   WHERE  YYYY > @IterationYear)
 END

SET @ReportColumnNames =
SUBSTRING(@ReportColumnNames,2,LEN(@ReportColumnNames))

PRINT @ReportColumnNames

-- Assemble final code
SET @DynamicSQL = CONCAT(N'SELECT * FROM (SELECT [Store (Freight Summary)]=S.Name,
                  YEAR(OrderDate) AS OrderYear,  Freight
FROM   Sales.SalesOrderHeader SOH
INNER JOIN Sales.Customer C ON SOH.CustomerID = C.CustomerID
INNER JOIN Sales.Store S ON C.StoreID = S.BusinessEntityID) as Header
PIVOT (SUM(Freight)
FOR OrderYear IN(', @ReportColumnNames, N'))  AS Pvt ORDER BY 1;')

PRINT @DynamicSQL; -- Testing & debugging

EXEC sp_executesql @DynamicSQL;
GO
```

Date Range Programming with Datetime Column

The time portion of a datetime column presents a big problem ("midnight bug") when looking for a time range of records (rows). The equal operator picks up only the midnight records, nothing beyond as demonstrated. Similar issue for the BETWEEN operator. Best solution is to use DATE (SQL Server2008) if time portion is of no interest. With datetime we cannot assume that the time portion is 00:00:00.000 since it may have been changed unintentionally.

```
USE tempdb;
SELECT * INTO SOH FROM AdventureWorks2012.Sales.SalesOrderHeader; -- Create test table
GO
-- (31465 row(s) affected)
SELECT COUNT(SalesOrderID), MAX(OrderDate) FROM SOH WHERE OrderDate = '2008-02-01';
-- 244    2008-02-01 00:00:00.000
SELECT COUNT(SalesOrderID), MAX(OrderDate) FROM SOH
WHERE OrderDate BETWEEN '2008-02-01' AND '2008-02-01';
-- 244    2008-02-01 00:00:00.000
-- Advance order date 1 second passed midnight
UPDATE SOH SET OrderDate = dateadd(ss, 1, OrderDate) WHERE OrderDate = '2008-02-01';
-- (244 row(s) affected)
-- Due to the non-zero time portion, no equal match
SELECT COUNT(SalesOrderID), MAX(OrderDate) FROM SOH WHERE OrderDate = '2008-02-01';
-- 0      NULL
-- The BETWEEN operator also fails
SELECT COUNT(SalesOrderID), MAX(OrderDate) FROM SOH
WHERE OrderDate BETWEEN '2008-02-01' AND '2008-02-01';
-- 0      NULL
-- A safe way to get all the sales - not the best performant if there is index on OrderDate
SELECT COUNT(SalesOrderID), MAX(OrderDate) FROM SOH
WHERE YEAR(OrderDate)=2008 AND MONTH(OrderDate) = 2 AND DAY(OrderDate) = 1;
--244    2008-02-01 00:00:01.000
-- Another way to get all sales - no performance issue in case of index on OrderDate
SELECT COUNT(SalesOrderID), MAX(OrderDate) FROM SOH
WHERE OrderDate >= '2008-02-01' AND OrderDate < DATEADD(dd,1,'2008-02-01');
-- 244   2008-02-01 00:00:01.000
-- Using the BETWEEN operator - performance issue in case of index on OrderDate
SELECT COUNT(SalesOrderID), MAX(OrderDate) FROM SOH
WHERE CONVERT(DATE, OrderDate) BETWEEN '2008-02-01' AND '2008-02-01';
-- 244   2008-02-01 00:00:01.000
GO
DROP TABLE tempdb.dbo.SOH;
```

Date Range Programming with Datetime Column

The BETWEEN Operator for DATE & DATETIME Ranges

```
-- BETWEEN dates implementation for datetime OrderDate
DECLARE @StartDate datetime ='20080201', @EndDate datetime = '20080205';
SELECT OrderCount=COUNT(*) FROM AdventureWorks2012.Sales.SalesOrderHeader
WHERE OrderDate >= @StartDate and OrderDate < DATEADD(DD,1,@EndDate);
GO
-- 502
```

```
-- BETWEEN dates implementation for datetime OrderDate using DATE data type
DECLARE @StartDate date ='20080201', @EndDate date = '20080205';
SELECT OrderCount=COUNT(*) FROM AdventureWorks2012.Sales.SalesOrderHeader
WHERE OrderDate >= @StartDate and OrderDate < DATEADD(DD,1,@EndDate);
GO
-- 502
```

```
-- Past midnight and next midnight
SELECT  dateadd(dd, datediff(dd, 0, CURRENT_TIMESTAMP)+0, 0),
        dateadd(dd, 1+datediff(dd, 0, CURRENT_TIMESTAMP)+0, 0)
-- 2016-10-23 00:00:00.000    2016-10-24 00:00:00.000
```

```
-- Orders for today (date range 1 day)
SELECT * FROM AdventureWorks2012.Sales.SalesOrderHeader
WHERE OrderDate >= dateadd(dd, datediff(dd, 0, CURRENT_TIMESTAMP)+0, 0)
  AND OrderDate <  dateadd(dd, 1+datediff(dd, 0, CURRENT_TIMESTAMP)+0, 0)
GO
```

```
-- Create a copy of the PurchaseOrderHeader (similar to SalesOrderHeader) table
USE tempdb;
SELECT * INTO POH FROM AdventureWorks2012.Purchasing.PurchaseOrderHeader
GO
-- (4012 row(s) affected)
```

```
-- Purchase order count for the entire month of MARCH 2008
SELECT COUNT(*) FROM POH WHERE OrderDate >='2008-03-01 00:00:00.000'
           AND OrderDate < '2008-04-01 00:00:00.000'
-- 313
```

```
-- Equivalent datetime or date comparison queries
SELECT COUNT(*) FROM POH WHERE OrderDate >='2008-03-01' AND OrderDate < '2008-04-01'
-- 313
```

CHAPTER 21: Advanced T-SQL Programming Topics

BETWEEN for Date Ranges cont.

```sql
-- SQL date between - performance issue due to CAST if OrderDate is indexed
SELECT COUNT(*) FROM POH WHERE
        CAST(OrderDate AS DATE) BETWEEN '2008-03-01' AND '2008-03-31';
-- 313
```

```sql
-- SQL datetime between with explicit inclusive lower and upper limits
/***** WORKS BUT NOT BEST PRACTICES *****/
SELECT COUNT(*) FROM POH WHERE OrderDate
BETWEEN '2008-03-01 00:00:00.000' AND '2008-03-31 23:59:59.997';  -- 313
```

```sql
/***** NOT BEST PRACTICES - WRONG RESULT IF TIME PART IS NOT 12:00AM *****/
SELECT COUNT(*) FROM POH WHERE OrderDate
        BETWEEN '2008-03-01 00:00:00.000' AND '2008-03-31 00:00:00.000' ; --313
SELECT COUNT(*) FROM POH WHERE OrderDate BETWEEN '2008-03-01' AND '2008-03-31';
-- 313
/*****************************************************************/
```

```sql
-- TIME PART assumed to be 12:00AM = 00:00:00.000 if not specified
SELECT COUNT(*) FROM POH WHERE OrderDate BETWEEN '2008-01-02' AND '2008-01-07';
-- 60
UPDATE TOP(1) POH SET OrderDate = DATEADD (second, 1, OrderDate)
        WHERE  OrderDate='2008-01-07';        -- (1 row(s) affected)
-- The 1 second passed midnight record is no longer included in the BETWEEN range
SELECT COUNT(*) FROM POH WHERE OrderDate BETWEEN '2008-01-02' AND '2008-01-07';
-- 59
```

```sql
-- BETWEEN is inclusive operator - it includes the limits
SELECT COUNT(*) FROM POH WHERE OrderDate
        BETWEEN '2008-01-02 00:00:00.000' AND '2008-01-07 00:00:00.000';  -- 59
```

```sql
-- Include midnight and midnight+1 sec records for 2008-01-07
SELECT COUNT(*) FROM POH WHERE OrderDate
        BETWEEN '2008-01-02 00:00:00.000' AND '2008-01-07 00:00:01.000';  -- 60
```

```sql
-- Date range query - good performance if OrderDate indexed ( SARGABLE)
SELECT [Sales]=COUNT(*) FROM Purchasing.PurchaseOrderHeader
WHERE OrderDate >= CONVERT(DATE,'20080301')
        AND OrderDate < CONVERT(DATE,'20080316');
-- 137
```

CHAPTER 21: Advanced T-SQL Programming Topics

4-Week 13 Month Calendar

The Christian (Gregorian, Western) calendar, used in most parts of the World, has been introduced by Pope Gregory in 1582. It appears to be irregular due to using 12 months instead of 13 months. While 13 month calendars were proposed in the past, its urgency rapidly increasing due to the expansion of Business Intelligence. 4 weeks 13 months calendar totals to 364 days, almost on the mark!

```
SELECT 4 * 7 * 13  -- 364
```

To include the remaining 1 or 2 (leap year) days, we have to make the last week of the year longer with 1 or 2 days, tentatively named **Earthday** and **Starday**. Each month starts with Monday. Therefore, each year starts with Monday. The new month is tentatively called **Undecimber** after undecim, Latin for 11. This naming follows the Latin number sequence starting with September (septem Latin for 7). The year ends two ways:

- Friday, Saturday, Sunday, Earthday (Undecimber 29)
- Friday, Saturday, Sunday, Earthday, Starday (Undecimber 30) - leap year
- January 1 is Monday in each year
- Each month calendar identical with Undecimber having an extra day or two

```
DECLARE @4week13month TABLE( ID INT IDENTITY(1,1),
 Mon char(3), Tue char(3), Wed char(3), Thu char(3), Fri char(3), Sat char(3), Sun char(3));
INSERT @4week13month VALUES ('MON', 'TUE', 'WED', 'THU', 'FRI', 'SAT', 'SUN'),
('1','2','3','4','5','6','7'), ('8','9','10','11','12','13','14'),
('15','16','17','18','19','20','21'),('22','23','24','25','26','27','28');
SELECT * FROM @4week13month ORDER BY ID;
```

MON	TUE	WED	THU	FRI	SAT	SUN
1	2	3	4	5	6	7
8	9	10	11	12	13	14
15	16	17	18	19	20	21
22	23	24	25	26	27	28

The SQL significance of such a calendar is immense: week can be used in GROUP BY summaries just like month. Currently week-based analysis is misaligned with month-based analysis. Some businesses do use 13-month calendars for business analysis and reporting.

> The **benefits of 13 month calendar** are presented at:
> http://en.wikipedia.org/wiki/International_Fixed_Calendar

CHAPTER 21: Advanced T-SQL Programming Topics

DDL Trigger on DATABASE CREATE

DDL trigger carries out action, in this instance just sending a message, when a new database is created. The screenshot segment shows the DDL trigger listing in SSMS Object Explorer.

```
USE master;
GO
CREATE TRIGGER trgNewDatabase
ON ALL SERVER  FOR CREATE_DATABASE  AS
BEGIN
DECLARE @database sysname, @event_data XML = EVENTDATA()
 SET @database = @event_data.value('(/EVENT_INSTANCE/DatabaseName)[1]', 'sysname')
 RAISERROR( 'trgNewDatabase DDL trigger message: %s DB has been created', 16,1, @database)
END
GO -- Command(s) completed successfully.
```

```
CREATE DATABASE zTest1;
GO  /* Messages
Msg 50000, Level 16, State 1, Procedure trgNewDatabase, Line 10
trgNewDatabase DDL trigger message: zTest1 DB has been created */
```

```
DROP DATABASE zTest1;
GO -- Command(s) completed successfully.
```

```
DROP TRIGGER [trgNewDatabase] ON ALL SERVER
GO -- Command(s) completed successfully.
```

Spatial Data Types: Geometry & Geography

The POLYGON & STLength() Functions

The geometry data type and geography data type are used for spatial and mapping applications. The geometry data type can store polygons. The perimeter of a polygon can be calculated by the STLength() spatial function and the polygon itself can be visualized in Management Studio Spatial results.

```sql
USE AdventureWorks2012;
-- Polygon length - square each side 10
DECLARE @Geomet geometry;
SET @Geomet = geometry::STGeomFromText('POLYGON((0 0,0 10,10 10,10 0,0 0))', 0);
SELECT @Geomet, LengthOfPerimeter=@Geomet.STLength(); -- 40
go

-- Polygon length - 5 sides
DECLARE @Geomet geometry=
  geometry::STGeomFromText('POLYGON((1 1, 1 7, 7 7, 20 20, 7 1, 1 1))', 0);
SELECT @Geomet, LengthOfPerimeter=@Geomet.STLength() -- 59.4065051772929
go

-- Polygon length - 6 sides
DECLARE @Geomet geometry;
SET @Geomet = geometry::STGeomFromText(
          'POLYGON((1 1, 1 7, 7 6, 6 11, 50 50, 20 1, 1 1))', 0);
SELECT @Geomet, @Geomet.STLength(); -- 152.43237011714
go
```

Polygon Difference & Intersection

The STDifference() and STIntersection functions will calculate the difference and intersection of two polygons. The example is for a small square inside a bigger square. The difference is displayed in Spatial results which is the dark area. The intersection coincidentally is the white small square.

```sql
-- Polygon difference and intersection
DECLARE @g geometry = 'POLYGON((10 10, 40 10, 40 40, 10 40, 10 10))';
DECLARE @h geometry = 'POLYGON((20 20, 30 20, 30 30, 20 30, 20 20))';
SELECT [Difference]=@g.STDifference(@h);
SELECT [Difference]=@g.STDifference(@h).ToString();
/* POLYGON ((10 10, 40 10, 40 40, 10 40, 10 10),
 (20 20, 20 30, 30 30, 30 20, 20 20))   */

SELECT [Intersection]=@g.STIntersection(@h).ToString();
go
-- POLYGON ((20 20, 30 20, 30 30, 20 30, 20 20))
```

CHAPTER 21: Advanced T-SQL Programming Topics

Spatial Data Types: Geometry & Geography

Geometry Area & CIRCULARSTRING Functions

```
-- Area of a polygon - triangle
DECLARE @Geomet geometry;
SET @Geomet = geometry::STGeomFromText('POLYGON((3 3,40 40, 80 3, 3 3))', 0);
SELECT @Geomet, AreaOfPolygon=@Geomet.STArea();
GO
-- 1424.5
```

The STBuffer() function "draws" the thick border.

```
SELECT geometry::Parse('CIRCULARSTRING(-2 2, 2 -2, 4 2, 2 4, -2 2)').STBuffer(.3);
```

CHAPTER 21: Advanced T-SQL Programming Topics

Working with geometry Data in Tables

```sql
IF OBJECT_ID ( 'dbo.GeometryTest', 'U' ) IS NOT NULL    DROP TABLE dbo.GeometryTest;
go

create table GeometryTest
(
        GeometryTestID int identity(1,1) primary key,
        Geom geometry ,
        GeomText as Geom.STAsText(),             -- computed column
        GeomDim as Geom.STDimension());          -- computed column
go

insert GeometryTest (Geom) values
        (geometry::STPointFromText ( 'POINT (85 115)',0)),
        (geometry::STPointFromText ( 'POINT (100 100)',0)),
        (geometry::STGeomFromText ('LINESTRING (70 70, 30 150,  150 150)', 0)),
        (geometry::STGeomFromText ('POLYGON ((0 0, 300 0, 300 300, 0 300, 0 0))', 0));

select * from GeometryTest
go
```

GeometryTestID	Geom	GeomText	GeomDim
1	0x00000000010C000000000040554000000000000C05C40	POINT (85 115)	0
2	0x00000000010C00000000000059400000000000005940	POINT (100 100)	0
3	0x000000000104030000000000000000008051400000000000008051400000000000003E400000000000C0624000000000000C062400000000000C0624001000000010000000010000000FFFFFFFF0000000002	LINESTRING (70 70, 30 150, 150 150)	1
4	0x00000000010405000000000000000000000000000000000000000000000000C0724000000000000000000000000000C072400000000000C0724000000000000000000000000000C07240000000000000000000000000000000000000010000000200000000010000000FFFFFFFF0000000003	POLYGON ((0 0, 300 0, 300 300, 0 300, 0 0))	2

```sql
declare @gmtry1 geometry,  @gmtry2 geometry, @combo geometry;
select @gmtry1 = Geom from GeometryTest where GeometryTestID=3
select @gmtry2 = Geom from GeometryTest where GeometryTestID=4
select @combo = @gmtry1.STIntersection(@gmtry2)
select Intersection = @Combo.STAsText();
go
```

Intersection
LINESTRING (150 150, 30 150, 70 70)

Spatial Data Types: Geometry & Geography

The geography Data Type in Map Application

Locating address in a rectangular Earth region based on the Person.Address table geo SpatialLocation column data.

```sql
USE AdventureWorks2012;

DECLARE @Rectangle geography;
SET @Rectangle = geography::STGeomFromText(
        'POLYGON((-50.0 50.0, -90.0 50.0, -90.0 25.0, -50.0 25.0, -50.0 50.0))',
        4326);
SELECT     s.BusinessEntityID
          ,s.Name                     AS Dealer
          ,a.AddressLine1
          ,a.City
          ,sp.StateProvinceCode
          ,a.PostalCode
 FROM Sales.Store s
      INNER JOIN Person.BusinessEntityAddress bea
              ON s.BusinessEntityID =bea.BusinessEntityID
      INNER JOIN Person.Address a
              ON bea.AddressID = a.AddressID
      INNER JOIN Person.StateProvince sp
              ON a.StateProvinceID = sp.StateProvinceID
 WHERE  a.SpatialLocation.STIntersects(@Rectangle) = 1
       ORDER BY Dealer;
GO  -- (240 row(s) affected) - Partial results.
```

BusinessEntityID	Dealer	AddressLine1	City	StateProvinceCode	PostalCode
2051	A Bicycle Association	6405 Erie Blvd. Hills Plaza	De Witt	NY	13214
354	Acclaimed Bicycle Company	830 Highway 499 So	Mcdonough	GA	30253
836	Active Cycling	Indian Mound Mall	Heath	OH	43056
1916	Active Life Toys	55 Standish Court	Mississauga	ON	L5B 3V4
1936	Active Transport Inc.	225200 Miles Ave.	North Randall	OH	44128
366	Activity Center	Factory Stores Of America	Crossville	TN	38555
1046	Better Bike Shop	42525 Austell Road	Austell	GA	30106
878	Bicycle Outfitters	Cherry Grove Plaza	Cincinnati	OH	45202
422	Bike Boutique	Polaris Town Center	Columbus	OH	43215
1924	Bike Products and Accessories	Regency Hilltop Shopping Cntr	Virginia Beach	VA	23451
698	Bike Rims Company	Edgewater Mall	Biloxi	MS	39530
622	Bikes and Motorbikes	22580 Free Street	Toronto	ON	M4B 1V7
424	Bikes Anyone?	Ames Plaza	Saugus	MA	01906
1162	Bikes for Kids and Adults	9900 Ronson Drive	Etobicoke	ON	M9W 3P3
510	Bikes for Two	63 West Beaver Creek	Richmond Hill	ON	L4E 3M5

CHAPTER 21: Advanced T-SQL Programming Topics

Surveying Spatial Locations in Person.Address with TABLESAMPLE

Since the limit is 5000 for Spatial results graphics, we use TABLESAMPLE random sampling. The outline of the Unites States is clearly visible in the spatial graphics. 4810 dots and partial results.

```
SELECT  Person.Address.City,
        Person.StateProvince.StateProvinceCode,
        Person.StateProvince.CountryRegionCode,
        Person.Address.SpatialLocation
FROM    Person.Address TABLESAMPLE (55)
    INNER JOIN Person.StateProvince
        ON Person.Address.StateProvinceID = Person.StateProvince.StateProvinceID
WHERE CountryRegionCode = 'US';
```

City	StateProvinceCode	CountryRegionCode	SpatialLocation
Concord	CA	US	0xE6100000010CA18642EB19FF4240E84C0794157B5EC0
Seattle	WA	US	0xE6100000010CCC2A6CCDCBCA474094427543D1995EC0
Torrance	CA	US	0xE6100000010C943F7FEBB1E440402956F3FF52A05DC0
Woodburn	OR	US	0xE6100000010CBF692502648C4640839FE7AD54AB5EC0
Puyallup	WA	US	0xE6100000010C827BF9CD1598474096246A5843935EC0

CHAPTER 21: Advanced T-SQL Programming Topics

Data Encryption & Decryption

Data encryption is an important part of keeping sensitive data, such as credit card numbers, safe. When we encrypt successively, the encrypted string varies.

```
USE AdventureWorks2012;
CREATE CERTIFICATE CertQ  ENCRYPTION BY PASSWORD = '007SkyFall$'
WITH SUBJECT ='CertQ',  START_DATE = '2012/01/01', EXPIRY_DATE = '2016/01/01';

DECLARE  @CypherText VARBINARY(MAX);
SET @CypherText = EncryptByCert(Cert_ID('CertQ'),'United States of America');
SELECT  @CypherText;
/*
0xDFAD2CABDDD07E75A74722CECF799B4AADBFE704D29F366DBF6F22C229E7EB6D94BC082BB2DFC7795C1AA92F7452D0AE2EF91
A2356B22F8508E37F7BC440CF926BC89C0FFCBBB04DF75206F2C6282FE87756D2003F40D738F92499674749BA8C9204A3BCAC9A7
8366939786A8D4E421DC71289E9D9D8140678EFD329BB5D7822
*/
SELECT Decyphered = CONVERT(VARCHAR(256),DecryptByCert(Cert_ID('CertQ'),
@CypherText,N'007SkyFall$'));
GO -- United States of America


DECLARE  @CypherText VARBINARY(MAX);
SET @CypherText = EncryptByCert(Cert_ID('CertQ'),'United States of America');
SELECT  @CypherText;
/*
0x77E17C2A7B30E68B3AA5792400842FBDA19E121F8BEFCF787F3C6F68D720CC6B992BBF1C27168CC7B5592359437494BF1F719FF
67A1B5131C5AA69EEEA539DC5AA261BBAEDC12201BDC2EC1E31280FD0B76E8773CDB57582BE857F24FD86997582ACFAE07028A9
0A0FA9D29A69FB53FC24261828F53884636A4452597A18A908
*/
SELECT Decyphered = CONVERT(VARCHAR(256), DecryptByCert(Cert_ID('CertQ'),
@CypherText,N'007SkyFall$'));
GO -- United States of America


 DECLARE  @CypherText VARBINARY(MAX), @cleartext varchar(256)='Yellowstone National Park ID, MT ,WY';
SET @CypherText = EncryptByCert(Cert_ID('CertQ'), @cleartext);   SELECT  @CypherText;
/*
0x386D15B848B3200CA2F0FD1341550AD16C61A19B71D2A14256B8C281249B5F9471EEB9C81DE9FA21CBE4602E099E1F7F363923
B8E0BF2960CAF13824D5EE0E852BA0B156532D50B336377648C6580BDFEB85453F34D722038FF6F7BD695343617E39E68259B05D
65F686CE63A68CFC795D86F94ADC75D0974882721A5083842C
*/
SELECT Decyphered = CONVERT(VARCHAR(256),DecryptByCert(Cert_ID('CertQ'),
@CypherText,N'007SkyFall$'));
GO  -- Yellowstone National Park ID, MT ,WY
```

CHAPTER 21: Advanced T-SQL Programming Topics

Database Backup

Full Database Backup with Verification

Full database backup and verify script for the AdventureWorks2012 database.

```sql
USE master;
GO
-- Backup database
BACKUP DATABASE [AdventureWorks2012] TO  DISK = N'F:\data\backup\AW2012.bak' WITH
NAME = N'AdventureWorks2012-Full DB Backup', STATS = 5;
GO
-- Verify database backup
DECLARE @backupSetId as int;
SELECT @backupSetId = position from msdb..backupset where
database_name=N'AdventureWorks2012' and backup_set_id=(select max(backup_set_id) from
msdb..backupset where database_name=N'AdventureWorks2012' );

IF @backupSetId is null begin raiserror(N'Verify failed. Backup info for DB
"AdventureWorks2012" not found.', 16, 1) end;

RESTORE VERIFYONLY FROM  DISK = N'F:\data\backup\AW2012.bak' WITH  FILE =
@backupSetId,  NOUNLOAD,  NOREWIND;
GO
```

```
/* Messages
5 percent processed.
10 percent processed.
15 percent processed.
.......
95 percent processed.
Processed 27920 pages for database 'AdventureWorks2012', file 'AdventureWorks2012_Data' on file 1.
Processed 80 pages for database 'AdventureWorks2012', file 'FSAlpha' on file 1.
Processed 2 pages for database 'AdventureWorks2012', file 'AdventureWorks2012_Log' on file 1.
100 percent processed.
BACKUP DATABASE successfully processed 28002 pages in 7.931 seconds (27.582 MB/sec).

The backup set on file 1 is valid.   */
```

Full Database Backup with Datestamp in Filename

```sql
DECLARE @BackupPathFile nvarchar(256)
 = N'f:\data\backup\AW2012_' + CONVERT(varchar, CURRENT_TIMESTAMP, 112) + '.BAK'
PRINT @BackupPathFile   -- f:\data\backup\AW2012_20121114.BAK
BACKUP DATABASE [AdventureWorks2012] TO  DISK = @BackupPathFile
```

Database Backup

Backup of a Single Table

Here is the list of options available.

- SELECT * INTO table2 FROM table1
- SSMS Script Wizard generates script with INSERTs
- SSMS execute SELECT query & the save the output to a file
- bcp table to a file
- SS Import/Export Wizard - export table to a table or file

The first one is the easiest, the last one is the most flexible. We have to pay attention that the export is reversible. For example, if we use CSV format then the strings should be enclosed in double quotes for example in order not to conflict with commas used for column separation. Execute the query.

SELECT * FROM Production.Product ORDER BY ProductNumber;

On upper left corner in results, right click, save results as, .csv (comma delimited). Sounds safe. But it is not because the some product names contain commas. That makes the data export irreversible, and probably useless for any application.

The SS Import & Export Wizard has option to specify Text qualifier for flat file destination.

CHAPTER 21: Advanced T-SQL Programming Topics

Setting SSMS Query Options to Include Double Quotes with Strings

There is a query option in SSMS setting to set double quote as text qualifier when saving in csv format. Click on Query, click on Query Options. Configure as shown.

The output will be proper csv file.

793,"Road-250 Black, 44",BK-R89B-44,1,1,Black,100,75,1554.9479,2443.35,44,CM ,LB ,14.77,4,R ,H ,U ,2,26,2006-07-01 00:00:00.000,NULL,NULL,1FF419B5-52AF-4F7E-AEAE-4FEC5E99DE35,2008-03-11 10:01:36.827

Database Restore

To restore a database backup to a new database we have to indicate the location (path & name) of the database files. FILE=1 refers to the first backup set in AW2012.BAK. A backup file can contain more than one backup.

```
USE [master]
RESTORE DATABASE [rptAdventureWorks2012] FROM  DISK = N'f:\data\backup\AW2012.BAK'
WITH  FILE = 1,
MOVE N'FSAlpha' TO N'F:\data\db\data\FSAlpha',
MOVE N'AdventureWorks2012_Data' TO N'F:\data\db\data\AdventureWorks2012_Data.mdf',
MOVE N'AdventureWorks2012_Log' TO N'F:\data\db\log\AdventureWorks2012_log.ldf',
NOUNLOAD,  STATS = 5
GO
```

/* Messages
5 percent processed.
10 percent processed.
15 percent processed.
.....
55 percent processed.
60 percent processed.
65 percent processed.
70 percent processed.
75 percent processed.
80 percent processed.
85 percent processed.
90 percent processed.
95 percent processed.
100 percent processed.
Processed 27920 pages for database 'rptAdventureWorks2012', file 'AdventureWorks2012_Data' on file 1.
Processed 2 pages for database 'rptAdventureWorks2012', file 'AdventureWorks2012_Log' on file 1.
Processed 81 pages for database 'rptAdventureWorks2012', file 'FSAlpha' on file 1.

RESTORE DATABASE successfully processed 28002 pages in 25.375 seconds (8.621 MB/sec). */

Restore of a Single Table

Restoring a table can be tricky. When exporting a table, basically the data content goes, and some metadata such as column names. SELECT INTO copies the data, column names, data types, sizes and the IDENTITY property if any. Constraints and indexes are not exported. Before restoring, the current table should be emptied. DELETE and TRUNCATE are not exactly the same. TRUNCATE is faster due to minimal logging. TRUNCATE also resets the IDENTITY SEED.

```
SELECT * INTO tempdb.dbo.Product
FROM Adventureworks2012.Production.Product;
GO   - (504 row(s) affected)
```

```
use tempdb;
CREATE UNIQUE INDEX idxProd on Product(Name);
GO
```

```
DELETE Product;  -- (504 row(s) affected)
DBCC CHECKIDENT(Product);
/*Checking identity information: current identity value '999', current column value 'NULL'.
DBCC execution completed. If DBCC printed error messages, contact your system
administrator.*/
```

```
TRUNCATE TABLE Product;
GO
DBCC CHECKIDENT(Product);
GO
/*Checking identity information: current identity value 'NULL', current column value 'NULL'.
DBCC execution completed. If DBCC printed error messages, contact your system
administrator.*/
```

```
-- Restore the content of table
INSERT Product
SELECT *
FROM Adventureworks2012.Production.Product;
/*Msg 8101, Level 16, State 1, Line 1
An explicit value for the identity column in table 'Product' can only be specified when a column
list is used and IDENTITY_INSERT is ON.*/
```

Database Restore

Repopulating Table with IDENTITY Column

IDENTITY is an obstacle in moving back the original data. We have to set the IDENTITY_INSERT flag and we have to specify all the columns in the INSERT statement. After repopulating we have to check if IDENTITY is seeded at the right value and rebuild the out-of-shape index.

```sql
SET IDENTITY_INSERT Product ON;
GO
INSERT INTO [dbo].[Product]
      ([ProductID],[Name]
      ,[ProductNumber],[MakeFlag]
      ,[FinishedGoodsFlag],[Color]
      ,[SafetyStockLevel],[ReorderPoint]
      ,[StandardCost],[ListPrice]
      ,[Size],[SizeUnitMeasureCode]
      ,[WeightUnitMeasureCode],[Weight]
      ,[DaysToManufacture],[ProductLine]
      ,[Class] ,[Style]
      ,[ProductSubcategoryID],[ProductModelID]
      ,[SellStartDate],[SellEndDate]
      ,[DiscontinuedDate],[rowguid],[ModifiedDate])
SELECT *
FROM Adventureworks2012.Production.Product;
GO
-- (504 row(s) affected)
SET IDENTITY_INSERT Product OFF;


DBCC CHECKIDENT(Product) ;
GO
/*Checking identity information: current identity value '999', current column value '999'.
DBCC execution completed. If DBCC printed error messages, contact your system
administrator.*/


ALTER INDEX [idxProd] ON [dbo].[Product] REBUILD;
```

> A good strategy is to save the table script with all related item scripts onto a disk .sql file.

That way we isolate table definition with constraints, defaults and indexes from table content.

CHAPTER 21: Advanced T-SQL Programming Topics

The Database Maintenance Plan Wizard

The SQL Server Maintenance Plan Wizard is an SSMS Object Explorer GUI tool to prepare a partial or complete maintenance plan for a database(s).

The Database Maintenance Plan Wizard

Follow the Plan Wizard Step by Step

Maintenance Plan Wizard

Select Plan Properties
How do you want to schedule your maintenance tasks?

Name: AW2012MaintenancePlan
Description:

Run as: SQL Server Agent service account

- ● Separate schedules for each task
- ○ Single schedule for the entire plan or no schedule

Schedule:
Not scheduled (On Demand)

Maintenance Plan Wizard

Select Maintenance Tasks
Which tasks should this plan perform?

Select one or more maintenance tasks:

- ☑ Check Database Integrity
- ☐ Shrink Database
- ☐ Reorganize Index
- ☑ Rebuild Index
- ☐ Update Statistics
- ☐ Clean Up History
- ☐ Execute SQL Server Agent Job
- ☑ Back Up Database (Full)
- ☐ Back Up Database (Differential)
- ☐ Back Up Database (Transaction Log)
- ☑ Maintenance Cleanup Task

ⓘ The Rebuild task reorganizes data on the data and index pages by rebuilding indexes. This improves performance of index scans and seeks. This task also optimizes the distribution of data and free space on the index pages, allowing faster future growth.

CHAPTER 21: Advanced T-SQL Programming Topics

One or More Databases Can Be Specified, Schedule Setup

The Database Maintenance Plan Wizard

Full Database Backup Specifications

Create the Maintenance Plan & Schedule the Jobs

Configure Stored Procedure As SS Agent Job & Schedule

SSMS Object Explorer GUI editor can be used to setup a new job with schedule. It can also be done programmatically. The EOWBatchProcessing job scripted.

```sql
USE [msdb];
GO

BEGIN TRANSACTION
DECLARE @ReturnCode INT;  SELECT @ReturnCode = 0;
IF NOT EXISTS (SELECT name FROM msdb.dbo.syscategories WHERE name=N'Database Maintenance' AND category_class=1)
BEGIN

EXEC @ReturnCode = msdb.dbo.sp_add_category @class=N'JOB', @type=N'LOCAL', @name=N'Database Maintenance'
IF (@@ERROR <> 0 OR @ReturnCode <> 0) GOTO QuitWithRollback
END

DECLARE @jobId BINARY(16)

EXEC @ReturnCode =  msdb.dbo.sp_add_job @job_name=N'EOWBatchProcessing',
                @enabled=1,                 @notify_level_eventlog=0,
                @notify_level_email=0,      @notify_level_netsend=0,
                @notify_level_page=0,       @delete_level=0,
                @description=N'Process all end of week jobs.',     @category_name=N'Database Maintenance',
                @owner_login_name=N'HPESTAR\Owner',                @job_id = @jobId OUTPUT
IF (@@ERROR <> 0 OR @ReturnCode <> 0) GOTO QuitWithRollback

EXEC @ReturnCode = msdb.dbo.sp_add_jobstep @job_id=@jobId, @step_name=N'EOWInventory',
                @step_id=1,                 @cmdexec_success_code=0,
                @on_success_action=1,       @on_success_step_id=0,
                @on_fail_action=2,          @on_fail_step_id=0,
                @retry_attempts=0,          @retry_interval=0,
                @os_run_priority=0, @subsystem=N'TSQL',             @command=N'exec uspInventoryEOW;',
                @database_name=N'AdventureWorks2018',               @flags=0
IF (@@ERROR <> 0 OR @ReturnCode <> 0) GOTO QuitWithRollback

EXEC @ReturnCode = msdb.dbo.sp_update_job @job_id = @jobId, @start_step_id = 1
IF (@@ERROR <> 0 OR @ReturnCode <> 0) GOTO QuitWithRollback

EXEC @ReturnCode = msdb.dbo.sp_add_jobschedule @job_id=@jobId, @name=N'EOWProcessingSATAM',
                @enabled=1,                     @freq_type=8,
                @freq_interval=65,              @freq_subday_type=1,
                @freq_subday_interval=0,        @freq_relative_interval=0,
                @freq_recurrence_factor=1,      @active_start_date=20181127,
                @active_end_date=99991231,      @active_start_time=40000,
                @active_end_time=235959,        @schedule_uid=N'0610654b-da58-46ff-9a96-39d69a0686a1'
IF (@@ERROR <> 0 OR @ReturnCode <> 0) GOTO QuitWithRollback

EXEC @ReturnCode = msdb.dbo.sp_add_jobserver @job_id = @jobId, @server_name = N'(local)'
IF (@@ERROR <> 0 OR @ReturnCode <> 0) GOTO QuitWithRollback
COMMIT TRANSACTION
GOTO EndSave
QuitWithRollback:
    IF (@@TRANCOUNT > 0) ROLLBACK TRANSACTION
EndSave:
GO
```

CHAPTER 21: Advanced T-SQL Programming Topics

FOR XML Clause

A SELECT query returns results as a table-like rowset. With a FOR XML clause the results are returned in XML format.

FOR XML RAW

The FOR XML RAW mode generates a single <row> element per row in the rowset that is returned by the SELECT statement. Tree structure can be generated by nesting queries.

```
SELECT *
FROM HumanResources.Shift
ORDER BY ShiftID
FOR XML RAW;
```

<row ShiftID="1" Name="Day" StartTime="07:00:00" EndTime="15:00:00" ModifiedDate="2002-06-01T00:00:00" />
<row ShiftID="2" Name="Evening" StartTime="15:00:00" EndTime="23:00:00" ModifiedDate="2002-06-01T00:00:00" />
<row ShiftID="3" Name="Night" StartTime="23:00:00" EndTime="07:00:00" ModifiedDate="2002-06-01T00:00:00" />

FOR XML AUTO

The FOR XML AUTO mode generates nesting in the resulting XML by using heuristics based on the way the SELECT statement is specified. You have minimal control over the shape of the XML generated. Tree structure can be generated by nesting queries.

```
SELECT *
FROM HumanResources.Shift
ORDER BY ShiftID
FOR XML AUTO;
```

<HumanResources.Shift ShiftID="1" Name="Day" StartTime="07:00:00" EndTime="15:00:00" ModifiedDate="2002-06-01T00:00:00" />
<HumanResources.Shift ShiftID="2" Name="Evening" StartTime="15:00:00" EndTime="23:00:00" ModifiedDate="2002-06-01T00:00:00" />
<HumanResources.Shift ShiftID="3" Name="Night" StartTime="23:00:00" EndTime="07:00:00" ModifiedDate="2002-06-01T00:00:00" />

CHAPTER 21: Advanced T-SQL Programming Topics

FOR XML EXPLICIT

The FOR XML EXPLICIT mode allows extensive control over the shape of the XML document. Attributes and elements can be freely combined in deciding the shape of the XML document. One of the options with XML EXPLICIT is the ELEMENT directive. The UNION ALL operator is used to assemble the tag and data information.

```
SELECT          1               AS Tag,
                NULL            AS Parent,
                ProductNumber AS [ProductHeader!1!ProdNo],
                NULL            AS [ProductDetail!2!ProductName!ELEMENT],
                NULL            AS [ProductDetail!2!ListPrice!ELEMENT],
                NULL            AS [ProductDetail!2!Color!ELEMENT],
                NULL            AS [ProductDetail!2!Size!ELEMENT]
FROM    AdventureWorks2012.Production.Product P WHERE ProductSubcategoryID is not NULL
UNION ALL
SELECT          2,
                1,
                ProductNumber,
                Name,
                ListPrice,
                Color,
                Size
FROM    AdventureWorks2012.Production.Product P  WHERE ProductSubcategoryID is not NULL
ORDER BY [ProductHeader!1!ProdNo], Tag   FOR XML EXPLICIT;
-- (590 row(s) affected) - Partial results.
```

```
<ProductHeader ProdNo="BK-M68B-46">
 <ProductDetail>
   <ProductName>Mountain-200 Black, 46</ProductName>
   <ListPrice>2294.9900</ListPrice>
   <Color>Black</Color>
   <Size>46</Size>
 </ProductDetail>
</ProductHeader>
<ProductHeader ProdNo="BK-M68S-38">
 <ProductDetail>
   <ProductName>Mountain-200 Silver, 38</ProductName>
   <ListPrice>2319.9900</ListPrice>
   <Color>Silver</Color>
   <Size>38</Size>
 </ProductDetail>
</ProductHeader>
```

FOR XML PATH

The FOR XML PATH mode together with the nested FOR XML query capability provides the flexibility of the EXPLICIT mode in a simpler manner. The example lists sales orders with detail line and header information.

```sql
SELECT TOP(100) S.Name                        AS '@Reseller',
       CONCAT(P.LastName, ', ', P.FirstName)  AS '@ContactName',
       SOH.SalesOrderID                       AS '@SalesOrderID',
       SOD.SalesOrderDetailID                 AS 'SOD/SalesOrderDetailID',
       SOD.OrderQty                           AS 'SOD/OrderQty',
       SOD.ProductID                          AS 'SOD/ProductID',
       SOD.UnitPrice                          AS 'SOD/UnitPrice',
       SOD.LineTotal                          AS 'SOD/LineTotal'
FROM   Sales.SalesOrderHeader AS SOH
       INNER JOIN Sales.SalesOrderDetail AS SOD
              ON SOH.SalesOrderID = SOD.SalesOrderID
       INNER JOIN Sales.Customer AS C    ON SOH.CustomerID = C.CustomerID
       INNER JOIN Person.Person AS P     ON C.PersonID = P.BusinessEntityID
       INNER JOIN Sales.Store AS S       ON C.StoreID = S.BusinessEntityID
ORDER BY SOH.SalesOrderID, SalesOrderDetailID
FOR XML PATH('SalesOrderLine'), ROOT('SalesOrdersReceived');
```

Results:

```xml
<SalesOrdersReceived>
  <SalesOrderLine Reseller="Better Bike Shop" ContactName="Hendergart, James" Sal...
    <SOD>
      <SalesOrderDetailID>1</SalesOrderDetailID>
      <OrderQty>1</OrderQty>
      <ProductID>776</ProductID>
      <UnitPrice>2024.9940</UnitPrice>
      <LineTotal>2024.994000</LineTotal>
    </SOD>
  </SalesOrderLine>
  <SalesOrderLine Reseller="Better Bike Shop" ContactName="Hendergart, James" Sal...
```

CHAPTER 21: Advanced T-SQL Programming Topics

Interesting T-SQL Scripts

Concatenation Loop With XML PATH

The FOR XML PATH clause makes it possible to do program looping within a query without requiring multiple statements. One way is to implement it as a correlated subquery.

```
Use AdventureWorks2012;
Go

SELECT  PM.Name AS Model
       ,(SELECT CONCAT(P.Name, ', ')
         FROM Production.Product AS P   WHERE P.ProductModelID = PM.ProductModelID
         ORDER BY P.Name FOR XML PATH('') ) AS ProductLineup
FROM Production.ProductModel AS PM ORDER BY Model;
-- (128 row(s) affected) - Partial result.
```

Model	ProductLineup
All-Purpose Bike Stand	All-Purpose Bike Stand,
Bike Wash	Bike Wash - Dissolver,
Cable Lock	Cable Lock,
Chain	Chain,
Classic Vest	Classic Vest, L, Classic Vest, M, Classic Vest, S,
Cycling Cap	AWC Logo Cap,
Fender Set - Mountain	Fender Set - Mountain,
Front Derailleur	Front Derailleur,
Full-Finger Gloves	Full-Finger Gloves, L, Full-Finger Gloves, M, Full-Finger Gloves, S,

A popular solution for the trailing comma issue is making it leading comma and taking it out from the first position with the STUFF function. Since the product name may contain commas, we use "|" as string list delimiter.

```
SELECT  PM.Name AS Model
       ,LTRIM(RTRIM(STUFF((SELECT CONCAT('| ', P.Name)
         FROM Production.Product AS P   WHERE P.ProductModelID = PM.ProductModelID
         ORDER BY P.Name FOR XML PATH('') ), 1, 1, ''))) AS ProductLineup
FROM Production.ProductModel AS PM
ORDER BY Model;
-- (128 row(s) affected) - Partial result.
```

Model	ProductLineup
ML Mountain Frame	ML Mountain Frame - Black, 40| ML Mountain Frame - Black, 44| ML Mountain Frame - Black, 48

CHAPTER 21: Advanced T-SQL Programming Topics

Interesting T-SQL Scripts

Challenging String Manipulations

```sql
-- Displaying hidden characters (whitespace) in a string; TAB character appears as space;
DECLARE @text varchar(64) = 'New'+char(9)+'York'+char(9)+'City'+char(9);
SELECT @text, CONVERT(varbinary(64), @text);
-- New York City 0x4E657709596F726B094369747909
```

```sql
-- Working with SUBSTRING & ASCII functions
SELECT      TOP (5)
            ProductNumber,
            MiddleOfString     =    SUBSTRING(ProductNumber,4,5),
            SecondChar         =    SUBSTRING(ProductNumber,2,1),
            ASCIIValue         =    ASCII(SUBSTRING(ProductNumber,2,1))
FROM AdventureWorks2012.Production.Product  ORDER BY NEWID();
```

ProductNumber	MiddleOfString	SecondChar	ASCIIValue
FR-R72R-44	R72R-	R	82
BK-R89B-48	R89B-	K	75
HN-4402	4402	N	78
LJ-1220	1220	J	74
BA-8327	8327	A	65

```sql
-- Compare empty string and NULL string
DECLARE @NullString varchar(32) = NULL, @EmptyString varchar(32)= '';
```

```sql
SELECT LEN(@EmptyString); SELECT LEN(@NullString);   -- 0  NULL
```

```sql
SELECT DATALENGTH(@EmptyString); SELECT DATALENGTH(@NullString);  -- 0  NULL
```

```sql
-- Testing for empty string and null string
SELECT 'Miami' WHERE @EmptyString = '';  SELECT 'Miami' WHERE @NullString is null;
-- Miami Miami
```

```sql
SELECT 'Miami' WHERE LEN(@EmptyString)=0;  SELECT 'Miami' WHERE LEN(@NullString) = 0;
-- Miami  (0 row(s) affected)
```

```sql
SELECT @EmptyString + @NullString+'Vegas';                      -- NULL
```

```sql
SELECT CONCAT(@EmptyString,@NullString, 'Vegas');               -- Vegas
```

CHAPTER 21: Advanced T-SQL Programming Topics

Interesting T-SQL Scripts

Date & Datetime Manipulations

```sql
-- Count business days for a date range
CREATE FUNCTION ufnWeekDaysCount ( @DateStart DATETIME, @DateEnd  DATETIME)
RETURNS INT AS   BEGIN
   IF ( @DateStart IS NULL OR @DateEnd IS NULL )
      RETURN ( 0 )
   DECLARE @i INT = 0;
   WHILE ( @DateStart <= @DateEnd )   BEGIN
      SET @i = @i + CASE
              WHEN datename(dw, @DateStart) IN ( 'Saturday', 'Sunday' )
              THEN 0    ELSE 1    END
      SET @DateStart = @DateStart + 1
   END -- while
   RETURN ( @i )
 END -- function
GO

SELECT dbo.ufnWeekDaysCount('2016-01-01', '2016-12-31');     -- 261

-- YEAR(), MONTH(), DATENAME() functions in aggregate query
SELECT  YEAR        = YEAR(OrderDate),
        MONTH       = MONTH(OrderDate),
        MMM         = UPPER(left(DATENAME(MONTH,OrderDate),3)),
        Sales       = FORMAT(sum(TotalDue),'c0','en-US'),
        OrderCount  = COUNT(* )
FROM    AdventureWorks2012.Sales.SalesOrderHeader
GROUP BY      YEAR(OrderDate),  MONTH(OrderDate),  DATENAME(MONTH,OrderDate)
ORDER BY      YEAR, MONTH;
GO -- (37 row(s) affected) - Partial results.
```

YEAR	MONTH	MMM	Sales	OrderCount
2008	5	MAY	$5,813,557	2386
2008	6	JUN	$6,004,156	2374

```sql
-- Month start/end is easy with EOMONTH() - Find month ending weekday
SELECT  DATEADD(DD,1,EOMONTH(GETDATE(),-2) )     AS FirstDayOfPreviousMonth,
        EOMONTH(GETDATE(),-1)                    AS LastDayOfPreviousMonth
-- 2016-11-01    2016-11-30

SELECT DATENAME(DW, EOMONTH(CURRENT_TIMESTAMP)) -- Monday
```

CHAPTER 21: Advanced T-SQL Programming Topics

Find Sprocs, Triggers, Functions & Views Where Column is Used

```sql
SELECT object_name(m.object_id) as ObjectName,
       left(definition, 256)    as Definition
FROM sys.all_sql_modules m inner join sys.objects o
                        on m.object_id = o.object_id
WHERE definition like '%SELECT%ListPrice%FROM%'
ORDER BY ObjectName;
```

	ObjectName	Definition
1	ufnGetProductDealerPrice	CREATE FUNCTION [dbo].[ufnGetProductDealerPrice](...
2	ufnGetProductListPrice	CREATE FUNCTION [dbo].[ufnGetProductListPrice](@Pro...
3	uspGetBillOfMaterials	CREATE PROCEDURE [dbo].[uspGetBillOfMaterials]
4	uspGetWhereUsedProductID	CREATE PROCEDURE [dbo].[uspGetWhereUsedProductI...

Designing the Query in GUI Query Designer

CHAPTER 21: Advanced T-SQL Programming Topics

Transforming Dynamic SQL Result Set into a View

A view is "clean", a dynamic SQL script can be pretty "messy". By wrapping dynamic SQL into a view, we get the best of both worlds: the power of dynamic SQL and the table-like access to a view.

```sql
USE AdventureWorks2012;
GO
CREATE PROC sprocListDepartment AS   BEGIN
DECLARE @SQL nvarchar(max) =
 'SELECT DepartmentID, Name, GroupName FROM HumanResources.Department ORDER BY DepartmentID DESC';
EXEC sp_executeSQL @SQL;
END
GO
```

```sql
CREATE VIEW vDepartment AS
SELECT * FROM OPENQUERY( HPESTAR, 'exec AdventureWorks2012.dbo.sprocListDepartment
WITH RESULT SETS  ((ID int, Department varchar(50), GroupName varchar(50)))');
GO
```

```sql
SELECT * FROM vDepartment;    -- (16 row(s) affected)
```

Accessing a View from Excel

A view can be accessed from Excel by logging in to SQL Server, choosing a database and picking the view.

CHAPTER 21: Advanced T-SQL Programming Topics

After Login the Data Connection Wizard Guides Us Through
The Data Connection Wizard requires network access and login to SQL Server.

The next popop window offers radio button selection for: Table, PivotTable and PivotChart & PivotTable; choosing Table.

CHAPTER 21: Advanced T-SQL Programming Topics

Querying the Database from a Client C# Program

The general program logic for SQL Server database access is very similar for other languages such as C++, VB or Java. First connection has to be established to SQL Server and the database, then a SQL query or stored procedure execution command is sent to the server, and finally the server returns a result set which has to be processed in a C# loop.

C# Code Listing

```
// C# database SELECT query demonstration
using System;
using System.Collections.Generic;
```

CHAPTER 21: Advanced T-SQL Programming Topics

Querying the Database from a Client C# Program

```csharp
using System.Text;
using System.Data;
using System.Data.SqlClient;
namespace DBTableDemo{ class Program {static void Main(string[] args){
// Database connection string
string ssConnectionString="integrated security=SSPI;data source=HPESTAR;" +
    "persist security info=False;initial catalog=AdventureWorks2012";
// Create a connection to SQL Server & database(catalog)
SqlConnection AW12Connection = new SqlConnection(ssConnectionString);
AW12Connection.Open();       // Open the connection
// SQL string to be sent to the server from this client
string SQL="SELECT * FROM HumanResources.Department ORDER BY DepartmentID";
// SqlCommand object
SqlCommand SQLCommand = new SqlCommand(SQL, AW12Connection);
// SqlDataReader object
SqlDataReader SQLCommandReader = SQLCommand.ExecuteReader();
// DataTable to hold the result dataset
DataTable DataTable = new DataTable();  DataTable.Load(SQLCommandReader);
// Print result set column headers & data rows to console with tabs
String RowsetColumn = string.Empty;
foreach (DataColumn column in DataTable.Columns)
   { RowsetColumn += column.ColumnName + "\t"; }
Console.WriteLine(RowsetColumn);   int MaxRow = 5;
for (int i = 0; i < MaxRow; i++)   { String Line = string.Empty;
foreach (DataColumn column in DataTable.Columns)
   {Line += DataTable.Rows[i][column.ColumnName] + "\t"; }
Console.WriteLine(Line);}
string PressEnter = Console.ReadLine();  // Wait for keyboard ENTER press
// Close the database connection
AW12Connection.Close();   }}}
```

Console Image with Data Display from HumanResources.Department

```
file:///C:/Users/Owner/AppData/Local/Temporary Projects/Project1/bin/Debug/Project1.EXE
DepartmentID    Name        GroupName           ModifiedDate
1               Engineering     Research and Development    6/1/2002 12:00:00 AM
2               Tool Design     Research and Development    6/1/2002 12:00:00 AM
3               Sales       Sales and Marketing     6/1/2002 12:00:00 AM
4               Marketing       Sales and Marketing     6/1/2002 12:00:00 AM
5               Purchasing      Inventory Management    6/1/2002 12:00:00 AM
```

CHAPTER 21: Advanced T-SQL Programming Topics

CHAPTER 22: In-Memory OLTP

SQL Server 2014 RTM In-Memory OLTP Sample

The sample T-SQL script can be download from:
http://msftdbprodsamples.codeplex.com/releases/view/114491

This sample demonstrates the In-Memory OLTP feature, which is new in SQL Server 2014. The sample script creates memory-optimized tables (new in SS14) and natively-compiled stored procedures (new in SS14), and can be used to run measurements on the performance benefit of in-memory OLTP. Documentation location for the In-Memory OLTP sample:
http://msdn.microsoft.com/en-us/library/dn511655(v=sql.120).aspx

CREATE TABLE script of one of the in-memory tables.

```
USE [AdventureWorks2012]
GO

CREATE TABLE [Sales].[SalesOrderDetail_inmem]
(       [SalesOrderID] [int] NOT NULL,
        [SalesOrderDetailID] [bigint] IDENTITY(1,1) NOT NULL,
        [CarrierTrackingNumber] [nvarchar](25) COLLATE SQL_Latin1_General_CP1_CI_AS NULL,
        [OrderQty] [smallint] NOT NULL,
        [ProductID] [int] NOT NULL,
        [SpecialOfferID] [int] NOT NULL,
        [UnitPrice] [money] NOT NULL,
        [UnitPriceDiscount] [money] NOT NULL CONSTRAINT
[IMDF_SalesOrderDetail_UnitPriceDiscount]  DEFAULT ((0.0)),
        [ModifiedDate] [datetime2](7) NOT NULL,
CONSTRAINT [imPK_SalesOrderDetail_SalesOrderID_SalesOrderDetailID] PRIMARY KEY NONCLUSTERED
HASH (  [SalesOrderID],
        [SalesOrderDetailID]
)WITH ( BUCKET_COUNT = 67108864),
INDEX [IX_ProductID] NONCLUSTERED HASH
(       [ProductID]   )WITH ( BUCKET_COUNT = 1048576),
INDEX [IX_SalesOrderID] NONCLUSTERED HASH
(       [SalesOrderID]  )WITH ( BUCKET_COUNT = 16777216)
)WITH ( MEMORY_OPTIMIZED = ON , DURABILITY = SCHEMA_AND_DATA )
```

SQL Server 2014 support inline index declaration, a new feature.

List of tables, views & stored procedures created by the sample script

```
select SchemaName=schema_name(schema_id), ObjectName=name,
       ObjectType = type, ObjectDesc = type_desc from AdventureWorks2012.sys.all_objects
where type in ('V','U','P') and name not like ('%diagram%') and
       object_id not in (select object_id from zorigAdventureWorks2012.sys.all_objects)
order by SchemaName, type_desc, name;
```

SchemaName	ObjectName	ObjectType	ObjectDesc
dbo	native_sp	P	SQL_STORED_PROCEDURE
dbo	usp_GenerateCKCheck	P	SQL_STORED_PROCEDURE
dbo	usp_GenerateFKCheck	P	SQL_STORED_PROCEDURE
dbo	usp_GenerateUQCheck	P	SQL_STORED_PROCEDURE
dbo	usp_ValidateIntegrity	P	SQL_STORED_PROCEDURE
dbo	DomainIntegrity	U	USER_TABLE
dbo	ReferentialIntegrity	U	USER_TABLE
dbo	UniqueIntegrity	U	USER_TABLE
Demo	usp_DemoInitSeed	P	SQL_STORED_PROCEDURE
Demo	usp_DemoReset	P	SQL_STORED_PROCEDURE
Demo	DemoSalesOrderDetailSeed	U	USER_TABLE
Demo	DemoSalesOrderHeaderSeed	U	USER_TABLE
Production	usp_DeleteProduct_inmem	P	SQL_STORED_PROCEDURE
Production	usp_InsertProduct_inmem	P	SQL_STORED_PROCEDURE
Production	Product_inmem	U	USER_TABLE
Production	Product_ondisk	U	USER_TABLE
Sales	usp_DeleteSpecialOffer_inmem	P	SQL_STORED_PROCEDURE
Sales	usp_InsertSalesOrder_inmem	P	SQL_STORED_PROCEDURE
Sales	usp_InsertSalesOrder_ondisk	P	SQL_STORED_PROCEDURE
Sales	usp_InsertSpecialOffer_inmem	P	SQL_STORED_PROCEDURE
Sales	usp_InsertSpecialOfferProduct_inmem	P	SQL_STORED_PROCEDURE
Sales	usp_UpdateSalesOrderShipInfo_inmem	P	SQL_STORED_PROCEDURE
Sales	usp_UpdateSalesOrderShipInfo_native	P	SQL_STORED_PROCEDURE
Sales	usp_UpdateSalesOrderShipInfo_ondisk	P	SQL_STORED_PROCEDURE
Sales	SalesOrderDetail_inmem	U	USER_TABLE
Sales	SalesOrderDetail_ondisk	U	USER_TABLE
Sales	SalesOrderHeader_inmem	U	USER_TABLE
Sales	SalesOrderHeader_ondisk	U	USER_TABLE
Sales	SpecialOffer_inmem	U	USER_TABLE
Sales	SpecialOffer_ondisk	U	USER_TABLE
Sales	SpecialOfferProduct_inmem	U	USER_TABLE
Sales	vSalesOrderDetail_extended_inmem	V	VIEW
Sales	vSalesOrderHeader_extended_inmem	V	VIEW

There are restrictions on constraints for in-memory tables. Therefore, the CK, FK & UQ checker stored procedures.

SQL Server 2014 RTM In-Memory OLTP Sample

Performance Comparison Of In-Memory & On-Disk Tables

SQL Server 2014 RTM In-Memory OLTP Sample creates a few in-memory tables with the _inmem suffix in AdventureWorks2012, including SalesOrderDetail_inmem. Following is a performance comparison.

```
DBCC DROPCLEANBUFFERS;
SET STATISTICS IO ON; SET STATISTICS TIME ON;
SELECT OrderQty, Freq=count(*) from Sales.SalesOrderDetail_inmem GROUP BY OrderQty
ORDER BY Freq DESC;
SET STATISTICS TIME OFF; SET STATISTICS IO OFF;
```

/* Table 'Worktable'. Scan count 0, logical reads 0, physical reads 0, read-ahead reads 0, lob logical reads 0, lob physical reads 0, lob read-ahead reads 0.
Table 'Workfile'. Scan count 0, logical reads 0, physical reads 0, read-ahead reads 0, lob logical reads 0, lob physical reads 0, lob read-ahead reads 0.

SQL Server Execution Times: CPU time = 47 ms, elapsed time = 54 ms. */

```
DBCC DROPCLEANBUFFERS;
SET STATISTICS IO ON; SET STATISTICS TIME ON;
SELECT OrderQty, Freq=count(*) from Sales.SalesOrderDetail GROUP BY OrderQty
ORDER BY Freq DESC;
SET STATISTICS TIME OFF; SET STATISTICS IO OFF;
```

/* Table 'Worktable'. Scan count 0, logical reads 0, physical reads 0, read-ahead reads 0, lob logical reads 0, lob physical reads 0, lob read-ahead reads 0.
Table 'Workfile'. Scan count 0, logical reads 0, physical reads 0, read-ahead reads 0, lob logical reads 0, lob physical reads 0, lob read-ahead reads 0.
Table 'SalesOrderDetail'. Scan count 1, logical reads 1246, physical reads 3, read-ahead reads 1277, lob logical reads 0, lob physical reads 0, lob read-ahead reads 0.

SQL Server Execution Times: CPU time = 78 ms, elapsed time = 204 ms. */

The on-disk elapsed time is almost 4 times that of the in-memory table. It is a very significant improvement in query performance in favor of the in-memory table. The in-memory OLTP technology frequently referred to as "Hekaton", the code name during development.

Memory Optimization Advisor

The memory optimization advisor can be applied to assist you migrating the disk-based database table to In-Memory OLTP. First we create a new in-memory OLTP database called RapidFire. Note the memory optimized filegroup declaration.

```sql
USE master;
CREATE DATABASE RapidFire
ON PRIMARY     (NAME = RapidFire_DATA,
                FILENAME = 'F:\RapidFire\Data\RapidFire_Data.mdf'),
FILEGROUP RapidFire_FG CONTAINS MEMORY_OPTIMIZED_DATA
                (NAME = RapidFire_CHKPOINT,
    FILENAME = 'F:\RapidFire\Checkpoint\RapidFire_CHKPOINT')
LOG ON         (NAME = RapidFire_LOG,
    FILENAME ='F:\RapidFire\Log\RapidFire_Log.ldf');
```

We create a new table in the database for migration.

```sql
USE RapidFire;
GO
CREATE TABLE Customer(
CustomerID INT PRIMARY KEY,
CompanyName nvarchar(100),
ContactFName nvarchar(30),
ContactLName nvarchar(30),
Email varchar(255),
City nvarchar(50),
State char(2),
ModifiedDate datetime);
GO
```

```sql
INSERT Customer VALUES
(1, 'Ajax Insurance', 'Jill','Smith', 'Jill@ajaxins.com', 'Juneau', 'AK', '20200201');
-- (1 row(s) affected)
```

There are restrictions on migration; among them FOREIGN KEY, CHECK & DEFAULT constraints cannot be migrated. The main article in BOL, In-Memory OLTP (In-Memory Optimization) http://msdn.microsoft.com/en-us/library/dn133186(v=sql.120).aspx, has hyperlinks to a number of specialized articles on the topic. Memory Optimization Advisor documentation: http://msdn.microsoft.com/en-us/library/dn284308(v=sql.120).aspx . The Customer table was designed specifically for smooth migration.

CHAPTER 22: In-Memory OLTP

Launching the Memory Optimization Advisor

Memory Optimization Advisor Welcome Screen

Table Memory Optimization Advisor

- Introduction
- Migration validation
- Migration warnings
- Migration options
- Primary Key migration
- Summary
- Migration progress

Welcome to the Memory Optimization Advisor

The Memory Optimization Advisor assists you in migrating your tables to memory-optimized tables.

You can use the Memory Optimization Advisor to:
- Discover and evaluate incompatibilities for memory optimization.
- Determine and note risks and caveats of memory optimization before migrating your table.
- Customize memory optimization options for your table.
- Optimized a fully compatible table in memory.
- Migrate data to new memory-optimized table.

To begin the script generation process, click Next.

☐ Do not show this page again

Memory Optimization Checklist

Memory Optimization Warnings

![Screenshot of Table Memory Optimization Advisor - Memory Optimization Warnings screen]

For more information, click on the link beside each warning.

	Warning	
ⓘ	A user transaction that accesses memory-optimized tables cannot access more than one user database.	More information
ⓘ	The following table hints are not supported on memory-optimized tables: HOLDLOCK, NOLOCK, PAGLOCK, READCOMMITTED, READPAST, READUNCOMMITTED, ROWLOCK, TABLOCK, TABLOCKX, UPDLOCK, XLOCK, KEEPIDENTITY, KEEPDEFAULTS, NOWAIT.	More information
ⓘ	TRUNCATE TABLE and MERGE statements cannot target a memory-optimized table.	More information
ⓘ	Dynamic and Keyset cursors are automatically downgraded to a static cursor when pointing to a memory-optimized table.	More information
ⓘ	Some database-level features are not supported for use with memory-optimized tables. For details on these features, please refer to the help link.	More information

Sidebar:
- Introduction
- Migration validation
- **Migration warnings**
- Migration options
- Primary Key migration
- Summary
- Migration progress

Memory Optimization Review

Review Optimization Options

Specify options for memory optimization:

- Memory-optimized filegroup: RapidFire_FG
- Logical file name: RapidFire_CHKPOINT
- File path: F:\RapidFire\Checkpoint
- Rename the original table as: Customer_old
- Estimated current memory cost (MB): 0

☑ Also copy table data to the new memory optimized table.

By default, this table will be migrated to a memory-optimized table with both schema and data durability.

☐ Check this box to migrate this table to a memory-optimized table with no data durability.

Sidebar navigation: Introduction, Migration validation, Migration warnings, **Migration options**, Primary Key migration, Summary, Migration progress

Memory Optimization PRIMARY KEY Configuration

Table Memory Optimization Advisor

Review Primary Key Conversion

- Introduction
- Migration validation
- Migration warnings
- Migration options
- **Primary Key migration**
- Summary
- Migration progress

Please choose the appropriate conversion for this primary key:

Column	Type	Collation
☑ CustomerID	int	

Select a new name for this primary key: Customer_primaryKey

Select the type of this primary key:

◉ Use NONCLUSTERED HASH index
   A NONCLUSTERED HASH index provides the most benefit for point lookups. It provides no discernible benefit if a query is running a Range scan.
   Bucket Count: 1000000
   The Bucket Count of a NONCLUSTERED HASH index is the number of buckets in the hash table. It is recommended to set the fill factor to 50 to 60% if the table requires a lot of space for growth. Bucket Count will be rounded up to the nearest power of two.

○ Use NONCLUSTERED index
   A NONCLUSTERED index provides the most benefit for range predicates and ORDER BY clauses. NONCLUSTERED indexes are unidirectional. It provides no benefit for ORDER BY clauses with orders different from the index.
   Sort column and order:

Column	Sort Order

[< Previous] [Next >] [Migrate] [Cancel]

Memory Optimization Migration Summary

Table Memory Optimization Advisor

Verify Migration Actions

- Introduction
- Migration validation
- Migration warnings
- Migration options
- Primary Key migration
- **Summary**
- Migration progress

- Generate memory-optimized table [Customer]
  - Rename table Customer to Customer_old.
  - Durability of the new memory-optimized table: Schema and data
  - Data will be migrated to the new table.
- Create primary key Customer_primaryKey on the new table.
  - NONCLUSTERED HASH Index, Bucket count = 1048576

Memory Optimization Migration Progress

Action	Result
Renaming the original table.	Passed
New name:Customer_old	
Creating the memory-optimized table in the database.	Passed
Adding index:Customer_primaryKey	
Copying data from the original table to the new memory-optimized table.	Passed

Memory Optimized Table Performance

CREATE TABLE Script for the In-Memory Table
The generated script for the optimized table.

```
USE [RapidFire]
GO

CREATE TABLE [dbo].[Customer] (   [CustomerID] [int] NOT NULL,
        [CompanyName] [nvarchar](100) COLLATE SQL_Latin1_General_CP1_CI_AS NULL,
        [ContactFName] [nvarchar](30) COLLATE SQL_Latin1_General_CP1_CI_AS NULL,
        [ContactLName] [nvarchar](30) COLLATE SQL_Latin1_General_CP1_CI_AS NULL,
        [Email] [varchar](255) COLLATE SQL_Latin1_General_CP1_CI_AS NULL,
        [City] [nvarchar](50) COLLATE SQL_Latin1_General_CP1_CI_AS NULL,
        [State] [char](2) COLLATE SQL_Latin1_General_CP1_CI_AS NULL,
        [ModifiedDate] [datetime] NULL,
CONSTRAINT [Customer_primaryKey] PRIMARY KEY NONCLUSTERED HASH
(        [CustomerID]  ) WITH ( BUCKET_COUNT = 1048576)
)WITH ( MEMORY_OPTIMIZED = ON , DURABILITY = SCHEMA_AND_DATA )
```

The graphical query designer helps us to generate query with JOINs for sample data.

```
SELECT   P.BusinessEntityID, P.FirstName, P.LastName, A.City, S.StateProvinceCode, P.ModifiedDate
FROM     Person.Address AS A INNER JOIN
         Person.StateProvince AS S ON A.StateProvinceID = S.StateProvinceID INNER JOIN
         Person.BusinessEntityAddress AS BEA ON A.AddressID = BEA.AddressID INNER JOIN
         Person.Person AS P ON BEA.BusinessEntityID = P.BusinessEntityID
```

CHAPTER 22: In-Memory OLTP

Populate the In-Memory Table with Dummy Test Data

```sql
USE RapidFire;
DELETE Customer WHERE CustomerID =1;  -- delete current record

SELECT CusomerID=ROW_NUMBER() OVER(ORDER BY (SELECT 1)), Company=
 CONCAT ('Company ',CONVERT(varchar(10), ROUND(RAND(CAST(NEWID() AS VARBINARY)) * 30000,0,-1))),
 P.FirstName, P.LastName, Email=
 CONCAT(P.FirstName, LEFT(P.LastName,1),convert(varchar(10),
 ROW_NUMBER() OVER(ORDER BY (SELECT 1))),'@ajaxins.com'),
 A.City, StateCode=LEFT(S.StateProvinceCode,2), P.ModifiedDate
INTO #StageCustomer
FROM AdventureWorks2012.Person.Address AS A INNER JOIN
    AdventureWorks2012.Person.StateProvince AS S
            ON A.StateProvinceID = S.StateProvinceID INNER JOIN
    AdventureWorks2012.Person.BusinessEntityAddress AS BEA
            ON A.AddressID = BEA.AddressID INNER JOIN
    AdventureWorks2012.Person.Person AS P
            ON BEA.BusinessEntityID = P.BusinessEntityID;

INSERT Customer SELECT * FROM #StageCustomer; -- 18798 row(s) affected)

SELECT TOP(3) * FROM Customer ORDER BY NEWID();
```

CustomerID	CompanyName	ContactFName	ContactLName	Email	City	State	ModifiedDate
3021	Company 6740	Glenn	Li	GlennL3021@ajaxins.com	St. Leonards	NS	2007-10-31 00:00:00.000
13728	Company 7518	Paula	Ruiz	PaulaR13728@ajaxins.com	Bellingham	WA	2007-03-16 00:00:00.000
3552	Company 20786	Terrence	Goel	TerrenceG3552@ajaxins.com	Lancaster	EN	2007-11-22 00:00:00.000

The on-disk Customer_old table is populated similarly with the script. The temporary table dropped.

```sql
DELETE Customer_old WHERE CustomerID =1;  -- delete current record
```

```sql
INSERT Customer_old SELECT * FROM Customer;  -- (18798 row(s) affected)
```

```sql
DROP TABLE #StageCustomer;
```

Both tables have identical structure and data population. We are ready for performance testing.

Memory Optimized Table Performance

Speed Comparison for GROUP BY Query

Even on a small table we can demonstrate the advantage of in-memory OLTP.

```
DBCC DROPCLEANBUFFERS;
SET STATISTICS IO ON; SET STATISTICS TIME ON;
SELECT City, Freq=count(*), LastMod=MAX(ModifiedDate)
FROM Customer GROUP BY City  ORDER BY Freq DESC, LastMod, City;
SET STATISTICS TIME OFF; SET STATISTICS IO OFF;
/*
Table 'Worktable'. Scan count 0, logical reads 0, physical reads 0,
Table 'Workfile'. Scan count 0, logical reads 0, physical reads 0,
SQL Server Execution Times:   CPU time = 15 ms,  elapsed time = 16 ms.
*/

DBCC DROPCLEANBUFFERS;
SET STATISTICS IO ON; SET STATISTICS TIME ON;
SELECT City, Freq=count(*) , LastMod=MAX(ModifiedDate)
FROM Customer_old GROUP BY City  ORDER BY Freq DESC, LastMod, City;
SET STATISTICS TIME OFF; SET STATISTICS IO OFF;
/*
Table 'Worktable'. Scan count 0, logical reads 0,
Table 'Workfile'. Scan count 0, logical reads 0, physical reads 0,
Table 'Customer_old'. Scan count 1, logical reads 293,
SQL Server Execution Times: CPU time = 16 ms,  elapsed time = 65 ms.
*/
```

Increase table sizes 10 fold for a new test.

```
;WITH CTE AS (
SELECT CompanyName, ContactFName, ContactLName, Email, City, State, ModifiedDate  FROM Customer_old
UNION ALL
SELECT CompanyName, ContactFName, ContactLName, Email, City, State, ModifiedDate  FROM Customer_old
UNION ALL
SELECT CompanyName, ContactFName, ContactLName, Email, City, State, ModifiedDate  FROM Customer_old
UNION ALL
SELECT CompanyName, ContactFName, ContactLName, Email, City, State, ModifiedDate  FROM Customer_old
UNION ALL
SELECT CompanyName, ContactFName, ContactLName, Email, City, State, ModifiedDate  FROM Customer_old
UNION ALL
SELECT CompanyName, ContactFName, ContactLName, Email, City, State, ModifiedDate  FROM Customer_old
UNION ALL
SELECT CompanyName, ContactFName, ContactLName, Email, City, State, ModifiedDate  FROM Customer_old
UNION ALL
SELECT CompanyName, ContactFName, ContactLName, Email, City, State, ModifiedDate  FROM Customer_old
UNION ALL
SELECT CompanyName, ContactFName, ContactLName, Email, City, State, ModifiedDate  FROM Customer_old),
idCTE AS (SELECT LastID=max(CustomerID) FROM Customer)
INSERT Customer
SELECT (SELECT LastID FROM idCTE)+ROW_NUMBER() OVER( ORDER BY (SELECT 1)), * FROM CTE;
-- (169182 row(s) affected)

TRUNCATE TABLE Customer_old; INSERT Customer_old SELECT * FROM Customer;  -- (187980 row(s) affected)
```

The same GROUP BY query test is repeated.
The in-memory table performs around 8 times faster.

```
DBCC DROPCLEANBUFFERS;
SET STATISTICS IO ON; SET STATISTICS TIME ON;
SELECT City, Freq=count(*), LastMod=MAX(ModifiedDate)
FROM Customer GROUP BY City  ORDER BY Freq DESC, LastMod, City;
SET STATISTICS TIME OFF; SET STATISTICS IO OFF;
/*
Table 'Worktable'. Scan count 0, logical reads 0, physical reads 0,
Table 'Workfile'. Scan count 0, logical reads 0, physical reads 0,
SQL Server Execution Times:   CPU time = 156 ms,  elapsed time = 150 ms.
*/
```

```
DBCC DROPCLEANBUFFERS;
SET STATISTICS IO ON; SET STATISTICS TIME ON;
SELECT City, Freq=count(*) , LastMod=MAX(ModifiedDate)
FROM Customer_old GROUP BY City  ORDER BY Freq DESC, LastMod, City;
SET STATISTICS TIME OFF; SET STATISTICS IO OFF;
/*
Table 'Worktable'. Scan count 0, logical reads 0,
Table 'Workfile'. Scan count 0, logical reads 0, physical reads 0,
Table 'Customer_old'.  Scan count 1, logical reads 4215,
SQL Server Execution Times:  CPU time = 203 ms,  elapsed time = 1243 ms.
*/
```

Increase the tables sizes 10 fold again with the same method and retest performance.

```
SELECT COUNT(*) FROM Customer;   -- 1879800
```

```
SELECT COUNT(*) FROM Customer_old;   -- 1879800
```

Customer in-memory table

SQL Server Execution Times: CPU time = 1514 ms, elapsed time = 1504 ms.

Customer_old on-disk table

 SQL Server Execution Times: CPU time = 1560 ms, elapsed time = 3109 ms.

In this instance the in-memory OLTP performance is twice better over on-disk technology.

Comparing Performance with WHERE Clause Present

WHERE clause in a query means searching through the table or index. The performance of in-memory table is more than 3 times better.

```
DBCC DROPCLEANBUFFERS;
SET STATISTICS IO ON; SET STATISTICS TIME ON;
DECLARE @Email varchar(255) = 'CedricW4585@ajaxins.com';
SELECT * FROM Customer WHERE Email = @Email  ORDER BY ModifiedDate, City, CustomerID;
SET STATISTICS TIME OFF; SET STATISTICS IO OFF;
GO
/*
SQL Server Execution Times:   CPU time = 858 ms,  elapsed time = 883 ms.
*/


DBCC DROPCLEANBUFFERS;
SET STATISTICS IO ON; SET STATISTICS TIME ON;
DECLARE @Email varchar(255) = 'CedricW4585@ajaxins.com';
SELECT * FROM Customer_old WHERE Email = @Email ORDER BY ModifiedDate, City, CustomerID;
SET STATISTICS TIME OFF; SET STATISTICS IO OFF;
/*
Table 'Customer_old'. Scan count 5, logical reads 29322,
SQL Server Execution Times:  CPU time = 610 ms,  elapsed time = 2805 ms.
*/
```

Create columnstore index on the on-disk table and compare performance. In-memory OLTP table beats on-disk table with columnstore index.

```
CREATE NONCLUSTERED COLUMNSTORE INDEX csindxCustomerOld ON Customer_old
(CustomerID, CompanyName, ContactFName, ContactLName, Email, City, State, ModifiedDate);
-- Command(s) completed successfully.  23 secs
```

Customer table

SQL Server Execution Times: CPU time = 889 ms, elapsed time = 878 ms.

Customer_old table

Table 'Customer_old'. Scan count 1, logical reads 5297,
SQL Server Execution Times: CPU time = 1139 ms, elapsed time = 1321 ms.

SQL Server 2014 clustered columnstore indexes are updateable to some degree:
http://msdn.microsoft.com/en-us/library/dn511016(v=sql.120).aspx

In-Memory OLTP Highlights

BOL page: http://msdn.microsoft.com/en-us/library/dn133186(v=sql.120).aspx

QUOTE: "New in SQL Server 2014, In-Memory OLTP can significantly improve OLTP database application performance. In-Memory OLTP is a memory-optimized database engine integrated into the SQL Server engine, optimized for OLTP. To use In-Memory OLTP, you define a heavily accessed table as memory optimized. Memory-optimized-tables are fully transactional, durable, and are accessed using Transact-SQL in the same way as disk-based tables. A query can reference both memory-optimized tables and disk-based tables. A transaction can update data in memory-optimized tables and disk-based tables. Stored procedures that only reference memory-optimized tables can be natively compiled into machine code for further performance improvements. The In-Memory OLTP engine is designed for extremely high session concurrency for OLTP type of transactions driven from a highly scaled-out middle-tier. To achieve this, it uses latch-free data structures and optimistic, multi-version concurrency control. The result is predictable, sub-millisecond low latency and high throughput with linear scaling for database transactions. The actual performance gain depends on many factors, but 5-to-20 times performance improvements are common."

In-Memory OLTP also introduces **natively compiled stored procedures**:
http://msdn.microsoft.com/en-us/library/dn133184(v=sql.120).aspx

QUOTE: "Natively compiled stored procedures are Transact-SQL stored procedures compiled to native code that access memory-optimized tables. Natively compiled stored procedures allow for efficient execution of the queries and business logic in the stored procedure. For more details about the native compilation process, see Native Compilation of Tables and Stored Procedures. For more information about migrating disk-based stored procedures to natively compiled stored procedures, see Migration Issues for Natively Compiled Stored Procedures.

 Note: One difference between interpreted (disk-based) stored procedures and natively compiled stored procedures is that an interpreted stored procedure is compiled at first execution whereas a natively compiled stored procedure is compiled when it is created. With natively compiled stored procedures, many error conditions (arithmetic overflow, type conversion, and some divide-by-zero conditions) can be detected at create time and will cause creation of the natively compiled stored procedure to fail. With interpreted stored procedures, these error conditions will typically not cause a failure when the stored procedure is created, but all executions will fail."

APPENDIX A: Job Interview Questions

Selected Database Design Questions

D1. What is your approach to database design?
D2. Some of our legacy databases are far from 3NF. Can you work in such an environment?
D3. Can UNIQUE KEY be used instead of PRIMARY KEY?
D4. Can a FOREIGN KEY be NULL?
D5. Can a PRIMARY KEY be NULL?
D6. Can a PRIMARY KEY be based on non-clustered unique index?
D7. Do you implement OrderQty > 0 condition as a CHECK constraint or in the application software?
D8. What is a heap?
D9. Can a table have 2 IDENTITY columns, 2 FOREIGN KEYs, 2 PRIMARY KEYs and 2 clustered indexes?
D10. Should each table have a NATURAL KEY or is INT IDENTITY PK sufficient?
D11. How can you prevent entry of "U.S", "USA", etc. instead of "United States" into Country column?
D12. How would you implement ManagerID in an Employee table with EmployeeID as PRIMARY KEY?
D13. How would you implement the relationship between OrderMaster and OrderDetail tables?
D14. Product table has the Color column. Would you create a Color table & change column to ColorID FK?
D15. Can you insert directly into an IDENTITY column?
D16. Which one is better? Composite PRIMARY KEY on NATURAL KEY, or INT IDENTITY PRIMARY KEY & UNIQUE KEY on NATURAL KEY?
D17. What is the lifetime of a regular table created in tempdb?
D18. How many different ways can you connect tables in a database?
D19. How would you connect the Vehicle and Owner tables?
D20. Can you have the same table names in different schemas?

Selected Database Programming Questions

P1. Write a query to list all departments with employee count based on the Department column of Employee table.
P2. Same as above but the Employee table has the DepartmentID column.
P3. Write an INSERT statement for a new "Social Technology" department with GroupName "Sales & Marketing".
P4. Same query es in P2, but the new department should be included even though no employees yet.
P5. Write a query to generate 1000 sequential numbers without a table.
P6. Write a query with SARGable predicate to list all orders from OrderMaster received on 2016-10-23. OrderDate is datetime.
P7. Write a query to add a header record DEPARTMENTNAME to the departments listing from the Department table. If there are 20 departments, the result set should have 21 records.
P8. Make the previous query a derived table in an outer SELECT * query
P9. Write an ORDER BY clause for the previous query with CASE expression to sort DEPARTMENTNAME as first record and alphabetically descending from there on.
P10. Same as above with the IIF conditional.
P11. The table-valued dbo.ufnSplitCSV splits a comma delimited string (input parameter). The Product table has some ProductName-s with comma(s). Write a CROSS APPLY query to return ProductName-s with comma and each split string value from the UDF as separate line. ProductName should repeat for each split part. 	ProductName	SplitPart
---	---
Full-Finger Gloves, L	Full-Finger Gloves
Full-Finger Gloves, L	L	
P12. You need the inserted lines count 10 lines down following the INSERT statement. What should be the statement immediately following the INSERT statement?
P13. What is the result of the second query? What is it called? SELECT COUNT_BIG(*) FROM Sales.SalesOrderDetail;   -- 121317 SELECT COUNT_BIG(*) FROM Sales.SalesOrderDetail x, Sales.SalesOrderDetail y;
P14. Declare & Assign the string variable @Text varchar(32) the literal '2016/10/23 10:20:12' without the "/" and ":".
P15. You want to add a parameter to a frequently used view. What is the workaround?
P16. When converting up to 40 characters string, can you use varchar instead of varchar(40)?
P17. Can you roll back IDENTITY seeds and table variables with ROLLBACK TRANSACTION?
P18. How do you decide where to place the clustered index?
P19. What is the simplest solution for the collation error: "Cannot resolve collation conflict..."?
P20. Which system table can be used for integer sequence up to 2^12 values?

APPENDIX A: Job Interview Questions

APPENDIX B: Job Interview Answers

Selected Database Design Answers

D1. I prefer 3NF design due to high database developer productivity and low maintenance cost.

D2. I did have such projects in the past. I can handle them. Hopefully, introduce some improvements.

D3. Partially yes since UNIQUE KEYs can be FK referenced, fully no. Every table should a PRIMARY KEY.

D4. Yes.

D5. No.

D6. Yes. The default is clustered unique index. Only unique index is required.

D7. CHECK constraint. A server-side object solution is more reliable than code in application software.

D8. A table without clustered index. Database engine generally works better if a table has clustered index.

D9. No, yes, no, no.

D10. A table should be designed with NATURAL KEY(s). INT IDENTITY PK is not a replacement for NK.

D11. Lookup table with UDF CHECK Constraint. UDF checks the Lookup table for valid entries.

D12. ManagerID as a FOREIGN KEY referencing the PRIMARY KEY of the same table; self-referencing.

D13. OrderID PRIMARY KEY of OrderMaster. OrderID & LineItemID composition PK of OrderDetail. OrderID of OrderDetail FK to OrderID of OderMaster.

D14. Yes. It makes sense for color to be in its own table.

D15. No. Only if you SET IDENTITY_INSERT tablename ON.

D16. Meaningless INT IDENTITY PRIMARY KEY with UNIQUE KEY ON NATURAL KEY is better.

D17. Until SQL Server restarted. tempdb starts empty as copy of model database.

D18. There is only one way: FOREIGN KEY constraint.

D19. With the OwnerVehicleXref junction table reflecting many-to-many relationship.

D20. Yes. A table is identified by SchemaName.TableName . dbo is the default schema.

Selected Database Programming Answers

P1. SELECT Department, Employees=COUNT(*) FROM Employee
   GROUP BY Department ORDER BY Department;

P2. SELECT d.Department, Employees = COUNT(EmployeeID) FROM Employee e
   INNER JOIN Department d ON e.DepartmentID = d.DepartmentID
   GROUP BY d.Department ORDER BY Department;

P3. INSERT Department (Name, GroupName) VALUES ('Social Technology', 'Sales & Marketing');

P4. SELECT d.Department, Employees = COUNT(EmployeeID) FROM Employee e
   RIGHT JOIN Department d ON e.DepartmentID = d.DepartmentID
   GROUP BY d.Department ORDER BY Department;

P5. ;WITH Seq AS (SELECT SeqNo = 1 UNION ALL SELECT SeqNo+1 FROM Seq WHERE SeqNo < 100)
   SELECT * FROM Seq;

P6. SELECT * FROM OrderMaster WHERE OrderDate >='20161023'
   AND OrderDate < DATEADD(DD,1,'20161023');

P7. SELECT AllDepartments = 'DEPARTMENTNAME' UNION SELECT Department FROM Department;

P8. SELECT * FROM (SELECT AllDepartments = 'DEPARTMENTNAME' UNION SELECT Name
   FROM HumanResources.Department) x

P9. ORDER BY CASE WHEN AllDepartments = 'DEPARTMENTNAME' THEN 1 ELSE 2 END,
   AllDepartments DESC;

P10. ORDER BY IIF(AllDepartments = 'DEPARTMENTNAME', 1 , 2), AllDepartments DESC;

P11. SELECT ProductName, S.SplitPart FROM Product P CROSS APPLY dbo.ufnSplitCSV (Name) S
   WHERE ProductName like '%,%';

P12. DECLARE @InsertedCount INT = @@ROWCOUNT;

P13. 121317*121317; Cartesian product.

P14. DECLARE @Text varchar(32) =
   REPLACE(REPLACE ('2016/10/23 10:20:12', '/', SPACE(0)), ':', SPACE(0));

P15. Table-valued INLINE user-defined function.

P16. varchar(40). It is a good idea to specify the length always. The default is 30.

P17. No. ROLLBACK has no effect on IDENTITY seeds or table variables. If an INSERT advanced the IDENTITY seed by 5 during the rollbacked transaction, it will stay that way after the ROLLBACK. It means a gap in the IDENTITY sequence.

P18. Business critical queries are the determining factor in placing the clustered index. Clustered index speeds up range queries.

P19. Place "COLLATE DATABASE_DEFAULT" on the right side of the expression.

P20. spt_values table.
SELECT N = number FROM master.dbo.spt_values WHERE type='P' ORDER BY N;

APPENDIX B: Job Interview Answers

INDEX of SQL Server 2014 Design & Programming

Index of the Most Important Topics

.

.sql script file, 555

@

@@DATEFIRST, 418
@@IDENTITY, 516
@@ROWCOUNT, 519
@@SERVERNAME, 58
@@SPID, 520
@@version, 58

3

3NF, 231
3-part name, 507
3-Part Name, 306

4

4-part name, 306
4-Week 13 Month Calendar, 723

A

a derived table, 477
a unique index, 438
Accent sensitive, 165
Accessing a View from Excel, 751
accessories, 1
Activity Monitor, 656
administration, 159
AdventureWorks, 1
AdventureWorks2008, 18
AdventureWorks2012, 19
AdventureWorksDW2012, 16, 17
aggregate, 81
aggregation, 8
Alberto Ferrari, 209
alphanumeric field, 447
ALTER TABLE, 176
ALTER TRIGGER, 620
American, 416
Amsterdam, 417
Analysis Services, 87, 621
analytic functions, 368
ancestors, 490
ANSI, 416
ANSI Date literal, 416
ANSI Style UPDATE, 526
ANSI UPDATE, 526
Arizona, 544
Ascii, 447
ASCII, 163
assignment, 665
assignment operator, 665
attribute, 13
Australia, 446
AVG(ListPrice), 69

B

BACKUP DATABASE, 60
backup filename with datestamp, 60
backup history query, 33
Backup of a Single Table, 733
batch, 99
Batch processing, 659
bcp, 558

BEGIN TRANSACTION, 541
Berlin, 417
BETWEEN, 447
BETWEEN Operator, 721
bill of materials, 491
BillOfMaterials, 552
binary number, 163
Binary String, 163
bit, 163
blocking, 520, 655
Bond, 250
Books Online, 60
Boolean, 163
brackets, 160
Brazil, 478
British, 417
browse, 626
B-tree, 137
bugs, 601
BULK INSERT, 595
business critical, 652
Business Rules, 616

C

C# Program, 753
cache memory, 635
calendar table, 360
Calendar table, 463
California, 544
CamelCase, 159
Canada, 446
cardinality, 393
Cardinality of CROSS JOIN, 401
cardinality of DISTINCT, 424
Cardinality of OUTER JOINs, 398
carriage return, 558
Cartesian explosion, 401
Cartesian Product, 393
CASE, 76, 447
Case insensitive, 165
case sensitive sort, 430
CAST, 416
category, 22, 71
Category, 10

Century, 452
CEO, 488
Chain of Command, 490
Character String, 163
CHARINDEX, 70, 421
CHECK constraint, 606
checkmark, 43
CHECKPOINT, 520
CHOOSE(), 361
chronological order, 403
Cinderella syndrom, 426
CIRCULARSTRING, 727
client, 89
client software, 99
Client Statistics, 651
Client-Server, 131
clustered index, 319, 320
Clustered index, 139, 182, 646
COALESCE, 421
COLLATE clause, 349
collation, 165, 349
Collation, 606
collation_name, 164
column alias, 378
columnstore index, 292
Columnstore Index, 291
comma delimited string, 72
Command Prompt, 593
COMMIT TRANSACTION, 541
Common Table Expression, 402
compatibility level, 298
Composable DML, 664
composite, 253
composite index, 137
composite PRIMARY KEY, 182, 319
composite **UNIQUE KEY**, 319
Compressed Index, 277
compression, 276
computed columns, 256
computer geeks, 6
CONCAT(), 361
Concatenation, 747
connection, 129, 655
constants, 69
context-sensitive, 107

Index of the Most Important Topics

Conversion, 449
CONVERT(), 449
COPY, 593
copy with headers, 97
correlated subqueries, 476
correlated subquery, 471
cost panels, 640
COUNT, 155
COUNT(), 155
COUNT(*), 347
COUNT_BIG(), 155
covering index, 137, 643
create a view, 391
CREATE DATABASE, 298
Create Partition Wizard, 290
CREATE SCHEMA, 168
credit card, 731
cross database, 507
CROSS JOIN, 401, 402
cross tabulation, 494
cross-reference, 245
Cross-reference, 12
crosstab, 494
crosstab listing, 495
CSV, 72
CTE, 84, 479
culture parameter, 354
currency format, 405
current session, 520
Cursors, 677

D

DATA ACCESS, 520
Data compression, 271
Data Compression Wizard, 278
Data Connection Wizard, 752
Data Dictionary, 12, 260
Data Modeling, 161
data sequence, 360
data type, 76
Data Types, 163
data warehouse, 624
Data Warehouse, 16, 17, 291, 360
data warehouse query, 16

data warehousing, 16
Database Administrator, 108
Database backup, 60
Database Backup, 732
Database Design Standards, 294
database engine, 159, 637
Database Engine Tuning Advisor, 660
Database Maintenance Plan Wizard, 738
database modeling, 205
Database Restore, 735
Database security, 718
DATALENGTH(), 9
date dimension, 360
Date Only, 454
Date sequence, 486
DATEFIRST, 418
dateformat, 417
DATEFROMPARTS(), 363
DATENAME(), 466
DATEPART(), 465
datetime2, 163
DATETIMEFROMPARTS(), 363
datetimeoffset, 163
DBA, 108
DBCC CHECKIDENT, 523
DBCC HELP, 660
DBCC USEROPTIONS, 420
dbo, 150
DDL Trigger, 724
dealer network, 1
debugging, 99
DECIMAL, 173
decompress, 271
Decryption, 731
default instance, 46, 59
default schema, 402
Default trace, 347
Deferred Name Resolution Process, 103
Delete (XML DML), 712
DELETE CASCADE, 183, 612
Delete Tables, 210
Demographic, 12
denormalization, 233
DENSE_RANK, 153
dependency chart, 335

derived table, 71
developer productivity, 199
Developer Reference, 64
diagram, 3
Diagram Design, 198
dimension tables, 16, 624
Dirty Reads, 691
disable constraint, 672
Display Line numbers, 120
DISTINCT, 75
distribution DVD, 60
distributor, 1
DMF, 30
DMV, 30
dmy, 417
Domain Integrity, 606
drill-down, 29
DROP COLUMN, 357
DROP TABLE, 178
drop-down, 185
duplicate, 603
duplicates, 75
duplicates removal, 603
duration, 635
Dynamic Management Function, 334
Dynamic Management Functions, 30
Dynamic Management View, 333
Dynamic Management Views, 30
Dynamic PIVOT, 718
dynamic SQL, 543, 751
Dynamic SQL, 718
dynamic tables, 652

E

eadability, 199
ECHO, 592
ecommerce, 541
empty string, 72
enable constraint, 672
Encryption, 731
end of batch, 157
English, 417
Enterprise-Level, 616
Entity integrity, 602

EOMONTH(), 364
EQUI-JOIN, 374
Error handling, 99
error message, 101, 128
Error Message, 224
Español, 487
European, 416
Evaluation Edition, 36
Exact Numerics, 163
Excel, 95, 751
EXCEPT operator, 83
exec sp_who, 520
Execute, 89
execution errors, 103
execution plan, 639, 640, 647
exist() Method, 708
explicit conversion, 10
export, 560
Exporting All Images, 599
Express Edition, 36
expression, 199
expressions, 69

F

fact tables, 16, 624
File, 92
FILESTREAM, 48, 265
FileTable, 48, 265
filter, 7
FIRST_VALUE(), 368
Fixed length, 163
Flat File, 95
floating point, 163
FOR XML AUTO, 744
FOR XML Clause, 744
FOR XML EXPLICIT, 745
FOR XML PATH, 746
FOR XML RAW, 744
FOREIGN KEY, 315
FOREIGN KEY constraint, 613
FORMAT, 71, 293
format file, 596
FORMAT(), 359
frames and parts, 1

France, 76, 447
Frequency, 423
FULL JOIN, 400
FULLSCAN, 654
full-text index, 331
Fulltext Indexes, 210
full-text search, 331
Full-Text Search, 631

G

Generate Change Script, 214
geography, 164
Geography, 725
geometry, 164
Geometry, 725
German, 464
Germany, 447
Globally Unique Identifier, 163
GO, 89
gold key, 189
gourmet food, 1
graphical, 111
Gregorian, 723
Grid, 90
GROUPING(), 669
GUI, 87
GUID, 163

H

HAVING, 15
HAVING clause, 82
HAVING count(*), 69
heap, 182
Hekaton, 757
Hex, 453
hierarchical, 243
hierarchyid, 18, 163, 164, 244, 713
hierarchyid functions, 716
Hijri date, 451
Hong Kong, 417
Hovering, 127, 128
Hungarian, 464

Hungarian naming, 159

I

Identifier, 159
identifiers, 159
IDENTITY SEED, 736
IIF, 444
IIF(), 363
Implementation Hierarchy, 262
implicit conversion, 97
Implicit conversion, 10
implicit looping, 11
import, 574
index, 137
index fragmentation, 645
index scan, 647
index seek, 647
indexed view, 143
Information Services, 5
INFORMATION_SCHEMA, 155, 324
INFORMATION_SCHEMA.TABLES, 155
inherited, 502
Inline Function, 684
inline index declaration, 755
inline user-defined function, 546
In-Memory OLTP, 352, 758
in-memory tables, 757
INNER JOIN, 71, 681
inner query, 471
Insert (XML DML), 711
INSERT Data, 698
INSERT EXEC, 518
INSERT SELECT, 515
INSERT VALUES, 513, 514
Install, 51
installation, 37
Installing Books On Line, 60
Integration Services, 87, 621
IntelliSense, 99, 127
internal storage, 453
international standard, 451
INTERSECT operator, 83
interview question, 671
INVALID DATE, 462

Invalid object name, 224
invalid table reference, 103
ISDATE(), 462
ISNUMERIC, 70
ISO 8601 format, 451
ISO date time, 416

J

Japanese, 417
job, 109
job management, 47
JOIN keys, 199
JOIN on non-key columns, 28
JOIN predicate, 380
junction table, 26, 245, 313

K

Ken Sanchez, 488
keyword, 328

L

LAG(), 367
LANGUAGE Turkish, 464
Last Word of a String, 446
LAST_VALUE(), 368
Latin, 513
Latin1_General_CS_AI, 430
LEAD(), 367
leading space, 9
leading zeros, 293
LEFT, 421
LEFT JOIN, 395
Leipzig, 447
LEN(), 9
less than JOIN, 385
License terms, 43
LIKE operator, 661
line feed, 558
list price, 22
lists installation options, 44
literals, 69

local variable, 157
logical data model, 161
London, 24
Lookup table, 12
Lookup Tables, 251
Los Angeles, 447
LTRIM(), 9

M

Madrid, 478
magyar, 487
maintenance, 159
major key, 83
Major sort key, 384
Management Studio, 87
many-to-many JOIN, 387, 388
master system database, 30
master-detail tables, 247
MAX(OrderQty), 78
Maximum Capacity Specifications, 651
maximum storage size, 163
mdy, 403, 417
meaningful names, 159
memory optimized, 758
memory-optimized. *See*
MERGE, 650
Messages, 99
metadata, 12, 155, 338
metadata query, 263
Miami, 447
midnight, 720
midnight bug, 426, 720
MIN(OrderQty), 78
minor key, 83
Minor sort key, 384
missing indexes, 652
model database, 32
modify() Method, 710
money, 163
MONEY, 173
Moscow, 417
Mountain-100, 74
msdb, 33
multidimensiona, 626

multidimensional, 628
multi-level totals, 669
multi-part identifier, 128
multiple WHERE conditions, 414
multiplication table, 402
München, 447

N

named instance, 46, 59
Natively compiled, 772
natively-compiled, 755
NATURAL KEY, 320
nchar, 164
Nested CTEs, 483
New York, 417
New York City, 421
newid(), 76
NEWID(), 323
NEWSEQUENTIALID(), 323
Niagara Falls, 544
NOLOCK, 692
nonclustered index, 646
nonclustered PRIMARY KEY, 182
non-correlated subquery, 477
Nondeterministic, 452
nondeterministic CTE, 408
Northwind, 23
not null, 69, 176, 241, 266, 297, 299, 305, 363, 395, 400, 438, 442
ntelliSense, 122
ntext, 164
NTILE, 153
NULL, 13
Nullability, 606
NULLIF, 421
numbering, 389
nvarchar, 164, 351

O

Object Explorer, 30
Object Explorer Details, 328
OBJECT_DEFINITIION(), 329

OFFSET FETCH, 366
OLAP reports, 621
OLTP, 1, 16
OLTP query, 20
ON, 5
ON clause, 386
On Line Transaction Processing, 1
OPENQUERY, 520
OPENROWSET, 512
Optimistic Concurrency Control, 700
Optimization, 635
optimizer, 641
ORDER BY, 5
ORDER by newid(), 14
ORDER BY NEWID(), 76
Organizational Chart, 488
orgchart, 715
outer query, 471
Outline Numbering, 716
OUTPUT clause, 517, 664
OVER clause, 78, 672

P

pad, 293
Padding, 293
Padding with leading zeros, 293
PAGE-LEVEL compression, 272
parameter sniffing, 650
parameterized view, 546
paramount, 375
parent table, 619
Parent-Child Tables, 698
PARSE(), 354
partition, 81
PARTITION BY, 74
Partition Function, 282
Partition Scheme, 282
Partitioned Table, 282
Pascal case, 159
PATINDEX, 467
PATINDEX string function, 467
PATINDEX(), 663
pattern match, 663
Pattern Matching, 467

performance improvement, 640
Pessimistic Concurrency Control, 701
PIVOT Operator, 494
PivotChart, 752
PivotTable, 627, 752
Plan Caching, 650
Planning, 37
Polish, 464
POLYGON, 725
populated table, 176
Portland, 447
poster, 333
PowerShell, 687
PowerShell commands, 688
PowerShell script, 330
predicate, 80, 649
prefix, 421
prime numbers, 545
PRINT, 540
prioritizing, 652
product photos, 600
Product table, 20
productivity, 159
Profiler, 134, 636
Programming Standards, 294
project team, 294
pubs, 23

Q

Quality Assurance, 5
queries, 134
query, 1, 155
Query Designer, 111, 314, 682
Query Editor, 87
query optimization, 233, 643
query performance, 271, 292
query() Method, 705
queryout, 558
Queso, 71
QUOTENAME(), 350
Quotient, 1

R

RAISERROR, 540, 699
random sort, 76
range query, 320
RANK, 153, 154
ranking functions, 78
READ UNCOMMITTED, 691
readability, 199
reads, 635
real, 164
Recursive, 552
Recursive CTEs, 485
Recursive Query, 490
red squiggly, 129
red wave underlining, 127
relationship diagram, 315
relationships, 198
REPEATABLE READ, 693
Reporting Services, 87, 621
rerunnable script, 557
reserved keywords, 429
Restore of a Single Table, 736
Results to File, 94
Results to Text, 93
REVERSE, 422
reverse engineer, 207
reversible UPDATE, 528
RIGHT, 427
RIGHT JOIN, 396
right-click, 185
Rio de Janeiro, 417
Road Bikes, 14
ROLLBACK, 699
ROLLBACK TRANSACTION, 541
row count, 347
ROWGUIDCOL, 21
ROW-LEVEL compression, 273
rowversion, 702
RTRIM(), 9
Running total, 666
runtime, 103
Russian, 464

Index of the Most Important Topics

S

SalesOrderHeader, 19
sample database, 1
SARGable, 80, 648, 649
scalar user-defined function, 547
schedule, 109
schema, 168, 169
schema_name, 15
SCHEMA_NAME(), 169
SCOPE_IDENTITY(), 516
scripting options, 336
search box, 328
Seattle, 24, 447
Security, 592
SELECT INTO, 431, 445, 446, 449, 497
SELECT statement, 5
self-join, 387
SELF-JOIN, 619
semi-structured data, 312
sequence, 360
SERIALIZABLE Isolation, 695
Server Configuration, 47
Server Dashboard, 658
SERVERPROPERTY, 58
session, 129
SET LANGUAGE, 418
SET TRANSACTION ISOLATION LEVEL, 690
set-based logic, 677
signed integer, 163
Single-valued SQL queries, 11
single-valued subquery, 475
smalldatetime, 163
smallint, 163
smallmoney, 163
SNAPSHOT Isolation, 696
software engineering, 635
software engineers, 294
Software standards, 294
South Africa, 544
sp_addextendedproperty, 260
sp_dropextendedproperty, 260
sp_help, 338
sp_helpconstraints, 263
sp_helpdb, 337
sp_helptext, 226, 338
sp_rename, 177
sp_tables, 509
sp_tables_ex, 509
sp_updateextendedproperty, 261
sp_who2, 520
Spain, 478
Spanish, 464
Spatial Data Types, 725
Spatial Indexes, 210
spt_values, 31
spt_values table, 31
SQL, ii, 1, 5, 12, 23, 28, 29, 30, 32, 33, 87, 158, 159, 160, 161, 163, 166, 167, 168, 169, 171, 176, 178, 223, 233, 244, 265, 267, 270, 271, 291, 294, 298, 356, 358, 359, 361, 362, 363, 364, 376, 381, 389, 394, 398, 400, 401, 403, 411, 414, 415, 417, 418, 497
SQL Injection, 718
SQL Server 2005, 1, 479
SQL Server 2008 R2, 332
SQL Server Agent, 109
SQL Server Analysis Services, 621
SQL Server Data Tools, 621
SQL Server instance, 58
SQL Server Profiler, 134
sql_variant, 164
SQLCMD, 555
sqlps, 687
square brackets, 160
Squiggly red line, 130
SS Version, 58
SSAS, 87, 621
SSDT, 621
SSIS, 87, 621
SSIS Import/Export Wizard, 561
SSMS, 87
SSMS Object Explorer, 59
SSRS, 87, 621
staging tables, 201
standard cost, 22
Standard Reports, 657
star schema, 17
stealth, 148
stealth behavior, 616

STLength(), 725
Stock, 250
stored procedure, 366
String Date Format, 417
String literal, 21
string literals, 417
structured programming, 84
STUFF, 451
STUFF(), 72
style number, 449
subcategory, 22
Subcategory, 10
subquery, 71
SUBSTRING, 427
SUM, 422
Summary of Isolation Levels, 697
Sweden, 76, 544
Sybase, 23
synonym, 448
syntax errors, 102, 103
sys.databases, 31
sys.dm_db_index_physical_stats, 645
sys.objects, 15, 158, 322
sys.sql_modules, 343
sys.synonyms, 448
sys.sysforeignkeys, 15
syscomments, 343
syslanguages, 419
sysname, 164
system databases, 29
system tables, 158, 331
system views, 135, 137, 145, 148, 158, 160, 331
systems analyst, 262

T

table alias, 477
Table alias, 431
table editor, 346
table population, 516
table scan, 647
Table Value Constructor, 513
table variable, 540
Table variable, 157
TABLESAMPLE, 730

Table-valued parameters, 673
tabs, 489
Technet Article, 650
tempdb, 34
Template Explorer, 683
temporal, 416
temporary table, 641
Temporary table, 34
Texas, 544
Text, 92
THEN, 447
THROW, 362
TIES, 74
tinyint, 163
titles table, 27
Tokyo, 417
TOP 10, 74
TOP clause, 74, 413
TOP n by group, 86
Toronto, 544
Touring-1000, 1
trailing spaces, 9
transaction, 689, 698
Transaction, 698
TRANSACTION ISOLATION LEVEL, 690
translate, 251
tree hierarchy, 18
trigger, 616
TRY...CATCH Block, 689
TRY_CONVERT(), 356
TRY_PARSE(), 358

U

UDF CHECK constraint, 341
UK-Style, 417
underscore, 159
UNICODE, 163, 240
UNICODE Chinese, 663
UNION ALL, 85, 478
unique, 75
UNIQUE, 320
unique index, 182, 603
UNIQUE KEY, 320
uniqueidentifier, 163

UNIQUEIDENTIFIER, 323
United Kingdom, 446
United States, 446
UNPIVOT, 495
update PRIMARY KEY, 672
UPDATE STATISTICS, 652
us_english, 487
user-defined function, 686
US-Style, 417

V

Valid Range, 468
value() Method, 707
varbinary, 163
varbinary(max), 265
varchar, 163
Variable-length, 163
version-stamping, 163
violation of 3NF, 319
Visio Forward Engineer Addin, 209
Visual Studio, 87

W

WHEN, 447
WHERE clause, 73
WHERE condition, 11, 644

WHILE, 540
wildcard, 5, 328
window function, 78
WITH CUBE, 73
WITH RESULT SETS, 370
WITH ROLLUP, 73
with xp_cmdshell, 592
worksheet, 97, 98
writes, 643

X

xml, 163
XML data, 312
XML data type, 503
XML Indexes, 210
XML PATH, 72, 747
XML PATH clause, 72
xp_cmdshell, 592
Xquery, 705

Y

ydm, 417
YEAR(OrderDate), 19
Yellowstone, 544
ymd, 416, 417
YYYYMMDD, 416